A READER'S COMPANION TO THE SHORT STORY IN ENGLISH

Edited by
Erin Fallon, R. C. Feddersen,
James Kurtzleben, Maurice A. Lee,
and Susan Rochette-Crawley

*Under the Auspices of the
Society for the Study of the Short Story*

GREENWOOD PRESS
Westport, Connecticut • London

Library of Congress Cataloging-in-Publication Data

A reader's companion to the short story in English / edited by Erin Fallon . . . [et al.] ;
under the auspices of the Society for the Study of the Short Story.
    p.   cm.
   Includes bibliographical references and index.
   ISBN 0–313–29104–7 (alk. paper)
   1. Short stories, American—History and criticism. 2. Short stories, English—History and
criticism. 3. American fiction—20th century—Dictionaries. 4. Commonwealth fiction
(English)—Dictionaries. 5. English fiction—20th century—Dictionaries. 6. Authors,
American—20th century—Biography—Dictionaries. 7. Authors,
Commonwealth—Biography—Dictionaries. 8. Authors, English—20th
century—Biography—Dictionaries. I. Fallon, Erin, 1971– II. Society for the Study of the
Short Story.
PS374.S5R43   2001
813'.0109—dc21   00–025113

British Library Cataloguing in Publication Data is available.

Library of Congress Catalog Card Number: 00–025113
ISBN: 0–313–29104–7

First published in 2001

Greenwood Press, 88 Post Road West, Westport, CT 06881
An imprint of Greenwood Publishing Group, Inc.
www.greenwood.com

Printed in the United States of America

The paper used in this book complies with the
Permanent Paper Standard issued by the National
Information Standards Organization (Z39.48–1984).

10 9 8 7 6 5 4 3 2 1

CONTENTS

Contents

PREFACE

The extraordinary output of short stories in the English-speaking world has led several scholars and critics to suggest that the genre will be recognized as the preeminent form in the twentieth century in the same way that the novel was in the nineteenth. This is not to say that the novel did not have its share of superior practitioners, but in almost every case novelists were or are also short-story writers, and in many cases the short stories in their integrity and coherence are better formed than the novels and likely will be remembered longer—those of Sherwood Anderson, for example, Ernest Hemingway, D. H. Lawrence, Katherine Anne Porter, or Eudora Welty, to name just a few that come to mind.

The stories discussed in this volume were, with one exception, written in the latter half of the twentieth century, most deriving from 1960 to the present. This was the time when degrees in creative writing multiplied (exponentially, I sometimes think) until almost every English department in the academy established an M.F.A. and/or Ph.D. program in the field. Writing workshops punctuated summer sessions around the world. In these programs, those interested in fiction mainly pursued their interests in writing short stories since novels are not easy to handle in workshops and are seldom undertaken. It is not surprising, then, that many an emerging writer's first publication is a collection of short stories. Thus the university was not only hiring writers and producing writers skilled in the form but also training readers. In this way, the academy created a reading public knowledgeable in how to read a short story—a necessary prerequisite, as Poe first declared when he suggested that readers need to read "the tale" with an art "kindred" to that employed by the writers themselves.

The latter half of the twentieth century also saw an important move toward diversity in the literary canon. In fact, never has there been so sweeping a change in the canon common to the English-speaking world as the one that took place in the last thirty or so years of the twentieth century. Certainly previous eras evidenced their share of changes, but not without battle. Scholars in our not-too-distant past, for example, argued over whether American literature ought to be the focus of serious study in academia at all; and some debated whether contemporary literature was distanced sufficiently for aesthestic judgments to be effective. But the recent changes in the canon made in the name of diversity and multiculturalism occasioned little overt argument among academics, likely since ethical values were an important, if submerged, part of the motivations for change.

In the late 1960s and during the decade of the 1970s, all of us were looking for literature written by black Americans to include in our syllabi. Publishers were just beginning to include stories and poems by authors most of us had never heard of. I remember the first time I encountered one such story ("Karintha" by Jean Toomer). I had been lying on the sofa with my head propped up and a stack of recently released anthologies by my side. I read the story with increasing admiration for the author and annoyance that I had never heard of Toomer in all my student and professional life. My first question was why I hadn't and my first answer was that my mentors had not instructed me. My second thought came quickly. "Karintha" went out of print almost as soon as it was published. My mentors knew as little as I did. Who then to blame? The answer was simple: all of us who accepted the existing canon without question. A similar feeling of dismay came over me in the next few years. I was teaching a course in Faulkner when I reread what I had written on *Sanctuary* in my 1950 master's thesis. I accepted at the time without question what others had said. Temple was raped, yes, but it was her own fault since she displayed herself to all the men gathered around her. This time my dismay was tempered and then overshadowed by remorse. This time I had to recognize not only my own complicity but also the moral dimensions of that complicity.

Broadly speaking, then, what started in the United States somewhat more than two decades ago as a tepid backburner concern for most educators has moved to the front burner and become a bubbling cauldron demanding more and more attention. In the mid- to late 1970s, the major faculty effort toward diversity included placing a sampling of writings by black Americans and by women into textbooks in an effort to diversify the canon. The 1980s saw both an increasing number of books and courses wholly dedicated to gender studies and a broadening of interest in issues of ethnicity and cultural diversity. By the late 1980s, race/ethnicity studies had begun to highlight a panoply of choices for the literature curriculum: African-American literature, Native American literature, Hispanic-American literature, Asian-American literature, Anglo-American literature, and Euro-American literature. By the 1990s, multiculturalism had become our creed, the global community our consciousness. With multiculturalism in mind, we sought stories written in English by natives of postcolonial countries and, in translation, stories by writers from Eastern Europe and Asia.

For every anthology there are limitations, and editors need a principle of selection. The editors here have limited their selection to chapters about contemporary writers of short stories in English, particularly those whose major output occurred in the 1960s and thereafter. They were able thus to include commentary on some of the most respected voices from various Third World and postcolonial countries (including Canada) as well as stories by Americans with different ethnic backgrounds.

This volume's table of contents is by no means inclusive and will be less inclusive in the future as more voices join existing ones in what is becoming a rising swell of diversity in the short story. The cauldron, we must remember, is no longer a melting pot but rather a hearty stew where each ingredient retains its characteristic texture and flavor while blending a part of itself into the tasty and much richer sauce.

Of the 22 American writers included in the text, more than half can be identified as belonging to historically marginalized groups: Jewish Americans, African Americans, Native Americans, Asian Americans, Latin Americans; in addition, two writers are from Africa, four from Great Britain, five from Canada, one from Ireland, five from the West Indies, one from Australia, two from New Zealand, four from India, and one from South Africa. Overall, 29 are female and 18 are male, not a surprising number since the short story in the twentieth century attracted a large number of women to its fold, perhaps because the essential form denies closure and accepts ambiguity as central to its being. The present volume aims to introduce these writers to the reading public—to teachers and students who find them on their reading lists but know little about them, and to lay readers who seek more information about the ever-widening spectrum of contemporary literature. Each chapter contains biographic material, a brief review of existing criticism, a lengthier analysis of specific works, and a selected bibliography. Readers will also find a detailed introduction to the short-story genre itself, from the time of its inception to the late twentieth century. An annotated bibliography and "About the Contributors" complete the volume.

Stories are integral to human interaction. In our earliest history, humans gathered around each other to tell stories. Before we had written language, humans scratched picture stories onto rocks and/or kept tales alive through word of mouth. Stories record human acts. They surround us in our everyday lives as well as in our dreams. We are told stories when we are too young to read; we read stories as we grow older; and we tell stories to our children and grandchildren. Our memories work in story language, and our dreams involve us in different kinds of narratives, including those that defy commonsense perceptions in time and space. The modern short story derives from fairy tales and myths and thus takes us back to our origins and forward to the present day. It is no wonder that short stories are central to our being.

Mary Rohrberger, Executive Director
Society for the Study of the Short Story

ACKNOWLEDGMENTS

We are grateful to Julie Garrett, Marc LaPorte, and Aaron Nitzkin for help with copyediting from first to last and to Kelly Grant who undertook the task of indexing, a not inconsiderable endeavor. Our grateful acknowledgment also goes to George Butler, our editor at Greenwood who showed remarkable patience, to Charles Eberline, for his careful and knowledgeable copyediting, and to Betty Pessagno who graciously ushered our book to press.

INTRODUCTION: A GLANCE AT THE HISTORY OF THE SHORT STORY IN ENGLISH

R. C *Feddersen*

Storytelling, it is widely assumed, originated somewhere in the misty dawn of language itself. While it seems a platitude to repeat this idea, the truth is that locating the origins of story is probably as hopeless a task as identifying humankind's earliest coherent utterance. Creation stories, the mythical stories informing ritual, folk and fairy tales, fables, and legends—the oral traditions of all cultures—underscore the primacy of narrative in our shared perceptions, our values, and our notions of reality. This organizing power of narrative—to shape our collective sense of experience and the world—has recently prompted psychologists to examine how children's experiences with stories may help to form the individual's development of language, cognition, and perception of reality. In the introduction to the 1989 Lohafer/Clarey compilation of recent essays, *Short Story Theory at a Crossroads*, noted critic and theorist Susan Lohafer states that "both psychologists and discourse analysts have come to regard 'storying' as a form of cognition, highly privileged and discrete in the set of human adaptations to experience" (Lohafer and Clarey 210).

Whether they bespeak the bases and values of culture in myth and folktale or foster a sense of right and wrong in fables, stories organize and transmit sequences of human events and experiences into meaningful units. The most fragmentary of tales still suggests some relationship between present, past, and future. As Lohafer and Clarey say, "Story is a human frame for experience" (211).

Fortunately, we need not fathom the abyss of the origin of language to sketch some important moments in the development of the short story as a literary form. Despite the fact that James Cooper Lawrence in 1917 claimed the short story to be the oldest of all "literary types" and the basis for both ballad and epic (65–66), many critics today make clear distinctions between the modern literary short story and earlier short narratives. A brief overview of the history of the tale may help us to put the development of short fiction as an identifiable genre into perspective.

Short narratives have for centuries served several purposes; they have preserved, explained, entertained, and instructed. Oral accounts of battles and other human trials have regaled listeners and provided vivid living memories of people and events. Other tales have given meaning and order to life by explaining origins or dramatizing human purposes and values. Short narratives abound in religious texts of most cultures. Stories in the Bible, from Cain and Abel to the parables of Christ, define the history of a people's relationship to God and each other. Among the ancients, we find the fables of the Greek slave Aesop, which date from the sixth century B.C. Endowing animals with human characteristics, fables teach moral lessons, and we still find them not only in children's stories and animated cartoons ("The Three Little Pigs") but perhaps also in George Orwell's *Animal Farm*. Fables were plentiful during the Middle Ages, a period during which the didactic function of stories (and literature in general) was emphasized.

After the fall of Rome in the fifth century A.D., many classical tales (including those of Ovid's *Metamorphoses*) were submerged or Christianized, but short didactic tales thrived in medieval times (often transmitted orally) and encouraged religious devotion. The *contes dévots*, believed to have originated with the early Christians, were pious tales in French verse meant to succor the lagging spirit. Later, *exempla* (short narratives used to illustrate sermons) became latter-day parables for the clergy. In the thirteenth and fourteenth centuries, *exempla* were compiled into volumes and indexed, and Ann Charters reminds us that a collection of these didactic prose tales about five hundred years ago was apparently the first book ever printed (Charters 1600).

Not all medieval short narratives were religious or moral in the strictest sense. French translations of Celtic fairy tales and romances of various lengths flourished. By the twelfth century, English ballads narrated dramatic accounts of love and death simply and directly. Again, James Cooper Lawrence concluded in 1917 that these must originally have been oral prose tales that (perhaps for memorizing and reciting) became preserved in verse: "They were merely short stories in rhythmical form." In fact, most short narratives of the Middle Ages were versed, but by the fourteenth century, short prose narratives called *novellae* were being written in Italy, most notably by Giovanni Boccaccio, whose *Decameron* is still printed and read in English translation today. Some of these tales are related to *exempla* in that they appear to convey a moral lesson, but others demonstrate a marked secular trend and perhaps more closely resemble another type of medieval tale, the *fabliau*. Like *contes dévots* and *lais*, *fabliaux* probably first appeared in French verse, but instead of spiritual or moral concerns, *fabliaux* tended to celebrate an earthier side of life. Humorous and often satiric, these realistic—but usually bawdy and exaggerated—tales seemed to counterbalance the extreme piety of the didactic tales.

Several examples of these types of short narrative were brought together by

Boccaccio's English contemporary, Geoffrey Chaucer, whose *Canterbury Tales*, like Boccaccio's *Decameron*, is a collection of tales within a framework, that of fictional pilgrims telling stories to their host. Unlike Boccaccio's tales, Chaucer's narratives are mostly in verse instead of prose. According to Henry Canby, Chaucer's pilgrims provide examples of several types of medieval tale: *exempla* ("The Pardoner's Tale" and "The Monk's Tale"), *fabliaux* ("The Miller's Tale" and "The Reeve's Tale"), and the beast-fable *fabliau* ("The Nun's Priest's Tale").

Although short narratives, including *exempla* and long and short romances, continued to circulate on the Continent and in Britain through the fifteenth, sixteenth, and seventeenth centuries, tales began a new form of existence during the eighteenth century. At about the time that the newer, more realistic novel was distinguishing itself from the earlier romance, the development of publishing as a business was helping to redefine the notion of authorship. Writers and publishers could now earn money from the printing and selling of prose fiction. Periodicals began to publish short narratives, essays, and sketches, including satires and gothic tales, which had to conform to length constraints in order to fit their allotted spaces in the publications. Thus in the ages of the novel, a combination of influences in the 1700s—trends in public taste and literature and the technology of publishing—helped to prepare for the advent of the short story as a modern genre. The eighteenth-century essay, especially those published in Addison and Steele's *Spectator*, may have been a major force in the development of the narrative style that would combine with elements of folktale to produce the early short story. It was in the next century, most theorists agree, that the form we now recognize as the literary short story emerged.

Around the turn of the nineteenth century, the British romantic movement was displacing neoclassical rationalism with a shift toward the affective aspects of human experience and an organic view of nature and creativity. The romantics reprised many of the concerns and forms of the Middle Ages, including a new fascination with gothic literature. Some German writers of the eighteenth century had been producing *novellae* that often depicted unusual experiences or even the supernatural. The romantics' interest in the nonrational—dreams and imagination—and their new self-consciousness as artists gave rise to an organic theory of art wherein form was not imposed from without, but arose from within the growth of a work of art. Once this way of looking at poetry and prose became entrenched, the season had come for a new genre.

While critics do not completely agree on exactly whom to credit with writing the first literary short story, they generally acknowledge that something happened around the time that Washington Irving was transplanting German folktales into the new American soil. With the publication of tales like "The Legend of Sleepy Hollow" and "Rip Van Winkle," Irving moved the folktale into a particular mode of telling in which the dramatized narrator becomes a subjective presence—a particular consciousness through which the tale filters. As Charles May has noted, Irving may have been combining the older mythic folk narrative with something like the narrative style of Addison and Steele in their *Spectator* essays of the eighteenth century (*The Short Story* 6, 8). This is a significant step toward the modern short story, because Irving's realistic narrator can relate mythic elements in some realistic detail. However, because Irving's narrator seems to be essentially a casual, anecdotal storyteller functioning to add verisimilitude, certain descriptive passages in Irving's stories are more characteristic of longer narratives like the novel or the romance. In short, as Mary Rohrberger has pointed out, these narratives lack "unity of effect with its concomitant freedom from excrescence" that theorists and critics commonly ascribe to definitive examples of the genre (*Hawthorne* 12). Irving's tales remain "tales" rather than short stories because they lack the tightly woven structure and taut economy of language that characterize the true short story.

A short time after Irving published his *Sketchbook* (1819), three writers, two Americans and a Russian, came on the scene with what are widely believed to be the earliest examples of short stories as we know them today. As always, the question of whom we credit with being first depends on several factors, and perhaps we should simply give credit to all three. After all, literary developments are fluid processes sometimes involving the interconnections of seemingly unrelated ideas among many different people. In other words, similar ideas occur to different people in different places at the same time. In the case of Nathaniel Hawthorne, Edgar Allan Poe, and Nikolai Gogol, the idea seemed to be to blend elements of folktale, romance, and often the supernatural into a realistic fictional world to produce early short stories.

Frank O'Connor and others believe that Gogol's "The Overcoat" (1840) was the first clear example of the short story, and very few critics would disagree that this is a remarkable example of the early short story. "The Overcoat" exhibits many of the same characteristics found in both Poe's and Hawthorne's tales: a single character engaged in a "real" world, but generally, a somewhat unusual conflict and a plot that includes supernatural or dreamlike elements. Indeed, Gogol's protagonist, a poor copyist, is extraordinary because he is so unremarkable amid a bureaucratic world that threatens to swallow the human spirit. When he reluctantly faces the exigency of buying a new coat that he can ill afford, his life seems to change for the better—but only for a short time, until the coat is stolen. In his desperate attempt to get back his coat, the copyist is killed, but in the end, he becomes a mythical figure, a ghost, who seems to haunt the city in his quest to recover his overcoat.

In America, the combining of the mythical, romantic story with a realistic world begins with Irving, but in the hands of Hawthorne and Poe, the narratives achieve a precise, tight construction. When Irving's Rip Van Winkle falls asleep for twenty years, long descriptions of the countryside reflect a general atmosphere of languor and dreaminess. Such things also happen in Poe's and Hawthorne's stories, but with a degree of compression and focus that evokes not simply a loose atmospheric effect, but suggests and reinforces characters' affective and psychic states as well. Descriptive details interlink into patterns of imagery and symbol on several levels at once so that the outer world is analogous to an inner world. Compression and unity are the result of patterns of detail meshing closely with plot and characterization toward a concerted impact—and this, for Poe, is the hallmark of the well-written tale.

In fact, Poe's review of Hawthorne's *Twice-Told Tales* in 1842 stresses the focus and unity of the well-made tale, and his remarks have been taken by many as one of the earliest attempts to formulate a short-story theory. Poe is quite explicit in stating the requirements of an artful story: incidents in the story should contribute to a single effect, and "in the whole composition there should be no word written, of which the tendency, direct or indirect, is not to the one pre-established design" (48). Thus every element, even every word, functions toward a particular effect. But Poe's point here goes beyond unity—a quality that aestheticians insist must inhere in any work of art—to emphasize the importance of detail in influencing by direct or indirect means the total work. Further, in order to derive the fullest satisfaction from such a story, the reader should contemplate it with a "kindred art," attentive to all levels of suggestion in each word and detail. As Mary Rohrberger points out in *Story to Anti-Story*, far too little attention has been paid to Poe's assertion that "beneath the surface of the stories, 'a strong undercurrent of suggestion runs continuously' " (2).

Of course, none of Poe's notions about the tale would have surprised Hawthorne, whose work exemplified (though not always) what Poe believed made a story work. Hawthorne was also aware of his tendency toward "allegory," as he playfully suggests in the remarks preceding "Rappaccini's Daughter." But while Hawthorne (like Poe) often incorporated mythic elements of older forms (romance and folktale), his stories do not resolve into simple allegories, but rather seem to hover between the "real world" and the mythical, so that concrete details resonate in the half-light between symbolism and allegory. As Rohrberger explains, "*Every thing in a short story tends to stand for something else, and* because it does meanings can multiply even though *the story is usually limited to a single major character involved in a single action*" (*Story to Anti-Story* 3; emphasis added). Hawthorne explores psychological reality through symbolic details making up the surface of his stories. Setting and plot form patterns that mirror inner struggles of which the characters are often not consciously aware. To come to grips with Hawthorne's stories, to understand, for instance, why young Goodman Brown in the story of the same name appears to resist the evil of the black mass in the forest and yet lives and dies a miserable man, we must read, as Poe suggested, with a "kindred art."

While by the 1840s both Poe and Gogol had written stories that critics today recognize as early examples of the short-story genre, some of Hawthorne's tales and sketches of the 1830s demonstrate the focus and texture of true short stories. "Young Goodman Brown" (1835), "My Kinsman, Major Molineux" (1832), and "Roger Malvin's Burial" (1832) exemplify typical short-story unity—focused plot and narrative, tightly knit patterns of symbolic detail, brevity. Hawthorne's stories tend to retain a romantic cast, but as Rohrberger has shown, one of his earlier "sketches," "The Hollow of Three Hills," prefigures the twentieth-century type of short story that effects unity of impression through taut symbolic structure but relies much less on plot than the typical tale of this period.

For the most part, both Hawthorne's and Poe's stories adhere to the dramatic plot development associated with the well-crafted play. Setting, situation, and character are established through exposition; the plot then introduces complication; and the action rises toward a climax or crisis after which the action descends toward some sort of resolution. Besides this traditional plot structure, Poe's and Hawthorne's stories involved unusual protagonists in very unusual conflicts and situations. In Poe's "A Cask of Amontillado," the first-person protagonist succeeds in exacting a scheme of revenge by luring his enemy into his family's wine cellar/burial vault, then burying him alive by bricking him into a small chamber. In Hawthorne's stories, protagonists appear to meet the Devil ("Young Goodman Brown") or to search the world for the unpardonable sin ("Ethan Brand"). Often these plots, because they fuse the allegory and myth with realistic elements, raise questions about the difference between reality and illusion. As is typical of romantic literature in general, dream—or often, nightmare—and other suprarational forces seem to subvert rational experience of ordinary reality.

Perhaps we should also mention one other American short-fiction writer who came upon the scene a decade or so after Poe and Hawthorne. Herman Melville is often cited as an important influence upon the development of the short story because in "Bartleby the Scrivener" he moved the short story a little more toward realistic depiction of events and characters and away from the mythical, archetypal, or obsessed figures of Poe and Hawthorne. Thus the narrator in "Bartleby" exists in a realistic place and time, and his reactions appear to stem from a credible, everyday psychology—he appears as a "real" person. Critics like Ann Charters and Charles May point to this story as an example of the short story's movement away from what Charters (following Northrop Frye's definition) calls the "tale" toward a story in which the protagonist's characterization and conflict appear real (Charters 1602–3). Charles May, describing this step toward the "as-if-real" story, cites the narrator's "practical and prudent world of the law office," but also notes that Bartleby himself is "a metaphoric figure rather than a realistic one" (*The Short Story* 35). May maintains that in contrast to the realism of the novel, the short story has throughout its development maintained some affinity for the transcendent and mythic despite its movement toward realism.

Later in the nineteenth century, particularly after the Civil War, realism became a dominant mode in American literature, and its impact on the short story can be seen in the works of writers like Mark Twain, William Dean Howells, and Bret Harte, who placed their characters in mimetic fictional worlds where conflicts and complexities arise from the interactions with the external realm, especially social forces. Notable short-story writers in this period—Willa Cather, Kate Chopin, Stephen Crane, Henry James, and Edith Wharton—wrote stories of clear detail and finely crafted plot. Many of these stories involved objective narration and crisp irony derived chiefly from plot, but complex ironies also emerged from nuances in point of view or narrative stance. In Chopin and Wharton, narrative distance and ironic subtleties invite readers to judge characters while, at the same time, questioning the certainties of such judgments. In James's first-person stories, articulate narrators seem to be authorial surrogates, but often hold attitudes toward and reach conclusions that seem to be undercut by larger patterns of irony.

Eventually, the realistic, "well-made" story became formulaic as magazines bought up scores of plot-driven stories that turned on ever-simpler ironic twists. Around the turn of the twentieth century, the popular market, the taste for realism and ironic reversal, and a simplified theory of craft developed from Poe's famous dictum insisting upon focused effect led to a period of decline for the short story. Critics began to declaim the moribund state of the form: in 1917, Herbert Ellsworth Cory in the *Dial* bemoaned the increasingly self-conscious technique of the short story as the "mortal foe of originality" (qtd. in Rohrberger, *Story to Anti-Story* 5). It would require a new generation of writers rejecting the emphasis on plot of the late nineteenth century to revitalize the genre in the modern short story of the early twentieth century.

Before taking up this next stage in the development of the short story in English, perhaps we should pause to discuss briefly why the early period in the development of the short story is long on American and short on British writers. Various critics have offered explanations as to why the short story seemed to thrive in America but not in England. H. E. Bates points to the dominance of England's Victorian novel with its massively ornate verbiage and weighty moral underpinnings; others suggest the lucrative availability of the American magazine market as a stimulus to American writers to produce stories. But despite the fact that there were many more notable American short-story writers in the nineteenth century, we must mention two British writers who contributed to the form. While Robert Louis Stevenson is best remembered for his longer works, he also wrote some noteworthy short stories. Stevenson admired the work of Poe and Hawthorne, and Valerie Shaw suggests that, being part of a regional culture, Stevenson may have found in the American writers "support for his belief that fiction should constantly return to its primitive origins in fable and fireside entertainment" (32). In "A Lodging for the Night" (1882), Stevenson combines "shrewd selectivity" with "Poe-like grotesqueries" (Shaw 34). While Stevenson's short-story output was "uneven," Stevenson's ideas about fiction departed from the Victorian notions of the time; he asserted the primacy of the subject in fiction and believed that setting should be revealed not so much in exposition as in action. In short, Stevenson's ideas about fiction are more conducive to producing the economy and taut unity of the short story than the lavish prose of the Victorian-style novel; "A Lodging for the Night" was both a popular story and an influence on later British short fictionists.

The English short-story writer who most readily comes to mind as the bridge figure between the nineteenth and twentieth centuries is probably Joseph Conrad. A Pole by birth, Conrad spent time in the British merchant marine and became a proficient writer of English prose. In short works like "Youth," "Typhoon," "The Secret Sharer," and his short novel *Heart of Darkness*, Conrad demonstrated his ability to combine a realistic sense of setting and narrative with symbolic substructure through densely metaphoric prose. Characters' deeper conflicts are often externalized in realistically rendered landscapes and situations. Conrad also seemed to anticipate the thematic concerns of modernism; thus protagonists often find themselves vaguely uncertain, alone in psychological realities that question absolutes and idealistic nineteenth-century notions of progress.

One of the writers for whom Conrad had great admiration was France's Guy de Maupassant, one of the two brilliant short-story writers outside the United States and Britain who helped delineate the development of the form before the modernist period. Both Henry James and Kate Chopin, among others, expressed keen admiration for Maupassant's deft craftsmanship and objective narrative style. Some critics contend that his influence reached even to the works of Sherwood Anderson and Ernest Hemingway. But while Maupassant's intricately crafted plots, finely etched realistic detail, and deft sense of irony endeared him as an excellent story writer, it was Russia's Anton Chekhov who is most often cited as the harbinger of a new era in the short story.

The reasons Chekhov is so much associated with the protomodernist short story stem from his narrative tendency to let tonal qualities supersede any emphasis on action. In this particular, he differentiates himself clearly from the lesser followers of Maupassant—the hordes of writers selling formulaic plot stories to popular magazines. Chekhov's short stories are vibrant with what an anonymous reviewer in 1903 called "impressionism" (May, *The Short Story* 51). Plots are less definitive, and while surface details are less distinct, they are far more suggestive. For example, in "The Lady with the Pet Dog" (1899), the narrator's lyrical narrative voice describes the sea both as bespeaking "the eternal sleep awaiting us" and yet also hinting "a pledge of our eternal salvation" to suggest the primal uncertainty and promise in the love affair developing between his characters as they stand alone listening to the rumble of the waves. Patterns of association weave themselves into affective nuances, and descriptive images move toward symbolism. Plot conflicts and irony yield to ambiguities and tensions between emotional and cognitive states.

Chekhov and Maupassant have been seen by theorists as representing two distinct impulses in the development of short fiction. Maupassant has been seen as the "realist" (distinctive plot and crisp irony), while Chekhov has been thought of as the "impressionist" (lyrical tone, subtle image patterns). But perhaps we should not be too quick to conclude that these two tendencies began only in the latter half of the nineteenth century. In fact, just as Hawthorne prefigured the less plot-driven structure of the modernist story in some of his sketches, so did Poe show us the contrast between the plot-irony story and the image-symbol story. "A Cask of Amontillado," with its narrator obsessed with executing revenge, is noted for its plot and its complex ironies. On the other hand, "The Fall of the House of Usher" is often seen as a richly symbolic story in which tone and imagery produce a surreal texture depicting the narrator's psychic state while the plot shows the collapse of a possibly incestuous aristocratic family. Both these stories are perennially anthologized and show the short-story craft at its best. However, the two narrative strains of Maupassant and Chekhov point to a divergence of much larger scope, and the movement toward Chekhovian modes of expression reflected not simply a change in taste so much as a conscious effort by several writers to breathe new life into a genre that after the turn of the twentieth century began to seem rigidly formulaic. The popular short story had become predictable and simplistic, relying on one-dimensional twists of plot. Chekhov's use of tone and suggestion recalled the genre's romantic beginnings, but also marked not so much a return to the past as the opening of a door to changes in technique and structure that would accommodate innovation as well as the subjective uncertainties and anxiety of the modern experience.

Just after the turn of the twentieth century, three writers all working in English but separated by nationality began to produce stories considered quintessentially modern. Sherwood Anderson of the United States, James Joyce of Ireland, and Katherine Mansfield of New Zealand all wrote short stories considered to be among the best ever written in English. Because of Chekhov's earlier work and immense stature, many critics assume that he directly influenced all modernists after him. However, as suggested before, perhaps it is better to think of "influence" in some cases as a wider, less direct (and much more complex) force that permeates rather than moves in straight lines. While all three—Anderson, Joyce, and Mansfield—admired Chekhov's work, evidence suggests that both Joyce and Mansfield were writing stories indicative of their development as modernist writers before they read Chekhov. In any event, Anderson, Joyce, and Mansfield were engaged in a creative reaction against the formulaic short story. Mansfield disdainfully spoke of plotty stories, and Anderson clamored for form, not plot in the short story.

Typically, these writers produced new stories that eschewed the outworn emphasis on plot; they dispensed with the older structure of exposition, complication, climax, and resolution. Instead, they favored beginning their stories in the "middle," in medias res, and building intensity not through overt action, but by accumulating force of imagery to suggest the inner tensions of protagonists. In Joyce's and Mansfield's stories, realistic surfaces fuse details into webs of association from which meaning emerges. Rather than a traditional climax, these "new" stories end abruptly in a moment charged with impact, a convergence of rhetorical force that fuses cognition and affect in symbolic resonance. Sometimes the concluding passages coincide with a character's sudden realization or intuitive insight. We call this type of closure an "epiphany," the term Joyce used to describe bits of ordinary experience that seemed especially revealing. In this sense, the word *epiphany* retains some sense of its religious meaning of "revelation" or "showing through." Sometimes stories end with characters only on the verge of insight or in an emotional state that they themselves do not fully understand. We still call these moments epiphanies even though the realization may take place more in the mind of the reader than in that of the protagonist. Given this new emphasis on suggestion and density, this period in the development of the short story obviously demanded that readers participate in special ways in the construction of meaning; more than ever, the short story asked to be read as Poe had suggested, "with a kindred art."

Despite the new story's movement away from realism to lyricism and suggestion, the modern short story retained certain realistic aspects. For one thing, modern stories tend to draw on our putative sense of everyday reality rather than the uncanny or extraordinary. Instead of stories like "Young Goodman Brown," wherein the protagonist, either in a dream or in actuality, meets the Devil and attends a black mass, we get stories like Katherine Mansfield's "The Fly," in which the plot revolves around unextraordinary events: a man is visited at his office by an old friend and then, while he is alone at his desk, drowns a fly in ink. Of course, this simple summary does little or nothing toward giving a sense of what "The Fly" might be about. This is a crucial point about many modernist short stories: because they work through suggestion at several levels, key conflicts may be discernible only by examining how elements other than plot fit together. In the case of "The Fly," a somewhat more detailed synopsis will reveal how the possible conflicts may be signified through several aspects of the story.

"The Fly" begins in medias res with the protagonist (who is called only "the boss") and his friend, Woodifield, already in conversation in the office. The boss is a man so caught up in his work identity that his pride in his newly refurbished office suggests that "office" has displaced "home." When old Woodifield (who has recently had a stroke) turns the conversation to Belgium, where both men's sons, victims of World War I, are buried, we find that the boss has never visited his son's grave. Once his visitor leaves, the boss gives orders not to be disturbed because he wishes to grieve—as he had many times in the past—for his son, who has been dead now for several years. But the boss is surprised to find that he cannot cry. When his attention is diverted to a fly struggling in his inkwell, he removes it to safety, but then becomes fascinated by the fly's resilience to adversity. As the boss continues to challenge the fly by dropping ink on it, the fly persistently strives to clean itself, but finally it dies, immobilized in a sticky mass of ink. The story ends with an epiphany when the boss, seized "by such a grinding feeling of wretchedness" that he is "positively frightened," discards the fly and calls his secretary for fresh blotting paper. After his blotting paper is delivered, the boss sits alone again, but cannot now remember what he had been thinking. The last line of the story reads, "For the life of him he could not remember" (348).

One problem for the reader of "The Fly" is to come to terms with the last sentence in connection with the boss's intense feelings of wretchedness only a few minutes before. Perhaps the reader may notice the rhetorical focus—and possible ambiguity or irony—of the last line, "For the life of him he could not remember." The echo of the familiar expression "for the life of me" fits the perfectly quotidian situation the boss is left in, but because it is rendered "for the life of him" through the distance of third-person narration, the reader may think about the boss's life—particularly the fact that his life had been defined solely in terms of the son before his death. In recalling other details, such as the fact that the boss has never visited his son's grave, and that he always pictures the boy's body perfectly preserved as if asleep, the reader may begin to sense that the story foregrounds questions about life and death. In other words, the perceptive reader is compelled to review other details whose significance intensifies in light of the story's ending. We might, for example, connect the two deaths, that of the son and that of the fly; but we may also note that as a central symbol, the fly may refer to other characters in the story as well, including the boss, his friend Woodifield, and even the boss's secretary. In a sense, all of these characters are struggling to survive against certain limitations of life. The web of associations that emanate from the fly is highly suggestive and, at the same time, ambiguous. The fly may suggest transcendence (it can fly) and also tenacity and courage (even the boss cheers its struggle to survive); its prosaic insignificance may also imply the meaninglessness of its life and death.

Many critics have offered different readings of "The Fly." We need not present a detailed analysis here; the central issue is that a sense of knowing what the story is about requires some series of interpretive moves on the part of the reader. Without this active cognitive participation, the reader may still experience an affective response, because as a modern short story, "The Fly" works at this level also. But without bringing some integration of cognitive and affective aspects to the level of understanding, the reader may well be left in the same sort of puzzled state as the protagonist himself, who experiences powerful but vague feelings one minute, but forgets or represses his responses the next.

Some have suggested that the modernist period with its questions of identity—the growing sense of isolation of the self, both from modern society and the natural world—was especially conducive to the production of excellent short stories. Others suggest that the reception of the short story during this era was enhanced by the emergence of New Criticism and its insistence upon looking closely at single texts. We might add that this critical approach emphasized methods of reading that fit extremely well with the aesthetic strategies of the writers themselves. Discussing *Understanding Fiction* (1943), a classic textbook by New Critics Robert Penn Warren and Cleanth Brooks, Lohafer notes that the formalist features of "compression, economy, irony, and tension . . . just happen to be the definitive characteristics of the literary short story" (Lohafer and Clarey 5). Nevertheless, as most critics freely admit, some of the most valuable and explicit statements of short-story theory can still be found in the comments of short-story writers themselves—practitioners whose concerns are generally aesthetic, not analytical. In 1961, Flannery O'Connor underscored the importance of compression by asserting that the short-story writer's problem is "how to make the concrete work double for him. . . . [Therefore], certain of the details will tend to accumulate meaning" and "become symbolic in the way they work" (1546). In statements like this, short-story writers not only suggest what the shortness of the form necessitates—selection rather than inclusion—but also the importance of this process in yielding the "impressionistic" (and subjective) texture of the short story necessary to a compelling and "realistic" portrayal of modern experience. Often, this portrayal of experience with its questions of identity and its existential uncertainties—both ontological and experiential—begins to seem disconnected. It is no wonder then that many critics comment on the "fragmentation" of experience in the modern short story that "arises precisely out of a sense that life can only be rendered in fragments and compressed subjective episodes which stimulate instead of drugging the mind" (Shaw 43).

Despite this sense of fragmentation, many modernist writers derived a powerful sense of continuity from the artistic impulse itself, that is, aesthetic coherence and unity provided a source of wholeness. Within less than a decade, Mansfield, Joyce, and Anderson had all published collections of stories that are interrelated in such a way that the individual stories accumulate additional force in resonance with each other. While a few such collections had appeared before, notably Sarah Orne Jewett's *The Country of the Pointed Firs* (1896), the early years of the twentieth century saw several of these unified collections, including Mansfield's *In a German Pension* (1911), Joyce's *Dubliners* (1916), and Sherwood Anderson's *Winesburg, Ohio* (1919); later, both Ernest Hemingway (*In Our Time*) and William Faulkner (*Go Down, Moses*) would add to the list. Not really novels and more than mere story collections, these volumes are what most critics now call short-story *cycles*. Robert Luscher prefers the term *sequences* because it emphasizes how the "reader successively realizes underlying patterns of coherence by continual modifications of his perceptions of pattern and theme" (148). Whatever we call such integrated collections, the cumulative effect of the whole is greater than the sum of the individual stories. The reader of such collections, Luscher says, combines the pleasures of experiencing "the patterned closure of individual stories and the discovery of larger unifying strategies that transcend the apparent gaps between stories" (151).

The stories in Sherwood Anderson's cycle *Winesburg, Ohio* focus on the individual members of a small midwestern town around the turn of the twentieth century. Each of these characters is unique—and "grotesque," as the narrator tells us—because each is a separate being, an experiential sensibility interacting with other members of the community. They share certain aspects of small-town life but also individually retain the "aloneness" of their individual and private psychological realities. For example, "Hands" is the story of Wing Biddlebaum, a character known and liked by Winesburg residents, but as the story unfolds, we find that Wing's residence here is essentially an exile from the original

Pennsylvania town where he was a schoolteacher. Mistaking Wing's idealistic love of his young male students as sexual advances, the inhabitants of his hometown drove him away to assume a new but estranged life in Winesburg, where Wing lives on the edge of town—and the margins of society. Throughout the story, Anderson's image patterns subtly intertwine suggestions of flight and transcendence with religious motifs linking Wing to Christ and even the Holy Spirit. Ironically, he is nicknamed "Wing" because his hands are never still; they flutter like wings. While this ties in with the notion of transcendence, it also reminds us of why Wing is driven into his present state of alienation: because these same hands had expressed transcendent love through gentle but misunderstood caresses. Moreover, despite his marginal acceptance within this small community, almost no one knows the pain of Wing's past or the loneliness of his present. For each character in Winesburg, limited private experience becomes forceful reality embedded in repeated patterns that participate in a larger sense of unity from story to story.

Much has been written about the "encoded" (or even esoteric) nature of modernist literature. While some of these arguments offer valuable new perspectives on modernism as an intellectual movement, they sometimes understate the individual visions of the writers and their relation to modernist aesthetics in embodying those visions. Today, almost every student of literature can identify the common themes of modernism—fragmentation, alienation, and the anxiety of living in an increasingly mechanized, denatured world. But we should remember that these helpful generalizations simplify creative works that were, both to readers and to the writers themselves, unique artistic responses. While it is true that modernist short stories tend to be complex, they are not always more complex than the stories of Hawthorne and Poe. Rather, they are complex in different ways. A comparison of representative stories from both periods indicates similarities as well as differences.

Exemplary stories of both periods show a concern with characters' subjective worlds and inner struggles, and to some extent, the fictive world reflects these. As we have seen, Poe's "Fall of the House of Usher" incorporates gothic elements and surreal imagery to suggest the narrator's unwitting psychic association with other characters, and his tortured inner struggle is mirrored in the external details of setting and plot, moving the entire story toward the level of nightmare. Hawthorne's "My Kinsman, Major Molineux" and "Young Goodman Brown" also rely upon a dreamlike quality that, consistent with the romantic impulse of the period, often includes intimations of the supernatural. Traditional or "public" symbols of innocence, authority, ritual, and good and evil invest the dream texture with cultural—or often, as some suggest, archetypal—underpinnings. Nevertheless, Poe and Hawthorne retain their distinctive individualities as story writers.

Modern short stories sometimes incorporate traditional symbols, but they often derive their significance just as much through the context of the story as through tradition. Thus in Joyce's "Araby," religious imagery (priests, halation, and figures of speech suggesting prayer) becomes skewed, almost darkly ironic, as we find that the young protagonist actually elevates his profane sexual stirrings to the level of the sacred. In a parallel but contrasting way, in Mansfield's "The Wind Blows," a lyrical narrative voice associates the wind with the unseen and disruptive power of Matilda's awakening sexuality. The instability of the outer world signifies the disturbing emotional changes threatening the security of Matilda's childhood serenity. As in earlier short fiction, settings, plots, and characters may all take on symbolic significance in focusing meaning. But in the modernist story, human identity is grounded in experiences of the world that appear less projective and more impressionistic. Sensory details are selected and emphasized through processes psychological and secular. Although Mansfield, Joyce, Anderson, and later, Ernest Hemingway, William Faulkner, Eudora Welty, Katherine Anne Porter, and James Baldwin share certain approaches to the craft, each of these writers responded to experience and cultural context with his or her distinctive vision.

As noted earlier, the most noticeable difference between the later and earlier short story is in the function and structure of plot. Dispensing with the exposition and resolution stages of dramatic development, modernist stories focus experience in a much flatter plot trajectory. Stories begin in the middle of things, show little rising action, and then end with epiphany rather than climax; falling action is usually minimal or nonexistent, so that resolution is left either implied or "open," in the sense that the story closure focuses on an intensity left suspended by the text. Another difference between the modernist story and previous ones arises from the treatment of time, which in the later stories is often psychological rather than chronological. The technique of "stream of consciousness" can shift narratives back and forth in time, and single moments of experience may expand to become almost spatial configurations of image patterns mapping a character's psychic reality that is paradoxically disconnected from the external world.

While critics still often point to modernist stories as quintessential examples of the short-story form, by the 1960s, the short story (like other genres) was undergoing another stage of change. Some suggest that the modernist method, like the irony-realism of previous expressions, was becoming formulaic; others suggest that the new developments of the 1960s really represent just an extension of modernism, perhaps in the same way that second-generation Romantics Keats and Shelley were in many ways quite different from their forebears, Wordsworth and Coleridge, but nonetheless still "Romantics." Richard Kastelanetz notices lesser, more subtle changes within what we are calling the modernist period. He claims that some post–World War II writers like Flannery O'Connor and Carson McCullers moved a little back toward plot and irony; during the 1960s, then, short fictionists returned to modernist impulses in very extreme ways—inscribing nihilism and suggesting that "there is a gaping pit in life." Kastelanetz further stresses the continuity of modernist and postmodernist aesthetics when he says, "Open form, as many critics have noted, is characteristic of an age that feels it does not have a strong hold on experience" (224).

Whether or not the postmodern impulse arises from modernism or represents a clean break from the past is under debate. What seems not to be in question is that the metafictional stories of the 1960s are distinctly different from what came before. Modernist stories had often developed single moments or experiences into layers of meaning that expanded almost spatially; symbols derived much of their force from context. In postmodern short stories, symbols become even less determinate and often turn in upon themselves. The fictive world itself loses much of the texture of representing a "realistic" world—the story world is sometimes like a hall of mirrors in which distortion is relative and infinite regresses are normal. The "new" story, then, startlingly foregrounds epistemological problems and uncertainties. As Mary Rohrberger explains it in *Story to Anti-Story*, "Contemporary writers find no guarantee as to the authenticity of the real world" (7). Postmodern fictionists often see the perceived world (or "reality") itself as a fiction, a construction, and so narratives call attention to themselves as artifice "in an attempt to make authentic the act of knowing" (Rohrberger, *Story to Anti-Story* 7).

Besides the self-parodying mode of metafiction, some contemporary fictionists construct fictive worlds of fantasy in which narrative retains some of the texture of realism. "Magic realism" is generally associated with South American writers like Gabriel García Márquez or Isabel Allende, and some critics see a strong cultural influence. But in a larger sense, much contemporary fiction, both North and South American, posits "reality" as absurdly antithetical to ordinary rationalist frames or common sense about the extensional world. Valerie Shaw suggests that in attempting to chart a modern reality that is "essentially alien and baffling," the short-story writer faces the " 'irreality' of modern existence by positing alternative worlds—realms of order which perhaps exist only in fantasy, but which nonetheless express defiance of the way actual life squanders ideals" (229). While this may to some degree be true, the magic realism of Latin America also offers visions quickened by numinous mysteries that have long been a part of folk tradition and culture, even amid the advent of technology and rationalism. Early postmodern fictionists, like their very important precursor, Franz Kafka of Prague, began to produce stories in which alternative realities merged with traditional reality so completely that experience became indistinguishable from dream or nightmare. Unlike protagonists in the romantic dreamworlds of Poe and Hawthorne, protagonists in Kafka's existential nightmares do not awaken because "there is nothing for them to wake to" (Rohrberger, *Story to Anti-Story* 9). Plots become distorted or seemingly nonexistent; symbol and metaphor become involuted in self-reflexive parody. The story world so completely deconstructs ordinary experience that reality reveals itself to be nothing more than a regress of arranged but shifting representations or images constructing a world in which oasis is never distinguishable from mirage.

Metafiction is a narrative realm of extreme self-consciousness where boundaries blur between truth/illusion and fiction/reality. The modernist angst—the alienation of experience between inner and outer realities—is displaced by questions like, What can we call real? Is identity in any sense real? Writers like Vladimir Nabokov, John Barth, Robert Coover, and Donald Barthelme explore these questions in fictions that have been called "anti-stories." In Barthelme's stories, experience is fragmented into collage or a mosaic of reality, the pieces often incorporating the stuff of popular culture and media with myth so that all constructions of reality interpenetrate. As Jerome Klinkowitz notes later in this volume, Barthelme drew on "the detritus of a textually motivated society" to reveal that "reality itself is a manufactured apprehension."

Very often in these stories that subvert rationalist conceptions of the extensional world, conflicts of plot or antiplot are paralleled or overinscribed by seeming conflicts between narrator and the narrative itself. In Nabokov's "The Leonardo," the narrator opens the story by adverting directly to the artifice of the fictive world, where "[t]he objects which are being summoned assemble" (Rohrberger, *Story to Anti-Story* 589). The narrator, then, commands the coming into existence of the world by asserting a creative act of language. But as the story unfolds, we often find the voice of the narrator blending with the voice of the protagonist; eventually the narrative and its protagonist seem to get beyond the control and knowledge of the narrator. Romantowski appears to be a struggling scholar, a romantic figure—as his name suggests—tragically at odds with the weighty materialism of his antagonists and their totalitarian culture. In the end, however, Romantowski, after being stalked and murdered by his tormentors, turns out to be a counterfeiter who has fooled both his enemies and the narrator himself; in the absence of aesthetic order, beauty and harmony vanish, the fictive world dismantles itself, and whatever is left "irks" the narrator in its "variegated void" (596). To the extent that we as readers align ourselves with the narrator—who has seduced us just as much as the counterfeiter Romantowski has himself seduced us, his enemies, and the narrator—we also share in the central conflict, a larger struggle to give fiction and reality shape and meaning.

Other postmodern stories foreground the fictionality of "the real" by merging fictive world with objective reality or by blending both these with fantasy and the media images of popular culture. In the title story of John Barth's *Lost in the Funhouse*, the protagonist (thirteen-year-old Ambrose) seems to be a younger version of the narrator, who in turn seems an obvious extension of the author. The self-referential narrator in "Lost in the Fun house" clearly accomplishes nothing by following the rules of convention: "The more closely an author identifies with the narrator, literally or metaphorically, the less advisable it is, as a rule, to use the first-person narrative viewpoint" (109). The author narrates in third person, but ironically, character, narrator, and author are conflated to the point that these putatively discrete identities collapse through the boundaries that would separate them. Moreover, the "funhouse," which appears as a symbol of Ambrose's labyrinthine adolescence, may also be seen to stand for the outer reality (experience of the extensional world) and so life itself; but just as fundamentally, the funhouse is also the narrative itself—the world of story. In a somewhat different approach, Robert Coover's "The Babysitter" uses brief mosaiclike passages to conflate fragmented perspectives on a single incident—a teenage girl is babysitting and watching television—until narratives of "reality" merge with characters' fantasies and the images of the television screen. Finally, these versions cannot be separated or schematized; they simply blend into the fiction itself, another representation, just as valid as any other.

Metafiction, magic realism, and other postmodern styles are noticeable "breakaways" in recent short fiction, but other, perhaps subtler tendencies also exist. Besides the fractured experiences, the parodies of fantasy and myth, and the surreal fabulations we have mentioned, more and more critics are discussing the so-called minimalism of writers like Raymond Carver, Ann Beattie, and Bobbie Ann Mason. There is considerable divergence of opinion as to whether "minimalism" is really a movement, or a trend, or simply a tendency of what we might call "style" growing out of the late stages of modernism. In any case, some writers (Carver, for one) have objected to being labeled "minimalists" even though not all critics intend the term to be pejorative. While the exact meaning of "minimalism" seems to vary from critic to critic, general characteristics can be loosely noted. "Minimalist" stories tend to be highly selective of detail; sometimes the narrative seems stripped bare, relying on simple, straightforward prose uncluttered by figurative language. One of the difficulties in getting a clear fix on minimalism is that critics disagree as to whether or not its techniques are simply an extension of the Chekhovian trend that started early in the twentieth century. Ernest Hemingway is sometimes cited as a "protominimalist" whose "iceberg theory" (the greatest mass of an iceberg remains out of view) illustrates his commitment to leaving as much out of a story as possible, so that the participatory reader must fill in the gaps. Chekhov also believed it better to err on the side of selectivity rather than inclusion. Charles May, who sees minimalism as a late extension of modernism, also sees Hemingway (and his Russian precursor Isaac Babel) as a legacy of Chekhov and Turgenev (*The Short Story* 18). On the other hand, Ann Charters thinks that Hemingway, like other Americans of the time, was influenced by Maupassant as well as Chekhov (1640). In any case, minimalism is generally regarded as having the texture of realism; while it may retain certain mythic features, both symbolic resonance and affective qualities are often flattened or minimized.

Despite the fact that many successful short-story writers have been called "minimalists," some critics and even some short-story writers suggest that in its extreme form, the minimalist impulse may lead to sterility, especially as fiction workshops in many universities tend to encourage stylistic traits. One of the more noticeable differences between many minimalist stories and earlier modernist stories is that in the earlier mode, the compression of rhetorical and affective force was accomplished in metaphors and symbols that derived from larger cultural contexts skewed into focus by the context of the story itself. As has already been indicated, Joyce's "Araby" relies upon religious imagery to foreground the very difficult conflict of a young boy's confusion of adolescent feelings with sacred adoration. The chief issue for the critics of minimalism is that the so-called minimalist story selects its sparse details—which often do become referents of a sort—from the ever-changing details of contemporary life, especially popular culture: television, fast-food franchises, department-store chains, and shopping malls. According to these critics, the illusion of "realism" in minimalism lies in the fact that it encodes, in a simplistic way, details understood only by a select group of readers, for whom the fact that a protagonist wears polyester suits and shops at K-Mart is characterization enough. This issue was addressed by writer Bharati Mukherjee at the Second International Conference on the Short Story in English (June 4, 1992). Mukherjee expressed her concern that people outside a certain time and culture are excluded by such stories; on the other hand, readers around the world enjoy Chekhov's stories even in translation because they more fully develop human feeling with suggestive details accessible to readers across cultures and generations.

Is minimalism a trend or a movement? Is it the last phase of modernism or just a name? Is it really inimical to the short story as a form? These are difficult questions that will have no easy answers. Certainly, some outstanding recent short-story writers—Raymond Carver, Bobbie Ann Mason, and Ann Beattie—have been called "minimalists" (whether they would agree or not). Another intriguing question is whether American minimalism represents a comment upon the culture at large—a new kind of intertextuality of television and popular culture displacing the once-familiar staples of American ethos. However our speculations run, we should remind ourselves that as long as skilled writers continue to evoke our interest and admiration through their craft and vision, we generally accept their methods as appropriate and valid.

Reading this brief sketch, one might suppose that contemporary short-story writers produce only two types of stories, "minimalist" or "postmodern." As any editor who selects and publishes short stories will tell you, nothing could be further from the truth. Today, short-story writers produce every imaginable type of story: minimalist, postmodern and experimental, traditional plot-irony, and lots of modernist epiphany stories. Many practitioners of the form seem to be combining two or more of these approaches into a synthesis of technique.

One of the exciting developments of the short story in English today is the emergence of many new ethnic American writers representing different cultures, infusing their craft with the experience and vision of otherness. In one sense, this may be a revivifying return to the source—to myth and folktale—as these writers incorporate (and sometimes reinscribe) folk stories from their cultures into their personal visions. Such writers include not only African Americans, where we had previously seen substantial representation, but also Asian Americans (for example, Maxine Hong Kingston, Amy Tan, and Gish Jen), Hispanics, Latinas, and Latinos (for example, Sandra Cisneros, Arturo Arias, and Rudolfo Anaya), and Native Americans (for example, Louise Erdrich, Leslie Marmon Silko, and Dianne Glancy). Immigrants from different countries have also made their appearance with stories written in English (for example, Bharati Mukherjee and Salman Rushdie). Since their appearance has been relatively recent, few scholars have engaged in serious study of their work in the short story.

An avenue for exploring history-in-the-making of the short story that both includes and challenges "postmodern" storytelling methods is that of following the path currently being blazed by so-called postcolonialist writers from the West Indies, New Zealand and Australia, India, the Philippines, and Polynesia. In their fiction, the historical quest is often renewed, as many of these literatures follow either a pattern of oral to written tale or else break with traditions altogether. Because this is a recent and evolving portion of the history of the short story, it is not surprising that no comprehensive history of it has been attempted, although comments have been made on the fictions of particular nations.

The editors of the present volume hope that by including a large section of writers from different cultures, we will have taken a step toward familiarizing readers with a group of writers not previously recognized. We also hope to shed new light on a selection of writers already well known to the contemporary reading public. Our aim is to pique the interest of students, as well as critics, in a genre that offers a wealth of theoretical possibilities not yet explored.

Finally, we should recall how Frank O'Connor's "The Lonely Voice" told us many years ago that the creative impetus for the short story often comes from submerged figures "wandering about the fringes of society" (87). Voice—a quality so ineffably a part of the short story—is often the affirmation, and sometimes the discovery, of identity itself.

WORKS CITED AND CONSULTED

Barth, John. *Lost in the Funhouse*. New York: Doubleday, 1968; New York: Anchor Books, 1998.

Bates, H. E. *The Modern Short Story: A Critical Survey*. New York: Nelson, 1941.

Canby, Henry Seidel. *A Study of the Short Story*. New York: Holt, 1913.

Charters, Ann, ed. *The Story and Its Writer: An Introduction to Short Fiction*. 4th ed. Boston: Bedford, 1995.

Kastelanetz, Richard. "Notes on the American Short Story Today." May, *Short Story Theories* 214–25.

Lawrence, James Cooper. "A Theory of the Short Story." May, *Short Story Theories* 60–71.

Lohafer, Susan, and Jo Ellyn Clarey, eds. *Short Story Theory at a Crossroads*. Baton Rouge: Louisiana State University Press, 1989.

Luscher, Robert M. "The Short Story Sequence: An Open Book." Lohafer and Clarey 148–67.

Mansfield, Katherine. "The Fly." *Stories*. New York: Alfred A. Knopf, 1956; New York: Vintage, 1991. 343–48.

May, Charles, ed. *Short Story Theories*. Athens: Ohio University Press, 1976.

———. *The Short Story: The Reality of Artifice*. New York: Twayne, 1995.

O'Connor, Flannery. "Writing Short Stories." Charters 1544–49.

O'Connor, Frank. "The Lonely Voice." May, *Short Story Theories* 83–93.

Poe, Edgar Allan. "Review of *Twice-Told Tales*." May, *Short Story Theories* 45–51.
Rohrberger, Mary. *Hawthorne and the Modern Short Story*. The Hague: Mouton, 1966.
————, ed. *Story to Anti-Story*. Boston: Houghton Mifflin, 1979.
Shaw, Valerie. *The Short Story: A Critical Introduction*. London: Longman, 1983.

CHINUA ACHEBE
(November 16, 1930–   )

Charles Dameron

BIOGRAPHY

Chinua Achebe was born in the village of Ogidi in eastern Nigeria in 1930 and was baptized Albert Chinualumogu Achebe. His father, who graduated from a teachers' college in 1904, was an early convert to Christianity and a lifelong Christian educator. He sent young Chinua to the local Church Missionary Society primary school. Yet Achebe himself notes that part of the village, including one of his father's brothers, was not Christian, and so "what was important to me then was that I was exposed to two different ways of seeing the world" (Samway 684). The interplay or tension between traditional Igbo culture and colonial culture would become a central concern for him in his writing. In 1948, he enrolled at University College, Ibadan, where he intended to pursue a career in medicine. He soon shifted to the program in arts, however, and was among the university's first graduates in 1953. (Wole Soyinka, the distinguished Nigerian man of letters, was an acquaintance and fellow undergraduate.)

Achebe began a career in radio broadcasting in 1954, working for the Nigerian Broadcasting Service until 1966. During this time, he launched his literary career with *Things Fall Apart* (1958), which soon became the classic novel of the African colonial experience. Following in quick succession were a second novel, *No Longer at Ease* (1960); a small collection of stories, *The Sacrificial Egg and Other Short Stories* (1962); two more novels, *Arrow of God* (1964) and *A Man of the People* (1966); and a children's book, *Chike and the River* (1966). On the eve of the Biafran War (Nigeria's civil war), Achebe resigned his broadcasting position. During the war, he worked for the Biafran government and then began teaching at the University of Nigeria at Nsukka. After the war, Achebe turned away from long fiction and published several volumes of poetry, several collections of essays, and a full collection of stories, *Girls at War and Other Stories* (1972). He also started a literary journal, *Okike: A Nigerian Jour-*

nal of New Writing, in 1971, which he edited for a number of years. He published his fifth novel, *Anthills of the Savannah*, in 1987, and since then he has published two collections of essays. In addition to his several teaching stints at the University of Nigeria at Nsukka, he has taught at a number of universities in the United States.

CRITICISM

Widely viewed today as one of Africa's finest writers, Achebe shot into prominence with his remarkable first novel, *Things Fall Apart*. In this work, he provides a powerful account of the colonial incursion into the region that would become Nigeria and portrays the irreversible consequences of this incursion on the region's traditional cultures. Over a span of five novels, he has moved through the colonial experience and into the postcolonial world of modern Nigeria, recording the cultural conflicts that have caused social values to become unstable and corruption to become all too common. Employing a realistic storytelling approach, Achebe has created memorable characters whose destinies are forged in the heat of cultural conflict, and the weaknesses in each cultural value system contribute to the tragedies that occur. Gerald Moore reflects the admiration that many critics have expressed for Achebe's style when he speaks of Achebe's "mastery of language . . . where he is on the whole felicitous in his introduction of Igbo words and proverbs into the flow of the text" (130).

While Achebe's novels represent his most enduring contribution to literature, he has been active in other genres, producing significant collections of essays, short stories, and poems, as well as several children's books. Many of his prize-winning poems express his painful reflections on the Biafran War, while his essays reflect his views on modern literature and on Nigerian culture. Bernth Lindfors points out that Achebe "believes that the African writer should be a teacher dedicated to explaining to his people how and why their world came to be the way it is today," and Lindfors sees his essays, novels, and children's stories as efforts to provide such instruction ("Chinua Achebe" 8).

In *The Sacrificial Egg, and Other Short Stories* (1962), a slim collection of five stories, Achebe included two stories from his student days and three written after his first two novels. In his introduction to the collection, M.J.C. Echeruo sees the earliest stories as containing important themes (conflict and failure, idealism and failure) that would be explored at greater length in Achebe's second novel, *No Longer at Ease*. Echeruo observes that in two of the more recent stories, Achebe creates modern fables that seem to "bridge the gulf between the innocence of Amos Tutuola and Ekwensi's sophistication" (6), references here to two other fine Nigerian storytellers.

All the stories in *The Sacrificial Egg* were included in the collection of thirteen stories published in 1972 as *Girls at War and Other Stories*. Writing in 1980, Gerald Moore pointed out that this collection "represents a thin harvest for two decades and indicates clearly enough that the short story has never been

Achebe's favorite medium" (140). That observation appears to be even more true now, twenty years later, since *Girls at War* continues to serve as his one full collection. Yet Moore asserted that three of the stories—"Girls at War," "Vengeful Creditor," and "Civil Peace"—"are of high interest" (140).

The most extensive analysis of Achebe's short stories can be found in F. Odun Balogun's critical study, *Tradition and Modernity in the African Short Story: An Introduction to a Literature in Search of Critics*. As Balogun's subtitle suggests, he argues that too little attention has been given to the African short story. After providing a general overview of the short story in Africa, Balogun identifies two stylistic trends, realistic and experimental, and then analyzes in depth the works of two writers who represent these trends and have created "the best examples of the African experience in this genre": Achebe (realistic) and Taban lo Liyong (experimental) (58). Echoing Moore's assessment of Achebe's style, Balogun asserts that "Achebe is the undisputed master of the realistic story conveyed through irony and a lucid, simple, proverbial language that at times reaches the height of poetry" (60). In two chapters, he examines closely each of the stories in the second edition of *Girls at War*. He then devotes a third chapter to the ironic implications of the story he considers Achebe's strongest, "The Madman," which he calls a prose-poem because of the story's poetic rhythms and compressed metaphorical qualities. While Achebe's principal creative energies have gone into his long fiction, his single full volume of stories contains a number of powerful, well-crafted stories that continue to be worthy of close critical attention.

ANALYSIS

Achebe's contributions to the short story are much the same as his contributions to the novel: stylistic innovations, such as his frequent use of traditional proverbs and his precise handling of pidgin English and school English, and thematic insights into traditional culture, the clash of cultures, and postindependence culture. When *Girls at War and Other Stories* was published in 1972, it contained thirteen pieces, including two short works that are clearly sketches rather than stories. Both "Polar Undergraduate" and "In a Village Church" were originally published in the Ibadan student magazine and display the undergraduate Achebe's clever wit, tinged with sarcasm. In the first, Achebe spoofs university students who claim to be so diligent in their studies that they get little sleep at night, yet they often snooze through their classes. In the latter, he chronicles the comic elements of one church service—the off-key singing, the snore-punctuated sermon—while slyly suggesting that nodding parishioners, like napping students in the library, may nevertheless absorb knowledge from the atmosphere itself. These sketches provide evidence of Achebe's precocious early talent but are out of place in a serious collection of stories. Wisely, Achebe removed these sketches and substituted a recent story in the collection's American edition (1973) and in Heinemann's second edition (1977).

In four of his stories, Achebe explores powerful myths and taboos of traditional Igbo culture. In two of these, "Uncle Ben's Choice" and "The Sacrificial Egg," Achebe blends the moralistic ending of the folktale with the realism of the traditional short story. "Uncle Ben's Choice" recounts an experience that occurred in 1919, when the narrator, at a much younger age, narrowly escaped from the inviting arms of Mami Wota, the Lady of the River Niger. According to legend, a man who succumbs to Mami Wota's spell will become wealthy, but he will never marry and father a family. Uncle Ben eluded Mami Wota, who went on later that same night to ensnare a white merchant. Proud of his family, Ben notes pointedly that the merchant accumulated wealth but never married. Thus social continuity is favored over an individual's material success.

In "The Sacrificial Egg," the siren of the river is evoked again, this time in describing some of the beautiful women who visit the popular market in Umuru on the River Niger. According to the mother of the protagonist's girlfriend, these women appear to be human, but they are "mammy-wota," or river spirits. The port marketplace has become too commercial, a spawning ground for superficial values. As a consequence, Kitikpa, an evil god who brings smallpox, visits the village to punish the people for their neglect of their traditional responsibilities. One evening, Julius, the young clerk who is the protagonist, accidentally steps on and crushes an egg left on the riverbank as a sacrificial offering to Kitikpa—an action that portends bad luck. Fatefully, or coincidentally, he discovers soon afterwards that his girlfriend and her mother have both contracted smallpox. In these stories, Achebe presents these traditional myths dramatically, without irony; they still play vital roles in a culture that believes in them.

In "Akueke," however, a traditional taboo is challenged and overcome, and Achebe lets the reader sort out the surprising conflicts at the end. Akueke, a young woman with six older brothers, attracts a flock of suitors after her sensational dancing at the first public performance of her age-grade. Her brothers, anxious to marry her off properly (they are responsible since their parents are both dead), become disturbed when Akueke refuses suitor after suitor. Consequently, the omniscient narrator tells us, "now her protective spirit despairing of her had taken a hand in the matter and she was stricken with this disease" (33), a swollen stomach. Medicine men are called in, but their ministrations are ineffective. The neighbors warn the brothers of the danger to the community of this abomination, especially if Akueke should die within the compound. The brothers do the appropriate thing, carting her off to the "bad bush" to die. When they return three days later and find her body missing, they assume that wild animals have dragged it off, and they continue with the necessary purification rites. Several months later, however, when they visit their aged grandfather in a distant village, they are shocked to encounter Akueke in his home. He tells them that Akueke has now become his daughter and is named Matefi, and "as for your purification rites you may carry on because Akueke is truly dead in Umuofia" (36). The grandfather's disgust for their actions is obvious, but technically he accommodates traditional belief by letting Akueke "die" and creating a new daughter, Matefi. Ultimately, of course, the young woman lives, apparently through her own efforts rather than those of the local medicine men (the reader is not told how she manages to reach her grandfather's village and become cured).

The failures of traditional ways emerge even more starkly in "The Madman," one of Achebe's finest stories. On his way to the Eke marketplace, a naked and genuinely mad wanderer steps off the broad black highway to find a drink of water and happens upon Nwibe, a man of high standing in his village, bathing in a stream. A remarkable and unintended switching of identities occurs. The madman, mistaking Nwibe for other men who have treated him abusively in the past, laughs at Nwibe and mocks him. Infuriated, Nwibe gives chase after the madman puts on Nwibe's loincloth. As Nwibe rushes naked onto the road toward the market, screaming at the escaping thief (who, now clothed, seems normal), he takes on the appearance of being mad himself. Several men from his village, who are on their way to the market, try in vain "to stop him setting foot irrevocably within the occult territory of the powers of the market" (10). After violating the taboo against nakedness in the market, Nwibe is caught and led back to his village, where a series of local medicine men try to cure him of his "madness." One pronounces him incurable because of the gravity of his action; a second treats him, unsuccessfully, while acknowledging cynically to himself that "if doctors were to send away every patient whose cure they were uncertain of, how many of them would eat one meal in a whole week from their practice?" (11). A third claims that he has cured Nwibe, and he "became overnight the most celebrated mad-doctor of his generation" (11). Poor Nwibe's humiliation, however, now prevents him from being accepted for initiation into the village's community of titled men, who treat him politely but remain wary of their unreliable neighbor. As a result of their rejection, Nwibe never becomes even "partially restored" (12) to his former self. Achebe thus creates another victim of the fraudulent healers and pompous elders who can be found in the traditional culture.

Three other stories illustrate the fruits of conflicts between cultures. "Marriage Is a Private Affair" explores the generational conflict over intertribal marriages, a conflict that also pits the mores of modern Lagos against the mores of interior villages. When Nnaemeka and his non-Igbo girlfriend, Nene, who live in Lagos, decide to marry, Nnaemeka learns that his father, back in his Igbo village, has already found an Igbo woman for him. But Nnaemeka marries Nene anyway, and his father refuses to see either of them for the first eight years of their marriage. When his daughter-in-law writes and tells her father-in-law that his two grandsons want to see him, however, he realizes that he will have to give in. Achebe wrote this story during his student days, and it likely captures tribal tensions that he observed in relationships between fellow students in Ibadan.

In "Chike's School Days," more sketch than story, Achebe presents a Christian family that is at odds with those in the village who follow the traditional ways. Chike, the young son, is brought up by his parents to refuse the "heathen" food of traditional Igbos, an action that goes against the community's shared sense of responsibility for the welfare of children. Yet Chike's family is subject to veiled ostracism because his Christianized father Amos married Sarah, an *Osu*, traditionally "a slave to one of the many gods of the clan." An *Osu* "could not marry a free-born, and he could not take any of the titles of his clan. When he died, he was buried by his kind in the Bad Bush" (38). When Amos had told his mother of his intention to marry Sarah, she had rushed to a diviner "of great power and wisdom" (39) who had performed his ritual incantations and then had pronounced a cure. Yet Amos had married Sarah as planned, despite the diviner's interventions. Achebe again exposes the failure of a traditional ritual, perhaps because the ritualist is either corrupt or incompetent, or perhaps because the power of the ritual has diminished as members of the tribe have shifted allegiance to a new system of Christian rituals. The story concludes with an account of some of Chike's experiences at primary school, "tackl[ing] the mysteries of the white man's learning" (40). Chike loves stories and songs and hates arithmetic. The enormous possibilities of strange words fire Chike's imagination, as the concluding sentences of the story confirm: "The first sentences in his *New Method Reader* were simple enough and yet they filled him with a vague exaltation: 'Once there was a wizard. He lived in Africa. He went to China to get a lamp.' Chike read it over and over again at home and then made a song of it. It was a meaningless song. 'Periwinkles' got into it, and also 'Damascus.' But it was like a window through which he saw in the distance a strange, magical new world. And he was happy" (42). This passage contains the potential for a conflict that Chike may well experience when he becomes mature: the tension between his fondness for the English language and his dismay at the distortions of African culture that outsiders have created while using the English language. Certainly Achebe has himself lived with this tension, crafting award-winning fiction and poetry in English while judging Joyce Cary's *Mister Johnson* an "appalling" novel about Africa and Joseph Conrad's *Heart of Darkness* a work of "racist slander" (*Hopes and Impediments* 58, 20–21). In this story, however, we see the young boy absorbed in the dreamy happiness of his linguistic innocence.

In "Dead Men's Path," the best of Achebe's undergraduate stories, he examines another instance of the collision between traditional ways and Christian ways. Michael Obi, an enthusiastic young Christian Nigerian, is appointed headmaster of Ndume Central School in 1949 and is charged by the Mission with making the school more progressive. He quickly establishes two goals: increase the quality of teaching and make the school's grounds more attractive. While he is beautifying the compound, he soon discovers that local villagers occasionally use a footpath from the village to the adjacent bush, and this footpath now interferes with his newly planted flowers and hedge. Obi learns that the footpath leads to the traditional burying ground; the local priest tells Obi that "the whole life of this village depends on [the path]. Our dead relatives depart by it and our ancestors visit us by it. But most important, it is the path of children coming in to be born" (*Girls at War* 73). Obi, who has had heavy sticks planted across the path and has secured them with barbed wire, tells the priest that "the whole purpose of our school . . . is to eradicate just such beliefs as that" (73). The priest, unwilling to reroute the path around the school, insists that the path be reopened so that both beliefs can coexist, and offers this proverb: "Let the hawk perch and let the eagle perch" (74). Obi stubbornly refuses to budge, and when a young village woman dies during childbirth two days later, a local diviner calls for "heavy sacrifices to propitiate ancestors insulted by the fence" (74). The next morning, Obi finds that the hedges have been uprooted all along the perimeter, the flowers have been destroyed, and one school building has been torn down. A visiting white supervisor reports to his superiors that a "tribal-war situation" exists and blames the overzealous headmaster. Though he overstates the situation, the supervisor nevertheless correctly recognizes a standoff that could have been avoided with some compromising on both sides. Neither position, Achebe implies, is blameless.

In the five other stories in the collection, Achebe examines the Nigerian world at the point of independence and thereafter and finds that its values are being compromised by widespread corruption. In "The Voter," democratic governance has resulted in the people of Umuofia electing Marcus Ibe, "a not too successful mission school teacher" (14), as their representative in the capital. After five years, Ibe has acquired two luxury cars and has built the largest house in the area, which he had the Archbishop bless upon its completion. During his re-election campaign, his workers compete with his opponent's campaign workers to buy the influence and votes of the village elders through none-too-subtle negotiations. One of Ibe's lieutenants, the bright young Rufus Okeke, is the protagonist of the story. His opponent's people manage to induce him to promise to vote for their man, Maduka, by offering a substantial bribe; Okeke knows that the opponent will not have nearly enough votes to win, so he believes that he will do no harm by putting his vote in the other man's box. They also pull out "a clay pot with feathers stuck into it" (18), an *iyi* from Mbanta that will ominously take note if Okeke fails to vote for Maduka. On election day, however, Okeke suffers a crisis of conscience in the voting booth: How can he betray his boss? Yet how can he double-cross the *iyi*? He solves his dilemma by tearing his paper vote in two, verbally asserting that he is voting for Maduka, and then putting one half in each box. He then leaves the voting booth "as jauntily as he had gone in" (21). Yet, as Achebe demonstrates, Okeke's corruption is really no worse than that of the very representatives of the community's institutions of moral leadership: Minister Ibe, the Archbishop, the village elders.

Achebe depicts the corruption of the new class of civil servants, who have become the privileged elite, in several other stories. "Vengeful Creditor," based on the short-lived experiment with free primary education in Nigeria that lasted from 1957 to 1958 (Munro 85), contrasts the arrogance of the elite against the plucky determination of a village widow and her daughter. Mr. and Mrs. Emenike, obviously representatives here of the privileged elite, focus no farther than their pampered comfort extends; Mrs. Emenike, the narrator tells us, "hated the words 'free primary' which had suddenly become part of everyday language, especially in the villages where they called it 'free primadu' " (56). At their leisure, she and her husband rail against the stupidity of the policy, which is finally suspended three months after its inception. When the Emenikes, who have lost a series of servants to free education, seek out and employ ten-year-old Vero to look after their year-old child, Vero's mother, Martha, is thrilled at the prospect of additional income, though she is disappointed that her daughter will have to drop out of school now that a fee is required. Vero, who has loved attending school, mistakenly understands that she will be able to return to school when the baby is a bit older. After some months, however, when it is clear that she will not be going to school anytime soon, she takes revenge by making the baby drink red ink. Mrs. Emenike beats her and then has her husband drive her home. The story ends with a confrontation scene between an outraged Martha and the Emenikes; but when Martha realizes what her daughter did to the baby, she grabs Vero and takes her home in deep anger. Clearly Vero's actions were wrong, but Achebe shows how economic desperation merges with class arrogance to create the constricting circumstances that Vero feels driven to rebel against.

"Girls at War," the title story and one of the best in the collection, characterizes the corruption of the civil-servant class during the Biafran War. Reginald Nwankwo of the Ministry of Justice is accustomed to the perks of power: an expensive car, first pickings of relief supplies, easy access to accommodating women. He willingly attends lively parties thrown by his colleagues, but he refuses to dance: this is his one pathetic sacrifice to the horrors of the war. He has a third encounter with Gladys, a beautiful young woman who first hitched a ride with him to join the militia and then later searched his car scrupulously as a member of Civil Defense. Now, however, Gladys works in the Fuel Directorate, and she is tarted up with her "high-tinted wig and a very expensive skirt and low-cut blouse" (106). Nwankwo, whose wife and children are safely removed to an interior location, is stunned by this "tragic" development, Gladys's loss of idealism, but he soon gives in to his lust and appropriates her for the day and night, during which they make love and attend a party that is well stocked with meat and drink and live music. The following morning, Nwankwo acknowledges that Gladys "was just a mirror reflecting a society that had gone completely rotten and maggoty at the centre" (116). But he is wrong, as the reader discovers in the final pages, when Nwankwo picks up a hobbled soldier while returning Gladys to her home and then the car is strafed by an enemy airplane: Gladys and Nwankwo rush toward the bush, but when the soldier is unable to get his door open and flee, Gladys turns back to save him. The car explodes, the soldier and Gladys are killed instantly, and Nwankwo "let out a piercing cry and fell down again" (120). Gladys emerges as the most powerful agent of right action in these stories, a scarred woman whose instincts are true, who risks her life (while Nwankwo guards his) and suffers the truly tragic consequences. In analyzing the story, Donald Burness forcefully asserts that Gladys "is of heroic proportions. She is among the most unforgettable women to have graced the pages of African literature" (67).

In "Sugar Baby," the story Achebe substituted for the two sketches he withdrew from the first edition, he uses one of his rare first-person narrators to tell another tale of greed and corruption among civil servants during the Biafran War, though this story is comical. Mike, the narrator, worked closely with his friend Cletus at the Propaganda Directorate during the last eighteen months of the war, and he observed firsthand Cletus's agony when he was deprived of sugar, to which he is addicted. With Cletus present, he now tells several of their friends about Cletus's wartime struggles with shortages of sugar. Once Cletus managed to secure a batch of artificial sweetener, but he gagged over its cloying taste and heaved the remaining tablets into the weeds beyond his house. Mike describes a visit to the Caritas relief stores, where an exhausted Irish priest offered to fill their needs until Cletus asked for sugar. The priest exploded at Cletus's selfishness: " 'Sugar! Sugar!! Sugar!!!' he screamed in hoarse crescendo. Sugar when thousands of God's innocents perished daily for lack of a glass of milk!" (96), and then he chased the two out of the building. When Mike was sent abroad on government business, he bought Cletus some sugar and presented it to him upon returning. But when Cletus's girlfriend happened to reach into the packet and began to put a few sugar cubes into her purse, Cletus tried to rip them from her fist; she threw them into his face and ran away. At the end of his account, Mike makes a joke about the clause that will have to be inserted in Cletus's marriage vows to exclude sugar from the worldly goods he is willing to share. On the one hand, Mike's narrative provides welcome relief from the painful memories that he and his friends obviously experienced during the war. Humor can take the sting from tragedy. On the other hand, the callous request to the Caritas priest parallels Nwankwo's abuse of the relief supply effort, albeit finally at Cletus's own expense.

In "Civil Peace," Achebe describes what occurred in the villages when the Biafran War ended and notes the corruption in the rural setting. Jonathan Iwegbu, his wife, and three of his four children have survived the war, and Jonathan also has the bicycle that he buried for safekeeping a year earlier. He begins taxiing people from their camp to the main road for their journey home and accumulates a nice stack of money in the process. Then he discovers that miraculously his own modest home is intact, and he and his family return home themselves. His wife begins preparing breakfast meals for sale, and Jonathan opens a bar. He even applies for and receives twenty pounds as an ex-gratia reward for turning in rebel money. Late that night, however, thieves arrive at his house and bang loudly at his door, demanding money to promote "civil peace." They fire their automatic weapons in the air to make their point, and neither the police nor the Iwegbus' neighbors come forward to intervene. Jonathan convinces them that all he has is the twenty pounds in ex-gratia money; he hands it through a window to the thieves, and they depart. In the morning, he is philosophical in describing the night's events to neighbors as he and his wife work away at their normal tasks: "Did I depend on it last week? Or is it greater than other things that went with the war? I say, let *egg-rasher* [ex-gratia] perish in the flames! Let it go where everything else has gone. Nothing puzzles God" (88). Though he is a victim of circumstances, a powerless and simple man caught in the winds of destruction and social upheaval, Jonathan takes life day by day and does what is needed to survive. He is a modern, and modest, hero, a rural counterpoint to the doomed Gladys—not a tragic hero, that is, but a comic one, in the classical sense. The Iwegbus are about the business of re-establishing order in their society, and Achebe clearly implies that they will succeed in their efforts, despite the corruption and confusion that whirl around them.

Through these effective stories, Achebe augments the historical portrait of an African people that he has elaborately created in his sequence of novels. To his short fiction he brings his concise style, his honed irony, and his gift of characterization. One wonders, finally, why Achebe has not written (or published) more short stories than these.

WORKS CITED AND CONSULTED

Primary

Achebe, Chinua. *Anthills of the Savannah*. London: Heinemann, 1987; New York: Anchor/Doubleday, 1988.

———. *Arrow of God*. London: Heinemann, 1964; New York: John Day, 1967.

———. *Beware, Soul–Brother, and Other Poems*. Enugu, Nigeria: Nwankwo-Ifejika, 1971. Revised and enlarged as *Beware, Soul Brother: Poems*. London: Heinemann, 1972; Enugu, Nigeria: Nwamife, 1972. Republished as *Christmas in Biafra and Other Poems*. Garden City, NY: Anchor/Doubleday, 1973.

———. *Chike and the River*. London and New York: Cambridge University Press, 1966.

———. *The Drum*. Enugu, Nigeria: Fourth Dimension, 1977.

———. *The Flute*. Enugu, Nigeria: Fourth Dimension, 1977.

———. *Girls at War and Other Stories*. London: Heinemann, 1972; Garden City, NY: Doubleday, 1973. (Page references are to the Anchor edition.)

———. *Hopes and Impediments: Selected Essays 1965–1987*. London: Heinemann, 1988. Republished as *Hopes and Impediments: Selected Essays*. New York: Doubleday, 1989.

———. *A Man of the People*. London: Heinemann, 1966; New York: John Day, 1966.

———. *Morning Yet on Creation Day: Essays*. London: Heinemann, 1975; Garden City, NY: Anchor/Doubleday, 1975.

———. *No Longer at Ease*. London: Heinemann, 1960; New York: Obolensky, 1961.

———. *The Sacrificial Egg, and Other Short Stories*. Onitsha, Nigeria: Etudo, 1962.

———. *Things Fall Apart*. London: Heinemann, 1958; New York: McDowell, Obolensky, 1959.

———. *The Trouble with Nigeria*. Enugu, Nigeria: Fourth Dimension, 1983; London: Heinemann, 1984.

————. *The University and the Leadership Factor in Nigerian Politics*. Enugu, Nigeria: Abic, 1988.

Achebe, Chinua, and Robert Lyons. *Another Africa*. New York: Anchor, 1998.

Achebe, Chinua, and John Iroaganachi. *How the Leopard Got His Claws*. Enugu, Nigeria: Nwamife, 1972; New York: Third Press, 1973.

Secondary

Balogun, F. Odun. *Tradition and Modernity in the African Short Story*. New York: Greenwood Press, 1991.

Bardolph, Jacqueline. "Langue et identité dans 'Uncle Ben's Choice' de Chinua Achebe." *Visions Critiques* 3 (1986): 87–97.

Burness, Donald B. "Solipsism and Survival in Achebe's 'Civil Peace' and 'Girls at War.' " *Ba Shiru* 5.1 (1973): 64–67.

Carroll, David. *Chinua Achebe*. 2nd ed. New York: Macmillan, 1990.

————. "Chinua Achebe." *Current Biography Yearbook*. 1992 ed. 1–5.

Echeruo, M.J.C. Introduction. *The Sacrificial Egg, and Other Short Stories*. By Chinua Achebe. Onitsha, Nigeria: Etudo, 1962. 3–6.

Elias, Mohamed. "Time in Achebe's *Girls at War.*" *Commonwealth Quarterly* 2.6 (1978): 17–23.

Ezenwa-Ohaeto. *Chinua Achebe; A Biography*. Bloomington: Indiana University Press, 1997.

Innes, C. L. *Chinua Achebe*. Cambridge: Cambridge University Press, 1990.

Innes, C. L., and Bernth Lindfors, eds. *Critical Perspectives on Chinua Achebe*. Washington, DC: Three Continents, 1978.

Killam, G. D. *The Writings of Chinua Achebe*. Rev. ed. London: Heinemann, 1977.

Kothandaraman, Bala. "Telling: Writing: Printing—Orality in Achebe's Short Stories." *South Asian Responses to Chinua Achebe*. Ed. Bernth Lindfors and Bala Kothandaraman. New Delhi: Prestige, 1993. 155–60.

Lindfors, Bernth. "Chinua Achebe." *Encyclopedia of World Literature in the 20th Century*. New York: Ungar, 7–9.

————. *Early Nigerian Literature*. New York: Africana, 1982.

————, ed. *Conversations with Chinua Achebe*. Jackson: University Press of Mississippi, 1997.

Moore, Gerald. *Twelve African Writers*. Bloomington: Indiana University Press, 1980.

Munro, Ian H. "Chinua Achebe, *Girls at War.*" *Cowries and Kobos: The West African Oral Tale and Short Story*. Ed. Kirsten Holst Petersen and Anna Rutherford. Aarhus, Denmark: Dangaroo, 1981. 84–88.

Nnolim, Charles E. "Structure and Meaning in Achebe's 'The Madman.' " *Ofirima* 1.2 (n.d.): 29–33.

Samway, Patrick H. "An Interview with Chinua Achebe." *America* June 29, 1991: 684–86.

Wilkinson, Jane, ed. *Talking with African Writers*. London: James Curry, 1992.

AMA ATA AIDOO
(March 23, 1942–   )

Susan Rochette-Crawley

BIOGRAPHY

Ama Ata Aidoo was born in Ghana to Nana Yaw Fama, a chief of Abeadzi Kyiakor. She was raised in the royal household and attended the Wesley School for Girls in Cape Coast. She later enrolled in the University of Ghana, Legon, where she graduated with a B.A. in English. She was a research fellow of African studies at the University of Ghana and attended the Stanford University Advanced Creative Writing Course in California. Her formal education gave her an intellectual background in drama and literature; her life in the royal household introduced her to oral stories and storytelling rhythms.

One of Aidoo's first publicly performed and disseminated works was the play *The Dilemma of a Ghost* (1965). It was followed in 1970 by the play *Anowa* and the short-story collection *No Sweetness Here*, written during an eight-year span that covered the "crucial period just before and immediately after the 1966 military overthrow of the Kwame Nkrumah government" (Odamtten 80). One of her best-known works, *Our Sister Killjoy; or, Reflections from a Black-eyed Squint* was first published in London in 1977. A section of its highly experimental blend of verse, prose, and epistolary form, "The Plums," appeared in Angela Carter's collection *Wayward Girls and Wicked Women*. Aidoo's second collection of short stories for children, *The Eagle and the Chickens and Other Stories*, was published in 1986. *Changes: A Love Story* was published in 1991. Aidoo has written extensively on the role of the African writer; her work is the subject of a growing body of criticism.

CRITICISM

Aidoo is a highly experimental short-story writer whose work arises from the convergence of the oral and the written tale. The diversity of critical interest in her work reflects the breadth of its imaginative range. Chimalum Nwankwo, in "The Feminist Impulse and Social Realism in Ama Ata Aidoo's *No Sweetness Here* and *Our Sister Killjoy*," for example, explores the connection between patriarchal thinking and colonialist mentality in Aidoo's fiction, while Denise Chussy, in the collection *Short Fiction in the New Literatures in English*, addresses Aidoo's use of the short-story form in *No Sweetness Here*. Aidoo's innovations in narrative voice, point of view, and oral/literary narrative blends continue to inspire critical interest.

ANALYSIS

According to Lloyd Brown in his *Women Writers in Black Africa*, Aidoo's stories are both literate forms and oral performances (100). Her collection *No Sweetness Here* reveals the extent to which this is true.

In the first story, "Everything Counts," the protagonist, a young African woman considering the female custom of wearing wigs to disguise real hair, reflects that

[s]he had always known that in her society, that is traditionally, men and women had had more important things to do than fight each other in the mind. It was not in school that she had learnt this. Because you know, one did not really go to school to learn about Africa. . . . As for this, what did the experts call it? War of the sexes? Yes, as for this war of the sexes, if there had been any at all in the old days among her people, they could not possibly have been on such a scale. These days, any little "No" one says to a boy's "Yes" means one is asking for a battle. O, there are just too many problems. (2–3)

In this short excerpt, several features of Aidoo's individual style are apparent. First, there is the blend of social realism and folk expression in the first sentence, in which the protagonist complains that there are more important things to do than "fight each other in the mind." Aidoo continues with her social critique by calling up the image of a "war between the sexes," but she makes it clear that this concept, worded by the "experts," is, or should be, distanced from African everyday life. Her admission that one does not go to school to learn about Africa implies the presence of neocolonial indoctrination and also suggests that the oral tradition is the tradition whereby one "learns about Africa." To reinforce this oral component to the tale, Aidoo concludes her paragraph with the invocation of the oral chorus in the line "O, there are just too many problems."

This excerpt, then, reveals in part Aidoo's complex interweaving of the oral and the written tale to create a story that, in terms of experimental impact, places her work at the forefront of contemporary short-story form as well as within the tradition of the *fefewo*, or complete dramatic narrative (Odamtten 81). It also reveals her standing commitment to both experimentalism and social realism. This commitment to both strands of narrative technique reflects her passion for giving voice to contemporary African life as well as her own highly educated background. The relation between the written and the oral tale in Aidoo's work does not obscure another very important facet of her short stories: the search for a genuine self, a self that, like the sexes, may be at "war" with itself yet nevertheless must find a vitality of its own.

The second story in Aidoo's collection, "For Whom Things Did Not Change," is a fine example of how this search for self, for both individual and communal black identity, both asserts itself and finds itself repressed, depending upon whom one is dealing with. Zirigu, the black man of a household in which another black man is the master, can speak very eloquently and forcefully when he is speaking to his wife, who is glad that she has only sons and no daughters, because life for women in her community is much more psychologically dangerous. But when Zirigu ministers to his "Massa," a young, educated black man who prefers to see himself as a guest in the government-run African household, his language becomes broken, and he reverts to a self-deprecating reference to himself as a servant. The question of black identity is confounded in the narrator's reflection that "when a black man is with his wife, who cooks and chores for him, he is a man. When he is with white folk for whom he cooks and chores, he is a woman. Dear Lord, what then is a black man who cooks and chores for black men?" As Odamtten has pointed out, the obverse question—"What then is a black man who lets a black man cook and do his chores for him?"—is simultaneously being asked (85). The story ends with the young black man, the guest of the government house, eliciting from Zirigu the story of how he, an elderly black man, came to become and to see himself as the servant of other black men. Zirigu makes it clear that the process, while it is a complicated one, amounts to the fact that in the "New Africa" the educated black man such as the narrator has simply become a replacement for the white man.

In the third story, "In the Cutting of a Drink," the collusion of oral and written tale with the theme of the search for self is very clear. The story is told in the manner of a folktale. The narrator of the story, a Fante tribesman who has gone to the city in search of his sister, who has not been home in twelve years, speaks in direct address to an uncle whom one assumes has become the head of the Fante brother's household. In relating his story in oral form to the uncle, the brother adopts an epistolary tone of voice. The refrain, "cut me a drink," is repeated many times within the story, usually with reference to the licentiousness of city life where the Fante narrator seems to discover his sister, who has now become one of the "bad women" of the city. "Any kind of work," she tells him, "is work." "Cut me a drink," the narrator responds, seeming to find in his sister another side of himself, a side he reveals to the uncle and tries to explain through appeal. The gap between city and village looms for both the brother and the sister and in many ways not only explains the sister's definition of herself but threatens to implicate the hitherto-solidified sense of self borne by the tribesman into the alien underside of city nightlife. The oral origins of the phrase "cut me a drink" converge with the narrator's verbally composed epistle to the uncle describing the disintegration of the sister's sense of self-worth.

"The Message" is told strictly in dialogue and concerns Maami Amfoa, an African mother who must travel to Cape Coast to—she thinks—shroud her daughter who must have died in childbirth, giving birth as she did "through the stomach," or by cesarean section. When she finds that her daughter is alive, she regards the medical treatment her daughter has received as miraculous. The cloth she has brought to shroud her daughter becomes a symbol of wholeness and life, rather than a symbol of the cut cloth of social conflict that in African literature often reflects the tensions between northern and southern African life.

The next story, "Certain Winds from the South," however, does not view the conflict between north and south from a favorable stance. This story is told primarily through the narrative eyes of M'ma Asana, whose daughter, Hawa, has also just given birth. Yet the occasion, which should be a joyous one, is marred by the son-in-law, Issa, deciding that he must go south to find work to support his family. He leaves before his child's navel has completely healed. The unhealed navel signifies the cut cord and unhealed relationship between the Africans in the north and those in the south. The tragedy is that Issa must go to the south to find menial work that could as easily be done in the north but that pays nothing there. Issa leaves while his wife and child are still asleep, telling only his mother-in-law of his intentions. When the daughter wakes, the mother must reveal to her the news and comfort her in her lamentations. This effort to comfort precipitates M'ma's relating to her daughter at last the same journey that her father made many years before. He, unlike Issa, went south to become a soldier. He was sent to fight the Germans in World War I, and he did not return.

In this story, Aidoo weaves the immediate story of Issa and Hawa with the story-within-the-story of Hawa's father. The framing of oral tale within oral tale reinforces the epistemological method of knowledge being passed down orally from generation to generation. This interweaving of oral tales contrasts the linear tales of Hawa's husband and Hawa's father having to travel to the south—a region that bears similarity to the imperialist West—to find employment and identity. The story concludes with M'ma insisting that she will find at the market good food for them both to eat. The market thus becomes a focal point for the conditions of the world outside their village. Good food can be gotten in the north only so long as the political and economic situations in the south remain stable: that is, as long as the system of exploitation whereby husbands must travel away from their families to find work remains the same. M'ma goes off to the market just as Issa leaves for the south. In the meantime, the recovering mother Hawa and her child Fuseni remain themselves the most vulnerable unit of the overall economic structure.

The title story of the collection, "No Sweetness Here," follows the message and represents a dramatic shift in tone and focus. The story is told through the voice of the "chicha," or teacher, in the Fanti village. Because the teacher is not herself a Fanti, she is in essence an "outsider," and this position puts her in solid narrative relation to the story she is undertaking to tell, the story of the death of the beautiful boy Kwesi by snakebite while he is on the school grounds. Kwesi's fate is linked to his mother's divorce suit, which goes through just as Kwesi is discovered to be bitten and then to die. The implication is dual: the Ghanian woman seeking a reprieve through the white way of divorce is punished on the very grounds, literally, that she implicates her son in Western ways of learning that discount the still-powerful natural and social forces of African life.

The title of the next story, "A Gift from Somewhere," articulates the dilemma of the story itself, a story that in many ways both mirrors and subverts the theme of the story "The Message." The "gift from somewhere" is the gift of life given to Maami Fanti's fourth-born child, who, unlike her other children, survives. It is not clear where, if anywhere in particular, the gift of life for her child comes from. In this story, there are no "medical miracles," and the religious representative prays to Allah not for the child's life but for his own reputation as a holy man should the child die, which, to him, seems inevitable. Thus this is not a story of faith, either in modern science or in religious and folk practice.

The power of the story resides not only in the fact that the child lives, but also in Maami Fanti's belief that fate will take its course. The title "A Gift from Somewhere" reflects the indeterminacy of the source of fate as it governs all lives. The symbol of the cloth, so important in the previous stories, takes on a new meaning here. Not only does the cloth, as the child is wrapped in it, represent continuity and the effort to keep the cloth of African heritage uncut, but it also represents, in Maami Fanti's refusal to rend her own cloth even in grief and desperation, the contiguity of African wholeness of spirit with love and faith.

Three stories of the collection, "Two Sisters," The Late Bud," and "Something to Talk About on the Way to the Funeral . . . ," constitute what Odamtten considers the "fourth phase" of the *fefewo* composition of the collection. In "Two Sisters," the Bird of the Wayside, the name Odamtten gives to the use of the omniscient narrator, tells the story of Connie, the elder sister, confined to an unhappy marriage. The story as a whole is satiric and thus moves from being an inherently folk tale to becoming a folk retailoring of a familiar story between two sisters.

In "The Late Bud," Odamtten asserts that the story is told chiefly through the agency of the Bird of the Wayside, or the overhearing omniscient or "bird's-eye" view of the narrator. This interest in the Bird of the Wayside as a narrative device and a folk tradition is interesting for the implications that it has in Aidoo's collection as a whole, but in this phase in particular. As "the bird of the wayside," the ambulant and transient narrator can, like the crow, fly a straight and high line over the drama of the story and alight at significant intervals throughout the unfolding of events.

The last two stories in the collection, "Something to Talk About on the Way to the Funeral . . ." and "Other Versions," reflect complementary storytelling methods, as well as further the already-prevalent themes of African sisterhood and oral storytelling. The story "Something to Talk About on the Way to the Funeral . . ." features a first-person narrator who, when relating the story about her sister and herself, recedes into the background and allows the other sister to take over the voice of the story. In this way, the "real" narrator's voice is muted by the overprevalence of the first sister's voice. Stylistically, this makes the story a very interesting one, if only for the fact that the "active," or perceiving, narrator of the story in fact becomes the voice through which we hear the story of Aunt Araba, or the "good woman who does not rot."

In the final story of the collection, "Other Versions," the reader is given to understand that there are "other versions" to the neocolonial story as we commonly know it. The main character in this story takes the reader through a labyrinth of description and exculpation to arrive finally at the point of seeing the postcolonial vision through the eyes of the repatriated son who knows the price at which his freedom of expression has been bought.

WORKS CITED AND CONSULTED

Primary

Aidoo, Ama Ata. *Anowa*. Harlow, UK: Longman's, 1970; Washington, DC: Three Continents, 1980.
———. *Changes: A Love Story*. London: Women's Press, 1991.
———. *The Dilemma of a Ghost*. London and Accra: Longman's, 1965; New York: Collier, 1971.
———. *The Eagle and the Chickens and Other Stories*. Enugu, Nigeria: Tana, 1986.
———. *No Sweetness Here*. Harlow, UK: Longman's, 1970; Garden City, NY: Doubleday, 1971.
———. *Our Sister Killjoy; or, Reflections from a Black-eyed Squint*. London: Longman's, 1977; New York: NOK, 1979.

Secondary

Booth, James. "Sexual Politics in the Fiction of Ama Ata Aidoo." *Commonwealth Essays and Studies* 15.2 (Spring 1993): 80–96.
Brown, Lloyd W. *Women Writers in Black Africa*. Westport, CT: Greenwood, 1981.
Chetin, Sara. "Reading from a Distance: Ama Ata Aidoo's 'Our Sister Killjoy.' " *Black Women's Writing*. Ed. Gina Wisker. New York: St. Martin's, 1993. 146–159.
Coussy, Denise. "Is Life Sweet? The Short Stories of Ama Ata Aidoo." *Short Fiction in the New Literatures in English*. Ed. Jacqueline Bardolph. Nice: Fac. de Lettres, 1989. 285–90.
Davies, Carol Boyce, and Anne Adams Graves, eds. *Ngambika: Studies of Women in African Literature*. Trenton, NJ: Africa World Press, 1986.

Horne, Naana Banyiwa. "Ama Ata Aidoo." *Dictionary of Literary Biography*. Ed. Bernth Lindfors and Reinhard Sander. Vol. 117. Detroit: Gale Research, 1992. 34–40.

Jones, Elred Durosimi, ed. *Women in African Literature Today*. Trenton, NJ: Africa World Press, 1987.

MacKenzie, Clayton G. "The Discourse of Sweetness in Ama Ata Aidoo's 'No Sweetness Here.' " *Studies in Short Fiction* 32 (Spring 1995): 161–170.

Needham, Anuradha Dingwaney. "An Interview with Ama Ata Aidoo." *Massachusetts Review* 36 (Spring 1995): 123–33.

Nwankwo, Chimalum. "The Feminist Impulse and Social Realism in Ama Ata Aidoo's *No Sweetness Here* and *Our Sister Killjoy*." *Ngambika: Studies of Women in African Literature*. Ed. Carole Boyce Davies and Anne Adams Graves. Trenton, NJ: Africa World, 1986. 151–59.

Odamtten, Vincent O. *The Art of Ama Ata Aidoo*. Gainesville: University Press of Florida, 1994.

Ogede, Ode. "The Defense of Culture in Ama Ata Aidoo's 'No Sweetness Here.' " *International Fiction Review* 21.1 (1994): 76–84.

Pieterse, Cosmo, and Donald Munro, eds. *Protest and Conflict in African Literature*. New York: Africana Publishing Co., 1969.

Saamantrai, Ranu. "Caught at the Confluence of History: Ama Ata Aidoo's Necessary Nationalism." *Research in African Literatures* 26 (Summer 1995): 140–57.

Willey, Elizabeth. "National Identities, Tradition, and Feminism: The Novels of Ama Ata Aidoo Read in the Context of the Works of Kwame Nkrumah." *Dialogues on Third World Women's Literature and Film*. Ed. Bishnupriya Ghosh and Brinda Bose. New York: Garland, 1997. 3–30.

JESSICA ANDERSON
(September 25, 1916–   )

Selina Samuels

BIOGRAPHY

Jessica Anderson was born Jessica Queale in 1916 in Gayndah, a small town 350 kilometers northwest of Brisbane, Australia. Her father was the son of Irish immigrants, and her mother was English; their marriage caused a family rift that never healed. In her autobiographical work *Stories from the Warm Zone*, Anderson writes that she and her siblings were forbidden to enter the house of their maternal grandmother. These stories also reveal a side to her intellectual parents that would have contrasted strongly with the suburban Brisbane of the period: her parents were not only Labour party members, but also atheists, or "free thinkers."

The Queale family moved to Brisbane during the 1920s, where Jessica grew up in the suburb of Yeronga. After attending Brisbane State High, she studied art at Brisbane Technical College Art School. In 1935, she moved to Sydney; the evocative images of that city feature in much of her fiction and indicate her affinity with and affection for her adopted home. Before attaining notoriety as a novelist, Anderson worked for many years in radio, adapting works by writers such as Charles Dickens, Henry James, and Martin Boyd and writing her own radio plays and stories, published under a pseudonym.

Anderson's first novel, *An Ordinary Lunacy*, was published by Macmillan in 1963. *Tirra Lirra by the River* (1978), the first of her novels published in Australia, is her most famous and acclaimed work. It won the prestigious Miles Franklin Award in 1978 as well as the Australian Natives' Association Literary Award. *The Impersonators* (1980) also won the Miles Franklin Award along with the New South Wales Premier's Award. Her most recent work is *One of the Wattle Birds*, published in 1994.

Stories from the Warm Zone and Sydney Stories (1987) is Anderson's only collection of short stories. It has been critically eclipsed by the national enthusiasm for *Tirra Lirra by the River*, which is included on a number of school syllabi. The first part of this collection of stories, *Stories from the Warm Zone*, is Anderson's only deliberately autobiographical work. It concentrates on the development of Bea between the ages of four and nine. The "warm zone" of the title refers to Queensland, more specifically Brisbane, and the stories are richly evocative of that part of Australia during the 1920s. The second section of the collection, *Sydney Stories*, contains three stories set in Sydney during the 1980s that center primarily on the pain of adult life: divorce, independence, love, and death. Anderson has been married and divorced twice (Anderson is the name of her second husband) and has one daughter, the screenwriter Laura Jones.

CRITICISM

Jessica Anderson is best known as a novelist. The majority of criticism of her work centers on her novels, particularly *Tirra Lirra by the River*. Critics have discussed the theme of expatriation in her novels ("The Expatriate Vision of Jessica Anderson" by Elaine Barry) and the tension within her novels between the old world and the new ("Of Rhinos and Caryatids: The Dialogic Imperative in Jessica Anderson" by Barbara Garlick). Anderson's literary models have tended to be English and American. She has said in an interview with Jennifer Ellison, in *Rooms of Their Own*, "I did read Australian novels but they didn't supply much for me. They were mostly blokey and outback. They don't supply much for a girl or a woman. Women were either mates, or martyrs in the kitchen . . . chopping the wood or killing snakes" (34). This statement is an indication of the male-dominated concerns of the Australian literature of the nineteenth and early twentieth centuries. Nevertheless, Anderson's writing can be seen as distinctly Australian, though arguably in a more modern and more female form. Her stories illustrate clearly her fascination with location by describing in lyrical terms two Australian cities, Brisbane and Sydney, and featuring place in all the stories as a primary character. Like place, Anderson perceives gender to be a determinant of self; *Stories from the Warm Zone* delicately conjures the partic- ular constraints imposed upon the developing female consciousness.

ANALYSIS

I have described *Stories from the Warm Zone and Sydney Stories* as a col- lection of short stories, but that is not entirely accurate. The first section, *Stories from the Warm Zone*, is a short-story cycle comprised of five stories that, while self-sufficient (at least four of them have been published independently), are linked by theme, place, character, and time. This section is also autobiograph- ical; its story-cycle form mirrors the flashbacks of memory when one remembers certain events separately and distinctly from occurrences that preceded and fol- lowed them. *Stories from the Warm Zone* is an unusual bildungsroman, with the development of the protagonist occurring in an episodic, fractured form, similar to that employed in Alice Munro's *Lives of Girls and Women* and *Who Do You Think You Are?* In *Fabricating the Self*, Elaine Barry discusses Anderson's short-story cycle as an example of a distinctly female autobiography: its form emphasizes the minutiae of daily life rather than the development of independence, the relatedness and family rather than isolation and difference.

Anderson's fictional autobiography, like a number of other autobiographies by women, is nonlinear in structure. Life is described not as a journey with a beginning and end, but as a series of interrelated but fragmented episodes. In this context, the short story, more specifically the short-story cycle, can be seen to be an appropriate form for an autobiographical bildungsroman by a woman writer, altering and subverting the linear conventions of the genre.

The second section of the collection contains three separate stories located in Sydney. These stories are not so much interwoven as contrasting. "The Milk" and "Outdoor Friends" both concern divorce, while "The Late Sunlight" presents a portrait of a happy marriage. In an interview with Ray Willbanks, Anderson explained that she added the middle story to create a balance. Indeed, the two parts of the collection as a whole maintain a balance between contrasts: Brisbane in the 1920s and Sydney in the 1980s; childhood and adulthood; family stability and family instability; a short-story cycle and a short-story collection. This balance is accentuated by the movement away from home and its certainties toward a wider world. During the course of *Stories from the Warm Zone*, Bea develops a sense of her own autonomy, her separateness from the rest of her family that culminates in her perception of her existence through the eyes of the aviator. She moves from feeling trapped under the house in the first story to waving to the aviator and the wider world in the final story of the cycle. In *Sydney Stories*, characters move apart from family in more obvious ways, through divorce or migration. Anderson juxtaposes the crises of childhood with those of midlife, highlighting the cycle of life as well as the cyclic form of the narrative.

Unlike much of Anderson's other fiction, *Stories from the Warm Zone and Sydney Stories* is set entirely in Australia, with the Viennese countess in "The Late Sunlight" providing the only reference to exile or expatriation. As the title indicates, the stories center on two places, Brisbane and Sydney, and in describing them, Anderson rewrites the Australian literary tradition. Her affectionate descriptions of both cities do engage in a process of mythmaking, but they resist the great Australian obsession with the landscape. Anderson concentrates on domestic detail rather than on capturing wide sweeps of the outback; with the exception of "Under the House," her portrait of Australia is largely urban. Thus Anderson is not only expressing her own experience but that of the vast majority of the population, a fact usually overlooked by Australian writers and filmmakers. Descriptions of houses feature vividly in her short fiction, particularly in *Stories from the Warm Zone*, where distinctive Queensland architecture evokes not only a place but also a specific time frame.

The first story, "Under the House," opens with a description of an "under-the-house" unique to Queensland where a four-year-old Bea has been left behind by her sisters, Rhoda and Sybil. Bea feels trapped under the house, a response that indicates early in the narrative her developing sense of independence and separateness from her family. The narrative voice is that of the adult Bea, but the point of view is that of the child. This dual perspective allows the narration to move fluidly through time: events are mentioned in one story but not elaborated upon until a later story. Thus Anderson ties the stories together and mimics the episodic, fleeting quality of memories. She juxtaposes a sharp childhood memory with a rapid description of the consequences of it, contrasting the clarity of the moment with the subsequent blurred passage of time.

In "Under the House," Bea's world is dominated by her elder sisters, who have told her to wait under the house for a visitor, a favorite game for the children isolated in rural Mooloolabin. Rhoda is described with particular affection, and it is with shock and alarm that the reader registers the news casually embedded in a description of Bea's mother: "At that time she must have been in her early forties, about the age at which Rhoda died" (9). Indeed, throughout *Stories from the Warm Zone*, Bea's relationship with her family is central. When the "visitors" arrive, they are Rhoda dressed in elaborate style and with a voice befitting a society lady, and the middle sister, Sybil, dressed as Johnny Pumper and wearing older brother Neal's prized medals on her chest. Bea is mystified by the sweets Rhoda produces, but is even more troubled by her inexplicable hat, the mystery of which is never solved. In the opening story, Anderson celebrates the mysterious and poignant memories of childhood. She also introduces into the cycle features that will characterize Queensland throughout the subsequent stories: the cool darkness of under-the-house, the sense of living on the edge of a wilderness, and the children's mimicry of adult gentility.

The second story, "The Appearance of Things," is the longest story in the cycle. In this story, Bea is eight years old, and the family has moved to the suburbs of Brisbane. Bea's perspective in this story has expanded to include her entire family, and she is described listening to the conversations of her parents while sitting under the kitchen table. In this story, speech is central, and each member of the family is defined by what he or she says and how he or she speaks. Bea's beloved sister Rhoda has decided to go to church, much to the alarm of their atheist parents. The title of the story refers to Rhoda's apparent religious sentiments, motivated largely by infatuation with Mr. Gilliard, the minister, and a fascination with the theatricality of the religious ceremony. Bea, similarly, is excited by the prospect of baptism and choosing a new middle name. Only Sybil, the middle sister and Bea's less favorite, persists in her devotions. In a characteristic Anderson flash through time, we discover that despite the aggressive skepticism of Neal, Bea's brother, he "was to become a Roman Catholic in his thirties" (38). The predominant tone of the story is ironic and gently comic, but the resonance changes when the narrator remembers talking to Rhoda's widower soon after her death. He mentions that his wife had said, soon before she died, that she would only see a clergyman if it was Mr. Gilliard, and he asks Bea what the minister had been like. She replies by describing his physical appearance, only realizing afterwards that Rhoda's husband had not asked for that information at all. This conversation reflects the childhood preoccupation with the appearance of things; it also indicates the problematic role of the narrator and the complex nature of memories. Despite the fact that Anderson endeavors to tell her stories from the point of view of the child Bea, she cannot help but filter her memories through her adult eyes, imbuing the stories with the almost paradoxical combination of a childlike freshness and an adult poignancy.

In "The Appearance of Things," Bea's gradual break from her family, expressed more fully in the following three stories, is signaled. Her decision to be baptized, seduced by the attraction of choosing her own second name, causes her defection from the ranks of the skeptics headed by her father. Their particular rituals alter, marking the uneasiness Bea feels with her father until his death from emphysema when she is sixteen: "And though on many evenings afterwards I read over my father's shoulder, and filled and lit his pipe, I never resumed my inspection of his person, nor sat beneath the table while keeping his foot at a gentle jog" (35).

"Against the Wall" tells of Bea's stammer. Bea is persecuted by Miss Rickard, her teacher, and starts to play truant, going to the forbidden creek to play with Peggy and Des Kellaway, children of vagrants. Bea's stammer, as Elaine Barry notes in *Fabricating the Self*, is "part of a larger mystery of blocked communications . . . part of any child's growing awareness of the complexity of human communication" (124), and part of Bea's gradual definition of herself as a separate and autonomous being. Bea's growing sense of independence is expressed as both euphoric and painful. Anderson draws a wonderful scene of Bea's glorious day alone in the house while her parents consult people about her stutter. She revels in the mystery of the familiar, seen unexpectedly in the light of solitude and freedom: "In this treasured privacy I did nothing forbidden, but did even the most usual things with a rapturous deliberation" (64). The aloneness caused by the problems Bea finds with communication, however, is not entirely joyous. She discovers that the mysterious "speech-blocking emanation" that occurs in the classroom is also present when she talks to her father, a block in communication that the adult narrator tells the reader will persist until his death. At the end of the story, after Bea discovers that she will be spending a year away from school, her initial reaction of joy is tempered by a sense of entrapment and separateness: "I felt myself imprisoned in a region from which I would never again escape to the sharper air of insubordination" (66). Her desire to go to visit the Kellaways at the campsite of Budjerra Heights that closes the story epitomizes Bea's need for independence from her family, her desire for the illicit pleasure of defiance.

The fourth story in *Stories from the Warm Zone*, "The Way to Budjerra Heights," is a series of vignettes from Bea's year at home and her increasingly close relationship with her mother. The adult narrative voice links these memories with the more recent memory of a month spent with her mother, then in her eighties: "In our lives, there were two spans of time when she and I were alone in the house together every weekday, the first lasting for a school year, the second for only a month. They have become ravelled together, and deliberation is needed to untangle them" (79). The presence of Bea's mother in the house and the absence of her father and brother define it as an essentially female space, and while the child is unable to speak outside its boundaries, she is quite able to communicate within. By placing the relationship of the protagonist with her mother at the center of her fragmented bildungsroman, Anderson alters the traditional structure of that form, in which separation from the family and total autonomy tend to be the ultimate goals. Instead of privileging independence, Anderson celebrates the interdependence and communication between mother and daughter, linking the memories of each caring for the other. In addition, the memory of Bea's relationship with her mother pervades her, and by extension Anderson's, memories of Queensland. Just as Anderson defines the Brisbane of the prewar years as a city on the fringes of wilderness, she also defines it as a primarily female space.

Anderson signals Bea's gradual maturity in two vivid scenes. At the end of the story, Bea's mother takes her and her sisters for a walk in the bush, during which Bea attempts to discover the way to Budjerra Heights. During the walk, her mother tells the story of being sexually harassed as a young working woman in Brisbane. This story carries many threats of the dangers of adulthood for women and momentarily unites the adolescent Rhoda with her mother. At the end of the story, Bea has discarded her ambition to visit Budjerra Heights and has thus grown out of the petty rebellions of childhood. In another scene that occurs earlier in the story but that permeates the cycle, the narrator recalls the scene of her father's death when he spoke the first words she had ever heard him speak "untempered by the presence of 'one of the children' " (90). In "The Way to Budjerra Heights," Bea is beginning to realize that maturity and independence are born of incidents less glamorous than a trip to a forbidden camping ground.

The final story of Anderson's short-story cycle is the shortest, concentrating on one moment of revelation. Bea is sullenly contemplating her imminent return to school, an event that will deprive her of her freedom and of the company of her mother and Kenny Fry, a neighboring crippled boy. When she hears a plane overhead, she rushes into the backyard to wave a white cloth. The plane comes closer and closer until she can see the aviator wave at her. This wave and the smile she decides that she has also received create in Bea a sense of exhilaration, of euphoria that she must share with the neighborhood. Her recognition by the aviator is a metaphor for her recognition by the wider world; she is flushed with the sense of her own significance. This revelation is fleeting, and she is unable (or else too tactful) to convey the sensation accurately to Kenny. This story marks for Bea, however, a realization of her autonomy, while the plane is an image of her inevitable journey away from parochial Brisbane into the wide world, her progression out of childhood.

Like *Stories from the Warm Zone*, the unrelated stories about Sydney are concerned with change and flux, but in these three stories, Anderson concentrates on the crises of adulthood: sexual betrayal and divorce, loss and displacement, and the search for love. "The Milk," "The Late Sunlight," and "Outdoor Friends" are also evocative of three different parts of Sydney: the inner-city suburb of Newtown, the Botanical Gardens in the center of the city, and Rushcutter's Bay in the east. Anderson describes Brisbane as a city of the past, defined through memory and its brief brush strokes, while her portrait of Sydney is more concentrated and deliberate, revealing the perceptions and romanticism of adults rather than the unthinking acceptance of the child.

In "The Milk," Marjorie has left her husband following the 1976 amendments allowing no-fault divorce. She moves into a cheap flat in Newtown, determined to resume her career as an illustrator. Once again, Anderson concentrates on domestic detail: the sad flat in the inner suburbs of Sydney, which represents freedom to a middle-class woman. Her friend Carla dismisses Marjorie's decision as being a result of menopause, but Marjorie replies, "Why shouldn't it be? Why shouldn't change of life be like adolescence? The two great changes. So? The two great chances" (116). Anderson is mirroring the crises and changes of Bea's childhood with the more dramatic crises of adulthood. Marjorie sees middle age as an opportunity for change and an opportunity to assert a delayed female independence, but it is not a statement made without pain. She develops an ulcer and is told by the doctor to drink milk, but although she cleans the milk servery and leaves the exact change and a clean milk bottle there every night, the milkman refuses to leave her any milk. This refusal is symbolic of the powerlessness that she hoped to put behind her by the divorce, just as the ulcer is indicative of accumulated stress. When Marjorie finally realizes that the milkman cannot see the coins against the Marimekko paper lining the servery, she obtains relief for her ulcer and a sense that she is finally gaining control over her life. Similarly, she realizes that her drawing is better when it is motivated by the pragmatic need to feed herself than when it is fuelled solely by inspiration and euphoria. In "The Milk," the emphasis is on a clearly gendered story of survival and resilience in the face of change.

"The Late Sunlight" initially seems to be out of place in the second section of Anderson's collection. Despite its apparent discordance, however, this story, like "The Milk" and "Outdoor Friends," deals with people who are displaced and dislocated. Marjorie in "The Milk" and Owen in "Outdoor Friends" are forced, as a result of divorce, to make new homes and rebuild their lives. In "The Late Sunlight," both Gordon and the countess he meets in Sydney's Botanical Gardens are away from home. Gordon is a young historian from Canberra who is doing some research in the State Library of New South Wales. Crossing the gardens on his way home to his "chilly rented flat," Gordon sits momentarily on a bench to enjoy the sunshine and meets Vera, an elderly Viennese countess. Her unashamed snobbery offends his idealistic Australian egalitarianism, but he is nevertheless drawn to her and to her story of exile. She migrated during the Second World War and is now unable and unwilling to return to a Vienna that is merely a shadow of its former glory. Vera's disdain for her Australian son, the "little Australian doggie," also contrasts with Gordon's happy marriage and his desire to return to Canberra to be with his wife and children. On their third meeting, Vera gives Gordon a small box as a token of their new friendship, and when he opens it the next morning, he finds a pair of diamond and ruby earrings. Shocked and angry, he rushes to return the earrings, only to discover that Vera has died during the night, having orchestrated the distribution of certain prized possessions so that they would not go to her daughter-in-law. Gordon is shocked by the gift because it indicates that Vera saw in him something he cannot see and would adamantly reject: a "refinement." His return of the earrings is an indication of his much-prized integrity and of his desire to maintain the equilibrium of his marriage, which such a rich gift might disrupt. The gesture also indicates his rejection of Vera's perception of him and her European values. Underlying "The Late Sunlight," however, is the sense of the interaction between the past, Europe, and the present, Australia, which the chance meeting between Gordon and Vera illustrates. Both characters are more in the past than the present: Vera talks about the past, while Gordon thinks about his historical research. Moreover, neither character is at "home." They are both displaced and alone, meeting fleetingly in an oasis in the midst of the modern city—a gracious, colonial creation. Of the three stories in *Sydney Stories*, "The Late Sunlight" is most deliberately about Australia and what it means to be Australian.

The final story in *Stories from the Warm Zone and Sydney Stories* is a novella that balances "The Milk." Anderson writes from the point of view of Owen Thorbury, an intentional device to contrast with Marjorie's point of view in the former story. Owen leaves his wife, Linda, and the matrimonial home, but discovers that his much-coveted freedom is not all he had planned. The story of Owen's path to independence is vaguely absurd: despite his determination and Linda's hysterical reaction, she recovers more quickly than he does, and he continues to be worried about the reactions of his three children and his independent mother. Unlike Marjorie, who revels in her new home, Owen rents a new flat rather haphazardly and continues to live in a shambling, unsettled fashion. To make matters worse, Owen meets Freda, the mother of his new son-in-law, while he is walking in the park near both their houses and begins an affair with her.

Freda is satisfied with a sexual relationship, but Owen falls in love with her and finds the inevitable end of the affair difficult to accept. He is tied to his insufferably demanding children, in love with the wrong woman, and in the grip of a midlife crisis that was not diminished by divorce. "Outdoor Friends" is a comic and painful portrait of Owen's realization that a bid for independence and change is more difficult than he had imagined. Unlike Marjorie, who accepts the problematic nature of her new "freedom," Owen comes to realize that despite his age, he has grown neither wiser nor stronger. His final hope is that of reconnection: a photographic image of the extended family gathered for the christening of his new grandchild. This image, he realizes, will not reveal anything new to him, but in that moment he recognizes the importance of connections and the impossibility of true independence. In the final story, Anderson comes full circle, from Bea's defiant solitary stance in "Under the House" to Owen's acknowledgment in middle age of his impotence in the face of change.

WORKS CITED AND CONSULTED

Primary

Anderson, Jessica. *The Commandant*. London: Macmillan, 1975; Ringwood, Victoria: Penguin, 1981.

———. *The Impersonators*. South Melbourne: Macmillan, 1980.

———. *The Last Man's Head*. London: Macmillan, 1970; Ringwood, Victoria: Penguin, 1987.

———. *One of the Wattle Birds*. Ringwood, Victoria: Penguin, 1994.

———. *The Only Daughter*. New York: Viking, 1985.

———. *An Ordinary Lunacy*. London: Macmillan, 1963.

———. *Stories from the Warm Zone and Sydney Stories*. Ringwood, Victoria: Penguin, 1987.

———. *Taking Shelter*. Ringwood, Victoria: Viking, 1989.

———. *Tirra Lirra by the River*. South Melbourne: Macmillan, 1978.

Secondary

Baker, Candida. *Yacker 2: Australian Writers Talk about Their Work*. Sydney: Pan/ Picador, 1987.

Barry, Elaine. "The Expatriate Vision of Jessica Anderson." *Meridian* 3.1 (May 1984): 3–11.

———. *Fabricating the Self: The Fictions of Jessica Anderson*. St. Lucia: University of Queensland Press, 1992.

Blair, Ruth. "Jessica Anderson's Mysteries." *Island Magazine* 31 (1987): 10–15.

Ellison, Jennifer. *Rooms of Their Own*. Ringwood, Victoria: Penguin, 1986.

Garlick, Barbara. "Of Rhinos and Caryatids: The Dialogic Imperative in Jessica Anderson." *Journal of Narrative Technique* 29.1 (Winter 1991): 72–82.

Gilbert, Pam. *Coming out from Under: Contemporary Australian Women Writers*. Sydney: Pandora, 1988.

Salzman, Paul. "Warm Zones, War Zones: Reading Families." *Australian Book Review* 92 (July 1987): 8–10.

Sykes, Arlene. "Jessica Anderson: Arrivals and Places." *Southerly* 46.1 (1986): 57–71.

Whitlock, Gillian. "The Child in the (Queensland) House: David Malouf and Regional Writing." *Provisional Maps: Critical Essays on David Malouf*. Ed. Amanda Nettlebeck. Nedlands: Centre for Studies in Australian Literature, University of Western Australia, 1994. 71–84.

Willbanks, Ray. "A Conversation with Jessica Anderson." *Antipodes* Spring 1988: 49–51.

MARGARET ELEANOR ATWOOD
(November 18, 1939–   )

Linda H. Straubel and Gayle Elliott

BIOGRAPHY

Margaret Eleanor Atwood was born in Ottawa, Ontario, Canada, the daughter of Carl Edmund Atwood and Margaret Killam Atwood. The middle of three children, Atwood spent several months each year with her parents and brothers in the bush of northern Ontario and Quebec, where her entomologist father conducted field research. Atwood's childhood was, by her own account, happy, her family close-knit. Her parents encouraged intellectual and creative endeavor, with storytelling and practical query being favored activities. Atwood began writing poems as a child; at five, she illustrated and bound a collection called "Rhyming Cats." While she was enrolled at Leaside High School in Toronto (1952–57), she contributed poems and essays to the school's literary magazine. She first read her poetry publicly at the Bohemian Embassy, a Toronto coffeehouse, while she was a student at Victoria College (1957–61). Atwood wrote during the same period for *Acta Victoriana*, the college journal, and the *Strand*, the campus literary magazine. She graduated from the University of Toronto with honors in English language and literature in 1961; *Double Persephone* was published the same year and was awarded the E. J. Pratt Medal for Poetry.

Atwood won a Woodrow Wilson Fellowship and undertook graduate study at Radcliffe College, Harvard University, in 1961; she received her master's degree in English in 1962. Although she briefly returned to Toronto and worked for a market research company (1963–64), following this with a teaching stint at the University of British Columbia in Vancouver (1964–65), she eventually returned to Harvard to continue her doctoral work. Her literary success soon freed her to focus solely upon her writing, and she discontinued work on her dissertation in favor of her art. Her first major collection of poems, *The Circle Game*, was published in 1966 and received the Governor General's Award for

Poetry; this marked an important milestone in Atwood's literary life (Rosenberg 11–12).

Atwood taught literature at Sir George Williams University in Montreal (1967–68) and published *The Animals in That Country* in 1968. She went on to teach creative writing at the University of Alberta during the 1969–70 academic year, and her first novel, *The Edible Woman*, was published in 1969. With the publication of *The Journals of Susanna Moodie* and *Procedures for Underground* (both in 1970) and *Power Politics* (1971), Atwood established herself as a poet of major literary significance.

Since the publication of *Surfacing* (1972), which established Atwood as a major North American writer worthy of serious scholarly attention, Atwood's work has been widely translated, read, and critiqued and has earned her a distinguished position in feminist and Canadian canons, as well as increasing international acclaim. As Judith McCombs observes, *Surfacing* was hailed as "a mythic and Canadian landmark" (*Critical Essays* 6). The publication of *Survival: A Thematic Guide to Canadian Literature* (also in 1972) further enhanced Atwood's reputation. *Survival*, Atwood's assessment of what constituted a distinctively Canadian literary tradition, distinguished her as one of Canada's foremost literary scholars. Critic Phyllis Grosskurth acclaimed the work as "the most important book ever to come out of this country. . . . [*Survival*] has seized me, a Canadian, by the shoulders and forced me to look unflinchingly into the mirror" (McCombs, *Critical Essays* 7). The simultaneous appearance of these two breakthrough books—which, in separate genres, examined the nature of both feminine and national identities—suggested a symbiosis between Atwood's creative and critical processes and underscored the correlation between Canada's national, feminist, and countercultural movements. As McCombs points out, "In the newly burgeoning fields of women's studies and Canadian studies, which countered New Criticism by proclaiming the personal and the literary as the political and the national, Atwood's works were evaluated, not as unique or peculiar artistic creations, but as voicing the hitherto-suppressed truths of women's and Canadians' lives" (*Critical Essays* 8).

By the mid-1970s, Atwood had established her place as a major figure in Canadian literature. Her novels are *The Edible Woman* (1969), *Surfacing* (1972), *Lady Oracle* (1976), *Life Before Man* (1979), *Bodily Harm* (1981), *The Handmaid's Tale* (1985), *Cat's Eye* (1988), *The Robber Bride* (1993), and *Alias Grace* (1996). Both *Surfacing* and *The Handmaid's Tale* were produced as films. She has published five collections of short stories: *Dancing Girls and Other Stories* (1977), *Bluebeard's Egg* (1983), *Murder in the Dark* (1983), *Wilderness Tips* (1991), and *Good Bones* (1992). Atwood has written two children's books, *Up in the Tree* (1978) and *Anna's Pet* (1980), as well as several volumes of poetry. She has also edited an "alternative cookbook," *The CanLit Foodbook* (1987). Her critical volumes include *Survival: A Thematic Guide to Canadian Literature* (1972) and a collection of critical essays entitled *Second Words: Se-*

lected Critical Prose (1982). Atwood currently lives in Toronto with novelist Graeme Gibson.

CRITICISM

Although Margaret Atwood is now renowned in an assortment of genres and critical roles and is firmly established as a novelist, short-story writer, and poet, as well as editor, political activist, and literary and social critic, it was not always so. The acclaim did not come automatically. In retrospect, Atwood's early work was bound to experience some criticism for its cold, "unfeminine" tone. Her Canadian themes were largely unnoted, and her work was often described as "disquieting and rather cold," "beautiful, but a little inhuman."

Appreciation of her work's Canadian themes also required, for the most part, the passage of time and a general critical shift from the focus on the "universal" (classical and Euro-American) themes of New Criticism to an anti-imperialist, Canadian-nationalist focus. Michael Ondaatje, however, as early as 1967, recognized and praised Atwood's independence of traditional mythology, as demonstrated in her poetry collections *The Circle Game* and *The Animals in That Country* (3).

As Judith McCombs informs us in her introduction to *Critical Essays on Margaret Atwood*, by 1970, Atwood's poetic *The Journals of Susanna Moodie* (based on the life of the Canadian pioneer heroine) received praise for its "eloquent Canadian identity," as well as its "literary gothic motifs." Yet McCombs notes, even then, fellow poet Peter Stevens, in comparing this volume to the poetry in *Procedures for Underground*, preferred the latter's "tentative affirming end" to the "restrictive Moodie voice," while A. W. Purdy tempered his largely favorable review by bemoaning the "death of love in author or character." Most important in the later recognition of Atwood's Canadian themes was Northrop Frye's greatly influential critical work, which codified and nurtured Canadian energies and a sense of a national literary tradition. He, too, praised *Journal*'s "Canadian sensibility" (qtd. in McCombs, *Critical Essays* 5).

Power Politics, Atwood's fifth volume of poems, garnered praise for its technical expertise and modernist insights, but was also labeled "cold and cruel," "powerful and disturbing" as a whole, yet "not quite attractive." Appreciation of its dexterity and "Laingian truths"—referring to R. D. Laing, the highly influential 1960s psychiatrist and author of such studies in psychopathology as *The Divided Self* and a volume of poetry on tangled relationships entitled *Knots*—vied with complaints against its "hard, cool language." At this time, a new element was added, as Elizabeth Brewster followed Atwood's critical lead to elucidate some of the mythic elements of the *Politics* poems (see McCombs, *Critical Essays* 5).

The 1972 publication of *Surfacing*, on the other hand, was a major turning point in Atwood's career and critical reception. She became Canada's preeminent, internationally famed and acclaimed poet/novelist. *Surfacing* was received as emblematic of the "new Canadian consciousness, rooted in its own place and realities, rejecting the unreal and mentally colonized internationalism of elder writers" (McCombs 6). Yet through much of 1972–73, readings of its themes became clouded and partly embroiled in the cause célèbre over Atwood's critical work on Canadian literature, *Survival: A Thematic Guide to Canadian Literature*. Controversy arose over the issues of victimization that Atwood saw as emblematic of the Canadian consciousness reflected in its literature. Some accused her of skewing Canadian literature to stress her own themes and ignoring "two hundred years of profound and iron stoicism" to do so. In 1973, Frank Davey, for instance, accused Atwood of "culture-fixing" and, in effect, privileging Ontario "WASP" writers over all other Canadian authors (qtd. in McCombs, *Critical Essays* 7–8). The "Survival shoot-out," as McCombs so aptly names it, peaked in 1973, after which a more conciliatory note was struck. By 1974, *Survival* had arrived as a work of paramount importance, although perhaps not to be considered all-inclusive in the study of Canadian literature, including Atwood's own fiction and poetry (8).

Atwood analysis has since become a "growth industry." To date, there are at least nine whole volumes dedicated exclusively to Atwood criticism and interviews, together with countless articles in Canadian and American journals alike. Like all brilliant art, Atwood's fiction, poetry, and criticism have engendered, and continue to engender, a dizzying plurality of approaches. This is no more than appropriate considering the richness of Atwood's work and the elaborate and dazzling thematic patterns she embroiders.

ANALYSIS

Most critical approaches to Atwood's work focus upon one of the following areas: the relationship between the United States and Canada, and their emblematic polarities of technology/wilderness and culture/nature; ecological and spiritual relation to nature; the yearning of the individual toward transcendence; a movement toward wholeness and reconciliation of opposites; the exploration, appropriation, and revision of fairy tales, folklore, myths, and gothic and popular literary genres and their "transformation" motifs; contributions to and revisions of Canadian literature; or sexual politics. Atwood's fiction complements the work of other feminists equally concerned with philosophical conflicts arising from the Western "bifurcation of consciousness."

A multitude of polarities arise from this basic dichotomy, and Atwood's landscape of the mind, her Cartesian hell, can be neatly superimposed thereon. Consider Atwood's direct expression of the mind/body split: "The trouble is all in the knob at the top of our bodies. I'm not against the body or the head either: only the neck, which creates the illusion that they are separate. The language is wrong, it should have different words for them." She continues to argue that this accidental constriction, this "lie" we call the neck, tells us that we can look down upon our bodies and move them around like "robots" or "puppets" (*Surfacing* 87). The related issues of divided self and the rifts it creates between self and others, men and women, Man and nature, reason and emotion, nation and nation, all emanate outward from this core problem of the fractured image.

Occupying the center space in this traditional humanistic model is Man, as embodied in each man, with his upper half afloat in metaphysics, and his spirit, mind, closer to the Mind of God. This is Man's thoughtful self. Man is divided, therefore, into two inverted pyramids, separate from himself and the world, seeing himself and the world around him according to the separate needs of his divided self. The upper, metaphysical self yearns for divine inspiration, religion. This heavenly sphere fulfills Man's immaterial longings and is exalted. The lower, carnal pyramid, debased, degraded, would, therefore, of necessity, dominate and debase all that would fulfill these humiliating needs of the body: Woman for sex, animals and plants for hunger. Woman and her natural locus, the physical landscape, since they cater to the baser half, are both inferior and necessary to survival; therefore, they should and must be dominated and exploited. The world, as thus divided by those having the power to enforce such a viewpoint, has congealed into our present hierarchical-aggression-ownership model of life.

Atwood's critique, then, begins with the mind/body dichotomy, then moves out into other forms of "knowledge" with which we cozen ourselves into believing that we (our minds) are, in fact, in charge here. Subsumed under "knowledge" and the control of reason are scientific texts such as archeology, referenced in such stories as "Significant Moments in the Life of My Mother" and "Hurricane Hazel," guidebooks to the wilderness (*Wilderness Tips*), handbooks to such frightening life processes as childbirth ("Giving Birth"), detective novels with their reassuring volubility in "Giving Birth" and "Bluebeard's Egg," gothic tales and the romantic trash fiction embedded within the larger fictive world of "True Trash," and the "fractured" fairy tales of "Bluebeard's Egg" and "The Man from Mars."

Besides examining the rift between men and women, "Bluebeard's Egg" inverts such traditional fairy-tale elements as the female curiosity and disobedience of the Bluebeard tradition (Grace, "Courting Bluebeard"; Godard; MacLulich). The locked room and the stained, telltale egg that betray two women are recast. Ed, the husband, becomes at once the closed, hard-shelled egg and the locked mysterious room. The mystery becomes a lie concocted by Ed himself that covers his duplicity with the fiction of his stupidity. Anna, his wife, collaborates in writing this fiction; it is a far more acceptable construct on which to build her life, since it grants the certitude of control. Along with tales and romances, the failed "life instructions manual" by which we try to run, and therefore, ruin our lives, abounds in Atwood's poetry, novels, and short-story collections.

While Atwood's short-story collections *Dancing Girls, Bluebeard's Egg*, and *Wilderness Tips* each has its own coherent thematic pattern, the map of her Cartesian hell is discernible through all. Lies and betrayals, as products of the divided self, for instance, are a particular concern in *Dancing Girls*: the narrator of "The War in the Bathroom" is a mind carried along by, and issuing orders to, "its" body: "She [puppet/body] walked along the street. . . . I [mind/narrator] gloated over the houses . . . as she passed them, fondling them. . . . now I could regard this street . . . as mine. . . . These trees were mine. . . . when the snow melted and the trees blossomed, the damp earth and the new leaves and the spring water running in the gutters would be mine" (*Dancing Girls* 4). The mind extends its reifying work from its dissociated body outward to the street and then, finally, to the passing of the seasons, the very processes of life, freezing them into graspable, ownable things. This avaricious mind has just moved into its new boardinghouse and tricks a sick old man out of his bathroom time. The mind lies to itself, translating this aggressive move as a defensive necessity, protecting its body's rights. Thus Atwood traces the process by which the lie of division engenders the "need" for domination.

Louise of "Polarities" tries to create a circle of friends on a mad mission to reunite a polarized city and is tricked and committed to a mental ward. The farm-wife/narrator of "When It Happens" knows that the world is about to end by the soothing classical music on the radio where there used to be news. Sarah of "The Resplendent Quetzal" sends her bird-watcher husband on a fool's errand, pretending to have seen an oriole in a bush. He, in turn, goes, pretending to believe and lying to avoid having to confront her with the truth because this "was one of the many lies that propped things up" (158). Annette ("A Travel Piece") is a travel writer weaving fantasies of perfect, Edenic vacationlands for the readers back home, a scrim of lies that come to "seem like a giant screen, flat and with pictures painted on it to create the illusion of solidity. If you walked up to it and kicked it, it would tear and your foot would go right through, into another space which Annette could only visualize as darkness, a night in which something she did not want to look at was hiding" (140). She is thrust through this screen, a flat system of lies, when her plane goes down and murder and cannibalism become necessary for survival.

Although embedded tales, particularly gothic and fairy tales, are featured in all three collections, *Bluebeard's Egg* makes especially extensive use of them. In the title story, for instance, the narrator, taking another dilettantish night course, is given the assignment of rewriting the Bluebeard tale. Atwood merges herself with her narrator in sharing various interpretations and writing strategies with her readers. The creative process of tale writing and "husband writing" merge as Louise shares her delusory blank-mysterious-egg version of her husband with the readers. This is story as a new sort of mimesis: one that not only mirrors and maps life, as is traditional in stories, but also adds fiction itself and the act of fictionalizing to the mirror image. Atwood, in equating "fact" and fiction, reminds us of the constructed nature of our "reality."

Wilderness Tips opens with a story of summer-camp boys spying on their waitresses sunbathing. One boy, Donny, is in danger of betraying himself and this male acculturation ritual by breaking the rules. He sees the women as titillating body parts, as do the other boys, yet he cannot help wondering about what they are reading. In another story, "Weight," Molly is a victim of her own hope, which can be seen as yet another of life's fictions, a construct that can either support or imprison. Molly and Curtis objectify each other, but Curtis takes this to the physical limit. The narrator, remembering her friend, calls her a "fixer" who thought that she could "fix things that were broken." Curtis, however, proves himself beyond even her skills, since he was "so broken he thought the normal state of the world was broken. Maybe that's why he tried to break Molly. . . . when he couldn't do it one way, he did it another" (227). This becomes one of Atwood's grisly puns when, a week after Molly left Curtis, "arms and legs started turning up" (231).

Atwood has provided a cogent examination of "a world-view and a science which, by reconceptualizing reality as a machine rather than a living organism, sanctioned the domination of both nature and women" (Merchant qtd. in McCombs, *Critical Essays* 4). Through her own work, she seeks a new, non-Cartesian way of thinking and writing. Our "life paradigm" must evolve, as Fritjof Capra has pointed out, into a view of a living universe in continual evolution, a single, organic whole "whose parts are essentially interrelated and can be understood only as patterns of a cosmic process" (Capra 78). Atwood's exposure of the constructed nature of our life paradigms implies that we can create new, more unified, and unifying, models. Atwood has drawn a map and marked it with an *x*. (You are *here*, and boy, is this place a mess!) Has she left us a trail? Shown us a way out? Is she hopeful? To get back to that old question, is her voice encouraging, warm, filled with unalloyed hope and joy? Nope. Is that her job?

WORKS CITED AND CONSULTED

Primary

Short Stories

Atwood, Margaret. *Bluebeard's Egg*. Toronto: McClelland & Stewart, 1983; New York: Ballantine Books, 1987.
————. *Dancing Girls and Other Stories*. Toronto: McClelland & Stewart, 1978; New York: Bantam, 1978.
————. *Good Bones*. Toronto: Coach House Press, 1992; London: Bloomsbury, 1992; as *Goodbones and Simple Murders*. New York: Doubleday, 1994.
————. *Murder in the Dark*. Toronto: Coach House Press, 1983.
————. *Wilderness Tips*. Toronto: McClelland & Stewart, 1991; New York: Bantam, 1993.

Novels

Atwood, Margaret. *Alias Grace*. Toronto: McClelland & Stewart, 1996.
————. *Bodily Harm*. Toronto: McClelland & Stewart, 1981; New York: Simon & Schuster, 1982.

————. *Cat's Eye*. Toronto: McClelland & Stewart, 1988; New York: Bantam, 1989.
————. *The Edible Woman*. Toronto: McClelland & Stewart, 1969; Boston: Little, Brown, 1970.
————. *The Handmaid's Tale*. Toronto: McClelland & Stewart, 1985; Boston: Houghton Mifflin, 1986.
————. *Lady Oracle*. Toronto: McClelland & Steward, 1976; New York: Simon & Schuster, 1976.
————. *Life Before Man*. Toronto: McClelland & Stewart, 1979; New York: Simon & Schuster, 1979.
————. *The Robber Bride*. New York: Doubleday, 1993.
————. *Surfacing*. New York: Simon & Schuster, 1972.

Poetry

Atwood, Margaret. *The Animals in That Country*. Toronto: Oxford University Press, 1969; Boston: Little, Brown, 1968.
————. *The Circle Game*. Toronto: Contact Press, 1966; Toronto: Anansi, 1967.
————. *Double Persephone*. Toronto: Hawkshead Press, 1961.
————. *The Journals of Susanna Moodie*. Toronto: Oxford University Press, 1970.
————. *Power Politics*. Toronto: Anansi, 1971; New York: Harper & Row, 1973.
————. *Procedures for Underground*. Toronto: Oxford University Press, 1970; Boston: Little, Brown, 1970.
————. *Selected Poems 1966–1984*. Toronto: Oxford University Press, 1976; New York: Simon & Schuster, 1978.
————. *Selected Poems II: Poems Selected and New, 1976–1986*. Toronto: Oxford University Press, 1986; Boston: Houghton Mifflin, 1987.
————. *True Stories*. Toronto: Oxford University Press, 1981; New York: Simon & Schuster, 1982.
————. *Two-Headed Poems*. Toronto: Oxford University Press, 1978; New York: Simon & Schuster, 1982.
————. *You Are Happy*. Toronto: Oxford University Press, 1974; New York: Harper & Row, 1975.

Criticism and History

Atwood, Margaret. *Days of the Rebels: 1815–1840*. Toronto: Natural Science of Canada, 1977.
————. *Second Words: Selected Critical Prose*. Toronto: Anansi, 1982.
————. *Strange Things: The Malevolent North in Canadian Literature*. Toronto: Oxford University Press, 1995.
————. *Survival: A Thematic Guide to Canadian Literature*. Toronto: Anansi, 1972.

Secondary

Brown, Russell. "Atwood's Sacred Wells [*Dancing Girls*, poetry, and *Surfacing*]." McCombs, *Critical Essays* 213–28.
Capra, Fritjof. *The Turning Point: Science, Society, and the Rising Culture*. Toronto: Bantam, 1983.

Godard, Barbara. "Tales within Tales: Margaret Atwood's Folk Narratives." *Canadian Literature* 109 (1986): 57–84.

Grace, Sherrill. "Courting Bluebeard with Bartók, Atwood, and Fowles: Modern Treatment of the Bluebeard Theme." *Journal of Modern Literature* 11.2 (1984): 245–62.

Grace, Sherrill, and Lorraine Weir, eds. *Margaret Atwood: Language, Text, and System.* Vancouver: University of British Columbia Press, 1983.

McCombs, Judith. "Atwood's Fictive Portraits of the Artist: From Victim to Surfacer, from Oracle to Birth." *Women's Studies* 12.1 (1986): 69–88.

———, ed. *Critical Essays on Margaret Atwood.* Boston: G. K. Hall, 1988.

Ondaatje, Michael. "*The Circle Game* by Margaret Atwood." *Critical Essays on Margaret Atwood.* Ed. Judith McCombs. Boston: G. K. Hall, 1988. 29–32.

Onley, Gloria. "Power Politics in Bluebeard's Castle [*Power Politics, The Edible Woman, Surfacing, Survival, Procedures for Underground*, and 'Polarities']." McCombs, *Critical Essays* 70–89.

Rosenberg, Jerome H. *Margaret Atwood.* Twayne's World Author Series: Canadian Literature. Ed. Robert Lecker. Boston: Twayne, 1984.

Vipond, Dianne. "The Body Politic in Margaret Atwood's 'True Trash.' " *Short Story* 3.1 (Spring 1995): 84–91.

TONI CADE BAMBARA
(March 25 1939–December 9, 1995)

Carol Franko

BIOGRAPHY

Bambara was born Toni Cade in New York City to Helen Brent Henderson Cade. She took the additional name Bambara from a signature on a sketchbook that she found in her great-grandmother's trunk. (Bambara is also the name of an African tribe). Bambara and her older brother Walter Cade grew up with their mother in Harlem, Bedford-Stuyvesant, and Jersey City, and she attended several public, private, and boarding schools in New York State, New Jersey, and the South. She received a B.A. in theater arts and English literature from Queens College in 1959, the same year that her first short story, "Sweet Town," was published in *Vendome* magazine. Bambara went on to earn an M.A. in American literature from the City College of New York; she also had training in theater, dance, and film in the United States and abroad.

Always a writer, educator, and political activist committed to both black nationalism and feminism, Bambara had a number of occupations: English instructor (at City College) and professor (at Livingston College and Rutgers and Duke universities), welfare investigator (in New York City), program director of a community center (New York City), and artist-in-residence (Spelman College). A further indication of the intertwining of education, writing, and activism in Bambara's life was her work with a number of black and women's studies programs in the United States as well as her creation of and participation in African-American writers' groups, writers' workshops, and community arts centers. Bambara's writing and editing career spanned several genres: essay, public address (at prisons, rallies, and so on), short story, novel, and scriptwriting for television and film. In the 1970s Bambara moved to Atlanta with her daughter, Karma. Bambara died of colon cancer in 1995. Posthumous publications include *Deep Sightings and Rescue Missions*, a collection of fictional and nonfictional work by Bambara edited and with a preface by Toni Morrison, and *Those Bones*

Are Not My Child, Bambara's fictional account of the Atlanta child murders of the early 1980s.

Bambara's commitment to individual agency, to family, and to community defines the thematic base of her art. Her commitment to social and political revolution was inseparable from these personal, local ties. In articles and dedications to her books, Bambara praised her mother for giving her the emotional and physical space to develop her creativity. She also credited what she enjoyed most in her work to her family: "the laughter and the outrage and the attention to language." Her family were "gifted laughers" who, through trips to the movies and to "Speakers Corner" in the neighborhood, taught her "the power of the word, the importance of the resistance tradition, and the high standards our community has regarding verbal performance" ("Salvation" 45–46). Fittingly, Bambara described her writing career as beginning when as a child she took the role of "neighborhood scribe" ("What It Is" 167), helping people to write personal and business letters, thus participating in the power of the word at a basic, social level.

Bambara was one of the first to bring together the black movement and feminism. In 1970, she edited and contributed three essays to *The Black Woman*, an anthology of varied writings by black women that demonstrates both the difference between and the solidarity among black women of the civil rights generation. In 1971, she edited *Tales and Stories for Black Folks*, which includes the first printing of her fine feminist story "Raymond's Run," two brief animal tales by Bambara (one coauthored), and her preface, "Our Great Kitchen Tradition," in which she tells African-American children to listen to the stories of their elders because this oral tradition, unlike racist stereotypes of blacks, tells "the truth" about their lives and heritage.

The Black Woman and *Tales* were followed by two collections of her short stories: *Gorilla, My Love* (fifteen stories, 1972) and *The Sea Birds Are Still Alive* (ten stories, 1977). *Gorilla, My Love* includes the stories Bambara wrote between 1959 and 1970, except for the two short animal tales in *Tales and Stories for Black Folks*. The stories in this first collection depict relationships among African Americans in the urban North and the rural South. Between the publication of *Gorilla* and *Sea Birds*, Bambara made trips to Cuba and Vietnam, where she met with women in resistance movements, and she relocated in Atlanta, where she became involved with several community arts programs while serving as artist-in-residence at Spelman College. These events left their mark on stories in her second collection, which is more explicitly political in theme than *Gorilla*.

Bambara's first novel, *The Salt Eaters*, was published in 1980 and won the American Book Award in 1981; her second novel was *If Blessing Comes* (1987). She also wrote award-winning screenplays for television and film documentaries. Her work is the subject of a growing body of criticism. Although *The Salt Eaters* is currently receiving the most attention, her two story collections are also critically acclaimed, and individual stories from them are frequently anthologized;

Bambara also based several screenplays on stories from both collections. *Gorilla, My Love* probably remains her most read and most loved book.

CRITICISM

Criticism of Bambara's short stories and of her first novel implicitly or explicitly focuses on how the "neighborhood scribe" became a writer who, as Ruth Elizabeth Burks suggests, acts for her community as a griot—a West African musician-entertainer whose performances include tribal histories and genealogies—or, as Elliott Butler-Evans suggests, as a storyteller rooted in oral tradition whose stories unify people and sustain values. Bambara herself might have named this writer function "truthteller," one who tells the truth about past, present, and possible futures of African Americans.

Discussions of her short stories emphasize their lyrical realism, their faithful rendering of Black English and black working-class experience, their structural resemblance to black art forms like jazz and the verbal performance of "signifying," and their ethnic and feminist themes. Ruth Elizabeth Burks, in "From Baptism to Resurrection: Toni Cade Bambara and the Incongruity of Language," identifies a paradox in Bambara's fiction, arguing that Bambara's rich use of idiomatic black speech is juxtaposed with the frequent theme that language is inadequate, and that characters' salvation lies in a wordless spiritual communion. In *Race, Gender, and Desire*, Elliott Butler-Evans sees the central paradox differently, focusing on the ideological tension between feminism and black nationalism in Bambara's stories. Butler-Evans argues that Bambara demythologizes black male characters with a deflating realism while remythologizing female agency through female characters' appropriation of traditionally male black practices, like the verbal performance of signifying (exchanging hyperbolic insults and other vivid dialoguing). While Butler-Evans's analysis is illuminating, it is also possible to see Bambara's short stories as effecting a feminist transformation of black revolution, one that aims to change destructive roles for both men and women and their families in the black community. Eleanor Traylor's study of both *The Salt Eaters* and the story collections in "Music as Theme: The Jazz Mode in the Works of Toni Cade Bambara" emphasizes the cultural work that Bambara accomplishes as a griot/storyteller/jazz artist. In her astute discussion of the title story in *Sea Birds*, Traylor argues that Bambara's fiction informs "modernity," the present moment that looks to a possible future, with "ancestry," the wisdom of the past.

Bambara herself was an intriguing commentator on her short stories. Writing in short fiction was an affirmation, both of her affinity for the form and of the necessity that she be able to combine writing with activism. The short-story form suited her temperament, Bambara commented, because "it makes a modest appeal for attention, allowing me to slip up alongside the reader on her/his blind side and grab'm." Further, Bambara thought of herself as "more sociable and street-based-work-committed than noveling permits" ("Salvation" 43). Bambara's contributions to the contemporary short story include experimentation in oral/literary and aesthetic/didactic narrative blends, in playful, anecdotal structures, in verb tense (especially the present tense), and in portrayals of epiphanies and/or threshold moments of individuals and communities.

ANALYSIS

"Writing for me is still an act of language first and foremost," said Bambara in a 1979 interview (Guy-Sheftall 236), and the phrase "act of language" is suggestive for considering Bambara as a writer of activist short stories. Although Bambara never considered fiction writing a substitute for political work, her short stories explore and affirm the struggle for agency of black people on an individual and communal level. Characters are presented both as acted on by and as actors within society—society including the black communities that are the focus of her stories and the dominant white culture that, when it appears, is depicted as an oppressive adversary and the reason why revolution is needed.

The often-noted importance of black oral and musical traditions to the form of her stories pushes her short fiction toward performance art, like the street-corner debates of her youth. Her frequent, complex use of the present tense, coupled with anecdotal flashbacks (which are also often in the present tense), adds to and complicates the sense of immediacy in her stories. Verbal and situational humor is another important feature. This performance mode is successful at portraying the personal and social discovery and affirmation of agency.

In her first collection, *Gorilla, My Love*, several stories show a first-person narrator (often a young girl named Hazel) performing her developing agency. Other stories in *Gorilla* make the first-person narrator more of a recording eye and ear who presents a vignette of the struggles for agency in a black urban or rural community.

The title story, "Gorilla, My Love," is a story of the young narrator's disappointment in and disapproval of broken promises, but it nonetheless portrays her agency within a supportive family. (The theme of keeping covenants is an important one to Bambara.) Hazel, the narrator, records a double disappointment. Currently she is outraged and saddened that an uncle who had promised to marry her is not only making plans to marry another, but has forgotten his promise and does not even apologize. This comic but poignant dilemma is paired with a triumphant incident when Hazel complains to the patronizing manager of a theater because the movie showing, *Gorilla, My Love*, features no gorillas and is a sappy religious film: "Just about anybody in my family is better than this god they always talkin about" (15). Hazel's moral outrage at how "grownups messin over kids just cause they little and can't take em to court" is juxtaposed with a description of her Mama, "her hat pulled down bad and that Persian lamb coat draped back over one hip on account of she got her fist planted there so she can talk that talk which gets us all hypnotized"—the talk being a scolding of teachers in Hazel's school who "start playin the dozens behind colored folks"

(17). Since the movie manager refuses to return Hazel's money, she starts a fire under the candy stand that closes down the theater for a week. Although her parents are about to punish her, they listen to her reasons and agree that this time she was justified.

The often-anthologized "Raymond's Run" is also narrated by a young Hazel; this story deftly combines Hazel's enactment of her agency with a feminist and socialist critique of the larger society's values: Hazel is a proud, fast runner in her urban neighborhood where even the grass "feels hard," and she is equally proud of her responsibility for caring for her retarded brother, Raymond. At the May Day races, Hazel scorns conventional notions of femininity that are inseparable from a profit-based and class-polarized society:

You'd think [my mother would] be glad her daughter ain't out there prancing around a May Pole getting the new clothes all dirty and sweaty and trying to act like a fairy or a flower or whatever you're supposed to be when you should be trying to be yourself, whatever that is, which is, as far as I am concerned, a poor black girl who really can't afford to buy shoes and a new dress you only wear once a lifetime cause it won't fit next year. (27)

Hazel affirms her prowess as a runner (she gets first place), but her achievement extends beyond this to embrace both her brother, whom she realizes shares her talent for running and whom she now plans to train, and Gretchen, another runner, who has previously hidden her hard work in training, but who now huffs and puffs "like a real pro." Hazel and Gretchen share a "big smile of respect between [them]," something Hazel has thought impossible for girls to do.

"The Lesson" extends the social critique of "Raymond's Run." A new, articulate woman in the neighborhood takes Hazel and her friends to Fifth Avenue and the F.A.O. Schwarz toystore, where the clowns cost thirty-five dollars (a sum, Hazel muses, that would pay any number of necessities in her family's life) and the toy sailboats one thousand. Hazel's mentor urges her to consider "what kind of society it is in which some people can spend on a toy what it would cost to feed a family of six or seven. What do you think?" Hazel goes off alone to "think this day through" and is determined that "ain't nobody gonna beat me at nuthin" (96).

While "The Lesson" shows black children being educated by an elder into the harsh social realities that call for revolution, "My Man Bovanne" (the first story in *Gorilla*) shows young black revolutionaries failing to appreciate their elders. An alternate Hazel persona, here an old woman, affirms her social consciousness and her sexuality in the face of her revolutionary children who "keep talkin bout what's proper for a woman [her] age" (7). "Old folks is the nation," Hazel quotes her activist children, "and I mean to do my part"—this as she takes home to gently seduce the old man Bovanne, former neighborhood jack-of-all-trades, whom her children have disparaged.

"Talkin bout Sonny" and "Basement" have first-person narrators who mostly function to record a significant problem in the black community. At a neighborhood bar, the narrator (a social worker named Betty) of "Talkin" and the man she is seeing (Delauney) discuss how a mutual friend, Sonny, recently snapped and stabbed his wife. Delauney empathizes with Sonny's one explanation, "Something came over me," and even seems to justify his friend's attack on his wife. The story is open-ended, merely indicating the connection between societal pressures on men and male violence against women. "Basement" comically yet seriously records the problem of child abuse while also showing adults taking responsibility to protect children. The young narrator learns from her friend's mother and aunt (Norma and Fay) that she shouldn't go into the basement of their apartment building because the superintendent and his friends might assault her. The story juxtaposes Norma's and Fay's comic, hyperbolic debate on the nature of men (Norma attacks, Fay defends) and Norma's wild chase after the supposedly culpable superintendent with both women's concern to inform and protect the narrator.

"The Johnson Girls," the last story in *Gorilla*, is a tour de force of Bambara's short-fiction/performance art. Agency is eloquently revealed as a communal project. Several women friends, including the younger narrator, gather around the admirable, independent Inez, who needs support and advice because she may be losing the best relationship with a man that she or perhaps any of her friends have known. Inez's friends try to make her see that Roy is a special man worth her breaking out of her usual strict respect of her own and others' autonomy. Each friend "performs" in vivid language her angle on life and male-female relationships. An ongoing feminist theme is the difficulty of strong women forming satisfactory relations with men, as the character Sugar explains: "A man, no matter how messy he is, I mean even if he some straight-up basket case, can always get some good woman, two or three for that matter, to go for his shit. Right? But a woman? If her shit ain't together, she can forget it unless she very lucky and got a Great Ma Drew working roots" (172). The young narrator is intrigued to see the Sugar whom she knows as a competent professional, the manager of a television studio, reveal this other side to her life. The point of "The Johnson Girls" is not that women only think about men but that women and men need one another and that women need their women friends. Beyond these themes, what is enduring in this story are the voices of Inez's friends as they valiantly and eloquently "speak their speak."

In Bambara's second collection, *The Sea Birds Are Still Alive*, her performance art is more explicitly political in its treatment of agency. While stories like "Medley" (a tour de force of anecdotal structure) and "Witchbird" are seen as similar to Bambara's art in *Gorilla*, some readers have also complained about the newly overt politics of many of these stories. Bambara herself commented that as short fiction, she found the tales of *Sea Birds* too "long and dense" (Guy-Sheftall 244). An alternate reading would see them as hybrid experiments that combine the lyrical realism of *Gorilla* with a critical utopian anticipation of who and what black people are and may become. Self-discovery is a political act in these stories; likewise, the discovery of and participation in the black movement and other revolutionary politics lead to new agency for the self.

The technical difficulty of the first story, "The Organizer's Wife," with its continual juxtaposing of past and present moments, exemplifies this experimental performance of agency. Virginia, the protagonist, is the wife of Graham, the leader of this rural community, who is currently in jail for opposing the sale of land for mining operations. As Virginia walks to town, carrying their newborn child, her memories of her meetings with Graham and falling in love seem to reveal her as an individual who wants to escape the poverty and hardship of her town and who has only reluctantly participated in its local revolution to keep the land and use it ecologically and fairly. But when she visits the preacher whose treachery got Graham arrested, Virginia's speech and actions reveal her to herself as someone now passionately involved in the community's struggles:

"Did you sell the land as well?" she heard herself saying, rushing in the doorway much too fast. "You might have waited like folks asked you. You didn't have to. Enough granite under this schoolhouse alone"—she stamped, frightening him—"to carry both the districts for years and years, if we developed it ourselves." She heard the "we ourselves" explode against her teeth. (18)

This personal transformation in the midst of social transformation where the I affirms herself or himself in a statement of "we ourselves" occurs variously in several other stories, including "The Apprentice," "Broken Field Running," "The Long Night," "A Tender Man," and "Christmas Eve at Johnson's Drugs N Goods."

"A Tender Man," the only story narrated by a male in either of Bambara's collections, complements "The Organizer's Wife" in its treatment of personal and social revolution. The narrator is about to participate in public activism (a student strike), but he gets caught up in a new relationship with a woman that returns him to a sense of responsibility for his daughter, the child of an unbalanced white woman, his former wife. As the narrator undergoes a difficult dialogue with the new woman in his life (who has considered adopting his daughter), he puts together his present self, active in black politics, with his past desire to be a "tender man" when he grew up. Both selves—public and private—are tentatively affirmed at the end of the story.

The title story of *Sea Birds* is set on a boat in Southeast Asia during a revolutionary war and thus enlarges the significant community beyond black urban and rural U.S. communities. It also enlarges the point of view to an omniscient one that juxtaposes a variety of oppressed and oppressor peoples. Here the agency of oppressed people in the midst of revolution is affirmed, while the assumptions of racists are satirized. The relative impersonality of this story is transformed at the end when the narrator takes us into the mind of a woman who has survived torture by the imperialist army opposing the people's rebellion.

"I write for a whole hour in my diary trying to connect with the future me and trying not to hear my daddy snoring." This passage from "Christmas Eve at Johnson's Drugs N Goods," the final story in *Sea Birds*, suggests how it is reminiscent of the Hazel stories in *Gorilla* while it encompasses the overt political themes more characteristic of *Sea Birds*. Candy, the first-person narrator, who lives with her aunt and uncle since her actress mother is on the road, is at a threshold in her life, poised between childhood and adulthood and between political naïveté and awareness. Familiar techniques in the story include an anecdotal or improvisational structure (anecdotes triggering memories that produce new anecdotes) and hyperbolic, "signifying" dialogues and descriptions. Candy and her coworkers at Johnson's drugstore while away the last working hour on Christmas Eve by engaging with two colorful shoppers, "vaudevillian" actresses. Candy admires these women, dressed in fur coats and verbally acute, but when they snub Obatale, the young man who works in the drug department, she changes her evaluation. Meanwhile, Candy's thoughts combine memories of her father, who is remarried and settled in another city, with recent doings in the drugstore. As she continues to hope that her father will visit her this holiday, she remembers how on her birthday last year they wordlessly said good night, squeezing each other's hands; she regrets that she did not speak the words of understanding and forgiveness that she was feeling—of how she knew "he feeling bad about moving away and all, but what can he do, he got a life to lead. Just like Mama got her life to lead. Just like I got my life to lead and'll probably leave here myself one day and become an actress or a director" (196–97).

Words that do get spoken become the "alchemy" of Candy's growth, and this process is performed in the story in the humorous/serious manner characteristic of Bambara's short fiction. Her Aunt Harriet, who is always doing crossword puzzles (and whose crossword vocabulary gives Candy the word "alchemy"), clashes with the white druggist at Johnson's (a man who reminds Candy of "Nazi youth") because, unlike the local healer, he refuses to explain the process he uses to make the drugs. A furious Aunt Harriet digs "down deep into her crossword-puzzle words," calls the druggist "a bunch of choicest names," and produces a line—"Medication without explanation is obscene"—that Candy and the other Johnson's employees imitate extravagantly for a week. When they are looking for an Aunt Harriet line to describe "the street riots in the sixties and so forth," the "new dude in Drugs" suggests "Revolution without Transformation is Half-assed" (200). This pithy statement leads Candy to make friends with Obatale, the "new dude," to find out what books he reads and look them up herself. So on this Christmas Eve, when the well-dressed and satirical shoppers make fun of the not-well-dressed Obatale, Candy makes a choice of which kind of person she wants to emulate and befriend. Obatale, in turn, invites her to an African holiday celebration; her acceptance makes the impression that Candy is about to enter a new community of blacks who are politically aware as well as being, as she comments, "nice people." This community, grounded in celebration of African heritages, will support Candy in ways that her family can no longer do, although her family has also contributed to the "alchemy" of her growing personal and social agency.

As a major African-American writer of the twentieth century, Toni Cade Bambara in her artful and political short fiction continues to enact the responsibility and the truthtelling that she saw as central to the "act of language."

> It's a tremendous responsibility—responsibility and honor—to be a writer, an artist, a cultural worker . . . whatever you want to call this vocation. One's got to see what the factory worker sees, what the prisoner sees, what the welfare children see, what the scholar sees, got to see what the ruling-class mythmakers see as well, in order to tell the truth and not get trapped. (Tate 14; ellipsis in original)

WORKS CITED AND CONSULTED

Primary

Bambara, Toni Cade, ed. [as Toni Cade]. *The Black Woman: An Anthology.* New York: New American Library, 1970.

——. "The Bombing of Osage." Screenplay. Produced by WHYY-TV Philadelphia 1986.

——. "Cecil B. Moore: Master Tactician of Direct Action." Screenplay. Produced by WHYY-TV Philadelphia, 1987.

——. *Deep Sightings and Rescue Missions.* Ed. Toni Morrison. New York: Pantheon, 1996.

——. "Epitaph for Willie." Screenplay. Produced by K. Heran Productions, Inc., 1982.

——. *Gorilla, My Love.* New York: Random House, 1972.

——. *If Blessing Comes.* New York: Random House, 1987.

——. "The Johnson Girls." Screenplay. Produced by National Educational Television, 1972.

——. "The Long Night." Screenplay. Produced by American Broadcasting Co., 1981.

——. "Raymond's Run." Screenplay. Produced by Public Broadcasting System, 1985.

——. *The Salt Eaters.* New York: Random House, 1980.

——. "Salvation Is the Issue." *Black Women Writers (1950–1980): A Critical Evaluation.* Ed. Mari Evans. Garden City, NY: Anchor/Doubleday, 1984. 41–47.

——. *The Sea Birds Are Still Alive: Collected Stories.* New York: Random House, 1977.

——. ed. *Tales and Stories for Black Folks.* Garden City, NY: Doubleday, 1971.

——. "Tar Baby." Screenplay based on Toni Morrison's novel. Produced by Sanger/Brooks Film Productions, 1984.

——. *Those Bones Are Not My Child.* New York: Pantheon, 1999.

——. "Transactions." Screenplay. Produced by School of Social Work; Atlanta University, 1979.

——. "What It Is I Think I'm Doing Anyhow." *The Writer on Her Work: Contemporary Women Reflect on Their Art and Their Situation.* Ed. J. Sternberg. New York: W. W. Norton, 1980. 153–168.

——. "Zora." Screenplay. Produced by WGBH-TV Boston, 1971.

Secondary

Butler-Evans, Elliott. *Race, Gender, and Desire: Narrative Strategies in the Fiction of Toni Cade Bambara, Toni Morrison, and Alice Walker*. Philadelphia: Temple University Press, 1989.

Burks, Ruth Elizabeth. "From Baptism to Resurrection: Toni Cade Bambara and the Incongruity of Language." Evans 48–57.

Deck, Alice A. "Toni Cade Bambara." *Dictionary of Literary Biography*. Vol. 38. *Afro-American Writers after 1955*. Ed. Thadious M. Davis and Trudier Harris. Detroit: Gale Research, 1985. 12–22.

Evans, Mari, ed. *Black Women Writers (1950–1980): A Critical Evaluation*. Garden City, NY: Anchor Press/Doubleday, 1984.

Guy-Sheftall, Beverly. "Commitment: Toni Cade Bambara Speaks" (interview). *Sturdy Black Bridges: Visions of Black Women in Literature*. Ed. Roseann P. Bell, Bettye J. Parker, and Beverly Guy-Sheftall. Garden City, NY: Doubleday, 1979. 230–49.

Mazurkiewicz, Margaret. "Toni Cade Bambara." *Black Writers*. Ed. Linda Metzger. Detroit: Gale Research, 1989.

Tate, Claudia. "Toni Cade Bambara" (interview). *Black Women Writers at Work*. Ed. Claudia Tate. New York: Continuum, 1983. 12–38.

Traylor, Eleanor W. "Music as Theme: The Jazz Mode in the Works of Toni Cade Bambara." Evans 58–70.

Vertreace, Martha M. "A Bibliography of Writings about Toni Cade Bambara." *American Women Writing Fiction: Memory, Identity, Family, Space*. Ed. Mickey Pearlman. Lexington: University Press of Kentucky, 1989. 168–71.

———. "A Bibliography of Writings by Toni Cade Bambara." *American Women Writing Fiction: Memory, Identity, Family, Space*. Ed. Mickey Pearlman. Lexington: University Press of Kentucky, 1989. 166–68.

———. "Toni Cade Bambara: The Dance of Character and Community." *American Women Writing Fiction: Memory, Identity, Family, Space*. Ed. Mickey Pearlman. Lexington: University Press of Kentucky, 1989. 155–66.

Who's Who among Black Americans. Ed. Iris Cloyd. Detroit: Gale Research, 1990–91.

JOHN SIMMONS BARTH
(May 27, 1930–   )

Terry J. Martin

BIOGRAPHY

John Barth was born in Cambridge, Maryland, near the eastern shore, the setting of many of his works. An opposite-sex twin, he has shown a lifelong fascination with doubling as a literary motif. He received his B.A. in 1951 and his M.A. in 1952 at Johns Hopkins University, where a job filing books in the Classics Library spurred his fascination with ancient Oriental tale cycles and made him "a critical pluralist for life" (*Friday* 9). Further formative influences on Barth's fiction include his training and occasional work as a jazz musician, which gained him an early appreciation for improvisation, and his many years of college teaching, which enhanced his knowledge of literary theory and tradition. Barth has taught at Pennsylvania State University (1953–65), the State University of New York at Buffalo (1965–69), and, more recently, Johns Hopkins University, at which he is now professor emeritus. In 1950, Barth married Harriet Anne Strickland, with whom he had three children. He was divorced in 1969, and in 1970 he married a former student, Shelly Rosenberg, with whom he has lived in the Baltimore area since 1973.

Barth claims that his books were written in pairs. His first two novels, *The Floating Opera* (1956) and *The End of the Road* (1958), have existentialist themes. The next two, *The Sot-Weed Factor* (1960) and *Giles Goat-Boy* (1966), show a growing fascination with myth, partly the result of his discovery of such noted myth critics as Lord Raglan, Otto Rank, and Joseph Campbell. In 1968, Barth published his first, widely influential book of short stories, entitled *Lost in the Funhouse: Fiction for Print, Tape, Live Voice*, followed in 1972 by *Chimera*, a collection of three novellas that won the National Book Award. Barth has since published mainly novels, including *LETTERS* (1979), *Sabbatical: A Romance* (1982), *The Tidewater Tales* (1987), *The Last Voyage of Somebody the Sailor* (1991), and *Once Upon a Time: A Floating Opera* (1994). However, in 1996, Barth published a second book of short stories, entitled *On with the Story: Stories*. In addition, Barth has published two books of collected essays: *The Friday Book* (1984) and *Further Fridays* (1995). In the former are collected two landmark essays, "The Literature of Exhaustion" (1967) and its companion piece "The Literature of Replenishment" (1980), in which Barth defines his own postmodernist aesthetic. He later reaffirmed and extended these views in "Post-modernism Revisited" (formerly titled "The Novelist as Critic" [1988]) and "4½ Lectures: The Stuttgart Seminars on Postmodernism, Chaos Theory, and the Romantic Arabesque" (delivered as a lecture in 1991, published in 1995), both of which appear in *Further Fridays*.

CRITICISM

Barth is generally either "praised or damned as postmodernist" (*Friday Book* 196), depending on the critic's aesthetic principles. The most common criticism of Barth's short fiction is that it is overly self-conscious, self-indulgent, and self-referential almost to the exclusion of any "realistic," external, or "objective" content. Indeed, Barth's essay "The Literature of Exhaustion" was widely mis-understood as saying that the possibilities of fiction had already been used up and that nothing was left for writers but to lapse into self-conscious parody. In addition, detractors such as John Gardner have gone so far as to pronounce Barth's stories fake and immoral because they depict life as absurd (94–96).

However, a growing number of critics have proclaimed Barth one of the most important and innovative writers of short fiction of the last few decades. Edward Walkiewicz, for example, defends Barth from the charge of excessive self-consciousness by pointing out that such criticism "fails to do justice to Barth's use of 'the narrative viewpoint' and 'the process of composition' as 'dramati-cally relevant emblems' " (97–98)   that is, it ignores how the medium itself dramatically forms the message in Barth's stories. Max F. Schulz has similarly praised "Barth's theoretical interest in fictional form . . . and genius for abstract manipulation of plot" (3), noting that "Barth's mature career as a fabulist begins with *Lost in the Funhouse*" (xiv). David Morrell cites the title story, "Lost in the Funhouse," as "the most important, progressive, trend-defining American short fiction of its decade" (96).

Although Barth distrusts labels, he has alternately described works such as *Lost in the Funhouse* as "mainly late-modernist" (qtd. in Tobin 89) and as "postmodernist" (*Friday Book* 203), putting his own spin on the sense of either term. Critics have found it difficult to categorize Barth's work. He has been variously labeled a metafictionist, a satirist, a fabulist, an antirealist, a regressive parodist, and a cheerful nihilist. In describing his work, Barth himself turns to oxymorons such as "passionate . . . farce" (*Friday Book* 59). Barth's fiction is indeed paradoxical. It intentionally makes use of many of the very conventions that it self-consciously rejects; although it is highly experimental and avant-garde, it is nevertheless conservatively rooted in traditional oral narrative; although it reflects the "Tragic View of Everything" (*Friday Book* 177), Barth's is "ineluctably the comic muse" (*Friday Book* 159); and so on. Even Barth's attitude toward the modern short story is paradoxical: a self-professed "congenital novelist" (*Further Fridays* 92), he decries the "hyperconstrictive, more or less constipative form" of the modern short story (*Further Fridays* 96), which he finds "claustrophobic" (98); nevertheless, he admits, "I was in love . . . with the short story" (*Further Fridays* 102). However one ultimately defines Barth's artistry, he has undoubtedly made one of the most original, brilliant, and provocative contributions to both the theory and the practice of short fiction.

ANALYSIS

Of *Lost in the Funhouse*, Barth has written, "[T]he most important . . . objective of most of these stories . . . is to try whether different kinds of artistical felt ultimacies and cul-de-sacs can be employed against themselves to do valid new work" (*Friday Book* 79), which is essentially Barth's view of postmodernism. Like Hawthorne, Barth is a literary revisionist, and his stories are twice-told tales containing elements of ancient myths and exhausted narrative conventions that are made to speak in new and complex ways. This strategy is especially well exemplified by the first story, "Frame-Tale," consisting of a modified Möbius strip with the words "ONCE UPON A TIME THERE WAS A STORY THAT BEGAN" on alternate sides of the same page. When the words are cut out, twisted, and joined beginning to end, they form a *regressus in infinitum* (i.e., ONCE UPON A TIME THERE WAS A STORY THAT BEGAN ONCE UPON A TIME . . .). Thus in Barth's postmodern rendering, a conventional fairy-tale opening is wrenched into a parodic and paradoxical self-reflexivity; instead of performing its traditional function of introducing a classic narrative, it loops back forever upon itself, thereby engendering an infinite number of frames and proclaiming itself as artifice. This is circularity "with a twist" (*Funhouse* vii), and in this fashion Barth co-opts and recycles old forms to create new meanings.

As an ironic frame for the other stories, "Frame-Tale" suggests the absurdity of the individual life cycle that the book as a whole constitutes. According to Barth, the life cycle is that of Ambrose Mensch. Given the potential "Everyman" sense of "Mensch" as well as Barth's acknowledgment that "ontogeny recapitulates phylogeny" (*Friday Book* 24), Ambrose is meant to be representative. Indeed, Barth's stories, like his early existentialist novels, typically depict the absurdity of life. The narrator of "Night-Sea Journey," for instance, declares, "[T]here is no sense, only senseless love, senseless death" (*Funhouse* 13). The characters in Barth's early stories must learn to live within the context of the paradox that it is "no meaningfuller to drown [one]self than to go on swimming" (*Funhouse* 13). Many feel an impulse toward suicide; none strongly affirms life. At best they opt, like Menelaus in "Menelaiad," to live for "the absurd, unending possibility of love" (*Funhouse* 167), or, like the unnamed narrator of "Anonymaiad," they find compensation in artistic endeavor. Yet Barth does not consider his stories "long-faced." He says, "They're pessimistic, but I hope they're entertaining" (*Friday Book* 74).

In Barth's stories, technical innovation, whether of narrative form, style, or point of view, is brilliantly wedded to theme and content. A self-proclaimed "romantic formalis[t]" (*Further Fridays* 289), Barth seeks to write fiction in which "the process of narration becomes the content of the narrative, . . . or the form or medium has metaphorical value and dramatical relevance" (*Friday Book* 79). Thus Barth's funhouse, like the labyrinth in Borges's *Labyrinths*, serves both as literary symbol and as structural paradigm. As the central symbol of the book, the funhouse represents the chaos and complexity of human experience. It refers to ironic self-consciousness (e.g., Ambrose "wondered at the endless replication of his image in the mirrors. . . . [H]e *lost himself in the reflection* that the necessity for an observer makes perfect observation impossible" [94]). It refers to the rite of passage into adulthood ("[E]veryone begins in the same place; how is it that most go along without difficulty but a few lose their way?" [79]). It refers to the intricacies of art ("[Ambrose] will construct funhouses for others and be their secret operator" [97]). It refers to the mysteries of sex and of the female anatomy ("[S]permatozoa . . . grope through hot, dark windings, past Love's Tunnel's fearsome obstacles. Some perhaps lose their way" [80]), and it potentially refers to many other meanings as well. Moreover, the funhouse gains added dramatical relevance by virtue of the comic, nonlinear, and labyrinthine structure of the narrative. For example, the plot of the story "Lost in the Funhouse," as Ambrose observes, "doesn't rise by meaningful steps but winds upon itself, digresses, retreats, hesitates, sighs, collapses, expires" (96). It is in fact impossible to determine what has actually occurred: a thirteen-year-old Ambrose may be on his way to the funhouse (or on his way back), or he may have lost his way in the funhouse where he lingers yet, or he may be an adult (married with children) looking back at his youthful experience, or he may have died, and so on. Like Ambrose, the reader is made to wander in a (textual) funhouse, and the story thus performs the very disorientation that is its subject matter.

In other stories, Barth experiments with a kind of antiplot in which the self-consciously announced absence of plot is what drives the narrative. For example, in "Title," the narrator's central problem is "to fill the blank" left by the exhaustion of such conventional narrative modes as "[p]lot and theme: notions vitiated by this hour of the world but as yet not successfully succeeded" (105). The narrative explores the narrator's options in the face of this narrative exhaustion, which include (1) the rejuvenation (somehow) of the short-story genre, (2) the invention of an entirely new narrative art form, (3) the paradoxical turning of "ultimacy, exhaustion, paralyzing self-consciousness . . . against [themselves] to make something new," or (4) "silence" (109–10). As in the case of the plot, the generic title ("Title") and substitution of grammatical terms such as "noun," "adjective," and "adverb" throughout the story call attention to themselves as blanks waiting to be filled. Paradoxically, the blanks are filled by the failure to fill the blanks. Similarly, for the narrator of "Life-Story," the desperate but futile search for a narrative "ground-situation" (117), with its figurative ontological sense, is met only by the discovery that there is no ground-situation; paradoxically, that discovery becomes his ground-situation. In both cases, a declared negation (i.e., there is no plot; there is no ground-situation) is wrenched into an affirmation.

Barth is equally innovative in the use of point of view. For example, he technically exploits ambiguities of point of view in "Echo," in which, as he explains in "Seven Additional Author's Notes (1969)," the words on the page could be "[Echo's], Narcissus's, Tiresias's, mine, or any combination of the series of the four of us's" (included in *Funhouse* but without pagination). The story in fact gains a different focus and significance depending on whom we conceive to be narrating: if the story is Echo's, it is about failed love; if Narcissus's, it is about the danger of self-love; if Tiresias's, it is about the burden of self-knowledge; if Barth's, it is about the paradoxical interplay of all four points of view. The ambiguity in point of view reflects the story's equally paradoxical theme: the self that we may know, possess, or love is always a misrepresentation—always Other—just as the Other that we may know, possess, or love is in reality a reflection of the self. Hence Echo's self is whomever she reflects, while Narcissus can only love himself as Echo (e.g., "[I]t was never himself Narcissus craved, but his reflection, the Echo of his fancy" [103]). For his part, Tiresias seeks to cure his own self-absorption by "telling the story over as though it were another's" (98), but the story of Narcissus, which is that of disastrous self-love, *is* the story of Tiresias, whose burdensome self-knowledge encompasses that of all other beings. Even Barth may be conceived as telling the story over "as if it were another's," for all of the characters are reflections of himself as viewed in the ironic mirror of postmodernist art. In "Echo," every step away from the self paradoxically leads back to it, and vice versa. Hence all of the characters and points of view ultimately merge into a larger and inextricable whole. As the narrative voice ponders, "Who's telling the story, and to whom? The teller's immaterial, Tiresias declares; the tale's the same, and for all one knows the speaker may be the only auditor. . . . [N]one can tell teller from told" (101–2). Even the reader is entangled willy-nilly in the story's problematic web of identity as the conventional relation between teller and told is inverted. Thus the ambiguous point of view both emblematizes and dramatically enacts this process.

Another innovation in narrative point of view is Barth's sophisticated use of framing. Like Borges, whom he is fond of quoting, Barth believes that stories within stories "disturb us metaphysically: When the characters in a work of fiction become readers or authors of the fiction they're in, we're reminded of the fictitious aspect of our own existence" (*Friday Book* 73). Nowhere does Barth use this device more extensively than in "Menelaiad," which set a new world's record in the number of frames. In it, Barth conceives a series of *"seven* concentric stories-within-stories, so arranged that the climax of the innermost would precipitate that of the next tale out, and that of the next, et cetera, like a string of firecrackers" (*Chimera* 32). In effect, the Chinese-box effect multiplies selves chaotically, and Peisistratus's urgent question "Which Helen?" (*Funhouse* 152) suggests how frame-bound human identity is. Moreover, Barth also seeks in this tale to reverse "the usual relation between container and contained" (*Chimera* 32). Thus the frames are invertible: characters from the inside frames may comment on characters in the outer frames, as when Proteus in the fourth frame says of Peisistratus in the second frame, "Ignore that fool" (154). Finally, many frames occasionally fuse at once into a single voice, as in Menelaus' question:

> " ' " ' "   " ' " '
> " ' " '   ' " '
>   Why?
> " ' "   " '
>   " '   ' (*Funhouse* 153)

As this quotation suggests, Menelaus has selves within selves that correspond to the multiple diverging frames of his narrative. The story is further complicated by the presence of Proteus, the prototypical shape-shifter and figure of the radical mutability of the self, who may jump frames, as it were, by assuming the identity of any other character in any other frame.

The use of frames problematizes the question of identity at the center of "Menelaid." Menelaus obsessively asks, "Who am I?" seeking to understand why from among so many other better-qualified suitors Helen has chosen him. Yet like Ambrose in the title story, "Lost in the Funhouse," he will at best discover only a series of inconsistent and shifting frames through which to view himself and Helen. Ambrose's use of the second person in "Lost in the Funhouse" generalizes this difficulty: "You think you're yourself, but there are other persons in you. Ambrose gets hard when Ambrose doesn't want to, *and obversely*. Ambrose watches them disagree; Ambrose watches him watch. In the funhouse mirror-room you can't see yourself go on forever, because no matter how you stand, your head gets in the way" (*Funhouse* 85). For Barth, true self-understanding is impossible, since subject and object can never coincide; there is only an infinite series of (literary) frames, which can never be grasped simultaneously.

The effect of many of Barth's experimental techniques is to deconstruct conventional moral dichotomies such as self/other, good/evil, rationality/irrationality, and so on. As Barth himself notes, "[T]here are no categories in Nature's warpless, woofless web" (*Friday Book* 22). An excellent example of this strategy is "Petition," a story in which the narrator, a Siamese twin, petitions the King of Siam to separate him from his brother because of the latter's alleged moral turpitude. Although the narrator insists on his own moral superiority, his claim is undermined by his evident hypocrisy: He accuses his brother of such things

as "guile" (62), "ignoran[ce]" (62), and "abuse" (66), yet he himself guilefully
fakes tears, willfully ignores others' criticism, and threatens to murder his
brother. The narrator's bad faith in requesting to be separated is revealed even
more by the fact that he is a twin. Barth notes that twins "usually signify the
'divided self,' our secret sharer or inner adversary—even . . . schizophrenia"
(*Friday Book* 3). As such, the narrator represents a fundamental split in consciousness, an interpretation supported by the many hints that the narrator lacks
an autonomous physical existence. Barth symbolically deepens and extends the
meaning of this split by alluding to Jungian psychology (e.g., "Me and My
Shadow" [68]) and to Oriental mysticism ("Yang and Yin" [70]). In light of the
archetypal images of unity and wholeness with which he is surrounded, the
narrator's love of division and of hierarchy seems misguided; his request to
achieve absolute autonomy by surgical incision, insane. What the narrator detests
above all is a blending and merging of categories; he states, "To be one: paradise! To be two: bliss! But to be both and neither is unspeakable" (71). Yet
"both and neither" remains, in Barth's view, the condition of all people. Barth
claims, "[W]e are all of us twins, indeed a kind of Siamese twins, who have
lost and who seek eternally our missing half. The loss accounts for alienation,
our felt distance from man and god" (*Friday Book* 3). Thus the narrator, whose
soul "lusts for disjunction" (66), and who asks to be attached to his own navel,
is the victim simultaneously of a disabling dualism and of a suicidal solipsism
for failing to open himself to the mystery of interrelatedness, or of paradoxical
Being. Barth's fiction, however, moves to embrace this mystery; his stated goal
as a writer is to transcend categories, and Barth has appropriately affirmed that
the best possibility for doing so lies in "passionate, mysterious farce" (*Friday
Book* 59)—the very genre of the story "Petition."

Unlike *Chimera*, whose geometric paradigm is the spiral, *Lost in the Funhouse* is circular and cyclical in construction, and the last story, "Anonymaiad,"
brings the book full circle—yet (as always) "with a twist." If the spermatozoan
narrator of the first story, "Night-Sea Journey," is the "tale-bearer of a generation" (9), initiating the life cycle and carrying its "heritage" (3), the narrator of
"Anonymaiad" is its mature and seasoned product. He, too, like his progenitor,
becomes the "tale-bearer of a generation," casting his heritage-filled amphorae
into the sea to seek communication with the world (or with himself), but also,
in a larger sense, to engender new narrative worlds. Thus Barth equates biological and artistic conception, both of which occur in an unceasing economy of
exchange: life for death, new narrative worlds for old. What matters in this
process is not the name or specific identity of the narrator (who remains unnamed), but the act of creation itself. If life is absurd, writing nevertheless
functions as a means of giving it order and meaning, even if that order and
meaning are themselves transfused with chaos. In coming full circle, the narrator
of "Anonymaiad" is no longer at the same point as the more desperate and
nihilistic narrator of the earlier "Night-Sea Journey"; rather, the later narrator is

committed to the life of his tale and is content in the knowledge that "an anon-ymous minstrel . . . Wrote it" (*Funhouse* 201).

Barth's more recent volume, *On with the Story*, is a short-story cycle framed by a couple vacationing at their "last resort" (4), who engage in intellectual banter, Joycean wit ("sinequanonsense" [201]), and passionate midlife reflection. Though the narrator is male, he is loosely modeled on Scheherazade, whom Barth regards as one of the four greatest literary inventions. Formally, *On with the Story* exhibits many of the same features as *Lost in the Funhouse*, including ironic self-reflexivity, ambiguity of reference, stories within stories, and meta-physical conundrums. Nevertheless, it is innovative in its structural and thematic application of the ideas of quantum mechanics and of chaos theory to literature, which can only be briefly suggested here. From the former, Barth figuratively incorporates such concepts as the participatory anthropic principle, which holds that "the observer is as essential to the creation of the universe as the universe is to the creation of the observer" (102); this principle is the burden of the story "Love Explained." Barth also includes the concept of loops in time, as when a character in "Stories of Our Lives" paradoxically reads the selfsame page of text that constitutes the ending of his own story before that ending has, in a manner of speaking, yet occurred (173). In addition, Barth makes use of Hei-senberg's uncertainty principle, which states that the more we know about a particle's position, the less we know about its momentum, and vice versa. In the narrator's words, "To the extent that anything is where it is . . . , it has no momentum. To the extent that it moves, it isn't 'where it is.' Likewise made-up characters in made-up stories; likewise ourselves in the more-or-less made-up stories of our lives" (86). The title story, "On with the Story," especially illustrates this paradox in action, in which the chief character Alice cannot tell whether she is still or moving.

From chaos theory Barth borrows the concept of the fractal, a geometric structure with an uneven shape repeated on an ever-larger scale, just as each of the uneven, open-ended stories can be said to give rise fractally to the book as a whole. Barth similarly incorporates the concept of the strange attractor, a force that produces patterns of nonlinear dynamics. As the narrator observes, "More than Freudian psychology, more than Marxist ideology, quantum mechanics has been the Great Attractor of the second half of this dying century" (101)—cer-tainly it is the strange attractor that has shaped the structure of *On with the Story* in terms of both the narrator's explicit and the author's implicit fascination with chaos theory itself. In addition, chaos theory provides the concept of self-organized criticality, which holds that "many composite systems naturally evolve to a critical state in which a minor event starts a chain reaction that can affect any number of elements in the system" (qtd. in *Further Fridays* 338). Self-organized criticality is evident in the number of small butterfly-wing–like move-ments that contingently motivate the plot in *On with the Story*. For instance, in " 'Waves,' by Amien Richard," a minor "swerve" (131) in the "particles" (120)

Amy and Richard leads them by chance simultaneously away from the swimming pool in which their child drowns, subsequently motivating all the future action by means of their mutual guilt. Finally, the conclusion to *On with the Story* is itself an exemplary application of chaos theory to literature, for it both expressly acknowledges and enacts the role of contingency in human relationships. In a book containing so many references to things that are, as the narrator admits, no laughing matter—sickness, death, rape, genocide, to name a few—Barth nevertheless achieves a comic triumph by means of the narrator's and his lover's fortuitous, chaotic, unpredictable, self-organized, healthy, gut-wrenching laughter.

WORKS CITED AND CONSULTED

Primary

Barth, John. *Chimera*. New York: Random House, 1972.

———. *The End of the Road*. New York: Avon, 1958.

———. *The Floating Opera*. New York: Avon, 1958.

———. *The Friday Book: Essays and Other Nonfiction*. New York: Putnam, 1984.

———. *Further Fridays: Essays, Lectures, and Other Nonfiction, 1984–1994*. Boston: Little, Brown, 1995.

———. *Giles Goat-Boy*. New York: Doubleday, 1966.

———. *The Last Voyage of Somebody the Sailor*. New York: Doubleday, 1991.

———. *LETTERS: A Novel*. New York: Putnam, 1979.

———. *Lost in the Funhouse: Fiction for Print, Tape, Live Voice*. Garden City, NY: Doubleday, 1968.

———. *On with the Story: Stories*. Boston: Little, Brown, 1996.

———. *Once Upon a Time: A Floating Opera*. Boston: Little, Brown, 1994.

———. *Sabbatical: A Romance*. New York: Putnam, 1982.

———. *The Sot-Weed Factor*. Garden City, NY: Doubleday, 1960.

———. *The Tidewater Tales*. New York: Ballantine Books, 1987.

Secondary

Bowen, Zack. *A Reader's Guide to John Barth*. Westport, CT: Greenwood, 1994.

Fogel, Stan, and Gordon Slethaug. *Understanding John Barth*. Columbia: University of South Carolina Press, 1990.

Gardner, John. *On Moral Fiction*. New York: Basic, 1978.

Morrell, David. *John Barth: An Introduction*. University Park: Pennsylvania State University Press, 1976.

Schulz, Max F. *The Muses of John Barth: Tradition and Metafiction from "Lost in the Funhouse" to "The Tidewater Tales."* Baltimore: Johns Hopkins University Press, 1990.

Tobin, Patricia. *John Barth and the Anxiety of Continuance*. Philadelphia: University of Pennsylvania Press, 1992.

Walkiewicz, Edward P. *John Barth*. Boston: Twayne, 1986.

DONALD BARTHELME
(April 7, 1931–July 23, 1989)

Jerome Klinkowitz

BIOGRAPHY

Donald Barthelme was born in Philadelphia, where his father (Donald Barthelme, Sr.) was studying at the University of Pennsylvania to be an architect. In 1933, the family moved to Houston, Texas, where the elder Barthelme pursued his career and later taught at Rice University. Here young Donald grew up in a self-consciously artistic family, living in a modernistic home his father designed that attracted much curious attention. As a student at the University of Houston, Barthelme wrote for and edited the student newspaper. Leaving the university as a junior, he worked as a reporter for the *Houston Post*, where part of his duties involved reviewing stage shows and movies; his catalog of trivia from American popular culture dates to these years. Between 1953 and 1955, he served in the U.S. Army, stationed in Japan and Korea as a service newspaperman. In 1955, he returned to civilian life and his job at the *Houston Post*, but soon after resigned to take a position writing publicity releases for the University of Houston News Service. Here he not only responded to the academic and intellectual life, but furthered it through his founding of the quarterly journal *Forum*, which he edited from 1956 through 1961. Having been named acting director of Houston's Contemporary Arts Museum in March 1961, he resigned from the university on August 1 to become the museum's permanent director. A year and two months later he left both Houston and the museum to become managing editor of the art and literature journal *Location* in New York, a project directed by the eminent art critics Harold Rosenberg and Thomas B. Hess. At this same time, his first short story, "The Darling Duckling at School" (later collected as "Me and Miss Mandible"), was published in the little magazine *Contact*. But from 1963 through his death in 1989, the vast majority of his work appeared in the *New Yorker*, where it educated a mainstream audience to the radically new disruptions of innovative fiction. During the last years of his life,

Donald Barthelme divided his time between writing in New York and teaching at the University of Houston's creative writing program. He died of a previously diagnosed cancer thought to be in remission.

CRITICISM

In the collection of writing published posthumously as *The Teachings of Don B.* (1992), Donald Barthelme's editor Kim Herzinger describes him as one whose work substantially redefined American short fiction for our time. It was his almost unique position as an experimentalist being published in broadly commercial venues that interested critics. Whereas other innovators such as Ronald Sukenick, Clarence Major, and Steve Katz were making their marks in literary quarterlies and little magazines by attacking the conventions of socially mannered realism, only Barthelme was able to do so within the very bastion of that style, the *New Yorker* magazine, where such conventions had been established by John O'Hara years before and where now Barthelme's self-consciously curious stories appeared side by side with more traditional works by John Updike and John Cheever. "If literature at one time presumably reflected life," Lois Gordon wrote in the first book-length study of the author in 1981, "Barthelme reverses the formula" (20–21). Gordon reflects the early fascination with Barthelme's materials, drawn as they are from the detritus of a textually motivated society, including bits of advertising slogans, fashion images, and superficially intellectual talk. Later critics, especially Maurice Couturier and Regis Durand in their own *Donald Barthelme* (1982), draw on postmodern theory to show how the author is manipulating signs to show how reality itself is a manufactured apprehension. Although there has been an attempt by Charles Molesworth (in *Donald Barthelme's Fiction*, 1982) to reduce such technique to simple irony and a campaign by Richard F. Patteson and others (*Critical Essays on Donald Barthelme*, 1992) to recast the author's reputation as less innovative and more traditionally mainstream, Barthelme's importance as a radical innovator survived his death and continues to influence the shape of the American short story.

ANALYSIS

The innovative nature of Donald Barthelme's career is apparent from his first published story, which appeared in 1962 as "The Darling Duckling at School" and was collected in *Come Back, Dr. Caligari* (1964) as "Me and Miss Mandible." Here the narrator confronts his reader with a circumstance at once as preposterous as a modernist Kafka nightmare yet as familiar as anything in real life. The scene is a sixth-grade classroom, filled with all the appropriate twelve-year-olds bursting with hormones and curiosities. Among them is something equally understandable, an insurance adjuster aged thirty-five. What is astounding is that despite his feelings to the contrary, the students and their teacher are perceiving him as a normal member of the class. In telling the story, this narrator establishes many of Barthelme's practices, such as interpreting the world in terms of its popular-culture icons (movie magazines, romance gossip of the Eddie Fisher–Debbie Reynolds variety) and delivering it all in a straight-faced, deadpan manner. But most important is the story's metafictive impulse, involving the reader as it does in the almost certain knowledge that Kafka's Gregor Samsa has already told this type of tale, albeit without the comedy. Thus is the author able to question his format even as he exploits it for maximum worth.

By the time of his second collection, *Unspeakable Practices, Unnatural Acts* (1968), Donald Barthelme had established himself as a wry and sometimes-satiric commentator on his times. His novel *Snow White* (1967) perfected the method of comic interfacing from "Me and Miss Mandible" by retelling the Grimm brothers' fairy tale in hip, topically 1960s settings, and stories such as "The Indian Uprising" and "The Balloon" extended the method conceptually, to the point that abstract philosophies could be encountered like obstacles in the street. This collection is also famous for a character's self-appraisal in "See the Moon," a confession that "fragments are the only form I trust." Here was the first overt comment on the author's own method, one practiced in "Robert Kennedy Saved from Drowning," a story presenting bits and pieces of the politician's life in the manner of cinematic outtakes or rejected photographic proofs—none of them especially significant in themselves, but forming in their juxtaposition a collagist's view of reality.

City Life (1970) is the collection that most emphatically foregrounds Barthelme's collagist method. "Views of My Father Weeping" is written in much the same manner as the Robert Kennedy story, segmenting brief paragraphs written in notebook fashion to approximate a narrator's sense of confusion and loss. In "At the Tolstoy Museum," the author employs collages themselves, taking nineteenth-century engravings and by deft cuttings and pastings (in the manner of artist Max Ernst's collagist novel *Une semaine de bonté*) makes visual commentary on his text, itself a series of fragmentary paragraphs telling more about Tolstoy in their juxtapositions than by themselves. This method, or rather the attitude behind it, is transferred to language itself in "Paraguay," where silence is sold in stores, art is recycled from dumps back into the mainstream of life, and terminologies from radically disparate disciplines (stereophonic reproduction, anthropological groupings, technological miniaturization) are mixed together, each retaining its own identity yet combined to form a single complex grammar and syntax.

In the stories of *Sadness* (1972), Barthelme presents his most convincing argument: that common, daily life itself is lived not by any natural order but according to the semiologies we as social beings devise. "Critique de la Vie Quotidienne" is the author's funniest story, devoted as it is to the predicaments that could have dogged any reader of the *New Yorker* at this time. "Our evenings lacked promise," the narrator laments, having remarked how they are spent with him reading the *Journal of Sensory Deprivation* while his wife Wanda so empathizes with her copies of *Elle* that she begins looking like the European film stars in its features. Here again collage is a factor, but much more subversively so, for it has been in almost subliminal fashion that Wanda has allowed herself to be recast by the cosmetics, coutures, diets, and designs of this magazine. Not that her husband is any better, lining up his fifteen drinks each evening on the side table while navigating himself into a life of blissful haziness, to be disrupted by his young daughter's demand that they find room in their small apartment for a horse. Each member, it turns out, is consumed by such social signs. When the family unit breaks up, it is to disappear into similar semiological systems: Wanda into poststructuralist French thought, the child to a pedagogically fashionable school, and the narrator into his endless supply of J&B scotch.

Readers may find their clearest insights into Barthelme's methods by considering the volume of short works he collected not as stories but as parodies, satires, and fables. *Guilty Pleasures* (1974) reaches back a dozen years to reprint *New Yorker* material passed over for the author's first four collections. Among them are his initial contributions to this prestigious magazine, which were not full-fledged stories in the journal's front pages but rather back-of-the-book exercises on such idiosyncrasies as *Time*-style journalese ("Snap Snap"), the odd attitudes of new-wave Italian cinema ("L'Lapse"), the Hobbesian language of demoralization and decay in the judgments of *Consumer Reports* ("Down the Line with the Annual"), and the send-up of pop anthropologist Carlos Castaneda's *Teachings of Don Juan: A Yaqui Way of Knowledge* ("The Teachings of Don B.: A Yankee Way of Knowledge"). Here is Barthelme's favorite cosmos, the world of texts, especially texts whose forms are defined by the sign systems they encapsulate. As he did with the hilarious "And Now Let's Hear It for the Ed Sullivan Show!" the author may have kept such stories out of his regular collections for fear that their close topicality might date them. In fact, there is such a close correspondence between the subject text's intentional methods and Barthelme's satire of them that even one-third of a century later, there is no need of footnoting or other explanation; should *Consumer Reports* ever become a thing of the distant past, the fun Barthelme has with it in "Down the Line with the Annual" is evident from its very language that the author makes his own. Reviewing both the disappointments of his own life and the magazine's dreary reports on the soundness of so many consumer products, he can only lament that "the world is sagging, snagging, scaling, spalling, pilling, pinging, pitting, warping, checking, fading, chipping, cracking, yellowing, leaking, stalling, shrinking, and in dynamic unbalance, and there is a mildew to think about, and ruptures and fractures of internal organs from lap belts, and substandard brake fluids, and plastic pipes alluring to rats, and transistors whose estimated batter life, like the life of man, is nasty, brutish, and short" (8). As for Ed Sullivan, it is writing such as Barthelme's, constructing fragment by fragment a collage of the once-famous host's television show, that captures the essence of such spectacle well enough that it outlives memory and can be reformed in the reader's appreciation. It is in such satires and parodies, whose methods carry over into the author's more serious short stories, that Donald Barthelme shows himself closest to actual daily life. Yet his genius is not in transcribing that life in realistic fashion, but in showing how such existence is constructed.

Although *The Dead Father* (1975) is classified as a novel, it indicates the next direction in Barthelme's short fiction as well: a talent for constructing narratives from almost pure dialogue, exchanges of language in which the speaker need not always be identified. *Amateurs* (1976) collects several stories of this type, including "You Are as Brave as Vincent Van Gogh" and "The Captured Woman." By the time of *Great Days* (1979), this method has been refined to the point that lines of dialogue can be set off not in quotes but by dashes (in the European manner). Here the advantage is that language can be bounced off itself like improvisations among jazz musicians, as a passage from "The New Music" indicates:

—Momma didn't 'low no clarinet played in here. Unfortunately.

—Momma.

—Momma didn't 'low no clarinet played in here. Made me sad.

—Momma was outside.

—Momma was *very* outside.

—Sitting there 'lowing and not-'lowing. In her old rocking chair.

—'Lowing this, not-'lowing that.

—Didn't 'low oboe.

—Didn't 'low gitfiddle. Vibes.

—Rock over you damn foot and bust it, you didn't pop to when she was 'lowing and not-'lowing.

—Right, 'course, she had all the grease.

—True.

—You wanted a little grease, like to buy a damn comic book or something, you had to go to Momma.

—Sometimes yes, sometimes no. Her variously colored moods.

Though each subject reference is recognizable, the story's point is not to relate information but to play with the way such data are created and defined. The two conversationalists—never characterized or even identified—are not just reconstructing a memory but playing a game with each other in bouncing language shapes off each other, just like jazz musicians trading lines in a jam session. Much innovative fiction of the American 1960s and 1970s shares this quality with jazz, in which the ongoingness of improvisation is more important than the summation of any result.

It is in the materials of *Overnight to Many Distant Cities* (1983) that Barthelme makes his strongest claims for language itself. Its dozen short stories, their style familiar from earlier collections, are separated each in turn by a brief, italicized interchapter drawn from the type of writing *Guilty Pleasures* had identified as satirical, parodistic, or fabulative. The volume's obvious precedent is Ernest Hemingway's *In Our Time*, and like Hemingway's interchapters, Barthelme's are untitled (in the table of contents, they are identified by just their initial words followed by an ellipsis). As a result, two styles of work are combined to make the collection a new whole, for the interchapters not only comment on the more conventional stories but remind readers that nuances of language stand behind everything the author does. This collection dates from the beginning of Barthelme's work in the creative writing program at the University of Houston; in the 1980s, he returned there frequently and eventually established two homes, dividing his year between Texas and New York. This homecoming of sorts to the university where he had been a student writer and later staff publicist and journal editor rekindled his interest in somewhat-folksy stories of the modern Southwest. These he contrasted with his customarily impolite notices of Greenwich Village pseudosophistication, with his collection's interchapters there as a reminder of how the root of all this interest was an understanding of how language use shaped both styles of life.

Such attitudes characterize his last novels, *Paradise* (1986) and *The King* (1990), which, despite their apparent exoticisms (a divorced man sharing his apartment and sex life with three attractive young women, England's Battle of Britain retold in Arthurian dress), are in fact the closest the author came to writing realistic fiction. Yet even here the characters' doings are clothed in the forms of popular culture's language, especially its languages of style and design. These fascinations are best expressed in the posthumous collection *The Teachings of Don B.* (1992), in which even satires rejected for *Guilty Pleasures* take on fresh pertinence among the author's more recent parodistic reflections. One such example is an early *New Yorker* contribution, "Man's Face: A New Novel in Forty Coaxial Chapters," all of which appears within the space of just a few pages, given that its form is that of *TV Guide*'s program notes. Here one is also reminded that the greater number of Barthelme's graphic collage stories were never collected; as restored to the canon, they correct the impression from the monumental volumes *Sixty Stories* (1981) and *Forty Stories* (1987) that the author may have become more socially discursive in his work.

The bulk of Donald Barthelme's fiction shows him to have been an intellectually astute writer, noticing the things of life not for their content or even for their form, but for how they are made and what makes them. At their best, his short stories replicate this process for the reader, making the otherwise-humdrum world seem as fascinating and hilarious as it must have been to him.

WORKS CITED AND CONSULTED

Primary

Barthelme, Donald. *Amateurs*. New York: Farrar Straus & Giroux, 1976.
————. *City Life*. New York: Farrar Straus & Giroux, 1970.

————. *Come Back, Dr. Caligari*. Boston: Little, Brown, 1964.

————. *The Dead Father*. New York: Farrar Straus & Giroux, 1975.

————. *Forty Stories*. New York: Putnam, 1987.

————. *Great Days*. New York: Farrar Straus & Giroux, 1979.

————. *Guilty Pleasures*. New York: Farrar Straus & Giroux, 1974.

————. *The King*. New York: Harper & Row, 1990.

————. *Overnight to Many Distant Cities*. New York: Putnam, 1983.

————. *Paradise*. New York: Putnam, 1986.

————. *Sadness*. New York: Farrar Straus & Giroux, 1972.

————. *Sixty Stories*. New York: Putnam, 1981.

————. *Snow White*. New York: Atheneum, 1967.

————. *The Teachings of Don B*. New York: Turtle Bay Books, 1992.

————. *Unspeakable Practices, Unnatural Acts*. New York: Farrar Straus & Giroux, 1968.

Secondary

Couturier, Maurice, and Regis Durand. *Donald Barthelme*. London and New York: Methuen, 1982.

Gordon, Lois. *Donald Barthelme*. Boston: Twayne, 1981.

Klinkowitz, Jerome. *Donald Barthelme: An Exhibition*. Durham, NC: Duke University Press, 1991.

————. *Keeping Literary Company: Working with Writers since the Sixties*. Albany, NY: SUNY Press, 1998.

Klinkowitz, Jerome, Asa B. Pieratt, Jr., and Robert Murray Davis. *Donald Barthelme: A Comprehensive Bibliography and Annotated Secondary Checklist*. Hamden, CT: Shoe String Press, 1977.

Molesworth, Charles. *Donald Barthelme's Fiction: The Ironist Saved from Drowning*. Columbia: University of Missouri Press, 1982.

Patteson, Richard F., ed. *Critical Essays on Donald Barthelme*. New York: G. K. Hall, 1992.

Stengel, Wayne B. *The Shape of Art in the Short Stories of Donald Barthelme*. Baton Rouge: Louisiana State University Press, 1985.

Trachtenberg, Stanley. *Understanding Donald Barthelme*. Columbia: University of South Carolina Press, 1990.

ANN BEATTIE
(September 8, 1947–   )

Michael W. Young and Troy Thibodeaux

BIOGRAPHY

The only child of James A. and Charlotte (Crosby) Beattie, Charlotte Ann Beattie grew up in Washington, D.C., where her father was an administrator for the Department of Health, Education, and Welfare. Beattie's description of the experience of growing up as an only child resonates with the dominant qualities of her writing: "I just wasn't up to a lot of things that I was experiencing; I was taken along and hovered over. It made me a watcher" (Samway 469). The position of the watcher, the careful observer—faintly puzzled, at times perhaps nonplussed, yet ever curious about what she sees—is the characteristic perspective of Beattie's narrative vision.

Although a predilection for observation may have entered Beattie's life early on, her literary aspirations developed much later. Discontentment with her high-school experience led to a lackluster performance in the classroom, and her high-school grades were below average. Despite this unpromising start, Beattie managed to gain admission to American University, where she briefly studied journalism before changing her major to English literature. She completed her B.A. in 1969, taking only three years to finish her degree, and then accepted a teaching assistantship at the University of Connecticut to pursue graduate study in English. She received her M.A. in 1970 and continued her work toward the Ph.D. until 1972. It was not until graduate school that Beattie started writing fiction, and her creative work began as a diversion from the boredom of graduate study and a way to renew her interest in literature. As her abilities as a fiction writer grew, however, so did the seriousness of her pursuit, and with the encouragement of one of her professors, J. D. O'Hara, Beattie began to submit her stories for publication.

Beattie's first publication, the short story "A Rose for Judy Garland's Casket," appeared in *Western Humanities Review* in 1972; that same year she withdrew from the Ph.D. program without completing her degree. Her first major short story, "Victor Blue," was published the following year in *Atlantic Monthly*, but the publication that truly sparked her career was "A Platonic Relationship," which appeared in the *New Yorker* in 1974. Her first successful submission to the magazine after a string of twenty-two rejections, this story began a decade-long relationship between Beattie and the *New Yorker* that would provide the foundation for her reputation.

In 1976, Beattie's first collection of short stories, *Distortions*, was published simultaneously with her first novel, *Chilly Scenes of Winter*. This dramatic double debut contributed much to Beattie's sudden celebrity and announced her status as a major new voice in American fiction. Since that time, she has published five additional collections of short stories and five more novels, numerous uncollected stories and essays, introductions to books of photography, an extended creative-critical essay in response to the work of the painter Alex Katz, children's stories, and a telescript version of one of her stories for PBS. She also edited *The Best American Short Stories 1987* and was a guest editor for *Ploughshares* (Fall 1995), contributing an introductory essay for each of the volumes she edited. Beattie's latest collection of short stories is *Park City* (1998), which contains selections from each of her previous five collections as well as eight new stories.

Beattie has taught at Harvard (Briggs-Copeland Lecturer in English, 1977–78) and at the University of Virginia, Charlottesville (visiting lecturer and writer, 1975–77; visiting writer, 1980). She received a Guggenheim Fellowship in 1977, was named a distinguished alumna by American University in 1980, and received an honorary doctorate of humane letters from that university in 1983. She received the award for excellence in literature from the American Academy and Institute of Arts and Letters in 1980 and was elected to membership in the academy in 1992. She and her second husband, the artist Lincoln Perry, currently divide their time between Maine and Key West, Florida.

CRITICISM

Critics have often sought to place Beattie as a member of a "school" of fiction or to find a definitive label for her work. While many of these labels may be helpful in describing some aspect of Beattie's work or career, no single label has proven sufficient to describe her work without in some way also reducing it. Her frequent appearances in the *New Yorker*, for example, have led several critics to draw comparisons with her direct predecessors in that magazine, such as John Cheever and John Updike, discovering in their work common themes and situations that would determine a school of "*New Yorker* fiction." The surface resemblances between Beattie's stories and Cheever's are significant enough to prompt Pico Iyer to claim that "one might almost read [Beattie's stories] as a sequel ('Son of Cheever' perhaps). For although her characters swallow pills instead of booze; although they flee to California instead of Europe; although their hassles are those of cohabitation instead of marriage—they might well be the progeny of Cheever's well-heeled lonelyhearts, raised on expectations they frequently let down" (548).

Although Beattie readily acknowledges the importance the *New Yorker* held for her early career, asserting, "I don't mind [the label]. It's not offensive," she also claims that her reaction to the label "depends on what you want to imply. It applied more when Cheever was publishing there" (telephone interview). In addition, she considers the stories that appeared in the *New Yorker* to have been "mavericks" in that magazine: "If I had been calculating," she recalls, "I would not have thought they sounded or looked or felt like '*New Yorker* fiction' " ("Collecting Myself" 3). One might also claim that the label "*New Yorker* writer" is founded on a circular argument: Beattie's frequent contributions to the magazine would of necessity define the very title by which some critics have wished to limit her. Finally, Beattie's work has appeared in the *New Yorker* with decreasing frequency since the late 1980s, reducing the extent to which her relationship with that magazine has characterized her later career.

Other efforts to categorize Beattie's fiction have focused less on the means of publication for her stories and more on their thematic and stylistic elements. The closely circumscribed realm of actions in which so many of Beattie's characters dwell, their benumbed, postexistential lassitude, their irresolution (seconded by the openness of Beattie's endings), and the flat, stark prose in which their stories are told have led critics to group Beattie with other contemporaries such as Raymond Carver, Bobbie Ann Mason, and Frederick Barthelme in a school of "literary minimalism." Beattie has frequently expressed her admiration for the work of each of these writers, and indeed it is not difficult to discern a certain literary consanguinity among them. The insufficiency of this label thus lies more in the intention of its wielders than in the term itself. As applied to the visual arts, "minimalism" named a specific movement that represented a conscious response to abstract expressionism; the term was descriptive and, largely, affirmative. Literary critics who have adopted the term have used it, however, in a pejorative sense. In a frequently quoted article entitled "Less Is Less," for example, Joshua Gilder attacks Beattie and other "minimalist" writers, defining "minimalist fiction" as "those little stories which seem to grow even smaller as you read. By the end (you know it is the end because you've come to the last page) the story has dwindled down to almost nothing, a mere wisp of melancholic vapor scattered by the first breeze" (78). As Beattie explains, critics such as Gilder who used the term to describe her work were "saying that there were empty spaces. Bad empty space, not good empty space" (Seshachari 199). It is possible, of course, to describe Beattie's work as "minimalist" in a more positive sense, and many critics have indicated the extent to which the strength of Beattie's stories lies in her use of nuance, the suggestiveness of the telling detail that alludes to what remains unspoken (perhaps necessarily so).

Neither Beattie's influences nor her intended effects are limited, however, to the American tradition of literary minimalism. In fact, Beattie compares her own open endings to the open ending of Joyce's "The Dead" and his concept of a character having a moment of revelation, or epiphany. She has called "The Dead" her "favorite" short story (telephone interview), even acknowledging that occasionally, her use of snow imagery is an "homage" to the final scene of that story (Montresor 227). Beattie believes that the writer must make sure that in any ending or epiphany "you've accomplished more than a quick resolution" (telephone interview). For each character at any point throughout the story, as happens throughout "The Dead," an epiphany will have "personalized the world greatly" for that individual (telephone interview). Thus it may not be so much a revelation but, to Beattie, the reidentification of the character's own sense of existence.

Both this use of direct revelation through significant detail and her unadorned, "deadpan" style place Beattie in a tradition that stems, at least in part, from the work of Ernest Hemingway, a tradition critics have referred to as "neorealism" or social realism. Beattie has mentioned an early attachment to Hemingway's works, claiming, "The first writer I read, really read, was Hemingway. He was a kind of model. I admired his understatement, the way things left unsaid become the main focus of his stories. The real story happens at the periphery" (Parini 23). She has also listed the "Nick Adams stories" among those works that have influenced her most ("The Hum inside the Skull" 1), and she has paid further homage to Hemingway by naming her copyright-holding corporation Irony and Pity, Inc., a reference to a line in *The Sun Also Rises*. Despite rare excursions into fantastic plots or postmodern narrative devices, Beattie's work has remained largely true to her model, constantly in touch with the world, seeking the evocative through the mundane. In fact, Christina Murphy, the first critic to publish a monograph on Beattie's work, claims that "Beattie has done more than any other writer to redefine the neorealist movement and to influence contemporary literature away from metafiction or surfiction and toward realism" (118).

One means by which Beattie has created a viable neorealist context for her stories is her use of references to popular culture. She frequently incorporates allusions to popular songs, name brands, television programs, and other artifacts of contemporary life. This aspect of her style has received both praise and blame from critics: praise for her realist attention to detail, her ability to generate psychologically complex portraits from the detritus of mundane affairs, and blame for being period-bound, for creating stories that date themselves (and thus become "dated") at the moment of publication.

Closely associated with this realist method is the image of Beattie as a sociologist creating a fictional record of her age. More specifically, perhaps, she is often described as a portraitist of the people who *are* her age. The label most commonly applied to Beattie, the one from which she has most consistently attempted to distance herself, is the title "voice of her generation." The very ability that may, in large part, have been responsible for Beattie's early success—her ability to strike a chord with people who came of age in the 1960s—

has also invited some of the harsher criticism she has received. As Jaye Berman Montresor points out, because her characters seemed representative of the disaffected ex-radicals of the post–Vietnam War era, Beattie became an unwitting spokesperson for her generation: "Beattie was seen as a chronicler, like Fitzgerald and Hemingway, of young people whose shattered idealism leaves them numb, unable to establish successful relationships or engage in meaningful work. As a result, the critical response to Beattie's fiction was at times as much (and sometimes more) a response to her cultural moment and milieu as it was to her creativity and skill as a writer" (Introduction to *The Critical Response to Ann Beattie* 7). Beattie's response to this characterization of her work has always been that it is a reductive approach that fails to take into account the nuances of her method. When she was asked by Patrick Samway how she would like her peers to remember her, Beattie's response was clear: "I would like my fellow . . . writers to see the larger implications of what I do and to judge me as being astute about human behavior" (471).

ANALYSIS

Several critics have noted that Beattie's strength lies in the short-story form rather than in the novel, and Beattie herself has admitted to being more at ease writing shorter pieces. One reason her shorter fiction has been generally more successful may be that her nuanced realism, her capacity for drawing a story from the most unprovocative people in the most banal situations, is crystallized in the concentration of the shorter form but strained to breaking in a longer piece. As Blanche Gelfant points out, "The short story will be sustained by trivia; a sudden revelation of the significance they have hidden, as a hostess hides liver in an hors d'oeuvre, will surprise and satisfy. But the novel becomes monotonous when insignificant details multiply and recur" (23). Perhaps another reason for this discrepancy lies in Beattie's characteristic tone. The emotionless, flat prose that has become her trademark seems better adapted to the shorter form. Within a short story, a string of simple sentences in which a key word is repeated works to underscore the significance of the word; in a longer piece, in which a great number of words receive the same emphasis, any possible significance is blurred, and the effect becomes more tedious.

The thirty-six stories selected for *Park City* provide an excellent cross-section of Beattie's work to date and attest to her mastery of the short form. The title of Beattie's third collection of stories, *Secrets and Surprises*, could be used to describe almost all of the stories in *Park City*; as Beattie states, "Surprise is what good writing is all about, and readers are attuned to it" (Introduction to *The Best American Short Stories 1987* xiii). What seems to surprise Beattie most in these stories are human relationships—the rather inscrutable decisions and actions by which relationships are defined and the even more enigmatic means by which they are sustained. This capacity for surprise at human relationships is at the heart of Beattie's narrative method, defining not only her attenuated plots and her impenetrable characters, but also the very means by which these plots and characters are built. Pico Iyer provides an apt description of this method: "Upon beginning one of her stories, it always takes a while to determine the relations between the floating soap bubbles; a child can easily be mistaken for a boy friend, a gay lover for a brother or a son. For the family circle of middle-class America has apparently imploded, and its domestic structure has been distorted and distended. . . . Everybody cares about 'relating' to everybody else, in part, perhaps, because relatives are unknown" (550).

"Vermont," a story from Beattie's first collection, *Distortions*, splices together brief episodes that revolve around just such complex familial relationships. The story opens as the narrator and her husband, David, try to comfort their neighbor Noel, whose wife has just left him for John Stillerman, another resident in their high-rise building, who, coincidentally, has recently been left by his own wife. "John's wife had a mastectomy last fall, and in the elevator she told Susan [Noel's wife] that if she was losing what she didn't want to lose, she might as well lose what she did want to lose. She lost John—left him the way popcorn flies out of the bag on the roller coaster" (137). The image of popcorn flying out of a bag is particularly telling in relation not only to the characters in this story, but to the characters in much of Beattie's fiction. Beattie's curiosity draws her to characters whose actions are most difficult to comprehend; they act with no apparent motivation, as though prodded by some ambiguous force, centripetal and centrifugal, into new combinations that offer no apparent advantage over the previous arrangement.

After Noel has gone back to his own apartment, the narrator lies in bed with David thinking, "One of us should have gone with Noel. Do you know your socks are still on? You're going to do to me what Susan did to Noel, aren't you?" The series of thoughts is pure Beattie, consistent with her conviction that the moments of life-altering revelation come unheralded, among dirty socks and afterthoughts. When eventually David does leave, the event is announced in absolute deadpan: "Later in the month, it happens" (139). The lack of agency apparent in this description pervades the entire story. John's wife leaves John, Susan leaves Noel, David leaves the narrator—all with only the most tenuous reasons given. Nor is there any greater sense of willfulness in the forming of new relationships: Noel and the narrator seem merely to fall together over the course of the story, despite the narrator's admission that she does not love Noel and Noel's contention that no one has ever loved him.

The vignettes continue, chronicling the growing relationship between Noel and the narrator as their lives become more intertwined, and coming full circle to culminate in a visit by David and his new girlfriend to the country house Noel and the narrator now share. Among these half scenes, one in particular seems to reflect something of Beattie's narrative method as a whole. Noel has become fascinated with a story about one of the narrator's former lovers, Michael, "who pushed his furniture into the hall and threw his small possessions out the window into the backyard and then put up four large, connecting tents in his apartment" (149). Noel asks her to tell the story time and again, and each time he urges her to remember more details. She provides a catalog of objects in the tent: Franco-American spaghetti, bottles of good wine, a flashlight, comic books, a lemon-meringue pie, a bottle of Seconal. No amount of detail seems enough for Noel; the facts are not sufficient to explain Michael's actions, and the end of her story offers no resolution:

We used to make love in the tent. I'd go over to see him, open the front door, and crawl in. That summer he collapsed the tents, threw them in his car, and left for Maine.

"Go on," Noel says.

I shrug. I've told this story twice before, and this is always my stopping place.

"That's it," I say to Noel.

He continues to wait expectantly, just as he did the two other times he heard the story. (148–49)

In this narrative moment folded within the greater disjunctive narrative, Noel is given the reader's role. He gathers in the details of the story, fully expecting their significance to cohere, expecting that some formal resolution or psychological explanation will give the story its closure, and like the reader of the larger narrative (and of Beattie's stories in general), he finds his expectations thwarted, his belief in causal relations undermined.

Perhaps an even more striking study in the inscrutability of motivation is "Wolf Dreams," the second selection from *Distortions* included in *Park City*. Cynthia, the protagonist, is almost wholly devoid of self-awareness. Having been married twice, first to a man who preferred the company of his army buddies to hers and preferred lifting barbells to having sex with her, and then to a man who viciously insulted her intelligence on their wedding night (comparing the inside of her head to a string of rattling Indian beads), she is now preparing to marry a third time. Despite her parents' protests against a third marriage, despite the insomnia she experiences over the decision, despite her inability to understand what was wrong with her previous marriages—or perhaps in some sense because of these same obstacles—Cynthia has agreed to marry Charlie Pinehurst. She insists, however, that before she will marry him, she must lose twenty pounds and save enough money for a suitable wedding dress.

Like a weight-conscious Penelope, then, Cynthia begins to spend her days obsessed with dieting and her insomniac nights compulsively eating, undoing the day's dieting. During one such night, she considers the decision she has made:

She asked herself why she was getting married. Part of the answer was that she didn't like her job . . . and also she was thirty-two, and if she didn't get married soon she might not find anybody. . . . It was getting late if she intended to have a baby. There was no point in asking herself more questions. Her head hurt, and she had eaten too much and felt a little sick, and no matter what she thought she knew she was still going to marry Charlie. (*Park City* 157)

In this paragraph, Beattie teases with predictable motivations, creates a parody of a rational process of choice, and then veers away at the last minute back into the inexplicable realm of human actions in which her stories find their home. In the process, she calls into question any apparently logical explanation for the characters' actions: she allows no recognizable distance between the process of rational thought and the process of rationalization.

Several critics have recognized in this aspect of Beattie's work a repudiation of traditional conceptions of a unitary consciousness. Beattie resists a definition of identity that rests in an individual, autonomous self that is hidden behind a socially influenced surface. As Sandra Sprows argues, the individuality of Beattie's characters "is usually portrayed as a function of their cultural/social positions rather than as an expression of an inner essence bubbling under the surface" (141). If Beattie's fictions resist the closure of a final revelation, if her characters rarely if ever come to know their true selves, perhaps it is because her characters contain no depths to be revealed. The illusion of depth that is so crucial in fiction since Henry James has been exploded here: characters like Cynthia are made of nothing but surfaces. The final image of "Wolf Dreams" underscores this fact: "Her eyes are closed. A picture comes to her—a high, white mountain. She isn't on it, or in the picture at all. When she opens her eyes she is looking at the shiny surface of the table. She closes her eyes and sees the snow-covered mountain again—high and white, no trees, just mountain—and she shivers with the coldness of it" (*Park City* 165). Faced with an internal landscape as inscrutable as the surfaces of the world around her, Cynthia has no more privileged access to herself than she has to the external world.

At times, in fact, the world of things seems more cordial to Beattie's characters than the world of human relationships, and characters thus frequently turn to the things in their lives for the certainty that the people in their lives (including themselves) cannot provide. As David Wyatt notes, Beattie's career "can be read as an attempt to explore the loss of the realm we call the personal amidst the white noise of things. Beattie has not yet stopped imagining characters for whom the possession of things serves as diversion from possession in and by love" (148). For example, in "A Vintage Thunderbird," the car that gives the story its title also becomes a replacement focus for the failed romance of the story's two main characters. Unable to adjust to the new terms of his relationship with Karen, Nick becomes fixated on Karen's car, which begins to represent not only the chance he has lost with Karen but the sense of regret that he harbors about his life in general. Beattie's spare prose is at its best evoking this lost world in the simplest language and from the smallest objects: "Her key ring was on the table. If he had the keys, he could be heading for the Lincoln Tunnel. Years ago, they would be walking to the car hand in hand, in love. It would be her birthday. The car's odometer would have five miles on it" (*Park City* 220).

At the story's conclusion, Karen has revealed that she has sold the car, and Nick is certain that she has been conned into doing so. Nick is enraged by her carelessness, by her inability to comprehend the value of this rare car, by her willingness to abandon what the car had come to represent for him. Karen makes a final gesture toward recovering what is now irretrievable, both emotionally and materially. This desire to regain what is lost haunts the characters in much of Beattie's work. They appear amid what James Plath has called "fictions of aftermath"—fictions set during a time after the real moment of crisis (which more likely than not has passed without sufficient recognition) in which characters deal with the wreckage of their lives by indirection and emotional displacement (360).

An excellent example of this emotional displacement is "Shifting," a story that, like "A Vintage Thunderbird," is focused around an automobile that has become fraught with symbolic weight. Here the car in question is a 1965 Volvo that has made an unexpected appearance in the lives of Natalie, the story's protagonist, and her husband, Larry. Natalie, a much-neglected housewife, has inherited the car from her uncle. Although she has agreed with Larry to sell the car, and although its lack of automatic transmission prevents her from even driving it, Natalie decides to keep the car, turning away several interested callers.

The Volvo becomes bound up with the other significant objects in Natalie's life (a piece of sculpture and a Calder mobile in the local museum she regularly visits), and it stands in opposition to the objects that surround her. When her husband demands that they take inventory of the things in their apartment and photograph them for insurance purposes, Natalie replies, "What's worth anything?" sparking "their first argument in almost a year" (*Park City* 230). Natalie, like the vast majority of Beattie's characters, is an alien in her own daily world. Beginning perfunctorily to photograph the possessions Larry has deemed worthy, Natalie ends by photographing parts of her own body, an act of coming to know herself through a process of defamiliarization, an attempt to answer her own question about the value of anything she has. The act is also related to her thoughts concerning Andy, a friend of Larry's who lost part of his leg in Vietnam; the disjunction between the wholeness of her body and the incompleteness of her life seems irreconcilable.

Natalie's single act of revolt against the emptiness of her life grows into a series of small rebellions. She begins to take driving lessons from a sixteen-year-old boy named Michael, and the intimacy of their secret lessons builds into the only romantic encounter Natalie has experienced with any man other than Larry (whose accidental first kiss had made them childhood sweethearts). In the story's conclusion, Natalie takes inventory of her own life, comparing her imperfect, overheated body to the cool, gray stone of her favorite sculpture:

If she were the piece of sculpture and if she could feel, she would like her sense of isolation.
    This was in 1972, in Philadelphia. (*Park City* 237)

The double conditionals of her thought seem almost equally unlikely: she is as far from feeling anything fully (or from understanding what she feels) as she is from being an impassive sculpture. The final line, appearing almost as an after-thought, reveals one of the great ironies of Beattie's work: despite the time-bound quality of her narratives and her overriding concern with the specifics of time and place, Beattie consistently weaves fictions around characters who have been set adrift, characters who themselves have only a tenuous grasp on their own place and time.

For many of Beattie's characters, all that remains of their sense of time is a fruitless marking of it. The passing of time no longer promises change. "Jack-lighting," published in one of Beattie's strongest collections, *The Burning House*, is an excellent example of this element in Beattie's work. The story is set during an annual gathering of a group of friends who, as is frequently the case in Beattie's work, function as a loosely defined extended family. The aftermath they face follows the loss of a central member of the group, the beloved, free-spirited, wise, and fearless Nicholas. The gathering takes place on Nicholas's birthday, the year following his death, at his brother Spence's country house. The "Jacklighting" of the title is a term for a type of illegal night hunting in which poachers shine bright lights into the eyes of their prey, making easy targets of the stunned animals. Although this practice is not mentioned until the final line of the story, the image of stunned paralysis, the feeling of being caught in the headlights, looms throughout the story. None of the characters seem to be able to move on. They refer to love affairs that seem meaningless; Spence sublimates his anger by making jam; they meet in remembrance of Nicholas's birthday, yet no one seems able to talk about him. The narrator captures the essence of this gathering in one of the most memorable lines in Beattie's work: "I get depressed and think that if the birds could talk, they'd say that they didn't enjoy flying" (*Park City* 305).

In strong contrast to the pervasive and debilitating lassitude of this gathering are the narrator's memories of Nicholas himself. In particular, he is credited with an uncanny capacity for seeing the world: "He'd find pennies on the side-walk when the rest of us walked down city streets obliviously" (*Park City* 302). When he was alive, Nicholas had challenged his friends to develop their ability to see the world. He had invented a game in which the friends would stare at something and then close their eyes and try to reenvision that thing in detail. The narrator, in tribute to Nicholas, attempts to play this game again, only to realize "that you can look at something, close your eyes and see it again, and still know nothing—like staring at the sky to figure out the distances between stars" (305). Here Beattie's epistemological skepticism reaches its apex; the narrator is even denied the consolation of an emotional displacement into the world of things.

One of the most compelling instances of Beattie's art of displacement is the frequently anthologized "Janus." In this story, the talisman is a bowl; vari-ously described as being "perfect," as having "real presence," and as being "a paradox of a bowl," it has become an object of obsession for the story's main character, a real-estate agent named Andrea. The bowl has assumed inordinate importance in her professional life—each time she shows a house, she places the bowl in some opportune location and, in effect, recenters the house around this object. It has begun to consume her personal life as well; she has begun to dream of the bowl, and its importance has become a constant secret she keeps from her husband. She begins to think of her connection with the bowl as "a relationship of some kind," and consequently she begins to be haunted by "the possibility of disappearance" (*Park City* 354).

Late in the story, the bowl's origin is revealed, providing at least a partial explanation for Andrea's obsession: the bowl had been a gift from her (previously unmentioned) lover. Although she had been drawn to the bowl from the first, she had been reluctant to buy it. The lesson of the bowl's purchase becomes the lesson of losing her lover: "Her lover had said that she was always too slow to know what she really loved" (*Park City* 355). When she fails to decide between her husband and her lover, the lover leaves: "It was a decision meant to break her will, to shatter her intransigent ideas about honoring previous commitments" (355). "Janus" thus provides a rare moment of identifiable psychological symbolism in Beattie's work. Not only has this object become the site of transference of her attachment to her lost lover, but it may also reflect Andrea's sense of her life's hollowness and sterility (the bowl is "meant to be empty").

As the psychological symbolism of "Janus" indicates, Beattie has begun, in her last three collections, to venture beyond the reticence of her earlier fiction, allowing her narratives to indicate a realm of meaning that resists the chain of displacement that dominates the earlier stories. The opening of "In the White Night," for example, directly confronts the studied denial in which her characters typically indulge: " 'Don't think about a cow,' Matt Brinkley said. 'Don't think about a river, don't think about a car, don't think about snow' " (*Park City* 356). The very impossibility of the "Don't-Think-about-Whatever game" that Matt encourages the story's main couple, Carol and Vernon, to play reveals the inadequacy of emotional displacement—the repressed term will inevitably reassert itself. Carol and Vernon are struggling with the grief of losing their daughter, and at times they must simply avoid their pain in order to live with it. Unlike Beattie's other fictions of aftermath, however, "In the White Night" does not itself engage in indirection. Instead, it directly examines the "necessary small adjustment[s]" (360) the couple must make to cope with their loss. The result is an uncharacteristically tender story that contains one of the most graceful gestures in Beattie's fiction. Seeing that Vernon has fallen asleep on the sofa with her jacket spread over him, and recognizing his collapse as a sign of emotional exhaustion, Carol takes his overcoat from the closet and curls up beside him on the floor.

Such moments are necessarily rare, even in Beattie's more recent work. Even as Beattie has begun to work on a larger canvas, both in terms of emotional range and in terms of plot, she has remained true to her vision of human relationships, refusing to reduce their maddening complexity in exchange for a comfortable narrative structure. Without compromising her skepticism concerning human motivations and without compromising her capacity for surprise, Beattie occasionally finds ways to show that even in the absence of knowledge, there lies a possibility for understanding.

WORKS CITED AND CONSULTED

Primary

Short Stories

Beattie, Ann. *The Burning House*. New York: Random House, 1982.
———. *Distortions*. Garden City, NY: Doubleday, 1976.
———. *Falling in Place*. New York: Random House, 1980.
———. *Park City: New and Selected Stories*. New York: Alfred A. Knopf, 1998.
———. *Secrets and Surprises*. New York: Random House, 1978.
———. *What Was Mine*. New York: Random House, 1991.
———. *Where You'll Find Me*. New York: Simon & Schuster, 1986.

Novels

Beattie, Ann. *Another You*. New York: Alfred A. Knopf, 1995.
———. *Chilly Scenes of Winter*. Garden City, NY: Doubleday, 1976.
———. *Falling in Place: A Novel*. New York: Random House, 1980.
———. *Love Always: A Novel*. New York: Random House, 1985.
———. *My Life, Starring Dara Falcon*. New York: Alfred A. Knopf, 1997.
———. *Picturing Will*. New York: Random House, 1989.

Essays, Introductions, and Interviews

Beattie, Ann. *Alex Katz*. New York: Harry N. Abrams, 1987.
———, ed. *The Best American Short Stories 1987*. Boston: Houghton Mifflin, 1987.
———. "Collecting Myself." *San Francisco Chronicle* May 24, 1998, Rev. 1: 3.
———. "The Hum inside the Skull—A Symposium" *New York Times Book Review* May 13, 1984, late ed., sec. 7: 1.
———, ed. *Ploughshares*. Fall 1995.
———. Telephone interview with Michael W. Young. April 11, 1995.
Maynard, Joyce. "Visiting Young Ann Beattie." *New York Times Book Review* May 11, 1980: 39.
Miner, Bob. "Ann Beattie: 'I Write Best When I Am Sick.' " *Village Voice* August 9, 1976: 33–34.
Montresor, Jaye Berman. "This Was in 1992, in Iowa City: Talking with Ann Beattie." *The Critical Response to Ann Beattie*. Ed. Jaye Berman Montresor. Critical Responses in Arts and Letters, 4. Westport, CT: Greenwood, 1993. 219–54.
Parini, Jay. "A Writer Comes of Age." *Horizon* 25 (December 1982): 22–24.
Plath, James. "Counternarrative: An Interview with Ann Beattie." *Michigan Quarterly Review* 32.3 (1993): 359–79.

Samway, Patrick H. "An Interview with Ann Beattie." *America* 162.18 (1990): 469–71.
Seshachari, Neila. "Picturing Ann Beattie: A Dialogue." *Weber Studies: An Interdisciplinary Humanities Journal* 7.1 (Spring 1990): 12–36. Rpt. in *The Critical Response to Ann Beattie*. Ed. Jaye Berman Montresor. Critical Responses in Arts and Letters, 4. Westport, CT: Greenwood, 1993. 187–204.

Secondary

"Ann Beattie." *Contemporary Authors*. Ed. Frances Carol Locker. Detroit: Gale, 1979. 41–42.
"Ann Beattie." *Current Biography* 46 (1985): 3–5.
Clark, Miriam Marty. "Postmodernism and Its Children: The Case of Ann Beattie's 'A Windy Day at the Reservoir.' " *South Atlantic Review* 61.1 (1996): 77–88.
Gelfant, Blanche. "Ann Beattie's Magic Slate; or, The End of the Sixties." *New England Review*. 1979. Rpt. in *The Critical Response to Ann Beattie*. Ed. Jaye Berman Montresor. Critical Responses in Arts and Letters, 4. Westport, CT: Greenwood, 1993.
Gilder, Joshua. "Less Is Less." *New Criterion* 1.6 (February 1983): 78–82.
Husten, Larry. "On Ann Beattie." *Salmagundi* 40 (1978): 160–64. Rpt. in *The Critical Response to Ann Beattie*. Ed. Jaye Berman Montresor. Critical Responses in Arts and Letters, 4. Westport, CT: Greenwood, 1993. 15–18.
Iyer, Pico. "The World According to Beattie." *Partisan Review* 50.4 (1983): 548–53.
Montresor, Jaye Berman, ed. *The Critical Response to Ann Beattie*. Critical Responses in Arts and Letters, 4. Westport, CT: Greenwood, 1993.
Murphy, Christina. *Ann Beattie*. Boston: Twayne, 1986.
Opperman, Harry, and Christina Murphy. "Ann Beattie (1947–   ): A Checklist." *Bulletin of Bibliography* 44.2 (1987): 111–18.
Sprows, Sandra. "Frames, Images, and the Abyss: Psychasthenic Negotiation in Ann Beattie." *The Critical Response to Ann Beattie*. Ed. Jaye Berman Montresor. Critical Responses in Arts and Letters, 4. Westport, CT: Greenwood, 1993. 141–54.
Taylor, David M. "Ann Beattie." *Dictionary of Literary Biography Yearbook 1982*. Detroit: Gale, 1983. 206–12.
Wyatt, David. "Ann Beattie." *Southern Review* 28.1 (1992): 145–59.

MORLEY CALLAGHAN
(February 22, 1903–August 25, 1990)

Grant Tracey

BIOGRAPHY

Morley Callaghan is one of Canada's most distinguished short-story writers. Writing in a direct, nonjudgmental style, without figurative language, he has published over one hundred short stories, thirty-nine in the *New Yorker*. For fourteen consecutive years (1928–41), a Callaghan story appeared in J. Edward O'Brien's *Best Short Stories* annual. In 1973, James T. Farrell observed that of all the writers of their generation, "I think now that he may be the best writer of the lot."

Callaghan was born in Toronto, Canada, in 1903 to Irish Catholic parents. In 1921, he entered St. Michael's College at the University of Toronto, and while he was earning a degree, he worked as a reporter for the *Toronto Star*. At the *Star*, Callaghan befriended Ernest Hemingway, and often the two retreated to the *Star* library to exchange stories and discuss writing philosophy. When Hemingway became a *Star* correspondent in Europe, he circulated Callaghan's fiction and placed "A Girl with Ambition" in a Paris journal, *This Quarter* (1926). It was Callaghan's first published story.

After graduating from the University of Toronto with a B.A. in 1925, Callaghan completed course work at Osgoode Hall Law School, but he never practiced law. Instead, he decided to commit himself to his fiction. Two Callaghan stories, "Soldier Harmon" and "A Predicament," were eventually published in *Scribner's* in July 1928. On the issue's cover, a yellow band read: "New Fiction Star—Morley Callaghan." Inside the issue, editor Maxwell Perkins introduced the young star: "It will be remembered that on the other occasion when we presented two stories in the same number the writer was Ernest Hemingway." Thus, indirectly, Perkins began the long association among critics between Callaghan and Hemingway. Although both writers use a reporter's spare style and colloquial speech, Callaghan's training in law and philosophy imbues his characters with a deeper metaphysics and interiority. Hemingway was concerned with feats of physical courage; Callaghan moral.

Callaghan's first collection of stories, *A Native Argosy*, was published in 1929. Following this success, he and his bride, Loretto Florence Dee, honeymooned in Paris, where their relationship with Hemingway became strained. During a "friendly" sparring match, Callaghan dropped the much bigger Hemingway with an uppercut. Hemingway's pride was hurt, and thus so was their friendship. However, the event did not seem to hurt Callaghan's career. He published six novels in the 1930s and a second collection of short stories, *Now That April's Here* (1936). In 1959, Macmillan reprinted most of these stories in a rather definitive *Morley Callaghan's Stories*.

From 1937 to 1948, Callaghan neglected his fiction and devoted time to radio programming. In 1948, Callaghan's story "The Little Business Man" was re-worked and expanded into the juvenile novel *Luke Baldwin's Vow*, and he began drafting *The Loved and the Lost*, which received the Canadian Governor General's Award for Fiction in 1951. Although he wrote several more novels, he virtually stopped writing short stories in 1953. He died on August 25, 1990.

CRITICISM

When I was an undergraduate at Trent University, I asked a Canadian literature professor, the son of a famous Prairie writer, why there were no Callaghan works assigned for the survey course. He grinned and dismissed the question with a curt "Oh, he's sentimental." That professor's opinion was not unique; rather, it was reflective of a pervasive Canadian attitude toward Callaghan that both revered and decried the writer's achievement. A debate blossomed in 1960 after Edmund Wilson, fiction editor for the *New Yorker*, declared Callaghan one of the century's great unknown writers, a star on the level of Turgenev and Chekhov (Wilson, *Morley Callaghan* 113). Wilson speculated that perhaps Canadians could not see the prophet within their midst, and that his novels were overlooked because several ended in "annihilating violence" (Wilson 118). George Woodcock and other professors held a different view. They regarded Callaghan's novels as "pretentious," the prose "flabby" and at times "excruciating" (Woodcock, *Morley Callaghan* 88–103). Even the admirers of Callaghan's short stories questioned the flattened style. Margaret Avison contended that by the conclusion of "A Cap for Steve," the repetition without variation of "cap" rendered the object meaningless (Avison, *Morley Callaghan* 76). Similarly, Mary Colum believed that Callaghan had a deeper understanding of human experience than either of his peers, F. Scott Fitzgerald or Ernest Hemingway, yet his prose style was "queerly pedestrian" (Colum, *Morley Callaghan* 53).

Callaghan's prose style reflects his generous, democratic spirit. The artist believed that prose should be transported in order to convey reality directly to the reader. But the effect of Callaghan's choice to eschew simile and metaphor not only reveals the inherent truth of the object but aligns readers more fully with the sensibilities of the people he represents: common men and women working in lunch counters or department stores searching for love and dignity. "Dignity" is one of Callaghan's favorite words and its placement in stories embodies an authorial attitude. Callaghan's narrative presence moves alongside characters, not above them, and the dignified tone perfectly mirrors the love and tolerance his largely Depression-era people search for and achieve. Wyndham Lewis first recognized this central theme when he stated that Callaghan's solutions to the problems of life are respect for individual dignity, patience, and understanding love (Lewis, *Morley Callaghan* 57). Callaghan loves the people he writes about, and his democratic spirit—what Lewis defines as "his fairness of mind" (57)—refuses readers the right to finalize characters. His characters are complex, and though rendered in a somewhat standard three-act structure (exposition, deflection, and resolution), Callaghan frequently forces readers to revise and reconsider earlier assessments. His vision is moral: readers, narrator, and characters are equal.

ANALYSIS

Callaghan's first story, "A Girl with Ambition" (1926), presents a culture clash between well-heeled Harry and lower-working-class Mary Ross. To gain Harry's respect, Mary seeks fame on the stage, but the futility of her quest is revealed through Harry's apparent ambivalence about her. At a roller rink, Harry's friend, Chuck, "roguishly" states, "Hello. I know you because Harry has told me a lot about you" (*Stories* 243). Callaghan's discriminate use of the adverb implies a less-than-noble assessment of Mary among Harry and his friends.

Mary's quest fails, but the narrative resolution grants her grace. Although she is unsuccessful on the stage, she enacts a final performance that moves Harry to reassess her: "Leaning on the veranda rail, he saw that her slimness had passed into the shapelessness of her pregnancy and he knew why she had been kept off the stage that night at the La Plaza. She sat erect and strangely dignified on the seat of the grocery wagon. They didn't speak" (246). Mary rejects Harry, afraid that she appears to be a fallen woman. Harry, who had treated her lightly, suddenly recognizes in her expectant motherhood the dignity she had always possessed.

Callaghan's often-anthologized "All the Years of Her Life" and his first *New Yorker* publication, "The Faithful Wife" (December 28, 1929), invoke similar ironic conclusions. The first story presents Alfred, a troubled adolescent who is caught stealing toiletries from his boss's mom and pop store. Alfred tries to appear tough, "like a swaggering big guy who could look after himself, yet the old childish hope was in him" (*Stories* 2–3). Neither boy nor man, Alfred faces castigation from Sam Carr, who judges him "a fool" and threatens to call the police. As they await the arrival of his mother, Alfred assumes that she will arrive tearfully. Her entrance surprises him: she carries herself with "a calmness and dignity" (3). Carr, too, is surprised and a "bit ashamed" by her "understanding gentleness" and kind, "patient dignity." (4) He agrees to drop the charges.

Surprised by his mother's strength, Alfred reassesses her character in the narrative's conclusion. Once home, banished to his room as punishment for his crime, he contemplates her "smooth" resolve with Carr. He wants to thank her for intervening on his behalf and walks toward the kitchen. Unseen, he watches as she sips tea with trembling hands. In a sudden moment of recognition, Alfred realizes that he has always been a tremendous burden on his mother. This knowledge redeems him for the reader and forces him to accept responsibility. Through the distilled image of trembling, Alfred crosses over into adulthood.

"The Faithful Wife" more fully develops Callaghan's desire to create characters that resist the readers' judgment. George works at a lunch counter, where he gazes with empathy at a customer: "She was about twenty-eight, pretty, rather shy, and dressed plainly and poorly in a thin blue-cloth coat without any fur on it" (*Stories* 164). After a walk along the lakeshore, George returns to the diner to find that the woman has telephoned and asked for him to stop by her apartment. The plot's deflection, the phone call, forces the reader to reevaluate the woman. Her earlier description filtered through George's naïveté appears faulty. "She had on a red woolen sweater, fitting her tightly at the waist" (166), and she "[breathed] deeply every time he kissed her" (166). As George's kisses become too eager, she stops the encounter, and he notices "a red ring mark on her finger."

Just as readers prepare to dismiss her as wanton and adulterous, Callaghan forces another look: "My husband, he's at a sanitarium. He got his spine hurt in the war, then he got tuberculosis. He's pretty bad. They've got to carry him around. We want to love each other every time we meet, but we can't" (*Stories* 167). Readers now recognize her need for tolerance and love, but George is not sympathetic. "Do you have a lot of fellows?" (167) he asks, and when she does not want to go further with the affair, he threatens. The readers' condemnation switches from the woman to George, and we are forced to question the integrity of his earlier empathetic gaze. Finally, he, too, redeems himself for the reader as he accepts her refusal: "He knew he could not spoil it for her" (*Stories* 168).

Callaghan's "fairness of mind" follows a discernible pattern: exposition (establishing mood and conflict), deflection (a strange event that redirects the character on a new adventure), and resolution (a discovery for the deflected character). Callaghan's tripartite narratives often center around a fixed setting: a park, a cathedral, a diner. "Mr. and Mrs. Fairbanks" is one such story.

The circular plot to "Mr. and Mrs. Fairbanks" ends with an ironic inversion. After the couple discovers that Helen (Mrs. Fairbanks) is pregnant, they stroll through the park. Bill Fairbanks, oblivious to her fears, "feels more expansive, more abundant" (*Stories* 227), and tells Helen that she is "soft and plump and kind of all glowing" (228). She is not reassured. In the story's deflection, Helen approaches an old man on a park bench and offers him a quarter, which he refuses. "He just turned his eyes up and looked at her steadily with simple dignity and then turned away" (229). His dignity shames her. Humiliated and embarrassed for categorizing him as "a bum," Helen displaces her anger on Bill, and the fears hinted at in the exposition resurface. She worries about growing old and finding the means for raising a child during the Depression. She and Bill briskly quarrel, and the argument escalates as they recross the old man's path. He understands their quarrel and smiles with concern. His rapport fills Helen with "humility," and she returns his grin. Earlier, his pride had humbled her; now, in the resolution, his grace reconciles her to her husband. She walks alongside Bill and shares his earlier joy, feeling "all soft and glowing" (232).

Callaghan's narrative voice can be compassionate or detached, but it is always tolerant. A wistful ironic tone pervades such stories as "An Escapade" and "A Predicament." The first story, according to Conron, can be read as a religious parable (*Morley Callaghan* [1966] 45). When Rose Carey drifts from her Catholic faith and attends a Protestant service as an observer, she is seeking to discover what the women in the bridge club find so fascinating without allowing herself "to take [the] religious notions seriously" (*Stories* 125). But next to her, a man begins crying; he has just lost his brother and is moved by the pastor's words. Rose, jarred from her detachment, gets involved: "She was sorry for him" (126). The deflection evolves when suddenly he holds her hand and she does not let go. Quickly, spiritual kinship becomes sexual: "Her cheeks were warm. She tried to stop thinking altogether" (127). Alarmed by her emotions, Rose, who entered the church wanting "to go unnoticed" for avoiding her own faith, exits, "erect and dignified," feeling the need to displace her sudden and inexplicable sexual passion. In the resolution, she hops a streetcar and returns to Father Conley's cathedral. There she says a series of prayers, "thinking of her husband at home." Callaghan ends her journey with some deft self-deception: "She prayed for half an hour, feeling better gradually till she hardly remembered the man in the theatre, and fairly satisfied, she got up and left the Cathedral" (128).

"A Predicament" also deals with self-deception and moral courage. Young Father Francis, "very interested in confession" (*Stories* 17), has his voyeuristic pleasures shattered when a drunken man stumbles into his confessional. Mistaking the priest for a bus driver, the man insists, "I wanna get off at King and Yonge Street" (17). Agitated and afraid that a disturbance would get into the papers, Father Francis avoids the problem by turning to another penitent. As a young woman admits to a series of "white lies," the priest grows more and more agitated, his mind returning to the drunken man: "The man was drunk—drunkenness, the over-indulgence of an appetite" (18). Distracted, the priest harshly tells the young woman, "They are lies, lies, lies, just the same" (18).

He eventually turns this judgment inward. After counseling the young woman, he finds the man on the other side of the confessional still waiting for his stop. As Father Francis opens the confessional half-panel, "the grating noise" that sounds like a door on a bus inspires him. "Step lively there; this is King and

Yonge. Do you want to miss your stop?" (*Stories* 19). The ruse works, the man leaves, but the priest is remorseful: "He had descended to artifice in the confessional to save himself from embarrassment" (19). He had accused the young woman of the very sin he himself has just committed. Later, at dinner with the other priests, he says nothing about the incident, convincing himself that the matter first had "to be settled in his own conscience." Despairingly, he realizes his self-deception and mocks himself: "Then perhaps he would tell the bishop" (19).

The Lost and Found Stories of Morley Callaghan assembles work discovered in 1985 by Morley's son, writer Barry Callaghan. None of the selections had previously appeared in the 1959 collection, and the best of them deal with coming-of-age themes. "A Pair of Long Pants" concerns Tony, a fourteen-year-old who is mistaken by a truck driver for a young adult and decides to go along for the ride. During the adventure, he tastes his first beer, experiences his first brush with the opposite sex, and perceives for the first time an open future somewhere beyond his town. "Hello, America!" is a Depression-era allegory about an English immigrant, Henry, who works at a roadside diner and offers soup to struggling Joes traveling the rails and looking for work. Henry's boss, Herrmann, disapproves, and the youngster decides to leave the "Levite" for the open road. "I want to thank you, Mr. Herrmann. . . . You've helped me make a lot of friends and I feel I've sort of got to know the country, I like it" (*Lost and Found* 244–45).

"With an Air of Dignity" tells of Steve, a young man learning to respect himself, and Rita, a maid who works for Steve's parents. Three years prior, Steve sent a local hooligan, Kersh, to jail by informing police of his robbery plans. Upon his release, Kersh has sought revenge by periodically beating up on Steve. Rattled by the encounters, Steve resolves to defend himself with a weapon. When Kersh arrives one day drunk and threatening, Steve grabs a gun, but before he can use it, Rita intervenes—she dons lipstick and distracts Kersh by encouraging him to take her to a bar. Though Rita compromises her reputation for Steve, Pauline, Steve's sister who disparages Rita's lower-class origins, is unimpressed. "A girl like Rita can always handle a man like Kersh" (*Lost and Found* 155). Pauline dismisses Rita as a bad-girl type, but Steve feels indebted to her and heads to the bar to return the favor. While there, he refuses to fight Kersh and thus suffers a savage beating until the bully, confused by Steve's passivity, gives up and leaves. Rita is confounded by Steve's behavior, but in the aftermath of the fight, the two share a moment that crosses class boundaries. "As they walked in step, their shoes squeaked in the hard snow. The street was long. It ran into the prairie, and the prairie into the cold sky. They were both watching the ribbons of light on the rim of the prairie sky" (*Lost and Found* 160).

"Two Fisherman," a story Callaghan selected as his favorite in 1942, according to Conron, considers a typical Callaghan theme of justice through a series of ironic contrasts (*Morley Callaghan* [1966] 105). The idyllic community of

Collingwood on Georgian Bay with "its smooth lake water" and "blue hill" is the backdrop for a hanging (*Stories* 209–10). Thomas Delaney, a citizen much beloved by the town, killed a man who molested his wife. K. Smith ("Smitty"), the hangman and public official, is a small gentle fellow, a family man with five children who likes to fish. Michael Foster, an aspiring reporter, unfairly judges the little man and the demands of law.

Michael visits Smitty fishing to confront him about his role in the hanging. But Smitty defends his decision, explaining, "The job hasn't been so disagreeable." Although he knows that "he ought to be ashamed of himself" (*Stories* 212), he does not feel ashamed because he has a job to do. As they continue to fish, Michael's opinion changes; he reaches an understanding, yet he cannot share that feeling with the community:

As Michael rowed the boat around to the boat-house, he hoped that Smitty wouldn't realize he didn't want to be seen walking back to town with him. And later, when he was going slowly along the dusty road in the dark and hearing all the crickets chirping in the ditches, he couldn't figure out why he felt so ashamed of himself. (*Stories* 213)

The shame Michael tried to force on Smitty he now, in typical Callaghan complexity, turns on himself.

All of Callaghan's characters seek love and tolerance, but the strongest element of his work is the reworking of the Christian admonishment "Let him who is without sin cast the first stone." "Two Fishermen" makes the reference clear. After Smitty hangs Delaney, he carries "himself with a strange cocky dignity" (*Stories* 214) and then gives Michael two fish he had caught in the morning. Rejecting the hangman and the fish, Michael disappears into the crowd gathered outside the jailyard. Another fisherman hurls a small rock, then seizes the fish and heaves them at the hangman.

Callaghan's explanation of the hangman's character can be extended to define all of the characters in Callaghan's fictional world: "The hangman, a necessary figure in society, a man definitely serving the public and the ends of justice, was entitled to a little human dignity. In fact he saw himself as a dignified human being" (Conron, *Morley Callaghan* [1966] 105).

WORKS CITED AND CONSULTED

Primary

Callaghan, Morley. *The Lost and Found Stories of Morley Callaghan*. Toronto: Lester & Orpen Dennys/Exile Editions, 1985.

———. *The Loved and the Lost*. Toronto: Macmillan, 1951.

———. *Luke Baldwin's Vow* (juvenile). Toronto: Winston, 1948; Toronto: Scholastic, 1974.

————. *Morley Callaghan's Stories*. Toronto: Macmillan, 1959; Toronto: Laurentian Library, 1967.

————. *A Native Argosy*. New York: Scribner, 1929; Freeport, N.Y.: Books for Libraries, 1970.

————. *Now That April's Here and Other Stories*. New York: Random House, 1936.

————. *That Summer in Paris: Memories of Tangled Friendships with Hemingway, Fitzgerald, and Some Others*. New York: Coward-McCann, 1963.

Secondary

Avison, Margaret. "Callaghan Revisited." *Morley Callaghan*. Ed. Brandon Conron. Toronto: McGraw-Hill Ryerson, 1975. 74–77.

Colum, Mary. "The Psychopathic Novel." *Morley Callaghan*. Ed. Brandon Conron. Toronto: McGraw-Hill Ryerson, 1975. 49–55.

Conron, Brandon. *Morley Callaghan*. New York: Twayne, 1966.

————. "Morley Callaghan as a Short Story Writer." *Journal of Commonwealth Literature* 3 (July 1967): 58–75.

Lewis, Wyndham. "What Books for Total War." *Morley Callaghan*. Ed. Brandon Conron. Toronto: McGraw-Hill Ryerson, 1975. 56–61.

Tracey, Grant. "One Great Way to Read Short Stories: Studying the Character Deflection in Morley Callaghan's 'All the Years of Her Life.'" *Short Stories in the Classroom*. Ed. Carol Hamilton and Peter Kratzke. Urbana, IL: NCTE, 1999. 67–71.

Wilson, Edmund. "Morley Callaghan of Toronto." *Morley Callaghan*. Ed. Brandon Conron. Toronto: McGraw-Hill Ryerson, 1975. 106–19.

Woodcock, George. "Lost Euridice: The Novels of Callaghan." *Morley Callaghan*. Ed. Brandon Conron. Toronto: McGraw-Hill Ryerson, 1975. 88–103.

ANGELA (OLIVE) CARTER
(May 7, 1940–February 16, 1992)

Erica Benson

BIOGRAPHY

Angela Olive Stalker was born in Eastbourne, Sussex, England, the daughter of Hugh Alexander Stalker, a journalist, and Olive (Farthing) Stalker. Before Carter entered grammar school, her family moved to South London, where she was to spend most of her life. From 1958 to 1961, Carter worked at the *Croydon Advertiser*, where she wrote record reviews and features. In 1960, Carter married Paul Carter, an industrial chemist. The following year, they moved to Bristol. In 1962, she began studying medieval literature at Bristol University, graduating with a B.A. in English in 1965. Following her separation from her husband in 1969 (they divorced in 1972), Carter went to Japan, where she lived until 1972. From 1976 to 1978, Carter was an Arts Council Fellow in creative writing at the University of Sheffield. She was a visiting professor of creative writing at Brown University in Providence, Rhode Island, from 1980 to 1981. In 1984, Carter was writer-in-residence at the University of Adelaide, Australia. On February 16, 1992, Carter died of lung cancer. She is survived by her second husband, Mark Pearce, and her son, Alexander.

Carter began writing as an undergraduate and published her first novel, *Shadow Dance* (1966), soon after graduating. Over the years, she tried her hand at a number of forms: poetry, novel, short story, children's literature, radio play, screenplay, and critical essay. A dedicated and productive writer, Carter published works nearly every year until the year after her death. She was awarded a number of literary prizes, including the John Llewllyn Rhys Prize in 1968 for *The Magic Toyshop* (1967, novel); the Somerset Maugham Award in 1969 for *Several Perceptions* (1968, novel); the Cheltenham Literary Festival Award in 1979 for *The Bloody Chamber and Other Stories* (1979, short stories); the Maschler Award in 1982 for *Sleeping Beauty and Other Favourite Fairy Tales*

(1982); and the James Tait Black Memorial Prize in 1985 for *Nights at the Circus* (1984, novel).

CRITICISM

Carter has gained recognition in a number of genres: novel, short story, critical essays, and children's literature. The focus of this chapter is her contribution to the short story. Carter's short fiction has been published in many periodicals and anthologies, in addition to being assembled into four collections that have been published and republished in Great Britain and the United States.

Carter has been compared to Proust, Borges, Hoffman, Poe, Polanski, and others, "but she can be more brilliant than all of them," boasts Richard Orodenker in the *North American Review* (72). Through rich, descriptive prose, Carter masterfully weaves speculation, myth, and reality with gothic elements. While Carter has been admired for her detailed description, she has often been criticized for overdoing it. Two words that pepper criticism of Carter's short stories are *disturbing* and *imaginative*. Grace Ingoldby, in "Putting on the Style," describes Carter's short fiction as "much easier to admire than to enjoy" (cited in *Contemporary Literary Criticism* 41: 121).

Many of Carter's pieces, particularly her retellings of European fairy tales, explore gender roles, sexual behavior, and social expectations and, therefore, have been interpreted as having a feminist perspective. Mary Kaiser, in "Fairy Tale as Sexual Allegory," suggests that Carter uses wide-ranging intertextuality to challenge the general assumption that fairy tales are eternal myths, only for children, with little relevance to the real world (35). While most critics agree that these pieces challenge gender roles and social expectations, they dispute the point of view as feminist. Peter Faulkner notes, "Some feminists objected to the terms of the rewriting, finding the depiction of women politically incorrect" (112). Indeed, Patricia Duncker, in "Re-Imagining the Fairy Tales," states: "Carter envisages women's sensuality simply as a response to male arousal. She has no conception of women's sexuality as autonomous desire" (cited in *Contemporary Literary Criticism* 41: 118). Without question, Carter's four collections confront readers, making them contemplate preconceived notions of the world.

Her first collection, *Fireworks: Nine Profane Pieces* (1974), also published as *Fireworks: Nine Stories in Various Disguises* (1981) and *Fireworks* (1987), contains nine pieces that Carter herself calls gothic tales. In the "Afterword," she notes that the short story recounts everyday happenings, whereas the tale "interprets everyday experience through a system of imagery derived from subterranean areas behind everyday experience, and therefore the tale cannot betray its readers into a false knowledge of everyday experience" (*Fireworks* 133).

Carter's second collection of short fiction, *The Bloody Chamber and Other Stories* (1979), also published as *The Bloody Chamber* (1979), won the Cheltenham Literary Festival Award in 1979. This collection is composed entirely of adult retellings of ten familiar fairy tales from "Red Riding Hood" to "Blue-beard."

The nine stories in Carter's third collection, published in Great Britain as *Black Venus* (1985) and in the United States as *Saints and Strangers* (1986), are based on real people—Lizzie Borden; Edgar Allan Poe and his mother; Jeanne Duval, Baudelaire's Creole mistress—and fictional characters set in the Old World and the New World. These stories are thematically and stylistically similar to those in *The Bloody Chamber and Other Stories*.

Carter's fourth collection, *American Ghosts and Old World Wonders*, was published posthumously in 1993. The nine tales in this collection are characteristically Carter: descriptive, speculative, imaginative, gothic. The tales are not bound to each other by time or space and span centuries and cultures from Lizzie Borden to Cinderella to Mary Magdalene.

A complete collection of Carter's short fiction appeared in 1995, three years after her death. This collection, entitled *Burning Your Boats: Stories* (1995) and also published as *Burning Your Boats: The Collected Short Stories*, is introduced by Salman Rushdie and contains a few stories not found in Carter's other four volumes of short stories.

ANALYSIS

Carter's passion for description, compulsion for speculation (about gender roles, sexual behavior, and social expectation), and obsession with appearances predominate in the thematically diverse pieces of her first collection, *Fireworks*. The tales were written between 1970 and 1973, and though their order may seem haphazard to the reader, they appear in the order in which they were written. One of the major undercurrents in nearly all of these pieces is the opposition between reality and appearance, between essence and facade. In an interview with Anna Katsavos, Carter contemplates appearances: "How do we know what is authentic behavior and what is inauthentic behavior? It's about the complex interrelation of reality and its representations" (Katsavos 16).

The first piece in the collection, "A Souvenir of Japan," weaves a European woman's impressions of Japan with accounts of her relationship with a younger Japanese man. The anonymous narrator's ruminations on the relationship alternate with her observations of the hypocrisy of Japanese society and its obsession with appearances: "To look at a samurai, you would not know him for a murderer, or a geisha for a whore" (*Fireworks* 11). Carter proposes that appearances are short-lived and void of essence, and she illustrates this view by a comparison of Japanese society to a "hall of mirrors which continually proliferated whole galleries of constantly changing appearances, all marvelous but none tangible" (*Fireworks* 10).

The narrator is guilty of such hypocrisy herself by holding the appearances before the reality and believing that perhaps the appearances will become the reality, knowing, however, that they never will. For example, her physical appearance is in stark contrast with those around her—she is tall and has a fair complexion, blue eyes, and blonde hair—yet she assumes that if she acts like everyone else, she will fit in. Furthermore, although she elaborately describes the appearance of her lover (a clearly feminine image)—he has an "elegant body," an "androgynous grace," "pectorals like the breasts of a girl approaching puberty," "blunt, bee-stung lips"—the description is illusive. It reveals little about his character—not even his real name—beyond his possession of "an unearthly quality" and "an inhuman sweetness" (*Fireworks* 6–7). The reader is even teased with the statement "I thought I was inventing him as I went along, however, you will have to take my word for it that we existed" (*Fireworks* 9). Unearthing the facade of feeling between the lovers, the narrator asks, "How far does a pretense of feeling, maintained with absolute conviction, become authentic?" (*Fireworks* 11). When does the appearance become reality? In the end, the reader learns, such folly is doomed to failure.

Hypocrisy also plays a central role in the next tale, the disturbing "The Executioner's Beautiful Daughter." In a small, primitive highland village, the lone executioner beheads his incestuous son, then later "makes love" to his beautiful daughter on the bloody chopping block. Although incest is illegal and carries the punishment of decapitation, the executioner, who always wears his black leather mask, knows that "there is nobody to cut off his head" (*Fireworks* 22). Carter describes in extensive, elaborate detail the verminous, stunted villagers, repressed and sexually obsessed, as well as the deplorable surroundings in which they live. The only inhabitant immune to the conditions is Gretchen, the executioner's sensitive, attractive daughter, "on whose cheeks the only roses in these highlands grow" (*Fireworks* 17).

In the third piece, "The Loves of Lady Purple," the boundaries between the worlds of the living and the imitation of living are crossed several times when a marionette subjects her puppeteer to the same fate as her previous lovers. As the tale reveals, Lady Purple, once a remorseless prostitute of the East, with a penchant for arson and murder, has become a marionette. An Asiatic professor found her wooden puppet and took to telling her story on the traveling stage, transmitting to the puppet the passion harbored inside his socially isolated, lonely shell of a life: "She was nothing but a curious structure until the Professor touched her strings, for it was he who filled her with necromantic vigor" (*Fireworks* 28). One night when the puppeteer is putting his beloved doll in her custom-made case, he kisses her as always, but this time "she sucked the breath from his lungs . . . sunk her teeth into his throat and drained him" (*Fireworks* 38). Before she steps out of the theater, she purposely knocks over a candle and never looks back at the inferno behind her.

Lady Purple was once a real woman; on the stage, "she did not seem so much a cunningly simulated woman as a monstrous goddess at once preposterous and magnificent," yet she was only wooden until that fateful night (*Fireworks* 28). Carter teases the reader with the question: "Had the marionette all the time parodied the living or was she, now living, to parody her own performance as a marionette?" (*Fireworks* 39).

In contrast to the two previous works, "The Smile of Winter" is a touching and reflective story depicting a lonely European woman in a small Japanese beach town in the middle of winter. The anonymous narrator wears "the smile of winter," which is hardly a smile at all but a metaphor for sadness and loneliness. This tale relies solely on Carter's descriptive prose to paint tranquil, forsaken images. At the end of the tale, Carter ironically explains: "Do not think I do not realize what I am doing. I am making a composition using . . . elements . . . inimical to my loneliness because of their indifference to it. Out of these pieces of inimical indifference I intend to represent the desolate smile of winter" (*Fireworks* 49–50).

The next story, "Penetrating to the Heart of the Forest," is a loss-of-innocence tale set in a utopian village covered with flora and fauna, bordered by an abundant forest. Dubois, a well-traveled botanist, settles in the area with his twins, one boy, one girl. The central characters are the fearless twins, who live in harmony with nature, are sexually intimate with each other, and are born explorers. They are carefree descendants of former slaves who have never been compelled to explore the forest and have created a myth of a deadly tree to justify their lack of adventure. Emile and Madeline, however, decide that nothing less than penetration into the heart of the forest will satisfy their curiosity. For the first time in their lives, they discover hostility there when a "perfectly white and innocent" water lily bites Madeline as she attempts to pick it. This incident precedes the feeling of shame Emile and Madeline feel in each other's nakedness for the first time in their lives: "The confusion . . . made their blood sting" (*Fireworks* 63). As they continue, the forest grows ever more enchanting and richer with exotic plants until they come upon a tree with fruit resembling apples. Carter leaves no doubt that this tale is an allegory of the loss of innocence in the Garden of Eden. When Dubois first arrives in the area, he declares, "Dear God! It is as if Adam had opened Eden to the public!" (*Fireworks* 53). At the conclusion, Madeline picks the applelike fruit: " 'It tastes so good!' she said. 'Here! Eat!' . . . He took the apple; ate; and, after that, they kissed" (*Fireworks* 66).

"Flesh and the Mirror" is the ultimate tale of appearances, "flesh" being the true essence of reality and "the mirror" reflecting an image of reality. The poignancy the anonymous narrator, a married British woman, experiences on her return to Tokyo when her lover fails to meet her at the pier thrusts her into a state of self-reflection and deep contemplation about her life. Carter switches between first- and third-person narration as the woman speaks from her true essence, her conscience (I), and from the appearance of the life she leads (she). The woman faults herself for living too much in the image of reality and not in reality: "It was as if I never experienced experience *as* experience. Living never lived up to the expectations I had of it" (*Fireworks* 69).

In addition, the narrator believes that women and mirrors conspire "to evade the action I/she performs that she/I cannot watch, the action with which I break out of the mirror, with which I assume my appearance" (*Fireworks* 71). The narrator's true essence, her conscience, wins out; she ends the affair, admits that her outward appearance reveals nothing about her true self, but, nevertheless, recognizes how difficult "acting naturally" can be.

The next piece, "Master," is in marked contrast to the previous tale. It is set in the Amazon forests; a third-person narrator recounts the relationship between a British adventurer who has a talent for killing animals and ravaging women and a pubescent girl of a native tribe, whom he has bought for the spare tire on his jeep. The master, sick with malaria, and the girl, whom he calls Friday, venture through the tropics, where he satisfies his rage by killing animals and physically and sexually abusing her. His most satisfying prey is the jaguar, which coincidentally (or not) is the spirit of the girl's tribe.

Carter adeptly portrays the girl as a metaphor for animalkind and perhaps for mother earth herself. Initially described as having a smile like that of a cat and eyes that see in the dark, the girl gradually embodies the spirit of her people: she grows long claws and whiskers, eats raw meat, and develops amber and brown spots. When the master is delirious with fever, she seizes the opportunity, shoots him, briefly feasts on his flesh, then trots into the forest on all fours. Perhaps this is a sign of victory: "The prey had shot the hunter" (*Fireworks* 87), but would it not have been more satisfying to know that the master had suffered as others had suffered at his expense?

The next story, "Reflections," is a hauntingly surreal tale about a two-way mirror that is the door between "mirror" worlds: one is the opposite image of the other, such that right is left, light is dark, and backward is forward. Carter's prose impeccably depicts these worlds such that anything but feeble attempts to reproduce them is impossible. As the story opens, a male narrator (the only one in the collection) walking in the woods is taken at gunpoint by a young woman, Anna, after he finds a peculiar shell that belongs in the mirror world. He is taken to the house of the mirror, where Anna's immobile aunt, an androgyne (half male, half female), constantly knits. The narrator is forced to enter the mirror world, where "I could not, for the life of me, make up my mind which world was which" (*Fireworks* 106). The narrator is dominated and raped by Anna and must kill her to escape the mirror world. Upon his return, the andro-gyne decrees that the narrator—the male—has irreparably damaged the connec-tion she has been knitting between "this world and that world" (*Fireworks* 111).

The final story, "Elegy for a Freelance," is markedly different from the other stories in the collection because it deals with political conspiracy, assassination, and bombs. The plot centers on a small group of London revolutionaries who plan to kill a member of the cabinet. It falls upon the assumed leader of the group to carry out the act; however, his cultivated indifference turns to fear, so he decides "to practice" on the old, blind landlord. The narrator, his girlfriend, discovers the crime, drugs him with sleeping pills, and consults with the others in the group, who hold a mock trial and hang him the following night. The next

day, while they are arguing about what to do with the dead landlord, they hear
on the radio that the army has taken power.

While all this is going on, there is a semblance of normalcy. To begin with,
none of the inhabitants of the building have a notion that anything strange has
been going on in the basement, where the group builds and tests bombs; moreover, no one notices that anything has happened to the landlord. Furthermore,
a girlfriend of one conspirator gives birth in the basement after the landlord has
been killed. What is ironic, however, is that the group was oblivious to the plot
of the army, whose coup would have greatly overshadowed their assassination
attempt anyway.

As in many of the previous tales, the main characters remain nameless; they
are identified, however, with letters: A, B, C, X. Curiously, the narrator, retelling
the story years later (the army is still in power, and she has served her time),
shifts between the second-person pronoun of address, *you*, and the third-person
pronoun, *he*, to refer to her former lover.

The multifaceted themes and distinctive style Carter employs in *Fireworks*
(1974) recur in her later collections. Interestingly, many of the stories in Carter's
later short-story collections focus on well-known real as well as fictional characters. *The Bloody Chamber* (1979), Carter's definitive work in the short-story
genre, contains ten stories based on European fairy tales, for example, "Bluebeard," "Beauty and the Beast," "Puss in Boots," "Snow White," and "Red
Riding Hood." The retellings are not for children and, for the most part, remain
in a world apart from our own. They are, on the one hand, erotic, animalistic,
violent, and disturbing; on the other hand, they are family-centered. In "The
Bloody Chamber," the masterpiece of this collection, the Bluebeard tale acquires
a new twist when the mother-in-law of the rich Marquis (i.e., Bluebeard) gallops
in and shoots him dead, just as he is about to decapitate her daughter (who
betrayed the Marquis by going into the room where the remains of his former
wives are kept). In "The Courtship of Mr. Lyon" and "The Tiger's Bride," both
based on "Beauty and the Beast," a father is responsible for giving his daughter
to an animal beast—in one story a lion, in the other a tiger—with different
results: When Beauty returns to the gravely ill Mr. Lyon, he turns into a handsome, healthy young man, while the tiger's bride ultimately submits to the
caresses of his tongue, which transform her into a tiger. The wolf, the epitome
of the wild animal beast as depicted in fairy tales, takes center stage in the final
three stories in the collection: "The Werewolf," "The Company of Wolves," and
"Wolf-Alice." In addition to revealing the universal animal nature of humans,
the stories in this collection challenge the universality of gender roles.

The stories in Carter's next two collections are more diverse thematically,
stylistically, and geographically than those in *The Bloody Chamber*. In *Black
Venus* (1985), also published as *Saints and Strangers* (1986), and in *American
Ghosts and Old World Wonders* (1993), the reader is taken to France, Central
Asia, England, New England, the Wild West, a Mexican border town, and Hol-
lywood and traverses the worlds of fantasy and reality, encountering abuse,

murder, incest, and illusion. Although Carter continues to create worlds of fantasy and fable in some of the stories (e.g., "Peter and the Wolf," "In Pantoland," "Ashputtle *or* The Mother's Ghost") the majority of the stories in these collections are based in reality, that is, the world as we more or less know it. A number of these stories examine the lives of famous (and infamous) historical figures, most of whom are female, for example, Lizzie Borden, Jeanne Duval (Charles Baudelaire's mistress), and Mary Magdalene. For example, two stories examine the life of Lizzie Borden before she murders her father and stepmother. "The Fall River Axe Murders" curiously begins and ends in the family house on the early morning of the murders; the bulk of the story details Lizzie's behavior on that treacherously hot, fateful day. "Lizzie's Tiger" portrays Lizzie as a young girl who runs off on her own to see the circus in town.

Burning Your Boats (1995), a complete collection of Carter's short stories, contains, in addition to the stories from her four collections—*Fireworks* (1974), *The Bloody Chamber* (1979), *Black Venus* (1985) and *American Ghosts and Old World Wonders* (1993)—six previously uncollected stories. Three of the stories—"The Man who Loved a Double Bass," "A Very, Very Great Lady and Her Son at Home," and "A Victorian Fable (with Glossary)"—were published between 1962 and 1965; two—"The Scarlet House" and "The Quilt Maker"— were published between 1977 and 1981; and one—"The Snow Pavilion"—was previously unpublished. Although each of these six stories bears some relation to other stories by Carter, they do not share a collective theme. For example, in "The Man Who Loved a Double Bass" (1962), when the personified double bass "Lola" is destroyed in a bar fight, her owner commits suicide; however, in "A Victorian Fable (with Glossary)," a "Jabberwocky"-like presentation with a glossary three times as long as the tale, a seedy neighborhood overrun with prostitution, crime, drunkenness, and illness is depicted.

WORKS CITED AND CONSULTED

Primary

Short Stories

Carter, Angela. *American Ghosts and Old World Wonders*. London: Chatto & Windus, 1993; London: Vintage, 1994.

———. *Black Venus*. London: Chatto & Windus, 1985. Published in the United States as *Saints and Strangers*. New York: Viking, 1986; New York: Penguin, 1987.

———. *Black Venus's Tale*. London: Next Editions, 1980.

———. *The Bloody Chamber and Other Stories*. London: Victor Gollancz, 1979; New York: Penguin, 1987. Published as *The Bloody Chamber*. New York: Harper & Row, 1979, 1981. Published as *The Bloody Chamber, and Other Stories*. New York: Penguin, 1993.

———. *Burning Your Boats: Stories*. London: Chatto & Windus, 1995. Published as *Burning Your Boats: The Collected Short Stories*. New York: H. Holt, 1996.

————. *Fireworks: Nine Profane Pieces*. London: Quartet, 1974; New York: Penguin, 1987. Published as *Fireworks: Nine Stories in Various Disguises*. New York: Harper & Row, 1981. Published as *Fireworks*. London: Chatto & Windus, 1987; London: Virago, 1987.

Novels

Carter, Angela. *Heroes and Villains*. London: Heinemann, 1969; New York: Simon & Schuster, 1969; New York: Pocket Books, 1972; London: Penguin, 1981.

————. *The Infernal Desire Machines of Doctor Hoffman*. London; Rupert Hart-Davis, 1972; New York: Penguin, 1994. Published as *The War of Dreams*. New York: Harcourt Brace Jovanovich, 1974; New York: Avon Books, 1977.

————. *Love: A Novel*. London: Rupert Hart-Davis, 1971. Rev. ed. London: Chatto & Windus, 1987; New York: Penguin, 1988. Published as *Love*. London: Picador, 1988.

————. *The Magic Toyshop*. London: Heinemann, 1967; New York: Simon & Schuster, 1968; London: Virago, 1981, 1992; New York: Penguin, 1996.

————. *Nights at the Circus*. London: Chatto & Windus, 1984; New York: Viking, 1985; New York: Penguin, 1986.

————. *The Passion of New Eve*. London: Victor Gollancz, 1977; New York: Harcourt Brace Jovanovich, 1977; London: Virago, 1982; London: Bloomsbury, 1993.

————. *Several Perceptions*. London: Heinemann, 1968; New York: Simon & Schuster, 1968; London: Virago, 1995.

————. *Shadow Dance*. London: Heinemann, 1966, 1968; London: Virago, 1994; New York: Penguin Books, 1996. Published in the United States as *Honeybuzzard*. New York: Simon & Schuster, 1967.

————. *Wise Children*. London: Chatto & Windus, 1991; New York: Farrar Straus & Giroux, 1992; New York: Penguin, 1993.

Secondary

"Angela Carter." No author. Segal, David, ed. *Short Story Criticism* 13. Detroit: Gale Research, 1993. 1–37.

Bristow, Joseph, and Trev Lynn Broughton, eds. *The Infernal Desires of Angela Carter: Fiction, Femininity, Feminism*. New York: Longman, 1997.

Contemporary Literary Criticism, Vols. 5, 41, 76. Detroit: Gale Research, 1976, 1987, 1993.

"Carter, Angela," no author. Vol. 5. 101–3.

"Angela (Olive) Carter," no author. Vol. 41. 109–22.

"Angela Carter," no author. Vol. 76. 322–31.

Day, Aidan. *Angela Carter: The Rational Glass*. Manchester, UK: Manchester University Press, 1998.

Faulkner, Peter. "Carter, Angela." *Reference Guide to Short Fiction*. Ed. Noelle Watson. Detroit: St. James Press, 1994. 111–13.

Gamble, Sarah. *Angela Carter: Writing from the Front Line*. Edinburgh: Edinburgh University Press, 1997.

Kaiser, Mary. "Fairy Tale as Sexual Allegory: Intertextuality in Angela Carter's *The Bloody Chamber.*" *Review of Contemporary Fiction* 14.3 (1994): 30–36.

Katsavos, Anna. "An Interview with Angela Carter." *Review of Contemporary Fiction* 14.3 (1994): 11–17.

Lee, Alison. *Angela Carter*. London: Prentice Hall International, 1997.

Müller, Anja. *Angela Carter: Identity Constructed/Deconstructed*. Heidelberg: Universitätsverlag Carl Winter, 1997.

Orodenker, Richard. "Nine Story Tellers." *North American Review* 268 (1983): 68–72.

Peach, Linden. *Angela Carter*. New York: St. Martin's Press, 1998.

Sage, Lorna. *Angela Carter*. Writers and Their Work Series. Plymouth, UK: Northcote House with the British Council, 1994.

———, ed. *Flesh and the Mirror: Essays on the Art of Angela Carter*. London: Virago, 1994.

Tucker, Lindsey, ed. *Critical Essays on Angela Carter*. London: Prentice Hall International, 1998.

RAYMOND CARVER
(May 25, 1938–August 2, 1988)

Hilary Siebert

BIOGRAPHY

By the time of his death at age fifty in 1988, Raymond Carver had established a prominent position as a distinctive writer of short stories known for their restrained prose and their focus on the lives of ordinary blue-collar Americans. Born Raymond Clevie Carver, Jr., in Clatskanie, Oregon, he was the first of two sons. His parents, Ella Beatrice Casey and Clevie Raymond Carver, lived a difficult life marked by poverty, alcoholism, and the struggles of working-class survival. In his four autobiographical essays opening the collection *Fires*, Carver makes it clear that in his adulthood, he fell victim to many of the same pressures his parents—and his father in particular—had faced.

Four years before Carver's birth, his father, a "farmhand-turned–construction worker," rode freight trains from Arkansas to Washington State in search not of dreams but of steady work, eventually finding employment in the sawmills of Oregon and Washington. After years of struggle, amid the pressures of work and family, alcohol came to dominate his life ("My Father's Life," in *Fires* 13–14).

Yet it was not Carver's childhood that affected him so much as his adulthood that followed his father's patterns: transience, low-paying jobs, bill collectors, and, finally, alcoholism. As Carver explains it, the biggest influences on his writing took place after he was twenty ("Fires," in *Fires* 32). At nineteen he had married the sixteen-year-old Maryann Burk, and by October of his twentieth year they had two children. After working with his father in a sawmill and then on his own as a deliveryman, Carver borrowed money to move his family and in-laws to Paradise, California, where he began part-time study at Chico State College. It was his good fortune to enroll in Creative Writing 101 with John Gardner, an unpublished writer at the time, who cultivated Carver's enthusiasm for writing short fiction. Carver's first published story, "The Furious Seasons," appeared in the college's literary magazine. At this time, Carver was writing stories, poems, and plays, as he did at various times throughout his career. He transferred to Humboldt State College and received an A.B. degree in 1963.

After a year's study in the Writers' Workshop at the University of Iowa, Carver returned to California. In 1967, he and his wife filed for bankruptcy, and later that year his father died. Also that year, Carver met Gordon Lish, who at the time was fiction editor for *Esquire*. Lish later accepted several of Carver's stories and exerted his influence over many years on the "lean" style of Carver's prose. By the early 1970s, Carver was beginning to achieve recognition for his stories and poetry, while at the same time his personal life was disintegrating. Alcoholism took its toll on his marriage to Maryann, and in 1976 they separated. In that same year, *Will You Please Be Quiet, Please?* appeared, his first major collection of short stories.

The year 1977 marked a turning point in Carver's life and, gradually, in his art. Carver gave up drinking after being hospitalized several times, and he met the poet Tess Gallagher, whom he later married. In 1979, Carver and Gallagher began living and writing together, as they did until Carver's untimely death of lung cancer nine years later. *What We Talk About When We Talk about Love*, edited by Lish, appeared in 1981.

Carver's next collection, *Cathedral* (1983), demonstrated a change in his writing style, one he and critics came to label as "more generous" both in the amount of dialogue between characters and the narrative stance toward them. An avid reviser, he began reshaping earlier stories, many of which appeared in *Where I'm Calling From: New and Selected Stories* (1988), the final collection published before his death later that year.

During his lifetime, Carver published several volumes of poetry as well as the story volumes and received many distinguished awards. These include a Guggenheim Fellowship, a National Endowment for the Arts Discovery Award for Poetry, a National Endowment for the Arts Fellowship for Fiction, and the Mildred and Harold Strauss Living Award. The O. Henry Award and the Pushcart Prize were awarded to several of his stories.

CRITICISM

Throughout the 1980s, Carver's prose style provoked heated critical debate. Terse in expression, with a focus on the lost lives of ordinary Americans, his stories prompted some readers to be captivated with the silence around his characters, while others blamed him for creating a world of helpless victims, living, at best, for moments of revelation that they themselves often could not perceive. Reviewers such as James Atlas and Madison Bell attacked Carver for leading a supposed "movement" in what was termed "minimalist fiction," while Carver himself resisted the label and the assumptions behind it. The claim was that Carver bore a responsibility for the fate of the characters he described, leaving them helpless, the inarticulate, confused victims of poverty, alcoholism, and the incoherence of contemporary American life. It was asserted that Carver's tone toward these characters was one of superiority.

Despite these claims, Carver's style has been widely studied, imitated, and praised. Among the many creative writers who have expressed appreciation for Carver's work, Tobias Wolff describes his stories as giving "a new picture of America, in a voice never heard before" ("Appetite," in Stull and Carroll 241); he describes a "spiritual restlessness" behind Carver's characters (Halpert 3) and says that Carver "has penetrated a secret about us and brought it to the light" (Halpert 11).

Literary critics have expressed a variety of reasons for finding meaning and value in Carver's style. Champions of the postmodern (e.g., Chénetier, Herzinger, Saltzman) have seen in the "flatness" of Carver's prose an example of how language is always inadequate to coherently "represent" the reality to which it refers, and how critics' search for determinate "meaning" in Carver's stories participates in the totalizing myths of humanistic readers and writers.

At the same time, other critics have offered aesthetic justification for Carver's style. Susan Lohafer and Randolph Paul Runyon are among those who have found in the careful restraint of Carver's prose an invitation for readers to enter into spaces within the sentences, between the sentences, and between the stories (Runyon 1). For such readers, what Carver omits serves the aims of a lyrical style, akin to Hemingway's, in which readers fill in the emotions and understandings left patterned but unstated by the writer. Daniel W. Lehman and Ewing Campbell have each demonstrated that Carver's stories are tightly, though subtly, crafted.

One central point of controversy that has yet to be resolved concerns the assessment of Carver's earlier and later styles. Carver himself described a "fuller, more generous" prose style beginning with the *Cathedral* collection (Kasia Boddy interview in Gentry and Stull 199), a change that has been variously attributed to his recovery from alcoholism, his companionship with Tess Gallagher, his concern over the "minimalist" label, and a change in American social attitudes. As Adam Meyer describes his style, there are actually three "phases": an early stage of relative expansiveness, an "arch-minimalist" period of intense reduction, and a final period of widening.

The later phase was marked not only by new stories but by significant revision of notable earlier stories. In these revisions, Carver made characters more articulate than they had been and gave them new opportunities for insight or healing. Such alterations seem heavy-handed to some readers, while others admire their warmth. Typical of these changes is the revision of a traumatic, existential helplessness in "The Bath" into a kinder, gentler world of sacraments and forgiveness in "A Small, Good Thing." Critical debate has not been as strong over the new stories themselves. Among them, "Cathedral," "Fever," and "Blackbird Pie" create a potential for characters' insight and recovery that is rare not only in Carver's previous work but in the history of the short story in general.

Assessment of the phases in absolute terms seems impossible, since reaction to them depends both on the reader's social values and aesthetic tastes. For one thing, readers who valued a "postmodern" discontinuity in the earlier stories have criticized what they see as a sentimental "humanism" in the later work. For another, critics such as Lehman point out that any "postmodern" discontinuity in characters' lives should not be confused with Carver's rhetorical control of meaning, which is in fact tightly maintained through symbolic images in the early stories as well as the late ones. Campbell suggests that readers who prefer "A Small, Good Thing" may not only prefer the redemptive outcome but may prefer a style that is more easily accessible, since Carver's more minimal style demands careful attention to patternings of repetition, parallelism, and opposition (*Raymond Carver* 52).

Beyond the arguments of critics, another assessment of Carver's work comes in the form of very personal tributes written about him by friends and by readers unknown to him. *Remembering Ray*, edited by William L. Stull and Maureen P. Carroll, illustrates the very human connection readers of all kinds have felt for Carver's characters and the situations he portrayed. Quoting the narrator in a story by Isaac Babel, Carver once observed, "No iron can pierce the heart with such force as a period put just in the right place" ("On Writing," in *Fires* 24).

ANALYSIS

Because the entire range of Carver's work is important to a study of his short stories, no one story collection can be considered representative. In addition, readers of the fiction may wish to consult his volumes of poems, since several stories and poems derive from the same incident (see Stull interview in Gentry and Stull 179). The focus here will be devoted to individual stories selected for their importance to critical debate and Carver's narrative style.

In responding to much of Carver's work, critics have sought biographical connections between the struggles of his characters and specific struggles Carver faced in his personal life. While such connections may be of general value in cultural analysis of the texts, they tend to distract readers from the reality of the stories themselves. As one example in the first major-press collection, *Will You Please Be Quiet, Please?*, "Nobody Said Anything" may at first appear to be an autobiographical portrait of Carver's childhood. The story portrays the fractured life of a dreamy adolescent boy, captured in images of sexual fantasy, family squabbles, and, at closure, the glowing, silvery image of a grotesquely green fish, itself cut in half and brought home as a trophy to a raging father who yells, "throw it in the goddamn garbage!" (*Please* 59).

What Carver suggests about this story is that it is true to a feeling about his childhood that he had "tapped into," rather than being true to the actual events (Kay Bonetti interview in Gentry and Stull 60–61). The final image of half a fish, simultaneously beautiful and grotesque, seems to capture the moment of adolescence in the boy. He is himself divided between the pleasures of his trophy and his fantasies, on the one hand, and the frustrations of a dissolving home life and an unloving world, on the other.

The issue of "silence" in the world of Carver's characters has also been prominent in the criticism. "Nobody Said Anything" is a title that reflects the symptomatic inability of characters to communicate. The boy's feelings receive no response throughout the story, and both he and the reader are left to dwell silently on the closing image of the fish (Meyer 44–45). Graham Clarke makes the important point that such a "syntax of silence," rather than muting the characters, allows readers to momentarily "glimpse" and feel the implications of these silences for the characters affected (100). "Fat," the first story in Carver's first collection, shows another such "glimpse." The "fat" man in this story becomes, in his fatness, an image of "otherness" to the narrating waitress who serves him. As Campbell argues, the story then creates openings in which the narrator glimpses moments of this otherness in herself. Through such moments of recognition, the story opens the possibility for the transformation of her own life through her connection to someone else (*Raymond Carver* 13).

By means of Carver's restrained style, then, readers are able to feel the absences faced by his characters, rather than just reading about them. When Carver's characters then see themselves in another person, as in "Fat," we witness a means by which they move beyond the immediate confines of their lives. "Neighbors," another story in the first collection, explores an overt voyeurism in which Bill and Arlene Miller pretend to each other that they are taking turns feeding the neighbors' cat and watering their plants when actually they are secretly rummaging through the personal belongings of their vacationing neighbors. By the end, they seem to have renewed their married lives by trying on their neighbors' clothes, masturbating in their bed, and vicariously living their lives. Just at this point, they are locked out of the neighbors' house and must face life on their own. Carver portrays this moment of final isolation to emphasize the Millers' desire for the vitality of their neighbors' lives. The image of their embrace outside the locked door suggests an Edenic banishment, in which they have "braced themselves," "as if against a wind" (*Please* 16; Meyer 38–39).

The question of an absent connection and a connection to others appears in modified terms in the story "So Much Water So Close to Home" in *Furious Seasons*, Carver's second collection. In this story of a married couple, Stuart and Claire Kane, Stuart has returned home from a four-day fishing trip. Only grudgingly, he explains to his wife that on the first night he and his buddies found the body of a drowned young woman and left it there until they returned to town at the end of their trip to notify the sheriff. For Claire, her husband's inability to feel anything for the "girl" highlights her own inability to feel any connection to him; he feels only annoyance at his public predicament. On the other hand, she feels explicit empathy with this girl who has been raped and murdered and lies "floating face down, eyes open" (Campbell, *Raymond Carver* 38).

This story also exemplifies Meyer's notion of an "hourglass" pattern to Carver's work, since this story reappears much condensed in *What We Talk About When We Talk about Love* and again, in an expanded version close to the original, in *Fires*. It is Meyer's judgment that in the shortened version, "Carver has gone a bit too far in his reductions" (104), and, based on his final version, Carver seems to have agreed. However, evaluation of this story's merit in its differing versions raises an important question about reader taste in reference to the determinacy of meaning.

As with "The Bath" and "A Small, Good Thing," readers who expect or need a writerly path toward meaning may struggle with the shorter version of "So Much Water"; interpretation depends highly on reader inference and is therefore less highly determined. Furthermore, the fact of indeterminacy leaves Carver's characters less connected to social structures that explain or relieve their suffering. In "So Much Water," the shortened version requires readers to infer meaning where the author has not stated it explicitly: exposition of background has been cut, as has any explanation as to why and on what terms Claire finally accepts her husband's sexual advances. Since nothing has changed between them and she is still grieving for the girl, the shorter version suggests a desperate acceptance of her own rape at his hands. In the final version, however, both husband and wife overtly mimic conventional behaviors and attitudes toward gender. The wife recalls an earlier threat of "violence" from her husband and recoils from it; the husband's physical behavior toward his wife demonstrates his violence; and the wife, assuming an empowered role, not only expresses extended empathy with the raped and murdered girl, but separates herself from her husband's callousness both verbally and physically. This version ends not with his sexual advances but with her statement, "For God's sake, Stuart, she was only a child" (Campbell, *Raymond Carver* 40–41).

"The Bath," one of Carver's most famous "minimalist" stories, also appeared in *What We Talk About*. This story exemplifies what Carver once described as a "sense of menace" in his work ("On Writing," in *Fires* 26). Menace is the force that seems to surround the world of the Weisses in this story. As their boy, Scotty, walks off to school on his birthday with a friend, he is knocked to the ground by a passing car. He manages to come home alone, shaken, to a mother who tries to comfort him but seems to sense impending trouble. After the boy falls into a coma and is hospitalized, the husband and wife find themselves helpless to comfort each other or receive comfort from the doctor. Husband and wife take turns going home for the physical and spiritual cleansing of a bath, but as each tries to unwind, each is disturbed by harassing phone calls. Calls to the husband come from the baker, who is stuck with the birthday cake Scotty's mother had ordered. The story ends with a menacing call to the anxious mother from someone—probably the baker—who says, "It has to do with Scotty, yes" (*Talk* 56). Nothing in this story relieves the private nature of the pain felt by the husband, the wife, and even the baker.

In revising "The Bath" as "A Small, Good Thing" for the later collection

Cathedral, Carver took perhaps his starkest portrait of human suffering and clothed it in redemptive imagery. Using what Campbell terms "Raymond Carver's Therapeutics of Passion," the new story now portrays the husband and wife supporting each other: they discuss having prayed for Scotty, and the wife realizes that she "felt glad to be his wife" (68). In the remaining events, the boy clearly dies in this version, but his parents find relief by confronting the baker about his phone calls. After expressing their anger, the Weisses are invited into the bakery, and the baker sits them down for warm rolls and coffee. The story ends on a moment of communion and sacrament, in which the characters break bread together and find refuge in a shared sense of grief.

Among other noteworthy stories in *What We Talk About*, "Gazebo" merits discussion because it exemplifies a first-person narration in the present tense that is distinctive for its colloquial voice. The story opens:

That morning she pours Teacher's over my belly and licks it off. That afternoon she tries to jump out the window.

I go, "Holly, this can't continue. This has got to stop." [. . .] She goes, "Duane, this is killing me." (*Talk* 21).

While such readers as William Gass have ridiculed this present-tense style for its quirky, mannered tone, it captures well the idiom of these characters' speech and the chaotic immediacy of their lives. Holly and Duane are supposed to be managing a motel, but their marriage has reached a point where they can barely go on. Duane has been sleeping with one of the maids in the rooms, and Holly cannot get over it. Both turn to alcohol regularly. In the present moment of the story, both characters are despairing: Holly wants out, and Duane would like her to give him another chance. Something has to change; Carver uses the present tense as well as the brevity of the story form to highlight the pathos, the trauma, and also the absurdity of the situation.

As Meyer suggests, the use of the present tense contributes to the ambiguity of the moment: we do not know whether this is the end of the relationship or the end of a horrible tension within it (94–95). Yet we do see how terrible and how crazy this moment is. Carver accomplishes this effect in several ways. First, he contrasts images of their present desire to escape with an idyllic scene of a country home where guests are welcome. While Holly and Duane neglect the guests knocking at the door of the motel office downstairs, Holly recalls the image of a "[d]ignified" house with a gazebo they used to visit; and she explains how she used to feel that when they were older, they too would live "in a place. And people would come to our door" (*Talk* 28).

To make this contrast clear, Carver reveals such decay in the present scene that the effect is one of a "dark humor" that Carver described in some of his work, when the situation leaves laughter as the only alternative to tears (Sexton in Gentry and Stull 131). Duane "stopped cleaning the pool," and it "filled up with green gick so the guests wouldn't use it anymore" (*Talk* 26). While the phone rings away downstairs, Duane and Holly have gotten out the scotch and snack on "cheese crisps from the machine" (*Talk* 27).

The title story of the next collection, *Cathedral*, represents what many critics view as Carver at his best. While the narrator-husband exhibits personality traits such as a sense of inferiority that typify Carver's struggling characters, the story portrays an event through which the narrator learns to see beyond his fears. At first he appears small-minded, jealous of his wife's life that does not include him. He acts hostilely toward the planned visit of his wife's blind friend, Robert, and feels intruded upon: "A blind man in my house was not something I looked forward to" (209).

After the three spend an awkward evening together, the wife falls asleep, leaving Robert and the husband to talk. Robert, whose wife has just died, is so accepting of the husband's quirks of behavior that the two manage to get along. The husband finds himself glad to have company as he watches television and smokes pot late into the night, his usual activities. As the television plays a documentary on the history of cathedrals, the narrator relaxes with Robert to the point that he tries to help Robert understand what a cathedral looks like. By the end of the story, the narrator is avidly drawing for Robert the features of a cathedral, with Robert's hand on top of his own and, eventually, with his own eyes closed. The earlier feeling of intrusion is replaced with a feeling of transcendence: "I was in my house. I knew that. But I didn't feel like I was inside anything" (228).

Carver's use of the short-story form is at once traditional and innovative. Working within the Joycean tradition of epiphany (Campbell, *Raymond Carver* 7–8), Carver's stories before *Cathedral* typically bring his characters to a point where they should gain insight into their lives, but the stories end before the reader can see how much insight has been gained or what will come as a result of it. Insight is left suspended, pending reader or character ability to perceive the lyrical effects of images that have been subtly patterned to show, rather than assert, the truth of a character's life. Even if such awareness is achieved, in the world of Carver's characters before *Cathedral*, insight does not clearly pave the way to a future; it is often limited to the stark fact that, as in "Gazebo," life has not turned out right, it has bottomed out, and something must change—though the means of change is not at hand.

With such stories as the title story and "Fever" in *Cathedral*, Carver makes the stark truth a background, taking his characters by the hand, if necessary, and providing transformative experiences. Epiphany, once it is realized, provides moments not only of insight but of cathartic experience for character and reader. The "lonely voices" and "submerged population groups" Frank O'Connor (*Lonely Voice* 18) once described as common to the short story appear in Carver's early stories with the shortest of horizons; in the later stories, characters' horizons are surprisingly large, given their plights.

After *Cathedral*, Carver's final stories in *Where I'm Calling From* show both earlier patterns and new directions. "Boxes," "Intimacy," and "Menudo" portray characters whose lives need change in situations where the possibilities for change seem limited. "Whoever Was Using This Bed" recalls the "menacing" phone calls in "The Bath," but this time the caller's plight is potentially a source for empathy, as the narrator's desire to unplug the phone is juxtaposed with the discussion between him and his wife as to whether either of them should be "unplugged" if they become terminally ill. In "Blackbird Pie," the narrator recounts accusations made by his wife in a letter when she left him; while he seems to be strangely denying the truth of the letter's authorship, he is at the same time acknowledging the emotional truth of her departure, and, as Meyer puts it, "[h]e realizes what is in store for him for the rest of his life" (159).

"Errand," Carver's last published story, pays tribute to the aesthetic concerns of Anton Chekhov, a writer he greatly admired. Entering the biographical situation of Chekhov's death—an entirely new type of setting for a Carver story— he focuses attention not on the author but on an overwhelmed delivery boy who strives to pick up a champagne cork that has been dropped while Chekhov's wife gives detailed instructions he does not understand. Again, in classic short-story form, Carver shows us how to see oblique meanings in life. Quoting V. S. Pritchett's definition, Carver observed, "A short story 'is something glimpsed from the corner of the eye, in passing.' . . . First the glimpse. Then the glimpse given life" ("On Writing," in *Fires* 26).

WORKS CITED AND CONSULTED

Primary

Raymond Carver. *Cathedral*. 1983. New York: Vintage, 1984.
———. *Fires. Essays, Poems, Stories*. 1983. New York: Vintage, 1989.
———. *Furious Seasons and Other Stories*. Santa Barbara, CA: Capra, 1977.
———. *No Heroics, Please: Uncollected Writings*. Ed. William L. Stull. New York: Vintage, 1992.
———. *Short Cuts: Selected Stories*. New York: Vintage, 1993.
———. *What We Talk About When We Talk about Love*. 1981. New York: Vintage, 1982.
———. *Where I'm Calling From : New and Selected Stories*. 1988. New York: Vintage, 1989.
———. *Will You Please Be Quiet, Please? The Stories of Raymond Carver*. 1976. New York: Vintage, 1992.

Secondary

Atlas, James. "Less Is Less." *Atlantic Monthly* June 1981: 96–98.
Bell, Madison. "Less Is Less." *Harper's* April 1986: 64–69.
Campbell, Ewing. *Raymond Carver: A Study of the Short Fiction*. New York: Twayne, 1992.

————. "Raymond Carver's Therapeutics of Passion." *Journal of the Short Story in English* 16 (Spring 1991): 9–18.

Chénetier, Marc. "Living on/off the 'Reserve': Performance, Interrogation, and Negativity in the Works of Raymond Carver." *Critical Angles: European Views of Contemporary American Literature*. Ed. Marc Chénetier. Carbondale: Southern Illinois University Press, 1986. 164–90.

Clarke, Graham. "Investing the Glimpse: Raymond Carver and the Syntax of Silence." *The New American Writing: Essays on American Literature since 1970*. Ed. Graham Clarke. New York: St. Martin's, 1990. 99–122.

Gass, William H. "The Unspeakable State of Soliloquy." *Harper's* May 1984: 71–74.

Gentry, Marshal Bruce, and William L. Stull, eds. *Conversations with Raymond Carver*. Jackson: University Press of Mississippi, 1990.

Halpert, Sam, ed. *When We Talk about Raymond Carver*. Layton, UT: Gibbs Smith, 1991.

Herzinger, Kim A. "Minimalism as a Postmodernism: Some Introductory Notes." *New Orleans Review* 16.3: 73–81.

Lehman, Daniel W. "Raymond Carver's Management of Symbol." *Journal of the Short Story in English* 17 (Spring 1991): 43–58.

Lohafer, Susan. *Coming to Terms with the Short Story*. Baton Rouge: Louisiana State University Press, 1983.

Meyer, Adam. *Raymond Carver*. New York: Twayne, 1995.

O'Connor, Frank. *The Lonley Voice: A Study of the Short Story*. New York: Meridian, 1965.

Runyon, Randolph Paul. *Reading Raymond Carver*. Syracuse: Syracuse University Press, 1992.

Saltzman, Arthur M. *Understanding Raymond Carver*. Columbia: University of South Carolina Press, 1988.

Stull, William L. "Beyond Hopelessville: Another Side of Raymond Carver." *Philological Quarterly* 64 (1985): 1–15.

Stull, William L., and Maureen P. Carroll, eds. *Remembering Ray: A Composite Biography of Raymond Carver*. Santa Barbara, CA: Capra, 1993.

SANDRA CISNEROS
(December 20, 1954–   )

L. M. *Lewis*

BIOGRAPHY

Sandra Cisneros was born in Chicago, the only girl in a family with six boys. Her father, from a Mexican family with some status but little wealth, was college educated but worked as an upholsterer. Her mother was a first-generation Mexican American with Amerindian lineage. The family often moved from Chicago to Mexico City and then back, as Cisneros says, on an almost predictable schedule. Until the family bought its first house when Cisneros was eleven, each return to Chicago meant a new apartment in a new neighborhood with new friends. This alternating sense of transience and stability provided the material for her first stories.

The University of Iowa Writers' Workshop, which Cisneros attended after her graduation from Loyola University, has become a standard topic for interviews. She worked there with a number of modern poets, including Donald Justice and Louise Gluck. However, she characterized some of the faculty as aloof, even unkind, and considered the program itself elitist. The writing community, she said, did not seem "supportive," and her classmates often adopted voices that were "distilled" and "esoteric" and, thus, alien to her (Satz 170). Cisneros still speaks of her resentment, but credits the workshop with allowing her to uncover a "truly distinct" voice after earlier years during which she "floundered from one imitation to the next" (Binder 61–63). In particular, seminar discussions of Gaston Bachelard's *The Poetics of Space* made her realize that her "communal knowledge" and "archetypes" were not those of her peers or teachers. With that epiphany, she turned from Walt Whitman to Aztec poetry, Latin American magic realism, and the Boom writers. During the last year of the workshop, she began the autobiographical sketches that would become *The House on Mango Street*, originally published in 1984 by Arte Publico and subsequently reissued by Vintage Books of Random House (1991). Her acceptance by a major New York publishing house was important to Cisneros, and she often notes it in interviews.

After her study in Iowa, Cisneros returned to Chicago to work in an alternative high school in a Mexican-American barrio. As she gained political experience and professional reputation, she found herself teaching more than she wrote, but she did publish her first book of poetry, *Bad Boys*, in 1980. With money from a National Endowment for the Arts grant, she was able to travel to Europe and completed *The House on Mango Street* in 1983.

In 1985, Cisneros moved to San Antonio to work with a Hispanic arts center and teach creative writing in local elementary schools. A second volume of poetry, *My Wicked, Wicked Ways*, was published in 1987. Cisneros claims that it is "chronological," tracking her uncertain years from twenty-one to thirty, and that the "wickedness" was "a woman appropriating her own sexuality," thus challenging patriarchal limits (Rodriguez Aranda 68, 74). *Loose Woman* (1994), her latest volume of poetry, is her expression of strength, power, and peace, with even more enthusiastic sexual themes (Rodriguez Aranda 74).

Cisneros's 1991 volume of short stories, *Woman Hollering Creek*, experiments with voices "as divergent and dissimilar as possible from her own" (Ganz 25). She has adapted two of the stories for the stage, directing and performing as well. In her continuing efforts to develop new forms and voices, she published a children's book, *Hairs/Pelitos* (1994), which was adapted from *The House on Mango Street*. Because of the distractions of her public life, Cisneros struggled to complete her forthcoming novel, *Caramelo*, for several years. More recently, the terminal illness of her father has further postponed publication.

Quite conscious of her identity as "the first Chicana to enter the mainstream of literary culture" (Ganz 27), Cisneros feels an obligation to the Chicana community; she is determined that her success should lead to theirs. As the character Esperanza says in the last line of *The House on Mango Street*, "I have gone away to come back. For the ones I left behind" (110). Cisneros affirms a particular loyalty to the community of Chicana writers and will not be satisfied, she says, as "the only one that's getting published by Random House" (qtd. in Ganz 27).

CRITICISM

The bulk of the criticism treats Cisneros almost exclusively as an ethnic writer—Chicana or Chicana feminist. In the short stories, women and girls appear marginalized because of gender, class, race, and ethnicity. As Mexicans, they are mestizo—a mix of Spanish and native Indian that recalls Cortez's shameful conquest of the Aztecs. As Mexican Americans, they are considered subordinate to white American society, and if they attempt to elevate themselves, they are considered traitors—as *pochas* (mixed and thus not authentic) or *agringadas* (Hispanic, copying Anglo ways). As women, they are subordinate again, suffering from the "universal oppression that comes from being female" and, more particularly, from the Mexican-American "male-dominated cultural heritage" (Rocard 130). That is why, Cisneros often says, so many of her stories feature women who are in pain and angry. Cisneros's contribution to the genre of Chicana feminism is her portrayal of women who not only establish identities for themselves, but also develop an independent, confident, even exultant sexuality. After periods of painful growth, they are finally able to love men as they wish and to establish "sisterhoods," mutually supportive relationships with other women.

Few critics have attended to Cisneros's style, except to note in general that it is rich or intense. There are occasional asides about her excesses and comments that her voice may be more cute or precious than penetrating. She is certainly expansive in her use of metaphor, which may support the themes or play independently of them. Almost every review article about her books features a selection of her striking language. Ilan Stavans is disturbed by what he considers the "uncritical deification" of Cisneros's work (32), characterizing her themes as oversimplified, her voice as "condescending," and her style as "sleek and sentimental, sterile and undemanding" (31). His quarrel is less with the author than with the indiscriminate "national obsession" with diversity, multiculturalism, and "the politics of inclusion" (30).

There is one sharp exchange about Cisneros's use of cultural material. In an article that is not widely accessible, Juanita Luna-Lawhn claims that Cisneros incorporates unflattering stereotypes that Chicanos have worked hard to dismantle (3). Cisneros seems to be aware of her vulnerability to such criticism, but declines to engage in the argument, claiming that her characters are realistic (Milligan 15). Joan Carabin responds directly to the accusation, charging that Luna-Lawhn has not looked carefully at the ways Cisneros uses memory.

There is little treatment of Cisneros's themes beyond the dominant ones of Chicana feminism. However, metaphors of space—particularly of house and neighborhood—have garnered attention in several articles, including Julian Olivares's "Sandra Cisneros' *The House on Mango Street* and the Poetics of Space." In addition, the code switching in *Woman Hollering Creek* is sometimes cited as validating the Chicana experience. The function of Cisneros's discoursive strategy, however, merits a great deal more attention than it has generated so far. Narrative voices, speech patterns of characters, the ways speakers acquire and value dialects, and Cisneros's own language in dedication and acknowledgment pieces all exhibit sly and purposeful play.

In recent years, a number of important articles have considered Cisneros's use of mythic and folkloric characters in *Woman Hollering Creek*. These articles have focused largely on the story "Never Marry a Mexican," which evokes the figure of La Malinche, Cortez's native mistress. Villainized for her role in the conquest, this figure came to represent the treachery and inconstancy of women. Yet, as Mary Louise Pratt has noted, by the 1970s, Mexican-American women began to "redefine or resymbolize La Malinche as part of a process of formulating Chicana identities and cultural politics" (860).

Many critics address the issue of form in *The House on Mango Street* and *Woman Hollering Creek*, variously considering the works as novels, short stories, prose poems, or vignettes. Cisneros herself has called the pieces "lazy poems," stories "hovering in that grey area between two genres" ("Do You Know Me?" 79). Some works in *Woman Hollering Creek*, she admits, were intended as "performance pieces" and do not "work well on the page" (Lecture). Most consistently, however, critics classify the two collections as bildungsromans, stories that characterize an adolescent hero's coming of age. Armed with artistic visions, Cisneros's heroines (appearing with different names in different stories) struggle against a number of obstacles to arrive at a sexual and emotional maturity.

ANALYSIS

The House on Mango Street is a collection of forty-four stories told in the voice of a young girl, Esperanza. The contexts suggest that she is about fourteen years old, seemingly no older in the last stories than she is in the first. Many stories recount her sexual awakening, and in one story she is raped. However, there is no real sense of sexual growth or maturity beyond a cynical view of men, already well established in early stories.

Esperanza exhibits greater maturity in her realization that women are limited to roles determined by men and in her desire for her own identity. Evoking the collection's dominant metaphor, she "had to have a house. A real house" (5), a "home in the heart" (64), not the "sad red house" on Mango Street where she lives but chooses not to belong (109–10). She sees that within all the buildings she knows, the neighborhood women are restricted to dreaming of what had been possible before their marriages. Ruthie, for example, could have done many things and "had lots of job offers" but "got married instead" (68–69). Esperanza's mother can sing opera and recalls the days when she was a "smart cookie," but today she only sings along with records while she stirs the morning oatmeal. Her great-grandmother, from whom Esperanza inherits her name, had been "a wild horse of a woman, so wild she wouldn't marry." She was stolen, was forced to become a wife, and after that, "sorry she couldn't be all the things she wanted to be," she sat in her house and "looked out the window her whole life" (11).

Married women are often virtual prisoners, like Rafaela, who "gets locked indoors" when her husband is away because he thinks that "she is too beautiful to look at" and might run away (78). Sally got married young and is happy in a way, with a house, a husband, and money to buy pillowcases and plates— when her husband will give her money. But he will not let her talk on the telephone, and "she is afraid to go outside without his permission," which is not likely because he does not even "let her look out the window" (101–2). Daughters are also expected to take "a woman's place": Alicia is attending college in order to escape a "life in a factory or behind a rolling pin," but according to her father, she must rise with the "tortilla star" so that she can cook for the family before she leaves for her classes. It is inappropriate, her father thinks, for her to study all night, or even to be afraid of mice (31–32).

Men in *The House on Mango Street* are generally portrayed as leaving home or coming back to it only in order to eat, sleep, and make decisions for their wives and daughters. Sometimes they never return or they die, leaving women and children without support and without experience at being independent. Some Mango Street men are abusive. They beat their wives and daughters, kick in doors when they are angry, and throw rocks through windows when their wives lock them out. The story "No Speak English" demonstrates the entitlement one man feels and the assumption he makes to justify his authority in the home. He moves his wife and child to Mango Street from Mexico after he had labored alone at two jobs to prepare a home for them. However, his wife never feels as if she "belongs" because Mango Street is not home for her. His reaction is one of disgust and anger because she is ungrateful and cannot understand that he defines home as the place where he is (78).

Outside the home, beyond their fathers' observation, the adolescent girls discover gender and sexual identities. Esperanza seems to be both a girl and a young woman at once. She is certainly more knowledgeable than her younger sister, Nenny, who lives in a world Esperanza and her friends "don't belong to any more" (52), but Esperanza does not yet understand the kissing games that the older girl, Sally, initiates (96–97). The girls discover that they actually have legs of their own, "good to look at and long" even if they are still skinny and still scabbed from childhood accidents (40). They wake up one day with hips (49). All the sexual information comes from older girls: Alicia tells them that hips "let you know which skeleton was a man's . . . and which a woman's" (50); Rachel teaches them how to walk in high heels so that men will not look away. (40); Marin knows how women get pregnant and how to tell when boys are thinking about them (26–27); Sally teaches them how to paint their eyes "like Cleopatra" (81). Of course, fathers regard sexual curiosity as dangerous and wish to limit what the girls can discover, fearing that when they become beautiful, they will not resist boys who pursue them (93).

Esperanza's sexual activity is largely limited to an intense, but unnamed tension. After she sees Lois and her boyfriend disappear into an alley, she watches with anxious curiosity: "Where does he take her?" She describes her feelings as everything "holding its breath inside" and "waiting to explode" while she imagines what she cannot see (73). When there is actual sexual contact, Esperanza does not choose the conditions. An old man at her first job asks for a birthday kiss, then grabs her face and kisses her "hard on the mouth and doesn't let go" (55). She uses the same language to describe her rape: she did not want to be touched, but the boy with the sour breath and dirty fingernails "wouldn't let her go" (99–100).

There is a sense in *The House on Mango Street* that women eventually form supportive relationships and even communities with each other. In the early stories, Esperanza indicates her need for a "best friend," someone to listen to her secrets and understand her jokes (9). Importantly, women often support one another by sharing the poetry they write. In one of the last stories, a group of three women who call themselves *Las comadres* remind Esperanza of her responsibility, though she does not fully understand at the time. She must remember to come back to Mango Street, they say, for "the others," those "who cannot leave as easily" as she can (105). That will be her contribution to what they call the "circle" (105).

A final thread, one that appears in *Woman Hollering Creek* as well, is the theme of women who betray their own. Sally's mother is probably intended to be representative. She cannot intervene on her daughter's behalf when she is punished for talking to boys; the best she can do is help disguise the bruises that come from the father's beating (92). The older girls are traitors because they model behavior that reinforces patriarchal assumptions without question or challenge. Marin, for example, who "knows lots of things," still assumes that some day a boy will arrive in her life to change it (27). Sally, who is named more than once as Esperanza's "friend," promised that sex with a boy would be magical, but "lied" about it and abandons Esperanza to her rapist (99–100).

Woman Hollering Creek is obviously a kind of sequel to Cisneros's first collection, though it begins with girls who are eleven or twelve years old. Some of the same characters reappear, including the best friend, Lucy, and most of the same themes appear again more fully developed. The twenty-two stories form another bildungsroman sequence in which women characters struggle against cultural definitions in order to establish identities for themselves as independent women with sexual dimensions and as authentic Chicanas. There is greater development of male characters, and there are even a few narratives from the male point of view. However, these boys and men almost always represent antagonistic patriarchal forces, or, in Stavans's words, they are "patently satanic" (32). On occasion, however, men or boys are treated more sympathetically because they are suppressed in the same way that women are.

Houses, the controlling metaphor in *The House on Mango Street*, are expanded in *Woman Hollering Creek* to include all the features that define personal space and the movement of characters beyond limits of houses, neighborhoods, and nations. In many stories, a new theme emerges: time like an onion, "with each year inside the next one" (6–7), or history as a snake with the future "swallowing its tail" (126). Two stories in particular, "*Bien* Pretty" and "Eyes of Zapata," are structured according to this "onion" time. Cisneros also makes extensive use of Chicano mythology and folklore, noting how women's roles are neglected or distorted.

The extensive reference to the Malinche myth marks Cisneros's effort to restore women to positions of respect in the mythology. Malinche, an Indian woman traded from tribe to tribe as a child, aided the Spaniards in their conquest of Montezuma. After being turned over to the Spaniards, she converted to Christianity and accepted the name Doña Marina. She became Cortez's confidante, representative, and eventually his lover, bearing him a son. Thus in mythology she has become both a Mexican Eve and the snake in Eden. She is known pejoratively as both *la vendida* (one who sells out) and *la chingada* (one who is fucked), who allows herself to be raped, mothers a bastard race, and turns her country over to invaders. Clemencia, in "Never Marry a Mexican," is a character with few ethnic or gender loyalties, and she willingly takes on the name of Malinche.

In the last story, Lupita is more practical about her loyalties. She recognizes that syncretism is a natural force, even if it does create tension. When one cultural group dominates another, she understands, the weaker one may be altered, but it is never obliterated. The dominant culture, no matter how ruthless, must adapt itself to the values of the culture it subsumes. Similarly, in "Little Miracles, Kept Promises," Rosario is able to find compromise between forces she had once considered antithetical: the sedate Christian Virgincita de Guadalupe and the fierce Aztec goddess Coatlaopeuh. Ultimately, she accepts her identity as both her "mother's daughter" and her "ancestor's child" (128). In these ways, Chicanas are able to establish their roles as women who enable two cultures to share values rather than as Malinches who betray one culture to another.

It is always dangerous to speculate about matters of influence, but readers of Simone de Beauvoir will surely note a number of parallels in the growth of Cisneros's women. The characters can also be seen as advancing through evolutionary phases that Elaine Showalter analyzed in nineteenth-century English fiction and suggested as typical of all "literary subcultures" (36). In this sequence, women first recognize, imitate, and internalize the values of the dominant patriarchy. Then, recognizing the inequities of the culture, they express resentment of their victim status and advocate minority rights. Finally, women are "freed from the dependency of opposition" to find confidence and comfort as they define themselves in communities of their own (39). Showalter names these stages as feminine, feminist, and female. At least one other critic arrives at a similar conclusion, noting how current Chicana writers recognize the destructive elements in their culture's definition of gender roles and then become confident in the "love of Chicanas for themselves and each other as Chicanas" (Yarbro-Bejarano 140). In *The House on Mango Sweet*, Esperanza is learning the roles of women, but is always resolved, at some level, that she will "not grow up tame like the others" (88); by the end of *Woman Hollering Creek*, Lupita has resolved that she will love herself more, and that she will associate with "real women" who "live their lives the way they were meant to be lived" (161–63).

The early stories of *Woman Hollering Creek* portray patriarchy as comforting, even seductive, though always dominant. Fathers are absent or ineffective at critical times, yet their appearance signals celebration and security. In "Eleven," for example, the birthday cake is saved for "when Papa comes home from work"

(9). The "best part" for children in "Mexican Movies" is when Mama and Papa carry them asleep to bed, and, half-awakening, they anticipate a Sunday morning with an intact household (13).

However, such comfort is purchased with submission to the father's values and to those of other males who assume entitlement. In "Mexican Movies," the father disburses money, determines moral limits, and assigns the care of a younger child to the girl. When Kikki cries, she must take care of him because "Papa doesn't move when he's watching a movie" (13). Micaela's brothers in "Mericans" define her roles—even at play. She wants to be a "flying feather dancer," but Keek insists that she be a German fighter pilot, then Ming the Merciless, then Tonto. She acquiesces, she says, because otherwise they "might not play with me at all" (18).

While these girls work at incorporating the values of the patriarchal culture, they are simultaneously beginning to perceive the injustice of its dictates and to refuse to submit to limits. Micaela, playing the roles assigned to her, still desiring her own role, wants to cry but does not, refusing to let the tears come because, she says, "[c]rying is what *girls* do" (19). Rosario, a more mature character in "Little Miracles, Kept Promises," faces the same expectations. As a girl, she is expected to play hostess, to get married, and to have children. Yet the life she desires for herself is more contemplative, creative, and solitary. For choosing such an alternative, she is willing to face the ridicule of her male relatives and her mother's indirect complicity with them. Rosario is personally resolute, but she confronts the patriarchal forces almost alone, with only a sense of a possible sisterhood when she struggles to a recognition of "power in her mother's patience" and "strength in her grandmother's endurance" (128).

"One Holy Night" is a transitional story, one of sexual initiation that also explicitly concludes that male superiority is a fiction. The young woman protagonist, gone to visit Chaq Uxmal Paloquin to be instructed, even anointed, referred to him as a "great and mighty heir" who would make her noble, perhaps divine. She found instead that sex was "no big deal. It wasn't any deal at all" (30). Lovemaking was not mystical; it was not "coming undone like gold thread, like a tent full of birds" (28). Instead, it was being roughly handled by a rude man with dirty hands (28), reminiscent of the rape in *The House on Mango Street*. Instead of being blessed, the girl felt bitten and gave out a cry, as if the person she had been but could not be any longer "leapt out" (30). Every claim that Chaq had made for himself turned out to be false, and his controls were painful.

After her initiation, the girl recognized that she had become part of a sisterhood: women who were still powerless, but who knew about men. On the way home from the encounter, she "thought about all the world," and how she had become "a part of history," and she wondered if all the women she passed on the street could tell that she had become one of them. They "were all the same somehow, laughing behind [their] hands" at what the world—and by implication, the world as determined by the opinion of men—had made over "nothing"

(31). What a "bad joke" it is, she thinks, to consider "the perfection of man" (35).

Cleófilas in the title story also goes through an initiation, but she encounters a competent sisterhood, a community of women who act against the excesses of the patriarchy, for themselves and for each other. However, Cleófilas never becomes part of the empowered group that rescues her. She discovers that Sequin, Texas, is not as "far away and lovely" as she thought it might be (45). It is, in fact, as ugly as her home in Mexico, where she was responsible to her six "good for nothing brothers" and had to endure her father's complaints. Life with a husband was only a different sort of submission. She endured one difficult pregnancy and took care of the child because her husband "couldn't be bothered." She endured his infidelity, and though she never would have thought it of herself, she endured his beatings—without fighting back, without breaking into tears, and without running away as she had once imagined she would. She did not even holler. She was willing to risk another difficult pregnancy because her husband did not understand, or did not care, that the baby might be turned around "and split her down the center" (53). In order not to embarrass him, she agrees not to ask her father for money and promises not to tell the doctor where her bruises came from. This is a long catalog, but typical of the privileges Cisneros's male characters have claimed for themselves. Cleófilas accepts them all. She has internalized patriarchal values: in recounting the abuses in an almost thoughtful voice, her strongest reaction is one of curious surprise.

Felicia, a member of the Chicana sisterhood who rescues Cleófilas, has established her own rules. She does not have a husband. She drives a pickup that she is paying for herself. What is more, she says what she wishes, even hollers just because she wants to—not because she had been instructed or permitted to do so, and not in response to a beating. In particular, she hollers to celebrate crossing a creek, the only feature in town, except for virgins, that is named after a woman.

These two stories—"One Holy Night" and "Woman Hollering Creek"—mark a point in Showalter's paradigm. Both protagonists have internalized the values of patriarchy or at least have submitted to its force. One responds passively, without remark; the other is also passive, but sees the pretense. Both stories feature sisterhoods: one is powerless but informed; the other is independent and competent. The girl in "One Holy Night" joins the powerless sisterhood; Cleófilas remains outside, able to laugh with the strong ones, but only on occasion and from a distance.

Clemencia, in "Never Marry a Mexican," has made a more significant break. Instead of submitting to abuse, she rejects men, announcing at once, "I'll *never* marry. Not any man. I've known them too intimately" (68). What she has known is the betrayal of her married lover, Drew, whose love defined her, but who was always gone in the morning when she awoke. She remembers his control: "Beautiful, you said. You said I was beautiful, and when you said it, Drew, I was." She felt honored and "worth loving" because of his attention (74–76). At some point, Clemencia realizes the fiction and does not react passively, as others had. Instead, she cultivates her anger for nineteen years until she can punish her old lover by seducing his son. She delights in her power, making the boy hunger and twist in his sleep for her, ultimately considering sexual mutilation, a time when she might take the boy in her mouth and snap her teeth (82). As satisfying as the vengeance may seem at first, it is counterproductive. Clemencia emphasizes the fact that she is a victim and strikes out against the man who wounded her, but in doing so, she perpetuates the oppression for Drew's son and wife, affirming his patriarchal assumptions that members of a man's family are not independent agents, but are his property or extensions of himself. In her obsession, Clemencia celebrates, and thus perpetuates, her status as victim.

In *"Bien* Pretty," the last story of *Woman Hollering Creek*, Lupita is at first as angry as Clemencia had been, but eventually achieves a measure of freedom. She had "always been in love with a man," and without her lover, Flavio, she considered herself "ugly" (160). During their lovemaking, she became almost an infant in his arms while he would coo to her (154). Thus, with that kind of dependency, she collapsed when Flavio left her. His departure "wore all her prettiness away" (137). Because Lupita still defined roles according to patriarchal values, her first reaction was to blame herself because she had never asked Flavio's forgiveness or told him often enough that she loved him (160). Her next reaction was an "uncontrollable desire" for revenge: she would drive to his house and "bash in his skull" (157). Finally, and most productively, she removes his memory, burning almost everything that has a connection to him. Thus intact, she is able to discern the sisterhood, the community of women she has known all her life—*"Las* girlfriends. *Las comadres"* and all of their "mamas and *tias"* (161). From that perspective, women can love with the power and passion that had been reserved for men, no longer to be considered as only "volatile and evil, or sweet and resigned" (161). For most readers, it is not necessary to note that Lupita is not rejecting heterosexual love, but is revising the conditions for it. With that freedom, she is able to enter a community of strong women.

In an evolution that parallels gender and sexual growth, characters in *Woman Hollering Creek* must also define themselves according to ethnic and linguistic conditions. In early stories, there are conflicts in language, and characters are uncertain or anxious about their ethnicity. By the last story, Lupita has resolved these issues.

In "Mericans," Micaela, along with her brothers, is visiting her grandmother in Mexico. Communication is difficult because the grandmother does not understand English and Micaela understands Spanish only when she is "paying attention" (19). A woman tourist encounters the children playing outside the church and speaks to them in "Spanish too big for her mouth" (20). The children reply in English and must literally identify themselves as "Mericans," obviously no longer Mexican, but evidently not yet considering themselves fully American. Patricia, in "My *Tocoya,"* is scorned by her namesake because she affects a "phony English accent" (37) to escape her subservient role as a girl in a traditional Mexican-American family. The status of Cleófilas in the title story is even more complex. She is an outsider in a community of outsiders. Moving from her father's home in Mexico to a Mexican-American community in Sequin, Texas, she can speak no English. Her neighbors can speak both languages, but their English is "gruff" (46), and their Spanish is "pocked with English" (55). Even with their deficiencies, they feel superior to Cleófilas and scold her for assimilating so slowly. Thus Cleófilas and her neighbors are both aliens in their language communities.

Clemencia is the most tortured character because her ethnicity and language betray her in all her environments. Her father, a Mexican from a proud and settled family, had "married down" when he wed a Mexican-American girl "who couldn't even speak Spanish" (68–69). Of course, had she been blonde, her language would have been forgiven. Clemencia's mother had an affair with an Anglo man and married him after her husband's death, shifting her attention from her own daughters to her stepsons. Clemencia's lover, Drew, was married to a "redheaded Barbie doll" whom he would not leave (79); he would never marry Clemencia under any circumstances because she was Mexican (80).

Perhaps in an effort to belong to more than one group, Clemencia works sometimes as a translator, but she feels incompetent with English idioms: she can never "get the sayings right" (73). Her neighborhood is not appropriately ethnic either. There may be "more signs in Spanish than in English," but by day the barrio is only *Sesame Street* "cute," and at night it grows threatening (72). She has rejected Mexican men as lovers, along with a long catalog of other Hispanics (69). However, she takes an Anglo man as a lover because he can speak to her in Spanish. In that language, she can love herself and think herself "worth loving" (74). There is no appropriate social status for Clemencia either. She is "amphibious," escaping the middle class, but still "worlds apart" from the poor and only a kind of creative novelty to the rich (71–72). Nor does Clemencia have any sense of support from women or loyalty to them; she delights in sleeping with married men, particularly if their wives are in the process of "birthing babies" (76). After all, she says, they aren't brown like she is; they are not *her* sisters. Clemencia, as she sees herself, is a victim, scorned by men, women, parents, Mexicans, Mexican Americans, Anglos, rich, and poor.

In "*Bien* Pretty," just as Lupita outgrows her anger at men, she resolves language and ethnic conflicts over time. She begins, like Clemencia, with a fear that she is not an authentic member of any group. She had learned her Spanish in public schools and from "crazy Graham," who was Welsh "and had learned his Spanish running guns to Bolivia" (153). Her Chicano politics came from Eddie, who left her for someone else, without the "decency to pick a woman of color" (142). Flavio Mungia seemed an ideal Hispanic man for her since his family came from Michoacan and he must thus be in direct contact with both Aztec and Spanish influences. He could teach her, she thought, native dances, Amerindian mythology, and Mexican folklore. Flavio, however, was both reluctant and unqualified. Though he was the first man to love her whose "*first* language was Spanish" (153), he declined to be her ideal Mexican, noting that his cultural connections went only as far back as his grandmother. He insisted on switching linguistic codes and wearing yuppie shirts, confident that he was authentic without a sarape or sombrero (151). His ultimate betrayal was to leave Lupita for Mexico, not in pursuit of cultural legitimacy, but because of obligations to wives he had not admitted to having before.

Lupita, who wanted to be Mexican and suffered because she was not (151–52), must finally accept the mixedness of her life as more authentic than any imagined purity. She recognizes that she must identify herself by the catalog of things she chooses to carry with her from one house to another: her futon, work, *molcajete* (mortar), flamenco shoes, *huipiles* (chemises), *rebozos* (shawls), Tae Kwon Do uniforms, new-age crystals, Latino tapes, and copy of the *I Ching* (141). Her home, located in San Antonio's King William district and filled with "Southwest funk," is equally impure. It belonged to a Hispanic poet on a Fulbright grant who traveled with her husband, who was a real *curandero* (folk healer) (139–40). Lupita never speaks directly of her epiphany, but it becomes clear when she accepts a compliment about her shawl, which was Peruvian and "*bien* pretty," whether it came from a Mexican supermarket in San Antonio or from Santa Fe or New York (161–62). Identity and function matter, not origin, she decides. Besides, it is no longer possible to determine origins or maintain fidelity to them.

WORKS CITED AND CONSULTED

Primary

Cisneros, Sandra. *Bad Boys*. San Jose, CA: Mango, 1980.
———. "Do You Know Me? I Wrote *The House on Mango Street*." *Americas Review* 15.1 (1987): 77–79.
———. *Hairs/Pelitos*. New York: Apple Soup Books, 1994.
———. *The House on Mango Street*. Houston: Arte Público Press, 1984; New York: Vintage Books, 1989.
———. Lecture. University of Texas-Pan American. March 9, 1994.
———. *Loose Woman*. New York: Knopf, 1994.
———. *My Wicked, Wicked Ways*. Berkeley: Third Woman Press, 1987.
———. *Woman Hollering Creek and Other Stories*. New York: Vintage Books, 1992.

Secondary

Binder, Wolfgang, ed. "Sandra Cisneros." *Partial Autobiographies: Interviews with Twenty Chicano Poets*. Erlangen: Verlag, Palm, and Erlagan, 1985. 54–74.
Carabin, Joan Cook. "Allusions Not Conclusions: Another Look at Stereotypes in Sandra Cisneros' Fiction." *Palo Alto Review* 2.2 (Fall 1993): 19–23.
Ganz, Robin. "Sandra Cisneros: Border Crossings and Beyond." *MELUS* 19 (Spring 1994): 19–29.

Luna-Lawhn, Juanita. "Las Dos Fridas: El Frito Bandito and Barbie-Q." *Palo Alto Review* 2.1 (Spring 1993): 3–10.

Milligan, Bryce. "Two Conversations with Sandra Cisneros." *Palo Alto Review* 2.1 (Spring 1993): 11–15.

Olivares, Julian. "Sandra Cisneros' *The House on Mango Street* and the Poetics of Space." *Americas Review* 15.3–4 (1987): 160–69.

Pratt, Mary Louise. " 'Yo Soy La Malinche': Chicana Writers and the Poetics of Ethnonationalism." *Callaloo* 16.4 (1993): 859–73.

Rocard, Marcienne. "The Chicana: A Marginal Woman." *European Perspectives on Hispanic Literature*. Ed. Genviève Fabre. Houston: Arte Público Press, 1988.

Rodriguez Aranda, Pilar E. "On the Solitary Fate of Being Mexican, Female, Wicked, and Thirty-Three: An Interview with Writer Sandra Cisneros." *Americas Review* 18.1 (Spring 1990): 64–79.

Satz, Martha. "Returning to One's House: An Interview with Sandra Cisneros." *Southwest Review* 82 (Spring 1997): 166–85.

Showalter, Elaine. *A Literature of Their Own: British Women Novelists from Bronté to Lessing*. Princeton: Princeton University Press, 1977.

Stavans, Ilan. "Sandra Cisneros: Form over Content." *Academic Questions* 9.4 (Fall 1996): 29–34.

Yarbro-Bejarano, Yvonne. "Chicana Literature from a Chicana Feminist Perspective." *Americas Review* 15.3–4 (1987): 139–45.

ROBERT COOVER
(February 4, 1932–)

Wayne B. Stengel

BIOGRAPHY

Robert Coover was born in Charles City, Iowa, in 1932. He attended Southern Illinois University for two years and then transferred to Indiana University, graduating with a B.A. in Slavic studies in 1953. On the day following his college graduation, Coover was drafted into the navy. He attended officer candidate school and served in Europe and the Mediterranean until 1957. From 1957 until 1960, he attended the University of Chicago, working on a master's degree in English, and then devoted several years to travel and study, publishing stories in small magazines such as *Evergreen Review, Cavalier*, and *Noble Savage*. In both 1958 and 1959, Coover made student charter trips to Europe, the second time to marry Maria del Pilar Sans-Mallafre, whom he had met while he was in the navy and she was a student at the University of Barcelona. During this period, Coover attended art school and wrote a number of the "Exemplary Fictions" from *Pricksongs and Descants*, as well as other pieces that were discarded or never published.

Although Coover did not receive his master's degree from Chicago until 1965, his three years in residence there at the end of the 1950s were formative for his aesthetic and intellectual development. At Chicago, Coover first read Samuel Beckett and envisioned him as a kind of literary father. In a first-rate essay, "The Last Quixote, Marginal Notes on the Gospel According to Samuel Beckett" published more than a decade later in 1971 in the *New American Review*, he acknowledged that it was Beckett's model that allowed him to continue making art in the absence of support or affirmation. It was Beckett's funny games with numbers, his academic gags, his abstruse puns, his rhetorical parody, and his overall virtuosity that inspired Coover. Also at Chicago, Coover became fascinated with courses in theology and the philosophy of religion. There he first encountered the philosophy of Karl Jaspers, who insisted that all of the

Christian miracles, including the Resurrection, should be interpreted metaphorically. Coover was also intrigued by Jaspers's contention that the only way
to struggle against the inflexibilities of myth was on a myth's own ground, by
reconceiving its metaphorical hold on its audience.

After Chicago, from 1962 to 1965, Coover lived in his wife's hometown,
Tarragona, Spain, where he did the major work on his first novel, composed
the original draft of his second, and wrote a number of the stories that would
find their way into *Pricksongs and Descants*. At this time, he turned to ancient
fictions, works by Ovid and *The Arabian Nights*, to see if he could apply their
conceptions of transformation to his own theories of fiction. Coover concluded
from his careful study of these works that the major struggle of all men and
women has been against metamorphosis, against the inevitability of transformation that overtakes all individuals. From the mid-1960s until 1980, Coover,
his wife, and their three children spent as much time living in Spain and England
(largely in Kent) as they spent in America, although the family frequently returned to the United States so that Coover could supplement his income with a
variety of teaching positions. A recipient of a Rockefeller grant in 1969 and
twice awarded Guggenheim grants in 1971 and 1974, Coover has taught at Bard
College, the University of Iowa, Washington University, Virginia Military Institute, Columbia, Brandeis, Princeton, and, since 1980, at Brown University.

CRITICISM

In 1966, Coover published his first novel, *The Origin of the Brunists*, about
the formation of a bogus religious cult following a mine accident in a small
midwestern town. Although the book won the William Faulkner Award for the
best first novel of the year and was admired by reviewers and academics, it took
Coover several more works before he developed a following of critics and students. In 1968, Coover's second novel, *The Universal Baseball Association, Inc.,
J. Henry Waugh, Prop.*, was published. Reaching a somewhat larger audience
and gaining an even more enthusiastic critical reception, this story about a tabletop baseball game and a man's obsession with his homemade myths and
fictions still seemed too narrow and claustrophobic a subject to build an audience
beyond those few critics, writers, and students interested in the metafictional
and fabulist writing that Robert Scholes described in his respected 1967 study,
The Fabulators. It was Coover's first short-story collection, *Pricksongs and
Descants* (1969), that established his reputation as a unique, innovative, and
highly talented modernist who was genuinely fascinated by experimentation, not
merely posing behind it.

Coover's next book-length publication was *A Theological Position*, a volume
of short plays that appeared in 1972. Coover's third novel was the purportedly
outrageous and controversial *The Public Burning*. In many ways, the publication
of this book, one that sees Richard Nixon's involvement in the Julius and Ethel
Rosenberg spy case as a kind of public saturnalia and carnival, a psychic cleans-

ing ritual for the savage paranoia of the American 1950s, was the watershed event of Coover's literary career. Owing to its angry, satirical tone about many then-living public figures, the novel was at once more accessible and immediate than anything Coover had previously published, but given its length—534 pages—and the density of Coover's prose, it was also more demanding than anything Coover had written. Following laudatory reviews by established critics like Geoffrey Woolf and Thomas R. Edwards and a nomination for the National Book Award, some literary pundits predicted that this novel, with its phantas-magorical vision of American history, would be regarded as one of the great breakthrough novels of the twentieth century, and that Coover would finally receive the extensive public recognition his talents had always deserved. These predictions have proved false. Although the manuscript of *The Public Burning* was completed in 1975, over two years elapsed before the novel was eventually published, after four publishers in this period rejected it for fear of libel suits and litigation. Following Viking Press's decision to print the book, few readers seemed to find its final form or its relatively sympathetic depiction of Nixon as outlandish, scatological, or daring as the prior publicity had suggested. Soon Coover's postmodernist carnival about the McCarthy era had settled into place as a difficult, interesting, and slightly obscure work of American fabulation or metafiction, and Coover had become another kind of underappreciated American artist, the writer's writer. Thus the rest of Coover's career has proceeded.

Without the fanfare surrounding the publication of *The Public Burning*, fewer critics and less of an audience seem to attend to each new Coover work. In 1980, *A Political Fable*, in which Dr. Seuss's Cat in the Hat runs for president, was published without enthusiasm or significant critical response. A similar fate greeted *Spanking the Maid* (1981), in which a single scene is repeated with endless variations. *In Bed One Night and Other Brief Encounters*, Coover's second short-story collection, followed in 1983, containing some stories that had been published in journals and literary magazines as early as the beginning of the 1970s. In 1986, Coover's *Gerald 's Party*, a novel he had been working on for much of the decade, was published and immediately attacked by critics for its opacity and emotional coldness. The next year saw the publication of *A Night at the Movies*, a short-story cycle in which Coover's individual stories parodied, inverted, and revised the classic movie genres and conventions of the 1930s and 1940s. *A Night at the Movies* contained the individual stories "Charlie in the House of Rue," a surreal vision of Charlie Chaplin, and "After Lazarus," both of which had been published in small magazines in 1980. The year 1987 also saw the book publication of *Whatever Happened to Gloomy Gus of the Chicago Bears?*, a revised version of a novella that first appeared in 1975 in the *New American Review* about a professional football player who displays a marked resemblance to Coover's depiction of Nixon in *The Public Burning*. In 1991, Coover published the novel *Pinocchio in Venice*.

Coover remains a tirelessly experimental, frequently provocative writer. However, due to the conservatism of the last twenty years in American culture and the trend away from the self-reflexive and the metafictional toward the realistic in writing tastes, he appears to many literary appraisers as a peripheral rather than a vanguard figure in American letters. Nonetheless, critics, students, and those readers interested in experimental fiction and the avant-garde remain intrigued by Coover's conceptions of the author, the text, and the reader.

With the possible exceptions of John Barth's short-story collection *Lost in the Funhouse*, William Gass's story cycle *In the Heart of the Heart of the Country*, and any of the short-story collections Donald Barthelme published from the mid-1960s until his death in 1989, no American short-story writer has contributed more to the development and possibility of innovative short fiction than Robert Coover. In only three short-story collections, *Pricksongs and Descants* (1969), *In Bed One Night and Other Brief Encounters* (1983), and *A Night at the Movies* (1987), Coover has used, expanded, and seriously challenged the nature of short-story form as demandingly as any contemporary American fiction writer. As metafictionist and fabulist (and long time friend and colleague of critic Robert Scholes), Coover conforms precisely to the definition of the fabulist writer in Scholes's seminal 1967 study of a then-new, landmark kind of fiction writer. According to Scholes's study, the fabulist is that author who successfully incorporates all the techniques of literary criticism into a work of fiction, thus blurring the boundaries between mimetic representation and an ongoing, self-conscious analysis of the work that continually interrupts and challenges its narrative. This self-reflexive writing style, whose subject is frequently the work itself, was the trademark of that loose grouping of writers in the American 1960s—Coover, Gass, Barth, and Barthelme, among many others—commonly called metafictionists. Yet the style and techniques of Coover's writing have always employed devices that set Coover's work uniquely apart from the metafictional movement with which it has too often been crudely lumped. As Larry McCaffrey succinctly summarizes Coover's career:

What Coover returns to again and again in all his works is the concept of man-as-fiction-maker. His characters are constantly shown in the process of inventing systems and patterns to help order their lives and give meaning to the world at large. In most of Coover's work there exists a tension between the process of man creating his fictions and his desire to assert that his systems are ontological rather than ideological in nature. For Coover this tension finally results in man losing sight of the fictional basis of his systems and eventually becoming controlled or entrapped within them. (106)

Thus all of Coover's writings, particularly his short stories, ask complex philosophical questions about the nature of language and knowledge, consciousness and the writing process, narrative voice and narrative control. In many of Coover's short stories, the dominant issue is that of authorial, masculine control: when does the controlling consciousness of a writer slip into self-consciousness and thus dramatize the aesthetic dismemberment that Roland Barthes describes in his essay "The Death of the Author"?

ANALYSIS

Coover's endless fascination with the man-made systems of language and art has made him question the larger foundational basis of all history, politics, and religion while seeking refuge in the limited, yet ideally existential freedom of ritual, myths, game, and sports. Building his novels, and frequently his stories, around obsessions with baseball, bogus religions, political celebrity, fairy tales, folklore, popular culture, and even some aspects of Christian miracle, Coover creates characters who find possibilities for order and meaning in a brand of ritual that lacks the gargantuan organization of sanctioned philosophy, metaphysics, or theology. For Coover, myth and ritual, finding their purest distillation in game and sport, reaffirm a philosophy of life as a series of disconnected instances. Freedom, he suggests, comes in finding a play, pattern, performance, or organizing principle that enables spontaneity within the framework of a particular moment. In Coover's writing, the underlying ontological question always becomes, where is the greatest amount of possibility, action, or reality within the artifice created?

The two greatest influences on Coover's writing—its style, syntax, and subject matter—have been Jorge Luis Borges and Samuel Beckett. One of Coover's best critics, Jackson Cope, has recognized Coover's obsession with Borgesian numerology, design, and self-reflexive architectonics as well as his similarly Borgesian desire to lose the self so as to reform the self, to destroy and create within the act of writing: "The impact of Borges upon Coover has probably been of major importance: They share an unremitting interest in the loss of self through the act of imaginative projection, and in the attempts to reconstruct (perhaps to recover) that self in the teasingly predictable forms of number and measure" (3–4). Coover's obsession with a numerological precision in or a geometrical shaping of many of his short fictions has parallels to his homage to the intricate articulation of consciousness that he finds in Samuel Beckett's fiction and that he patterns for his own. In his 1971 essay published in the *New American Review*, "The Last Quixote," Coover likens Beckett's art to that of a sculptor who slowly, persistently chips away at an ultimate human form, perfected geometrical design, or final mathematical purity. Beckett "is like those great sculptors who spend whole lives in the restless pursuit of some impossible quality, a glance, a gesture, a Pygmalion, a leg, who ends up giving us not so much objects, as a process, humbling, archetypal, perceptive" (Andersen 36).

Yet the quality of Coover's most characteristic short stories is finally not that achieved by the loss and recovery of identity in Borges's circular ruins, nor is it the droning, if comic, search for objects, relationships, and the ideal syntax that Beckett's endlessly futile, though absolutely necessary, art accomplishes. The prototypical Coover narrator/persona is the Adam figure in Coover's story "Beginnings," published first in *Harper's* in 1972 and later appearing as the longest story in his collection *In Bed One Night and Other Brief Encounters* (1983). For Coover, all writers are Adamic figures and the making of literature

is an Adamic quest of consciousness into a world constantly created and re-
created through acts of perception.

In Bed One Night was completely ignored by reviewers and scholars alike.
This collection of offhand, deadpan, and frequently amusing stories, however,
is a compelling illustration of what happens when an American fabulist, freed
from the more austere demands of European or South American postmodernism,
casually strolls across the page in search of beginnings for new stories. Here
Coover attempts at all costs to avoid forced literary resolutions, concluding that
just because honest, original beginnings and endings are hard to come by doesn't
mean that the death of literary realism, as previous audiences knew it, presup-
poses the emergence of an apocalyptic era in writing.

"Beginnings" is an Adam and Eve story that returns us to the genesis of all
art, all sexual and literary desire, and all naming. As in "The Magic Poker"
from *Pricksongs and Descants*, Coover invents an island—his paradise lost—
as a sort of primitive East Hampton atoll in which words, nature, children, Eve's
body, household duties, plots, endings, and beginnings of plots all compete for
this Adam's attention. These objects appear randomly, as equally important, and
assume no hierarchies of order, urgency, or meaning. After surveying his island,
its landscape, natives, and possible pleasures, this Adam's consciousness floods
with new beginnings, initial situations, and plot outlines for openings to short
stories only to find that once his aesthetic imagination follows these channels
of possibility, they become resolutions, endings, places where other writers have
laboriously tilled before and thus are no longer fresh, imaginative beginnings.
What emerges in this endlessly circular, geometrically wandering, geometrically
controlled articulation of Coover's consciousness is a funny, affectionate blueprint of Coover's mind and his own pursuit of an easygoing, frequently fumbling
American kind of postmodern fabulation:

An ordinary island then, with ordinary trees and bushes. . . . he recognized that there was
something suspicious about it, as though it might have been like the air he breathed, just
another metaphor. . . . Small wonder, then, that he took to inventing stories in which time
had a geography, like an island, place moved like the hands of a clock, and point of
view was a kind of punctuation. He assigned numbers and symbols to death, love, characters, unexpected developments, transitions, then submitted them to the rhythms of
numerologies. (*In Bed* 44–46, 49)

What one sees in this story is not only Coover elaborately parodying all the
techniques and wanderings of his own previous writing styles, but his authorial
recognition that all objects of consciousness, even the self, are finally made of
words and thus are capable of the mutations and drifting of all thought, speech,
and cognition. Indeed, a writer can easily, even willingly, be trapped within his
own words and his own mythmaking.

The great challenge of Coover's writing career, then, has been to find the
way out, to begin again, to start completely over in every story he writes. This

daunting, impossible impulse to create and destroy simultaneously finds its expression in "Beginnings" in the motivating premise of the story. The story's Adam/Prospero figure's search for his paradise lost, a brave new world of the imagination, comes after he has shot himself and our explorer/interpreter attempts to read, enact, or make sense of the patterns of blood and ink his body has splayed against his cabin wall: "It is important to begin when everything is already over. . . . Thus there were worse jokes his blood might have played on him. Its message might have read: All beginnings imply an apocalypse. . . . He awoke the next morning tangled in first lines like wrinkled sheets" (*In Bed* 40–41, 57–59). An almost violent insistence on highly original beginnings and endings, on a contrived sense of an apocalypse and bloodshed, has filled Coover's short fiction within the last decade, making his stories, despite their wit, sophistication, and philosophic elegance, unpalatable even to some postmodern tastes.

If "Beginnings" is in many ways representative of *In Bed One Night and Other Brief Encounters* (1983), "Gilda's Dream" exemplifies both the richness and difficulties of Coover's most recent work of collected short fiction, *A Night at the Movies* (1987). As Jackson Cope had observed, *A Night at the Movies* is both a collection of individual stories and a short-story sequence that attempts to reproduce the continuity and discontinuity of experiencing a night at the movies in America fifty years ago. We watch, in individual stories, the previews, the serial, the travelogue, the short subjects, and the cartoons. Then, what we came for: the western shoot-out, the poignant Chaplin slapstick, the romance of *Casablanca*, all reimagined from Coover's particularly angular perspective. Yet this night at the movies is finally, for Cope, about what the movies have frequently left out: the female spectator, who is often represented on the screen, but whose dreams and desires are most frequently merged with those of the men watching the movie beside her.

A Night at the Movies is Coover's Alice loose in Wonderland; she makes up everything that makes her up. But that comes again to beginnings and mergers, the collapsing of boundaries: There is a merger between the seer and the scenes. Projectionist and the projected fuse into all this linkage of the claw as the projector, the male force dominating the film image, out of control, until we focus upon the projectionist who "can feel his body, as though penetrated by an alien from outer space." But one of the ghost films behind all this existential terror is that of the ingenue, perhaps Pauline, Pearl White, but certainly in peril; and the projectionist fuses again with this image to become the child-woman himself visiting the foyer at intermission and meeting the alien figure escaped from the screen into her mythology of men; he seems, as she says, "a real dreamboat" (Cope 137–38).

In "Gilda's Dream," which consists of one page-length paragraph several episodes into *A Night at the Movies*, Coover is clearly rethinking Columbia Pictures' gaudy 1946 musical *Gilda* with Rita Hayworth and Glenn Ford, only in Coover's refantasized version, Rita Hayworth has become a transvestite nightclub singer in some south-of-the-border locale, "Argentina maybe," who finds herself doing a largely autoerotic striptease in a men's washroom for the men's-room attendant and a strange, frightening man hiding in the stall behind the louvered door and watching her through the slats. In Coover's telling of the scene, the drag queen Gilda sings not "Put the blame on Mame, boys," but "Put the blame on dames," "as he feels himself disintegrate into tiny little pieces, and not all of them seemed to be my own" (*Movies* 75). Coover's Gilda seems first haunted, then literally disintegrated by the objectifying male gaze that has so dominated and paralyzed Hollywood filmmaking. As he describes his dreams, his striptease "started from the bottom up, but my face remained completely covered. Except for my eyes, which stared out and somehow, at the same time, stared back at themselves: stared, that is, at their own staring" (*Movies* 74). This man in women's sexy clothing, ironically, the ultimate film fantasy femme fatale, only sees himself and his own gaze when, like the audience, he looks at the erotic, enticing Gilda. However, what most frightens Gilda in his dream is the strange man hiding in the stall staring at him behind the slats in the louvered door. Moreover, what almost frees Coover's Gilda from the hold of the camera and the male spectator in a way that the Hollywood Gilda has never been freed is his recognition that in some respects, he is this man who is watching. As Coover reads his Gilda's dream thoughts:

Who was this man who frightened me so, I knew he was watching me through the slots, because I could see myself through his eyes. From that perspective, I was both threatening and desirable, so I understood that the fear in the room belonged to the room itself and not to me. Suddenly I felt free, utterly free! (*Movies* 75)

Coover's transvestite nearly reassembles himself when he realizes that the fear and the gaze come from the room, from the entire, masculinized Hollywood film industry and its male visual positioning, even from an entire culture of moviegoers. But then, as Jackson Cope suggests, the projectionist projects himself into the picture, the man hiding in the stall takes a picture, and the iron claw of the projector, the masculine visual apparatus, clicks into place once again. The projectionist meets the ingenue, the heroine in distress, in the lobby, and the categories are thus disturbed: he must pretend to be completely masculine; she, a Hollywood starlet, must pretend to be a woman. Both projectionist and projected, as Cope notes, feel that their bodies are "as though penetrated by an alien from outer space" (138). The categories of sexuality have been disturbed. As Coover concludes in his account of "Gilda's Dream," "there would be no going home" (*Movies* 75); the movies must remain a world of myth and fantasy, not ever a world of authentic representation or social, political, or sexual reality.

In a world of man-made, mass-produced myths, a night at the movies, yesterday and today, serves as a huge narcotic. In "Gilda's Dream," as in all the other film remakes in *A Night at the Movies* as well as in many of the stories within *In Bed One Night and Other Brief Encounters*, Coover writes an essentially feminist parable in which characters are entrapped in narrow visions of male authority and control. Their only means of escape is through self-consciousness and self-correction, through a search for lost identity and the painful articulations of consciousness. Trapped within its "Beginnings" and "Gilda's Dream," Coover's short fiction over the last fifteen years has delighted those readers willing to chart the search for order and control within the minutiae of consciousness as myth and has befuddled or alienated those who find these searchings, however poignant or amusing, tedious and self-reflexively masculine.

By many estimates, Coover's *Pricksongs and Descants* is the author's most complete and assured fictional performance and one of the wittiest, most intricate short-story cycles published by an American short-story writer in the twentieth century. Although it is most often acknowledged as an exacting examination of the writing process and, with John Barth's *Lost in the Funhouse* (1968), William Gass's *In the Heart of the Heart of the Country* (1968), and Donald Barthelme's *City Life* (1970)—all published within a year and a half of *Pricksongs*—one of the definitive metafictional short-story sequences, *Pricksongs* is, finally, much more. Like Joyce's *Dubliners*, Hemingway's *In Our Time*, and J. D. Salinger's *Nine Stories, Pricksongs* is a reverberating progression of stories that builds novelistically, serially, and musically so that each of its twenty chordlike tales, juxtaposed against any other tale, retells and resounds its myths about the creative process. As *Pricksongs* spirals through its cycle, it asks, at least, the following questions: How do the source and energies of any short story germinate, expand, and develop? Why are folktales, mythological stories, biblical accounts, and their variants such enduring vehicles for telling and retelling, and why are they at once so pliable and so false? What does the male imagination desire to possess, control, or order through the stories that it systematizes into these mythologies, and what feminine perspectives have so much masculine fabulation excluded? Ultimately, how does all great storytelling contain destructive as well as creative energies, centrifugal as well as centripetal forces? Finally, who owns the proprietary right of interpretation or hermeneutics of any story: the author who envisions and creates it, the audience that responds and relates to it, or the societal consciousness, that zeitgeist, that the story mirrors and that supplies its medium of transmission and dissemination?

One of the best means to analysis of *Pricksongs* is an examination of its title. Coover himself has commented on its thematic significance for the work: " 'Pricksongs' derives from the physical manner in which the (Pre-Enlightenment) song was printed—the notes were literally pricked out; 'descant' refers to the form of music in which there is a cantus firmus, a basic line, and variations that the older voices play against it" (Gordon 92). If much of *Pricksongs* dramatizes the masculine thrust of narrative and the lyrical, feminine play around it, the work's overall conception of counterpoint is not easily achieved. Many of the twenty stories in this cycle are clearly about the war between masculine and feminine imaginations for power and control of narrative voice and narrative vision: what the bitter grandmother figure in the opening story of the cycle, "The Door: A Prologue of Sorts," calls "death-cunt-and-prick-songs," stories evolving through the endless conflicts of sex, violence, and death. This reference leads to the punning ironies of Coover's title, unexplored in his own explanation of its genesis. *Pricksongs and Descants* forever describes the song of the phallus and the resulting death of the vagina, hardly because Coover honors the sexual status quo, but rather because so much myth, system building, folklore, fairy tale, biblical narrative, and popular culture have presumed that this should be the way of the world. In his effort to destroy as well as to create in the writing process, Coover very much defies the historically presumptive masculine right to order, control, and dominate the strains of his own narratives or even those feminine desires represented within his text.

Perhaps this position is best ironized in three of the highly open-ended collage stories in *Pricksongs*, "The Magic Poker," "Quenby and Ola, Swede and Carl," and "The Babysitter." If *Pricksongs* contained nothing other than these three tales, it could still be regarded as a major work of American experimental fiction. Each of these stories builds a curvilinear, swirling Möbius strip of events and situations by atomizing each of its brief, episodic components into framelike particles that, separated by ellipses from the next frame, swirl back on, contradict, muddle, or complicate the meaning of the events that preceded it. Taking aesthetic directions from the cubism of Picasso and Gris, the filmic montage of Eisenstein, and the jagged editing style of Godard, as well as the alienation effect of Brecht, each of these stories becomes an effective parable on some aspect of the myth of the writing process, or the myth that envisions literature as a vocally unified, well-wrought urn.

"The Magic Poker," one of the best and most demanding stories in the book, a tale that Coover has recognized as a breakthrough story for the entire sequence (McCaffrey 114), presents a seemingly omnipotent Prospero figure who invents an island as his masculine enclave, domicile, and play space. He soon populates this brave new world with a once-majestic, now-dilapidated manor house; lush, almost menacing vegetation that threatens to subsume these human ruins; a Caliban figure, the son of a former caretaker who has reverted to an apelike, primitive existence on the island; and two beautiful sisters who arrive from the mainland and immediately stumble upon the magic poker he places in their path. This magic poker soon becomes either the wondrous, alchemical instrument of all transformation, the poetic, sensitive wand of literature and writing, a weapon for male domination and abuse of the female, or the penis, that symbol of male pride and potency, the fertile power of the entire story. With the alternating, contradictory frames of his collage, Coover takes great delight in never showing the magic poker for long as any one of these specific possibilities. At the story's end, the two sisters, the feminine agency of the story, wrest control of the magic poker from this Prospero, and struggling to leave the island with her sister in their boat, the other woman thrusts Prospero between her legs, withdrawing, only seconds later, the magic poker in his place. Thus a story about a sexual conflict becomes a story about the violence necessary to remove the poker, the pen, the privileged instrument of expression from the hold, control, and domination of the masculine imagination. Clearly, "The Magic Poker" exalts in the death, through sex and violence, of the all-powerful masculine consciousness as the presiding consciousness in postmodernist fiction, and Coover's tone is gleeful at its demise.

If "The Magic Poker" describes the myth of literature and the writing process from the perspective of the author, narrator, or God-like creator, "Quenby and Ola, Swede and Carl" examines literary perception from the perspective of the audience and the reader. In what is one of the most successfully realized pointillist short stories in contemporary fiction, Coover, again using the frames of film technique, adapts the dots and ellipses, the unsettlingly shifting light and perspectives of Georges Seurat's pointillism to the story of a city dweller hopelessly lost in his attempts to interpret or understand the family who runs a lakefront fishing lodge in backwoods Minnesota. In this tale, Carl is the alien urban interloper, the intruder as guest at a family-owned fishing camp in a verdant, isolated, and extremely rural upper Midwest. Judging from the dizzying, flickering, cross-circuiting frames of Coover's narrative, Carl may or may not have slept with Ola, the nubile, thirteen-year-old Lolita and daughter of his hosts, Quenby and Swede. He may or may not have consummated his desire for Quenby, his hostess at the camp, the baker of famous lemon pies for her husband and daughter, and though slightly overweight, the still voluptuously desirable wife of Swede. What is worse, Swede, the silent, morose Nordic owner of the lodge, may know of Carl's dalliance with either his wife or his daughter or both, and he may or may not be planning Carl's murder. But Swede is not talking.

Fortunately for Carl and for any reader of postmodern fiction, Coover insists that individual perspective and angles of vision create individual realities. Therefore, what should drive contemporary fiction, for Coover, is not so much the possibilities of narrative but the myriad positions from which we can view and interpret events. Ultimately, what activates and moves forward the frames of this Coover story are Carl's sexual drive for both women, actualized or not; his fear of and perverse attraction to the violence that might erupt from Swede's imputed knowledge of his supposed liaisons with both women; and Carl's endless, imaginative fascination with storytelling, be it about his own perhaps mythical adventures, or that story he hears repeatedly from Ola of Swede's sudden violent rage and shooting of the family cat for placing its paws in Quenby's homemade lemon pie. The frames and conflicting images of this story, like those of "The Magic Poker," are generated in the male drive for sex, violence, imaginative freedom, and the corresponding death of linear storytelling, born again in this disjunctive, atemporal mosaic of points of view. Finally, this story takes narrative control and narrative authority away from Carl as masculine audience, reader, and exegete of Swede and his family. Eventually, the story insists that all experience and all fictive representation of it are a sea of indeterminacy. In its beautifully, even realistically, rendered surfaces of light and shadow, moon glow and darkness, the story sees individual perception and all types of fiction as functions of the Heisenberg uncertainty principle. But why let one male observer—one reader as highly biased as Carl—interpret reality (or that of Quenby, Ola, and Swede) from his limited, myopic perspectives?

If "The Magic Poker" debunks male authorship and "Quenby and Ola, Swede and Carl" questions the reader response of an oversexed male urbanite lost in the woods and the words, "The Babysitter," one of Coover's most taxing and most frequently anthologized short stories, asks, what is the nature of that human consciousness into which writers send their signs and signifiers, their semiotics and their messages? Consequently, "The Babysitter" describes neither how the artist creates nor the way individuals perceive these dispatches, but rather those force fields that unite individual minds into that conglomerate buzz of responses called social perception. Coover brilliantly uses his montage framing devices, his brief bytes of thought, to create a vision of a variety of consciousnesses at work. In this tale, Coover as carefully shaping artist seems absent, and Coover as audience or interpreter of signs and significance is on hold. Instead, "The Babysitter" asks what the perimeters and boundaries of human consciousness are, the dimensions of this semipermeable envelope, if the obscure object of desire for a particular world is a fifteen-year-old nymphet, the babysitter. "The Babysitter" is a particularly harrowing story in its depiction of a near-totalitarian, mechanically behaviorist mental world in which all the male minds that Coover invades desire sex, nurturance, or intimacy with a young girl who, if physically desirable, is an emotional and intellectual void.

Harry Tucker, a middle-aged, maritally discontent suburbanite, leaves his wife at a cocktail party to return home for a fantasized, if unactualized, rendezvous with the babysitter. Mark and Jerry, two neighborhood teens, come to visit the babysitter with unlikely, eventually unrealized, desires to seduce or rape her. Concurrently, eight-year-old Jimmy Tucker precociously tickles and slaps the babysitter as she undresses him for his bath, and the babysitter slaps and tickles Jimmy in return. Meanwhile, the baby himself may be dead due to the indifferent, frazzled, or angry care of a babysitter too bombarded by the conflicting stimuli of each second to respond to the infant's hour-long cries for gratification.

Of all contemporary short stories, "The Babysitter" may be one of the most purely gestural and most thoroughly disassociated. While Coover records the frames of the masculine imagination as monads of desire futilely flying at the babysitter's body like so much random Brownian motion, the story superficially reproduces the trappings of Updike's or Cheever's upper-middle-class suburban milieu, but so consistently disrupts any conception of unified social or human consciousness as to make this setting virtually unrecognizable. Effectively destroying point of view, causing the reader to question whose mind or consciousness any particular cell of the story represents at any particular moment, the story's spiraling, conflicting, always-separate images purposefully confuse reality and illusion and merge the erotic with the grotesquely antierotic. Coover's

nervous, self-consciously shallow split-screen technique mimics the minimal attention spans of all the characters and parallels their efforts and failures to
process and assimilate signals. If memory, pain, desire, or laughter are nothing
more than a blip on the television screen or a quick flickering of the pinball
machine that the story's would-be teenage rapists hump before their simulated
attack on the babysitter, Coover implicitly questions how any human consciousness in the world he depicts can have the perspective or vision to understand
or appreciate aesthetic design—his or any writer's.

If the baby is the tragic victim of Coover's antitragedy and the terrifyingly
emergent consciousness of the story, the always-glowing cathode rays of the
color television set casting their red, green, and purple lights on the flesh of
both the babysitter and her charge must be the star, the axis, the focal point of
this world beyond chaos theory. Choreographed, geometric images of Astaire
and Rogers, of classic Hollywood westerns, even of vapid spy movies from fifty
and sixty years ago that the television screen only reproduces, cannibalized from
the movies, constitute the blank, harried babysitter's mind. They supply her with
emotional and sexual response mechanisms and offer her directions and frames
of reference for diapering the baby, slapping the eight-year-old's underwear,
slapping the baby, finding a pair of Mr. Tucker's underwear strewn on his bed
and wearing them, and sexually fantasizing. When the television screams violence, she imagines assault; when the television squeals romance, she channel-
surfs to daydreams of her boyfriend. Horrifyingly, Coover's babysitter is a
human television set herself, complete with knobs and antennae, easily pro-
grammed and controlled, quickly turned on and off.

Coover is a fabulist more than willing to cede narrative voice and desire to
the women portrayed in his fiction, yet his depiction of Dolly Tucker, Harry's
aging, lonely wife obsessed with her added pounds and her billowing figure,
becomes the truly dehumanized vision in the story, the victim of an actual
suburban party rape amid all the imaginary ones. Dolly wears a painfully tight
girdle to the neighborhood cocktail party. After a trip to the bathroom, she is
unable to get her body completely back into this torture chamber, so she is
literally buttered—forcibly bent, torn, and twisted out of her girdle and greased,
stretched, and yanked into some semblance of shape by most of the party guests
present, male and female. As always in Coover's art, sex or the antierotic leads
to a kind of violence that, in turn, suggests the death of an entire society and
much of the art that has attempted to represent it.

More than in any other story Coover has written, boredom and enervation
permeate the frames, ellipses, and spaces between the babysitter, the party
guests, the teenagers, the Tucker children, and Harry and Dolly themselves.
Accordingly, a desire for an imagined apocalypse, an end to the triviality, restlessness, discontinuity, and emptiness of their imaginations, haunts all the characters and many of the frames of "The Babysitter." In the story's last segment,
Dolly imagines, or perhaps discovers, that the cocktail party is ending as police
sirens sound nearby and another guest tells her that her children are murdered,

her husband is gone, a corpse is in her bathtub, and her house is wrecked. Dolly's only response to this almost wished-for annihilation is "Let's see what's on the late, late movie" (*Pricksongs* 239). Coover's penchant for the simultaneous creation and destruction of images, like that in Jean-Luc Godard's alternately exhausting and exhilarating *Weekend* (released in 1968 and possibly an influence on the story), makes the last ten of "The Babysitter's" thirty-plus pages hard going; but as is most often the case in Coover, this minute articulation of consciousness, or lack of it, has its visionary rewards.

Such is the case with many of the other stories in *Pricksongs*. The three stories grouped under the title "The Sentient Lens," "Scene for Winter," "The Milkmaid of Samaniego," and "The Leper's Helix," remain some of the most intricate, phenomenologically audacious accounts in English of the conflicts in literary representation between what the human eye perceives and what the lens of narrative has customarily reported, and of the myth that the two can ever be congruent. Similarly, most of the stories in the "Seven Exemplary Fictions of Pricksongs and Descants" inhabit terrain that remains, more than thirty years later, as philosophically and aesthetically adventurous as it was when the stories were first published together in 1969. Tales like "The Brother" and "J's Marriage" examine biblical miracle from the angle of vision of men abandoned, trapped, and destroyed by God's will and impulse: Noah's hapless brother, drowned in floodwaters, and Joseph, the Virgin Mary's spiritually perplexed, sexually deprived husband. In these stories, Coover asks whom myth denies and how creative omnipotence can be so cruel. With equal intelligence and assault, the exemplary fictions "The Marker," "In a Train Station," and "The Wayfarer" question how the conventions of fiction falsify both art and life and force us into dangerous assumptions and conclusions, be they the elegant speculations of prose that sounds like that of Alain Robbe-Grillet and the *roman nouveau*, a heightened version of Rod Serling's *Twilight Zone*, or an updated biblical parable. Coover demonstrates in every story of this unique, sumptuous work that unless a protean sensibility, like his own, constantly prods, investigates, and challenges its premises, the myth of literature and storytelling can be as coercive and totalitarian as a cop on the beat, a member of the thought police, or any writer who wants to tell you how to read and think.

WORKS CITED AND CONSULTED

Primary

Coover, Robert. *Aesop's Forest: The Plot of the Mice*. Ills. Michael McCurdy. Santa Barbara: Capra Press, 1986.
———. *After Lazarus: A Film Script*. Michigan: Bruccoli Clark, 1980.
———. *In Bed One Night and Other Brief Encounters*. Providence, RI: Burning Deck Press, 1983.
———. *Briar Rose*. New York: Grove Press, 1996.

————. *The Convention*. Northridge, CA: Lord John Press, 1982.

————. *Gerald's Party: A Novel*. New York: Linden Press, 1986.

————. *Ghost Town: A Novel*. New York: Henry Holt, 1998.

————. *Hair o' the Chine: A Documentary Film Script*. Michigan: Bruccoli Clark, 1979.

————. *John's Wife: A Novel*. New York: Simon & Schuster, 1996.

————. *A Night at the Movies*. New York: Simon & Schuster, 1987.

————. *The Origin of the Brunists*. New York: Viking Press, 1978.

————. *Pinocchio in Venice*. New York: Linden Press, 1991.

————. *A Political Fable*. New York: Viking Press, 1980.

————. *Pricksongs and Descants*. New York: E. P. Dutton, 1969.

————. *The Public Burning*. New York: Viking Press, 1977.

————. *Spanking the Maid: A Novel*. New York: Grove Press, 1982.

————. *A Theological Position: Plays*. New York: Dutton, 1972.

————. *The Universal Baseball Association, Inc., J. Henry Waugh, Prop*. New York: Random House, 1968.

————. *Whatever Happened to Gloomy Gus of the Chicago Bears?* New York: Linden Press, 1987.

Secondary

Andersen, Richard. *Robert Coover*. Boston: Twayne, 1981.

Barthes, Roland. "The Death of the Author." *Image, Music, Text: Roland Barthes*. Ed. and trans. Stephen Heath. New York: Hill & Wang, 1977.

Cope, Jackson I. *Robert Coover's Fictions*. Baltimore: Johns Hopkins University Press, 1986.

Gass, William H. *Fiction and the Figures of Life*. New York: Knopf, 1970.

Gordon, Lois. *Robert Coover: The Universal Fictionmaking Process*. Carbondale: Southern Illinois University Press, 1983.

Kennedy, Thomas E. *Robert Coover: A Study of the Short Fiction*. New York: Twayne, 1992.

McCaffrey, Larry. "Robert Coover." *Dictionary of Literary Biography*. Vol. 2. Ed. J. Helterman and R. Layman. Detroit: Gale Research, 1978. 106–21.

Oates, Joyce Carol. "Realism of Distance, Realism of Immediacy." *Southern Review* 7 (Winter 1971): 295–337.

Schmitz, Neil. "A Prisoner of Words." *Partisan Review* 40 (Winter 1973): 131–35.

————. "Robert Coover and the Hazards of Metafiction." *Novel: A Forum on Fiction* 7 (Spring 1974): 210–19.

Scholes, Robert. *Fabulation and Metafiction*. Urbana: University of Illinois Press, 1979.

ANITA DESAI
(June 24, 1937–   )

Minoli Salgado

BIOGRAPHY

Anita Desai, the daughter of a German mother and a Bengali father, was born and raised in India, where she attended Queen Mary's School in Delhi and Miranda House, University of Delhi, from which she graduated with a B.A. with honors in English. Her first piece of fiction, a short story, was published in 1946 and her first novel, *Cry the Peacock*, in 1963. Her oeuvre is extensive, covering several award-winning novels, books for children, critical essays and articles, and a volume of short stories, *Games at Twilight*, published in 1978. In the same year, she won the Winifred Holtby Award for her novel *Fire on the Mountain*, and in 1983 she was awarded the Guardian Prize for Children's Fiction for *The Village by the Sea*, a work serialized for television by the BBC. Her witty and ironic novel *In Custody*, published in 1984, was also made into a film. In the past few years, Anita Desai has spent much of her time in England, where she was made an honorary fellow of Girton College, University of Cambridge (1988), and the United States, where she was the Elizabeth Drew Professor at Smith College (1987–88) and the Purington Professor of English at Mount Holyoke College (1988–92).

CRITICISM

Anita Desai's work has been described as containing a "modern sensibility" (Ram, "Interview" 96), but the precise delineations of Desai's modernism have been the subject of critical debate over the years. While all her fiction foregrounds many of the formal and thematic constituents of modernism—subjectivity, formal fragmentation, temporal dislocation, and a quest for meaning, described by Desai herself as an "effort to discover, to underline and convey the true significance of things" (Sharma 12)—the development in her fiction has led some critics to claim that she is in fact more of a realist. The development is a clear and consistent one. From an early preoccupation with the fragmented individual (and usually female) consciousness in *Cry the Peacock* (1963) and *Voices in the City* (1965), Desai reveals an increasing concern with social and historical contingency in *Where Shall We Go This Summer?* (1975), *Fire on the Mountain* (1977), and *Clear Light of Day* (1980), and in her more recent novels, *In Custody* (1984) and *Baumgartner's Bombay* (1988), she gives primacy to a man's point of view and explores, rather than seeks to escape from, social contradictions.

This shift from the private to the public, from an exploration of the psychological effects of oppression to an emphasis on its social constituents, means that the critical reception of Desai's work needs to be placed firmly in its time. Hence K. R. Srinivasa Iyengar's claim in 1973 that Desai is an eminently psychological novelist (464) is based upon a reading of her early work, and Fawzia Afzal-Khan's argument in 1993 that Desai "ultimately subordinates her poetic and mythic imagination to her moral vision," which carries "the moral weight of realism" (60, 59), draws upon an awareness of her more recent fiction.

Games at Twilight, a collection of eleven short stories written at different times and published in 1978, is a transitional work. It reveals the ideological tensions of a predominantly modernist writer who seeks to reconcile her early celebration of the transforming power of the individual imagination with an increasingly urgent awareness of its limitations. It has been argued that Desai's exploration of "stages of awareness" in the short stories "is so obsessive that it sometimes violently separates the psyche from the social context" (Sharma 163). This claim is conditioned by a reading that privileges theme over form. The separation between individual awareness and social context is not so much the result of Desai's "obsessive" concern with subjectivity, a deliberate escape to the sanctum of the psyche, but rather, as I will show, a desire to explore the fundamental links between the personal, spiritual, and aesthetic and the social, historical, and material, within the demands imposed by the short-story form. Desai's exploration of moments of individual insight and, in particular, epiphanic awareness reveals as much about the modernist short story from India as it does about the middle stage of Desai's literary development. The following analysis of epiphany in Desai's short stories examines the interplay between the structural constituents of the stories and their thematic concerns and reveals the way in which her work opens up for scrutiny the complex relationship between epiphany and the short-story form.

ANALYSIS

Epiphany is a central concept in short-story criticism. Defined by James Joyce as a "sudden spiritual manifestation" (216), the idea of epiphany seems to be implicitly accepted by a range of critics as one of the key elements structuring the short story. Mary Pratt, for example, claims that "the moment of truth stands as the model for the short story the way the life stands as the model for the novel" (183), suggesting that the revelatory nature of epiphany is somehow supported by the short-story form and that it serves as a principle of composition for the writer. This view is qualified by Nadine Gordimer, who argues that "a discrete moment of truth is aimed at—not *the* moment of truth, because the short story doesn't deal in cumulatives" (180; emphasis in original). Yet is the short story indeed the vehicle of epiphanic moments, or might it be instead the instrument for their subversion? Clare Hanson's argument that the short story is "a form which hugs the unknown to itself" (30) suggests that the answer might lie somewhere in between: the short story, while promoting the desire for spiritual insight, might at the same time work implicitly toward denying the possibility of religious certitudes.

This subtle negotiation is evident in the work of Anita Desai. Her short stories bring into sharp relief the difference between epiphany as an underlying structural principle in the short story, provided for by what Hanson has called the "elisions and gaps" in the short story (25), and epiphany as a thematic concern. For while the stories in *Games at Twilight* show a common thematic concern with a moment of truth or insight, their textual construction works toward questioning the value of these insights. Therefore, in order to analyze the way in which Desai interrogates epiphany—a moment of spontaneous, sudden, and transforming spiritual insight—it is necessary to analyze her treatment of spiritual awareness as a whole. Indeed, only two of her stories describe epiphanies, "Studies in the Park" and "Surface Textures," but, as I will show, Desai's subversion of these epiphanies draws upon a broader subversion—one that questions the value of all insight—evident in nearly all the stories in the collection. After analyzing the thematic and structural discontinuities in her work, I will show how Desai localizes epiphany, giving this socially transcendent and universalizing experience a culturally specific bearing.

Illumination is the key theme of Anita Desai's short stories. Its real and metaphorical manifestations not only structure individual stories, but also serve to provide the collection's overall pattern, that element of fiction that Desai has claimed is of most concern to her (Ram, "Interview" 100). The stories move between the "light" of insight, however fleeting, and the "dark" of indifference, between a development toward a moment of truth and an acknowledgment of the elusiveness of individual vision. But as the very title, *Games at Twilight*, suggests, the stories describe potential and partial illumination. Desai conveys this partial illumination by yoking a character's renewed awareness to the twilight hours. Twilight is the time when Raghu learns about the ignominy of defeat in the title story; it is the hour of release for Basu as he finally gains some peace in "Pigeons at Dawn"; it is the best time for reviewing and reflection, as Suno discovers in "Studies in the Park"; it is the hour of conviviality both forced and genuine in "The Farewell Party." In all these stories the conjunction between time and renewed awareness is used to affirm a dream time, a time when the imagination is released, a time when Scheherazade can begin her work of storytelling. It is, in other words, a time for the suspension of belief. This is significant, for it allows Desai to throw into doubt the value if not the validity of the insights gained by her characters.

How does Desai succeed in creating ambiguity in her depiction of spiritual insight? A brief look at the way she combines formal disruptions with implicit social commentary provides an answer. Desai successfully uses a number of different methods to convey a twilight quality: the tense changes in the first-person narratives of "Studies in the Park" and "The Accompanist" emphasize developments in the state of mind of the central character, and the restless shift of focus from one character to another in "Games at Twilight," "The Farewell Party," and "Scholar and Gypsy" draws attention to the temporality and transience of a suspended state of consciousness. This fluid form destabilizes the potential for a unified focus or moral center to the texts. Yet Desai does not stop here. She highlights the divergence between twilight and daylight awareness, exploring the spiritual and emotional conflicts generated by the urge for the fulfillment of self-reflection and the need to meet social obligations and material demands.

This conflict is explored in the story of Mr. Bose, who continues to provide private tuition despite finding it "intolerable, all of it—except, . . . for the seventy-five rupees paid at the end of the month" (*Games* 16). He discovers that "the two halves of the difficult world he had been holding so carefully together, sealing them with reams of poetry, reams of Sanskrit, had split apart into dissonance" (17). The fragile harmony at the end is conveyed in suitably aesthetic terms, with literature and music providing the idiom for an uneasy reconciliation and acceptance: "The grammar re-arranged itself according to rule, corrected itself. The composition into quiet made quite clear the exhaustion of the child, asleep or nearly so. The sounds of dinner being prepared were calm, decorative even. Once more the radio was tuned to music sympathetically sad" (19).

The harmony created between Mr. Bose and his environment is quite clearly an aesthetic construct; his newly acquired tranquillity is described as a fabrication, "a composition into quiet," and it is this overt aestheticism that draws attention to the author's presence. It is as if Desai has stepped out from the shadows to reveal that Bose's state of mind is constructed from an awareness that lies outside his own. The passage provides a gloss of unity and harmony, delineating an aesthetic resolution of material conflict. Yet this exposure of the artifice that goes into the construction of a character's awareness not only draws attention to the external presence of the writer, thereby disrupting a hitherto-seamless narrative, but also emphasizes the very exteriority of this moment of reflection, calling into question its authenticity and value.

This technique for destabilizing individual insight through self-conscious aestheticism is carried over into Desai's treatment of epiphany. In "Studies in the Park," Suno, a stressed student, tries to concentrate on reviewing for his exams in a provincial park. There he sees something that, in his words, "burnt the surfaces of my eyes so that they watered" (31). The exact import of his insight is, significantly, left unclear; what dominates is the form his vision takes. It is a vision of a young woman whom he believes to be dying. The sight of her makes him feel as if he "were gazing at a painting or a sculpture, some work of art" (30). Suno compares the woman's face to "a flower, wax-white and composed, like a Persian lily or a tobacco flower at night," and sees in it "a beauty I had never come across even in a dream." He assumes that her paleness indicates that she is dying, and he even attempts a diagnosis—"she was very ill, with anemia, perhaps, or t.b."—and wonders if the old man accompanying her is "her husband, her father, her lover?" interpreting the intimacy between them as "inhuman" and "divine" (30). Upon this brief glimpse of strangers in the park rests an undefined insight that liberates Suno from his social responsibilities, leading him to abandon his forthcoming exams and his familial commitments.

There is clearly an ironic distance here between the immanent author and the central character, a disjunction allowed for by the use of a first-person narrative rich in hyperbole and melodrama. Although the epiphany is undoubtedly a genuine experience for the central character, Desai's depiction invites the reader to make judgments about it. Not only does she show the epiphany to be based upon a vast number of suppositions, but the overtly romantic rendition of his experience suggests that it is shaped by an aesthetic idealism that renders it immature and vacuous, the product of a highly romantic, self-serving imagination. What is more, Suno's vision of death in life so closely corresponds to his own sense of futility over his exams that it suggests that his epiphany draws upon a desire to escape from exam pressures.

This depiction of epiphany as an escape from social pressures is supported by Desai's treatment of spiritual awareness in general. In "Scholar and Gypsy," Desai wryly juxtaposes an American woman's self-discovery and newly awakened religious awareness with the rationalist perspective of her unimaginative husband. Pat, the American woman, describes her experience in typically extravagant terms as an "escape from India," an escape from "all those Hindu horrors" and all "the greasy Indian masses, whining and cajoling and sneering" (128). This escape involves a reductive, childlike impression of the mountain folk whose harsh life is idealized under Pat's new visionary awareness: "All they have is a black old kettle and a pack of wood on their backs, rope sandals and a few sheep, but they laugh and sing and go striding up the mountains like—like lords" (129).

Yet again Desai has developed a story line that upholds the importance of individual insight while simultaneously creating a formal dissonance that questions the value of this insight. What is more, Desai's contextualization of spiritual experience furthers this destabilization. If the only option for a spiritually transformed person like Suno is to opt out of society altogether (a pattern also found in the epiphanic story "Surface Textures"), it implicitly calls into question the viability of the spiritual experience to penetrate the real contradictions of existence. In "Studies in the Park," it is as if Desai self-consciously locates

Suno's epiphany in a tangibly godless world, exposing the experience as a self-indulgent fabrication and thereby subverting its transcendental potential to break the boundaries between spiritual and material worlds.

These boundaries form the subject of over half of the *Games at Twilight* stories, in which Desai repeatedly draws attention to a character's failure to find a link between spiritual and material worlds, exposing the fragmentation of experience that is the very antithesis of epiphanic awareness. Art and artifice, she suggests, can provide a means of overcoming this fragmentation. Yet even in stories such as "The Accompanist" and "Sale," in which Desai explores the liberating potential of an artist's awareness, she simultaneously reveals its limitations. In "Sale," for example, an artist who paints imaginary birds and flowers is shown to be hopelessly misunderstood by a couple of prospective clients. They withdraw with embarrassment upon interpreting his enthusiasm for personal anecdote as a sign of pressure to buy his paintings. When the painter crosses the boundary between solitary genius and ordinary man, his work, too, is called into question by these devotees of High Art who wish to maintain their romantic view of the artist as gifted genius despite the ample evidence of the symbiotic relationship between material and spiritual need. Art has been created out of the "rags and grime" of the city studio and is less an "inspired act of creation" (43) (as the prospective clients believe) than a habitual way of seeing, a way of surviving both physically and emotionally in the filthy city. The underlying logic of "Sale" is that the truth of imaginative insight, the path toward epiphany, must be publicly denied in order for the artist to achieve material success.

It has been seen that the depiction of spiritual awareness in Desai's short stories is destabilized through a combination of narrative emplotment—focusing on the failed attempts of an individual to permeate the boundaries between material and spiritual worlds—and disruptive formal techniques. This combination works to take the reader out of the text and dissipates the potential for creating the single, reunifying effect of epiphany. It is as if the compression imposed upon the short-story form invites not the integrative vision of epiphany but the dissipation of partial insights. This is substantiated by Desai's disavowal of epiphany in "Surface Textures." Here she brings together several of the techniques found in her treatment of spiritual awareness in a ruthless interrogation of the value of the sudden, spiritual revelation.

"Surface Textures" centers on Harish, a civil servant, who is permanently transformed when he observes the contours of a melon that his wife has brought for lunch: "From the start [he] regarded it with eyes that seemed newly opened. One would have thought he had never seen a melon before" (35). From then on, he is captivated by the sight and shape of everyday objects, paying no attention to anything else. His eyes "slide about" over the surfaces of things, "taking in things normally considered nondescript and unimportant [such as] the paving stones on which . . . feet momentarily pressed, the length of wire in a railing at the side of the road, a pattern of grime on the windowpane of a disused printing press" (36). This aestheticized awareness is clearly induced by an epiphany, yet it leads him not merely to lose his concentration—so that "the people in the queue outside went for another day without rice and sugar and kerosene for their lamps and Janta cookers" (36)—but also to lose his job, his wife, his family, and his home.

Harish's epiphany socially and psychologically dislocates him. His worship of surface textures induces a trancelike state that leads him, in turn, to be the object of devotion. He therefore comes to be socially relocated as a swami. Is Harish mad or is he a mystic? Desai's ironic detachment leaves us little room for doubt. Harish's exclusive contemplation of external reality, including the objects of devotion brought to him, and the contentment of his devotees to interpret his silent form as a manifestation of divinity reveal that both worshippers and worshipped are deluded by appearances. For Harish and his devotees, spiritual awareness is founded upon exteriority. By creating a disjunction between truth and the absolution of spiritual insight, between meaning and its individual interpretation, Desai seems to contend that all truths, including those that are founded upon epiphanic experience, are partial, personal, and plural. In "Surface Textures," Desai has not only made epiphany relative by exploring the difference between objective reality and subjective experience and creating an ironic dissonance between the two, she has contextualized it. In doing so, she has come to interrogate the cultural value placed upon manifestations of divine insight.

Seeing may be believing for the characters of Anita Desai, but the textual disruptions in her short stories question the possibility for lasting, meaningful insight. Indeed, her work seems to promote what Dominic Head has described in his analysis of Joyce as the multidimensional "non-epiphany," one in which epiphany becomes "a nexus of a *variety* of forces rather than a *single* effect" (54, 49; emphasis in original). Such a plural and disruptive form of epiphany may well be one that is imposed upon the short story by the exigencies of the form. Not only does the very length of the short story enforce omission and exclusion, liberating the text from the imposition of authorial commentary, but the very open-endedness—what Clare Hanson has described as the "tangentiality" (23)—of the short story seems to invite, and simultaneously to undermine, the possible rendition of a single-effect, unifying epiphany.

What is more, unlike the unifying, transcendent epiphanies that conclude her novels *Clear Light of Day* and *In Custody*, the relativized epiphanies of Desai's short stories invite the reader to question their meaning and worth. This interrogatory procedure transforms the epiphanies from passive principles—ones that extol the value of passive awareness in the character and passive acceptance in the reader—to an active force that invites the reader to inquire into the very possibility of finding true value. Further, Desai's consistent suggestion that the path to spiritual insight is at odds with social commitments, commitments whose power can seem overwhelming even to those who are familiar with the Indian social context, is revisionary. Through it, she promotes the individual's right to determine the course of his or her life. This right is no mere platitude. It gains real urgency and force when it is set within the Indian social context in which Desai has gone so far as to claim that the concept of the individual does not exist (Salgado 10, 312).

Whether this revisionary impact is the result of a conscious effort by the author is debatable. Desai has repeatedly drawn attention to the need to "compromise with life" and social reality (Salgado 302, 308–9). More important, perhaps, she has suggested that art, the act of writing, is itself a compromise between the experience of epiphany and its articulation:

A writer who wishes to capture the spirit of place requires not the power of observation so much as a burning intensity of vision. If his vision has such intensity, his gaze will become powerful as the magnifying glass that is held between the sun and a sheet of paper, compressing and generating enough heat to burn a ring through the paper. In the end, this is what a book is: the blackened remains of a fire lit by the writer. (Desai, " 'Feng Sui' " 109)

Her view that a book is composed of the residual ashes of a writer's visionary insight delineates the distance between aesthetic aspiration and its outcome. It serves as an emphatic reminder that the textual depiction of epiphany in the short story is characterized not by coherence and cohesion but by distance, discontinuity, and displacement.

WORKS CITED AND CONSULTED

Primary

Desai, Anita. *Baumgartner's Bombay*. London: Heinemann, 1988.
———. *Bye-Bye Blackbird*. Delhi: Orient, 1985.
———. *Clear Light of Day*. London: Heinemann, 1980; Harmondsworth: Penguin, 1982; New York: Harper, 1980.
———. *Cry the Peacock*. Delhi: Orient, 1980.
———. *Fasting, Feasting*. London: Chatto & Windus, 1999.
———. " 'Feng Sui' or Spirit of Place." *Essays in Post-Colonial Literatures*. Ed. Britta Olinder. Gothenburg: Gothenburg University Press, 1984. 101–9.
———. *Fire on the Mountain*. London: Heinemann, 1977; New York: Harper, 1977; Harmondsworth: Penguin, 1981.
———. *Games at Twilight*. London: Heinemann, 1978; New York: Harper, 1978; Harmondsworth: Penguin, 1982.
———. *In Custody*. London: Heinemann, 1984; Harmondsworth: Penguin, 1985.
———. "Indian Women Writers." *The Eye of the Beholder: Indian Writing in English*. Ed. Maggie Butcher. London: Commonwealth Institute, 1983.
———. *Journey to Ithaca*. New York: Knopf, 1995.
———. *The Village by the Sea*. London: Heinemann, 1982; Harmondsworth: Penguin, 1985.

———. *Voices in the City*. Delhi: Orient, 1968.
———. *Where Shall We Go This Summer?* Delhi: Orient, 1982.

Secondary

Afzal-Khan, Fawzia. *Cultural Imperialism and the Indo-English Novel: Genre and Ideology in R. K. Narayan, Anita Desai, Kamala Markandaya, and Salman Rushdie*. University Park: Pennsylvania State University Press, 1993.

Alcock, Peter. "Rope, Serpent, Fire: Recent Fiction of Anita Desai." *Anita Desai: The Woman and the Writer*. Spec. issue of *Journal of Indian Writing in English* 9.1 (January 1981): 15–34.

Asnani, Shyam M. "Anita Desai's Fiction: A New Dimension." *Indian Literature* 24.2 (March–April 1981): 44–54.

Butcher, Maggie, ed. *The Eye of the Beholder: Indian Writing in English*. London: Commonwealth Institute, 1983.

Dalmia, Yashodhara. "An Interview with Anita Desai." *Times of India* April 29, 1979.

Dudt, Charmazel. "Past and Present: A Journey to Confrontation." *Anita Desai: The Woman and the Writer*. Spec. issue of *Journal of Indian Writing in English* 9.1 (January 1981): 67–73.

Gordimer, Nadine. "The Flash of Fireflies." *Short Story Theories*. Ed. Charles E. May, Athens: Ohio University Press, 1976. 178–182.

Hanson, Clare. " 'Things out of Words': Towards a Poetics of Short Fiction." *Re-reading the Short Story*. Ed. Clare Hanson. Basingstoke: Macmillan, 1989. 22–33.

Head, Dominic. *The Modernist Short Story: A Study in Theory and Practice*. Cambridge: Cambridge University Press, 1992.

Joyce, James. *Stephen Hero*. London: Jonathan Cape, 1969.

Mukherjee, Meenakshi. "The Theme of Displacement in Anita Desai and Kamala Markandaya." *World Literature Written in English* 17 (1978): 225–33.

———. *The Twice Born Fiction*. New Delhi: Heinemann, 1971.

Pratt, Mary. "The Short Story: The Long and the Short of It." *Poetics* 10 (1981). 175–194.

Ram, Atma. "Anita Desai: A Bibliography." *Journal of Indian Writing in English* 9 (January 1981): 93–98.

———. "Anita Desai: The Novelist Who Writes for Herself." *Journal of Indian Writing in English* 5.2 (1977): 39–42.

———. "Interview with Anita Desai." *World Literature Written in English* 16 (1977): 95–104.

Salgado, K. Minoli. Personal interview with Anita Desai. "Towards a Definition of Indian Literary Feminism: An Analysis of the Novels of Kamala Markandaya, Nayantara Sahgal, and Anita Desai." Diss. University of Warwick, 1991. 10, 312.

Sharma, R. S. *Anita Desai*. New Delhi: Arnold-Heinemann, 1981.

Shirwadkar, Meena. *Image of Woman in the Indo-Anglian Novel*. New Delhi: Sterling, 1979.

Srinivasa Iyengar, K. R. *Indian Writing in English*. 2nd ed. New York: Asia, 1973.

Srivastava, R. K., ed. *Perspectives on Anita Desai*. Ghaziabad: Vimal, 1984.

Steinvorth, Klaus. *The Indo-English Novel*. Wiesbaden: Franz Steiner, 1975.

Varady, Evelyn. "American and British Responses to Anita Desai's *Games at Twilight and Other Stories*." *Journal of Indian Writing in English* 8.1–2 (1982): 27–34.

Walsh, William. *Indian Literature in English*. London and New York: Longman, 1990.

Weir, Ann Lowry. "The Illusions of Maya: Feminine Consciousness in Anita Desai's *Cry the Peacock*." *Journal of South Asian Literature* 2.6 (Summer–Fall 1979): 149–52.

(KAREN) LOUISE ERDRICH
(June 7, 1954–   )

Norma C. Wilson

BIOGRAPHY

Louise Erdrich, an enrolled member of the Turtle Mountain Chippewa, began at an early age writing stories and making them into books. Born in Little Falls, Minnesota, Erdrich was raised in Wahpeton, North Dakota. Her father, Ralph Erdrich, of German descent, taught at the Wahpeton Bureau of Indian Affairs (BIA) School. When Louise was beginning to write, he sometimes paid her a nickel for a story (Bruchac 78). Erdrich's mother, Rita Gourneau Erdrich, also an employee of the BIA, had grown up on the Turtle Mountain Chippewa Reservation in North Dakota, where Erdrich's grandfather, Patrick Gourneau, had served as tribal chairman (Peterson 87). Erdrich recalls that her mother encouraged her writing talent by weaving strips of construction paper together and stapling them into book covers for her stories (May 146–47). As a child, Louise often visited her mother's family, the Gourneaus, on the reservation, which would become the setting for much of her fiction.

Erdrich attended Dartmouth College, completing a B.A. in 1976. She taught in the Poetry in the Schools Program for the North Dakota Arts Council in 1977–78. In 1978, she received a fellowship to teach composition and creative writing at Johns Hopkins University. Erdrich completed her M.A. at Johns Hopkins in 1979. She then moved to Boston and edited the Boston Indian Council newspaper the *Circle*. In 1980, she was a MacDowell Colony fellow. She was a Yaddo Colony fellow in 1981 and received a National Endowment for the Arts Fellowship in 1982. Her novel *Love Medicine* won the National Book Critics Circle Award for the Best Work of Fiction for 1984. The novel has been published in ten foreign-language editions.

Erdrich married Michael Dorris, head of Dartmouth's Native American Studies Program, in 1981. Dorris had three adopted children, and three additional children were born to the couple. They had a collaborative writing relationship and coauthored a number of short stories and a novel, *The Crown of Columbus*. Erdrich, Dorris, and their children lived in New Hampshire, Montana, and Minnesota. The couple separated in 1995. Dorris took his life in 1997.

CRITICISM

Erdrich has received wide critical acclaim for her short fiction, which first gained attention from a large audience in 1982, when her story "The World's Greatest Fishermen" won the Nelson Algren Award from *Chicago* magazine. The story would become the first chapter of Erdrich's first novel, *Love Medicine* (1984). Her story "Scales," which would become another chapter of the novel, was included in *The Best American Short Stories* for 1983. Critic Suzanne Ferguson focused on four of Erdrich's prize-winning short stories—"Scales," "Saint Marie," also from *Love Medicine*, and "Fleur" and "Snares" from Erdrich's novel *Tracks*—in her article "The Short Stories of Louise Erdrich's Novels." Ferguson says that "in the short story, the reader is more likely to focus on theme and symbol, which allow us to process the text as a meaningful construct, rather than on verisimilitude" (541). Her discussion of the themes of the four stories is a convincing argument that "it is perhaps only when we incorporate the individual chapters [of Erdrich's novels] as 'short stories' that we most clearly perceive how the meaning and value arises from experience through the process of making it a story" (554).

When Erdrich was interviewed by Laura Coltelli, she credited Michael Dorris with helping her to make the transition from writing stories and poems to writing novels (49). According to John Purdy, "Anishinabe [Chippewa] literary motifs are found throughout *Love Medicine*: the westward road of the dead, the prevalence of water as a metaphor and allusion to tribal history, the image of fish and fishing, the respect and awe for people of power who possess obscure knowledge" (428). While Elaine Jahner acknowledges that *Love Medicine* "derives much of its complexity from its truth to the culture of the Turtle Mountain Chippewa Tribe in North Dakota," she recognizes the novel's universality: "It's compulsive fascination comes from the fact that she knows how to tell grand stories about characters whose intensity shatters banality and leaves us rethinking the whole matter of being human" (96).

Critic Carol Hunter compared the novel's structure to Edgar Lee Masters's *Spoon River Anthology* (474). Erdrich's narrative technique, using flashbacks, stream of consciousness, and multiple narrators, is also similar to that of William Faulkner. Her work is also like Faulkner's in its rather circumscribed locale and rural setting and in the centrality of the told story. Recognizing Erdrich's writing accomplishments early in her career, the editors of *Studies in American Indian Literatures* devoted the winter 1985 issue to her writing. An article in this issue by Linda Ainsworth compares *Love Medicine*'s structure to that of two Faulkner novels, *As I Lay Dying* and *Go Down, Moses*. Ainsworth explains that like *As I Lay Dying*, Erdrich's novel centers on a female character who dies early in the narrative; the following "chapters build upon remembrances of her"; and the other characters "distinguish themselves by their varying responses to her death and what kinds of memories they have of her" (27). She points out that "*Go Down, Moses*, like *Love Medicine*, is made up of several stories whose connections are never made explicit. Readers must puzzle out what links them together on their own." She further states that the novel is "made up of stories that have an integrity of their own. Stories are juxtaposed against other stories. Oftentimes they seem to collide with one another. Out of this collision emerges a new, more complex story—one that is never really 'told' " (27). Referring to Ainsworth's article, Purdy says that Erdrich's greatest strengths as a novelist and storyteller are "her complete absorption in one landscape and the people who inhabit it . . . and her ability to 'layer' points of view through a diversity of characters, a polyphony of voices speaking of this place and each other over a long period of time" (423–24).

Kathleen Sands describes *Love Medicine* as "metafiction, ironically self-conscious in its mode of telling, concerned as much with exploring the process of storytelling as with the story itself" (12). Sands distinguishes Erdrich from other Native American fiction writers, saying that "the storytelling process she draws upon is not the traditional ceremonial process of the reenactment of sacred myth, nor is it strictly the tradition of telling tales on winter nights. . . . The source of her storytelling technique is the secular anecdotal narrative process of community gossip" (14).

The thread of community gossip runs through Erdrich's later fiction as well. It informs the eleven short stories that Erdrich wove into her second novel, *The Beet Queen* (1986). The stories making up *The Beet Queen*, set between 1932 and 1972, are roughly contemporary with those in *Love Medicine*, but unlike her first novel, *The Beet Queen* focuses on the northern European immigrant population of Argus, a fictional small North Dakota town, and the people of the surrounding agricultural area, extending eastward to the Twin Cities. Over half of the stories making up this second novel had been published earlier as short stories.

The stories that make up Erdrich's third novel, *Tracks* (1988), describe the painful transitional period between 1912 and 1924 when the land of the Chippewa people was taken and exploited by the whites. Four of the chapters making up this novel had been published earlier as short stories. Purdy calls *Tracks* "a storytelling session in which Erdrich makes the invisible apparent to her readers, and the lesson it provides compelling." Referring to this novel, he points out that Erdrich's books "fit not only into the relatively recent tradition of written fiction by Native Americans, but also into the ancient traditions of spoken literature on this continent" (428).

In a new and expanded edition of *Love Medicine*, published in 1993, Erdrich included four stories that were not part of the original edition, "The Island," "Resurrection," "The Tomahawk Factory," and "Lyman's Luck." An additional section has also been added to her story "The Beads." Erdrich's new edition clarifies the historical and family background for the novel and prepares readers for her fourth novel, *The Bingo Palace* (1994). *The Bingo Palace* continues the stories of the characters in *Love Medicine*, though from more limited perspectives, alternating between the third-person perspective of someone living in the Chippewa community and that of Lipsha Morrissey.

Reviewer Peter Beidler compares *The Bingo Palace* to Erdrich's first novel, saying that before *Love Medicine*, Erdrich was "a writer of short stories who noticed one day that, hey, maybe she had a novel here" (274). However, after *The Bingo Palace*, he sees her as "a writer who knows what she has to offer to the world and offers it with boldness and love." Beidler points out the differences between Erdrich's and Faulkner's work, the most obvious being that "Faulkner's was a white world with a few Indians at the margins, while Erdrich's is an Indian world with a few whites at the margins" (272). He adds, "The importance of spirit, love and cooperation in Erdrich's imagined North Dakota world makes it quite different from Faulkner's Mississippi" (272).

In "Louise Erdrich's 'Scarlet Letter': Literary Continuity in *Tales of Burning Love*," Thomas Matchie emphasizes Erdrich's place in American literature, pointing out that Herman Melville, Flannery O'Connor, and Mark Twain have all influenced her work, but focusing on the influence of Nathaniel Hawthorne. In a psychological analysis of Erdrich's novel, Matchie compares the five women in *Tales of Burning Love* to the five selves of Hawthorne's Hester Prynne.

ANALYSIS

Erdrich's short fiction is characterized by the thematic ingredient of love medicine, the thread binding all her work. Subjecting her stories to constant revision and expansion, Erdrich has intricately connected them to each other. This pattern of stories is richly diverse in characters who are imagined whole, but in a non-linear time frame. They are Chippewa and European in ancestry, urban and rural, conservative and radical, traditional and modern, and they are always seen in relationship. The lone protagonist disappears in the web of characters that people Erdrich's stories.

In an interview with Joseph Bruchac, Erdrich said that she has an "urgent reason for thinking about women attuned to their power and their honest nature" (82). Such women fill her stories, from her first published to her most recent. A comparison of two of these stories, "The True Story of Mustache Maude" (1984) and "The Leap" (1990), illustrates the development of Erdrich's skill as a writer and the increasingly complex themes that rise from her stories.

Relationships between women are important in both stories, and in both, women settle down after a period of wandering to find meaning and relationship. The daughter of an "Italian Lothario" and a beautiful Chippewa woman named Mahngatosie (Loon Heart), Maude tells her life story. Her parents performed in a play, *The Traveling Legend of Pocahontas*. After her father's death from a heart attack, Maude wandered with her mother through Minnesota until one day, fording the Little Missouri River, Loon Heart "eased off her horse and began to float downstream." After telling Maude not to follow, she lifted into the air, circled three times, and "her mate joined her forever" (63). Orphaned Maude wanders, eventually becoming a cattle rustler who makes her home in the North Dakota Badlands, where she steals the "rare blue sow" and becomes the only friend of the Countess Svagmadda, another Badlands resident. The Countess appears one day to take back the hog, which by this time has proven such a bother that Maude wants to sell her back to the Countess. Instead, the Countess challenges Maude to a duel. As the women fight, wearing dresses that are armed with weapons, they happen to touch each other's softness, look into each other's eyes, and fall in love. Their "secret canyon" becomes a "love retreat," and the women live together until the Countess disappears after diving into the Garrison Reservoir. At the end of this tall tale, Maude finds comfort in the reflection of the sky in the water, which "asks blankness from all else" (67). She sees blankness in her own face, except for the whiskers that keep appearing and that she plucks out and shaves at the beginning and end of this amusing, though preposterous, spoof of Paul Bunyan.

"The Leap" is also about the relationship between women, a daughter and her mother who live in New Hampshire. The narrator is the daughter of Anna, the "surviving half of a blindfold trapeze act." As the story begins, Anna walks slowly through her house without upsetting anything or losing her balance, though she is blinded by cataracts. "I owe her my existence three times," the narrator says, proceeding to tell the three stories that make up the whole. Before the narrator was born, her mother was one of the Flying Avalons until the night lightning struck the main pole, causing the circus tent to buckle and Harry Avalon to fall to his death. Knowing that her husband's hands had not met her at the proper time, Anna, who was seven months pregnant, had torn off her blindfold, changed direction, and grabbed a heavy wire of "braided metal, still hot from the lightning strike" (66). Though her hands were severely burned, she was not seriously injured until an "overeager rescuer broke her arm" and caused a part of the tent to collapse, a buckle of which "knocked her unconscious." Anna's child was born dead, but while she was recuperating in the hospital, her doctor taught her to read. After that, Anna stopped flying on the trapeze and began flying by means of books. She married the doctor, moved to a farmhouse on land he had inherited, and gave birth to a daughter, the narrator.

The daughter's second story, like the first, illustrates her mother's courage and quick thinking. When she was seven, their farmhouse caught fire, and the burning stairs prevented the narrator from escaping her room. Arriving home with her husband to find the house in flames, Anna realized that her daughter was trapped, tore off her dress, used an extension ladder to climb to the branches of a tree, and then leapt from the tree to a new gutter attached to the roof of the house. "Hanging by the backs of her heels" from the gutter, she tapped on her daughter's window, motioning for her to prop it open. Then Anna crawled inside her daughter's room, gathered her into her lap, and jumped with her daughter into the firefighters' net.

In the third story, which contains the other two, the daughter returns to the house she grew up in after a "failed life where the land is flat" (67). By returning to the place where she had lived as a child, the narrator has been able to re-connect with the past, symbolized by her half sister's tombstone. Her father has died, and she has come home to read to her mother and to care for her, to turn off the stove when she smells smoke. The return has rekindled her love for her mother, illustrated in the last words of the story, in which the narrator recalls, "I felt the brush of her lips and heard the beat of her heart in my ears, loud as thunder, long as the roll of drums" (68). This statement unites the three stories with images that connect the daughter's love for her mother to their need for each other. It is this "love medicine" that is the thematic thread binding Erdrich's writings to each other.

To an extent that is unique among writers, Erdrich has revised and expanded her stories, even after they have been published. The pattern formed by the relationships between her characters is a midwestern patchwork of Chippewa and European. Though her stories have originated in wide-ranging settings, Er-drich has pieced them into the North Dakota landscape where she was raised.

In the first section of "The World's Greatest Fishermen," which would be-come the first chapter of Erdrich's novel *Love Medicine* (1984), we meet June Kashpaw, walking on the "morning before Easter Sunday" in the oil-boom town of Williston, North Dakota (*Love Medicine*, 1984 edition, 1). The year is 1981. "Killing time" (like the mythological trickster) while waiting to catch a bus, June responds to a man motioning to her from inside and enters a bar. Thinking that this man "could be different," she misses the bus and spends the evening drinking with him. Then they go parking on a country road. The man passes out on top of her, and June manages to push open the door and get out of his pickup. After feeling "a shock like being born," June begins to walk, not back toward Williston, but toward the Turtle Mountain Reservation, her home, over two hundred miles to the northeast. Caught in a blizzard, she dies, but not in spirit: "June walked over it [the snow] like water and came home" (*Love Medicine* 6).

June's niece, Albertine Johnson, narrates the remaining three sections of "The World's Greatest Fishermen." A nursing student at the university in Fargo, Al-bertine is upset with her mother, Zelda, because she failed to notify her of June's death so she could attend the funeral. After spring classes are over, Albertine returns to the reservation. Through her eyes, we are introduced to her extended family and learn of the family and tribal history. Though Albertine is young, she is strong, intelligent, and perceptive, with a sense of irony and humor.

Through the four scenes in this narrative, Erdrich introduces the reader to a wide range of characters. Some, like Albertine and her cousin Lipsha, try to make a meaningful pattern of their lives; others, like King and Gordie, are so miserably debilitated by alcohol and their loss of June that they cannot put the fragments back together. These characters reappear in the stories that follow. Approximately half of the novel's fourteen interconnected short stories were published either before or after the novel was issued. Covering a fifty-year time span, from 1934 to 1983, the stories, along with Erdrich's first book of poems, *Jacklight* (1984), initiated the themes, motifs, structure, and style Erdrich would use for her later fiction.

Erdrich's second novel, *The Beet Queen* (1986), focuses on the northern European immigrant population of Argus, a small North Dakota town, and the people of the surrounding agricultural area, extending southwestward to Rapid City, South Dakota, and eastward to Minneapolis and St. Paul, Minnesota. The eleven short stories pieced into the novel are set between 1932 and 1972, just a bit earlier than the time frame of *Love Medicine*. The one transitional character between these novels is Dot Adare, the daughter of Celestine James, a mixed-blood Chippewa, and Karl Adare, of German ancestry. Dot is the novel's Beet Queen.

Erdrich's meticulous attention to her craft is apparent when one compares the initial version of "The Air Seeder" to the version published in *The Beet Queen*. Between the story's initial publication and its inclusion as chapter 6 of the novel, Erdrich made a number of improvements, including character development. Dot's father, Karl Adare, who is trying to sell an air seeder, and the land speculator, Demeray Pfef, took on more clearly defined personalities. Nevertheless, the story did not undergo major changes before being pieced whole into the novel.

"The Air Seeder" humorously illustrates an Erdrich theme: the urgency and difficulty of forming relationships. This is especially apparent when two strangers like Adare and Pfef get together. Their initial encounter is a mundane meeting between two businessmen, but by the end of the story, the two have become sexual partners. Wanting to shock Pfef, who bores him because of his nervousness and sensitivity, Karl inadvertently makes himself vulnerable and breaks his neck trying to turn a somersault off the bed of his hotel room. No one can claim that in Erdrich's fiction nothing ever happens. The amazing thing is that the dramatic, often-bizarre things that are always happening to her characters make sense, even though their actions are as awkward and ill considered as those of average human beings.

The stories in Erdrich's third novel, *Tracks* (1988), reach back into the first quarter of the twentieth century. The novel's chapters are narrated by two characters, an unreliable mixed-blood named Pauline and an elderly Chippewa man, Nanapush. He narrates chapter 5, the central portion of which was initially published as "Snares" in the May 1987 issue of *Harper's Magazine* and was selected for *The Best American Short Stories* (1988). Set in 1924, "Snares" dramatizes the conflicts among the Chippewa people over a treaty with the U.S. government to cede a portion of their land. Nanapush tells the story of his own resistance, which coincided with his love affair with Margaret Kashpaw. The story begins and ends at the Catholic church, where Nanapush has an amusing conversation with Father Damien. "These benches are a hardship for an old man," Nanapush says. "If you spread them with soft pine-needle cushions I'd have come before" (60). The priest answers, "You must think of their unyielding surfaces as helpful. . . . God sometimes enters the soul through the humblest parts of our anatomies if they are sensitized to suffering." Not to be outdone, Nanapush counters, "A god who enters through the rear door . . . is no better than a thief." Nanapush decides, "Our original gods were better, the Chippewa characters who were not exactly perfect but at least did not require sitting on hard boards."

But the story gets serious when Nanapush and Margaret are captured on their way home by Morrissey and Lazarre, who signed the treaty and are angry at Margaret for speaking out against it. They tie Nanapush and Margaret up in a barn. Margaret fights back, biting Lazarre and drawing blood. Nanapush tries to talk their way out of captivity, mentioning, among other things, that Fleur Pillager, a powerful witch, is Margaret's son's wife. Nevertheless, Lazarre orders Morrissey to smash Nanapush. When he comes to, Nanapush sees that Lazarre has sliced off Margaret's long braids and is shaving her scalp. Her braids have been tied around Nanapush's mouth as a gag to silence him. When the two are finally released, they walk to Margaret's house and begin to plan their revenge.

By the end of the story, Nanapush and Margaret are planning to marry. Father Damien tells Nanapush that he should confess, and Nanapush details his sins, including that of snaring Morrissey like a rabbit and stealing the wire to do it from the priest's piano. He tells Father Damien that he will return the wire and will never again use his snares on humans. Lazarre has been caught anyway, his arm infection from Margaret's bite causing his death. "The Snare," placed at the center of *Tracks*, epitomizes the violent conflicts of the early twentieth century, not only between the U.S. government and the Chippewa nation, but among the Chippewa people themselves. Internal conflicts that continued throughout the century weakened relationships within the tribe.

Conflicts within families and within the tribe are evident in "The Tomahawk Factory," one of the four new stories Erdrich included in her expanded version of *Love Medicine* (1993). In this story, Lulu Nanapush and Marie Kashpaw, once rivals for former tribal chairman Nector Nashpaw, cause a riot in the tribe's new tomahawk factory. With the stories added to the new edition, Erdrich extends the time frame for the book and more firmly connects the first novel to her fourth, *The Bingo Palace* (1994).

Internal Chippewa conflicts are also evident in *The Bingo Palace*. Three of the novel's chapters were published separately as short stories. "The Bingo Van," which with slight alterations is chapter 7, was first published in the *New Yorker*. The story is narrated by the son of June Kashpaw and Gerry Nanapush of *Love Medicine*. Lipsha has lived an ambitionless, yet spiritual life, with mixed success as a healer. Good hearted, yet naïve, Lipsha finds his healing ability lessened once he begins charging for his services; and he finds that achieving the American Dream, via ownership of a bingo van, negatively affects his love medicine. Like most Americans, even a Chippewa man like Lipsha feels a certain amount of pressure to be viewed as materially successful. Lipsha attempts to rise in status, not out of pride, but in his effort to win Serena, the woman of his dreams. His quest is complicated by the fact that he works in a bingo hall for the financially successful Lyman Lamartine, his rival for Serena's affections and the father of her son Jason. Lipsha wins two hundred dollars by choosing a lucky number on a U-Pickem card, which gives him the courage to go out with Serena.

After spending a night with Serena, he gladly gives her the remainder of the money he has won to help her open a clothing-design shop. Soon he is lucky again, this time winning at bingo the van he has coveted. But after his initial high, riding around in the van, things go downhill, and Lipsha realizes that part of his loss is his own fault: "In that van, I rode high, but that's the thing. Looking down on others, even if it's only from the seat of a van that a person never really earned, does something to the human mentality" (in Lesley 92). When he first got the van, Lipsha could have offered to drive Serena's sick son to the clinic; instead he went out partying and wound up getting taken for a ride by some white guys from Montana. Lipsha was dumped at a tattoo parlor; he left with a tattoo of a little horse on his hand and wearing "big-waisted green pants" belonging to the tattooist. He found his bingo van "smashed on the sides, kicked and scratched, and the insides are scattered" (in Lesley 99). Nevertheless, part of the seat makes a bed for him, and the story ends, "Sinking away, I feel like everything worth having is within my grasp. All I have to do is put my hand into the emptiness" (in Lesley 99).

Thus, as he enjoys his rest, Lipsha affirms one of Erdrich's predominant themes. It is not the riches treasured by society that make life worth living, but rather the basic human understanding that enables one to be comfortable on this earth. Lipsha's van has been totalled, but it provides a plush bed, and that is what he needs. By telling the stories of Lipsha and other Chippewa characters, Erdrich not only affirms this native culture's survival in the modern world, but shows the rest of us what is truly important in life, how to better appreciate what we do have, how to preserve our sense of irony and humor, how to survive when it seems that we have lost everything.

Louise Erdrich's fiction can best be compared to a quilt or a beadwork design, with love medicine like a thread binding it. That relationships are to be nurtured as essential to community life is a prominent theme. This nurturing, so necessary to survival, is a component of tribal life too often neglected in the centuries since Europeans began to displace the tribes and take over the American land. The design of Erdrich's stories, both within and between her novels, is made of her characters' efforts to establish relationships and to maintain them. Her careful connections between characters and their stories as she has continued to write accentuate these relationships.

The love-medicine theme continues in Erdrich's novel *Tales of Burning Love* (1996), which returns in its first chapter to the scene described in the first section of "The World's Greatest Fishermen" from *Love Medicine*, but now with the focus on Jack Mauser, the man June meets in a Williston bar. Thinking that he is dead, four of Jack's former wives tell each other their tales of loving him.

Erdrich pieced seven previously published stories into this novel. One of them, "The Leap," was discussed earlier. In *Tales of Burning Love*, Erdrich severely fragments, expands, and transforms the story, changing its setting to North Dakota and shifting the love emphasis from that of mother and daughter to heterosexual love. Sensational in the extreme, this novel features, among other things, Anna's husband (now an undertaker) crawling into the crematorium after her death to be incinerated with her remains. Certainly this novel fits neatly within the larger quilt of Erdrich's fiction, but the short story, "The Leap," is the more powerful work of literature. Erdrich's ability to piece stories together in this novel and to keep the reader interested and engaged is admirable; yet it seems that the cutting and sewing involved in connecting her stories may have consumed too much of her creative energy in *Tales of Burning Love*.

Her next book, *The Antelope Wife* (1998), is more successful, perhaps because it is closer to the storytelling style of the Chippewa. Loosely constructed of related stories, the book presents a fictional history of the inhabitants of Erdrich's North Dakota and Minnesota relatives and neighbors. Though it is subtitled *A Novel*, it stretches the genre farthest of any of her works. Like many other Native American writers, Erdrich seems unbound by the traditional form of the English novel. In *The Antelope Wife*, Erdrich self-consciously uses beadwork as a metaphor for her construction of stories, fitting them into the framework of female artists sewing beadwork patterns. The stories begin with a myth in which twin sisters are sewing, "each trying to upset the balance of the world," and end with several questions and statements by the author, a feature of metafiction, in which Erdrich asks such metaphysical questions as "Who is beading us?" (240).

In between are some marvelously hilarious and horrific stories of relationships and conflicts going back more than a century. The reader marvels at Erdrich's storytelling abilities. After killing an Ojibwa woman in an attack on her village in 1862, Scranton Roy, a private in the U.S. Cavalry, is able to produce the breast milk so desperately needed by a baby he rescues. "Almost Soup," a white dog, explains how he was able to survive to old age only through what he calls "dog magic" (75). The stories in this book are as varied as life. They are urban and rural, historical and contemporary, third-person and first-person. The characters frustrate the gender stereotypes of Euro-American culture in that the most successful men are nurturers, and the most successful women are artists, students, and entrepreneurs. The most destructive character, Richard Whiteheart Beads, inadvertently causes his daughter's death and eventually takes his own life. The antelope wife of the title, also called "Sweetheart Callico," is finally freed from life in the city (*Gakahbekong* in Chippewa) when Klaus Shawano, the man who had kidnapped her years earlier, releases her on the flat land. Though none of the characters from her previous books reappear in *The Antelope*

Wife, the book is tied to the others thematically and is one of Erdrich's most complex and meaningful portrayals of the lives of Chippewa people.

WORKS CITED AND CONSULTED

Primary

Dorris, Michael, and Louise Erdrich. "A Baby between Us." *Redbook* 177.1 (May 1991): 50+.

————. *The Crown of Columbus*. New York: HarperCollins, 1991.

Erdrich, Louise. "The Air Seeder." *Antaeus* (Autumn 1985): 212–17.

————. "American Horse." *Earth Power Coming*. Ed. Simon J. Ortiz. Tsaile, AZ: Navajo Community College Press, 1983. 59–72.

————. *The Antelope Wife*. New York: Harper Flamingo, 1998.

————. *Baptism of Desire: Poems*. New York: Harper, 1989.

————. "The Beads." *North Dakota Quarterly* 52.2 (Spring 1984): 54–61.

————. "The Beet Queen." *Paris Review* 27 (Spring 1985): 10–26.

————. *The Beet Queen*. New York: Henry Holt, 1986.

————. "Best Western." *Vogue* May 1990: 288+.

————. *The Bingo Palace*. New York: HarperCollins, 1994.

————. "The Bingo Van." *New Yorker* February 19, 1990: 39–47. Rpt. in *Talking Leaves: Contemporary Native American Short Stories*. Ed. Craig Lesley. New York: Dell, 1991. 82–89.

————. *The Birchbark House*. New York: Hyperion Books for Children, 1999.

————. *Blue Jay's Dance: A Birth Year*. New York: HarperCollins, 1995.

————. "A Change of Light." *Redbook*. Under (pen-name) Milou North, a collaboration (October 1980).

————. "Chez Sita." *Minneapolis–St. Paul Magazine* August 1986

————. "Crown of Thorns." *Chicago* September 1984: 206+.

————. "Destiny:" *Atlantic Monthly* January 1985: 64–68.

————. "The Dress." *Mother Jones* July–August 1990: 50–54+.

————. "Flesh and Blood." *Ms.* November 1984: 74, 75+.

————. "Fleur." *Esquire* August 1986: 52–55+.

————. "Fleur's Luck." *Georgia Review* 47 (Winter 1993): 659–63.

————. "Flight." *American Short Fiction* 2.5 (Spring 1992).

————. "I'm a Mad Dog Biting Myself for Sympathy." *Granta* 34 (Fall 1990): 135+.

————. "The Island." *Ms.* January–February 1991: 38–42.

————. *Jacklight*. New York: Holt, Rinehart, & Winston, 1984; London: Abacus, 1990.

————. "Knives." *Chicago* August 1986: 108+.

————. *Last Reports on the Miracles at Little No Horse*. New York: HarperCollins, 1999.

————. "The Leap." *Harper's* March 1990: 65–68.

————. "Line of Credit." *Harper's* April 1992: 55–60.

————. "Listeners Unite." *Redbook*. Under (pen-name) Heidi Louise, a collaboration (October 1980).

————. "The Little Book." *Formations* Spring 1985.

————. *Love Medicine*. New York: Holt, Rinehart, & Winston, 1984. Expanded ed. New York: HarperCollins, 1993.

————. "Lulu's Boys." *Kenyon Review* no. 6.3 (Summer 1984): 1–10.

————. "Mary Stamper." *USA Today* July 22, 1994: USW8+.

————. "Matchimanito." *Atlantic* July 1988. Rpt. in *The Best of the West 2*. Ed. James Thomas and Denise Thomas. New York: Norton, 1988. 66–74.

————. "Mauser." *New Yorker* April 8, 1991: 38–42.

————. "Mister Argus." *Georgia Review* 39 (Summer 1985): 379–90.

————. "Naked Woman Playing Chopin." *New Yorker* July 27, 1998: 62–67.

————. "Nuclear Detergent." *New England Review and Bread Loaf Quarterly* 5.4 (Summer 1983): 593–601.

————. "Old Man Potchikoo." *Jacklight*. New York: Holt, Rinehart, & Winston; London: Abacus, 1990. 74–78. Also published in *The Oxford Book of Modern Fairy Tales*. Ed. Alison Lurie. New York: Oxford University Press, 1993.

————. "The Plunge of the Brave." *New England Review* 15 (Fall 1993): 57–70.

————. "Pounding the Dog." *Kenyon Review* no. 7.4 (Fall 1985): 18–28.

————. "The Red Convertible." *Mississippi Valley Review* Summer 1981.

————. "Saint Marie." *Atlantic Monthly* March 1984: 78–84.

————. "Satan: Hijacker of a Planet." *Atlantic Monthly* August 1997: 64–68.

————. "Scales." *North American Review* 267 (March 1982): 22–27. Rpt. in *The Best American Short Stories, 1983*. Ed. Shannon Ravenel and Anne Tyler. Boston: Houghton Mifflin, 1983. 141–154.

————. "Sita Kozka." *Ms*. August 1986: 52+.

————. "Snares." *Harper's Magazine* May 1987: 60–64. Rpt. in *The Best American Short Stories, 1988*. 60–64.

————. *Tales of Burning Love*. New York: HarperCollins, 1996.

————. *Tracks*. New York: Henry Holt, 1988.

————. "The True Story of Mustache Maude." *Frontiers* 7.3 (1984): 62–67.

————. "A Wedge of Shade." *New Yorker* March 6, 1989: 35–40.

————. "Where I Ought to Be: A Writer's Sense of Place." *New York Times Book Review* July 28, 1985: 6, 23.

————. "Wild Geese." *Mother Jones* October 1984: 21–22.

————. "The World's Greatest Fishermen." *Chicago* October 1982: 159+.

Secondary

Ainsworth, Linda. "Response to *Love Medicine*." *Studies in American Indian Literatures* 9.1 (Winter 1985): 24–29.

Beidler, Peter. "Review of *The Bingo Palace*." *American Indian Culture and Research Journal* 18.3 (1994): 271–75.

Bruchac, Joseph. *Survival This Way: Interviews with American Indian Poets*. Tucson: University of Arizona Press, 1987.

Chavkin, Allan Richard, ed. *The Chippewa Landscape of Louise Erdrich*. Tuscaloosa: University of Alabama Press, 1999.

Coltelli, Laura. *Winged Words: American Indian Writers Speak*. Lincoln: University of Nebraska Press, 1990.

Ferguson, Suzanne. "The Short Stories of Louise Erdrich's Novels." *Studies in Short Fiction* 33.4 (Fall 1996): 541–55.

George, Jan. "Interview with Louise Erdrich." *North Dakota Quarterly* 53.2 (Spring 1985): 240–46.

Gleason, William. " 'Her Laugh an Ace': The Function of Humor in Louise Erdrich's *Love Medicine." American Indian Culture and Research Journal* 11.3 (1987): 51–73.

Hall, Sharon K., ed. *Contemporary Literary Criticism Yearbook 1985.* Vol. 39. Detroit: Gale Research Co., 1986. 128–134.

Hower, Edward. "Magic Recaptured." Rev. of *The Bingo Palace. Wall Street Journal* January 4, 1994.

Hunter, Carol. "A Review of *Love Medicine." World Literature Today* 59.3 (Summer 1985): 474.

Jahner, Elaine. "A Review of *Love Medicine." Parabola* 10.2 (May 1985): 96, 98, 100.

Kroeber, Karl, ed. "Louise Erdrich." "Bibliographies of Fourteen Native American Poets." *Studies in American Indian Literatures* 9.1 (1985): 1–41.

Matchie, Thomas. "Louise Erdrich's 'Scarlet Letter': Literary Continuity in *Tales of Burning Love." North Dakota Quarterly* 63.4 (Fall 1996): 113–23.

May, Hal, ed. *Contemporary Authors.* Vol. 114. Detroit: Gale Research Co., 1985. 146–147.

Owens, Louis. *Other Destinies.* Norman: University of Oklahoma Press, 1992.

Peterson, Janet. "Louise Erdrich." *Native American Women.* Ed. Gretchen M. Bataille. New York: Garland Publishing, 1993. 87–88.

Purdy, John Lloyd. "(Karen) Louise Erdrich." *Dictionary of Native American Literature.* Ed. Andrew Wiget. New York: Garland Publishing, 1994. 423–29.

Rainwater, Catherine. "Reading between Worlds: Narrativity in the Fiction of Louise Erdrich." *American Literature: A Journal of Literary History, Criticism, and Bibliography* 62.3 (September 1990): 405–22.

Sands, Kathleen M. "Response to *Love Medicine." Studies in American Indian Literatures* 9.1 (Winter 1985): 12–14.

Stead, Deborah. "Unlocking the Tale." *New York Times Book Review* October 2, 1988: 41.

Strouse, Jean. "In the Heart of the Heartland." *New York Times Book Review* October 2, 1988: 1, 41, 42.

Walsh, Dennis M., and Ann Braley. "The Indianness of Louise Erdrich's *The Beet Queen." American Indian Culture and Research Journal* 18.3 (1994): 1–17.

Wiget, Andrew. "Louise Erdrich" (headnote). *The Health Anthology of American Literature.* Vol. 2. Ed. Paul Lauter et al. 2nd ed. Lexington, MA: D.C. Heath, 1994. 3133–34.

RICHARD FORD
(February 16, 1944–   )

Larry D. Griffin

BIOGRAPHY

Richard Ford was born on February 16, 1944, in Jackson, Mississippi, the only son of Parker Ford, a traveling salesman, and his wife, Edna, a homemaker. Ford grew up in Jackson, Mississippi, and Little Rock, Arkansas, then attended Michigan State University as an undergraduate. He studied law at Washington University in St. Louis, served briefly in the U.S. Marine Corps, and in 1970 received his M.F.A. from the University of California at Irvine, where he studied under E. L. Doctorow. In 1968, Ford married Kristina Hensley, who had a Ph.D. in city planning. During the 1970s he taught creative writing at Princeton, Williams College, and the University of Michigan. In 1977, he received a Guggenheim Fellowship, and a National Endowment for the Arts Fellowship followed in 1978. In 1987, he received the Mississippi Academy of Arts and Letters' Literature Award.

Several of Ford's stories in *Rock Springs* (1987) as well as the novel *Wildlife* (1990) are set in Montana, where the Fords moved when Kristina became the planning director of Bozeman, Montana. Currently, however, Ford divides his time among his leased plantation house in the Mississippi Delta, a house trailer in Chinook, Montana, a nineteenth-century Bourbon Street townhouse in New Orleans (where Kristina now works as the executive director of the City Planning Commission), and an apartment in Paris, France. Two of the three stories in his 1997 collection), *Women with Men*, are set mostly in France; the third is set in Montana.

In 1980, Ford received the American Academy and Institute of Arts and Letters Award for Literature. In 1995, he received the Rea Award for his contributions to short fiction, and in 1996, he received both the PEN/Faulkner Award and the Pulitzer Prize for Fiction for *Independence Day*.

CRITICISM

The landscape of Montana is an essential component in Richard Ford's collection *Rock Springs*. As Raymond A. Schroth suggests, the "stories and characters so spring from their landscapes and physical situations as to personify the spirit of the motels, roadside bars, lakes and highways where we encounter them" (227). In an interview with Kay Bonetti, Ford himself explains that "a place makes itself felt entirely through particulars" (71), elsewhere noting that "places don't have essences. They're too profuse and incalculable. Their essentialness and their appeal is in their specificity" (Ford, "Place" 68).

In characterizing the place of Sunburst, Montana, in the story "Children," Ford may be said to utilize a device termed by Richard Hugo as "the triggering town" (7). While Hugo's analysis applies specifically to poetry, its insight is applicable here because it suggests a distinction between the sense of a place and the essence of a place. The "triggering town," a fictional setting within which a poem (or story) unfolds, is a location in the imagination only. Without essence, it provides a source of "creative stability" and thus grants the author possession of the emotional resonance—or sense—of itself (12). Indeed, as Ford writes in "I Must Be Going," "imagination . . . thrives in us by extending partial knowledge to complete any illusion of reality" (104).

Ford suggests that his stories concern the accommodation of character to place (Green 72). Yet Phillip Orr, in his review of *Rock Springs*, insists that the stories in Ford's collection emphasize the individual's aloneness in the world. Perceiving a distance between the characters and their emotions, and a resulting inability to arrive at any redemption, he classifies the author as a minimalist. Bruce Weber, however, disagrees with this assessment. Ford's characters never give up, Weber argues; "they actively seek the high-minded solace that's available— in self knowledge, in the future, in love" (59). Ford, too, finds a measure of hopefulness in his work, proclaiming that writing itself "is an act of optimism" (McQuade 67).

Yet bad things do happen to Ford's characters, things that strip them down to their vital selves. As Dean Flower concludes, "Despite brief moments of grace, Ford's stories tend to confirm a sense of inexorable meanness at work in the world" (210). Vivian Gornick in "Tenderhearted Men: Lonesome, Sad, and Blue" describes Ford's characters as "pained and bewildered people driven by their own sad emptiness into prototypic American violence" (33). When Nick Norwood compares the short stories of *Rock Springs* to *Wildlife*, he writes, "Ford's characters are people who started life with nebulous dreams and who wind up suffering at the hands of bad luck or their own miscalculations" (86). Yet what Ford has said specifically of the stories "Fireworks" and "Rock Springs" in *Rock Springs* may also be applied to much of his work: "I think it's people on the edge; things could really get worse, or things could get a little better. That, I think, is where the two lines of dramatic action take place in all these stories" (Bonetti 95).

ANALYSIS

In *Rock Springs*, Richard Ford peoples his Montana with male characters: Earl, the car thief, whose arm is tattooed "FAMOUS TIMES" in "Rock Springs"; Jack Russell's sixteen-year-old son, whose mother leaves his father in "Great Falls"; Russ, whose experience includes driving his girlfriend's ex-husband to prison at Deer Lodge; George, whose best friend beats him out of a sexual encounter in "Children"; Lloyd Henderson, whose bad luck begins when one woman sleeps with him while her friend robs him in "Going to the Dogs"; Les Snow, whose wheelchair-bound best friend beats him out of a sexual encounter in "Winterkill"; Frank Brinson, whose father kills a man with his bare hands before his own son in "Optimists"; or Les, whose mother breaks off her relationship with her boyfriend in "Communist."

Many of the stories in *Rock Springs*, along with those in *Women with Men*, concern soulless sexual encounters or episodes of infidelity. In "Going to the Dogs," for example, when two women come to visit Lloyd Henderson, the narrator whose wife has left him, one seduces him while the other steals his wallet. Similarly, in "Empire," Sims recalls that Cleo, the girl next door with whom he slept while his wife Marge was in the hospital recovering from cancer, has "a tattoo of Satan's head on her ass" (128). Later, he spends the night with the lovely Sergeant Benton while traveling with his wife on a train (145).

Other stories depict lives of hardship and misfortune and bitterness. In "Winterkill," Les Snow, the unemployed narrator, and Troy, his wheelchair-bound, taxi-driver friend, go fishing and find a dead deer in the river. Considering why it fell, Troy lets his discontent bubble to the surface: " 'So a gimp man can catch it on a fishing rod in a shitty town,' Troy said and gasped with bitterness. Real bitterness. The worst I have ever heard from any man, and I have heard bitterness voiced, though it was a union matter then" (167). In "Communist," Les introduces Glen Baxter, another man down on his luck: "When he was around our life he worked wheat farms as a ditcher, and stayed out of work winters and and in the bars drinking with women like my mother, who had work and some money. It is not an uncommon life to lead in Montana" (216). In "Optimists," Frank Brinson begins his story with a catalog of misfortunes:

All of this that I am about to tell happened . . . in 1959, the year my parents were divorced, the year when my father killed a man and went to prison for it, the year I left home and school. . . . The year, in other words, when life changed for all of us and forever—ended, really, in a way none of us could ever have imagined in our most brilliant dreams of life. (171)

Instead of feeling cursed, however, many of Ford's characters attribute their misfortune to the unpredictability of life. After the accidental murder of Boyd

Mitchell, for example, Roy Brinson, Frank's father, remarks simply, "Bad things happen" (184). Frank too perceives that "the most important things in your life can change so suddenly" and is "taken up by the chanciness of all that's happened and by all that could and will happen next" (187). Similarly, in "The Newel Vignettes," Newel remembers that his father had once told him "that now and then things get away from you and you [can't] control events any more" (303).

For many of the characters in Ford's stories, in fact, misfortune, even criminality, seems inevitable, unavoidable. In "Sweethearts," Russ says of Bobby, his girlfriend's violent ex-husband, "There was nothing I could say then that would save him or make life better for him at that moment or change the way he saw things" (65). As Frank remarks in "Optimists," sometimes "situations have possibilities in them, and we have only to be present to be involved" (181). Yet while several characters in Ford's stories are desperadoes or criminals, they are never one-dimensional villains. Jack Russell, the narrator's hunter-father in "Great Falls," shows blatant disregard for the law when he sells the wild game he kills, but his transgression pales in comparison to his wife's infidelity and subsequent abandonment. Earl, the car thief in "Rock Springs," admits that he is "an offender in the law's eyes," but does not view himself as a criminal: "I always thought differently, as if I weren't no offender and had no intention of being one, which was the truth" (17). When a man sees Earl eyeing a car in the parking lot of the Ramada Inn, Earl puts the reader in the man's position and asks: "Would you think he was trying to get his head cleared? . . . Would you think his girlfriend was leaving him? Would you think he had a daughter? Would you think he was anybody like you?" (27). Such direct address collapses the distance between the characters and the readers and, in so doing, calls attention to the humanity of even the most flawed among us.

The involvement of "regular," multidimensional, often-sympathetic people in violent or criminal activity, then, invites readers to empathize with the characters, despite their imperfections and vulgarities. It acknowledges, moreover, the universal potential for violence and criminality. In "Great Falls," Jack Russell's son, admitting to lingering questions about the events of the night when his parents separated, concludes that there is coldness in each of us: "Possibly it— the answer—is simple: it is just low-life, some coldness in us all, some helplessness that causes us to misunderstand life when it is pure and plain, makes our existence seem like a border between two nothings" (49).

Indeed, many characters in Ford's stories, cognizant of their own helplessness and coldness, arrive at a sense of life as empty, "a border between two nothings." Frank Bascombe in *Independence Day* lives alone with his "ghostly self" in his ex-wife's house and concludes: "The poet was right again. 'Let the winged Fancy roam / Pleasure never is at home' " (108). In "Children," George says of the external world, "[It] was a place that seemed not even to exist, an empty place you could stay in for a long time and never find a thing you admired or loved or hoped to keep" (98). In "Sweethearts," warned by Bobby "to face that empty moment" (54), Russ decides that what is important about life was "never being in that place you said you'd never be in. And it was not about being alone. Never that" (68).

Yet for some in Ford's stories, being alone may be a positive experience, signaling independence and maturity. In "Children," for example, George remarks admiringly of Lucy, "She was already someone who could be by herself in the world" (94). In "Empire," when Sims looks out the train window, he revels in his solitude: "[He] felt alone in a wide empire, removed and afloat, calmed, as if life was far away now, as if blackness was all around, as if stars held the only light" (148). In "Jealous," the narrator, Larry, also feels stillness in his aloneness: "And for a long time then I sat very still and felt as though I was out of the world entirely" (144).

Richard Ford's characters demonstrate an extreme optimism, made more distinctly so by the difficulties they encounter in their lives. In the face of their adversities, they seek to live better, to love better, to know themselves better, so that they may enjoy a future better than the present one they now heroically endure. As Ford has told Kay Bonetti, the positive aspect of his stories is the accommodation of the feelings of men to the events in their lives: "I always was writing about . . . men trying to deal with their own sensitivity" (80–81). Yet Dean Flower writes of *Rock Springs* that "Ford never asks that we pity these characters" (209). Schroth agrees: "He focuses his camera on ordinary— and sometimes outlaw—lives, people who for the most part eschew self-pity and are slow to judge. Ford helps us, too, withhold judgement" (227). Sharing William Dean Howells's ambition to "create a literature worthy of America," Ford has said, "Everything counts, after all. What else do you need to know?" (Schroth 230).

WORKS CITED AND CONSULTED

Primary

Ford, Richard. "Going to the Dogs." *Triquarterly* 78 (1990): 125–131.

———. "I Must Be Going." *Utne Reader* 55 (1993): 102–104.

———. *Independence Day*. New York: Knopf, 1995.

———. "The Newel Vignettes."*Michigan Quarterly Review* 15.3 (1976): 298–307.

———. "Place qua Place: Missing the True Character of a Landscape—by a Country Mile." *American Film* 16.10 (1991): 68.

———. *Rock Springs*. New York: Atlantic Monthly Press, 1987.

———. "Shooting the Rest Area." *Paris Review* 16.2 (1975): 154–67.

———. "Snowman." *Triquarterly* 48 (1980): 214–24.

———. *The Sportswriter*. New York: Random (Vintage), 1986.

———. *Wildlife*. New York: Atlantic Monthly Press, 1990.

———. *Women with Men*. New York: Knopf, 1997.

Secondary

Bonetti, Kay. "An Interview with Richard Ford." *Missouri Review* 10.2 (1987): 71–96.

Flower, Dean. "In the House of Pain." *Hudson Review* 41.1 (1988): 209–17.

Gornick, Vivian. "Tenderhearted Men: Lonesome, Sad, and Blue." *New York Times Book Review* (September 16, 1990): 32–35.

Green, Michelle. "Transient Writer Richard Ford Lets His Muse Roam Free in *Wildlife.*" *People* July 9, 1990: 71–72.

Hugo, Richard. *The Triggering Town: Lectures and Essays on Poetry and Writing.* New York: Norton, 1979.

McQuade, Molly. "Richard Ford." *Publishers Weekly* 237.20 (1990): 66–67.

Norwood, Nick. "*Wildlife.*" *The Redneck Review of Literature* (Fall 1991): 86–87.

Orr, Phillip. "*Rock Springs.*" *Northwest Review* 26.2 (1988): 143–47.

Rushdie, Salman. *Imaginary Homelands.* London: Viking (Granta), 1991.

Schneider, Wolf. "*Bright Angel*: Richard Ford Ups the Ante." *American Film* 16.5 (1991): 50–51.

Schroth, Raymond. "America's Moral Landscape in the Fiction of Richard Ford." *Christian Century* March 1, 1989: 227–30.

Weber, Bruce. "Richard Ford's Uncommon Characters." *New York Times Magazine* April 10, 1988: 59–65.

JANET FRAME
(August 28, 1924–   )

Susan Rochette-Crawley

BIOGRAPHY

"It is little wonder that I value writing as a way of life when it actually saved my life" (Frame, *An Autobiography* 221). Eight years misdiagnosed as a schizophrenic, Janet Frame was headed for a lobotomy. Fortunately, for her sake and for the sake of all who have been enriched by her writing since, the surgery never took place. Her first collection of stories, *The Lagoon*, received the Hubert Church Award for best prose and rescued its author from a life of psychiatric paralysis. It also gave birth to a new literary voice with international, as well as local, appeal.

Janet Frame was born on August 28, 1924, in Dunedin, New Zealand. Her twin, who died a few days after birth, remains present in much of her work: many of her stories, particularly the early ones, are written with an "other" self in mind. In *The Reservoir*, for example, the narratives seem to address a kindred spirit in need of explanation. The reader, then, becomes the stand-in personality to whom the stories are directed. The effect is overwhelming. One feels that one has been taken into confidence.

Frame's early life, as reflected in *The Reservoir* stories and her autobiography, was marked by both poverty and magic. Her father's occupation as a railwayman kept the family poor and on the move, but poetry, art, and storytelling (her mother was a poet and her father supplied her with paper and pen and encouraged her to write) mitigated the squalor of their daily life. The 1989 movie *An Angel at My Table*, directed by Jane Campion, faithfully presents this era of her life, its joys as well as its sufferings.

Magic in Frame's early life also sprang in part from the great freedom that she enjoyed as a child. While the title story of *The Reservoir* depicts certain parts of the landscape as forbidden, for the most part, the exotic wildlife and countryside of coastal New Zealand were a playground for Frame and her companions, a backdrop for exploration and adventure. The intimate and detailed knowledge she acquired of the countryside, its unique flora and fauna, its magic and mystery, surfaces in her fiction as surreal imagery infused with depictions of ordinary life. The result is a unique brand of storytelling, one in which legend and everyday life coexist harmoniously.

After Frame was released from the hospital in New Zealand, she went to live with her sister, June. There she met New Zealand writer Frank Sargeson, then living an austere life in the New Zealand countryside. Sargeson offered Frame part of his living quarters, arranged for her to receive National Assistance, and set up a rigid schedule of writing, reading, and self-exploration. His encouragement, combined with her own dedication to her work, eventually led to a writing fellowship abroad. The award enabled her to leave New Zealand and travel first to London and then on to Spain. Since then she has been awarded the Robert Burns Fellowship and the New Zealand Literary Award, among others. She is an honorary member of the American Academy of Arts and Sciences and has seen her work flourish in popularity and acclaim.

CRITICISM

Most critics of Frame's work agree that she is New Zealand's greatest living writer; the growing body of scholarship on her work indeed reinforces this judgment. While many write about her several complex novels, recent criticism has considered her stories and autobiographies as well.

Jeanne Delbaere's collection of essays *Bird, Hawk, Bogie: Essays on Janet Frame*, along with Elizabeth Alley's *The Inward Sun: Celebrating the Life and Work of Janet Frame* and Gina Mercer's *Janet Frame: Subversive Fictions*, largely present New Zealand and Australian critics' assessment of the author's work. In 1977, G. K. Hall's Twayne Series published *Janet Frame*, authored by Patrick Evans. The year 1992 saw the publication of both Judith Dell Panny's study *I Have What I Gave: The Fiction of Janet Frame* and *The Ring of Fire: Essays on Janet Frame*, edited, again, by Jeanne Delbaere with a bibliography compiled by Alexander Hart. While much of the criticism of Frame's work focuses upon her novels, in "The Child Archetype in the Commonwealth Short Stories," K. Chellappan writes about the Commonwealth short story and its relation to the work of Janet Frame, Katherine Mansfield, and Mulk Raj Anand.

Many of these sources are currently available through New Zealand and Australian publishers. It is hoped that with the growing interest in Frame's work, more criticism will become available in the United States and the United Kingdom.

ANALYSIS

Janet Frame's first book of stories, *The Lagoon*, is not available in print at this time. Thus the volumes that will introduce most readers to Frame are *The*

Reservoir and *Snowman, Snowman*. This analysis of her work will focus on these two volumes and the great variety of short-story forms that they present.

Snowman, Snowman, a volume first copyrighted in 1962, is subtitled *Fable and Fantasies*. This subtitle seems to indicate that Frame was already experimenting with the short-story form. Indeed, the title story to the collection is an amusing and poignant invention: a dialogue between a "Snowman" and a "Perpetual Snowflake." The Snowman, the embodiment of the existentialist dilemma over being and nothingness, recognizes that his status is ephemeral, that his existence on earth is short-lived, and, moreover, that not all snowmen are found to be "equal"—some are endowed with features and powers that others are not. The Perpetual Snowflake warns the Snowman that he is in constant danger of ceasing to be—the natural and unavoidable elements of time will not work to preserve the snowman. The story ends with the Snowman vowing to wage a doomed yet valiant offensive against the powers that destroy it.

"Snowman, Snowman," in excess of one hundred pages, is perhaps more properly termed a novella. Its inclusion in a volume of "fables and fantasies," however, aligns it with the short-story form and thwarts conventional classification. Likewise, the remaining seventeen stories, many of which are no longer than two or three pages, challenge story length at the other end of the spectrum. The exceedingly short story "The Training of My Tigers," for example, contains a complete cycle of setting, rising action, climax, falling, action, and resolution within the confines of less than two thousand words. In it, the tigers retain their ferociousness, and it is the trainer, in the end, that is tamed.

Frame's "fables and fantasies" strain the boundaries of the realist story. Much of their imagery and poetic style contributes to that quality of "marvelousness" that Tzetsvan Todorov identifies in his structural analysis of the fantastic. Many invoke the myths and legends of the aboriginal Maori people to emphasize the fanciful quality of life. Frame's early style also aligns her work with the so-called magic realism frequently associated with South and Central American writing. Indeed, Frame's New Zealand, with its geographical distance from the north, provides a similar imaginative landscape, a "strange" and "exotic" territory on the fringe of the industrialized world. Additionally, Frame's stories in this volume are particularly well suited to postmodernist critical practice because they so explicitly concern the boundaries between the fabulous and the real.

Frame's next volume of stories, *The Reservoir*, published in 1963, contains stories of a more traditional and modernist ilk. The title story is a coming-of-age narrative in which local children learn the limits of adult prohibitions and the consequences of testing them. The plot follows the children as they explore the forbidden territory of the reservoir. Those brave enough to try to cross the reservoir must overcome a series of physical obstacles, the most treacherous of which is a log bridge. In the end, the ones who complete the passage find that there is nothing extraordinary about the reservoir itself.

"The Teacup," another story in *The Reservoir*, tells how a fellow boarder's teacup comes to assume great importance for the narrator. The teacup comes to symbolize all the narrator felt and hoped for her longtime friend, who eventually deserts the boardinghouse and leaves her behind. The boarder's special teacup, lost at his departure, is a grail to which the narrator gives complete devotion.

Typically, Frame's stories focus on a single image set within a single action and follow a single plot line. In contrast to the conventional modernist short story, however, Frame insists that the singularity of an experience not dominate her narrative: the teacup, the unifying symbol throughout the story, is an emblem of the fragility of a modernist story line. There is no final epiphany, the symbol of the teacup is lost forever, and the narrator is left with the realization that the adherence of symbol to meaning is tenuous at best.

Frame's greatest strength as a short-story writer lies in her ability to create and build upon metaphors and paradoxes. In her story "The Triumph of Poetry," for example, she opens with the following statement about the main character:

When he was born they named him Alan, meaning that in future the area of himself would be known as Alan. The area of oneself is like a drop of ink absorbed by blotting paper, gradually spreading, blurring at the edges, receiving upon it other blots in different shapes and colors until finally the original is dim, indistinguishable, while the saturated sheet of human upon which it lies is cast as worthless into the wastebasket, and another sheet, a clean sheet provided by the advertisers, is placed upon the desk. (*The Reservoir* 157)

By comparing the "area of oneself" to a drop of ink on blotting paper, Frame paints an image of the self as distinct, yet muddied by its interaction with others. She gives us a beautifully constructed metaphor of being that "defamiliarizes" what might otherwise be a mundane comparison.

In addition to her use of metaphor, Frame is attentive to the details of setting. The cutty grass and tinkertailor of the New Zealand countryside come to life in her fiction. She introduces her reader to the botanically and zoologically unique landscape of the "down under" in a way that allows the reader to observe the exotic and unusual without feeling excluded or outside of it. Part of Frame's strength as a writer lies in her original and skillful use of the short-story form to capture the barely glimpsed aspects of both the natural and spiritual worlds of her characters.

WORKS CITED AND CONSULTED

Primary

Short Stories

Frame, Janet. *The Lagoon*. New York: Braziller, 1951.
———. *The Reservoir*. New York: Braziller, 1963.
———. *Snowman, Snowman*. New York: Braziller, 1963.
———. *You Are Now Entering the Human Heart*. New York: Braziller, 1984.

Novels

Frame, Janet. *The Adaptable Man*. New York: Braziller, 1965.
————. *The Carpathians*. New York: Braziller, 1988.
————. *The Edge of the Alphabet*. New York: Braziller, 1962.
————. *Faces in the Water*. New York: Braziller, 1961.
————. *Intensive Care*. New York: Braziller, 1970.
————. *Living in the Maniototo*. New York: Braziller, 1979.
————. *Owls Do Cry*. New York: Braziller, 1957.
————. *Scented Gardens for the Blind*. New York: Braziller, 1963.
————. *A State of Seige*. New York: Braziller, 1966.
————. *Yellow Flowers in the Antipodean Room*. New York: Braziller, 1968.

Autobiography

Frame, Janet. *An Autobiography*. New York: Braziller, 1991.

Secondary

Alley, Elizabeth. " 'An Honest Record': An Interview with Janet Frame." *Landfall: A New Zealand Quarterly* 45.2: 154–68.
————, ed. *The Inward Sun: Celebrating the Life and Work of Janet Frame*. Wellington, New Zealand: Daphne Brasell, 1994.
Chellappan, K. "The Child Archetype in the Commonwealth Short Stories: Katherine Mansfield, Janet Frame, and Mulk Raj Anand." *Commonwealth Review* 1.1 (1989): 60–72.
Dalziel, Margaret. *Janet Frame*. Wellington: Oxford University Press, 1980.
Delbaere, Jeanne, ed. *Bird, Hawk, Bogie: Essays on Janet Frame*. Aarhus: Dangaroo Press, 1978.
————, ed. *The Ring of Fire*. Sydney: Dangaroo, 1992.
Evans, Patrick. *Janet Frame*. Boston: Twayne, 1977.
Mercer, Gina. *Janet Frame: Subversive Fictions*. St. Lucia: University of Queensland Press, 1994.
Panny, Judith Dell. *I Have What I Gave: The Fiction of Janet Frame*. Wellington, New Zealand: Daphne Brasell Associates Press, 1992.

ERNEST J. GAINES
(January 15, 1933–   )

Mary Ellen Doyle

BIOGRAPHY

Pointe Coupee Parish on the False River, near New Roads, Louisiana, land of cotton and sugar cane, land of French plantation owners, Creoles, Cajuns, black slaves, and their descendants—this is the land of Ernest Gaines's birth in "the quarters" of River Lake Plantation. The oldest son of field workers Manuel and Adrienne Jefferson Gaines, he was himself in the fields at age nine. Off-season, he was also in the one-room schoolhouse, where, according to people still there, he became a "scholar" who loved learning, studied into the night, and often read or wrote letters for the old people. When he was about eight, his parents separated, and he lived for a time with his great-aunt, Augusteen Jefferson, a woman crippled from infancy whose indomitable spirit, he says, "taught me to stand." The search for the absent father and for true manhood, the influence of wise older women, and the need for courage in the face of hardship infuse Gaines's work, all of it set in the South, a land that inspires both his loyalty and his imagination.

In 1948, at the age of fifteen, he joined his mother and stepfather, Norbert Colar, in California. There he experienced the diverse culture of a military base, the benefits of a public library, and the expansive world of books, a world that, he discovered, did not yet contain his familiar Louisiana land or people. He decided to write his own stories to fill in the gap.

After service in the army, he went to San Francisco State and Stanford universities, where he met open-minded, encouraging teachers. He studied Faulkner, Hemingway, and the Russians, from whom he says that he learned not the content of his stories, but methods of writing. The schools' literary magazines published his first short stories. Stanford was followed by ten years of part-time work and writing, with publication of four stories in literary journals, *Catherine Carmier* in 1964, *Of Love and Dust* in 1967, and a collection of five stories,

Bloodline, in 1968. In these years of lean earnings and mixed reviews, he was sustained by the courage, independence, and discipline learned from his aunt and by his loyalty to his Louisiana subject amid the pressure of the 1960s to write for social goals.

Success came with the publication of *The Autobiography of Miss Jane Pittman* in 1971 and its translation into film in 1974. Many interviews and public lectures followed. Succeeding novels are *In My Father's House* (1978); *A Gathering of Old Men* (1983); and *A Lesson before Dying* (1993). Numerous awards from universities and foundations include the prestigious MacArthur Genius Award in 1993. In 1981, Gaines joined the creative writing faculty at the University of Southwestern Louisiana in Lafayette and since then has divided his time among teaching, lecturing, and writing.

CRITICISM

Little criticism of Gaines's work appeared before the publication of *The Autobiography of Miss Jane Pittman*. Afterwards, criticism dramatically increased, and brief reviews expanded into substantive analyses. Although most criticism concerns the novels, it is useful for students of the short stories because it considers Gaines's main subjects and themes: issues of manhood, religion, and biracial identity; the relationships of fathers and sons, men and women, young and old, individuals and community; and the multiple ethnic cultures of southern Louisiana. The novels and short stories also share many characteristic techniques: first-person viewpoint, dialogue reminiscent of oral storytelling, and detailed settings.

Until now, little criticism has been done on the early, published but uncollected short stories of Ernest Gaines. A forthcoming book, however, considers all of them as the experiments with subject matter, themes, and narrative techniques (Doyle, *Voices*, chap. 2). It also considers why these works were excluded from the collection, *Bloodline*. That collection has drawn several substantive articles predominantly focused on the story "The Sky Is Gray" or on the stories as a connected sequence. Recent criticism reveals an emerging awareness of Gaines's special talent for and success with the short-story form. He himself has acknowledged his early preference for it and his belief that his short stories would make his name (Gaudet and Wooton 111). They may yet do so, especially if more criticism of *Bloodline* should encourage him to publish more stories and collections.

ANALYSIS

Of Gaines's earliest published but uncollected stories, three are independent tales of boys maturing ("The Turtles," "Boy in the Double Breasted Suit," and "My Grandpa and the Haint"). Another, "Mary Louise," introduces characters who later reappear in *Catherine Carmier*; the story, however, has no part in the larger work, but focuses on the constricted life and dashed hopes of a female character peripheral to the novel. Between 1972 and 1983, Gaines published five stories originally considered parts of novels in progress: Chapter One of *The House and the Field* (1972); Chippo Simon (1976); "In My Father's House" (1977); "The Revenge of Old Men" (1978); and "Robert Louis Stevenson Banks, aka Chimley" (1983). "Chapter One of The House and the Field," which presents a fairly stereotypical slavery situation, never became a novel. The others are interesting for analysis of the use that was (or was not) made of them in two novels, *In My Father's House* and *A Gathering of Old Men*.

Gaines's best short fiction appears in *Bloodline*, a collection that includes three previously published stories and two more ("Three Men" and "Bloodline") written specifically to create a connected sequence (Ingram 46–49). The linking theme is manhood: how it is developed, threatened, and destroyed or maintained, affirmed, and exercised in a world of historic and culturally ingrained racism. A male is the protagonist or central figure of each story; boys and men advance in age from early childhood to young adulthood and progress from shelter in the quarters to exposure to segregation and brutality in the town and wider world and, finally, into activism in the civil rights movement. Through experiences of family, of black and white communities and their expectations of black men, and above all, through their own reflections, these males confront the challenge of attaining genuine manhood, a status whose meaning emerges from the implications of each story taken with the others. Its definition clearly includes loyal, loving responsibility to one's family and one's "people," the courage to face danger and pain with dignity, and the strength to make decisions that assert one's own and others' full humanity, even when those others do not approve or even understand—all this without losing sensitivity or patience and without resorting to violence.

All the stories are told in the first person, a mode that Gaines favors for its high orality, and that flows most naturally from his experience of listening to the storytellers among his people. In the first four stories, the narrator is a single male; multiple narrators tell the final story. These narrators, however, do not seem to be telling remembered events or even talking to themselves (cf. Callahan); rather, the style of dialogue, diction, sentence patterns, and amount of detail suggest that they are registering sensation, thought, and feelings just as they occur. The result is directness, realism, and intensity, which render the outer world and inner responses beyond either a child's ability to articulate or a narrator's power to remember (Doyle, "Best" and *Voices*, chap. 3).

"A Long Day in November" was published both in *Bloodline* and, with appropriate revisions, as a child's story. It presents the quarrel and reconciliation of Eddie and Amy Howard from the viewpoint of their six-year-old son, Sonny. Eddie is preoccupied with his car, a symbol to him of manhood and freedom but representative to his wife of his diminished time for and attention to family, his diminished love. On one agonizingly "long day," Sonny follows his mother's return to her mother, who wants above all to break up a marriage she never approved, and his father's efforts, through various advisors, to get his wife home. The climactic destruction of the car to save the marriage takes place among the community of the quarters, with Granmon pronouncing Eddie "a man after all."

Not all critics concur in this judgment; some see Eddie both as emasculated by women who will not tolerate the little freedom and power he enjoys and as failing to model real manhood for his son (Burke 546–48; Bryant 112; Werner 37). Most critics, however, support the view that Gaines has achieved, in a comic mode, his most serious aim: to address the danger of separation and to emphasize the importance of bonds between husbands and wives and fathers and sons. Moreover, many have noted that this is the only story without an absent father (Gaudet and Wooton 60). This positive reading emphasizes the impact of the action on Sonny. From a disastrous morning at school brought on by his distress, Sonny returns at night to the security of home and two parents who will both now support his education. Not even Amy's insistence that Eddie beat her to prevent mockery for his submission mars Sonny's sense of their love (though the episode has generated much debate on Gaines's own view of the act and good judgment in creating it). Ultimately, the child is reestablished in a family and the family in a social circle.

The positive interpretation this story elicits also derives from Gaines's use of voice. Sonny's viewpoint, his childish vernacular, renders all his acute physical and emotional sensations with immediacy. His comic-ironic attempts to interpret his sensations assure us that his confusion and pain are temporary and that the adults around him have done well to resolve their differences so that he can grow up, too, happy and whole.

The same use of childish, immediate viewpoint and language, however, creates a serious tone in Gaines's most anthologized story, "The Sky Is Gray." Eight-year-old James is forced into premature manhood by the absence of his soldier father and by his mother's attempts to cope with grinding poverty and train him to survive with dignity. During another long day of cold and sleet, Octavia takes James to the dentist in town. Plot is minimal; the point of the story is what James learns from all his new experiences and the comparisons he makes to those he remembers. This hostile, segregated small-town world, where even blacks abuse each other over sex and religion, is more than a long bus ride from the shelter of the quarters. Here safety requires one to see and hear all but "make 'tend" not to, to say as little as possible to anyone but be ready for self-defense, to conceal one's cold and hunger but maneuver to get near heat or take food whenever possible, without compromising one's dignity.

Loved and popular as this story is, it has raised high winds of controversy, especially about its characterization of Octavia and its implied definition of manhood. Is Octavia really loving and wise, or is she herself damaged by experience and apt to damage James? Must she impose such emotional chill and severe behavioral demands on a child? Why can't a "man" turn up his collar against the sleet? Why can't her demands be explained? Above all, why can't a fatherless child display and receive signs of affection, at least in the security of private relationships? Whose side is Gaines on?

Technique again supports his characterizations and theme. The characters balance each other: Auntie and the Cajun Helena explain or soften Octavia's severity; the platitudinous minister and the nihilist student offset each other. The story's world is "gray" in theme as in setting: no racial culture is entirely admirable or threatening; head must be balanced with heart. The use of James's viewpoint, moreover, reveals that even if he is partially stymied by maternal sternness, he retains a sensitivity to the details of his surroundings (Gaines is famous for the meaningful detail in his settings), an emotional warmth, and a determination both to develop his mind and to love and care for his family— not a bad definition of early "manhood" in any culture.

As the first two stories attract readers with their child protagonists-narrators and hopeful endings, the next two challenge them to like or at least understand morally unattractive main characters in plots with ambivalent outcomes. In "Three Men," Proctor Lewis, the son of an absent father and a deceased mother, is nineteen years old; his world has expanded from the town night spot to its jail. After killing another black man in a brawl over a woman, he has turned himself in with the expectation of being bonded out as labor on a local plantation. His young manhood is on the verge of permanent destruction due to his faulty understanding and wrong choice.

Two others share his cell: Munford, an embittered old brawler, regularly in and out of jail to the amusement and contempt of whites, and Hattie, a homosexual despised by both of his cellmates but able to assert himself and possessed of a gentleness and kindness they lack. With inimitable vulgarity, Munford assures Proctor that he himself is the image of what the younger man will become if he accepts the false freedom of being "bonded out." Ironically, only when Proctor adopts something of Hattie's tenderness toward a youngster beaten and thrown in their cell for stealing food does he begin to take responsibility for his own character and embrace a true manhood.

Only a depth of viewpoint softens the reader's response to Proctor, who enters the story utterly amoral, disgustingly vulgar in speech, exploitative, and prone to violence in action. Women are his sex objects; "men" are those who can use them most easily and often. But an inner recorder follows his tortuous mental and emotional movement in and out of self-deception, into memories and honest loneliness, out of isolation, into true assessment of his situation and his choices. In the end, the reader sympathizes with and hopes for Proctor, almost even admires him.

In the title story, "Bloodline," Copper Laurent's moral ambivalence is far more difficult to interpret and evaluate, partially because he is not the narrator and, in fact, appears in only three of eleven sections of the story. His presence, however, is pervasive in the dialogue between Felix, the elderly black narrator, Amalia, the aunt of Copper's black mother, and Frank Laurent, the brother of Copper's white father. Copper, who has inherited his father's strength and arrogance, has now returned to claim his plantation. From the quarters, he conquers all efforts to bring him into the main house by the back door as a black servant. Through Felix's eyes, ears, and thoughts, readers perceive the bitter heritage of exploitative miscegenation and the current generational struggle. They see the gross injustices done to Copper's family and to all plantation blacks; they see the inhuman fanaticism of a self-proclaimed "soldier" who beats and chains the very men he has come to free, who is willing to make his aunt suffer before she goes through the front door, and who even threatens to bathe the scene in blood to get his share.

Whether the protagonist of this struggle is the seldom-seen but everywhere-felt Copper or the plantation system itself remains unclear. Old, sick, morally weak Frank or intolerant, loveless, possibly crazy Copper—if neither has the method to accomplish justly and peacefully the systemic change they both desire, then how will it occur, and who will be responsible? Felix cannot tell; the reader has to wrestle with the questions left behind when Copper goes away.

"Just Like a Tree," the final story, differs sharply from the first four in that it has multiple narrators, and the central male figure is not among them. The action of the story is merely the gathering of the quarters people to say farewell to old Aunt Fe, whose niece is taking her away for fear of the reprisals against local civil rights activists. Memories and feelings flow through the minds and hearts of ten narrators from three generations, blacks and whites, men and women, some who understand the motivations of both the niece and the activists, others who do not. Though each holds a piece of the meaning, all know that when this old woman is "jecked up" from her roots, the community's life will be irreparably diminished. Aunt Fe represents the older generation, especially the wise women, who have transmitted stories, courage, and convictions to the young. Aunt Fe, "Faith," will die before she can be moved; she will live on in Emmanuel, the "savior," one of the young activists who is sensitive and appreciative, rooted even as he moves. She and he, across generations and genders, have combined head and heart. This story, too, has small boys among its narrators; they will be influenced not only by surviving Aunt Clo and Aunt Lou but by Emmanuel and the men and women like him.

Bloodline began with a child learning to live with his people; it ends with an old woman dying among them. The collection's final statement seems to be that manhood is achieved only when one is fully part of a community that keeps, values, and transmits its own history and beliefs, its loyalty and courage, its hope and its love.

WORKS CITED AND CONSULTED

Primary

Gaines, Ernest J. *The Autobiography of Miss Jane Pittman*. New York: Dial, 1971; New York: Bantam, 1972, 1982.

————. *Bloodline*. New York: Dial, 1968; New York: Norton, 1976; New York: Vintage Books, 1997.

————. "Boy in the Double Breasted Suit." *Transfer* 3 (1957): 2–9.

————. *Catherine Carmier*. New York: Atheneum, 1964; San Francisco: North Point, 1981; New York: Vintage Books, 1993.

————. "Chapter One of *The House and the Field*, a Novel." *Iowa Review* 3 (1972): 121–25.

————. "Chippo Simon." *Yardbird Reader* 5 (1976): 229–37.

————. *A Gathering of Old Men*. New York: Knopf, 1983; New York: Vintage Books, 1984, 1992.

————. "In My Father's House." *Massachusetts Review* 18 (1977): 650–59. Rpt. in *Chant of Saints*. Ed. Michael S. Harper and Robert B. Stepto. Urbana: University of Illinois Press, 1979. 339–48.

————. *In My Father's House*. New York: Knopf, 1978; New York: Norton, 1983; New York: Vintage Books, 1992.

————. "Just Like a Tree." *Sewanee Review* 71 (1963): 542–68.

————. *A Lesson Before Dying*. New York: Knopf, 1993; New York: Vintage Books, 1994, 1997.

————. "A Long Day in November." *Texas Quarterly* 7 (1964): 190–224.

————. *A Long Day in November*. New York: Dial, 1971.

————. *Of Love and Dust*. New York: Dial, 1967; New York: Norton, 1979; New York: Vintage Books, 1994.

————. "Mary Louise." *Stanford Short Stories*. Ed. Wallace Earle Stegner and Richard Scowcroft. Stanford: Stanford University Press, 1960. 27–42.

————. "My Grandpa and the Haint." *New Mexico Quarterly* 36 (1966): 149–60.

————. "The Revenge of Old Men." *Callaloo* 1 (May 1978): 5–21.

————. "Robert Louis Stevenson Banks, aka Chimley." *Georgia Review* 37 (1983): 385–89.

————. "The Sky Is Gray." *Negro Digest* 12 (August 1963): 72–96.

————. "The Turtles." *Transfer* 1 (1956): 1–9. Rpt. in *Something in Common: Contemporary Louisiana Stories*. Ed. Ann Brewster Dobie. Baton Rouge: Louisiana State University Press, 1991. 89–97.

Secondary

Babb, Valerie Melissa. *Ernest Gaines*. Boston: Twayne, 1991.

Beavers, Herman. *Wrestling Angels into Song: The Fictions of Ernest J. Gaines and James Alan McPherson*. Philadelphia: University of Pennsylvania Press, 1995.

Bryant, Jerry H. "From Death to Life: The Fiction of Ernest J. Gaines." *Iowa Review* 3 (1972): 106–20.

Burke, William. "*Bloodline*: A Black Man's South." *CLA Journal* 19 (1976): 545–58.

Byerman, Keith. *Fingering the Jagged Grain: Tradition and Form in Recent Black Fiction*. Athens: University of Georgia Press, 1985. 67–103.

Callahan, John F. "Hearing Is Believing: The Landscape of Voice in Ernest Gaines's *Bloodline*." *Callaloo* 7 (1984): 86–112.

Charney, Mark J. "Voice and Perspective in the Film Adaptations of Gaines's Fiction." *Critical Reflections on the Fiction of Ernest J. Gaines*, Ed. David C. Estes. Athens: University of Georgia Press, 1994. 124–38.

Doyle, Mary Ellen. "The Best of *Bloodline*: 'Camcorder' Narration in Two Stories by Ernest Gaines." *Journal of the Short Story in English* 18 (1992): 63–70.

———. "Ernest Gaines' Materials: Place, People, Author." *MELUS* 15.3 (1988): 75–93.

———. "Ernest J. Gaines: An Annotated Bibliography, 1956–1988." *Black American Literature Forum* 24 (1990): 125–50.

———. *Voices from the Quarters: The Fiction of Ernest J. Gaines*. 1999. Manuscript Forthcoming by Louisiana State University Press.

Duncan, Todd. "Scene and Life Cycle in Ernest Gaines's *Bloodline*." *Callaloo* 1 (May 1978): 85–101.

Estes, David C. "Gaines' Humor: Race and Laughter." *Critical Reflections on the Fiction of Ernest J. Gaines*. Ed. David C. Estes. Athens: University of Georgia Press, 1994. 228–49.

Forkner, Ben. "Ernest J. Gaines." *Critical Survey of Short Fiction*. Vol. 4. Ed. Frank N. Magill. Englewood Cliffs, NJ: Salem Press, 1981. 1429–36.

Gaudet, Marcia. "Black Women: Race, Gender, and Culture in Gaines's Fiction." *Critical Reflections on the Fiction of Ernest J. Gaines*. Ed. David C. Estes. Athens: University of Georgia Press, 1994. 139–57.

———. "The Failure of Traditional Religion in Ernest Gaines' Short Stories." *Journal of the Short Story in English* 18 (1992): 81–89.

Gaudet, Marcia, and Carl Wooton. *Porch Talk with Ernest Gaines: Conversations on the Writer's Craft*. Baton Rouge: Louisiana State University Press, 1990.

Gaughan, Sara K. "Old Age, Folk Belief, and Love in Stories by Ernest Gaines and Louise Erdrich." *Louisiana Folklore Miscellany* 10 (1995): 37–45.

Hicks, Jack. *In the Singer's Temple: Prose Fictions of Barthelme, Gaines, Brautigan, Piercy, Kesey, and Kosinski*. Chapel Hill: University of North Carolina Press, 1981. 83–137.

———. "To Make These Bones Live: History and Community in Ernest Gaines's Fiction." *Black American Literature Forum* 11 (1977): 9–19.

Ingram, Forrest, and Barbara Steinberg. "On the Verge: An Interview with Ernest J. Gaines." *Conversations with Ernest Gaines*. Ed. John Lowe. Jackson, MS: University Press of Mississippi, 1995. 39–55.

Lowe, John, ed. *Conversations with Ernest Gaines*. Jackson: University Press of Mississippi, 1995.

Luscher, Robert M. "The Pulse of *Bloodline*." *Critical Reflections on the Fiction of Ernest J. Gaines*. Ed. David C. Estes. Athens: University of Georgia Press, 1994. 62–88.

McDonald, Walter R. " 'You Not a Bum, You a Man': Ernest J. Gaines's *Bloodline*." *Negro American Literature Forum* 9 (1975): 47–49.

Meyer, William E. "Ernest J. Gaines and the Black Child's Sensory Dilemma." *CLA Journal* 34 (1991): 414–25.

Pecile, Jordan. "On Ernest J. Gaines and 'The Sky Is Gray.' " *The American Short Story*. Vol. 2. Ed. Calvin Skaggs. New York: Dell, 1980. 452–58.

Puschmann-Nalenz, Barbara. "Ernest J. Gaines: 'A Long Day in November' (1963)." *The Black American Short Story in the 20th Century: A Collection of Critical Essays*. Ed. Peter Bruck. Amsterdam: Grüner, 1977. 157–69.

Roberts, John W. "The Individual and the Community in Two Short Stories by Ernest J. Gaines." *Black American Literature Forum* 18 (1984): 110–13.

Shelton, Frank W. "Ambiguous Manhood in Ernest J. Gaines's *Bloodline.*" *CLA Journal* 19 (1975): 200–209.

Simpson, Anne K. *A Gathering of Gaines*. Lafayette: Center for Louisiana Studies, University of Southwestern Louisiana, 1991.

Walker, Robbie. "Literary Art and Historical Reality: Ernest Gaines's Portrayal of the South in Transition." *Griot* 2 (Summer 1983): 1–9.

Washington, Mary Helen. "Commentary on Ernest J. Gaines." *Memory of Kin: Stories about Family by Black Writers*. New York: Doubleday, 1991. 38–42.

Werner, Craig Hansen. *Paradoxical Resolutions: American Fiction since James Joyce*. Urbana: University of Illinois Press, 1982. 34–40.

MAVIS GALLANT
(August 11, 1922–   )

Michael Trussler

BIOGRAPHY

Mavis Gallant was born in Montreal, Canada. Her father died when she was young, and her schooling took place at a number of institutions in Canada and the United States. She worked briefly for the National Film Board and then as a journalist for the *Montreal Standard* from 1944 until 1950, when she moved to Europe. After living in several cities, Gallant finally settled in Paris. Though she is reticent about her personal life, when she was asked by Geoffrey Hancock in the crucial *Canadian Fiction Magazine* interview (1978) whether her transmigratory background made "exile . . . the world condition in [her] stories" (46), she allowed that being "a refugee of a kind" forms the basis of much contemporary experience. Throughout her journalism and fiction, Gallant has focused on the dilemmas of ordinary individuals who, perplexed by the enormous political upheavals and changes of twentieth-century life, find that their worlds are contingent upon transition. Noting that Gallant's stories "reflect . . . the fragmentation of historical reality in the West over the past seventy years," Neil K. Besner maintains that "no other contemporary writer in English conceives of this recent past—the past as social, cultural, and political history and the past as recreated in individual and in cultural memory—in as varied and significant a manner as Gallant" (x).

Gallant is the author of several essays, a diary account of the May 1968 student uprising in Paris, and one drama, but her privileged forms are the novella and the short story. Most of her work is initially published in the *New Yorker*, a magazine with which she has been associated since the 1950s. Much of her early work, such as *The Other Paris* (1956) and *My Heart Is Broken: Eight Stories and a Short Novel* (1964), concerns characters who are unsettled, whose desires to be understood are at odds with their social environments. In *The Pegnitz Junction: A Novella and Five Short Stories* (1973), Gallant powerfully addresses how living in postwar Europe (especially from a German perspective) specifically requires an investigation into the experience of history. A prolific writer, Gallant has published collections of short stories every few years. Following *The End of the World and Other Stories* (1974) and *From the Fifteenth District: A Novella and Eight Short Stories* (1979), Gallant published *Home Truths: Selected Canadian Stories* (1981), which contains a valuable introduction by the author. *Overhead in a Balloon: Stories of Paris* (1985) has been favorably compared to Joyce's *Dubliners* for its extended treatment of Parisian life. *Paris Notebooks: Essays and Reviews* (1986) was succeeded by *In Transit* (1988), *Across the Bridge: Stories* (1993), and *The Moslem Wife and Other Stories* (1994), a retrospective collection of previous short fiction. Serious critical acclaim began in 1978 with the special issue on her work in *Canadian Fiction Magazine*. At first neglected, Gallant is now considered to be preeminent in Canadian letters; her work has become the subject of numerous critical studies and doctoral theses.

CRITICISM

Three book-length studies constitute an in-depth response to Gallant's writing. Neil K. Besner's *The Light of Imagination: Mavis Gallant's Fiction* (1988) clarifies Gallant's explorations of the dynamic relationship between individual memory and cultural historical remembrance. Besner offers a fleeting but concise stylistic analysis of the importance of genre to Gallant's fiction; for him, the short story's brevity creates a space in which "the play of Gallant's narration can reverberate more closely amidst its own echoes" (48). In *Reading Mavis Gallant* (1989), Janice Kulyk Keefer presents an incisive account of Gallant's work by interweaving her essays and journalism with interpretations of the fiction. While Keefer does not theorize the generic implications of Gallant's writing, her study valuably contextualizes the short fiction within the critical commentary, notably in terms of feminism. Her chapter "Social Narratives," an astute reading of the journalism, is an important contribution to the assessment of Gallant's work. *Figuring Grief: Gallant, Munro, and the Poetics of Elegy* (1992) by Karen E. Smythe is a sophisticated argument that perceives Gallant's short fiction as the attempt "to re-write modernity—to 'work through' modernism by confronting and challenging various of its tenets" (24). Short-story theorists might further Smythe's treatment of the fiction as a version of the late modernist "fiction-elegy"—texts that work out mourning as a process—by developing a finer understanding of the form's particular rendition of temporality. More than many short-story writers, Gallant has self-consciously addressed how the experience of temporality shapes our notions of historicity. Of considerable interest to both the short-story theorist and the general reader is Gallant's use of the form to investigate the reciprocity between private constructions of memory and the overall cultural imaginary that is historical remembrance.

ANALYSIS

In her *Canadian Fiction Magazine* interview, Gallant tells of her youthful interest in World War II refugees who had recently arrived in Montreal: "I used to try to write from their point of view; that is, seeing something familiar to me the way someone from an entirely different culture might see it" (Hancock 31). In many ways, this remark can be seen as a blueprint for her subsequent work. Intensely political without being didactic, acutely aware of how epistemological problems are immanent in the most ordinary aspects of daily life, committed to the belief that fiction can be used to probe the nature of the Other, Gallant extends the modernist emphasis on interpreting perspective as a phenomenon. When Mordecai Richler commends Gallant as "an astute, unsentimental observer" in his afterward to *The Moslem Wife and Other Stories*, maintaining that her "beautifully composed stories can also be read for the considerable pleasure of their incidental observations" (251), he speaks as one writer who esteems the artistry of another. Richler's comments, however, implicitly point to Gallant's desire to ground her work in the "here-and-now" of the contemporary. What authors communicate, she says, "is that something is taking place and that nothing lasts" (*Paris Notebooks* 177). Perhaps the most compelling element of Gallant's writing is her ability to engage and render intelligible the chaotic tumult of mid-to-late-twentieth-century experience in the West. A chronological survey of Gallant's short stories will intimate the range of her work.

Frequently anthologized, "The Ice Wagon Going down the Street," from *My Heart Is Broken*, depicts two expatriates, Peter and Sheilah Frazier, who have returned to Canada after failing to strike it rich in Europe and the Orient. Throughout much of the story, Peter contemplates the memory of his former employer in Geneva, a young woman also from Canada, Agnes Brusen. Brooding over a private childhood epiphany that Agnes has confided to him, Peter, in order to grant himself some measure of self-worth, appropriates Agnes's vision and makes it his own by inserting himself into her description of the ice wagon. To Smythe, Peter's "reconstruction of Agnes . . . is paradigmatic of the reader's involvement in the fiction-elegy" (42); we recognize that Peter's true failure consists in his desire to "substitute" another's understanding for his own. "The Ice Wagon Going down the Street" is prescient of Gallant's later work in the way that she compresses seemingly inconsequential narratives into the dominant story. In having Peter insult a friend's bride "who was freshly out of an Ursuline convent," for instance, Gallant intimates an undeveloped, though implied, narrative that creates a sort of subterranean tension that affects our understanding of the surface events pertaining to the Fraziers.

This technique of enfolding tacit narratives within a primary narrative plays a crucial part in "Malcolm and Bea," from *The End of the World and Other Stories*. A couple living on a NATO base in France that is about to be shut down, Malcolm and Bea seem to be in the final throes of their marriage. In that part of the story that takes place in the present, Malcolm aids another man,

Leonard, whose mistress has attempted suicide. The story of Malcolm and Bea's past courtship also unfolds. Keefer describes Gallant's fiction as having a dialectic between the progression of plot and the various "helices and spirals . . . that give her characters access to memory" (163). Leonard describes his psychic state by saying that "all of his life he thought he was going to Pichipoi," referring to an "unknown place" invented by Parisian Jews about to be deported by train to Germany during World War II. To these people, who exist in the story only through this imagined destination, Pichipoi offered the possibility of solace, since "it was a place that might not be any worse than the present." Keefer explains that in Gallant's desire "to incorporate catastrophic historical events and terms without turning them into kitsch," she offers momentary glances of these terrible events "to differentiate such history from, yet relate it to, the process of everyday living" (171). In contrast to someone like George Steiner, who tries to grapple with the horrors of Nazism by suggesting that they took place almost in a different "species" of time, Gallant uses her short fiction to reveal how terrible public events metamorphose into the private.

One of her most celebrated works, "The Moslem Wife," a story in *From the Fifteenth District*, also pivots on the uneasy distinction between personal occurrences and the disruptive features of major political events such as World War II. Netta Asher, a woman who cannot disengage herself from what Gallant calls "the prison of childhood" in the Linnet Muir stories, has been separated from her husband (and cousin) during the war. Jack Ross has spent the conflict in North America, while Netta has remained in their hotel in France during the Occupation. The story's present involves the couple's reunion, but the bulk of the text contains flashbacks to their mutual, cloistered childhood and early marriage, when Netta had been characterized as a submissive "Moslem wife." While a writer such as Somerset Maugham often employed a similar milieu to comment ironically on the foibles of the *bête humaine*, Gallant concentrates on problems of epistemology and historical reconstruction. Forced to confront the existential dimensions of her own experience, Netta finds in her memory a series of repeated images of the hotel that has been the site of so many drastic changes, afterimages that cannot be made to cohere. Besner observes that Netta is "confounded in her attempt to decide which experience—her own . . . haunted, historical experience, or her relationship with Jack, who would deny that memory links past with present—is real" (112).

Gallant herself has high regard for *The Pegnitz Junction*, a series of interconnected stories that unravel "the small possibilities [of fascism] in people" (Hancock 41). The title piece is an experimental tour de force that precludes paraphrase. Blending what Walter Benjamin would see as allegorical collage with penetrating psychological and social realism, "The Pegnitz Junction" recounts the seemingly endless return train journey from France of two German tourists, a man and a woman, and the man's son. Christine, the young woman, has the ability to perceive the thoughts of others, a technique that permits the juxtaposition of what Gallant calls numerous "short circuited" conversations

(Hancock 65) with various forms of discourse. Because the terrifying ambiguities of the "Hitler time" are omnipresent in the collection, we as readers "become cultural critics, responsible for reading history" (Smythe 90). One of our responsibilities is the requirement to think hermeneutically. The accumulation of minor details in the stories, such as Gallant's description in "Ernst in Civilian Clothes" of how an ex-POW had "put on his Hitler Youth uniform at seven" because it "was a great saving in clothes," lead us to recognize that trying to understand the present obliges us to be neighbors to a recent past that is as deeply foreign as it is familiar.

While Gallant is not an overtly metafictional writer, she often self-consciously sounds out contemporary problems in aesthetics. "Bonaventure," one of the "Canadians Abroad" stories in *Home Truths*, examines the formalist impulse of twentieth-century art. Alluding to the masters of High Modernism—Joyce, Woolf, and Mann, among others—the story ambivalently critiques the views of Adrian, a musician-ephebe who believes that "painters learn to paint by looking at pictures, not at hills and valleys (152). Opposed to Borges's brilliant (but occasionally arid) fictional essays, Gallant's text also takes on the vagaries of sexual and generational conflicts, rather than simply being an abbreviated reflection on theoretical issues.

The more recent "Speck's Idea," from *Overhead in a Balloon*, is a telling satire that implicates the commodification of culture. An art dealer, Speck struggles to restore the reputation of a forgotten painter in order to ensure the prosperity of his own gallery. By manufacturing a retrospective avant-garde, Speck colludes with the hyperreal cityscape of Paris: "The street resembled a set in a French film designed for export, what with . . . the lights of the bookstore, the restaurant, and the gallery reflected, quivering, in European-looking puddles." Smythe is right to argue that for Gallant, "this commodification has contributed to the decline of historical consciousness on a large scale" (77); one might add that "Speck's Idea" avoids Jean Baudrillard's sense of despair regarding Western culture's inundation by simulacra. The left, an "anxious, humourless audience in its costly fake working-class clothes," is pilloried beside Speck's "Fascist" penchant for "dictating and regulating taste" (Besner 143), suggesting perhaps that the rhetoric of contemporary critical theory is itself overblown.

In discussing their art, short-story writers—from Frank O'Connor to Nadine Gordimer to Charles Baxter—often suggest that the form's implicit distrust of the novel's tendency for "totalization" closely enacts the fragmentary nature of human cognition. One of Gallant's greatest contributions to twentieth-century short fiction is her use of the genre to probe how the philosophical and historical problems of our time can best be approached by attempting to understand the enigmatic nature of the concrete. Conveying the intricate, often absurd, nature of human experience with an attentive and disciplined eye, Gallant's writing is unwavering in its exactitude, never failing to startle.

WORKS CITED AND CONSULTED

Primary

Gallant, Mavis. *Across the Bridge: Stories*. Toronto: McClelland & Stewart, 1993.

———. *The Collected Stories of Mavis Gallant*. New York: Random House, 1996. Reprinted as *The Selected Stories of Mavis Gallant*. Toronto: McClelland & Stewart, 1996.

———. *The End of the World and Other Stories*. Toronto: McClelland & Stewart, 1974.

———. *A Fairly Good Time*. New York: Random House, 1970.

———. *From the Fifteenth District: A Novella and Eight Short Stories*. New York: Random House, 1979.

———. *Green Water, Green Sky*. Boston: Houghton Mifflin, 1959.

———. *Home Truths: Selected Canadian Stories*. Toronto: Macmillan, 1981. Reprint, New York: Random House, 1981.

———. *In Transit*. New York: Viking, 1988.

———. *The Moslem Wife and Other Stories*. Toronto: McClelland & Stewart, 1994.

———. *My Heart Is Broken: Eight Stories and a Short Novel*. New York: Random House, 1964.

———. *The Other Paris*. Boston: Houghton Mifflin, 1956.

———. *Overhead in a Balloon: Stories of Paris*. New York: Random House, 1985.

———. *Paris Notebooks*. Toronto: Macmillan, 1986.

———. *The Pegnitz Junction: A Novella and Five Short Stories*. New York: Random House, 1973.

———. *What Is to Be Done?* Dunvegan: Quadrant, 1983.

Secondary

Baudrillard, Jean, *Fatal Strategies*. Trans. Philip Beitchman and W.G.I. Niesluchowski. New York: Semiotext(e), 1990.

Benjamin, Walter. *Illuminations*. Trans. Henry Zohn. New York: Schocken Books, 1969.

Besner, Neil K. *The Light of Imagination: Mavis Gallant's Fiction*. Vancouver: University of British Columbia Press, 1988.

Hancock, Geoffrey. "An Interview with Mavis Gallant." *Special Issue on Mavis Gallant*. Spec. Issue of *Canadian Fiction Magazine* 28 (November 1978): 18–67.

Keefer, Janice Kulyk. *Reading Mavis Gallant*. New York and Toronto: Oxford University Press, 1989.

Merler, Grazia. *Mavis Gallant: Narrative Patterns and Devices*. Ottawa: Tecumseh Press, 1978.

Smythe, Karen E. *Figuring Grief: Gallant, Munro, and the Poetics of Elegy*. Montreal: McGill-Queen's University Press, 1992.

NADINE GORDIMER
(November 20, 1923–   )

Christine Loflin

BIOGRAPHY

Nadine Gordimer was born in Springs, South Africa. She is the daughter of Isidore and Nan Gordimer. In 1949, she married Gerald Gavronsky; they had one child and were divorced in 1952. She married Reinhold Cassirer in 1954; they have one child. Gordimer first published a collection of short stories, *Face to Face*, in 1949; her first novel, *The Lying Days*, came out in 1953. Since then, she has published ten novels and a dozen collections of short stories. In addition, Gordimer has published numerous essays, including two collections: *The Black Interpreters: Notes on African Writing* (1973) and *The Essential Gesture: Writing, Politics, and Places* (1988). An outspoken critic of the former apartheid government in South Africa, Gordimer is a member of the African National Congress (ANC) and a member of the Congress of South African Writers. She has won numerous awards and honors for her work, including the Nobel Prize for Literature in 1991; the Booker Prize for Fiction in 1974, for *The Conservationist*; and honorary degrees from Harvard University, Yale University, Smith College, Mount Holyoke College, and the New School for Social Research.

CRITICISM

Nadine Gordimer has been the subject of numerous book-length studies and innumerable articles. The great majority of these studies, however, have focused on her novels. In the criticism of her short stories, writers have analyzed her presentation of race relations, her political positions, and gender issues. Articles such as Jeanne Colleran's "Archive of Apartheid: Nadine Gordimer's Short Fiction at the End of the Interregnum" and Barbara Eckstein's "Pleasure and Joy: Political Activism in Nadine Gordimer's Short Stories" study Gordimer's representations of the ideologies of both apartheid and the antiapartheid movement in South Africa. In "Once More into the Burrows: Nadine Gordimer's Later Short Fiction," Alan Lomberg analyzes recurrent themes in Gordimer's work, including love affairs, employers and servants' relationships, and the reconsideration of youthful events in old age. Kevin Magarey's "Cutting the Jewel: Facets of Art in Nadine Gordimer's Short Stories" explores the poetic structure of her stories: "The best of Nadine Gordimer's stories have . . . a concentration and a coherence of experience as recorded, as selected, and as significant, that is hardly possible in the novel" (47).

Karen Lazar's "Feminism as 'Piffling'? Ambiguities in Nadine Gordimer's Short Stories" addresses the perennial question of Gordimer's problematic relationship to feminism. In part, Gordimer's resistance to feminism may be the result of early male critiques of her work that emphasized the "endless feminine sensitivity . . . so overpoweringly omnipresent in Miss Gordimer's writings that even Virginia Woolf might be a little alarmed" (Delius 24). Gordimer repudiates the idea that her sensitivity is specifically "feminine" and claims that "to me, feminist writing is about being female, it's the people who write about how many orgasms you are entitled to, about the meaning of childbirth, and so on. To me, this is a kind of specialized sidetrack in writing" (interview with Franca Cavagnoli 87). Despite Gordimer's overt dismissal of feminism, Lazar sees Gordimer's short stories in *Something Out There* (1984) as displaying "a high degree of sympathy for women and an indignation against their social position" ("Feminism" 103–4). Yet, Lazar asserts, Gordimer continues to contend "that any potential for ideological identification between women is 'cut right through' by differentials of race and class" (108–9).

In "Echoes from Elsewhere: Gordimer's Short Fiction as Social Critique," Graham Huggan claims that the literary techniques of the short story, its limited duration and its fragmentation, make it "an ideal vehicle for radical social critique" (63). In Gordimer's short stories, readers should look for a "submerged consciousness" (63) below the surface of the narrative, a story the narrator will not or cannot tell directly. Through her manipulation of the literary techniques of the short story, Huggan claims, Gordimer reflects the politics of repression in South Africa: "The absent presences of the text . . . become the invisible nodes around which the story coheres" (71).

ANALYSIS

In her early work, Gordimer often focuses on the reaction of an intelligent, sensitive consciousness (usually white, although not always) to encounters across racial barriers. In stories such as "Is There Nowhere Else Where We Can Meet?" and "The Catch," she explores the limitations that racial prejudice and expectations impose on interactions between the races. Many of her stories, including these two, take place in a kind of limbo, outside the rounds of everyday life. A couple is on a beach holiday, a woman takes a shortcut through the woods, a young girl goes to an interracial party, and they encounter someone from a different race, outside the places in which their roles would be carefully scripted.

In "Ah, Woe Is Me" and "Six Feet of the Country," Gordimer ends the story with an image of a white gesture across racial barriers that is ludicrously inadequate to the suffering and pain with which the white characters have been confronted. In "Ah, Woe Is Me," the white employer talks to her former maid's daughter, Janet, at the end of the story. Janet's mother is now unemployed, and Janet is forced to stay home to care for her. Janet's misery is the result of the situation of black domestic workers in South Africa, whose employers need not provide any health benefits or pension plans nor continue to employ them when they become ill; it is also the result of the white employer's own actions. Yet all the employer can do when she realizes that Janet is no longer going to school, no longer studying to be a teacher, is to fetch her some old clothes and a few shillings. At the end of the story, Janet is weeping; the white employer thinks, "What could I do for her? What could I do?" and gives her a handkerchief (*Selected Stories* 35). Through these scenes, presented without narrative comment through the perspective of the white employer, Gordimer exposes the inadequacy of the employer's sympathy and the unconscious limitations of her analysis of Janet's problems. She thinks of their lives as "unknown and unimagined by me, and therefore beyond my questioning"; she sees the children appear in ragged clothes and thinks, "I suppose they were getting poorer" (*Selected Stories* 31). Without a willingness to see either her own involvement in the family's poverty or the larger economic system that forces them below their previous standard of living, the employer is helpless to change their situation: all she can do is offer a handkerchief. This story is a powerful indictment of charitable feelings among whites who support apartheid; later in her career, Gordimer will become equally scathing about liberals who refused to see the need for revolution in South Africa and continued to call for gradual reform from within the system.

In "Is There Nowhere Else Where We Can Meet?" the white woman protagonist encounters a black man along a secluded path. There is a struggle; he seizes her bag, and she runs away. Despite its structure, however, this story suggests that this archetypal scene of interracial violence may be the result of the woman's own prejudices; at first, she passes him without incident. When he comes after her and moves in front of her, he does not touch her: "He was there in front of her, so startling, so utterly unexpected, panting right into her face" (*Selected Stories* 18). Their scuffle and his grab for her purse may be the result of her panic at being so near to him. At the end of the story, the woman, disheveled and tired, chooses not to turn in at the first house to report the incident. Instead, she thinks to herself, "What did I fight for? Why didn't I give him the money and let him go?" (20). This question does not resolve the nature of their struggle; perhaps she is just regretting that she did not give in more quickly. But the decision not to report this incident and her self-condemnation show that the protagonist sees herself as at least partially at fault. The woman turns away from the house gate and "went down the road slowly, like an invalid, beginning to pick the blackjacks from her stockings" (20). This last detail, like the question "What did I fight for?" suggests a new understanding and the possibility that the protagonist will reassess her own involvement in racism and violence; yet the reader is not quite sure that such a transformation has actually taken place. This ambiguity about the quality, the durability, or even the existence of a moment of epiphany is one of the hallmarks of Gordimer's short stories.

The encounter across racial barriers, the importance (and ambiguity) of the ending, and the significance of the title in "Is There Nowhere Else Where We Can Meet?" are all common features of Gordimer's short stories. In addition, a few of her stories, such as "A Bit of Young Life," "The Night the Favorite Came Home," and "Friday's Footprint," analyze the limitations of middle-class white lives in ways reminiscent of John Updike's dissection of white suburbia in America. In stories such as "The Bridegroom," Gordimer focuses on a moment in which the human costs and contradictions of life under apartheid are starkly revealed. The protagonist of "The Bridegroom," for example, realizes that his friendship with the black men he works for will have to end when his white wife arrives at the work camp: "They just mustn't hang around, that's all. They must just understand that they mustn't hang around" (*Selected Stories* 85). Without realizing it, he has crossed the boundaries of apartheid society and must retreat before his transgression is revealed to his bride.

Several stories focus on conflicts and ironies within the antiapartheid movement itself. In "The Smell of Death and Flowers," the protagonist makes her first action against apartheid in a march into a township by whites—a march reported ahead of time to the police and to the newspapers, so that it becomes a ritual of transgression, arrest, and witnessing. Tacitly, the story asks, what has been accomplished? Politically, the act is an insignificant protest; perhaps its most important result is the protagonist's momentary feeling of sympathy across racial lines: "And she felt, suddenly, not *nothing*, but what they [black township residents] were feeling at the sight of her, a white girl, taken" (144). In "Open House," a white woman on the fringes of the antiapartheid movement entertains a foreign reporter with a miscellaneous collection of old friends purporting to be the "real voice" of the people, while a member of the ANC quietly passes through, leaving a note in her kitchen: "HOPE YOUR PARTY WENT WELL" (397). This message, printed in capitals, brings into the open the white hostess's anxiety about what she is doing: is this party fraudulent, a misrepresentation of the feelings of the African people? Is she simply pandering to the journalist's desire to see "the real South Africa"? What would it mean for this party to "go well"? The message from the underground is mysterious, oracular; the ANC figure passes through the background of this story like a barracuda underneath a school of clown fish. "Open House," like her recent story "The Moment before the Gun Went Off," warns Gordimer's outside audience that South African news stories are reported by people who have only a fleeting understanding of the complexities of life in South Africa. Her stories suggest a way of reading that is cautious, even suspicious, looking for what has been, perhaps necessarily, left unsaid.

In her most recent collection, *Jump and Other Stories* (1991), Gordimer's work takes a new turn. From her earliest stories, Gordimer's work has always included violence, as in "Is There Nowhere Else Where We Can Meet?" Violence, however, is contained, controlled: typically, by the end of the story, someone is thinking about what has happened, is trying to put it into some kind of context. For example, in "An Intruder," a house is broken into, and belongings are strewn about in a particularly obscene way; suddenly, the pregnant wife realizes the significance of the contraceptive jelly displayed on the couch in the living room—the intruder must have been a lover of her husband's. The story ends, "She was grown-up, now, suddenly, as some people are said to turn white-haired overnight" (386). Gordimer implies that violent acts are powerful rhetorical acts, demanding interpretation. In several of these new stories, however, violence is uncontained, uncontrollable: people are killed accidentally, victims are chosen at random. Stories end at moments of division. In "Once upon a Time," a story in which a young boy is trapped in the razor-sharp security wire topping the walls around his house, Gordimer ends the story: "The bleeding mass of the little boy was hacked out of the security coil with saws, wire-cutters, choppers, and they carried it—the man, the wife, the hysterical trusted house-maid and the weeping gardener—into the house" (30). The violence cannot be contained within the interpretive system of the family; it is beyond their imagination that the fence, meant to harm intruders, would harm the son. The title, "Once upon a Time," implies that this is a fairy tale. It is not, however, like the sanitized, twentieth-century versions of the Grimms' fairy tales, but a return to the uncensored, frightening originals. As Jeanne Colleran comments, in "Jump," "Once upon a Time," and other stories, "wordlessness is the only response possible to the devastating sense that life has outstripped any ability to account for it" (242).

"Once upon a Time" is also a departure from realistic fiction, which links it to the metafictional story "Teraloyna," in which Gordimer imagines a mythical island whose population has spread around the world, intermarrying with both blacks and whites, linking enemies by blood ties. Some of these stories are set outside of South Africa, including "Jump," "Some Are Born to Sweet Delight," and "My Father Leaves Home." In "Some Are Born to Sweet Delight," Gordimer traces how a girl in England is seduced, is engaged to a terrorist, and then ignorantly carries a bomb with her onto a plane, which is completely destroyed. Again, the meaning of the violent act is beyond the comprehension of its victims: "Vera had taken them all, taken the baby inside her; down, along with her happiness" (88). The terrorist is not South African; *Jump and Other Stories* widens the scope of Gordimer's analysis of violence, revealing that while racism is the underlying cause of violence in South Africa, its roots grow elsewhere as well.

Published after the release of Nelson Mandela in 1991, Gordimer's tales can be read as her speculations about, and fears for, the future. Violence is no longer intentional violence against a specific person, but a force of its own that sweeps up the young boy in "Once upon a Time," the white farmer's black son in "The Moment before the Gun Went Off," and the morning jogger of "Keeping Fit." Parents maim and kill their children, onlookers are crushed in crowds, whole planeloads are killed at once.

A few of these stories have black protagonists. In the past, Gordimer has used this perspective rarely, limiting her presentation of black experience to third-person narration in most of her stories. In 1990, Gordimer published her first novel from the perspective of a South African person of color, *My Son's Story*. In *Jump and Other Stories*, "The Ultimate Safari" and "Amnesty" are told in the first person by a young black girl and a black woman, respectively. Both of these protagonists are rural, linked to major political events only through family relationships. In "The Ultimate Safari," Gordimer presents the emotions of a young girl who crosses through Kruger Park in northern South Africa to arrive at the refugee camps set up for her people. Civil war drives these people to flee over the border, but they are not allowed to make a new home for themselves there; they must wait in refugee camps until they are allowed to return home. Gordimer uses the young girl's perspective and her rationalization of her experience to explore the meaning of "home." Interviewed by a reporter, the girl's grandmother says that she will not go back: "There is nothing. No home." The young girl thinks, "Why does our grandmother say that? . . . After the war, if there are no bandits any more, our mother may be waiting for us. And maybe when we left our grandfather, he was only left behind, he found his way somehow, slowly, through the Kruger Park, and he'll be there. They'll be home, and I'll remember them" (46). She has eagerly picked up the implication of the reporter's questions—that there will be a time when she can go "home," back to her village. But "home" to her does not mean a place, but a people, and she idealistically populates her village with all the people she has lost. The reporter's naïve assumption that there will be a home to return to is exposed first by the grandmother's denial and then more poignantly by the young girl's utopian vision of home.

Similarly, in "Amnesty," Gordimer depicts the disruptions and adjustments that are necessary when a husband is released from Robben Island. The wife, sitting on a hilltop, muses over everything that has happened: her child's refusal to recognize her father, her husband's quick visits, followed by a new loneliness as he continues his political work. She describes herself as "waiting," a status shared by many of the characters in this anthology who wait in refugee camps, in hotel rooms, in airport lobbies, in safe houses. Through these images of waiting and the images of violence, these stories paint a vivid picture of life in the "interregnum," as Gordimer herself has called it—that uneasy space between one regime and another, when the outcome is still uncertain.

WORKS CITED OR CONSULTED

Primary

Short Stories

Gordimer, Nadine. *Face to Face*. Johannesburg: Silver Leaf Books, 1949.

———. *Friday's Footprint*. New York: Viking, 1960.

———. *Jump and Other Stories*. New York: Farrar Straus Giroux, 1991.

———. *Livingstone's Companions*. New York: Viking, 1971.

———. "Loot." *New Yorker* March 22, 1999: 104–5.

———. *Not for Publication and Other Stories*. New York: Viking, 1965.

———. *Selected Stories*. New York: Viking, 1976. Published in England as *No Place Like: Selected Stories*. London: Jonathan Cape, 1975.

———. *Six Feet of the Country*. New York: Simon & Schuster, 1956.

———. *Six Feet of the Country* (contains stories from previously published collections). New York: Penguin, 1982.

———. *The Soft Voice of the Serpent and Other Stories*. New York: Simon & Schuster, 1952.

———. *A Soldier's Embrace*. New York: Viking, 1980.

———. *Some Monday for Sure*. Portsmouth, NH: Heinemann Educational, 1976.

———. *Something Out There*. New York: Viking, 1984.

———. *Town and Country Lovers*. Los Angeles: Sylvester & Orphanos, 1980.

———. *Why Haven't You Written? Selected Stories, 1950–1972*. London: Penguin, 1992.

Novels and Nonfiction Prose

Gordimer, Nadine. *The Black Interpreters: Notes on African Writing*. Johannesburg: Spro-Cas/Ravan Press, 1973.

———. *Burger's Daughter*. New York: Viking, 1979.

———. *The Conservationist*. London: J. Cape, 1974; New York: Viking, 1975.

———. *The Essential Gesture: Writing, Politics, and Places*. New York: Knopf, 1988.

———. "The Flash of Fireflies." *The New Short Story Theories*. Ed. Charles May. Athens: Ohio University Press, 1994. 263–67.

———. *A Guest of Honour*. New York: Viking, 1970.

———. *The House Gun*. Farrar Straus Giroux, 1998.

———. *July's People*. New York: Viking, 1981.

———. *The Late Bourgeois World*. New York: Viking, 1966.

———. *The Lying Days*. New York: Simon & Schuster, 1953.

———. *My Son's Story*. New York: Farrar Straus Giroux, 1990.

———. *None to Accompany Me*. Farrar Straus Giroux, 1994.

———. *Occasion for Loving*. New York: Viking, 1963.

———. *A Sport of Nature*. New York: Knopf, 1987.

———. *A World of Strangers*. New York: Simon & Schuster, 1958.

———. *Writing and Being*. Cambridge, MA: Harvard University Press, 1995.

———. *A Writing Life*. Ed. Andries Walter Oliphant. London: Viking, 1998.

Secondary

Cavagnoli, Franca. "The Writer at Work: Interview with Nadine Gordimer." *Current Writing: Text and Reception in Southern Africa* 5.1 (April 1993): 85–92.

Colleran, Jeanne. "Archive of Apartheid: Nadine Gordimer's Short Fiction at the End of the Interregnum." *The Later Fiction of Nadine Gordimer*. Ed. Bruce King. New York: St. Martin's, 1993. 237–45.

Delius, Anthony. "Danger from the Digit: *The Soft Voice of the Serpent.*" *Critical Essays on Nadine Gordimer*. Ed. Rowland Smith. Boston: G. K. Hall, 1990. 23–25.

Driver, Dorothy, Ann Dry, Craig MacKenzie, and John Reed, comps. *Nadine Gordimer: A Bibliography of Primary and Secondary Sources, 1937–1992*. London: Hans Zell, 1994.

Eckstein, Barbara. "Pleasure and Joy: Political Activism in Nadine Gordimer's Short Stories." *World Literature Today* 59.3 (Summer 1985): 342–46.

Githii, Ethel W. "Nadine Gordimer's *Selected Stories.*" *Critique: Studies in Contemporary Fiction* 22.3 (1981): 45–54.

Huggan, Graham. "Echoes from Elsewhere: Gordimer's Short Fiction as Social Critique." *Research in African Literatures* 25.1 (Spring 1994): 61–73.

Jacobs, J. U. "Living Space and Narrative Space in Nadine Gordimer's 'Something Out There.' " *English in Africa* 14.2 (October 1987): 31–43.

Kinkead-Weekes, Mark. "Sharp Knowing in Apartheid? The Shorter Fiction of Nadine Gordimer and Doris Lessing." *Essays on African Writing, 1: A Re-evaluation*. Ed. Gurnah, Abdulrazak. Oxford: Heinemann, 1993. 88–110.

Lazar, Karen. "Feminism as 'Piffling'? Ambiguities in Nadine Gordimer's Short Stories." *Current Writing* 2.1 (October 1990): 101–16. Rpt. in *The Later Fiction of Nadine Gordimer*. New York: St. Martin's, 1993. 101–16.

————. "*Jump and Other Stories*: Gordimer's Leap into the 1990s: Gender and Politics in Her Latest Short Fiction." *Journal of Southern African Studies* 18.4 (1992): 783–802.

Lomberg, Alan. "Once More into the Burrows: Nadine Gordimer's Later Short Fiction." *The Later Fiction of Nadine Gordimer*. Ed. Bruce King. New York: St. Martin's, 1993. 228–36.

Maclennan, Don. "The South African Short Story." *English Studies in Africa* 13 (March 1970): 112–19.

Magarey, Kevin. "Cutting the Jewel: Facets of Art in Nadine Gordimer's Short Stories." *Critical Essays on Nadine Gordimer*. Ed. Rowland Smith. Boston: G. K. Hall, 1990. 45–74.

Trump, Martin. "What Time Is This for a Woman? An Analysis of Nadine Gordimer's Short Fiction." *Women and Writing in South Africa: A Critical Anthology*. Ed. Cherry Clayton. Marshalltown: Heinemann Southern Africa, 1989. 183–207.

PATRICIA GRACE
(August 17, 1937–   )

Pierre-Damien Mvuyekure

BIOGRAPHY

Patricia Grace was born in Wellington, New Zealand. Although she has been presented as a member of the Maori tribe, one of the New Zealand native tribes, Grace has multiple ancestry. She is a descendant of Ngati Raukawa, Ngati Toa, and Te Ati, and she is married to a Ngati Porou. She was educated in Wellington, first at Green Street Convent and then at St. Mary's College. After teaching in country schools in Northland and Porirua, she returned to Plimmerton, where she now lives with her husband and seven children.

Whether in anthologies or in introductory notes to her books, Grace is always described as the first Maori woman writer in English. She is mostly known for her short stories and novels, but also for her children's stories. In 1975, she published her first and acclaimed collection of short stories, *Waiariki*, followed by *Mutuwhenua* (1978), her first novel. There followed another collection of short stories, *The Dream Sleepers and Other Stories* (1980), and two children's books, *The Kuia and the Spider* (1981) and *Watercress Tuna and the Children of Champion Street* (1984). Subsequently, she published other works of fiction, including *Potiki* (1986), *Electric City and Other Stories* (1987), *Selected Stories* (1991), *Cousins* (1992), *The Sky People* (1994), and *Baby No-Eyes* (1998). Grace has received numerous awards, including ones from the Maori Purposes Fund Board and the New Zealand Literary Fund. Despite the fact that Grace's stories have appeared in numerous periodicals and anthologies, as yet, too few scholars and critics have approached her work.

CRITICISM

Although Grace has written novels and children's stories, she is best known for her short stories. However, she has been blamed for her manipulation of the

English language to present a Maori self. In his "A Maori Literature in English, Part I: Prose Fiction—Patricia Grace," Norman Simms divides the twelve stories of *Waiariki* into three categories: "Maori Tales" are "written in English words, but following Maori syntax and thought patterns"; "Macaronic Tales" are those written "with a high frequency of Maori words"; and "English Tales" are those stories that do not disturb the "English syntax beyond its normal bounds and [in which] the experience of Maoriness is made to flow through the narrative shape of a European story" (111). But a more damaging criticism is Simms's conclusion that "Patricia will ultimately be judged" upon the English tales and that "her success is partial and admirable, but that more remains to be done before the boundaries of the short-story as evolved for the European experience are adjusted fully to accommodate the Maori experience" (111). However, an analysis of the three collections of short stories reveals that Grace is even more successful in stories that use a high frequency of Maori words and thought patterns or those that blend prose and sung poetry. Thus the so-called manipulation of language can be said to be the strongest contribution that she makes to the short-story genre. It is worth noting that the textual strategies that Grace uses in her stories are known in postcolonial writing and theory as "abrogation" and "appropriation," respectively, "a refusal of the categories of the imperial culture" and the process whereby "the language is taken and made 'to bear the burden' of one's own cultural experience" (Ashcroft, Griffiths, and Tiffin 38).

In his review of *The Dream Sleepers and Other Stories*, David Norton charges Grace with writing with "minimal punctuation. Particularly in some of the earlier stories there is so little that reading is almost as difficult as making out a troublesome handwriting" (116). Other critical reviews of the three collections of short stories have focused on the fact that Patricia Grace is interested in presenting Maori people to a Pákehá (European) audience. But what clearly characterizes Grace's three collections of short stories, besides exquisite manipulation of the English language, is adumbrated in "Parade" when Grandpa Hohepa tells his granddaughter, who is reluctant to participate in a Maori parade, "It is your job, this. To show others [Pákehá] who we are" (*Waiariki* 88). Of course, showing who the Maori are includes blending sung poetry with fiction and inserting Maori words in stories as if they were English words, although *Waiariki* and *The Dream Sleepers and Other Stories* have a glossary at the end.

ANALYSIS

The introductory note to "Patricia Grace" in *Contemporary Literary Criticism* characterizes the author's work as employing "an unusual prose style based on Maori speech patterns" (Matuz 110). Critics of Grace have often failed to see that she does to the English language what postcolonial writers the world over have done. For example, many of Grace's short stories in *Waiariki* and *The Dream Sleepers and Other Stories* read like *The Palm-Wine Drinkard* by the Nigerian writer Amos Tutuola. Before becoming a classic, Tutuola's novel was blamed for its bad English, imitative of the speech and thought patterns of some of the Nigerian languages. Further, some Caribbean writers like Kamau Brathwaite have creolized English. In African-American literature, writers have manipulated the English language by writing in or using black dialect in novels, poems, and plays. It is therefore time to praise, not denigrate, Grace for her contribution to the short-story genre.

Waiariki chronicles the lives of Maori people by using Maori speech patterns and Maori words. It is worth noting that Grace matches language with the level of her characters' education. "A Way of Talking," the opening short story, is written in plain English because the protagonist, Rose, is a college student who has mastered the Pákehá language, English. She gets upset with Jane Frazer, a white dressmaker, because she does not mention her Maori scrub cutters by their names. In "Toki," Grace begins her use of Maori thought patterns and words. The story is about Toki, a fisherman who attracts a bride-to-be to him by bragging about his fishing skills. The protagonist and narrator of the story challenges Toki to the competition. At the end, waves crash Toki's boat, the bride goes back to the narrator, and Toki abandons fishing for big fish for "kina" (sea eggs) and "paua" (shellfish).

From the North he came, Toki, in his young days. Ah yes. A boaster this one, Toki the fisherman. "They are all there, the fish!" he said. "In the waters of the north. The tamure, the tarakihi, the moki, and the hapuku. And Toki, he has the line and the hand for all of them." Toki from the north, Toki the fisherman. (7)

This excerpt displays elements of oral traditions such as the use of "Ah," as well as the first sentence that might lead one to read it as a translation. An inversion of the subject pervades the story: "Long ago we had a mind for the same girl, Toki and I" or "Then he came Toki, and her head was turned until I showed him as a boaster" (6). The excerpt also shows the names of fish in Maori.

In "The Dream," the fifth story of the collection, Raniera awakes from a dream that he and his friends try to interpret in order to bet on horse racing. This short story challenges the reader by using full sentences in Maori:

"E Hika! He aha te moemoea?" [Hey! What's the dream?] called Ben as Raniera stepped from the taxi and waved to the driver.
    "What's the dream?"
    "E tama, he tuna!" [An eel, man]
    "Ei! Kia Tika ra!" [?]
    "Yeh! A big one this eel. Ka nui te kaita!" [Great in size] (20–21)

The sentences are followed by their "translation" in English, a technique known as "glossing" (Ashcroft, Griffiths, and Tiffin 61). That is, by paying attention to the conversation among characters, one is able to fathom the meaning of the

Maori phrases. This is carried on in "Holiday," the sixth short story of the collection, narrated by a young Maori who visits her Nanny Retimana. The language matches the story: the young girl worries that when she gets to her grandmother's, Retimana will have changed, just as her parents will have changed by the time she goes back home. Most important is the fact that the story is sprinkled with numerous words and phrases in Maori, like "A taure-kareka [a scoundrel]," "a parengo [a sea lettuce]," "haunga [stinking]," "Uncle's big pukee [Uncle's big stomach]" (27), and "You bring your wife next time, and bring my nokopuna [grandchildren]" (29). Of course, the reader has to go to the glossary pages to find the meaning of these Maori words and phrases. Norman Simms has noted quite rightly that "in this story the Maori words seem appropriate to the characters and the situation, but mostly as local colour, and can be justified mainly on the grounds of the child's unsophisticated reproduction of the surface situation around her" (112).

Grace's unique blend of the lyric and prose is clearly demonstrated in "And So I Go" and "Valley." "And So I Go" is an innovative short story in that it is told in double voice and is sprinkled with poetic lines. The narrator, whose voice is italicized, is asked why he is leaving his community (elders, brothers, sisters, and children) to go to another place. In a sense, the story recalls the "call and response" that one can observe in African-American churches, a technique also used in fiction, drama, poetry, and speeches by African Americans. The following excerpt illustrates both the double-voicedness and the infusion of poetic devices:

And you ask me shall I sing. I tell you this. The singing will be there within myself. Inside this body. Fleeting through these bones. Ringing in the skies of being. . . .
    Ribboning in the course of blood to soothe swelled limbs and ache bruised heart.
    You say to us our brother you will sing. But will the songs within be songs of joy? Will they ring? Out in the skies of being as you say? (45)

The language in this excerpt is metaphoric, imagistic, and lyrical. Further, the excerpt adumbrates the themes of relationships, land, and sea as signposts of the Maori cultural identity that permeates *Waiariki* and other collections of short stories. This inclusion of the lyrical is powerfully displayed in "Valley," a short story that spans four seasons, summer, autumn, winter, and spring. The story is narrated by a Pákehá schoolteacher who tries to make her Maori students aware of their lives through four seasons. The lyricism of the short story recalls Shakespeare's sonnets about summer, autumn, winter, and spring, with their respective imagery. Each season (or part of the story) contains at least one poem.

The use of Maori words and the blend of the lyric continue in *The Dream Sleepers and Other Stories*, Grace's second collection of short stories. The book is divided into two parts, with seven stories in the first part and five in the second. David Norton has characterized the stories in the second part as lacking in "focus of coherence" (116), but a closer reading reveals that not only do they have common themes like family relationships, but they also are held together by the same characters—Uncle Kep, Mereana, Lizzie, Charlotte, Macky, and Denny Boy. More important, such assessments ignore the extensive use of Maori and the lyrical within the prose lines to produce a coherent whole. Although the collection has fewer poems than *Waiariki*, one example from the first part will demonstrate how Grace blends poetry and prose. In "Letters from Whetu," Grace makes a point about the use of English through Whetu, who, bored by his classes, resorts to writing letters to Enny, Ani, Sef, and Andy during, respectively, English, mathematics, geography, and history classes. Further, Whetu makes his English teacher's life miserable by purposely using "yous" instead of "you" and by making fun of her fondness for "K.M.—KAY EM," or Katherine Mansfield, whom she knows by "HART (HALT ALL RACIST TOURS)" (30). Throughout the letters, Whetu is unable to remember two childhood songs, the " 'Shake-a-Shake-a' and the 'Culley bubba,' " but he remembers Iosefa's verse:

> Tasi lua tolu fa [one two three four—Samoan],
> Come a me a hugga hugga
> Shake-a-shake-a Shake-a
> Culley bubba longa-a long-a
> And
> Tangaroa Tangaroa [God of the Seas]
> Little fish belong-a he a
> Shake-a Shake-a. (31)

Life is meaningful to Whetu, then, only when he sings in Maori and creates songs that play on English, as in "rai-ai-ain," "Chi-I-ild," and "ea-ea-earth" (42). Blending poetry and prose reveals to what extent Grace breaks from regular sentences to verses and then back to regular sentences without any warning. This is what makes *Waiariki* and *The Dream Sleepers and Other Stories* more successful than *Electric City and Other Stories*. In effect, the last collection does not make extensive use of Maori words, nor does it blend poetry and prose. Perhaps Grace ultimately gave in to the pressure of literary critics, or maybe she thought that she had done enough with *Potiki*, her second novel, which also blends poetry and prose.

WORKS CITED AND CONSULTED

Primary

Grace, Patricia. *Baby No-Eyes*. Honolulu: University of Hawai'i Press, 1998.
———. *Cousins*. New York: Penguin Books, 1992.
———. *The Dream Sleepers and Other Stories*. Auckland: Longman Paul, 1980.
———. *Electric City and Other Stories*. Auckland: Penguin Books, 1987.
———. *The Kuia and the Spider*. Auckland: Longman Paul, 1981.
———. *Mutuwhenua: The Moon Sleeps*. Auckland: Longman Paul, 1978.

————. *Potiki*. Auckland: Penguin Books, 1986.

————. *Selected Stories*. Auckland: Penguin Books, 1991.

————. *The Sky People*. Auckland: Penguin Books, 1994.

————. *Waiariki*. Auckland: Longman Paul, 1975.

————. *Watercress Tuna and the Children of Champion Street*. Auckland: Longman Paul, 1984.

Secondary

Ashcroft, Bill, Gareth Griffiths, and Helen Tiffin. *The Empire Writes Back: Theory and Practice in Post-colonial Literatures*. New York: Routledge, 1989.

Bader, Eleanor J. "Ridiculous Things in Pakeha Kitchens." *Contemporary Literary Criticism*. Vol. 56. Ed. Roger Matuz. New York: Gale Research, 1989. 123.

Beston, John B. "The Fiction of Patricia Grace." *Contemporary Literary Criticism*. Vol. 56. Ed. Roger Matuz. New York: Gale Research, 1989. 119–21.

————. "Rev. of *The Dream Sleepers and Other Stories*." *Contemporary Literary Criticism*. Vol. 56. Ed. Roger Matuz. New York: Gale Research, 1989. 116–17.

Matuz, Roger, ed. *Contemporary Literary Criticism*. Vol. 56. New York: Gale Research, 1989.

Norton, David. "Rev. of *The Dream Sleepers and Other Stories*." *Contemporary Literary Criticism*. Vol. 56. Ed. Roger Matuz. New York: Gale Research, 1989. 116.

Pearson, Bill. "Witi Ihimaera and Patricia Grace." *Contemporary Literary Criticism*. Vol. 56. Ed. Roger Matuz. New York: Gale Research, 1989. 117–119.

Simms, Norman. "A Maori Literature in English, Part I: Prose Fiction—Patricia Grace." *Contemporary Literary Criticism*. Vol. 56. Ed. Roger Matuz. New York: Gale Research, 1989. 110–14.

Tutuola, Amos. *The Palm-Wine Drinkard and His Palm-Wine Tapster in the Dead's Town*. New York: Grove Press, 1953.

Wevers, Lydia. "The Short Story." *The Oxford History of New Zealand Literature in English*. Ed. Terry Sturn. New York: Oxford University Press, 1991. 201–68.

GISH JEN
(1955–   )

R. C. *Feddersen*

BIOGRAPHY

Gish Jen was born Lillian C. Jen to immigrant Chinese-American parents in New York City. She grew up in Yonkers and Scarsdale, New York. She earned her B.A. at Harvard and then studied at Stanford before attending the Iowa Writers' Workshop in the early 1980s. In a *MELUS* interview with Yuko Matsukawa (1993–94), Jen said that her interest in writing probably began with a fifth-grade project—a literary magazine—for which she submitted contributions in every category. Later, as an English major at Harvard, Jen took a prosody class with Robert Fitzgerald, who encouraged her to do something "literary" and helped get her a job in publishing with Doubleday (118). Although Jen was initially a business student at Stanford, she "spent the whole year writing novels and taking writing courses" (118). During the summer of 1982, between her first and second year at the Iowa Writers' Workshop, two of Jen's stories, "Bellying-Up" and "The Small Concerns of Sparrows," were accepted for publication under her legal name, Lillian C. Jen. Lillian Jen took her high-school nickname, "Gish" Jen (after Lillian Gish), as her pen name before the publication of "The White Umbrella" in 1984.

Gish Jen won national acclaim with the 1991 publication of her novel *Typical American*, which was nominated for a National Book Critics' Circle Award. However, it was Jen's skill with short fiction that first caught the interest of keen readers. Since she officially launched her career in 1982, Jen's stories have appeared in the *New Yorker*, the *Atlantic, Best American Short Stories*, and various anthologies. She has garnered several awards and honors, including the Henfield Foundation *Transatlantic Review* Award (1983), the prize from the Katherine Anne Porter Contest (*Nimrod*, 1987), and the prize from the Boston MBTA (Massachusetts Bay Transportation Authority) Urbanarts Project (1988). In addition, Jen has received fellowships from the Radcliffe Bunting Institute

(1986), the Copernicus Society (1986), the National Endowment for the Arts (1988), the Massachusetts Artists' Foundation (1988), and the Guggenheim Foundation. Her story "Birthmates" appeared in *The Best American Short Stories of the Century* (1999). Jen is married, has one son, and lives in Massachusetts.

CRITICISM

Although Gish Jen quickly demonstrated that she is an excellent short fictionist, she has not yet published a collection of stories. Nearly all critical attention (and much well-deserved praise) has focused on her novel. One article by Gerald Burns in the *Philippine American Studies Journal* examines Jen's "What Means Switch" with three other stories published in the May 1990 issue of the *Atlantic Monthly*. In "A Quartet of Voices in Recent American Literature," Burns discusses the common concerns of contemporary fiction and claims that "gender relations is a central subject and catalyst in recent American literature" (8). Burns argues briefly that even though "What Means Switch" is ostensibly concerned with cultural differences, it also foregrounds gender issues.

There can be little doubt that a writer of Jen's skill will stimulate much critical attention in the years to come, but for now, most commentary on her work must be gleaned from reviews of *Typical American*. A brief look at Jen's novel and the response to it will be useful for two reasons. First, the novel is about the Changs, a fictional Chinese-American family who first appeared as short-story characters; in fact, *Typical American* grew out of Jen's story "In the American Society" and incorporates parts of two other stories: "The Water-Faucet Vision" and "Grover at the Wheel." Second, the novel relates to the stories in that it develops one of Jen's central concerns as a fiction writer: the concept of personal identity in today's world.

Typical American has been lauded as an insightful look into the immigration experience and its inevitable clashes of culture in adapting to life in America. In particular, reviewers praised Jen's deft sense of language, rich irony, and wry, though sometimes dark, humor. An admirer of Jane Austen, Jen uses irony in complex and often subtle ways in the novel, as in much of her short fiction. While most of the Chang short stories are narrated by second-generation daughters Callie and Mona, the novel uses the more distant third-person narrative style of "Grover at the Wheel," a story that (with some changes) makes up two chapters. In the *New York Times Book Review*, A. G. Mojtabai extols the novel's "epigrammatic sweep and swiftness" in "line after stunning line." One dissenting opinion about narrative style is voiced in the *Women's Review of Books* by Vivian Gornick, who laments that contemporary American writing overemphasizes language craft; "skill not insight, voice not point of view." Gornick seems to find problematic something that Jen herself believes to be a strength, the use of "complex tone"—an ironic finesse that arises from seemingly indeterminate moral and emotional distance in narration. Jen credits this narrative tendency to her cultural background, where opposite qualities can exist simultaneously in the same thing, like yin and yang ("*MELUS* Interview" 119).

Nearly all commentators discuss *Typical American*'s concerns with adapting to a different culture, concerns that are also found in much of Jen's short fiction. Matthew Gilbert of the *Boston Globe* (unlike Gornick, who believes that the immigrant novel has been done better) praises the novel, noting that the traditional extended-family structure itself is eroded as characters developing private selves begin to keep secrets from each other; the "operative theme . . . is that freedom can be dangerous." Mojtabai cites greed—American materialism—as the transforming motivation. His only quibble with the novel's excellence is that characters could be rendered deeper and motivation developed more fully, faults that Vivian Gornick finds also.

Jen has said that one purpose in writing *Typical American* was to explore what it means to become "American." She suggests that Ralph Chang's struggle with American individualism—toward realization of a "grandiose self"—allegorizes a struggle of national identity, America's need to stop and assess the real nature of freedom and its limitations ("Writing" 133–34). The issue is not preserving the individual's heritage, but understanding and maintaining a sense of "self" that is difficult to define in contemporary life. Jim Bencivenga in the *Christian Science Monitor* discusses *Typical American*'s "cross-cultural perceptions of family life" in terms of the shifting cultural values that "sometimes freshen but often buffet relations." A mechanical engineer, Ralph's nineteenth-century ideas of fixity symbolize his reluctance to forsake traditional structures; but as family members adapt, they begin to "rely on bonds less visible, more emotional, and psychologically dense" (13).

Two critics who provide analytical insights into Jen's work are Patricia Storace and Manini Samarth. Storace, in the *New York Review of Books*, claims that dualities—"the notion of pairs, doubles, and the interplay of possibility and limitation"—inform the book. She also discusses the importance of sibling rivalry as a motivation for Ralph, whose idolization of capitalist rogue and third-generation Chinese American Grover Ding absurdly recalls the romantic individualism of another "Ralph," Ralph Waldo Emerson. Storace further believes that immigration is a metaphor in the novel, that birth, death, and passages of life are forms of immigration. Bilingualism emphasizes how self-concepts are influenced by language and how the Changs' adjustments to domestic family life may be seen as "translation" (11).

Manini Samarth's "Affirmations: Speaking the Self into Being" examines Jen's novel along with books by two other Chinese Americans, Frank Chin and David Wong Louie. Samarth praises *Typical American* as a "funny, probing," and "subtl[e] exploration of the immigrant's two polar realms of existence—his lighted, open world of assimilation and his darker, narrower world of myth" (93). Samarth believes that Jen conceptualizes the "self" in spatial metaphors, so that the house symbolizes the "private, mythic Chinese self" protecting the "not-dual" (and so one) identity: disintegrating houses and businesses advert to

the failing stability of the family's traditional structure (94). Samarth also notes
that the novel affirms Asian women, who rely not on superstructures and myths
but "meaning in little gestures" (95). Regarding language, Samarth claims that
as the Changs are forced to adapt, they slowly move from filtering America
"into the inner world of myth and selfhood" toward flexibility of experience and
expression; language becomes an "open space in which the Changs constantly
recreate themselves" (96).

In many ways, *Typical American* is intimately connected in its themes with
many of Jen's best short stories. The contemporary experience pushes characters
beyond previous identity questions of who one *is* to what it means to be *one* at
all. Besides family and parental influences, many facets of culture (myth, language, economics, social structure) contribute to the construction of reality in
which, and against which, the individual self emerges. In this novel (as in many
of Jen's stories), the automobile and driving become metaphoric of the mobile
(and unrooted) American "self," the externalized sense of empowerment that
can be exhilarating but dangerously fragile. Order and structure often contrast
with the ebb and flow of complex human relationships suggested by images of
fluidity and water. Jen considers *Typical American* to be a "tragi-comic" novel;
if so, then Ralph is the parodic tragic hero whose trajectory, whether Chinese
(as the patriarchal protector of family order) or American (as entrepreneur),
cannot rise to the level of his aspirations. As hero, he is undercut by decrepit
roofs, houses, and businesses, despite his engineering skills. Jen's irony shades
from light and dark comedy into the realm of tragic introspection.

ANALYSIS

"In the American Society" (1986) is one of Jen's most anthologized stories
and the story from which her novel (originally titled the same) grew. Although
this story centers on Ralph Chang, it is narrated by older daughter Callie, whose
mildly amused ironic distance is subtly blended with her sympathy for both
father and mother. The first section of the story (subtitled "His Own Society")
depicts Ralph as owner of a restaurant specializing in pancakes (not fried
chicken, as in the novel). The restaurant (Ralph's foray into the American
Dream) is very successful until Ralph thinks of his relationship to the business
as analogous to his grandfather's paternalistic relationship with his village in
China. Seeing himself as a kind of "godfather," Ralph begins to lose employees
who want only a job, not a place in Ralph's "society." More troubles arise when
Ralph hires illegal Chinese workers who flee the authorities owing him bail
money. Both Ralph and his wife keep secrets: he does not tell her about hiring
Chinese employees, and she does not tell him about her plans for joining the
country club.

Contrasts in settings carry much of the impact of this story. In the second
part (subtitled the same as the story), Ralph (at his wife's insistence) shops for
a suit to attend a party to meet some of the country-club set. When the Changs

finally arrive at the party, it is a patio affair; Ralph is conspicuously overdressed. The contrast between the structure of Ralph's world (with him at the center) and the informality of the party gathered around the pool foregrounds the culture/identity conflicts. Callie signals the contrast of structure and fluidity earlier when she says that she and her sister Mona are ready to leave the confinement of the restaurant; the late summer breezes, like her dreams, begin to be redolent of the ocean.

The water motif continues when Ralph is confronted near the pool by his drunken host, Jeremy (whom he has never met); after a dispute over an empty wine bottle, Jeremy drunkenly and repeatedly asks Ralph who he is, comically emphasizing the motif of identity. Things worsen as Jeremy attempts to apologize by giving Ralph his polo shirt; in removing Ralph's jacket, Jeremy finds and loudly announces the price from the still-attached tag. The contrast in clothing styles (polo shirt and suit) underscores the differences of externalized social identity roles projected by the two men. Finally, Ralph defiantly flings both the shirt and his jacket into the pool, and the Changs quickly depart.

Callie's extroverted younger sister Mona is impressed with her father's assertiveness, but everyone is disappointed when it is discovered that Ralph's keys (in the jacket pocket) are now at the bottom of the pool. His wife suggests that they wait at the restaurant (Ralph's world) until the party dies down. While this is essentially a comic story, Ralph's comment near the end that both Callie and Mona are "good swimmers" (unlike him) suggests the serious mediation between family and outside society that the daughters must enact as they develop their own personalities. Such navigation is not simple, and Callie's narrative tone makes this story subtler than it may first appear.

A much later story (but earlier in the life of the Changs), "Grover at the Wheel," again uses juxtaposition and setting for contrast. Ralph, Helen (wife), and Theresa (sister) attend a traditional Chinese dinner party to meet a prospective marriage partner for Theresa. But Grover Ding turns out to be Chinese only in appearance. As a third-generation Chinese American, he neither speaks the language nor knows Chinese customs. In fact, Grover is almost a type—the self-made American man who respects only his own resourcefulness. Grover is irreverent throughout the lavish seven-course meal. His attitude toward romance is as capitalistic as his attitudes toward material wealth, and he unabashedly flirts, not with Theresa, but with Ralph's wife.

When Ralph, Grover, and host "Old Chao" (an engineering professor whom Ralph obviously envies) go to look at Old Chao's new car, Grover takes Ralph on an unsanctioned, high-speed test drive, leaving Old Chao in dismay. As they leave the city, Ralph notices that Grover does not drive like other people who either sit hunched over the steering wheel or stiffly back from it; Grover is in facile accord with the car, "snaking" its way through the traffic. Without hesitating, he simply glances and passes. The convertible becomes an extension of Grover's ego—car and driver are a metaphor for the unanchored, unattached self that sees the stars as superficial personal comforts and trees as "opportunities."

In sharp contrast to the earlier meal, Grover and Ralph stuff themselves at a roadside cafe (which, it turns out, Grover owns). His and Ralph's "meal" is a perverse inversion of the earlier traditional dinner: they order dinner first, then lunch, then breakfast. Ralph stops short of entering the kitchen where Grover is (presumably) enjoying an after-hours sexual dalliance with the waitress—an absurd parody of the hoped-for courtship of Theresa. In a sense, Ralph is actually the one seduced by Grover. Finding that Grover, too, is familiar with *The Power of Positive Thinking*, Ralph begins to idolize Grover and to fantasize his own materialistic independence. Ralph temporarily escapes not only from the formality of the social occasion, but also from less clearly defined emotional responsibilities of his place in the family. The last line ambiguously undercuts Ralph's euphoric "liberation": "A sky opened out around him, a whole starry firmament, as he climbed the long staircase home" (37).

Two other stories about the Chang family explore tensions between traditional family structure and emotional attachment from the point of view of the older daughter, Callie, who must come to terms with life both inside the family and outside, in the larger and less certain world of American society. "The White Umbrella" (1984) and "The Water-Faucet Vision" (1987) depict the daughters' (especially Callie's) process of growing up in a bicultural experience and how it suggests the conflicts of personal identity.

In the first story, twelve-year-old Callie discovers that her mother has gone to work without telling her or her sister Mona even though the parents claim that they do not need the extra income—like the Lee family, the other Chinese family in town. Problems arise when the girls walk to piano lessons in a rainstorm, and Callie tries to keep her mother's secret. Even though she knows that many American mothers work, Callie uncritically accepts her parents' need to maintain "appearances," and the motif of appearances and "seeing" emerges early when Callie tells Mona that her glasses are dirty, and Mona retorts that Callie's own glasses need cleaning.

Callie is embarrassed when Miss Crosman notices that Mona's glasses are indeed "filthy," but her attention is drawn to a white umbrella near the piano. The white umbrella, which "glowed like a scepter on the blue carpet," is a central symbol that points to Callie's fantasy desire for an "American" identity; this association with the romantic American myth of femininity found in fairy tales temporarily offers escape from the conflict that Callie is experiencing, which includes acknowledging her family's "otherness." Callie believes that the umbrella was left by Eugenie Roberts, another student a year older than Callie. Eugenie is rumored to have a boyfriend in high school and seems to be Callie's image of all-American girlhood and sexuality: she has auburn hair, blue eyes, and "ballooning breasts" (402). Callie's desire for the umbrella is doubly strong because she knows that it is the kind of American "thing" that her mother would never allow her to have.

After the lesson, Callie conceals the fact that her mother is working by waiting outside in the rain even though Mona opts to go in with Miss Crosman. Callie pretends that her mother, who always runs late coming from work, will be picking them up any minute, just as earlier, she had lied to Miss Crosman that her mother was a concert pianist. Ironically, Miss Crosman turns out to be the owner of the umbrella and makes a present of it to Callie, who immediately senses "just what she wanted to hear": Callie tells Miss Crosman that she wishes that she were her mother (407).

The emotional conflict between Callie's immature but intuitive need to fill the emotional needs of others and trying to fulfill her own is ironically complicated by the ending of the story. Her mother does arrive, and Callie learns that she is up for a promotion at her job at the store. But the mother's sense of security outside the home is uncertain, as is suggested by the fact that she is prone to have car accidents. Callie—partly from guilt—conceals the umbrella under her skirt. When Mona (who seems much less concerned with appearances) asks what is under her skirt, their mother has a minor accident that leaves her head tilted back and her eyes closed in despair. This story's emotional peak occurs when Callie, fearing that her mother is dead, begins to cry. In the ensuing confusion, she throws the umbrella down a sewer.

Despite its obvious central symbol, "The White Umbrella" is not as simple as it may first appear, partly due to the narrative stance. Callie is telling this story from a distance in time, as a more mature person, but she offers little evaluation of her behavior. Her minimal commentary is brought into ironic relief by the fact that her judgment during the time of the story is undercut: she assures Mona that the clouds are only "cumulous," yet both of them get soaked in the rain. It is also rain that puts the umbrella in Callie's possession, even though her desire for the umbrella has little to do with its use. Like images of liquidity in other stories, the rainwater contrasts with structured order, this time, of "appearances." Despite Callie's attempts to ignore the rain, she cannot ignore her emotions—and the spontaneous flow of her own tears. The final irony is that Callie's act of contrition conceals a secret; her disposal of the umbrella is ambiguous and complex—is it cleansing or repressing her sense of guilt?

Callie's struggle with a romanticized sense of identity is also foregrounded in "The Water-Faucet Vision," which she again narrates from the standpoint of an adult. Callie quickly contrasts her own sensibility of life with that of her sister Mona, to whom "fighting was just fighting"; Callie "on the other hand was going to be a martyr" (81). Callie is an imaginative, but somewhat intrapunitive fifth-grader who becomes "morbid in Catholic school" (81). Callie finds some malachite beads near an aqueduct, and these quickly become a religious talisman that she clutches instead of her teddy bear. Both Callie and her friend Patty Creamer become pious, but only Callie aspires to sainthood. Patty prays for things like the dress that her mother buys her within a week, but Callie wants divine power for repairing human relationships. When Patty's father leaves her mother, the girls resort to asceticism; they deny themselves eating snacks, then looking at flowers, and even looking at boys.

The big tests come with two incidents of domestic discord. When a sobbing Patty tells Callie that her father left her mother to go to "Rio Deniro," Callie wants to restore him to his rightful place in the family. But the need for a miracle comes even closer to home when, during an argument with her father, Callie's mother somehow falls through an upstairs window. Despite the fact that the emergency-room entrance looks "like the gates of heaven," and the doctors speak of the "miracle" that Callie's mother escapes even a broken bone, Callie wants a "real miracle": "for the whole thing never to have happened" (87–88). A week later, Callie loses her "divine" beads when they accidentally fall down a sewer, and even though she had not cried during her mother's accident, she cannot stop crying about the lost beads. Soon she has a vision that tells her that the beads will be returned to her through the water system if she leaves all the water faucets running in the house.

Much of the irony in this story again stems from the distance in time from the actual events. For example, the older narrator undercuts Patty's lisping assertion that Callie would probably be doing "miracleth by seventh grade" by beginning the next paragraph with a one-word sentence fragment: "Miracles." Then she relates that today Patty laughs at her former devotion and has turned her attention to "rugs, and artwork, and antique Japanese bureaus—things she believes in" (82). Further, the adult Callie interrupts her main narrative to relate more recent events. She has sublet her apartment to a young married couple who leave notes to themselves that are actually prayers asking for such things as a job for the wife within a half-hour drive and dinner recipes that cost less than sixty cents. The laughable simplicity of praying for such pedestrian things (which require personal effort, not divine intervention) recalls Patty's prayers for material things, but also Callie's naïve faith in how human relationships can be fixed.

"The Water-Faucet Vision" provides a good example of a type of irony found in several of Jen's works in which seemingly irrelevant details and events in the story's objective world appear to comment ironically upon characters and their actions. In this story, while Patty is telling Callie of her father's desertion, a one-winged (hence, flightless) pigeon walks by and produces "a large runny dropping" (83). This detail undercuts Callie's ineffectual attempts to comfort Patty, but it also comically connects with Callie's observation a few paragraphs later that their prayerful efforts paid off: Patty's father returns a month later, bringing with him "nothing but dysentery" (84). While this small matter of the pigeon might be regarded as an absurd parody of a divine "sign," it may also suggest what psychologist Carl Jung termed *synchronicity*, the simultaneous occurrence of two events (or a thought and an event) that do not appear to be causally connected.

Reality seems to assert its existence in often-comic, but dramatic fashion in Jen's writings. This aspect of "reality" is also reminiscent of that inaccessible and uncanny realm that postmodern psychoanalyst Jacques Lacan called "the real"; Lacan's elusive "real" punctuates human experience with an absurd, sometimes-ironic force. This underlying sense of a "real" keeps Jen's fiction from verging into self-parodying metafiction. Despite Jen's conviction that reality is to a degree "artifice" ("Writing" 135), her fictive world, unlike those of post-modernists for whom the world is sheer artifice, retains some sense of reality, no matter how inscrutable.

This powerfully ironic sense of the "real" intensifies the motifs and images that echo throughout "The Water-Faucet Vision." The most noticeable pattern of interlinking details in this story is the one pertaining to water. From Callie's first finding the beads near an aqueduct to her losing them in a sewer, hints of water and water-related objects connect important episodes. The parents' fight starts over an accident that happened during the repair of a defective (and leak-ing) roof; Patty's father claims that he is going to Rio because he would rather look at water than his wife and child; Callie's younger sister, Mona, tells her mother that she is a "lucky duck-duck" for having survived the fall (88). Callie's absurd final "vision," predicting that her beads will be returned if she leaves all the water faucets running overnight, brings the water imagery into sharp ironic focus. But water as a symbol is not simple, but ambiguous; the loss of the beads in a sewer reminds us that not everything associated with water is "good."

Callie's act of leaving the water faucets open brings her secret into the open: when she is confronted by her mystified family, she, "like a puddlebrain" (89), tells them the truth. But in this instance, the truth reconnects Callie with the world, with family and friends, and Patty reminds her that miracles are not supposed to happen in "thewers" (90). Water here is opposed to fixed illusions and suggests the flux of human involvement. The loss of the beads in a sewer (a place for contaminated water to flow) ironically triggers a profuse flow of tears from Callie, something that did not accompany the trauma of her mother's accident. Her tears are a kind of purging, and although she laments the loss of her simplistic and escapist piety, the adult Callie understands a different kind of faith—the "grit of true faith" (90). Narrated four months after the death of her mother, the story ends with a focus on Callie's aging father and a wisp of nostalgia for the simpler time when a "heavenly father" could relieve any hurt.

Callie's less introverted and more worldly and practical younger sister, Mona, narrates "What Means Switch" (1990), the story of Mona's crush on Sherman, a new Japanese student in her eighth-grade class. The overtly comic surface of this story overlays serious implications about the complexity of identity. Jux-taposition foregrounds Mona's relationship with Sherman in terms of a bom-bardment of influences, direct and indirect, from family, parents, classmates, neighborhood, school, popular culture, and language. The Changs have recently moved to Scarsdale, an affluent, mostly Jewish community, and at this formative age, Mona has begun to use Jewish expressions, such as "Oy!" In fact, the title refers not to Sherman's broken English, but Mona's quick adaptation to the Jewish-American diction of her Scarsdale classmates. "Switch" is Mona's sim-plistically practical answer to changing affiliation from one culture to another. She tells Sherman that he can become American just as she could "switch" from being Roman Catholic to being Jewish. Mona thinks, "Maybe he doesn't get what means switch" (80). Indeed, Sherman, whose cultural identity is traditional Japanese, does not believe that "switching" is so easy.

This discussion of "switching" follows Sherman's story of how his father once apologized by bowing to his mother, raising another problematic issue of identity, that of gender. When Mona and Sherman finally speak of marriage, the issue of who will "switch" is, for Sherman, a foregone conclusion; but Mona refuses to accede, insisting that Sherman should become American. As simple as this puppy-love disagreement seems, Jen is raising an important question about how love relationships affect identity: intimacy brings risk to identity, and in the contemporary world, there are few guidelines as to how compromise should be reached. Gender matters permeate many areas of the story. When Mona first sees Sherman in class, she receives numerous notes from her class-mates. Her first impulse is to be cool, like Paul Newman, but a few minutes later she thinks of Miss America: "back straight, knees together, crying" (78). When Mona objects to Sherman's notebook with a white kitten in blue ribbons on the cover, she points to her own with its psychedelic cover. His response is to buy her a new notebook with a white kitten in pink ribbons.

The different levels of irony in this story range from comic to serious. The fact that Sherman's ethnicity is mistaken for Chinese by both Mona and her classmates obliquely suggests that racial characteristics actually mask more com-plex matters. When Sherman draws pictures to represent people of different ethnicities, his caricatures exaggerate stereotypical qualities: the American looks like John Wayne, the Jew resembles the "Wicked Witch of the West, only male," but both the Chinese and Japanese men look roughly like Sherman himself (80). When Mona asks how to tell them apart, the issue of nationalism moves this scene to a serious and emotional confrontation with Mona's mother. Sherman turns his figures so that the Chinese figure faces the American and the Jew, but positions the Japanese figure to face the Japanese flag, which he enlarges and places on the refrigerator. Revealing his self-concept within his version of reality in contrast to Mona's, Sherman refers to an earlier incident during which he and Mona are separated while shopping. " 'Chinese lost in department store,' " he says. 'Japanese know how go' " (80). When Mona's mother sees the flag, her memories of World War II and the Nanking massacre cause her to rip the drawing down and send Sherman home. Mona's American education, which has emphasized Japan's attack on Pearl Harbor, keeps her from understanding her mother's reaction; she wonders how "two people who don't really speak En-glish" can understand each other better than she does (80).

Through juxtaposing several ideas—naïve perceptions of cultural affiliation, the ambiguous notion of "American culture," the Scarsdale subculture, and Sher-man's traditional conservatism—Jen sets up ironies that deconstruct common conceptions of culture and identity. Another (and perhaps metaphoric) source of irony stems from the narrative technique that Jen uses in this story. Mona's voice tells the story in the present tense, but from a later time, as a mature adult.

We know of the narrator's time distance because Mona tells us that this is the 1960s, before "Orientals" are so numerous that they become "Asians." Moreover, when Mona tells us that a friend once suggested that her Chinese ethnicity is unusual and valuable like a special talent that Mona might make into a career, the adult Mona comments wryly, "Here is the irony: I am" (78). The effect of this narrative style of bringing the past into the present is suggestive of voiceover narration in film; even more, it suggests that Mona is reliving a past experience in the present tense, paradoxically inside the experience and outside it at the same time. This narrative "doubling" is an effect congruent with the motifs of the story—the tensions and disjunctions of trying to have "one" identity.

The relationship between "self" and the influences that shape a sense of identity is complex. Our access to these processes remains partial and distorted—something Mona unwittingly reveals through ironic contradiction. She says that her sister Callie is the "liar of the family" because she worries about appearances, and yet Mona obviously embellishes—and sometimes fabricates—for her classmates "facts" about Chinese culture: that Chinese women get pregnant from drinking tea, that she herself knows karate. These acts of speech enable Mona to create a persona for her peers, but the boundary between this Mona and any deeper sense of her own identity is blurred—a problematic aspect of contemporary experience.

Mona and Sherman must finally part, and their last interlude is perplexing. Sherman has been frustratingly slow in his advances; he has not tried to kiss Mona. As they wait outside Mona's house, he makes some overtures, but his awkwardness leaves little chance that Mona will get lost in passion. Nevertheless, when the top button of her blouse comes undone, Mona is not sure whether she meant it to or not. Sherman buttons it back. At this point, the narrative shifts to shorter segments that alternate between what Mona says to classmates about the final meeting and her reliving the events in the story.

Mona does not tell anyone what apparently really happens after Sherman buttons her blouse: A powerful sense of irony emerges as thirteen-year-old Mona and Sherman progress from sweaty hand-holding to his kissing her on the neck—until Sherman uses judo to flip her onto the ground. It is not clear whether Sherman's brutal response here is his conservative judgment of a girl with an unbuttoned blouse, or whether it is his anger at feeling a momentary loss of control with a girl whom he cannot marry because she will not "switch," a girl who "will never be Japanese," as he tells her later in a letter (84). Mona's jolt—the intrusion of the "real"—is ironic. Sherman's skill with judo had been the cultural identity marker that made him the envy of his male classmates, but now it informs the aggression that displaces the caresses of Mona's fantasy. The last segment of the story begins with Mona's recollection of seeing herself flipped onto the ground; she is shocked and her head is bleeding, but the emphasis is on her vivid sensation of the physical world: she "can't believe how many leaves there are on a bush—every one green and perky and durably itself. And past them real sky" (84).

After discarding mementos of Sherman, Mona wants to "switch" to a simpler identity and context; she wants to move to Chinatown. Her mother correctly guesses that this has to do with boy problems. Tradition and gender questions move to the fore again as Mona's mother tells her that she need not attend school every day because it is not good "for a girl to be too smart anyway" (84). Finally, Mona reflects that she would switch everything around if she could, but she now knows that switching (and perhaps defining one's identity) is not a simple thing. She enters the house where her father and mother are once again discussing whether or not to construct a wall to prevent cars from accidentally turning into their yard—a recurrent problem in their suburban neighborhood.

Just as the story opens with "Here we are, nice Chinese family" (76), its closure circles back to the family and returns to the tensions and paradoxes of what it means to have a sense of identity in an "open" culture that is not always "open," where freedoms, paradoxically, can become limitations. Mona's view from the hard ground makes her realize that leaves may belong to the same bush, but each is "durably" itself, striving to fulfill its own potential. The Changs live in a neighborhood with winding streets that are "charming" (76), not rigid or inhibited. But the Changs need a wall, a barrier against the mobility and freedom of others who may need straight streets and square corners to know where they are.

The problem of contemporary identity is also the subject of "Birthmates" (1994–95), but this story is not about the Chang family, nor is it as comic as much of Jen's earlier work. Art Woo is a Chinese American in a "dinosaur industry"—working for a minicomputer company that is losing ground in the market because of competition from personal computers. From the story's foreboding opening paragraph with Art waiting to enter a hotel that bars the doors at 9:00 P.M., "Birthmates" uses juxtaposition and imbricated ironies to reveal Art's central identity conflict. In addition, details interlink ideas of communication, culture, relationship, love, sex, birth, and death. Almost all aspects of the story, including the bicultural experience, may be read as fitting into contexts that superimpose symbolic levels on planes of irony. This story's rich subtlety, narrative sophistication, and dense compression suggest that Gish Jen is well on her way to establishing herself as one of our most important short-story writers.

WORKS CITED AND CONSULTED

Primary

Jen, Gish. "Birthmates." *Ploughshares* 20.4 (1994–95): 81–97. Rpt. in *The Best American Short Stories 1995; The Best American Short Stories of the Century*. Ed. John Updike and Katrina Kenison. Boston: Houghton Mifflin, 1999. 220–34.
———. "Eating Crazy." *Yale Review* 74 (1985): 425–33.
———. "Grover at the Wheel." *New Yorker* December 31, 1990. 32–37.

————. "In the American Society." *Southern Review* 22 (1986): 606–19. Rpt. in *New Worlds of Literature*. Ed. Jerome Beaty and J. Paul Hunter. New York: Norton, 1989; *The New Generation: Fiction for Our Time from America's Writing Programs*. Ed. Alan Kaufman. New York: Anchor Press, 1987. 79–95; *Imagining America: Stories from the Promised Land*. Ed. Wesley Brown and Amy Ling. New York: Persea Books, 1991.

————. "*MELUS* Interview: Gish Jen." By Yuko Matsukawa. *MELUS: The Journal of the Society for the Study of the Multi-ethnic Literature of the United States* 18.4 (1993–94): 111–20.

————. *Mona in the Promised Land* (novel). New York: Knopf, 1996.

————. *Typical American* (novel). New York: Plume, 1992.

————. "The Water-Faucet Vision." *Nimrod* 31.1 (1987): 25–33. Rpt. in *The Best American Short Stories 1988*. Ed. Mark Helprin and Shannon Ravenel. Boston: Houghton Mifflin, 1988. 81–90; *Literature and Ourselves; A Thematic Introduction for Readers and Writers*. Ed. Gloria Henderson, William Day, and Sandra Waller. New York: HarperCollins, 1994.

————. "What Means Switch." *Atlantic Monthly* May 1990: 76–84.

————. "The White Umbrella." *Yale Review* 73 (1984): 401–9. Rpt. in *Home to Stay: Asian American Women's Fiction*. Ed. Sylvia Watanabe and Carol Bruchac. Greenfield Center, NY: Greenfield Review Press, 1990. 153–61; *My Mother's Daughter: Stories by Women*. Ed. Irene Zahava. Freedom, CA: Crossing Press, 1991. 196–205.

————. *Who's Irish?* (stories). New York: Knopf, 1999.

————. "Writing about the Things That Are Dangerous." Interview. By Martha Satz. *Southwest Review* 78 (1993): 132–40.

Jen, Lillian. "Bellying-up." *Iowa Review* 12.1 (1981): 93–94.

Jen, Lillian C. "The Small Concerns of Sparrows." *Fiction International* 14 (1982): 47–55.

Secondary

Bencivenga, Jim. "Culture Contrast." Rev. of *Typical American*, by Gish Jen. *Christian Science Monitor* March 25, 1991: 13.

Burns, Gerald T. "A Quartet of Voices in Recent American Literature." *Philippine American Studies Journal* 3 (1991): 1–8.

Gilbert, Matthew. "The Americanization of Lai Fu." Rev. of *Typical American*, by Gish Jen. *Boston Globe* March 14, 1991: 80.

"Gish Jen: *Typical American*." *Contemporary Literary Criticism Yearbook 1991*. 69–77.

Gornick, Vivian. "Innocents Abroad." Rev. of *Typical American*, by Gish Jen. *Women's Review of Books* July 1991: 14.

Mojtabai, A. G. Review of *Typical American*. *New York Times*. March 31, 1991: 9.

Scrimarth, Manini. "Affirmations: Speaking the Self into Being." *Parnassus* 17.1 (1992): 88–101.

Storace, Patricia. "Seeing Double." Rev. of *Typical American*. *New York Times Review of Books*, August 15, 1991: 9.

CHARLES RICHARD JOHNSON
(April 23, 1948–   )

Scharron A. Shy-Clayton

BIOGRAPHY

Charles Richard Johnson was born to Benjamin Lee Johnson, a night watchman and construction worker, and Ruby Elizabeth (Jackson) Johnson, a teacher prevented from working due to health problems. Young Charles's interest in writing grew, thanks to his mother's fondness for literature and a house filled with hundreds of books waiting to be devoured. He received his first diary at the age of twelve; forty years later, he still practices the habit of journal writing.

Although much of the reading public was not familiar with Johnson's work until the publication of National Book Award winner *Middle Passage* in 1990, his early efforts attracted the attention of several notable teachers. At age fifteen, he found a personal mentor in illustrator Lawrence Lariar, and while he was an undergraduate journalism student at Southern Illinois University, he received political guidance from Amiri Baraka. These two influences resulted in the publication of two collections of political cartoons (*Black Humor*, 1970; *Half-Past Nation Time*, 1972) as well as hundreds of individual drawings that appeared in such publications as *Ebony*, the *Chicago Tribune*, and *Jet*. Later, while he was completing a master's degree in philosophy (also at Southern Illinois University), he worked as a photojournalist in Chicago and wrote fledgling novels aimed toward integrating philosophical reflections into depictions of black experience. During this time, he studied with author and writing teacher John Gardner, who enhanced both his aesthetic knowledge and his interest in moral issues.

Charles Johnson, now a practicing Buddhist, is professor of creative writing at the University of Washington. Aside from the National Book Award, he has earned the Washington State Governor's Award for Literature, the *Callaloo* Creative Writing Award, and a nomination for the PEN/Faulkner Award for *The Sorcerer's Apprentice*.

CRITICISM

Johnson received some early attention for addressing philosophical dilemmas within an African-American context (*Publishers Weekly*, 1974). His work also garnered praise for addressing the complexities of race and gender with a compelling combination of satire, allegory, and allusion. In a *New York Times* review article in 1975, however, Anne Gotlieb criticized Johnson for the number of academic in-jokes and erudite references that sabotage the magic in *Faith and the Good Thing*, a flawed but fabulous book.

Due to his tendency to dance between fictional narrative and abstract philosophy, classification of Johnson's work is extremely difficult (Moritz 1991). Moreover, he himself refuses affiliation with a "black literary genre" that he views as prescribed, limited, and not always inclusive or imaginative. Highly experimental, he mixes elements of the slave narrative, fantasy, folklore, Eastern and Western philosophies, realism, surrealism, and metaphysical experiences (Phillips, Penner, and Ventura) and distances himself from political imperatives (Little, "Interview").

In a 1988 nonfiction work, *Being and Race: Black Writing since 1970*, Johnson asserted that writers should be able to write in any form. This is an idea he has practiced as well as preached. *The Sorcerer's Apprentice*, eight short stories published in 1986, followed the novels *Faith and the Good Thing* and *Oxherding Tale*. The stories are reminiscent of back-porch tales spun by wise and experienced elders; they evoke the oral tradition of African-American storytelling, with keen focus on character development and moral lessons.

Since its publication, *The Sorcerer's Apprentice* has elicited varied assessments. Its stories have been commended both for their presentation of the cultural alienation of black Americans and for their integration of formal language and street vernacular. Michiko Kakutani applauded the author for his adeptness in avoiding the pitfalls of didacticism and his virtuosity in addressing, in a nonparochial way, questions of prejudice and assimilation (*New York Times Book Review* 24). Jonathan Penner, however, criticized *The Sorcerer's Apprentice* for attempting to showcase the author's—rather than his characters'—philosophical insight (*Washington Post* 8). Moreover, while Kakutani readily credits the author for his virtuosity, she nonetheless determines that his stories sometimes fail because of their insistence on a moral conclusion (as in "Exchange Value" and "Moving Pictures"). This moralizing ambition, she suggests, is destructive to Johnson's "conjugations of social detail and vernacular descriptions" and "robs" his characters of their individuality.

ANALYSIS

In 1986, Jonathan Penner described *The Sorcerer's Apprentice* as a work designed with wit and craft but not necessarily designed for "pleasure cruising." Its parable-like stories explore complex philosophical concepts from uncommon vantage points; its characters express themselves in unexpected and introspective ways. The first story, "The Education of Mingo," suggests that we can create our worst nightmares through pursuing self-centered interests at the expense of others. It depicts the well-intentioned, though paternalistic, aims of farmer Moses Green as he methodically embarks on the schooling—or indoctrination—of his slave, Mingo. A lifelong bachelor who seldom washes and is childless and without kinfolk, old farmer Moses is convinced that educating Mingo is a completely altruistic act; he fails to realize that it fills a void in his own life. The reader, however, can readily see that Moses' sense of self derives from his relationship to Mingo. His dependence on the slave eventually supersedes the moral imperative to free him, for to do so would be self-destructive. Yet Mingo's mimicry of farmer Moses, at first comic, turns tragic when he internalizes his master's thinking and becomes a "spitting image" of the slave owner. Ultimately, the education of Mingo accomplishes the enslavement of Moses as the two become reflections of each other.

In "Exchange Value," in which two thieves become the victims of their own greed, Johnson's desire to explore issues of moral choice, self-knowledge, and the philosophical implications of behavior is once again evident. As the protagonist, Cooter, describes a robbery of an elderly neighbor committed with his brother, Loftis, the reader is thrust into a world of sin and retribution where petty crooks suffer the unexpected consequences of their transgression. Cooter and Loftis anticipated finding a shoe box, perhaps, of saved money but discovered instead a large inheritance and other valuable objects. Cooter recognized that old Miss Bailey's belongings were like "raw energy" and that he and his brother, "like wizards, could transform her stuff into anything else at will. All we had to do, it seemed to me, was decide exactly what to exchange it for" (34–35). Yet ironically, as Loftis studied the situation, the mystical powers of the ill-gotten goods had already begun to transform him. He warned Cooter, "As soon as you buy something you lose the power to buy something" (36), thus suggesting that the essence of Miss Bailey has begun to inhabit his soul and raising the questions: What is the value of exchange? Is the transgression worth the price? Is the exchange of selfhood and identity for material goods too steep a price to pay?

"Menagerie, a Child's Fable" is a parable about racism reminiscent of Orwell's *Animal Farm*. Set in a pet store and narrated by a dog, it depicts the impact of oppression on a group of animals whose struggle for freedom turns into a nightmarish journey. Left to fend for themselves after the owner fails to return, the animals split into opposing camps—those who desire self-rule, those who seek a return to the past, and those who want to build community—and begin to compete for power and control. Ultimately, they destroy themselves. Reflecting on the devastating results of their discord, the dog disparages his peers' inability to accept their own diversity, lamenting, "We could have endured, we had enough in common—for Christ's sake we're all animals" (*The Sorcerer's Apprentice* 59).

Echoing the themes developed in "The Education of Mingo" and "Exchange Value," "China" returns to the notions of identity and change, depicting an aging man's search for a will to live and his wife's resignation to the inevitability of death. Rudolph, a fifty-four-year-old man who suffers from high blood pressure, flat feet, emphysema, and fainting spells, becomes a practitioner of the martial arts and learns to employ mental strength to break free of physical confinement. While Rudolph ascends to a higher level of self-awareness and acceptance, however, his wife, Evelyn, remains loyal to rational logic: "She would wait until he worked this thing out of his system, until Nature defeated him and he surrendered, as any right-thinking person would, to the breakdown of the body, the brutal fact of decay, which could only be blunted, it seemed to her, by decaying *with* someone" (*The Sorcerer's Apprentice* 75). Despite Evelyn's pessimism, however, Rudolph's success in effecting his own transformation ultimately suggests that one's identity and destiny are often self-directed.

In "Alethia," "Popper's Disease," and "The Sorcerer's Apprentice," a serious, thoughtful tone ushers the reader through an engaging setting only to arrive, ultimately, at a surreal scenario that demands a reexamination of beliefs. Influenced by Ralph Ellison's notion that the self is ephemeral and Hume's sense of its loss in the "other" and in objects, Johnson suggests again and again that identity is an illusion, that the self is merely a collection of memories, impressions, and sensations always in a state of development. This belief underlies his depictions of the postal worker who ascends to kung fu knight ("China"), the master who depends on his slave ("The Education of Mingo"), the thief who becomes an image of the miser he robs ("Exchange Value"), the professor who struggles with his alter ego ("Alethia"), the black doctor who suffers from the disease of being alien in a white culture ("Popper's Disease"), and the protagonist who obliterates himself ("The Sorcerer's Apprentice").

Johnson's intermingling of esoteric philosophy with black vernacular challenges stereotypical classifications of persons, thoughts, or ideas. His writings engage the total Self (black and American, answering W.E.B. Du Bois's question of being) and attempt to "bridge the gap" between the Western philosophical inheritance and the black experience.

WORKS CITED AND CONSULTED

Primary

Johnson, Charles Richard. *Being and Race: Black Writing since 1970.* Bloomington: Indiana University Press, 1988.
———. *Black Humor.* Chicago: Johnson Publishing Co., 1970.
———. *Faith and the Good Thing.* New York: Viking, 1974.
———. *Half-Past Nation Time.* Westlake Village, CA: Awareness Press, 1972.
———. *Middle Passage.* New York: Atheneum, 1990.

———. *Oxherding Tale*. Bloomington: Indiana University Press, 1982.
———. *The Sorcerer's Apprentice*. New York: Atheneum, 1986.

Secondary

Boccia, Michael. "An Interview with Charles Johnson." *African American Review* 30.3 (1996): 611–18.

Gleason, William. "The Liberation of Perception: Charles Johnson's *Oxherding Tale*." *Black American Literature Forum* 25 (Winter 1991): 705–28.

Gotlieb, Anne. "Faith and the Good Thing." *The New York Times Book Review* January 12, 1975: 6.

Johson, Charles. "Philosophy and Black Fiction." *Obsidian, Black Literature in Review* 6.1 (1980): 55–61.

Kakutani, Michiko. Review of "The Sorcerer's Apprentice." *The New York Times* February 5, 1986: 24.

Little, Jonathan, "Charles Johnson's Revolutionary *Oxherding Tale*." *Studies in American Fiction* 19 (Autumn 1991): 141–51.

———. "An Interview with Charles Johnson." *Contemporary Literature* 34 (Summer 1993):159–81.

Moritz, Charles, ed. *Current Biography Yearbook* 1991.

Penner, Jonathan. "Magical Mystery Tours." *The Washington Post* February 16, 1986: 11.

Phillips, J. J. Review of "The Sorcerer's Apprentice." *Los Angeles Times Book Review* March 30, 1986: 11.

Rushdy, Ashraf H. "The Phenomenology of the Allmuseri: Charles Johnson and the Subject of the Narrative of Slavery." *African American Review* 26 (Fall 1992): 373–94.

Ventura, Michael. "Voodoo and Subtler Power." *The New York Times Book Review* March 30, 1986: 7.

Weixlmann, Joe, ed. *Charles Richard Johnson*. Spec. Issue of *African American Review* 30.4 (1996): 517–689.

ELIZABETH JOLLEY
(June 4, 1923–   )

Brian Dibble

BIOGRAPHY

Elizabeth Jolley was born Monica Elizabeth Knight in Erdington (near Birmingham), England, to Charles Wilfrid Knight (1890–1977) and Margarethe Johanna Carolina (née Fehr) Knight (1896–1976). Her life from the beginning was marked by contrasts, bourgeois and unconventional by turn. Her father was a school science teacher who earned a B.Sc. and M.Sc. via correspondence school. He had a penchant for studying foreign languages, especially German, his wife's native tongue and the language spoken at home when Jolley was young. A Quaker when Jolley was born and once again a Methodist before World War II, Wilfrid was a lifelong pacifist who was jailed as a conscientious objector during World War I. His wife, the daughter of Catholic Austrians of aristocratic descent, experienced a complicated childhood; for example, her father married and remarried two more times as his wives died of illness, and his daughter was looked after by a series of women who apparently did not like her. She was therefore sent to convent school at an early age. She was a Montessori teacher and an ex-Catholic when, on a Quaker food-distribution mission after World War I, Wilfrid met and married her in Vienna in 1922. He was high-minded but unassuming, and she seems to have been high-handed and moody. He performed various charitable acts (feeding his poor students and visiting the aged and sick in hospitals) whereas she fretted over an economically restricted life in an alien land although she befriended German POWs and took refugees from Germany and Austria into their home.

Elizabeth Jolley's formal education was spotty, but she made much of it. After on-again, off-again enrollment in infant schools, she attended Bilston Girls' High School. At the age of eight, she began to study at home because her father feared that in public schools she might lose her innocence along with her ignorance. From late 1934 to mid-1940 she boarded and studied at Sibford, a

Quaker school near the Cotswolds. It was a time of further material privation and (initially) great loneliness, but also one of family feeling—she was cherished by some of her teachers, and her sister joined her there in 1939—and considerable learning (of French and German and of classic English authors). She says that she left boarding school "an idealist." If her own boarding-school life is lovingly parodied in her novel *Miss Peabody's Inheritance* (1983), and if the pain of schoolgirl awkwardness, envy, and cruelty is recounted in *My Father's Moon*, that period of her life nevertheless remains cherished.

Jolley started nurse's training at St. Nicholas and St. Martin's Hospital in Surrey in 1940 and was immediately introduced to the horrors of war-wounded civilians, British soldiers, and prisoners of war, which gave her medical knowledge, evoked her compassion, and developed her sense of life as a trial made more bearable, even rewarding, if it was directly or indirectly shared with another. Like boarding school, the conventlike strictures of nursing school further extended her sense of family belonging to one of community belonging, of affiliation with a group, and of special affection for some of its members. In that community, complexities of human relationships comparable to those in the family are found (love, envy, and so on), and thus it is not surprising that this period provides the setting and characters for much of her work.

While she was at St. Nicholas and St. Martin's, she met Leonard Jolley (1914–1994), a man almost ten years her senior who had been hospitalized there for two years with a "tubercular hip." A friendship ostensibly based on matters of the mind developed between them—he was a Quaker, he had an M.A. in English and German literature as well as a librarian's qualification from the University of London, and he had a windup record player and a good collection of classical music. In January 1943, she joined the Queen Elizabeth Hospital in Birmingham, where Leonard Jolley, the Selly Oak College librarian, was then living with his wife. She left in 1946 to keep house for a woman doctor in Birmingham and then to work in a progressive boarding school (Pinewood) in Hertfordshire, in a position that was called "matron" but was more like a jill-of-all-trades, including cooking, washing, and tending the children. In fact, Jolley was at Pinewood because she had had her first child by Leonard Jolley that year and thus was forced to leave nursing. Leonard was appointed librarian in the Royal College of Physicians in Edinburgh in the fall of 1950, and Elizabeth soon joined him there, where their second and third children were born. Next he became deputy librarian at the University of Glasgow in 1956. The Scottish years were cold and wet, the pay was low but they were happy years.

The couple migrated to Perth in 1959 when Leonard Jolley was appointed head librarian at the University of Western Australia. In Perth, Elizabeth Jolley agonized in the role of "faculty wife"; she was an unwilling committee member and dutiful if anxious dinner giver. Manifestly unsuited to the role, she preoccupied herself with a weekend retreat they bought in Wooroloo in November 1970, some forty miles east of Perth, a place generically giving the title to her book of short stories, *Five Acre Virgin* (1976), possibly also the setting for her first-published novel, *Palomino* (1980) and for the ending of her second novel, *The Newspaper of Claremont Street* (1981) and certainly the setting of her *Diary of a Weekend Farmer* (1993). In this same period, she took on a variety of part-time jobs that figure in her novels and stories—nursing-home nurse (*Mr. Scobie's Riddle* [1983]), salesperson ("The Travelling Entertainer"), and house-cleaner (the opening *Five Acre Virgin* stories, *The Newspaper of Claremont Street*). At this time, she also began to write with print publication in mind.

Although Jolley started writing as a girl, keeping a diary from when she was twelve and having a story ("The Adventures of George Henry the Caterpillar") read on the *Children's Hour Radio* (Midland Region) in her early twenties, writing success did not come quickly or easily to her in Perth. The odds did not favor women, especially Western Australian women, particularly ones who wrote the quirky, allusive stories Elizabeth Jolley did, apparently simple but disturbing for their thought-provoking lacunae. However, after many rejection slips, some of them quite cruel, she managed to publish ten stories in the 1964–74 period. Critics must also be aware of the fact that early in her career Jolley had many stories broadcast on BBC's World Service programing, a broadcast specially beamed for the "colonies"—virtually all of the stories in her first two books of short stories originally appeared in that format. In addition, in 1975 she submitted four radio playscripts to the Australian Broadcasting Commission in Sydney for a "Soundstage" competition, two of them highly commended ("Night Report," which was later incorporated into her novel *Mr. Scobie's Riddle*, and "The Performance").

In his review of Bird's *Off the Air*, Peter Craven exclaims, "What a culture we might have had if Elizabeth Jolley had been a great woman of the theatre" (15). In 1974, she was offered a position as a part-time tutor of "enrichment" classes in creative writing at the Fremantle Arts Centre, a position she held for some twelve years; Fremantle published her first book, *Five Acre Virgin*, in 1976. In 1978, she started teaching fiction at the Western Australian Institute of Technology (now Curtin University), going on to become a prolific and acclaimed writer.

Now, in her late seventies, she continues as Curtin's writer-in-residence and (since 1998) professor of creative writing. In addition, she continues volunteer work she started when she was a tutor for the Fremantle Arts Centre, namely, attending book clubs in Perth and visiting book clubs and writing groups in country towns (the latter a central feature of her novel *Foxybaby* [1985]). The death of her husband, Leonard, in 1994 meant that she no longer visited him daily in a nursing home, from where she would bring him back in his wheelchair to their home ten minutes away for the afternoon, where he had his own library and music and would stay for dinner (recurrent in *The Georges' Wife*). It also meant that she was freer to accept speaking engagements interstate and concentrate on her work.

Elizabeth Jolley is one of Australia's finest writers. Her output now comprises five collections of short stories, twelve novels, a collection of essays (edited by

Caroline Lurie), a collection of sketches (*Diary of a Weekend Farmer* [1998]), and more than one hundred interviews, articles, and reviews of others' books. Her titles are auctioned for six figures to publishers in New York, and her books are reviewed around the world and are translated into half a dozen languages. Films have been made of her stories and novels (e.g., *The Last Crop*, based on "A Gentleman's Agreement," was produced by the Australian Broadcasting Company [ABC] in 1991, and a film version of *The Well* was acclaimed at the 1997 Cannes International Festival of Film), an option is out on another (*Miss Peabody's Inheritance*), and a documentary has been made of her world (*The Night Belongs to the Novelist*, by Chris Wilcox [Yowie Films, 1986]). She has received most if not all of the significant Australian awards as well as a number of North American and European ones, her most recent Australian ones being a D.Litt. *honoris causa* from Macquarie University in Sydney in 1995 and honorary doctorates from the University of Queensland in 1997 and the University of New South Wales in 2000.

ANALYSIS

Elizabeth Jolley's first book was a collection of eleven short stories. The title, *Five Acre Virgin*, employs one of her conspicuous stylistic devices, a punning that constitutes functional ambiguity: the title refers to a block of uncleared land and also to Aunty Shovell/Cheryl Hurst, an unmarried woman of generous proportions. Other devices include images that are indeterminately metaphorical and literal, as in "we nearly killed ourselves laughing" (34) and "Howard's done wonders over the plastic toilet seat" (24). Jolley's reliance on such linguistic devices diminished over time and was largely gone from her writing by the late 1980s.

The collection's title also highlights one of Jolley's concerns, the ideal of owning land, as in "Bill Sprockett's Land" (although she is quite aware that Tolstoy's story "How Much Land Does a Man Need?" refers to a plot six feet long, four feet wide, and eight feet deep). Her interest in land, especially land in the country, is central in her early stories. It can give comfort and security; its tending is simple reciprocity and can be a form of practicing hope. Alone on the land, one can dwell on the present instead of worrying about the past and fearing the future. Moreover, a rural retreat can provide distraction from the haunting specter of powerful figures like children, employers, needy friends, and lovers.

The first six stories of the book constitute a discontinuous narrative that focuses on the life of the Morgan family—mother (cleaner), daughter (schoolgirl), and son (high-school dropout). (The father is in jail, in his wife's provocative metaphorical/literal term, "doing life"). These three (and, once, another sister) appear and reappear in the first six stories, as well as in one of Jolley's novels: the daughter is the protagonist of *The Newspaper of Claremont Street*, a cleaner in Perth who is hopeful of buying five acres in the country.

Five Acre Virgin would seem a parody of the pastoral if the characters in its stories were not so grimly, if manically, real—there is something of Balzac in them, something of Dickens. In conventional terms, they are losers, though, intriguingly, the term Jolley uses in her "Author's Note" for the characters in the first six stories is "Discarders" (the term "Discarded" might seem more appropriate). Yet "Discarders" (the word is used on page 33) well describes the characters in the other five stories, for there are unassertive people and pathetic couples among them, people who do not care for others and are hardly able to care for themselves—Jolley's arresting term for some of them is "feckless." However, in the margins of the society of the Discarders and the Discarded, there are some who are powerful for being oppositional, for asserting desire against all odds. Conspicuous among them are the women, for no man is more canny than they (although the Morgan son is more cruel).

In "The Jarrah Thieves," unmarried Martha Dobsova (there are many immigrants in the book—Dutch, German, Austrian, British) exercises power symbolically if not actually when she fires all of the male workers she suspects of stealing by shouting the order to them when they cannot hear it over the roar of their log trucks (90). She is satisfied, and she and the men can look forward to "next time" when the ritual is repeated. In "A Gentleman's Agreement," when Mrs. Morgan is forced to sell the land she has inherited from her father, she asks the doctor buying it to let her hold onto it until she puts in and takes off just one more crop. Against his lawyer's advice, the doctor agrees, and she plants jarrah trees that take a lifetime to mature. If such stories point overtly to basic power differences not only between the haves and have-nots but also between men and women, then "The Shepherd on the Roof" in *Five Acre Virgin* explores them more subtly in the marital context, the husband coming off badly and the wife coming off not well.

Jolley's second collection, *The Travelling Entertainer*, contains ten stories. Published three years after her first collection, the book might seem constrained in some ways, for instance, "The Fellow Passenger" had its first existence in the form of a radio story then called "The Worcester Sauce Queens" broadcast by the BBC in the early 1960s, and "The Performance" was broadcast nationally as a play by the ABC in 1976. Further, it shows how Jolley also reuses written materials; for example, it recycles characters from *Five Acre Virgin*, Uncle Bernard of "Outink to Uncle's Place" appearing again as the main character in "The Outworks of the Kingdom" and "The Agent in Travelling." Character types and situations are reused too—the Clarks who have Mr. Stannard as a boarder who wants a shed on the property in "The Shepherd on the Roof" are reiterated in the Pages who house Mr. Parker in a shed at the back of their block in "Mr. Parker's Valentine." Lines from one book recall ones in the other. Martha Dobsova's "poem of the seeds" (88) in the former is echoed by Uncle Bernard's "poem of the grapes" (43) in the latter; indeed, in the latter, words or lines from one story reappear in another—in "Winter Nelis," when Leonora chastises a hotel receptionist in Europe, she realizes that she has made "[a]n unbearable mistake. She remembered his pale eyes bulging as he looked in disbelief" (31), and in "Grasshoppers," when Peg does the same in India, "[s]he had made an unbearable mistake in speaking to him as she had. His pale eyes looked at her in disbelief" (161). Sometimes the humor is of the same change-room sort seen earlier—a cocktail-party joke has it that gynecologists greet each other with "At your cervix m'dear" and "Dilated to meet you" (*The Travelling Entertainer* 122).

At the same time, *The Travelling Entertainer* is a book of wider and deeper import for how it explores heterosexual and homosexual pairings, coming to understandings about relationships more than to conclusions about sexualities. A comparison of "The Shepherd on the Roof" from her first book with "Mr. Parker's Valentine" from her second, for example, shows Jolley once more contrasting a soft-hearted wife with a hard-headed man around the issue of a boarder. The husband is not comfortable in his household while another man is around, even an old man; and the wife cannot bring herself to dash the boarder's hopes (in the first story) or to turn him off the property (in the second one). The special complication of "The Shepherd on the Roof" is the postaccident arrival of an uncouth and in-love pair of teenagers (the girl a daughter of a friend of the wife) and the husband's refusal to take them in. Effectively, the husband says, "It's not our responsibility" (52), and the wife is unable or afraid to argue how and why it is. If he can grudgingly be respected for knowing his limits, she at least elicits sympathy for her stark realization that "it's my fault though I gave my husband the responsibility" (55). The special complication of "Mr. Parker's Valentine" is twofold: Eleanor Page's closer contact with Mr. Parker progressively infuriates Pearson Page, who cannot stand the old man's gardening advice; and in his anger and carelessness, he causes Parker's death during a tree-pruning exercise. Like Mrs. Clark, Eleanor Page knows that she "hid her feelings, so giving him [Pearson] full responsibility" (94). But she is able to see and obliquely name the cruelty in him (93), to feel "the burden of Pearson's anger and resentment," and to know that she could not ever "reach Pearson in his grim remorse" (94). The title refers to the fact that fifty years before, Mr. Parker received a valentine and was never bothered by the fact that he did not know the identity of the sender of the unsigned card. The story itself shows Eleanor Page for the first time comprehending something crucial about herself, her boundaries, and those of Pearson Page, a knowledge that is sobering because it implies the difficulty of knowing the self and the impossibility of knowing the other.

Wider and deeper still are the explorations of several other stories, in partic- ular, "Winter Nelis," "The Fellow Passenger," and "Grasshoppers." The first and the third introduce the concept of lesbianism, implicitly in the one and explicitly in the other. In "Winter Nelis," an impressionistic series of descrip- tions provides the basis for concluding that Leonora Brown had at least three lesbian affairs, a frantic one as a sixteen-year-old with her fashion-store boss Big Fancy, a passionate and perhaps promising one in a nursing-school setting

with Sister Haddon, and a quite unhappy, very unpleasant one with Miss But-
terick in Europe. Now married, ten years older than her husband, she suffers
vaguely from adonia and anomie, conditions briefly but artificially alleviated by
her discovery of a young neighbor-wife who comes home at midday and sobs
away the afternoon. She subjugates her own unhappiness to that of this other
woman who by dinnertime has put on a brave front: a depressive who has
learned that is wrong to give the appearance of love, she reaches out to someone
possibly in the same situation, but she is not making contact. In "Grasshoppers,"
Peg Mercer (divorced from a husband who was unfaithful with male lovers and
who left for a female one), newly involved with a younger lover, Bettina, is
experiencing the conflicting needs of passion that involve the need to care and
to be cared for. This leads the too-old, too-fat Peg—out of fear, out of hope—
desperately to put her mother and daughter at risk for the shallow, greedy Bettina, harming her mother and killing her daughter in the process. She is forced
to demonstrate and experience the humanness of sorrow, pietà-like. "Grasshoppers," in other words, is a story about being a mother.

    "The Fellow Passenger" explores same-sex attraction as a recent consideration
for the protagonist. Dr. Abrahams, a husband and father with a family name to
uphold, a medical doctor with a professional reputation to maintain, "was a sick
man and was keeping the sickness in his own hands" (72). He has taken his
wife and daughter on an ocean cruise, and, as if without warning and without
apparent reason, a much-younger man attaches himself to him, requiring him to
give him money, clothes, and luggage and to book and share a room with him.
The young man has a thigh wound, but that is beside the point insofar as the
doctor has a predisposition: years ago, when he was young and lost along his
way on horseback to treat a woman, he met a man on the road. "The man's
eyes shone as he patted the horse and Abrahams felt as if the intimate caress,
because of the way the man looked, was meant for him. He continued his
journey feeling this tiny heart bursting change into gladness, which is really all
the greatest change there is" (74). When the young desperado is arrested and
taken away, the doctor is at the end of a voyage of self-discovery, having learned
that he is both the hunted and the hunter, that in spite of his wife and daughter,
he is still in search of a relationship.

    Jolley's third collection of stories, *Woman in a Lampshade*, recalls the mix
of comedy and moral seriousness of the earlier collections ("Uncle Bernard's
Proposal," "The Play Reading," "Butter Butter Butter for a Boat," and "Wednesdays and Fridays"), as well as the way in which other stories to a greater or
lesser degree work with characters and situations from the novels ("The Pear
Tree" and *Newspaper*, "The Libation" and *Palomino*, "Dingle the Fool" and
Milk and Honey, and to a lesser extent "One Christmas Knitting" and *Newspaper*). Comparably, the transitional status of this collection is marked by the
authority of the technical and moral range of such stories as (to take only two
examples) "Adam's Bride" and "Hilda's Wedding."

    The residuum of a short novel that did not "work" for her early Fremantle publishers, "Adam's Bride" (titled "The Bench" when it was published in *Meanjin* in 1979) weaves together some of Jolley's central themes: the insistent plight of the "discarded," the evil pain of betrayal of love and/or trust, the longing for some fullness to living, the claustrophobia of a married relationship, and the wearying burden of the awareness of human suffering. The discarded in this tale is the slow-witted girl who is married off by her anxious mother to a traveling man who sees in the girl the chance to own some land. However, the betrayal that forms the center of the story (as betrayal does in many Jolley pieces) is not so much this marriage of necessity as it is the husband's inadvertent posturing to his wife as a writer—writing representing to each, in different ways, a hopefulness and significance. But the husband in fact writes nothing as the wife arranges the family farm life around his apparent activity. When, prompted by the gossipy shopkeeper who sold pen and paper to the husband, the wife discovers the pretense, the husband covers his shame in a burst of violence from which the woman flees in a panic that ultimately leads to the death of both the gossipy shopkeeper and the couple's child in a road accident. This story of betrayal(s) gains complexity and poignancy through being told, not as it unfolds, but as a court testimony by the husband in defense of his wife and in indictment of himself. He is heard by "The Bench," a man whose despair is suggested by his cryptic confidences to his young assistant both about the sentences he has given and about his empty marriage. Having heard Adam, he is nearly immobilized by "the inextricable mess of human misery standing before him" (38); he leaves the court, and the young assistant, having himself heard enough confidences, knows enough not to need to leave his work to investigate the meaning of the noise of a road accident outside. Typically, in "Adam's Bride" Jolley works through indirection, depending on symbolism and the skillful juxtaposition of detail to lead the reader to an apprehension of her vision of a world of human suffering mitigated by hope and compassion.

If in "Adam's Bride" the scale tilts toward suffering, in "Hilda's Wedding," suffering is surprised and contained by hope. Here Jolley reinvokes her comic strain, so that the improbable functions as an image of what is possible, given sufficient moral understanding and enough compassionate energy. The story is focused through apprehensions of a naïf, a relieving night nurse who, on the one hand, puzzles over the hospital myth that Night Sister Bean can hex a blood transfusion with a simple look and, on the other hand, enlists the night support staff of the hospital to arrange a wedding for the "always pregnant" (41) hospital kitchen maid, Hilda, to Boy—who quintessentially represents Jolley's "discarded" as being someone who "had no name and no one knew how old he was . . . [who] worked all night quietly . . . [and whose voice] no one had ever heard" (41). The relieving night nurse's investigation into the nature of evil is inconclusive—she stages a transfusion that invites Sister Bean's gaze, but it is not clear whether or not Sister Bean looks at the (successful) transfusion; and later Sister Bean asks, "[S]ince when did varicose veins get a transfusion nurse?" (46). Similarly, she successfully marries off Hilda to Boy minutes before Hilda gives birth in a hospital elevator, but at the moment in the makeshift ceremony when it is asked whether or not anyone has any objection, "Boy dropped something heavy, it sounded like a hod of coke" (44). The muddle of the leading character's effort to know evil and to do good is underscored by the passage that Casualty Porter Feegan, officiating at Hilda's wedding but lacking a Bible, reads out from a cricketer's manual: "The moral character of any pursuit is best estimated by its consequences to individuals and its effects upon society. If the absence of evil be not a permissible proof of innocence it ought to imply assent, when no positive evidence stands in opposition" (44).

Evil in Jolley's world is comprised by "the weariness and the contamination and the madness of suffering" (46). Such suffering that is not owing to mortality is typically the result of betrayals consequent on need (sometimes modulating to greed) and on ignorance (sometimes identified with innocence). If evil is understood this way—as need and/or ignorance—it is difficult to assign evil to others. Thus the story ends with the relieving night nurse speculating that when the ailing Night Sister Bean is admitted to surgery, "we would know once and for all the truth about this thing everyone said about her" (46). But in the absence of such knowledge, there remains not only the awareness of suffering and need, but also moments of living that are "surprisingly sweet and fresh," like the one the central character experienced at the end of the story when she stood at the doors of the hospital, "full of fresh milk and . . . took deep breaths of this cool air which seemed just now to contain nothing of the weariness and the contamination and the madness of suffering" (46).

These two pieces from Jolley's second-last collection illustrate several of the characteristics of her stories. Perhaps most notable is the way in which the narratives balance upon the edge of realism and something else—comedy, farce, melodrama. Technically, that balance is achieved in part through symbolism— for example, the doves (a recurrent image in many of her stories) in "Adam's Bride": " 'Mr. and Mrs. Dove in the roof!' [The Bench] said looking upwards. 'Safe suburban regularity! . . . Did you know, young Robinson, that if doves are put together in a cage they'll peck each other to death?' " (13). Technically, it is in part achieved through the deployment of what Jolley calls the "sophisticated space"—the filiation of details across the length of a narrative, requiring the reader to make connections and construct both the verisimilitude of the story and its larger significance. These devices—the symbolism and the sophisticated spaces—wed realism (the depiction of character in a believable situation) to not-quite-realism (the depiction of exemplars in boundary situations) and result in Jolley's philosophical narratives of desire and dependency.

WORKS CITED AND CONSULTED

Primary

Central Mischief: Elizabeth Jolley on Writing, Her Past, and Herself. Lurie, Caroline, ed. Ringwood, Victoria: Viking, 1992.

Jolley, Elizabeth. "Elizabeth Jolley." *Contemporary Authors: Autobiography Series*. Vol. 13. Ed. Joyce Nakamura. Detroit: Gale Research, 1991. 105–23.

Fellow Passengers: Collected Short Stories of Elizabeth Jolley. Milech, Barbara, ed. Ringwood, Victoria: Penguin, 1997.

———. *Five Acre Virgin and Other Stories*. Fremantle, Western Australia: Fremantle Arts Centre Press, 1976.

Off the Air: Nine Plays for Radio by Elizabeth Jolley. Bird, Delys, ed. Ringwood, Victoria: Penguin, 1995.

———. *Stories* (incorporating *Five Acre Virgin* and *Travelling Entertainer* and adding "Self-Portrait: A Child Went Forth"). Fremantle, Western Australia: Fremantle Arts Centre Press, 1984.

———. *The Travelling Entertainer and Other Stories*. Fremantle, Western Australia: Fremantle Arts Centre Press, 1979.

———. *Woman in a Lampshade*. Ringwood, Victoria: Penguin, 1983.

Secondary

Bedford, Jean. "Adversity in Detail." Rev. of *Five Acre Virgin and Other Stories*. *Australian* March 5, 1977: 8.

Bird, Delys, and Brenda Walker, eds. *Elizabeth Jolley: New Critical Essays*. Collins Angus and Robertson, 1991.

Burns, D. R. "Tales of Imagination and Realistic Horror." Rev. of *The Travelling Entertainer and Other Stories*. *Australian Book Review* April 1980: 20–21.

Burns, Graham. "Chronicler of Time's Slow Attritions." Rev. of *Stories*. *Age* July 14, 1984: 13.

Chishom, A. R. "Haloes around the Drabness." Rev. of *Five Acre Virgin and Other Stories*. *Age* February 5, 1977: 23.

Coover, Robert. "Dotty and Disorderly Conduct." Rev. of *The Well* and *Woman in a Lampshade*. *New York Times Book Review* November 16, 1986: 1+.

Dutton, Geoffrey. "A Talent Which Has Its Flaws." Rev. of *Stories*. *Bulletin* May 29, 1984: 97.

Eldridge, Marian. "Quirky Stories Well Worth Re-reading." Rev. of *Woman in a Lampshade*. *Canberra Times* April 9, 1983: 13.

Ellison, Jennifer. "Interview with Elizabeth Jolley." *Rooms of Their Own*. Ringwood, Victoria: Penguin, 1986. 174–91.

Forshaw, Thelma. "The Comic Muse." Rev. of *Mr. Scobie's Riddle, Woman in a Lampshade*, and *Miss Peabody's Inheritance*. *Quadrant* 28.4 (1984): 81–82.

Halliday, Bob. "Elizabeth Jolley's Well of Loneliness." Rev. of *The Well, Woman in a Lampshade*, and *Milk and Honey*. *Washington Post* November 2, 1986, *Book World*: 10–11.

Halligan, Marion. "Variations on Character." Rev. of *Stories*. *Canberra Times* September 29, 1984: 16.

Hildyard, Annette. "Bomb Nuts, Detectives, and Prisoners: Recent Australian Fiction." Rev. of *Woman in a Lampshade*. *Island Magazine* 18–19 (1984): 40–44.

Ikin, Van. "New Anthologies." Rev. of *Five Acre Virgin and Other Stories*. *Quadrant* 21.10 (1977): 79–80.

Kavanagh, Paul, and Peter Kuch, eds. "This Self the Honey of All Beings." *Conversations: Interviews with Australian Writers*. Sydney: Angus & Robertson, 1991. 153–76.

Keesing, Nancy. "Female Companions." Rev. of *The Travelling Entertainer and Other Stories* and "Palomino." *Australian Book Review* March 1981: 34–35.

————. "Lampshade Reflects Great Talent." Rev. of *Woman in a Lampshade. Weekend Australian* March 12–13, 1983: 16.

————. "Land as Obsession." Rev. of *Woman in a Lampshade* and "Mr. Scobie's Riddle." *Australian Book Review* April 1983: 6–7.

Lord, Gabrielle. "Exposing Truths and Myths." Rev. of *Woman in a Lampshade* and "Mr. Scobie's Riddle." *National Times* March 13–19, 1983: 32.

Milech, Barbara, and Brian Dibble. "Aristophanic Love-Dyads: Community, Communion, and Cherishing in Elizabeth Jolley's Fiction." *Antipodes: A North American Journal of Australian Literature* 7.1 (1993): 3–10.

Plunket, Robert. Rev. of *Stories. New York Times Book Review* April 24, 1988: 34.

Reid, Stuart, interviewer. "Dr. Elizabeth Jolley: Early Life in England; Migration to Australia 1959; Development as a Writer since 1960s; Publications to 1989; Tutoring and Lecturing in Creative Writing." A ninety-seven-page verbatim transcript of five hours of interviews of Elizabeth Jolley (May and June 1989) held in the J. S. Battye Library of Western Australian History.

Saari, Peggy. Rev. of *Stories. Antioch Review* 46.3 (1988): 393.

Salzman, Paul. *Elizabeth Jolley's Fictions: Helplessly Tangled in Female Arms and Legs.* St. Lucia: University of Queensland Press, 1993.

Webby, Elizabeth. " 'All the Qualities of Art': Circulating Some Shorts." Rev. of *The Travelling Entertainer and Other Stories. Meanjin* 40.2 (1981): 200–208.

Willbanks, Ray. "A Conversation with Elizabeth Jolley." *Antipodes: A North American Journal of Australian Literature* 3.1 (1989): 27–29.

Williams, Bruce. "Three Short Story Writers: Peter Cowan, Elizabeth Jolley, Justina Williams." Rev. of *The Travelling Entertainer and Other Stories. Westerly* 25.2 (1980): 104–7.

Windsor, Gerard. "The Importance of Being Old-fashioned." Rev. of *Stories. Australian Book Review* December–January 1984/1985: 17–18.

JAMAICA KINCAID
(May 25, 1949–   )

Hermine Lee

BIOGRAPHY

Jamaica Kincaid was born Elaine Potter Richardson in Antigua on May 25, 1949. She grew up with her mother, her stepfather, and three brothers. She later came to know her biological father, but was not able to call him "father" because her stepfather was the person to whom she was attached. Though her family was poor, Kincaid has said that she was "very well brought up." She attended school in Antigua but left before taking the examination required for high-school graduation. She came to the United States just after her sixteenth birthday with the hope of making a living and helping to support her family in Antigua. She stayed with a family in Westchester, New York, and took care of their children while attending school at night. She initially planned to become a nurse but soon changed her mind.

Kincaid left Westchester to attend the New School for Social Research, where she studied photography. She later attended Franconia College in New Hampshire, then returned to New York with an idea for a series of interviews with celebrities that won her a job at *Ingenue* magazine. Eventually, she met *New Yorker* columnist George Trow, who found her fascinating and began to write about her. Later, he suggested that she write stories for the magazine herself and introduced her to the editor, William Shawn. She became a staff writer for the *New Yorker* in 1976; most of her short stories were first published there.

Kincaid has said that since she was a child, she has always hated anything associated with colonialism. (Antigua was a British colony until its independence in 1981.) This hostility came almost instinctively, she believes, because it developed on its own before she understood the concept of imperialism. She hated the British patriotic songs that the colonists sang like "Rule Britannia" and the British anthem; she hated the name of her school, the Princess Margaret

School; she hated English cultural and social values. She even hated her name because she believed that it did not reflect her heritage; she was named for someone whom she felt exploited Antigua. This hostility toward Britain and its imperialism appears as a theme in many of her works; it is the major focus of *A Small Place* (1988), which presents a harsh criticism of Antigua during and after colonialism.

Kincaid's relationship with her mother also permeates her writings. A close bond in early years deteriorated as the author grew into adolescence; the estrangement continued into part of her adult life. Though amends were eventually made, the complexities of mother-daughter relationships continued to interest Kincaid; she explored them in her two autobiographic novels, *Annie John* (1983) and *Lucy* (1990), and in her short-story collection, *At the Bottom of the River* (1978).

Jamaica Kincaid is married to Allen Shawn, son of the former editor of the *New Yorker* magazine who once encouraged her writing. They have two children and live in upstate Connecticut.

CRITICISM

Kincaid's first book, *At the Bottom of the River*, received high praise. The *Village Voice* called her writing "sophisticated and precise." It won the Martin Dauwen Zabel Award from the American Academy and Institute of Arts and Letters in 1983. Her subsequent novels, *Annie John* and *Lucy*, were also well received. For many critics and readers, it was the lyricism of these early works that enchanted. But Kincaid eventually came to reject this style of writing, a style she saw as heavily influenced by English Romantic poetry, in favor of the more forthright tone. *A Small Place*, consequently, presents a critique unadorned by lyrical prose. Originally intended for the *New Yorker*, it was deemed by a new editor to be too harsh for its readership. Its language was praised as "musical" (*New York Times*) and "poetic" (*Los Angeles Times Book Review*), but anger emerged as its most compelling quality.

Jamaica Kincaid's works are highly experimental, which makes them at times difficult to understand. They shift from one voice to another, from past to present, and from reality to fantasy, often without alerting the reader. The element of "mystery" they introduce—a mystery tied to the protagonists' question "Who am I?"—has engendered various interpretations of her writings, many of which are rooted in psychology, Freudian, psychosocial, and psychohistorical. Yet while critics have tried to fit Kincaid into particular schools of writing, she has consistently resisted such efforts and has refused to belong to any group. Her early works, as she herself has stated, "were attempts to discard convention—my own conventions and conventions that exist within writing" (Vorda 25).

ANALYSIS

The common theme that runs through Kincaid's fiction is that of a fractured mother-daughter relationship. This fracture operates on two levels: at the literal level, the protagonist works through a troubled relationship with her mother; at the metaphorical level, the writer explores the ties between colony and "Mother Country." This is particularly true of her short stories.

In *At the Bottom of the River*, many images suggest the search for self. Water and light images are most frequent, though insects and reptiles, caves and holes also appear regularly. Water takes on several different meanings; it suggests a journey (17), the source for cleansing (3, 15), fertility and birth in the female (24), and finally, a source of enlightenment (75). Light generally symbolizes the epiphanies experienced by the protagonists. Caves, holes, animals, and insects refer to the primeval history from which the narrators draw heavily in their search for wholeness.

The sequence of the stories charts the progress of an identity quest, taking the reader through a series of formative experiences that culminate in self-understanding. Though the stories are more episodic than interconnected, there is enough of a thread to clearly follow the discovery. The first story, "Girl," opens with the protagonist recalling her mother's litany of advice on domestic matters. Besides dictating the practical housekeeping chores, the mother tells how to take care of a man—first her father, then her husband or lover: "This is how you iron your father's khaki shirt so it doesn't have a crease" (4), and later, "This is how to love a man and if this doesn't work there are other ways" (5). According to the maternal directives, then, a woman's primary obligation is to please the male; no attention is granted to developing the self as a separate entity. The long passage of admonition from the mother proceeds for over two pages with no periods—suggestive of relentless nagging—and the girl's two timid interjections convey the hopelessness and passivity she feels. Ultimately, then, "Girl" introduces the conflict between a well-intentioned but domineering mother and her seemingly obedient but frustrated daughter. Here the protagonist appears as a child who wishes to direct her life onto different paths than those onto which she is being guided.

The second story, "In the Night," has five sections, four of which recall sights, sounds, people, and happenings of the past. This is one of the few times a father appears, here as a night-soil man who removes sewage. (In *A Small Place*, Kincaid relates that one of the ills of the colonial government in Antigua is an underdeveloped sewerage system.) At night, like the other night-soil men, he sees supernatural creatures like the bird that is really a woman who has taken off her skin. The night-soil men are not the only ones to encounter the supernatural, however. Waking from a nightmare, the child protagonist sees lights on a mountain and asks what they are. The mother casually replies, "Oh, it is a jablesse," and tells of a person who can change her form as she pleases, but who especially likes to transform into a pretty woman. The mother warns the child to be careful of pretty women.

Such incidents point to a naturalness and ease with the folklore that the narrator and her family feel, a naturalness in conflict with their simultaneous hankering after things foreign. The father, after all, takes pride in his "brown felt hat which he orders from England, and brown leather shoes which he also orders from England" (10). Mr. Gishard, a neighbor, "appears" in his white suit that came from England long after his death. This tug between the local and the foreign, between folk superstitions and colonial rationality, is the dilemma of imperialism.

The story "At Last" presents a dialogue between a mother and a daughter now grown up. Divided into two parts, "The House" and "The Yard," it begins with the daughter questioning her mother about whether she was loved and about why doors in the house were kept closed. The line of questioning suggests that the girl has felt rejected, shut out from her mother's love. The mother proceeds to sketch moments from the early days, prompting the protagonist to ask, "The children?" to which the mother replies that they were not there yet.

The story to this point is straightforward until the mother relates that sometimes she appeared as a man and at other times as a hoofed animal and that she "left no corner unturned." With the birth of the children, however, she seemingly underwent a violent change. "What was the name—I mean the name my mother gave me—and where did I come from? My skin is now coarse. What pity. What sorrow. I have made a list. I have measured everything. I have not lied. But the light. What of the light? Splintered. Died" (17). Such language illustrates a rift not only in the mother-daughter relationship but also within the mother herself. It also suggests a parallel to another mother-daughter connection, that between mother country and colony.

In contrast to the confined spaces of the first section, "The Yard" begins with wide-open spaces, mountains, and children laughing. It is a return to the narrator's search for truth and self, this time through philosophical questionings, particularly related to death as the destroyer of all life. Toward the end of the story, symbols of primitive life abound—"the spotted beetle pauses then retraces its primitive crawl. Red fluid rock was deposited here and now the soil is rich in minerals"—emphasizing the universality of death and the interconnectedness of all things from the beginning of time (19).

"Wingless" is a story in six sections. Together, the passages present a girl growing into womanhood and wondering about her future. She feels that she is standing on the brink of "a great discovery" but wonders if, like Columbus, she will be punished for her findings. She attempts to "separate and divide" feelings (22), "to pin tags on them" and "register" them (23–24), but realizes that she cannot easily dictate emotions, her own or those of others. She begins to see aspects of herself that are not flattering; she is dishonest at times, despite the threat of punishment, and she does not always appreciate her mother. She cries out in frustration, "Where? What? Why? How then? Oh that! I am primitive and wingless" (24). The use of "wingless" here builds on an earlier metaphor: "Perhaps my life is as predictable as an insect's and I am in my pupa stage" (21). The narrator concludes that she is young and incapable of dealing with such a complex issue, a recognition that itself signifies growth.

"Holidays" is the first of the stories not set in the West Indies. Here a fireplace and deerflies are mentioned, and for the first time, the narrator revels in the joys of small things—the flies, a colorful book, the sun beating down on her back. Away from home, she seems to have left her troubles behind. Though she writes a letter to her family, she is deliberately superficial so as to keep the beautiful world to herself lest it become tainted like the other. Her contentment is interrupted only by one malicious jab at "the meek, self-sacrificing women" back home and the rituals of churchgoing. The narrator seems at this point to voice her determination not to fall into that category of women.

The story that follows, "Letter from Home," shifts between different spaces and times. Its tone is at first tranquil, but it soon builds to a frenzy to match the narrator's deepening anxiety as she awaits a letter from home. When she receives the letter, the contents of which are never revealed, it affects her deeply—"the wind blew hard, the house swayed" (39)—and she questions the Christian doctrine of Heaven and Hell and the lion lying down with the lamb. The images that follow are of life continuing in the order laid down by Nature. This section, in its portrayal of violent feelings, illustrates the continued upheaval of the narrator's emotions.

A dream cycle is the form used to tell the next story, "What I Have Been Doing Lately." As the narrator rests on her bed, she dreams of going on a journey. Shortly after she sets out, however, she encounters a body of water and must spend several years building a boat. When she finally crosses the water, everyone ignores her and the scenery begins changing. As in *Alice in Wonderland*, she comes upon a hole and decides to venture down it, but when she sees writings in a foreign language on the sides of the hole, she decides that she does not like the experience and wishes herself out. She continues the journey and meets a woman she at first thinks to be her mother. The woman asks her, "What have you been doing lately?" and she recounts her experiences with some significant differences. Among the new bits of information is a story of a monkey that threw a stone and hit her, but the cut healed immediately; "but now the skin on my forehead felt false to me" (44), she relates. She sees people across a "big body of water," "black and shiny," having a picnic and laughing and talking. She feels, "I would like to be with these people," but when she gets close, she finds that they are covered in black mud and are not laughing, and "the sky seemed far-away and nothing I could stand on would make me able to touch it with my fingertips" (44).

The images in this story suggest not only a psychological journey to one's beginnings but also the historical journey to cultural origins. The crossing of the water, the foreign language, the monkey, and the woman who seemed at first sight to be her mother all suggest a yearning to return to Africa, both spiritually and literally. In getting there, however, the narrator realizes that she is a stranger. The fantasy she had of the happy, fulfilling life that people enjoy there turns out to be just that, a fantasy. Through her disappointments, she comes to realize that her place is where her mother is and wishes, "If only I could get out of this. . . . If only just around the bend I would see my house and inside my house" (45). The narrator's journey begins and ends in the same place—at home in bed. This does not mean that she has not progressed; rather, it suggests that at the end she has a better understanding of where to seek her identity. While a literal journey will not bring the wholeness she needs, understanding her relationship to her personal and cultural past may. If this narrative can be taken as a reference to the writer's life, it may be worth noting that when she changed her name, she took one from the region of her birth, the West Indies, not from Africa.

"Blackness" is one of the more beautiful pieces of prose in the collection. It starts out with an overwhelming picture of blackness that surrounds the narrator and that is also part of her being. Because of it, she can no longer say her name and does not at once recognize her foot—references to a lack of self-knowledge. Images of objects "dashed and shattered" and her being in a boat and tossed by "the waves cruel and unruly" (48) continue the theme of a splintered psyche that has led to the agonizing search for the true self.

In the second part of the story, the narrator has a dream in which soldiers passed by her house and "blotted out the daylight and night fell immediately and permanently" (49). She could no longer see the beasts or smell the perfume of the flowers. The soldiers destroyed the foundations of her house and then left. The dream details the reason that she is unable to say her name. Continuing in the metaphorical vein, Kincaid suggests that the arrival of the British in Africa caused much psychological damage by their forcibly uprooting a people from their homeland and forcing a new identity on them. They lose their former selves but do not fully accept the other.

The narrator continues her story by telling of her child who is seemingly cruel to a playmate. She taunts him and "tugs at the long silk-like hairs that lie flattened on his back." She builds a hut for him on the cliff "so that she may watch him day after day flatten himself against a fate which he knows and yet cannot truly know until the moment it consumes him" (50). The child may be symbolic of the next generation that demands justice but also revenge. The British? The silk-haired boy realizes that the end of their reign is at hand and they are powerless to stop it. The passage ends on a note of hope and joy: "Oh. look at my child as she stands boldly now, one foot in the dark, the other in the light" (51). The child, unlike the mother who does not recognize her own foot, now stands with one foot in the light.

"Blackness" ends with the narrator coming to terms with the blackness that blocks her vision; abandoning hatred, she moves toward "the silent voice"—the ancestral voice. The blackness is erased in her: "The silent voice enfolds me so completely that even in memory the blackness is erased" (52). The wholeness is portrayed in the freedom and open spaces of the continents—the lions roam, the continents are not separated, the river flows uninhibited.

"Mother" relates the development of the new bond established between the narrator and her mother. Here the two are transformed into sea creatures, and when the narrator sees the mother extending affection to a fish, she becomes jealous. When her mother shows love for other creatures, she becomes increasingly bitter. One day, her mother puts her on a boat for a new island. Though she is heartbroken at the separation, she finds her mother in disguise in the new land, and they resume the close ties they once shared. This brings to a resolution the love-hate relationship between mother and daughter and, in so doing, resolves the questions of homeland, of colonial and ancestral bonds, and of the connections between life and death.

"At the Bottom of the River," the title story from the book, addresses the search for a personal and professional identity in the new land. There is no hearkening back to the past but a look to the future. The story opens with a description of a rugged, inhospitable terrain where a large stream with "deep ambition" (62) flows. It traverses the plain and comes to rest in a basin, where it awaits the arrival of someone to give its life meaning. The metaphor implies that although life in the new land may be difficult, it does present opportunities.

Kincaid then presents three scenarios through which she explores the meaning of life and death. The first depicts a man who lies on his bed and waits for something to happen to give his life meaning. The narrator says of this character, "He sits in nothing, in nothing, in nothing" (64). The second, in contrast, presents a man who has a devoted wife and daughter and a career that gives his life purpose. Yet although he seems content, he is troubled that eventually all things die, including the work of his own hands. Finally, in the third scenario, a worm finds pleasure in the joy and pain of living, treasuring every moment it experiences. When it, too, dies at last, the narrator hears her mother's voice saying that death is natural. The narrator, after examining each of these scenarios, concludes that, "Each moment is not as fragile and fleeting as I once thought" (69) and that the passive man had not lived, but the active one with his doubts can die only once. "Inevitable to life is death and not inevitable to death is life" (72).

The last two sections of "At the Bottom of the River" show the narrator at the river's edge, looking in. At the bottom of the river, she sees a house surrounded by green grass; at the edge of the grass are many white-gray pebbles and, beyond them, flowers. Then she notices that everything is illuminated, and as she wonders what it all means, a woman appears at the door of the house and shields her eyes as if looking into the future. The narrator joins her in looking and, with some effort, at last sees what the woman sees: a world with no shadows, a utopia to the narrator. As she longs to go there, she is suddenly transformed into an unreal being, "made up of will and over my will I had complete dominion" (79), and in an enlightened moment, she realizes her strength.

The final epiphany occurs when she enters a lit room and sees among other things some books, a chair, a table, and a pen. These are the tools of her trade— writing. She also realizes that to be human is to live with the past and with death: "And as I see these things in the light of the lamp, all perishable and transient, how bound up I know I am to all that is human endeavor, to all that is past and to all that shall be, to all that shall be lost and leave no trace. I claim these things then—mine—and now I feel myself grow solid and complete, my name filling up my mouth" (82).

WORKS CITED AND CONSULTED

Primary

Stories

Kincaid, Jamaica. "The Apprentice." *New Yorker* August 17, 1981. 25–26.

———. "The Circling Hand." *New Yorker* November 21, 1983. 50–57.

———. "Cold Heart." *New Yorker* June 25, 1990. 28–40.

———. "Columbus in Chains." *New Yorker* October 10, 1983. 48–52.

———. "Dates and Comments." *New Yorker* October 17, 1977. 37–39.

———. "Figures in the Distance." *New Yorker* May 9, 1983. 40–42.

———. "The Finishing Line." *New York Times Book Review* December 2, 1990. 18.

———. "The Fourth." *New Yorker* July 19, 1976. 19–23.

———. "Gwen." *New Yorker* April 16, 1984. 46–52.

———. "Have Yourself a Gorey Little Christmas: Nine Writers Create Stories for Edward Gorey's Christmas Illustrations." *New York Times Book Review* December 2, 1990. 18.

———. "The Long Rain." *New Yorker* July 30, 1984. 28–36.

———. "Lucy." *New Yorker* September 24, 1990. 44–56.

———. "Mariah." *New Yorker* June 26, 1989. 32–38.

———. "Notes and Comment." *New Yorker* January 3, 1983. 23–24.

———. "Poor Visitor." *New Yorker* February 27, 1989. 28–30.

———. "The Red Girl." *New Yorker* August 8, 1983. 32–38.

———. "Somewhere, Belgium." *New Yorker* May 14, 1984. 44–51.

———. "The Tongue." *New Yorker* October 9, 1989. 44–54.

———. "A Walk to the Jetty." *New Yorker* November 5, 1984. 45–51.

Books

Kincaid Jamaica, *Annie, Gwen, Lily, Pam, and Tulip*. New York: Knopf, 1986; Whitney, 1989.

———. *Annie John*. New York: New American Library, 1985.

———. *At the Bottom of the River*. New York: Farrar Straus Giroux, 1978; Plume, 1992.

———. *Lucy*. New York: Farrar Straus Giroux, 1990.

———. *My Brother*. New York: Farrar Straus Giroux, 1997.

———. *My Favorite Plant: Writers and Gardeners on the Plants They Love*. New York: Farrar Straus Giroux, 1998.

———. *My Garden (Book)*. New York: Farrar Straus Giroux, 1999.

———. *A Small Place*. London: Virago Press, 1988.

Kincaid, Jamaica, and Robert Atwan, eds. *The Best American Essays*. Boston: Houghton Mifflin, 1995.

Shorter Fiction, Essays, and Nonfiction

Kincaid, Jamaica. "Antigua Crossings." *Rolling Stone* June 19, 1978.

———. "Biography of a Dress." *Grand Street* 11.3 (1992). 92–100.

———. "Erotica." *Ms.* January 1975.

———. "Jamaica Kincaid's New York." *Rolling Stone* October 6, 1977.

———. "On Seeing England for the First Time." *Translations* 5.1 (1991). 32–40.

———. "Ovando." *Conjunctions* 10 (1989).

———. "The Ugly Tourist." From *A Small Place. Harper's* September 1988.

Secondary

Bonneti, Kay. "An Interview with Jamaica Kincaid." *Missouri Review* 15 (1992): 125–142.

Chodorow, Nancy. *The Reproduction of Mothering: Psychoanalysis and the Society of Gender.* Berkeley: University of California Press, 1978.

Cudjoe, Selwyn R. "Jamaica Kincaid and the Modernist Project: An Interview." *Callaloo* 12 (1989).

Dance, Daryl C., ed. *Fifty Caribbean Writers: A Bio-bibliographical Critical Sourcebook.* Westport, CT: Greenwood, 1986.

Dutton, Wendy. "Merge and Separate: Jamaica Kincaid's Fiction." *World Literature Today* 63 (1989): 406–10.

Ferguson, Moira. *Jamaica Kincaid: Where the Land Meets the Body.* Charlottesville: University Press of Virginia, 1994.

Leavitt, David. "Review of *At The Bottom of the River." Village Voice* January 17, 1984.

O'Connell, Alex. "Review of *At The Bottom of the River." New York Times* January 3, 1998.

Solomon, Charles. "Review of *At The of the River." Los Angeles Times* January 12, 1992.

Vorda, Allan. "An Interview with Jamaica Kincaid." *Mississippi Review* 20 (1991): 7–27.

MAXINE HONG KINGSTON
(October 27, 1940–   )

Jennie Wang

BIOGRAPHY

Maxine Hong Kingston was born in 1940 in Stockton, California. Her parents, fictionalized in many of her works, originally came from Canton, China. Her father, Tom Hong ("The American Father" in *China Men*), was a village teacher; he sailed for America in the 1920s out of curiosity for the sea and the desire for adventure. Her mother, Chew Ying Lan (Brave Orchid in *The Woman Warrior*), remained in China with two children for fifteen years because of U.S. immigration law that excluded the entry of Chinese women. A strong, independent, and modern woman, she went to medical school, obtained her diploma, and worked for a time as a medical doctor in her village; eventually, she managed to come to America by herself.

Kingston is the first of the six children born after her mother joined her father in America. Throughout the 1940s and 1950s, her parents, like many Chinese immigrants, labored in the fields, laundry, and casino, yet despite their hardship, they raised their children to value literacy and learning. Kingston's father taught her Chinese language, poetry, and history, and her mother nurtured in her a taste for Chinese opera, Chinese folklore, and folk storytelling, which the author later translated into her own "talkstories."

Kingston is one of the few major American writers to demonstrate the benefit of bilingual education in her literary achievement. Attending both public school and Chinese school, she finished her education successfully and went on to the University of California, Berkeley. She first majored in engineering; then, enchanted by the power of language, she switched to English. She received her B.A. in 1962 and a teaching certificate in 1965. Throughout the 1960s, she was actively involved in the civil rights movement and the peace movement, which set the historical context as well as the major themes of her work. She married Earll Kingston, an actor, had a son, went with him to Hawaii, and lived there for seventeen years. While she was working as a schoolteacher, Kingston began to research Chinese immigrant history and wrote her first two books, *The Woman Warrior* and *China Men*, whose exuberant narrative power and originality amazed audiences in North America.

The Woman Warrior, subtitled *Memoirs of a Girlhood among Ghosts*, tells the story of Kingston's own experience growing up female and Chinese in America; she traces her Chinese cultural heritage through the strong presence of her mother and her "talkstories." *China Men* is a metafictive history of the Chinese immigrant experience from the late nineteenth century to the contemporary period. Here Kingston searches for the lost legacy of both her own father and "The Fathers"—the forefathers of Chinese immigrants, who built the transcontinental railroads in the Sierra Nevada Mountains, planted in the cane fields of Hawaii, and fished in Alaska and Cuba.

The Woman Warrior was published in 1976 and *China Men* in 1980. Both books brought Kingston immediate recognition and considerable fame. Reviewers predicted that *China Men* "will come to be regarded as one of the classic American works on the experience of immigration" (*Los Angeles Herald Examiner*). The book won the American Book Award in 1981 and was named to the American Library Association Notable Books List. *The Woman Warrior* won the National Book Critics Award in 1976 and was one of *Time* magazine's top ten "nonfiction" works of the decade. Her short stories, articles, and poems have appeared in the *New Yorker, New West, Ms.*, and *American Heritage*. Among many honors and awards, Kingston also received the *Mademoiselle* Magazine Award in 1977, the Anisfield-Wolf Race Relations Award in 1978, and the Stockton Arts Commission Award in 1981. She was offered a number of fellowships, including a Guggenheim Fellowship (1981) and a fellowship from the National Endowment for the Arts (1989) that enabled her to write full-time. Her third book, *Tripmaster Monkey*, was published in 1989 and introduced an archetypal figure named Wittman Ah Sing—an unemployed, fifth-generation, Asian-American, college-educated, avant-garde artist, activist, poet, and playwright confronting the "military-industrial-educational-complex" in San Francisco and the Bay Area in the 1960s. The book is rated the best novel about the 1960s.

Since 1988, Kingston has been teaching creative writing at the University of California, Berkeley. The 1990 fire at Berkeley Hills unfortunately burned a working manuscript. In an interview with Bill Moyers, she related that she is engaged in an effort to invent "a language of Peace," which she hopes will "heal our national wound from the war in Vietnam." In order to write her next book, *The 5th Book of Peace*, she has conducted "lab work" with Vietnam veterans— who have gathered in a commune in the mountains of France under the supervision of a Buddhist monk. The time and efforts Kingston puts into writing may explain the weight in her work. As a writer, she is as ambitious and self-conscious as Joyce declared he was in *A Portrait of the Artist as a Young Man*: "I go to encounter for the millionth time the reality of experience and to forge in the smithy of my soul the uncreated conscience of my race." Like Joyce, Kingston has a lofty sense of Self and a strong sense of duty to the people and the community about whom she writes and for whom she speaks. Not surprisingly, critics have compared her works with Joyce's *Portrait* and *Ulysses*. Considering the time gap between *Ulysses* and *Finnegans Wake*, it can be predicted that an American "phoenix" in the wake of the *Wake* may arise from the ashes of her burnt manuscript when she publishes her next book.

CRITICISM

The first Asian-American writer accepted in the canon of American literature, Kingston, in a decade and a half, is reported to be one of the most widely taught living American authors on college campuses today, together with Toni Morrison and Leslie Silko. In 1991, to meet the demand of curriculum instruction, the Modern Language Association published *Approaches to Teaching Kingston's The Woman Warrior*, edited by Shirley Geok-Lin Lim, which includes pages of references to books, articles, interviews, films, video productions, and recordings for Kingston study.

Kingston's influence on contemporary women writers and ethnic-minority writers can be said to be monumental. However, Kingston criticism in the past suffered from ethnocentric and phallocentric readings that underestimated the surrealistic elements in her fiction and her postmodern narrative strategies and often misdirected its criticism against the "Chinese," "sexism in China," and the "Chinese patriarchy." The problems of misinterpretation are well documented, exemplified, and criticized by Kingston herself in an essay on "Cultural Misreading by American Reviewers."

The development of postmodern and postcolonial theories since the late 1980s has opened new perspectives in Kingston study. Linda Hutcheon's theory of "postmodern historiographic metafiction" at last places Kingston's work in a proper tradition. Malini J. Schueller's book *The Politics of Voice: Liberalism and Social Criticism from Franklin to Kingston* recognizes Kingston's radicalism and also her unique position as a woman writer who destabilizes the concept of gender, and questions racial definitions. Such a position is well examined in Donald C. Goellnicht's study on "Tang Ao in America: Male Subject Positions in China Men" (see Lim and Ling). Meanwhile, the emergence of Asian and Asian-American critics in the literary academy led by Elaine Kim, Frank Chin, Sau-Ling Wong, Amy Ling, Shirley Geok-Lin Lim, King-Kok Cheung, and David Leiwei Liu has produced several more substantial readings of Kingston's works.

Kingston's works contain an encyclopedia of genres and textual materials. A mixture of fiction and reality, fantasy and memory, dreams and imagination, legends and history, and bilingual sources of literary references and folklore weaves the tapestry of her textuality. Kingston's powerful imagination, her freedom in self-fashioning through imaginary projections, and her self-projection as self-emancipation have opened infinite possibilities for storytelling. Yet because her first two works were published as "nonfiction," critics have had difficulty classifying them.

Arguably, Kingston's three major works may all be classified as short-story sequences. She herself describes *The Woman Warrior* as "five interlocking pieces and each one was like a short story or an essay"; similarly, *China Men* consists of eighteen essayistic fictions, each containing "a myth, and then a modern story and then a myth." *Tripmaster Monkey*, published as a novel, consists of chapters that stand on their own as short stories. For students and scholars of the short story as a genre, perhaps it will make sense to view *The Woman Warrior* in the tradition of Joyce's *Dubliners*, Faulkner's *Go Down, Moses*, and John Barth's *Lost in the Funhouse*. Kingston virtually wrote a female narrative in the tradition of a contemporary male genre—metafiction.

Characteristic of metafiction, the idea of an "essay," as she emphasizes, is most important in analyzing her works. Her stories are indeed essayistic, speculative, self-conscious, full of paradoxical statements and contradictions, constantly canceling the surface of meaning and challenging the reader's logic and reasoning; they are, in Mary Rohrberger's term, "anti-stories." They make up a novel, as Kingston points out, with "a coherent long, long structure" and "interlocking themes." Such a structure and thematic development are often invisible, absent from the printed page, linked by the author's implicit arguments and ideas. A comprehensive understanding of Kingston's works can be reached only through a revelation of such structure and interlocking themes—the "ghost of Idea" behind the story. The following pages offer such a reading of *The Woman Warrior* as an example.

ANALYSIS

The Woman Warrior is a sequence of five short stories. The five stories stand for five different stages in Kingston's search for a female identity. Like an essay, "No Name Woman" evokes the topic of what will become of a daughter from a Chinese family if she pursues sexual liberty with a "stranger." Kingston recalls her mother's story about an aunt in pre-revolutionary China who committed adultery with a "stranger," disgraced her family, and threw herself into the family well. This sensational story, with its popular motifs of sex, violence, and mystery, as well as its Orientalist stereotype of the grieving Asian woman, is only a preamble, "a story within a story," used to provoke the very question of such an identity. For the adolescent girl, whose sexual identity is awakening, her "no name" aunt serves as a mirror image of her own reality. Like her aunt, she is faced with a choice between individual sexual liberty, which is what the mainstream white culture has to offer in the 1960s, and the preservation of her name, her place in her family and her ethnic community. Through the aunt's story, Kingston's mother issues a warning not to repeat the "family curse" in a country of "strangers," describing the consequence of "adultery"—adultery between worlds.

Kingston's strength lies in her ability to escape the modernist dilemma of "exile" from community and to reinvent native tradition in her search for a new identity. Instead of "adultery," Kingston chooses "marriage"; in Chinese tradition, as she tells us in *The Woman Warrior*, "marriage promises to turn strangers into friendly relatives" (12). Instead of choosing between worlds, Kingston chooses to be a medium between worlds, a translator between cultures.

"White Tigers" therefore invokes the heroic tradition of Chinese women drawn from Chinese history and legends: "We could be heroines, swordswomen" (19). Casting herself in the role of Fa Mu Lan, a "Woman Warrior," who took her father's place to be drafted to fight wars in ancient China, Kingston explores an ideal identity through dreams and fantasy. She envisions herself as a commander of an army and a comrade to her husband, capable of giving birth to a son in the battlefield and returning home a dutiful daughter to her parents and in-laws. She conceives of herself as a leader of her community; "The villagers would make a legend about my perfect filiality." Her ideal projection of an ideal female identity modeled upon Chinese heroic tradition is dispersed when her conscious mind returns to the level of reality: "My American life has been such a disappointment" (45).

"Shaman" heals the gap between the ideal world and the real world. In it, Kingston examines the model of her mother as a modern Chinese woman in 1930s China combating the "ghosts" of traditions, liberating herself and other women as well as the sick and poor in her village.

"At the Western Palace" brings the reader back to America, only to see her mother's heroic spirit defeated once she is displaced from China. The story deals with defeat, denial, the displacement of authentic identity of Chinese women, and their cultural alienation. Brave Orchid's sister Moon Orchid comes to America to join her husband and is denied by him, since he has already married another woman, a Chinese-American woman. Brave Orchid exhausts her wisdom and power in helping her own sister Moon Orchid to claim her legitimate identity. She fails completely because she has no control of the language, law, and way of life in the white world. The idea that the legitimate wife from China ends in a state mental asylum "at the Western Palace" reveals the tragic consequence of "adultery" and "infidelity." On the other hand, it suggests that the domestic tradition from China cannot be preserved; new roles and new identity have to be self-made in America, re-created in a new land.

In "A Song for a Barbarian Reed Pipe," Kingston continues to explore the theme of cultural and linguistic deprivation manifest in the form of silence, the silence of Chinese women in the public realm of American life. The idea of the story is to break the silence of oppression by speaking up, creating a voice as a spokeswoman, finding "words" to express the Chinese-American woman's experience. So she makes up a story with words she invents, with bilingual black humor and Chinese jokes, that her mother "cuts her frenum" to let her tongue loose, so that she "would be able to move in any language . . . speak languages that are completely different from one another" (164). To preserve her mother's talent in storytelling, she speculates on her career choice and is determined to search for words to translate her "mother tongue."

She ends her search on a high note, a story translated from a Chinese classic, the story of Ts'ai Yen, a poetess born in A.D. 175. Like Kingston, Ts'ai Yen was the daughter of a Chinese scholar, Ts'ai Yung, who was well known for his library collection. During a war, Ts'ai Yen was captured by a chieftain of the Southern Hsiung-nu. For twelve years, Ts'ai Yen was married to the chieftain and had two children born in a "barbarian" land, "who did not speak Chinese." After the war was over, Ts'ai Yen was ransomed to return to China and remarry. On her way back, she wrote on horseback a sequence of tragic songs about the war, about her life in a barbarian land. These poems have been passed down as "Eighteen Stanzas of a Barbarian Reed Pipe," the title Kingston borrows for her story. Through imaginary juxtapositions of a woman writer with the woman warrior, daughter of China and wife of two worlds, mother of foreign sons and companion to foreign soldiers, Kingston eventually creates a unique female role—a translator of literary texts and cultural identities, a transnational woman writer. The lost legacy of her "mother tongue" is restored, "entitled" in her story through translation into a new language. Thus if "No Name Woman" is an evocation, "White Tigers" can be read as an initiation story or a provocation, "Shaman" as an exposition, and "At the Western Palace" as a painful revelation, while "A Song for a Barbarian Reed Pipe" reaches a conclusion in the search for a Chinese female identity.

WORKS CITED AND CONSULTED

Primary

Kingston, Maxine Hong. "Cultural Mis-reading by American Reviewers." *Asian and Western Writers in Dialogue: New Cultural Identities*. Ed. Guy Amirthanayagam. London: Macmillan, 1982. 55–65.

———. *China Men*. New York: Knopf, 1980.

———. *Hawai'i One Summer, 1978*. San Francisco: Meadow Press, 1987.

———. *Tripmaster Monkey: His Fake Book*. New York: Knopf, 1989.

——— *The Woman Warrior: Memoirs of a Girlhood among Ghosts*. New York: Knopf, 1976.

Secondary

Cheung, King-Kok. *Articulate Silences: Hisaye Yamamoto, Maxine Hong Kingston, Joy Kogawa*. Ithaca, NY: Cornell University Press, 1993.

Cheung, Kink-Kok, and Stan Yogi. *Asian American Literature: An Annotated Bibliography*. New York: MLA, 1988.

Chin, Frank. "This Is Not an Autobiography." *Genre* 18.2 (1985): 109–30.

Hutcheon, Linda. *A Poetics of Postmodernism: History, Theory, Fiction.* New York: Routledge, 1988.

Kim, Elaine H. *Asian American Literature: An Introduction to the Writings and Their Social Context.* Philadelphia: Temple University Press, 1982.

Klucznik, Kenneth B. " 'It Translated Well': De Man, Lacan, Kingston, and Self at the Borderline of Other." *Symploke* 1:2 (Summer 1993): 177–94.

Lim, Shirley Geok-Lin, ed. *Approaches to Teaching Kingston's The Woman Warrior.* New York: MLA, 1991.

Lim, Shirley Geok-Lin, and Amy Ling, eds. *Reading the Literatures of Asian America.* Philadelphia: Temple University Press, 1992.

Ling, Amy. *Between Worlds: Women Writers of Chinese Ancestry.* New York: Pergamon, 1990.

Moyers, Bill. *The Stories of Maxine Hong Kingston.* New Jersey: Films for the Humanities, 1994.

Schueller, Malini Johar. *The Politics of Voice: Liberalism and Social Criticism from Franklin to Kingston.* New York: State University of New York Press, 1992.

Skandera-Trombley, Laura E., ed. *Critical Essays on Maxine Hong Kingston.* New York: G. K. Hall, 1998.

Skenazy, Paul, and Tera Martin. *Conversations with Maxine Hong Kingston.* Jackson: University Press of Mississippi, 1998.

Wang, Jennie. "The Myth of Kingston's 'No Name Woman': Making Contextual and Intertextual Connections in Teaching Asian American Literature." *The CEA Critic* 59 (Fall 1996): 21–32.

———. "*Tripmaster Monkey*: Kingston's Postmodern Representation of a New 'China Man,' " *MELUS* 20.1 (Spring 1995): 101–14.

Wong, Sau-Ling Cynthia. "Autobiography as Guided Chinatown Tour? Maxine Hong Kingston's The Woman Warrior and the Chinese–American Autobiographical Controversy." *American Lives: Essays in Multicultural American Autobiography.* Ed. James Robert Payne. Knoxville: University of Tennessee Press, 1992.

———. *Reading Asian American Literature: From Necessity to Extravagance.* Princeton: Princeton University Press, 1993.

———, ed. *Maxine Hong Kingston's* The Woman Warrior. New York: Oxford University Press, 1998.

DORIS LESSING
(October 23, 1919–   )

Rick Oehling

BIOGRAPHY

Born in Kermanshah, Iran, in October 1919, Doris Lessing lived for the first five years of her life there before settling with her family in Southern Rhodesia (now Zimbabwe). Lessing's father, Alfred Cook Taylor, lost a leg in "the Great Unmentionable" (World War I) and was nursed back to health by Emily Maude McVeagh, Lessing's mother. Their courtship and marriage did not significantly alter their relationship of patient and nurse: he remained a baffled, unhappy survivor, and she centered her life around his. In Rhodesia, Taylor took up farming, but never proved wholly successful at it.

Although Lessing rebelled against her parents, she also inherited two strong characteristics from them: her father's skepticism and her mother's industry. Around the period of World War II, Lessing swung into the very cycle she had once disavowed: dancing and drinking with "the crowd," two unsuccessful marriages, young motherhood. The breakup of a conventional first marriage was followed by a period of engagement in left-wing politics and another marriage, this time to a German Communist expatriate. In 1949, she left Rhodesia and Africa and sailed to England with her third child, Peter, and the manuscript of her first novel, *The Grass Is Singing* (1950).

Lessing was remarkably prolific during the next decade, publishing three collections of short stories and novellas, reviews, journalism, plays, and five novels, including the first three volumes of the *Children of Violence* novel series. Readers wondering about the autobiographical feel of the early stories and of the *Children of Violence* novels will find that her autobiographical writings—*Going Home* (1957), *In Pursuit of the English* (1960), *Particularly Cats* (1967), *African Laughter: Four Visits to Zimbabwe* (1992), and *Under My Skin: Volume One of My Autobiography, to 1949* (1994)—clarify what is taken from life and what is invented.

Lessing has lived in London since 1949. Over the past fifty years, she has published thirty-five books, including six volumes of short stories and novellas. Her recognition as a writer increased dramatically with the publication of *The Golden Notebook* in 1962. Around this time, Lessing became interested in the Mohammedan mystic system, Sufism, and also began to write in greater detail about madness in the individual and the collective (a concern evident even in her first book, *The Grass Is Singing*). Throughout the 1970s and 1980s, she experimented with a variety of genres and forms; she followed a visionary novel of "inner space" (*Briefing for a Descent into Hell*, 1971) with a realistic novel of midlife crisis (*The Summer before the Dark*, 1973). Her ventures away from traditional realism lost her some older readers but gained her many younger fans, especially among science-fiction readers. Although none of Lessing's writings can be termed conventional science fiction, several of her works display affinities with the more experimental strains of the genre (Philip K. Dick, J. G. Ballard, and Ursula LeGuin, for example).

In the early 1980s, after the *Canopus in Argos* speculative fiction series, Lessing wrote and published two works of quiet realism under the pseudonym "Jane Somers." In the preface for a later edition published under her own name, she explained that this was done in part to escape the role of "Author Doris Lessing" and in part to test the reputation-driven publishing and reviewing industries. In October 1994, on her seventy-fifth birthday, she published the first volume of a planned three-volume autobiography that reexamines her past without sentimentality, underscoring a statement she made in 1980: "Once upon a time, when I was young, I believed things easily, both religious and political; now I believe less and less. But I wonder about more" (preface to *The Sirian Experiments*). Lessing published the second volume of her autobiography in 1997 and a longer science fiction novel entitled *Mara and Dann* in 1999.

Lessing was the guest of honor at the 1988 World Science Fiction Convention. Other honors include the Somerset Maugham Award for *Five: Short Novels* (1954), the Prix Medicis, the Austrian State Prize for Literature, the Shakespeare Prize (Hamburg), the W. H. Smith Award for *The Good Terrorist* (1985), and the James Tait Black Prize for *Under My Skin* (1995).

CRITICISM

Doris Lessing is often cited as one of the major writers of the post–World War II era; several hundred reviews and articles have been written about her work, as well as several book-length studies. Lessing is cited in most literary histories of the era and, because of the impact of *The Golden Notebook*, is particularly featured in surveys of modern women writers. She is widely regarded as a masterful short-story writer, and some readers feel that the stories represent her best work. The collections have appeared throughout her career and share themes and formal concerns with the novels, plays, and nonfiction.

There is no book-length study devoted exclusively or even largely to Doris

Lessing's short fiction. Michael Thorpe's *Doris Lessing* (1973) addresses the African stories, and Mona Knapp's *Doris Lessing* (1984) includes chapters on both the African and English stories. Two of the best books on Lessing—Lorna Sage's *Doris Lessing* (1983) and Betsy Draine's *Substance under Pressure: Artistic Coherence and Evolving Form in the Novels of Doris Lessing* (1983)— deal with the novels almost exclusively; however, both present synthesizing approaches that are helpful in creating a context for the short stories. Throughout the 1970s and 1980s, an overwhelming percentage of the articles written on Lessing focused upon *The Golden Notebook* and to a lesser extent upon the concluding volume of the *Children of Violence* series, *The Four-gated City* (1969). Selma R. Burkom's "Only Connect: Form and Content in the Works of Doris Lessing" makes the story "Dialogue" central to its argument for an over-arching philosophical impulse toward integration in Lessing's work. This discussion is then amplified and applied to several new stories in Nancy Neufield Silva's "Doris Lessing's Ideal Reconciliation." Nancy Shields Hardin explores the influence of Sufi parable on Lessing's themes and narrative forms in "Doris Lessing and the Sufi Way." While the short stories have not received the critical attention that the novels have, some of Lessing's most astute readers—Virginia Tiger, Claire Sprague, Clare Hanson, and Ellen Cronan Rose—began in the 1980s to redress this imbalance.

Where do Lessing's stories appear on a hypothetical map of the modern short story? Because the stories range so greatly, it is difficult to define a "characteristic" Lessing story. Certain strengths, however, are consistent: the plain, vernacular style, the rapid but effective sketching in of character, the use of setting and atmosphere, and the disdain for sentimentality and exquisite writing. Her narratives are especially skillful in rendering subtle shifts in a character's state of mind: few writers could so quickly and convincingly communicate psychological breakdown as Lessing does in "To Room Nineteen" and "The Temptation of Jack Orkney." Some of her most powerful epiphanies rise out of the self's obliteration into the larger, darker forms of its environment. Lessing is skilled in the representation of those spaces that outlast the human lives that so fleetingly occupy them: vast African skies, rooms in a London boardinghouse, a planet freezing over and turning an Eden into an iceball.

Lessing's experiments with the short story have often involved expanding realism to integrate it with other, more visionary modes. She writes with a realist's curiosity about ordinary people and common social practices, yet she often turns this curiosity inward to explore the submerged lives of her characters, rendering in exact and telling detail their dreams, desires, and premonitions. In a review of Lessing's *Stories*, novelist Margaret Drabble maintains that Lessing's particular genius combines a keen journalistic sense with an uncommonly clear eye for manifestations of the unconscious. Drabble writes, "It is the combination of the two gifts that makes her one of the great writers of our time" (56).

ANALYSIS

This Was the Old Chief's Country (1951) was the second book Doris Lessing published and her first collection of stories, the only original collection to have an exclusively African setting. The title signals the theme of dislocation and exile that runs through the volume. Characters are exiled from the land, from each other, from themselves. This *was* his country, but now when the Old Chief encounters a fourteen-year-old white girl on the road, it is uncertain who holds rank. Wives brought out to the veldt find themselves married to strangers; a white woman feels compelled to abandon her relationship with a black child when she begins to raise her own children ("Little Tembi"). A note of baffled disbelief is recurrently struck in these stories as characters come to feel that there is something fundamentally bogus about this socially determined reality.

The theme of feeling spiritually exiled in one's own country finds its strongest expression in the collection's concluding story, "Winter in July." The title, referring to the seasons of the Southern Hemisphere, also alludes to the conflict between actuality and desire. The story's central relationship is the bond between two brothers and Julia, a woman with whom they are both involved. However, rather than having all her needs satisfied by the two brothers, Julia finds that her restlessness is doubled. Kenneth, the brother who understands her and shares her nihilist beliefs, is too close for comfort; Tom, whose nature is more alien and more accepting, provides her breathing room. Ultimately, each of the characters wants it both ways; that is, each wants both winter and July. Julia wants both familiarity and foreignness; the men desire Julia and want to be alone with each other. Each scenario is sampled and each is unbearable; the impossibility of resolving the conflict between desire and actuality parallels Julia's lifelong sense of exile: "Emotionally, there was no country of which she could say: this is my home" (249). In the end, Julia's kindred spirit, Kenneth, turns upon her, saying, "Do stop fussing. . . . [S]top making us all miserable over impossibilities. . . . It's not much fun being the fag-end of something, but even that has its compensations" (249). This concluding note of compulsory self-estrangement is particularly ironic because it is struck by a prospering white farmer—one who has claimed the old chief's country for himself. Only seventy-five years after colonization, it already feels like "the fag-end of something."

Throughout her career, Lessing returns to these kinds of situations where characters insist that they are trapped by reality and yet are haunted by the sense that this reality is inauthentic or impossible. Single-minded ideologies like apartheid depend upon faith in a single reality, but Lessing's title announces a counterreality: *This Was the Old Chief's Country*. The collision of Lessing's progressive sympathies with the reactionary apartheid state perhaps contributed to the sense of utopian counterrealities shadowing much of her fiction. In her writings, Doris Lessing seeks to bridge impossible contradictions through imaginative thought; she maintains that where abstract thought and categorizations end, human nature begins. Although some readers complain that Lessing, like

Julia, seems to enjoy "making us all miserable over impossibilities," she often appears cheered by contradictions and bemused by her own evidence that the entire world and everyone in it is secretly mad. The result often reads as if Turgenev had conspired with Lewis Carroll in creating a fiction of ersatz realities rendered in a scrupulously realistic method, a sort of realism of unrealities.

It is interesting that this sense of unreality peeking through the conventionally real is also manifest in Lessing's earliest stories set in England, most notably in "The Other Woman" from the novella collection *Five: Short Novels* (1953). In this story set during the Blitz (the bombing of England during World War II), the main character, Rose, decides that the nightmarish things happening to her simply cannot be real. When a policeman finds her sitting in her bombed-out basement and warns her that the whole weight of the house is lying on her cracked ceiling, she responds, Isn't that how it has always been? Frightened of living alone in the world, Rose enters into an affair wherein she is forced into the role of "the other woman." This conventional phrase seems absurd applied to prim Rose, who did not know of the marriage and who wants only conventionality and order for herself. In the end, Rose and the wife hammer out a new set of conventions for all parties to live by. The sense of unreality that had threatened to undo Rose's sanity is sublimated into a new code and a new conventionality. In one sense, Rose and the wife are right to see themselves as "realists," not because they see the world realistically, but because they have conspired to make their corner of reality conform to how they want it to be.

There is a comic tone to several of the stories in *Five* that makes the folly of the characters seem appealingly quixotic. The father's quest for gold in "Eldorado" seems somewhat foolish, but sets him apart from the true antagonist of Lessing's early fiction—the stolid, unimaginative human herd. However, this bedrock of idealism and goodness is nowhere evident in the bleak sequence of stories that make up *The Habit of Loving* (1957). Where the central characters in *Five* were unrealistic, the figures in this collection are unreal, a menagerie of mimes and manics. Many of the stories are short, harsh, and expressive of a bitter parodic vision that also surfaces in Lessing's drama from this period. Lessing's parodic fictions are sometimes her grimmest, her dark wit pursuing dark visions. In the concluding novella of *The Habit of Loving*, entitled "The Eye of God in Paradise," we are introduced to the figure of Dr. Kroll, the administrator of an insane asylum in post–World War II Germany, who for six months of the year heads the hospital and for six months locks himself within it. As "head" of the hospital, Kroll is efficient and cultivated, his asylum laid out like a concentration camp; but during his confinement, he covers canvases with Boschian visions of apocalyptic war. His paintings reveal a puritan soul obsessed with an angry God, fluctuating between maniacal egotism (the I of God) and maniacal self-abasement (the Eye of God). The use of an Alpine setting in Lessing's story implies that Europe's "heart of whiteness" is a spiritual void.

One of Lessing's best stories from the 1950s is "The Black Madonna," which first appeared in *Winter Tales 3* (1957) and later in *African Stories* (1964). Several features make the story emblematic of Lessing's short fiction: it begins as an essay but slips effortlessly into a tale; its tone is dry, ironic, and mock-respectful of "conventional wisdom"; its characterizations, settings, and plot are all drawn rapidly; and although it initially reads as satire or even parody, "The Black Madonna" draws the reader toward a dark, distressing close.

Trapped in the imaginary state of Zambesia during the last months of World War II, an Italian prisoner of war named Michele is ordered to use his skills as an artisan to create a mock village that the Zambesian army can then destroy in a celebratory display of might. A Zambesian army captain is ordered to supervise Michele's work. While the two men meet as stereotypes of their conflicting cultures and professions—Michele's is a warm-hearted and sensuous temperament, while the Captain's manner is dry and officious—their relationship soon becomes a marriage of contraries, with Michele painting and listening while the Captain drinks red wine in the sun and tells Michele of all the impossible contradictions of his life, including his jealous relationship with his white wife and a second "impossible" relation with a black woman, his "bush-wife."

By day, the mock village that Michele constructs appears as a senseless jumble of lathes; however, when the jeep's headlights are trained on it at night, a village appears. Completing the task weeks early, Michele decorates the interior of the mock church with frescoes while the Captain goes on a "holiday from himself," confessing that he hires detectives to spy on his wife, who in turn taunts him with nicknames like "Storm-trooper" and "Little Hitler." (The ironies of a white supremacist state at war with Nazi Germany were not lost on Lessing: her fiction set during the war is saturated with an awareness of ubiquitous asininity.) The Captain moves into an emotional part of himself that has been shut down for decades. Like "a man suffering a dream," he watches the transubstantiation of white plaster into "black Madonnas, black saints, black angels."

On the night of the military show, the searchlights reveal that Michele has painted red crosses on the mock village. The loudspeakers announce that the program has been changed: this is an English village that is about to be shelled by German artillery. The red crosses continue a symbolic pattern that has run throughout the story, with color symbolizing the rich variety of life that the "colour bar" tries to whitewash away. The Captain suffers a "nervous breakdown," his conventional self's way of restoring what Michele has broken down. Visiting him in the hospital, Michele finds the old walls restored and, stung, offers his friend a mock salute and departs with his rejected gift—a painting "of a native woman with a baby on her back smiling sideways out of the frame." The Captain turns his face to the wall to weep, fearful that the white-clad nurses will hear.

White-clad nurses, white walls: these images of an annihilating whiteness are not met by parallel images of blackness as void; rather, black is set gemlike at the very center of Michele's canvases, enhancing the other hues of his palette.

In the Captain's old world, forms appeared ghostly under a varnish of whitewash but are restored to life through the bold colors of Michele's art—in red crosses, gold halos, black madonnas. By showing aesthetic harmony created out of the blending of distinct colors, the story undermines the apartheid fear that "mixing" will muddy purity and individuation will be lost. Like complimentary colors on the color wheel, the natures of Michele and the Captain generate a happy marriage of opposites. Sadly, the Captain's failure of will necessitates that the story's conclusion is a slow fade to white.

The year 1962 saw the publication of *The Golden Notebook*, in which Lessing interpolates newspaper clippings, journals, dreams, short stories, novellas, and an entire novel ("Free Women") into the larger narrative frame. In the light of the short fiction, it is interesting to see how the novel's mini-narratives, like wheels within wheels, move the whole forward. Many episodes in the novel can be read as self-contained short stories; in parallel terms, certain stories in Lessing's next collection, *A Man and Two Women* (1963), would not be out of place in *The Golden Notebook*, particularly "How I Finally Lost My Heart," "A Room," and "A Dialogue."

The sense in *The Habit of Loving* that the habits of modern living have exiled us from nature and natural feeling is reiterated in *A Man and Two Women*. However, the later collection also displays a keener sense of the fantastic rising out of mundane circumstances, as when the narrator of "A Room" finds herself visited by sensations and dreams that appear to be residual from previous occupants. More disturbing is the manifestation of the ginger-haired demon in the garden of Susan Rawlings, the protagonist of "To Room Nineteen." This story opens by stating that it concerns "a failure of intelligence"; yet it is clear that Susan Rawlings does not lack intelligence in any conventional sense of the word. Rather, the failure lies in the Rawlings' faith in a certain type of intelligence, a reasonable, rational intelligence that consigns forebodings and apparitions to the realm of pathology.

In 1972, Jonathan Cape (London) published Lessing's *The Story of a Non-marrying Man and Other Stories*; the collection was simultaneously published in the United States by Knopf under the title *The Temptation of Jack Orkney and Other Stories*. As different as these two title stories are, they are both about men who travel away from "safe society" and into spiritual solitude. John Blakeworthy, the non-marrying man, is a white man who "goes native," providing an image of what might have happened to the Captain had he not lost his nerve. Jack Orkney is a more troubling case; his story is one of the most unsettling and haunting of Lessing's works. Spurred by the death of his father, Orkney is drawn into a spiritual netherworld marked by desolating dreams, a loss of his old faiths, and profound loneliness. In midlife, he catches up with his name, the Orkney Islands being remote islands off the coast of Scotland, many of which are uninhabited. Like other Lessing characters from the early 1970s, Jack Orkney undergoes a spiritual crisis that moves him into areas of himself that he was unaware even existed—uninhabited islands of the inner sea.

During this period, Lessing was also examining the punishments exacted by society upon individuals who attempt to break from the herd. In "An Old Woman and Her Cat," Hetty refuses to go to the housing estate for the elderly, where she would have to give up her cat; instead, she follows her companion into a vagrant existence in abandoned houses. Mrs. Fortescue, the elderly prostitute in the story of the same name, is easy prey for a puritanical but sex-driven boy because her profession excludes her from protection. Spiritual vagrants like Jack Orkney are safeguarded by status and class from the indignities suffered by these two old women, but they find themselves profoundly isolated from friends and family.

Balancing such depictions of loneliness and alienation, a number of stories in this collection are written out of a love of solitude. This is especially true of a number of pieces that resemble notebook entries or sketches—"A Year in Regent's Park," "Lions, Leaves, Roses," "The Other Garden"—each of which celebrates daily routine and the pleasures of solitary activities like walking in the park and gardening. There is no effort to "plot" these stories; rather, the narratives borrow their shape from what is observed and where observation leads the imagination. The most remarkable is "Lions, Leaves, Roses," an evocation of an afternoon in the park that is also a meditation on varieties of perceptual experience: there is the "crazy"woman whose "cracked mind let[s] the sunlight through," the policeman whose vision is blinkered by convention, and the stone lion who conjures the image of a real lion, "eyes unblinking, with no need to swat away thoughts, words, feelings, for he was everything he saw." This last phrase, "for he was everything he saw," reiterates a theme that goes back as far as *The Grass Is Singing*: that nature is animated by presence and a type of "collective unconscious" from which humans have unwisely exiled themselves. In this context, Lessing quotes Vladimir Mayakovsky's "Not a man, but a cloud in trousers," and "Lions, Leaves, Roses" culminates in a vision of the trees breathing and the earth spinning: "Leaves, words, people, shadows, whirled together toward autumn and the solstice."

It was roughly twenty years before Lessing's next collection of new stories, *London Observed: Stories and Sketches*, appeared in 1992 (it was published a few months later in the United States under the title *The Real Thing: Stories and Sketches*). During this interval, however, stories appeared in periodicals and magazines, and her non-African tales were collected in *Stories* (1978). This period also saw the publication of several extremely powerful short novels— *The Making of the Representative for Planet Eight* (1982), *The Diary of a Good Neighbour* (1983), and *The Fifth Child* (1988)—a form in which Lessing excels.

As the subtitle indicates, *London Observed* is composed of both "stories" and "sketches." In the sketches, Lessing spins narratives out of such mundane activities as sparrows scavenging in a courtyard cafe and cars piling up in a traffic jam. The fullest of these sketches is "In Praise of the Underground," a fascinating, discursive portrayal of London written from the perspective of a seasoned subway rider. The piece blends everything from the history of local streets to the observation that "never has there been a sadder sartorial marriage than saris with cardigans." Two characteristics that come through clearly in these sketches are Lessing's abiding open-mindedness (particularly about life in London after the implosion of the British Empire) and her curiosity about every aspect of her environment.

It is interesting that in several of the "stories" ("Debbie and Julie," "The Pit," "The Real Thing"), Lessing's irony is more savage and her vision of the world more frightening than in the "sketches." But the stories are also more elusive and shifting. The title phrase of "The Real Thing" refers to Henry James's ironic tale of how "illusion" and "reality" are slippery notions that often reverse themselves. In James's version, an aristocratic couple who come upon hard times offer to model for an artist. While they "appear" perfect, every sketch turns out stiff and artificial-looking. In the counterclockwise universe of the canvas, it is the artist's working-class models who appear as authentic aristocrats. Lessing has similar fun with this nebulous image of "the real thing" in her story of a husband and wife who, after divorcing, are more amicably and intimately bound than ever. Jody, the brash new American wife of the ex-husband, hates their phony British civility and seems at first to be more authentic; however, she too reveals herself as an actress playing a role. As in James's tale, there is no exit from this hall of mirrors.

London Observed: Stories and Sketches is possibly Lessing's most varied collection. A grim story of a teenager giving birth in an abandoned shack ("Debbie & Julie") is followed by a lighthearted sketch of a café refilling after a rainstorm. In "Storms," an entire life story is revealed between the lines of a cabdriver's monologue, as he drives the narrator home from the airport after a rainstorm. Glinting through the cabdriver's narration—and, indeed, throughout all of the stories—are flashes of London and its mercurial skies. It is interesting to note that, while some of Lessing's early story collections like *The Habit of Loving* can seem claustrophobic, her recent stories communicate a sense of openness and wonder. It almost seems as if Doris Lessing in her eighties is a more curious and speculative creature than the writer who emerged in the gray 1950s.

The fecundity and range of *London Observed: Stories and Sketches* indicate that Doris Lessing is continuing to discover stories and revelations in every walk of life and in every new direction her speculating mind takes her. While other short-story writers sometimes seem to be repeating or perfecting themselves in their later works, Lessing is always striking out into new territory. In this light, it is intriguing to note that Lessing's 1999 novel *Mara and Dann* was intensely episodic, as if it were a patchwork of stories in the guise of a (science fiction) novel. It is interesting to note, too, that *Mara and Dann* represents Lessing's first long fiction in thirty years that is set entirely in Africa. Lessing expressed her passion for the short story as a form in her "Preface" to the *African Stories* where she betrayed the fact that she would continue to compose short stories "even if there really wasn't any home for them but a private drawer." This statement reveals what an instinctual drive storytelling is for Lessing—that she would write them even if they could not find a reader. This is the sense that many readers take from Lessing's writings: that they are necessary and true and beyond the realm of fashion and mores. When we read her, a window is opened, and we are grateful that this tale has made its way into the vast world beyond the private drawer.

WORKS CITED AND CONSULTED

Primary

Lessing, Doris. *African Stories*. New York: Simon & Schuster, 1965.

———. "The Black Madonna." *Winter Tales 3*. London: Macmillan, 1957. 132–56.

———. *Five: Short Novels*. London: Michael Joseph, 1953.

———. *The Habit of Loving*. London: MacGibbon & Kee, 1957; New York: Crowell, 1957.

———. *London Observed: Stories and Sketches*. London: HarperCollins, 1992. U.S. edition published as *The Real Thing*. New York: HarperCollins, 1992.

———. *A Man and Two Women*. London: MacGibbon & Kee, 1963; U.S. edition published as *A Man and Two Women; Stories*. New York: Simon & Schuster, 1963.

———. *The Making of the Representative for Planet Eight*. St. Albans: Grenada, 1982.

———. *Mara and Dann*. New York: HarperFlamingo, 1999.

———. *The Sirian Experiments: The Report by Ambien II, of the Five*. New York: Vintage, 1980.

———. *The Story of a Non-marrying Man and Other Stories*. London: Jonathan Cape, 1972. U.S. edition published as *The Temptation of Jack Orkney and Other Stories*. New York: Knopf, 1972.

———. *This Was the Old Chief's Country*. London: Michael Joseph, 1951; New York: Crowell, 1952.

———. *Walking in the Shade: Volume Two of My Autobiography, 1949–1962*. New York: HarperCollins, 1997.

Secondary

Burkom, Selma R. "Only Connect: Form and Content in the Works of Doris Lessing." *Critique* 11 (1968): 51–68.

Draine, Betsy. *Substance under Pressure: Artistic Coherence and Evolving Form in the Novels of Doris Lessing*. Madison: University of Wisconsin Press, 1983.

Drabble, Margaret. "Revelations and Prophecies." *Saturday Review* (May 27, 1978): 54–57.

Hanson, Clare. "Each Other: Images of Otherness in the Short Fiction of Doris Lessing, Jean Rhys, and Angela Carter." *Journal of the Short Story in English* 10 (1988): 67–82.

Hardin, Nancy Shields. "Doris Lessing and the Sufi Way." *Contemporary Literature* 14 (1973): 565–81.

Knapp, Mona. *Doris Lessing*. New York: Ungar, 1984.

Rose, Ellen Cronan. "Crystals, Fragments, and Golden Wholes: Short Stories in *The*

  Golden Notebook." Re-reading the Short Story. Ed. Clare Hanson. New York: St. Martin's, 1989. 126–37.

Sage, Lorna. *Doris Lessing.* London: Methuen, 1983.

Silva, Nancy Neufield. "Doris Lessing's Ideal Reconciliation." *Anonymous: A Journal for the Woman Writer* 1 (1974): 72–81.

Sprague, Claire. "Genre Reversals in Doris Lessing: Stories like Novels and Novels like Stories." *Re-reading the Short Story.* Ed. Clare Hanson. New York: St. Martin's, 1989. 110–25.

Thorpe, Michael. *Doris Lessing.* Harlow, Essex: Longman Group, 1973.

Tiger, Virginia. " 'Taking Hands and Dancing in (Dis)Unity': Story to Storied in Doris Lessing's 'To Room Nineteen' and 'A Room.' " *Modern Fiction Studies* 36.3 (1990): 421–33.

BERNARD MALAMUD
(April 26, 1914–March 18, 1986)

Begoña Sío-Castiñeira

BIOGRAPHY

Bernard Malamud, the elder of the two sons of Max and Bertha Fidelman Malamud, was born in Brooklyn, New York. His mother died in 1929, when Bernard was in his teens; her loss was a crucial event in the author's life that ultimately determined the nature of his women characters and his general conception of the feminine world. In 1932, he graduated from Erasmus Hall High School, and in 1936, he received his B.A. from the City College in New York. After several temporary positions at department stores, he worked for a while teaching English to immigrants who had come to the United States to escape Hitler's concentration camps in Europe. He then got a teaching position at Erasmus Hall High School in Brooklyn, where he worked in the evenings between 1940 and 1948 as a permanent substitute. His thesis, entitled "Thomas Hardy's Reputation as a Poet in American Periodicals," earned him an M.A. degree in 1942 from Columbia University. His first short stories were published in 1943 in the magazines *Threshold, New Threshold, American Prefaces*, and *Assembly*.

Malamud married Ann de Chiara in 1945, a Gentile woman of Italian origin. His first son, Paul, was born in 1947, and between 1948 and 1949 he taught at different high schools in New York City. In 1949, he was hired as an instructor of freshman composition at Oregon State College in Corvallis, Oregon, where he later was appointed associate professor. In 1952, his daughter Janna was born in Corvallis, where his first novel, *The Natural*, was written.

In 1956, he received a *Partisan Review*–Rockefeller grant that allowed him to travel in Europe and stay in Italy for a year. In 1957, his second novel, *The Assistant*, was published, and he subsequently received the Daroff Memorial Award. His first collection of short stories was published in 1958, under the title *The Magic Barrel*. In the same year, he received the Rosenthal Foundation

Award of the National Institute of Arts and Letters for his second novel. He received the National Book Award for *The Magic Barrel* in 1959.

His third novel, *A New Life*, was published in 1961, the year he was hired at Bennington College, in Vermont, as a professor in the Division of Language and Literature. His second collection of short stories, *Idiots First*, came out in 1963, a year he spent traveling in England and, again, in Italy. In 1964, he was appointed a member of the National Institute of Arts and Letters of the American Academy. He traveled in the Soviet Union, Spain, and France in 1965, and in 1966 his fourth novel, *The Fixer*, was published. In 1967, he was awarded both the National Book Award and the Pulitzer Prize (for *The Fixer*); the next year he visited Israel.

His fifth novel, *Pictures of Fidelman: An Exhibition*, was published in 1969, when he received the O. Henry Short Story Award. His sixth novel, *The Tenants*, came out in 1971, and in 1973 he published his third collection of stories, *Rembrandt's Hat*. After the publication of his seventh novel, *Dubin's Lives*, in 1979, he received the Vermont Council Award. He was also the president of PEN American Center between 1979 and 1981. He published his eighth novel, *God's Grace*, in 1982, and his personal selection of stories, *The Stories of Bernard Malamud*, for which he was awarded the Gold Medal for Fiction, in 1983. He died on March 18, 1986. In 1989 an unfinished novel, *The People*, and several unpublished stories were collected and published posthumously under the title *The People and Uncollected Stories*.

CRITICISM

Despite his valuable contributions to the twentieth-century North American literary landscape and the critical acclaim he received during his lifetime, there is no comprehensive study of Malamud's work. This fact should trigger further study, as Rita Kosofsky observes in *Bernard Malamud: A Descriptive Bibliography*, the most up-to-date compilation of the critical production on Malamud's work so far. As Joel Salzberg points out, bibliographic study has been impeded by Malamud's widely known reluctance to facilitate the study of his private life.

Critical response to Malamud's short stories and novels has been produced in two different forms: major works in the form of books or extended essays and short articles or reviews. The following critics have written major works that evaluate and analyze Malamud's fiction: Sidney Richman, who in 1966 offered a partial study of the first three novels and the first two story collections; Sandy Cohen, whose 1974 book reviews Malamud's fictional work up to *Pictures of Fidelman*; Robert Ducharme, who, in the same year, published a comprehensive study of themes and techniques; Sheldon Hershinow, whose 1980 contribution is still one of the clearest and richest approaches to the writer's short stories; Iska Alter, who in his 1981 book investigates the traces of social criticism contained between lines of Malamud's texts; Robert Solotaroff, who published a general study in 1989 that analyzes the stories, including those in *Pictures of Fidelman*, which had been previously regarded as a novel; and Edward Abramson, who in 1993 offered a newly revised thematic approach to Malamud's novels and some of the most famous stories.

Of the short articles and reviews appearing in periodicals, several hundred are gathered together in Kosofsky's bibliographic study. As she accurately points out, Bernard Malamud has often been considered a member of the Roth-Bellow-Malamud "trilogy," both for affinities in their technique and in their subject matter. Malamud's work has also been viewed as a reflection of earlier writers such as Kafka, Dostoyevsky, Joyce, Hemingway, and Henry James (Kosofsky xii).

In 1988, Richard O'Keefe offered a useful analysis of the different critical responses to Malamud, citing four distinct tendencies (240–50). The first one—typified by the criticism of Robert Kegan—regards Malamud as a primarily philosophic writer; this view focuses on the recurrence of certain existential themes such as freedom (illustrated through symbols like the prison, alienation, suffering, and anxiety). The second group of critics—exemplified by Robert Ducharme, Mark Schultz, Robert Alter, or Beth and Paul Burch—considers Malamud a mythic author. The third group includes critics Charles Alva Hoyt and Jackson Benson, who study Malamud as a cultural critic, interested in such traditional themes as American innocence abroad and the ensuing abuse of "inferior" types. The fourth group, the most extensive one, regards Malamud as an ethnic writer. In this category appear all the arguments defending Malamud's Judaism and his interest in such motifs and themes as the Holocaust, the use of Yinglish, and the importance of the Jewish traditional culture and the Hebrew religion. Leslie A. Field and Ruth R. Wisse are two of the most important contributors to this set of ideas.

As Sheldon Hershinow has observed, Malamud's critics generally agree on several points. They regard irony and humor as the main resources of his storytelling technique. In addition, they point to the existential humanism of Martin Buber, the presence of the fantastic in an otherwise crudely realistic or naturalistic setting, the significant use of symbolism, and a highly personal vision of redemption through suffering.

ANALYSIS

Although from the beginning of his literary career Malamud always combined the production of novels and short stories in a balanced way, the author often acknowledged having been longer in love with short fiction: "If one begins early in life to make up and tell stories he has a better chance to be heard out if he keeps them short" (Malamud, *Stories* x). It was his belief that the great obstacle the short-story writer has to face is the need to say it all and yet say it fast—as if two people met at a bar or train station and one of them had only a minute to tell the other that both of them are human beings, and that the story about to be told will be faithful to that principle (Hicks 31). In Malamud's view, the literary event called "story" comes close to Wojaechowski's notion that meaning is revealed as a specular fragment or burst of lightning (Wojaechowski 204–5). In the preface to his collection of selected stories, Malamud states:

I love the pleasures of the short story. One of them is the fast payoff. Whatever happens happens quickly. . . . a short story packs a self in a few pages predicating a lifetime. The drama is tense, happens fast, and is more often than not outlandish. In a few pages a good story portrays the complexity of a life while producing the surprise and effect of knowledge—not a bad payoff. (*Stories* xii)

If we examine the nature of the twenty-five stories that comprise *The Stories of Bernard Malamud*, his personal anthology published in 1983, we find a diverse picture. On the one hand, the anthology contains pieces that dwell in the grounds of the "old" stories of tradition revolving around a single and simplified conflict whose action is slowly developed by means of a sequential process. Such is the case of the stories from the 1950s and most of the ones from the 1960s, like "The Cost of Living" and "The First Seven Years." On the other hand, we find stories rich with the elements that demonstrate Malamud's final leap into modern paradigms. The narrative structure of these latter stories seems to disappear completely from the eyes of the reader or appears only in fragmentary form, as in "Talking Horse."

Two different types of stories can be found in Malamud's own collection. The first group, of which "The Loan" is a good example, describes a complete process in which a myth is presented and explored; ambiguities are addressed as they appear and are finally resolved. The second group contains initiation stories in which readers face a problem conveyed through a central character or the narrator provided with selective omniscience. These initiation stories take the character on an individual pilgrimage toward the knowledge of evil or the problem of human limitations. Often, characters face a crossroads at which they realize that the most appropriate way to face up to dilemmas is, first, to acknowledge their existence and, second, to come to terms with the fact that the way out of them is not necessarily granted beforehand. An excellent example of this second group of stories is "Rembrandt's Hat."

In the following analysis, I have grouped texts from *The Stories of Bernard Malamud* thematically, while also acknowledging the chronology of their creation, since chronology can demonstrate Malamud's literary trajectory and evolution. Focusing on the stories from the anthology that were first collected in *The Magic Barrel*, the first thematic group contains characters in search of fulfillment through human caring: Feld, the shoemaker in "The First Seven Years" (1950) and Leo Finkle in "The Magic Barrel" (1954). Despite all the criticism written about the first text, regarding it as one of Malamud's most valuable stories, the second merits attention for a variety of reasons: it demonstrates more impressively the use of technical innovations such as myth and irony, as well as a transparent parallelism in subject matter between the story and one of Malamud's finest novels, *The Assistant*. This last feature of the story renders it a strategic piece, located between the novelistic activity of the author and his short-story work.

Sobel, a thirty-five-year-old Polish refugee, devotes his entire life to work for Feld, the shoemaker, in order to, someday, conquer the love of Miriam, his daughter. Although the story contains a powerful plot and displays some of the most refined Malamudian characteristics, scholarship has barely dealt with it. Malamud was deeply aware of the importance of education in human life and, furthermore, of its relevance in achieving some kind of earthly happiness. Miriam chooses education, and as a result, her future will be clouded with material scarcity; she discards the convenience of the capitalist universe that Max, the student, has the potential to offer her. "The First Seven Years" is, in essence, a realistic text: the events narrated in it belong to the world of ordinary existence, although the somber tonalities nevertheless appear stylized and crafted.

The setting does not contain naturalistic elements that signal an overtly naturalistic approach, as do those in the stories published after the 1960s. The action takes place indoors, and the outside is contemplated at a distance or in a blurred way. Description of places is kept to a minimum in order to favor the focus on the human beings portrayed. Their characteristic features are a lack of affection, as well as constant anxiety and nostalgia over a sterile past that, though missed, has contributed nothing positive to the present condition of life. The story reveals a three-part structure based upon a presentation of the conflict, a central section where the conflict is played out, and a resolution of the conflict, the sections lasting four, five, and three pages, respectively, with dialogue and summary forms prevailing.

The situation portrayed through Feld's family and the shoemaker's relationship with Sobel corresponds to Richard Sennett's sociological analysis of the modern family as a product of industrialism and capitalism. According to Sennett, the modern individual is the product of an intensive family in which an implicit set of rules renders its members incapable of facing up to basic problems, with the result that they remain isolated from each other. The result is a fear-ridden society that cultivates laziness and emotional sterility to avoid the confusion and dizziness resulting from fighting conflicts (18, 153). Malamud's implicit social criticism can be perceived by studying the opposite figures of Feld and Sobel. Whereas Feld is an assimilated Jew, far away from the European ghetto, blind to the I–thou relationship, Sobel appears directly transplanted from the ethnic ghetto, from where he still retains appreciation for close relationships that reinforce community bonds among the citizens.

Like Chekhov, Malamud uses a kind of narrative neutrality in presenting his characters. Both basic instincts and high virtues are acknowledged as natural constituents of human nature. The distance kept between the implied author and Feld is evenly controlled throughout the story in such a way that it never becomes excessive or scarce. The resulting text, far from being artificial or improbable from excess of realism, can be enjoyed as a piece of fine art through the perception of a sharp use of irony. On the one hand, Malamud lets the reader know how Feld misreads Sobel's thinking, inarticulate reasoning, and actions by means of an omniscient narrator who remains far away from the protagonist's point of view. On the other hand, the omniscient narrator-commentator gives up his "wisdom" at those moments when he allows us to see facts focalized through Feld, and it is then that the ironic touches become noticeable. Here is an obvious example: "He had once asked him, Sobel, why you read so much? He read, he said, to know. But to know what, the shoemaker demanded, and to know, why? Sobel never explained, which proved he read so much because he was queer" (Malamud, *Stories* 22–23). This focalized view allows for the reader to look at the main character with a sarcastic distance through the use of irony.

Much could be written about the use of myth and symbol in the story. A brief overview of these elements would include the physical weakness of Feld's heart, which corresponds to his lack of sensitivity on a nonphysical level; the O and X written down on Max's shoes by the shoemaker, pointing at the student's belonging to the capitalist system where the human being's productivity is used as animal force; and the use of the number seven and the presence of magic in the weird character of Sobel, subtly depicted halfway between the divine and the human.

The second thematic group focuses around Buber's concept of responsibility between I and thou. The anthology contains four stories related to the issue: "The Bill" (1951), "The Loan" (1952), "The Mourners" (1955), and "Take Pity" (1958). "The Loan" is a study of human conduct in the face of oppressive social structures. Malamud wrote "The Loan" at a moment when capitalist social structures were at the highest stage of their historical growth. The story's three characters must face not only the suffering inflicted on them by the Holocaust, but a more fundamental, underlying sense of powerlessness that they experience in the face of modern capitalism. Despite all the difficulties faced by Lieb, Bessie, and Kobotsky in their lives, it is only the female character who proves unable to grow enough to achieve generosity. Malamud seems to have aimed to make a distinction between her and both male characters regarding qualities of suffering. In view of how Lieb and Kobotsky fare in the story (the baker would be happy to part with the money, and Kobotsky has come so low as to humiliate himself and ask him for a loan to buy a stone for his wife's grave), we can affirm that suffering is for them redemptive because it involves their mutual responsibility for each other. Lieb suffers for Kobotsky and Kobotsky suffers for Dora, but Bessie suffers for nobody. She is earth centered, wrapped up in herself, and her suffering has nothing to do with her Jewishness. Lieb and Kobotsky are Malamudian heroes, and, as Fairchild chose to express it, Bessie plays the villain character from beginning to end (Fairchild 24).

In a brilliant essay on Jewish identity and Jewish suffering, David H. Hirsch examines the controversy and complexity of Malamud's use of suffering. He claims that Malamud, "an American Jew seeking his Jewish identity in Jewish suffering, has not been able to find that necessary ingredient in the American experience" (50). In support of Hirsch's argument, it should be noted that some of Malamud's characters suffer not because they are Jews but because they are the victims of a socioeconomic system beyond their control, a claim that can be sustained throughout Malamud's work, from Morris Bober in *The Assistant* to Feld in "The First Seven Years" and Albert Gans in "A Silver Crown."

If "The First Seven Years" shows a comic rise of the main character, "The Loan" dramatizes the fall of the feminine character from a situation that lacks harmony at the beginning to an existential abyss, a fall that is caused by the lack of a fundamental virtue: the capacity to give. There is a single line of action in the story. Smells play a crucial role in framing the plot as they match the thematic structure: sweet smells, related to the softness of bread, ultimately correspond to the sweetness of love, found in Lieb, and are opposed to the smell of charred corpses, more tuned in with the bitterness of Bessie and her refusal to provide a way out.

"Angel Levine" (1955) may be considered the core of the third and final thematic grouping, critiquing as it does the role of religion in the life of the individual. The story's satiric point of view and its skepticism about the possibility of divine "collaboration" with human beings have no precedent in any of the formerly published stories. Malamud uses character pairing as a tool to dramatize Buberian mutuality, a technique that is more noticeable than ever in a story that confronts two racial groups that were facing one of the worst stages in their social relationships during the 1950s: Jews and blacks.

Of central importance in this story is a distinction between the real and the unreal. Manischevitz is a character whose "existence" is never doubted. Yet his metaphysical connotations, linked to his search for the self, make him nevertheless come close to a different world. In presenting a parody of mystical experience, the story makes no distinction between the supernatural and the allegorical. Both levels are blended in the shape of an unusual parable. On the first level of the parable, the superficial one that considers the literal plot, we see a man who receives a visit from another man, who claims to be an angel and who offers his host assistance in his tribulations. On the second level, resulting from the transcodification of the allegory, we ascend from the heights of an apparent magical scheme to a metascheme that transcends fantasy. On this allegorical level, we witness a pilgrimage of the body in search of the soul as it travels the traditional three mystic "paths," paths that recall the Spanish mystic tradition in the literary texts by San Juan de la Cruz or Saint Teresa of Jesus. The classic pattern of an allegorical journey is subverted in the end through the final blindness of the protagonist to what should be a recognition of the unity of body and soul.

As with *The Magic Barrel*, Malamud's first collection, the stories from the 1960s, collected in *Idiots First*, show a concern with the individual's search for communion with the "other." The depressing tonality of these later stories is made more noticeable through the constant presence of failure and frustration, generally caused by an excess of pride. Technically, realism predominates; the stories contain more detailed settings, graphically constructed with particular street names, recognizable social atmospheres, and political periods. All in all, Malamud grows up to be "a much angrier writer than appears to be understood, especially by himself" (Leibowitz 38).

Among these stories, "The Jewbird" (1963), examining the theme of the good master, goes beyond realism and stands out for its uniqueness among all of the short stories written by Malamud. In his postmodern effort to get back to narrativity, to return to the synthesis of novelistic contraries—form and content—Malamud finds his best tool in the mixture of fantasy and reality. The story can be viewed as an experiment in what has been called "magic realism," a term that in its first stages played a pivotal role in defining the new Latin American novel that was born around the 1940s. We are told the story of a three-membered Jewish family that receives a sudden visit from an old black talking bird that claims to be named Schwartz and speaks in a Yiddish dialect.

In order to speak about magic realism, we must, first of all, be able to distinguish two different, conflicting, yet separately coherent perspectives, "one based on a rational view of reality and the other on the acceptance of the supernatural as part of everyday reality" (Chanady 21, 22). In "The Jewbird," Malamud combines natural and supernatural viewpoints: the Cohen family provides a natural, realistic context, while a supernatural one appears with Schwartz, the talking bird, who represents the vital force for this family. We must consequently look for the resolution of the antinomy between the natural world of the family and the supernatural world of Schwartz on the level of textual representation (Chanady 69). Even though the reader recognizes the two conflicting logical codes on the semantic level, he suspends his judgment of what is rational and what is irrational in the world of fiction. The final step into magic realism and out of the merely fantastic in the story results from the absence of authorial intrusions. The existing antinomy on the semantic level is resolved in the act of reading (textual level) only if the focal character does not perceive the conflict and if the narrator, by describing both kinds of phenomena in the same way, annuls the contradiction. Both conditions are fulfilled in this story.

Malamud published fifteen stories between the release of *Idiots First* and his death in 1986. Eight of them were collected in *Rembrandt's Hat* (1973). A qualitative change takes place in these late stories. All the optimism gained by the escape to ideal or fantastic worlds is abandoned. The common note now is the author's pessimism in respect to the communicative task among human beings, in spite of the hunger for contact that all the characters, in different degrees, show.

A thematic group stands out in this collection, three stories dealing with the wall of failed communication between father and son: "My Son the Murderer" (1968), "The Silver Crown" (1972), and "The Letter" (1972). The first one of the trilogy, one of the best stories in the collection, contains not only depth in the treatment of the theme and characterization but also a new technical method that does away with the exhaustive traditionalism that pervaded the former stories. The story presents Leo, Harry's father, who tries with feverish insistence to unblock the silence in which his son is wrapped up in order to show him his love, an attitude that only achieves violent reactions from the son. In his technique, Malamud returns to the aesthetic methods of such expressionist artists as Kokoschka, Kandinsky, and Van Gogh. His interest is in the expressionist image that renders essential features of characters' attitudes.

Several aspects connect "My Son the Murderer" to expressionism, not only in respect to technique, but also in relation to theme. Among others, we could mention the presence of interior vision of characters played out through multifocalization, something that has no precedent in Malamud's former stories. This is a story that portrays emotional states and vital reactions, pernicious sometimes, when a character who abandons traditional paths of behavior such as resignation and patience then adopts attitudes of chaotic subjectivity or aggression. Other expressionist elements are the abstract use of color and, particularly, the subject of the relationship between father and son, which captures in the story the violence and the intensity of age confrontation—a theme reflected in many books from the period of World War I.

As happens to the protagonist in *A Dream Play* (1902) by Strindberg, Harry is characterized by means of his symbolism and fragmentation. Although Malamud does not use the dream tool, Harry is divided, multiplied throughout seven different images that Leo perceives of his son whereby he expresses all he cannot understand about him. We see him vanish only to see him reappearing again and capture him once more in a new blurred fashion. In the construction of Harry as a character, as happens to Strindberg's characters, "there are no . . . scruples, no laws. There is neither judgment nor exoneration, but merely narration" (Dahlström 177).

The purpose of reviewing "God's Wrath" (1972) here is to hint at the personal war that the author silently made against a society that has endlessly and permanently ignored women as individuals, particularly within the Jewish community. Most of the protagonists of the stories in *The Stories of Bernard Malamud* are masculine: Feld, Leo Finkle, Manischevitz, Nat Lime, Newman, and many others who, in the opinion of many critics, embarrassingly minimize the number of women. The women, far from being provided with self-identity in the collection, are perceived from a distance and generally fulfill the instrumental role of antagonists or crisis promoters.

In "God's Wrath," Lucille Glasser takes the lead of the feminine rebellion timidly started by other prostitutes of Malamud's like Stella Salzman and continued in a stronger way by Esmeralda, Evelyn Gordon, and Mary Lou Miller. Luci Glasser unveils the falseness of an outdated and empty system of values, incarnated in her father, that deprives human beings of basic affection and throws them down into the emptiness of hopelessness and irreversible devaluation. Luci goes out into the streets in search of love; for Malamud, love was an acquired condition and "a gift of life" (Leelavathi Masilamoni 36).

Malamud wrote this story in the historic context of a liberal society, the 1960s in North America, when the morality of single motherhood and feminism were no longer questioned except on particular grounds. Luci corresponds to the definition that W. I. Thomas, in *The Unadjusted Girl*, offers of the "type." The sociologist emphasizes that the prostitute becomes a natural product of the conflict created when the psychology of the individual, the current system of values, and the lack of a cohesive community collide with each other (119–20). Luci causes her father's catharsis. Glasser, the "pious" hypocrite, who spends his life praying at the synagogue, is responsible for his daughter's profession, for her having turned into a vampire seeking revenge ("cocksucker"), a participant in fighting the corrupted morality and false values that go with it.

Malamud keeps Luci at a distance, something achieved by means of choosing a selective omniscient narrator who focalizes facts through Glasser without allowing us access to Luci's mind or feelings. In her refusal to accept "resurrection," or reintegration into a kind of life more in accordance with the norm, Luci Glass changes her second name, thereby giving us to understand that her choice of profession is the product of her father's actions (Glasser). To her, the brothel becomes therapeutic; it signifies a rejection of the "real" world. Malamud, then, does not condemn any of his prostitutes. On the contrary, he makes them reflectors of his philosophy of life, "dancing at the moment," and enables them to make whatever choice suits them to gain a little bit of happiness.

WORKS CITED AND CONSULTED

Primary

Malamud, Bernard. *The Assistant*. New York: Farrar, Straus & Cudahy, 1957; New York: Avon, 1980.

———. *The Complete Stories*. Ed. Robert Giroux. 1st Ed. New York: Farrar Straus Giroux, 1997.

———. *Dubin's Lives*. New York: Farrar Straus Giroux, 1979; New York: Viking Penguin, 1979.

———. *The Fixer*. New York: Farrar Straus Giroux, 1966.

———. *God's Grace*. New York: Farrar Straus Giroux, 1982; New York: Viking Penguin, 1995.

———. *Idiots First*. New York: Farrar, Straus, 1963; New York: Farrar Straus Giroux, 1986.

———. *The Magic Barrel*. New York: Farrar, Straus & Cudahy, 1958.

———. *The Natural*. New York: Harcourt, Brace, 1952; New York: Farrar Straus Giroux, 1984.

———. *A New Life*. New York: Farrar, Straus & Cudahy, 1961; New York: Farrar Straus Giroux, 1988.

———. *The People and Uncollected Stories*. New York: Farrar Straus Giroux, 1989.

———. *Pictures of Fidelman: An Exhibition*. New York: Farrar Straus Giroux, 1969.

———. *Rembrandt's Hat*. New York: Farrar Straus Giroux, 1973; New York: Farrar Straus Giroux, 1986.

———. *The Stories of Bernard Malamud*. New York: Farrar Straus Giroux, 1983.

———. *The Tenants*. New York: Farrar Straus Giroux, 1971; New York: Viking Penguin, 1994.

Secondary

Abramson, Edward. *Bernard Malamud Revisited*. New York: Twayne, 1993.

Alter, Iska. *The Good Man's Dilemma: Social Criticism in the Fiction of Bernard Malamud*. AMS Studies in Modern Literature, no. 5. New York: AMS Press, 1981.

Chanady, Amaryll Beatrice. *Magical Realism and the Fantastic: Resolved versus Unresolved Antinomy*. New York and London: Garland, 1985.

Cohen, Sandy. "From Eros to Caritas." *Bernard Malamud and the Trial by Love*. Ed. Robert Brainard Pearsal. Amsterdam: Rodolphi, 1974.

Dahlström, C. Leonard. *Strindberg's Dramatic Expressionism*. Ann Arbor: University of Michigan, 1930.

Dembo, L. S. *The Monological Jew*. Madison: University of Wisconsin Press, 1988.

Ducharme, Robert. *Art and Idea in the Novels of Bernard Malamud: Toward "The Fixer."* The Hague: Mouton, 1974.

Fairchild, Terrance LeRoy. *Life and Art: The Short Fiction of Bernard Malamud*. University of Iowa Press, 1990.

Hershinow, Sheldon. *Bernard Malamud*. Modern Literature Monographs. New York: Frederick Ungar, 1980.

Hicks, Granville. "His Hopes on the Human Head." *Saturday Review* October 12, 1963. 31–32.

Hirsch, David. "Jewish Identity and Jewish Suffering in Bellow, Malamud, and Philip Roth." *Saul Bellow Journal* 8 (Summer 1989): 47–58.

Ji-Moon, Koh. *Major Themes in the Contemporary American Novel*. Seoul, Korea: 1984.

Kosofsky, Rita N. *Bernard Malamud. A Descriptive Bibliography*. Westport, CT: Greenwood, 1991.

Leelavathi Masilamoni, E. H. "Bernard Malamud: An Interview." *Indian Journal of American Studies* 9.1 (1979): 33–37.

Leibowitz, Herbert. "Malamud and the Anthropomorphic Business." *Bernard Malamud*. Ed. Harold Bloom. New York: Chelsea House, 1986. 37–40.

O'Keefe, Richard. "Bibliographical Essay: Bernard Malamud." *Studies in American Jewish Literature* 7 (Fall 1988): 240–50.

Richman, Sidney. *Bernard Malamud*. New York: Twayne, 1966.

Salzberg, Joel. *Bernard Malamud: A Reference Guide*. Boston: G. K. Hall, 1985.

Sennett, Richard. *The Uses of Disorder: Personal Identity and City Life*. New York: Knopf, 1970.

Solotaroff, Robert. *Bernard Malamud: A Study of the Short Fiction*. Twayne's Studies in Short Fiction, no. 8. Boston: Twayne, 1989.

Thomas, W. I. *The Unadjusted Girl: With Cases and Standpoint for Behavior Analysis*. Boston: Little, Brown, 1925.

Wojaechowski, Konstanty. "Powiesa a nowella" (letters by E. Orzeskowa and P. Chimilowsky). *Pamietnik Literacki* (Lwow) 12 (1913): 204–5.

BOBBIE ANN MASON
(May 1, 1940–   )

Cheryl Roberts

BIOGRAPHY

Bobbie Ann Mason was born on May 1, 1940. She spent her childhood with her family on a dairy farm in rural Kentucky, an experience she draws on in her fiction writing. As a teenager, she became first a fan and then national president of the Hilltoppers Fan Club. Some of her activities included writing the organization's newsletter and traveling throughout the Midwest to concerts, experiences that brought her into contact with a large world.

In 1958, Mason entered the University of Kentucky, where she developed a love of literature. Upon receiving her B.A. in 1962, she moved to New York City and put her earlier interests and experiences to use by writing for various fan magazines. In 1966, she earned her M.A. from the State University of New York at Binghamton and then entered the University of Connecticut English graduate program. She married a fellow graduate student, Roger Rawlings, in 1969.

Mason received her Ph.D. in 1972; her dissertation on Vladimir Nabokov was revised and published in 1974 as *Nabokov's Garden: A Guide to "Ada."* In this work, she analyzes symbolism and the imagery of nature in *Ada*. From 1972 to 1979, she worked as an assistant professor of English at Mansfield State College in Pennsylvania. There she continued her nonfiction writing with the 1975 publication of *The Girl Sleuth: A Feminist Guide*. This drew on her childhood love of the popular children's series and, again, on her experience with popular culture. While she acknowledges their earlier positive influence as models of independence, she notes that these characters today are stereotypical, even cliché.

In the late 1970s, Mason began to move toward fiction writing. While she was clearly able to write nonfiction, she found greater satisfaction in her fiction—first a novel and then short stories. She submitted her short stories to the *New Yorker* magazine and, receiving encouraging comments, focused further on the short-story genre. Her twentieth submission, "Offerings," was published in 1980. She has gone on to publish short stories in the *New Yorker* as well as the *Atlantic Monthly, Redbook, Washington Post Magazine*, and others. She has also published several anthologies of her stories. In addition to her short stories, Mason has written several novels: *In Country, Spence + Lila*, and *Feather Crowns*. Her novel *In Country* was made into a movie starring Bruce Willis and Emily Lloyd.

CRITICISM

In a *New York Times* article, Michiko Kakutani states that Mason's stories are "finely crafted tales that manage to invest inarticulate, small-town lives with dignity and intimations of meaning" (309). Rather than engaging in lengthy description, Mason uses details economically; she is more concerned about how the words sound in a down-to-earth Anglo-Saxon way than about using sophisticated, Latinate vocabulary. She has been praised for her ability to write authentic dialogue; her stories explore the daily lives of rural Southerners in a rapidly changing environment, both physical and societal. According to David Quammen, her basic themes include deprivation, disappointment, and disorientation of lives in transition (7). Mason's pop background may account for the wealth of references to modern cultural icons: the Beatles, Elvis, *The Joy of Cooking* cookbook, K-Mart, Burger Chef, and above all, television: *Gunsmoke, Phil Donahue, Charlie's Angels, M*A*S*H**.

There are symmetry and symbolism in the choices her characters make. Mack Skaggs in "The Rookers" crafts a card table for his wife on their twenty-fifth anniversary; in creating the tabletop out of wood scraps, he is also assembling the pieces of their marriage together, into some kind of coherent whole. Peggy Jo in "Detroit Skyline, 1949" journeys to the North in a classic search of self-identity, yet never actually arrives and only sees Detroit's skyline on television (Wilhelm 308). In other stories, truck drivers are seekers, and construction workers and seamstresses attempt to build new selves. On a larger scale, in "Big Bertha Stories," Mason compares the U.S. role in Vietnam to strip mining.

Thulani Davis finds Mason's work to have a "fitful quality . . . an odd tension" (306), and Lorrie Moore agrees that there is a looseness of direction, a diffusion in her work. Stories in *Love Life* have beginnings and endings that do not match. For example, "Piano Fingers" starts with a sexually bored husband and ends with a father's gift to his daughter of an electric keyboard. Elements and themes may be introduced and then dropped. Moore, however, interprets this as an exciting unexpectedness, and Mason herself believes that her stories tend to end "at a moment of illumination" (Mason, Lyons, and Oliver 258). Moore believes that Mason's greatest achievement is in her collections, where each story contributes another layer, cumulating in a rich "community of contemporary lives" (309).

ANALYSIS

The characters in Mason's first collection of short stories, *Shiloh and Other Stories*, illustrate her themes of disorientation and insecurity. In "Shiloh," Norma Jean Moffit has responded to changes in rural Kentucky by making changes herself; she begins with bodybuilding and continues with taking courses at the local community college. Her feelings of restlessness and confinement, in part resulting from her domineering mother and fifteen-year marriage to Larry, find their release as she remakes herself for the future. Yet "Shiloh" is not Norma Jean's story. It is Larry's, the truck driver who is disabled as a result of an accident and whose continual presence at home may be what motivates Norma Jean to move in the direction of change. Larry, on the other hand, sees his homecoming as a chance to begin the marriage anew. The loss of a child early in their marriage has never really been processed; he wonders if they should talk about it. He feels "unusually tender about his wife" and "sees things about Norma Jean that he never realized before" (2, 7). But it appears that Norma Jean has moved beyond him.

Larry Moffit, the driver who can no longer drive, stays home and makes models. He has even bought plans for a log cabin, a new home to build for his wife, a new life perhaps, by returning to the past. Representing an even more direct connection to the past is a trip to the Confederate battleground of Shiloh. Norma's mother and father eloped there, and though her husband died when Norma was ten, Mabel insists that the "young couple" go there as a sort of second honeymoon. While Norma rejects the honeymoon appellation, she agrees to go. Neither she nor Larry appreciates or is even interested in the history of Shiloh; they see it as a large park, filled with families of campers. Away from the domination of her mother, with just Larry as her opponent, Norma states her intention to leave Larry. In a marijuana-induced haze, Larry finally makes a connection between the past and the present, the continuity of generations, the graveyard of white markers and the cemetery of his marriage. This profound moment, though illuminating, is not transforming. Larry realizes that he "is leaving out the insides of history. . . . And the real inner workings of a marriage, like most of history, have escaped him" (16).

Yet the story does not end in despair. We have no doubt that Norma Jean is a survivor; at the end of the story, she has run to the top of a cliff and waves at or to Larry. Larry, while recognizing the foolishness of his house-building plans, retains hope and responds to her wave by running to her, the goldfinch falling yet spreading his wings to catch himself and fly again.

In "The Retreat," another unhappily married woman, Georgeann Pickett, longs for escape from a confining marriage. Shelby, her husband, has gone from high-school delinquent to called minister at rural churches in western Kentucky. The move from the country to the city, and from religion to consumerism, has caused many small churches to die and makes it necessary for Shelby to work as an electrician during the week. Shelby's life, and that of his wife and two children, is regulated by rules "which come out of nowhere," like rubbing "baking soda onto his gums after brushing his teeth" (133). His rigidity is further revealed by his insistence on giving a sermon on alcohol on a wintry Sunday when the intended object of the sermon did not attend.

Georgeann's mother originally disapproved of the marriage, but insists to Georgeann that marriage is forever, and "a preacher's marriage is longer than that" (137), so that Georgeann feels the forces of tradition and society arrayed against her. Still, she strikes out in small ways. As the minister's wife, she performs many typical duties such as playing piano, preparing communion, and typing up the bulletins. One Sunday, she switches the musical offerings and is later chided by her husband, who likes to have an accurate record of each Sunday's service. Rather than protest, she pencils in the changes before filing the bulletin. Another example of her efforts toward selfhood can be seen in her refusal to accompany her husband to a funeral and, further, in cleaning out the henhouse in his absence, clearly breaking the rule of no work on the Sabbath. While these small efforts seem pathetic, they are not portrayed in a mean-spirited manner. Mason permits her character to act out in the limited ways available to her.

The central event of the story is attending the annual retreat, which Georgeann used to love, but now tries to evade. Unable to parlay a bout with body lice into a reason to stay home, she goes and finds some small measure of escape not in the workshop on "seven categories of intimacy" and "marriage enhancement," but in playing a video game in the basement, attacking and defending herself from space aliens—opponents that she can identify and strike out at. All too soon, however, she and Shelby return home to find that Shelby is being transferred yet again. Her refusal to accompany him is met with denial and prayer on his part and, sadly, capitulation on her part. With no education, no job skills, and no outside support, she is simply unable to break the rules of her society.

In Mason's second collection of short stories, *Love Life*, her stories become more complex, and her characters are more richly composed. Themes of dissatisfaction and disorientation again predominate. In the title story, Opal is an aging, unmarried, retired algebra teacher who retains strong ties to the past both in her attitudes and her surroundings of quilts, muumuus, and verandas. Jenny, her niece, has returned to live with her and brings a sense of newness and change. Yet in some ways they are alike: both seek solitude, Opal through MTV and peppermint schnapps and Jenny through buying a tract of land to camp out on. Both reflect on the men in their lives and know that men cannot offer what they lack. Both "sit on the veranda and observe each other. They smile, and now and then roar with laughter over something ridiculous" (8). Neither confides in the other.

The quilts in "Love Life" carry the theme of the loss of history. While the quilts fascinate Jenny, Opal is simply reminded of "a lot of desperate women ruining their eyes" (10). In a direct rejection of the past, Opal asserts that she will begin aerobic dancing or perhaps motorcycle riding. Yet she is destined to be a spectator of the changes around her. Her time is spent watching MTV. Jenny, on the other hand, asks to see the quilts repeatedly and insists on seeing the burial quilt, a dark background of white shapes with names and dates. "Don't you go putting my name on that thing," Opal says (15), as Jenny wraps it in plastic to take with her. Jenny can afford to be morbid about death and the past, yet her interest is more of a seeking for roots: "I'm looking for a place to land" (13). The restlessness of the "new South" is clearly in evidence.

"Hunktown," another story from *Love Life*, combines changes in the rural South with midlife crises. Cody Swann, divorced father of grown-up children, remarries Joann, whose husband of eighteen years left her for another woman. She has a good job at the post office and a small farm inherited from her father. Cody, laid off from his job at an electrical-parts plant, has decided to try to make it big in music and wants her to sell the farm and move to Nashville with him. The conflict for Joann is over relinquishing a secure life for the uncertain success of Cody, a move that might preserve the marriage.

Yet Joann's ambivalence runs deeper. She has grown up knowing the difference between mustard and turnip greens. She collects dried beans to save for seed. Tilling and planting are natural to her, while the world of nightclubs and bars depresses her with its country songs filled with clichés. Cody is impatient with her, impatient with the old and known. He wants to seize the opportunity to make a record and have it distributed, but predictably, Phil Donahue has exposed such deals on television. As in others of Mason's stories, finding a new place in the changing South is difficult, and it seems more difficult for her male characters than the females. Yet change is less a choice than an inevitability: in a world where sweet potatoes are sold from the back of the truck, the black farmer advises Joann to "lay them in a basket. . . . The sweet will settle in them, but if you disturb them, it will go away" (37).

"Big Bertha Stories" describes a Vietnam veteran with posttraumatic stress syndrome who works at a strip mine and goes home to his family for sporadic visits. There, he tells Big Bertha stories to his son, stories that combine the large strip-mining crane and Paul Bunyan, stories that are about the rape and destruction of Vietnam. Both his son and his wife long for him to be home, but his behavior becomes increasingly erratic, the stories cause his son to have nightmares, and eventually, at Donald's suggestion, Jeannette drives him to the VA hospital. Like many who stayed home, and especially those a little younger than most vets, Jeannette believes that it is "unhealthy to dwell on it so much. He should live in the present" (118). She considers escaping through divorce and getting a job, but there are not many around, and like most of Mason's characters, she has little education or wider vision. And she truly loves Donald. His institutionalization frees Jeannette to get a job and live independently with her son, but at the end of the story, she seems to have identified with Donald's stories of Big Bertha. The story is, like so many of Mason's, not despairing, not satirical, not damning. It is merely real.

WORKS CITED AND CONSULTED

Primary

Mason, Bobbie Ann. *Feather Crowns*. New York: HarperCollins, 1993.

————. *The Girl Sleuth: A Feminist Guide*. Athens, GA: University of Georgia Press, 1975, Reprinted 1995.

————. *In Country*. New York: Harper & Row, 1985.

————. *Love Life*. New York: Harper & Row, 1989.

————. *Nabokov's Garden: A Guide to "Ada."* Ann Arbor, MI: Ardis, 1974.

————. *Shiloh and Other Stories*. New York: Harper & Row, 1982.

————. *Spence + Lila*. New York: Harper & Row, 1988.

Secondary

Anderson, Nancy G. "Bobbie Ann Mason." *Dictionary of Literary Biography Yearbook* 1987: 351–59.

Davis, Thulani. "Rednecks, Belles, and K-Mart Women: Southern Women Stake Their Claim." *Voice Literary Supplement* 42 (February 1986): 10–13. Excerpted in *Short Story Criticism* 4 (1990): 306–7.

Kakutani, Michiko. "Watching TV and Being Rootless in the South." *New York Times* March 3, 1989: C35. Excerpted in *Short Story Criticism* 4 (1990): 308–9.

Mason, Bobbie, Bonnie Lyons, and Bill Oliver. Interview in *Contemporary Literature* 32 (Winter 1991): 449–70. Rpt. in *Contemporary Literary Criticism* 82 (1994): 250–58.

Moore, Lorrie. "What Li'l Abner Said." *New York Times Book Review* March 12, 1989: 7, 9. Excerpted in *Short Story Criticism* 4 (1990): 309–10.

Quammen, David. "Plain Folk and Puzzling Changes." *New York Times Book Review* November 21, 1982: 7, 33. Excerpted in *Short Story Criticism* 4 (1990): 299.

Wilhelm, Albert E. "Making Over or Making Off: The Problem of Identity in Bobbie Ann Mason's Short Fiction." *Southern Literary Journal* 8 (Spring 1986): 76–82. Excerpted in *Short Story Criticism* 4 (1990): 307–8.

JAMES ALAN McPHERSON
(September 16, 1943–   )

James Kurtzleben

BIOGRAPHY

James Alan McPherson was born in the diverse, older section of Savannah, Georgia, a place he would later call "a black lower-class" section of town. His father, James Allen McPherson, Sr., was a master electrician, and his mother, Mabel Smalls McPherson, worked as a maid in a white home. His parents' strong work ethic encouraged him to see beyond the limitations of his present circumstances and strive for something better. In addition to their example of perseverance, E. J. Smith, the family physician who delivered him and encouraged him throughout his youth, inspired McPherson to achieve.

In segregated public school, the disciplined, proud, self-reliant black teachers—represented in his fiction by Esther Clay Boswell—taught McPherson about the strength of the human spirit. Later, a part-time job at the M&M Supermarket—likely the stage for his coming-of-age story "A Matter of Vocabulary"—further deepened his understanding of human nature. Though McPherson grew up during some of the darkest times for African Americans in the twentieth century, he recalled that most adults he knew during his childhood did not dwell on the sad realities of racism and segregation. Optimism seemed to pervade his community, a community that had its shortcomings but that remained, in his view, "rich in possibilities for the future" (Cox 311, 312).

In 1961, McPherson enrolled at Morris Brown College in Atlanta. During successive summers, he worked as a dining-car waiter on the Great Northern Railway, work that surely gave him the inspiration for his story "A Solo Song: For Doc." From the older "Doc-like" waiters, he learned the art and joy of storytelling; from his travels across the country, he gained a broadened and receptive perspective of American culture.

McPherson spent two years at Morgan State University in Baltimore, then returned to Morris Brown in 1965 to complete his B.A. The following fall, he enrolled in Harvard University Law School, believing that "a lawyer was a good guy who helped people" (Shacochis 16). The more he learned at Harvard, however, the more he believed that the college "brought in the sons and daughters of the middle class to perfect their skills to be moved into law firms to help those great fortunes pass from one generation to the next," skills not very useful to African-American communities (Shacochis 16). Moreover, while he was working on a district attorney project as a student in the Boston courts, he found that his creative impulses distracted him from the tasks at hand. He began to recognize narrative patterns in the real-life legal dramas he witnessed and to empathize with the litigants he represented. Ultimately, he found that he could not practice criminal law comfortably (Cox 313).

During this period, he supported himself as a janitor in an apartment building in Cambridge. There, he said, he "had the solitude, and the encouragement, to begin writing seriously" (Cox 312). This building was to become the setting for "Gold Coast." After the *Atlantic Monthly* awarded this short story first prize in its creative writing contest, one of McPherson's respected law professors, Paul Freund, mentioned to McPherson, "Oh, you're the one who writes for the *Atlantic*. You've gone beyond the law." His offhand remark directed McPherson onto the path of a career in writing (Cox 312).

McPherson completed his LL.B. in 1968, then spent the summer industriously writing stories in Cambridge. The next year, the *Atlantic Monthly*, in conjunction with Little, Brown, published these stories in the collection *Hue and Cry*. The following September, McPherson enrolled in the Writers' Program at the University of Iowa. There he wrote feature articles for the *Atlantic Monthly* and accepted a position as contributing editor, a post he still holds (Cox 313).

After earning his M.F.A. from Iowa, McPherson continued to write while serving on the faculties of the University of California, Santa Cruz; Morgan State University, Baltimore, Maryland; and the University of Virginia, Charlottesville. He was awarded a Guggenheim Fellowship in 1972–73 and published his second collection, *Elbow Room*, in 1977, for which he earned the Pulitzer Prize. In 1981, he received a MacArthur "Genius" Fellowship and accepted employment as a professor in the University of Iowa's Writers' Program, where he still teaches today. Among McPherson's celebrated works are *Railroad: Trains and Train People in American Culture*, (1976), *Confronting Racial Differences*, co-edited with DeWitt Henry (1990), his memoir *Crabcakes* (1998), and most recently a book of essays also coedited with DeWitt Henry, *Fathering Daughters: Reflections by Men* (1998).

CRITICISM

Critical response to McPherson has been varied. Some critics see him as presumptuous for trying to speak for so many different cultural groups; some accuse him of essentialism; some find that his work lacks any traditional definitions of the African-American culture as a whole. Few, however, would deny the honest analysis he provides of a broad range of American subcultures.

In his review of *Hue and Cry*, Granville Hicks applauds McPherson's "universal human sympathy and craftsmanship" and agrees with Ralph Ellison's jacket-cover statement that McPherson transcends "those talented but misguided writers of Negro-American cultural background who take being black as a privilege for being obscenely second rate." Believing that African Americans can write literature that is aesthetically pleasing without submitting to pressures that a black man write stories of protest, they praise McPherson's focus on the vast range of the American cultural scene (Hicks 47, 48).

Irving Howe groups McPherson with young black writers he considers unnationalistic and nonseparatist, calling them "a decidedly individualistic lot." Howe emphasizes McPherson's dedication to writing *great* short fiction, characterizing the author as one "who works hard on every sentence, thinks lucidly about his effects, and knows that in art meaning, even salvation, depends on craft." McPherson's writing, he asserts, is "beautifully poised" (130, 135).

Ronald Christ does not see such aesthetic appeal in McPherson's work. He labels McPherson's writing "flat, almost clinical" and complains that the African-American writer was obliged to protest, but did not. McPherson, he maintains, is preoccupied with making compromises and balancing the two sides of his stories and does not respect the established traditions of black literature (570). In a review of *Hue and Cry*, Robert Gross is more tolerant. His comparison of McPherson to his contemporaries locates the author within an African-American literary tradition concerned with a "quest for authentic communication between people, the effort to make sense out of a meaningless world" (94, 96, 98).

The debate over McPherson's status within the community of African-American writers often overshadows responses to the aesthetics of his work. When Robie Macauley wrote in the *New York Times* that McPherson was a writer and black, but not a "black writer," Ruthe T. Sheffey disagreed, arguing that the narrative structures and patterns of his stories evoke the trickster persona of African-American folklore. Moreover, she suggests that McPherson's distinctively African-American voice is most powerful when it draws upon his experiences in the South (Macauley 31; Sheffey 122–31).

William Domnarski argues that critics who praise the diversity of McPherson's stories but criticize his repression of blackness misread the author's work. Those who claim that McPherson's stories compromise the positions of blacks, he asserts, miss their subtle suggestions. His stories are really about demonstrating the challenges presented to blacks in a dominantly white culture (37–44). Other critics suggest that McPherson is a spokesperson for a subset of African-American culture about which little has been written. Edith Blicksilver, for example, writes that McPherson's stories describe the dilemma confronting African-American intellectuals who are attracted to what white society has to offer but are simultaneously repulsed by that society's racist tendencies ("Image of Women" 390–401).

Some critics recognize McPherson for contributing to the "worklore" of American culture. Rosemary M. Laughlin notes that Doc Craft, "the waiter's waiter," as some call him, is in good company among the other folk heroes and heroines of the workplace (222). Others have focused on the unique mythic quality of McPherson's literary technique. Jon Wallace, for example, discusses how three of McPherson's narrators employ language to shield themselves from society ("Politics" 17–26). Recalling Sheffey's suggestion that the structures and patterns of McPherson's work evoke the trickster persona, Wallace also argues that McPherson's examples of the waning of societal norms and mores demonstrate that form and structure in a story are as important as the content ("Story" 447–52). Perhaps this recent focus on McPherson's ability with language, form, and dialect foreshadows an end of criticism that concerns itself with the intentions of the artist rather than the quality of his art.

ANALYSIS

In his first collection of short stories, *Hue and Cry*, McPherson quotes Pollock and Maitland's *History of English Law* before the time of Edward I: "When a felony is committed, the hue and cry (*hutesium et clamor*) should be raised." These klaxons of alarm never ring so loudly as when McPherson's characters are in danger of losing their identities.

The first piece, "A Matter of Vocabulary," portrays a young man's loss of innocence. After witnessing the theft of the Sunday offering by church elders, Thomas Brown begins to reassess his own morality. Later, when his brother is humiliated at the grocery store where they both work, he arrives at a deeper understanding of others' situations. Eventually, even the mysterious, drunken Barefoot Lady who cries for Mr. Jones at the closed doors of the local funeral home begins to make some sense to him. He understands how she can feel that there is no other choice, no other way to be made.

Other stories in the collection consider similar themes. "A Solo Song: For Doc," for example, describes how a waiter loses his identity to the capitalist culture that first helped him forge it. The autobiographical piece "Gold Coast" introduces a janitor/narrator who initially feels a kinship with the outcast of his story, James Sullivan, but rejects him to remain part of the group. The title story of the volume depicts the failures of human beings in relationships. "On Trains" tells a story of blatant racism suffered calmly by an old black man who simply wants to do his job, the job he has always done. Again and again, then, these stories demonstrate how individuals can readily lose their identities to others in power, and how one can even exile oneself.

If at times the characters in *Hue and Cry* appear more "fence-straddling" than complex, those in McPherson's second collection, *Elbow Room*, emerge as authentic participants in the trials of life. Conflicted, ambivalent, inconsistent, they deny any easy identification. Rather, their stories seem to say to the reader, "It's time you asked yourself what you *believe.*" From a Southern black who enjoys honky-tonk music to an interracial couple with second thoughts about the identities our culture offers them, *Elbow Room* presents a cast of characters who defy traditional stereotypes and hence break the tired formula of American fiction as predictable, closed, and complete.

In "A Sense of the Story," McPherson's depiction of a man who kills his boss for treating him as expendable calls into question the justice of the U.S. judicial system. In "The Story of a Scar," the narrator identifies with a scarred woman he meets in a doctor's office, but although he is first proud for befriending someone so deformed, in the end he condemns himself for not having even asked her name. The main character of "The Faithful," a preacher/barber unwilling to accept the role thrust upon him by a newly enlightened community, inflicts exile on himself rather than give up the self-destructive identity with which he feels most comfortable. "Problems of Art" depicts characters who create identities to suit the moment and hence appear to the narrator to have no identities at all. Together, these stories shake the foundations of selfhood and ultimately suggest that identity is a construct.

A character who makes assumptions about Japanese people in "I Am an American" encourages readers to see people as individuals, first through coarse joking, then through his own shame. In "The Story of a Dead Man," a robust, reckless Billy Renfro plays doppelgänger to his refined and educated cousin William, who wants to leave the South for sophisticated northern Chicago. Billy and William are complementary halves of a whole identity: together, they express the duality of human nature.

In "Just Enough for the City," McPherson's narrator is a Jesus figure who demonstrates to the modern-day Pharisees how religion can destroy the moral order it seeks to create when it denies personal and individual complexities. "A Loaf of Bread" carefully examines opposing sides of a conflict between members of a lower-class black neighborhood and the white grocer who owns the only grocery store in the area. Here, as with all of the stories in *Elbow Room*, McPherson is especially skillful in making the arguments of the antagonist and protagonist equally important and valid.

James Alan McPherson's short stories explore the no-man's-land where diametric and polemic oppositions arise out of the diversity, conflicts, and contradictions of our culture. By examining the shared complexities of the human condition, McPherson's art often seems to transcend stereotypical labels. McPherson writes penetrating stories that refuse to let the reader off the hook; hence they are not for the reader who looks for generalizations or answers, especially answers that offer comfort or relief. As McPherson himself explains: "The short story is the only indigenous American [literary] form. You don't have any great novels coming out of this country because it's too fragmented, made up of too many different groups. Who can see the whole picture? All you can do is give little reports from this section, that section" (Shacochis 27).

WORKS CITED AND CONSULTED

Primary

McPherson, James Alan. *Elbow Room*. Boston: Atlantic–Little, Brown, 1977.
———. *Hue and Cry: Short Stories*. Boston: Atlantic–Little, Brown, 1969.

Secondary

Beavers, Herman. "I Yam What You Is and You Is What I Yam: Rhetorical Invisibility in James Alan McPherson's 'The Story of a Dead Man.' " *Calaloo* 9.4 (Fall 1986): 565–77.
———. *Wrestling Angels into Song: The Fictions of Ernest J. Gaines and James Alan McPherson*. Philadelphia: University of Pennsylvania Press, 1995.
Blicksilver, Edith. "The Image of Women in Selected Stories by James Alan McPherson." *CLA Journal* 22 (June 1979): 390–401.
———. "Interracial Relationships in Three Short Stories by James Alan McPherson." *CEA Critic* 50 (Winter–Summer 1987–88): 79–88.
Bone, Robert. "Black Writing in the 1970's." *Nation* 227 (December 16, 1978): 677–79.
Christ, Ronald. "Review of *Hue and Cry*." *Commonweal* 89 (September 1969): 570.
Cox, Joseph T. "James Alan McPherson."*Contemporary Fiction Writers of the South: A Bio-Bibliographical Sourcebook*. Westport, CT: Greenwood, 1993.
Domnarski, William. "The Voices of Misery and Despair in the Fiction of James Alan McPherson." *Arizona Quarterly* 42.1 (Spring 1986): 37–44.
Fikes, Robert. "The Works of an 'American' Writer: A James Alan McPherson Bibliography." *CLA Journal* 22 (June 1979): 415–23.
Fuller, Hoyt. "Some Other Hue and Cry." *Negro Digest* 18 (October 1969): 49, 50, 88.
Gervin, Mary A. "Developing a Sense of Self: The Androgynous Ideal in McPherson's 'Elbow Room.' " *CLA Journal* 26.2 (December 1982): 251–55.
Gross, Robert A. "The Black Novelists: Our Turn." *Newsweek* June 16, 1969: 94, 96, 98.
Hicks, Granville. "Literary Horizons." *Saturday Review* May 24, 1969: 47–48.
Howe, Irving. "New Black Writers." *Harper's* December 1969: 130–46.
Laughlin, Rosemary M. "Attention, American Folklore: Doc Craft Comes Marching In." *Studies in American Fiction* 1 (Autumn 1973): 220–27.
Llorens, David. "Hue and Cry." *Negro Digest* 19 (November 1969): 86–87.
Macauley, Robie. "White and Black and Everything Else." *New York Times Book Review* September 25, 1977: 31.
Shacochis, Bob. "Interview with James Alan McPherson." *Iowa Journal of Literary Studies* 4.1 (1983): 7–33.
Sheffey, Ruthe T. "Antaesus Revisited: James A. McPherson and 'Elbow Room.' " *Amid Visions and Revisions: Poetry and Criticism on Literature and the Arts*. Ed. Burney J. Hollis. Baltimore: Morgan State University Press, 1985. 122–31.
Wallace, Jon. "The Politics of Style in Three Stories by James Alan McPherson." *Modern Fiction Studies* 34.1 (Spring 1988): 17–26.
———."The Story behind the Story in James Alan McPherson's 'Elbow Room.' " *Studies in Short Fiction* 25.4 (Fall 1988): 447–52.

LORRIE MOORE
(January 13, 1957–   )

Robin Werner

BIOGRAPHY

Lorrie Moore was born Marie Lorena Moore on January 13, 1957, in Glens Falls, New York. Both her father, an insurance-company executive who came from a family of academics, and her mother were avid readers. Lorrie Moore was first published in *Seventeen Magazine* as a winner of a writing contest at the age of nineteen. She did her undergraduate work at St. Lawrence University, graduating summa cum laude in 1978. In 1982, she received her M.F.A. in writing from Cornell University. She is a member of Phi Beta Kappa, the Associated Writing Programs, and the Authors' Guild. Currently Moore is an English professor at the University of Wisconsin and lives in Madison with her husband and son.

Lorrie Moore's first short-story collection, *Self-Help*, was published in 1985, followed shortly thereafter by her first novel, *Anagrams* (1986). She has published two other short-story collections, *Like Life* (1990) and *Birds of America* (1998). Moore has also published a second novel, *Who Will Run Frog Hospital?* (1994), and a work for children, *The Forgotten Helper* (1987). Her work frequently appears in *Fiction International, Ms.*, the *New York Times Book Review, Paris Review*, the *New Yorker*, and other magazines. Moore's awards include an O. Henry Award, a Rockefeller Foundation Fellowship (1989), and a Guggenheim Fellowship (1991). She was a recipient of the National Endowment for the Arts Award in 1989 and was included in Debra Spark's acclaimed anthology *20 under 30*.

CRITICISM

Much of the criticism of Moore's work focuses on her use of humor. Moore's humor has been described as "wry" and "apt," but as Ralph Sassone discusses in his article "This Side of Parody," her use of humor produces dramatic effect: "Although a cursory reading of her work might make it seem coolly satirical, its aftereffect is the memory of palpable pain. . . . Funniness is simultaneously a leavening agent for her wrenching narratives, a temporary paregoric for her characters, and a distancing device that perpetuates their alienation" (15). In a review of Moore's first collection, *Self-Help*, the *Library Journal* describes her wit as "quicksilver" and "self-protective" (73). The *New York Times* describes Moore's style in *Self-Help* as possessing "some fine, funny and very moving pictures of contemporary life" (Kakutani, "Books" C21). Overall, reviews critiqued the stories as lacking in coherence and depth, a fault that Moore corrected in her second collection.

Criticism of Moore's second short-story collection, *Like Life*, continues to reflect a focus on the author's dark humor. Sassone claims that in this collection, "she proves that although her natural gift is for kinetic prose about the bright and wired, she can also write understated stories in which the mood is closer to a hush" (15). This collection presents a broader range and deeper emotions than *Self-Help*. John Casey of the *Chicago Tribune* describes Moore's writing in *Like Life* as a mix of "comedy and sadness, wisecracks and poignancy" (3). This collection is more self-reflexive, probing deeper into the condition of life. The humor and language games serve to intensify the dark elements of the tales.

Moore's latest collection, *Birds of America*, furthers this intensification. While her humor still sears throughout, this is a dark book. Moore's style is vivid. Her sentences are described by the *New York Times* as "fluid, cracked, mordant, colloquial"; they "hold, even startle, us as they glide beneath the radar of ideological theories of behavior to evoke the messy, god-awful behavior itself" (McManus 6). Although in a few instances the dialogue seems to degenerate into wisecracking, overall this collection articulately depicts the pain and humor of contemporary existence: "It will stand by itself as one of our funniest, most telling anatomies of human love and vulnerability" (6).

ANALYSIS

Criticism that focuses on Moore's use of humor occasionally implies that because her works are funny, they do not merit serious examination. Moore defends her use of humor by pointing out that the world is funny, and individuals spend much of their time attempting to be humorous: "If you're going to ignore that, what are you doing? You're just saying that part of the world . . . doesn't exist. And of course it exists" (Garner). Throughout Lorrie Moore's work, it is apparent that this dark humor, and the pain it masks, are part of her intense contemplation of contemporary existence. Beginning in *Self-Help*, Moore presents characters that will become typical in her work—individuals who are sarcastic, witty, and secretly vulnerable. These characters, usually women, populate all three of Moore's collections of short stories.

In "How to Be the Other Woman," the first story in *Self-Help*, the style is fragmentary, modeled on an instruction manual, filled with lists and witty snatches of dialogue. This style is repeated in several other stories in this collection, the distanced narration contrasting sharply with the emotional upheaval of the events being narrated. On the surface, the story's title suggests a tale of a woman having an affair, but it reveals a word game typical of Moore's style, brought out later when the narrative instructs:

Wonder if you are getting old, desperate. Believe that you have really turned into another woman:
    your maiden aunt Phyllis;
    some vaporish cocktail waitress;
    a glittery transvestite who has wandered, lost, up from the Village. (17–18)

In "How to Become a Writer," Moore addresses the frustrations of pursuing this vocation. Again the style is instructive, but here the content seems to contain hints of autobiography despite Moore's assertion that her work is fictional. In this tale, the protagonist seems reluctantly propelled into creative writing and arrives at realizations like "writers are merely open, helpless texts with no real understanding of what they have written and therefore must half-believe anything and everything that is said of them" (124). Throughout this collection, it is the small details that poignantly recall the realism of these frustrated lives. Crisp and episodic, *Self-Help* presents a humorous examination of futility and desperation.

In *Like Life*, Moore's writing style is more subdued. Here her objects of study range from a woman having affairs with two men ("Two Boys") to an examination of a pestilential urban hell ("Like Life"). Once more the interspersed humor intensifies the frustration and pain, but in *Like Life* there are more mingled notes of compassion and tenderness. The tenderness of passages like this love scene in "The Jewish Hunter," "He was a kisser, and he kissed and kissed. It seemed the kindest thing that had ever happened to her," are interspersed with failed communication as religiously as the love scenes in this story are followed by Holocaust documentaries (124).

In the title story "Like Life," which concludes the collection, Moore moves into a familiar, yet alien urban world. In a dreamlike slum that seems to echo Orwell's *1984* and where the heroine's response to a diagnosis of precancer is "Isn't that . . . like *life?*" Moore once more depicts a failing relationship (152). In this, perhaps the darkest story in the collection, poverty and disease become a condition of life as the heroine searches for escape through her dreams of an old house.

Birds of America, Moore's latest collection, continues to focus on the breakdown of connections between people. A further refinement and intensification, *Birds of America* still contains elements of dark humor, but the subject matter tends toward more serious crises. Stories like "Which Is More Than I Can Say about Some People" and "Charades," which won an O. Henry Award in 1993,

depict family relationships both strained and evolving. Perhaps the most acclaimed story from this collection is "People Like That Are the Only People
Here," a narrative of a couple dealing with their infant's cancer. Once again,
Moore's writing seems to veer into autobiography, reflecting her own similar
experience, but she insists that the story is not "straddling a line between nonfiction and fiction." Moore asserts: "It was fiction. . . . I re-imagined everything.
. . . Fiction can come from real-life events and still be fiction. It can still have
that connection, that germ" (Garner 2).

In "People Like That Are the Only People Here," Moore's imagery is striking:
moments like a mother finding a blood clot in her baby's diaper are described
as "a tiny mouse heart packed in snow" (212). As the story follows this family
through the traumatic series of events to the uncertain ending, Moore's gift for
mixing tenderness, wit, sadness, and realism is revealed. This story is the highlight of the collection and of Moore's work so far.

Lorrie Moore's work displays intelligence, wit, and pathos. At their best, her
short stories are poignant reflections of the human spirit on trial. Alternately
hilarious and distressing, Moore's fiction takes the reader into a life that is often
disturbingly familiar and communicates a kind of self-reflection of which her
characters are often incapable.

WORKS CITED AND CONSULTED

Primary

Moore, Lorrie. *Birds of America*. New York: Knopf, 1998.
————. *Like Life*. New York: Penguin, 1991.
————. *Self-Help*. New York: Knopf, 1985.

Secondary

Casey, John. "Eloquent Solitudes: The Short Stories of Lorrie Moore Address Life's
    Essential Loneliness." *Chicago Tribune* May 20, 1990, sec. 14: 3.
Garner, Dwight. "Moore's Better Blues: Lorrie Moore Finds the Lighter Side of Ordinary
    Madness in 'Birds of America.' " *Salon Magazine* October 27, 1998. http://
    www.salonmagazine.com/books.int/1998.
Kakutani, Michiko. "Books of the Times." *New York Times* March 6, 1985: C21.
————. "Observations on Failures in Passion and Intimacy." *New York Times* June 8,
    1990: C28.
"Lorrie Moore: *Self Help.*" *Library Journal* March 15, 1985: 73.
McManus, James. "The Unbearable Lightness of Being: Lorrie Moore's Stories of People
    in Dire Predicaments Are Underpinned by a Comic Sensibility." *New York Times*
    September 20, 1998, sec. 7: 6.
Sassone, Ralph. "This Side of Parody: Lorrie Moore Gets Serious." *Village Voice Lit-
    erary Supplement* June 1990: 15.
Schumacher, Michael. *Reasons to Believe*. New York: St. Martin's, 1988.

BHARATI MUKHERJEE
(July 23, 1940–   )

Sherry Morton-Mollo

BIOGRAPHY

Bharati Mukherjee was born in preindependence India in a suburb of Calcutta and was raised in a well-to-do though "circumscribed" (as she describes it) environment. Her family ran a successful pharmaceutical factory, and her father was a prize-winning chemist. Her upbringing combined Bengali Brahmin tradition with Western influences. She was partly educated by Irish nuns, yet she observed Hindu practices—a paradox that may have influenced the themes of both her short fiction and her novels. It might even be argued that her childhood experiences fostered her talent for visualizing the many sides of a cultural "collision" and capturing their contradictions and incongruities in narrative form.

Indeed, Mukherjee is herself a twice-transplanted immigrant (from India to Canada, and then from Canada to the United States) and has, appropriately, "transformed" herself in many ways and in many environments. Although she had already received a master's degree in both English and ancient Indian culture at the Universities of Calcutta and Baroda, she visited the United States in 1961 and pursued further academic training. Her initial interest in the Iowa Writers' Workshop led to a master's of fine arts and a doctorate in English at the University of Iowa. She currently teaches at the University of California at Berkeley.

The iteration of this distinguished academic career hides within it the complex nature of Mukherjee's emigration to the United States, a journey she made after frustrating and humiliating experiences with racial prejudice in Canada, where she lived for some time with her husband, writer Clark Blaise. During the years 1962–80, she divided her time among Canada (her husband's homeland), the United States, and summer visits to India. In an interview with Mukherjee, Alison B. Carb relates how the author "actively protested what she saw as a pattern of bigotry against Canadians of Indian descent through published essays such as 'An Invisible Woman' and in short stories which were later included in

Darkness" (646). This collection of short stories was completed in 1984 while the author was writer-in-residence at Emory University in Atlanta, Georgia.

After the publication of *Darkness*, Mukherjee settled in New York City, where she was an instructor at Columbia and New York universities. During this time, she coauthored with her husband an investigative report on the 1985 Air India plane crash (Bombay to Toronto), an event that figures in her short story "The Management of Grief" (*Middleman*) and that culminated in the nonfiction work *The Sorrow and the Terror* (1987). The following year saw the publication of Mukherjee's award-winning *The Middleman and Other Stories* (1988), a collection of varied stories that demonstrate and examine the many problematical facets of the immigrant experience. This collection won the National Book Critics Circle Award and focused international attention on the author. The issues explored in *The Middleman* are unified and transmogrified in her subsequent novel *Jasmine* (1989), perhaps her quintessential statement on the alienation and emotional displacement of the immigrant and the need for new definitions of selfhood that accommodate the individual immigrant's experience as a "stranger in a strange land."

Mukherjee's other novels include *The Tiger's Daughter* (1972), which grapples with the conflicts of an "enlightened" young Indian woman who must deal with an unenlightened environment that manipulates cultural standards to victimize her; *Wife* (1975), which chronicles the alienation and eventual madness of a female Indian immigrant psychologically stranded in New York City with her engineer husband; and *The Holder of the World* (1993), which expands the issues raised in all her fictional works in imaginative ways that not only manipulate narrative time (as did *Jasmine*) but include a sort of time cross-sectioning involving two females, a seventeenth-century Puritan American and a twentieth-century Mughal Indian.

Bharati Mukherjee is an impressive woman in person: those who meet her find their attention arrested by her personal grace and self-confidence. She seems not only a writer with an artistic mission, but one who truly contains a multitude of selves and worlds within her. Her work continues to generate discussion as she expands not only the boundaries of her subjects, but the very means by which she illuminates them. She depicts disorienting cultural collisions and the subtle ironies, humorous and grotesque, that accompany them.

CRITICISM

Bharati Mukherjee envisions herself as a spokesperson for the immigrant and a chronicler of a century in which cultures clash, populations shift, and a new global mentality must be forged. In several lengthy interviews, she speaks of her intention to explore the disturbing but undeniable conclusion that one must remake or "reinvent" oneself in the process of entering and becoming a vibrant force within another culture.

Critical commentary on Mukherjee has often accompanied the author's own assessments of her fictive themes and purposes. Many important observations by critics can be found amid the interviews in which Mukherjee speaks for herself. An interview with Mukherjee conducted by Michael Connell, Jessie Grearson, and Tom Grimes, for example, asserts that "the idea of transformation, of life being a process of almost constant and radical evolution" (8), persists as one of her major themes. Certainly her short stories support this conclusion, as does her novel *Jasmine*, which presents the tale of an Indian woman, capable of many transmutable selves, who transforms herself upon emigrating to America. Mukherjee, who has suffered psychically as a result of racial prejudice, has applied this experience to her works and the characters that people them, extending "psychic damage" to an entire globe of people who live amid an informational and electronic overload of world terrorism, violence, and human-produced evil. Her characters, like the ever-shifting world they inhabit, are always scrambling to remold and remake themselves. In short, her characters, as immigrants and "middlemen," must remain fluid entities.

Another recurring issue identified by critics of Mukherjee is feminist conflict as it occurs within the immigrant's framework. Both of her novels *The Tiger's Daughter* and *Wife* primarily deal with particular females interacting with amorphous, changing cultural roles. In the first, the heroine loses her culturally defined status as a "lady"; in the second, adrift in a bewildering alien environment, the heroine plunges into insanity and murder. In an article on Mukherjee's heroines, Sant-Wade and Radell discuss *The Middleman* collection and state, "The author indicates in all the stories . . . [that] it is impossible to adapt to life in the New World without sustaining some kind of wound to one's spirit." Furthermore, these critics indicate that it is "a deeper wound for the women of the Third World, who are engaged in the struggle to fashion a new identity for themselves in an alien culture" (11).

Another theme identified by critics and acknowledged by Mukherjee herself is the theme of building a new America. Mukherjee has stated in a televised interview with Bill Moyers that "we have come not to passively accommodate ourselves to someone else's dream of what we should be, we have come, in a way, to take over, to help build a culture" (*A World of Ideas*). This emphasis on a rebuilding or remolding of America in a new image is part and parcel of Mukherjee's work and has become part of an unstated controversy regarding it. Although her consummate skill as a writer and social observer is unchallenged, the role of her fiction as concomitant force in a redefinition and remaking of the term "multiculturalism" is still in question. Nonetheless, Mukherjee's stature in both the academic world and the larger world of humanists and artists seems to assure her enduring importance and relevance.

ANALYSIS

In a 1993 *Toronto Star* article that reviewed her novel *The Holder of the World*, Bharati Mukherjee is quoted as saying, "The art of compression is very important to me. I want to squeeze the entire world in a single sentence." Indeed, Mukherjee's stated purpose in her fictional works "to make my intricate and unknown world comprehensible to mainstream American readers" (Moyers 1990) is primarily achieved through her ability to "compress" the difficult and disorienting immigrant experience into metaphorical, yet concretely jarring stories that explore the ramifications of our rapidly changing global population.

In collections like *The Middleman and Other Stories* and *Darkness*, Mukherjee's tightly woven tales of "process" may be viewed as concise parables about the nature of cultural change and the overwhelming violence to self it can entail for the individual member or "soul" of a particular culture. "Orbiting," for example, depicts the discomfiting plight of an Afghani refugee who, after circling several airports, finds himself forced to accommodate an uncomprehending America, befuddled by his scars and his suffering. Meanwhile, the narrator of the tale internalizes the huge gap between cultures (as does the reader via the narrator) and finds a way to ameliorate the sense of dislocation and displacement she observes through the medium of love.

Mukherjee's sense of a need for compression is illustrated in a myriad of ways in her short stories—a genre eminently suited to the author's mode of providing glimpses into the many-sided immigrant experience. For example, through the eyes of her narrator in "A Wife's Story," readers perceive the palpable foreignness of a stranger sitting next to her in a New York theater: "Under the bright blue polyester Hawaiian shirt sleeve, the elbow looks soft and runny" (25). In this one, simple, concretized image, the alien culture has become emblematized in a physical item—the elbow of a stranger. Instantly, the reader is plunged into the narrator's world of disconnectedness because not only has the elbow been separated from the person to whom it belongs, its description ("soft and runny") tellingly captures its repulsive nature. The elbow, like the narrator (and, by extension, the reader), is caught between categories that are clearly anomalous—both elbow and nonelbow, an alien, almost obscene, fleshy, partially cooked egg. In this one rendered detail, Mukherjee has encapsulated all the disorientation of the foreigner who tries to accommodate a culture she finds both unsettling and unaccepting.

Although self-reinvention and identity transformation, feminism, and the concept of a vibrantly infused new America are evident themes in all Mukherjee's fictional works, it is her narrative process that most empowers her style as a writer. In her short stories, Mukherjee achieves a narrative process that duplicates the violent and transformational aspects of global cultural confrontations. These confrontations always remain personal (through her finely drawn characterizations) and at the same time universal because they not only reflect the alienation inherent in any immigrant experience, they also actively involve the reader in the immigrant journey—the process of moving into, adapting to, and influencing a new and unfamiliar culture.

Additionally, Mukherjee's narrative technique incorporates a rich and interlocking host of symbolic and situational elements—elements that include profound and refractive symbols, such as the molting caged parrot in "The Middleman" or the tradition-charged Thanksgiving turkey in "Orbiting" whose carving alludes to both the scarred refugee and the skills (at survival, at adapting) that he possesses. Other elements that enrich Mukherjee's detailed, yet also metaphorically infused text include specific plots that depict immigrant journeys and escapes ("escapes" that take on double meanings as both a transformation and a finding of freedom) or provide example upon example of disintegrating or evolving cultural stances. Stories such as "The Middleman," "Orbiting," "The Tenant," and "Buried Lives" not only explore the nature of their characters' state of "in-between-ness," but also signify in their very titles a sense of their peculiar instability and flux. Her characters, Mukherjee emphasizes, "take risks they wouldn't have taken in their old comfortable worlds to solve their problems. As they change citizenship, they are reborn" (Carb 654).

Through her distinctive use of language and metaphor, Mukherjee effectively replicates the individual immigrant experience and, by depicting her characters as process, in effect, leads the reader inside, through, and out of culture clashes. Often her use of language results in grotesqueries that seem to "deconstruct" (and thereby elucidate) the position of the displaced person. Incident and language are utilized in these stories to highlight the predicament of the immigrant who is literally and figuratively caught in the middle between lifestyles, between cultural categories, between old and new perceptions of what constitutes the very essence of their identities. Mukherjee's characters are neither insiders nor outsiders, they are in-betweeners: perhaps, in some ways, they are more lost (and yet perhaps more creatively challenged) than any so-called marginalized group. They are simply individual pieces of a larger worldwide grouping—not, however, part of a conglomerate "new mosaic" or obliterated "melting pot," but a new "majority" of dynamic global travelers.

For the most part, Mukherjee's story lines portray characters that must demonstrate an energy, vitality, and resilience necessary to successfully (often ironically) undergo what must be undergone in order to survive and transmute culture in the modern world. Mukherjee states herself that her characters are survivors—not necessarily whitewashed martyrs, but beings "filled with a hustlerish kind of energy" (Carb 654). As the reader views their conflicts and process, Mukherjee's characters fluctuate and persist in environments that frequently demand paths of dramatic acculturation and metamorphosis. This metamorphosis may take on many forms and may or may not be disappointing, painful, or violent, but such vast transformations always depict a truth about the immigrant experience.

In "Orbiting," the narrator, an American-Italian female who is dating an Afghani refugee named Ro, enacts before the reader's eyes a kind of alternating mental alienation-accommodation process that demonstrates both sides of a cultural clash, with both poignant and humorous effect. In this comfortably jarring story, Mukherjee presents a magnificently incongruous clash between a tortured man who attends a traditional Thanksgiving dinner with the narrator's parents:

" 'He was born in Afghanistan,' I explain. But Dad gets continents wrong. He says, 'We saw your famine camps on TV. Well, you won't starve this afternoon' " (Middleman 68). The scene increases in poignancy as a culture of pain clashes with one of comfort: "Ro's talking of being arrested for handing out pro-American pamphlets on his campus. Dad stiffens at 'arrest' and blanks out the rest. . . . Ro was tortured in jail. Electrodes, canes, freezing tanks. . . . Dad looks sick. The meaning of Thanksgiving should not be so explicit" (72–73). Not only is the character Ro "foreign" to the narrator's parents, his entire lifestyle—based on attempting to obtain what they already have and take for granted—is alien. Through the lens of the narrator Renata (who is discovering her love for Ro), the reader feels what the family is feeling when it observes the tangibility of difference. The narrator, with the reader alongside her, becomes strained, hyperconscious of her new position inside—and outside—both cultures, watching their comingling: "I see what she is seeing. Asian men carry their bodies differently. . . . Each culture establishes its own manly posture, different ways of claiming space" (70).

Both Ro and Renata possess a dynamism that facilitates their survival in the new multicultural world. They are capable of changing and expanding their consciousnesses; they possess the ability to transform themselves and their perceptions of a world that is delimited by cultural standards and definitions. An alternate "American" is being created, a transposed and reinvented one: the daughter of Italian immigrants befriends, falls in love with, and visualizes in innovative ways the soon-to-be new American—a composite of pain, scars, and far-away political struggles, the embodiment of another way of "claiming space."

In several stories in *Middleman*, Mukherjee's characters become "alienating" in the midst of their own alienation. Oftentimes they are not only alienated from their cultural identities in a new environment, they are alienated from what may be perceived as standard moral values: that is, values themselves become subject to loss and reinvention. In "Jasmine" (*Middleman*), the Trinidadian heroine accommodates to American life by half submitting to and half willing an adulterous affair with the husband of her employer. In the last line of this disquieting story, Mukherjee undercuts the excitement of Jasmine's newfound independence with her unique use of language, subtly mixing positive and negative sensations: "It felt so good, so right, that she forgot all the dreariness of her new life and gave herself up to it" (135). The inclusion of "dreariness" in a sentence with a series of positive adjectives like "new," "good," and "right" emphasizes the compromised—exhilarating but painful—experience of the immigrant finding his or her way. In story after story, Mukherjee repeatedly utilizes this technique of mixing alternating impulses or using terms in ways that make them seem commonplace and yet foreign at the same time. Her diction, her symbolic landscape, and her choice of metaphors all underscore her thematic concerns and her "message" that not only are the survivors of a massive global immigration those that are capable of being "in process," but that they are the process by which a new America is reinvented and revivified.

Other stories exhibit the extreme effects of the loss of values that results in a kind of moral wasteland or demonstrates the destructive effects of violently mixing cultures. In "Fathering" (*Middleman*), the Vietnamese child of an American soldier chaotically disrupts his family and its fundamental relationships when she comes to live with her father. Father and child are able to forge a new bond, one born out of the terrible pain of the child who saw her grandmother murdered and who, in moments of stress, presses quarters so insistently into her arm that blood pools under the skin. Here Mukherjee duplicates the sense of the arbitrary benefit of such a bond that goes beyond shared DNA and dissonant cultures by inserting a qualifying adjective: "Then, as in fairy tales, I know what has to be done. . . . I jerk her away from our enemies [the child's doctor and the narrator's wife]. My Saigon kid and me: we're a team. In five minutes we'll be safely home in the cold chariot of our van." The wonderful juxtaposition of "safely" and "cold" and "chariot" (as metaphor) expresses simultaneously the positive and negative aspects of the narrator's decision to break up his home. In this example, the "chariot" (which is a metallic, modern van) seems to predict a rosy future for the father-daughter pair, and yet it is undercut not only by its modifier "cold" but by the implication that all is illusory, a mere hoped-for "fairy tale."

This aspect of mixing contradictions and incongruities in order to emphasize the "ambivalence" of the immigrant who must reinvent his or her self has also been identified by Sant-Wade and Radell. In their article "Refashioning the Self: Immigrant Women in Bharati Mukherjee's New World," they discuss the "rebirth" of identity as akin to birth itself, both painful and inevitable. They also note that Mukherjee's characters seem to possess the ability to step back, watch their own process, and react to it with wonder and ambivalence: "Mukherjee weaves contradiction into the very fabric of the stories: positive assertions in interior monologues are undermined by negative visual images; the liberation of change is undermined by confusion or loss of identity; beauty is undermined by sadness" (12).

The universe of Mukherjee's short stories is multicultural and transitional, a universe of infinite variety and flux. Her characters are people in process, and her narrative techniques—in which mixtures are created, juxtaposed, and compounded so deftly that the reader is often caught unaware between cultures in a disorienting grip of alienation—are techniques that make manifest her themes. Her powerful and subtle narrative style enables Mukherjee to employ the short story not only as a vehicle of "compression" but as a refracting lens that showcases her characters, and it is her characters that grip us so fully. The wife reinventing herself before a mirror ("A Wife's Story"), the small-time hustler importing Third World women to American bridegrooms ("Danny's Girls"), the Tamil-born Indian escaping riots and crooked captains ("Buried Lives"), a Trinidadian girl in search of herself ("Jasmine"), a female Indian immigrant fighting for her identity in a new world amid old ways and discovering that she is a "freak" of sorts ("The Tenant")—these are the voices and images of Mukherjee's text. The sense of "evolution," "process," and "becoming" is the way of life for her characters, and her process as writer and immigrant becomes our process as the readers of her text and citizens of a changing world.

WORKS CITED AND CONSULTED

Primary

Stories

Mukherjee, Bharati. *Darkness*. New York: Fawcett Crest, 1992.
———. *The Middleman and Other Stories*. New York: Grove Press, 1988.

Novels

Mukherjee, Bharati. *The Holder of the World*. New York: Knopf, 1993.
———. *Jasmine*. New York: Grove Weidenfeld, 1989.
———. *The Tiger's Daughter*. Boston: Houghton Mifflin, 1972.
———. *Wife*. Boston: Houghton Mifflin, 1975.

Nonfiction

Mukherjee, Bharati, Blaise, Clark, and Bharati Mukherjee. *Days and Nights in Calcutta*. Garden City, NY: Doubleday, 1977.
———. *The Sorrow and the Terror*. New York: Viking, 1987.

Secondary

Carb, Alison B. "An Interview with Bharati Mukherjee." *Massachusetts Review* 29 (1988–89): 645–54.
Connell, Michael, Jessie Grearson, and Tom Grimes. "An Interview with Bharati Mukherjee." *Iowa Review* 20.3 (Fall 1990): 7–32.
Hancock, Geoff. "An Interview with Bharati Mukherjee." *Canadian Fiction Magazine* 59 (1987): 30–44.
Low, Gail Ching-Liang. "In a Free State: Post-colonialism and Post-modernism in Bharati Mukherjee's Fiction." *Women: A Cultural Review* 4.1 (Spring 1993): 8–17.
Marchand, Philip. "Writer Bharati Mukherjee's Work Never Strays Far from the Harsh Realities of Our Wired-up Global Village." *Toronto Star* October 23, 1993, Weekend section. L1.
Moyers, Bill. "Bharati Mukherjee Talks about the New Conquest of America." *A World of Ideas*. PBS. WNET, New York. June 3, 1990.
Nelson, Emmanuel S. "Kamala Markandaya, Bharati Mukherjee, and the Indian Immigrant Experience." *Toronto South Asian Review* 9.2 (Winter 1991): 1–9.
Pandya, Sudha. "Bharati Mukherjee's Darkness: Exploring the Hyphenated Identity." *Quill* 2.2 (December 1990): 68–73.

Rustomji-Kerns, Roshni. "Expatriates, Immigrants, and Literature: Three South Asian
    Women Writers." *Massachusetts Review* 29 (1988–89): 655–65.
Sant-Wade, Arvindra, and Karen Marguerite Radell. "Refashioning the Self: Immigrant
    Women in Bharati Mukherjee's New World." *Studies in Short Fiction* 29.1 (Win-
    ter 1992): 11–17.
Steinberg, S. "Bharati Mukherjee." *Publishers Weekly* August 25, 1989: 46.

ALICE MUNRO
(July 10, 1931–   )

J. R. (Tim) Struthers

BIOGRAPHY

In southwestern Ontario, a little east of Lake Huron, a little outside the town of Wingham, on her parents' nine-acre farm, past which flowed, she states in the brief essay entitled "Everything Here Is Touchable and Mysterious," "a short river the Indians called the *Meneseteung*, and the first settlers, or surveyors of the Huron Tract, called the Maitland" (33): This is where a bright, attractive, and poor girl of Scotch-Irish descent named Alice Laidlaw, later to be known as Alice Munro, grew up. Beyond the town proper and beyond the edge of that other part of town: "that straggling, unincorporated, sometimes legendary non-part of town," Alice explains, "called Lower Town (pronounced Loretown)" (33). The places, the people, the names and languages and even pronunciations here, she will tell you, all make a difference; they make *all* the difference. "We believed there were deep holes in the river. We went looking for them, scared and hopeful, and never found them, but did not stop believing for that. Even now I believe that there were deep holes, ominous beckoning places, but that they have probably silted up. But maybe not all" (33). Year after year and story after story, Alice has gone on looking for, has gone on delving for, these familiar yet mysterious places.

In September 1949, Alice Laidlaw left home to attend the University of Western Ontario in London—"not the real London," remarks Del Jordan, the narrator/protagonist of Munro's semiautobiographical *Lives of Girls and Women*, with some degree of apology, "but a medium-sized city in western Ontario" (142). In April 1951, when scholarship money ran out after her second year at Western, Alice Laidlaw discontinued her university studies, but not without signaling her literary prowess by publishing her first three stories, "The Dimensions of a Shadow," "Story for Sunday," and "The Widower," in *Folio*, Western's student-run little magazine of the period. At the end of 1951 she got married for the first time, to Jim Munro, with whom she immediately traveled west to Vancouver, where they settled for just over a decade before moving in 1963 to Victoria, on Vancouver Island. Here Alice lived with Jim for another decade, helping to start and to operate Munro's Books and raising their three daughters; another daughter (the second born to them) had died after just two days of life.

Then, in 1973, Alice and Jim separated and after many years of returning in imagination and in memory and sometimes in fact to her very special world in southwestern Ontario, Alice moved home. For two years she lived in London, including eight months in 1974–75 as writer-in-residence at the University of Western Ontario, and then went to live in Clinton, a town forty-five miles north of London. Clinton was the hometown of Gerald Fremlin, soon to become Alice's second husband, whom she had first met nearly twenty-five years earlier when he was a young air-force veteran, a student at Western Ontario at the time she was a student there, and, like Alice, a contributor to *Folio*. Now, in 1974, the distinguished editor-in-chief of the newly published fourth edition of *The National Atlas of Canada*, Gerald Fremlin had very recently returned to live in his hometown, reintroduced himself to Alice when she was writer-in-residence at Western and was joined by Alice in Clinton. Returning to take up residence again in her native region, Alice was struck most forcibly, she says, with "how life is made into a story by the people who live it, and then the whole town sort of makes its own story" (Munro in Struthers, "The Real Material" 33). She began composing *Who Do You Think You Are?* (published in the United States and England under the title *The Beggar Maid: Stories of Flo and Rose*), a book that replicates in its pattern, but of course partly reinvents in its detail, the life story to this point—upbringing in southwestern Ontario, departure for and residence on the West Coast of Canada, followed by return to southwestern Ontario—that we might be tempted to call phase one of "the Munro myth."

With the publication of the stories in *Who Do You Think You Are?* came an important advance in reputation, not to mention a significant if modest increase in income for Munro. The first of the stories in *Who Do You Think You Are?*, entitled "Royal Beatings," was published in the *New Yorker* in 1977, the beginning of a steady stream of stories by her to be published there. "Royal Beatings," which Munro has described as "a *big* breakthrough story" (Munro in Struthers, "The Real Material" 21) for her in terms of her exploration of the short story as a form, opened and charted a way forward in her subsequent stories and books of stories. "It's like that comment by Flaubert," Munro told Catherine Sheldrick Ross (author of the brief but insightful biography *Alice Munro: A Double Life*) about what we might choose to call phase two of "the Munro myth": " 'Live an orderly way like a bourgeois so that you can be violent and original in your work' " (16). Indeed, it is precisely these qualities—violence and originality, representation and transfiguration, truth and beauty—that profoundly challenge and ultimately reward the most discerning of Munro's readers.

CRITICISM

As for short-story writers, so for their critics: real breakthroughs—most impressively, perhaps, in James Carscallen's monumental and mythic study *The Other Country: Patterns in the Writing of Alice Munro*—come through finding a form and a style that will suffice. A substantial number of critics have responded strongly and astutely, though often very differently from one another, to the challenge of Munro's work. E. D. Blodgett, in his book *Alice Munro*, and Ildikó de Papp Carrington, in her book *Controlling the Uncontrollable: The Fiction of Alice Munro*, argue very perceptively, but in quite different ways from each other. Blodgett states: "Thus *Who Do You Think You Are?* marks an important and profound change in the development of Munro's thinking because of its desire not to yield to the possibilities of metaphor and analogy, but to probe their limits. We are made to know that translation—the Latin word for metaphor—possesses danger, particularly as it makes possible the interchange of lives and the loss of self that is part of the transaction" (107). As a result, Blodgett notes, we see that "Translation is also a trope, a method of transposing texts, which constantly turns upon the same core of material" (107). Consequently, Blodgett remarks, "the turning may illuminate the absence of a core, that point where the real is lost in the acting and speaking, in the discourse by which it is hoped to be recaptured" (107). Carrington remarks of the same book—more specifically, of "Royal Beatings"—that "the shameful revelations in this story include a significant addition to the adults' behaviour: Rose's pleasurable complicity in her own beating" (44). This dramatic situation, Carrington observes, is followed by hints of indolent satisfaction among all participants that generate "distinctly postcoital interpretations" (45).

Fascinatingly, too, Magdalene Redekop, in her book *Mothers and Other Clowns: The Stories of Alice Munro*, and Ajay Heble, in his book *The Tumble of Reason: Alice Munro's Discourse of Absence*, offer radically different yet equally penetrating views of Munro's overpowering and inexhaustible story "Meneseteung" from *Friend of My Youth*. Redekop remarks: "By the time Munro is done, the decorated surface of this story and the multiplying slogans such as 'Salt of the Earth' will be a disguising that allow us access to a grief more intense than what is felt in any other story by Alice Munro" (271). Heble observes how Munro, by openly acknowledging the narrator's own involvement in the telling of "Meneseteung," "turns what might, after the fashion of 'Walker Brothers Cowboy,' be a story about an unfulfilled relationship into a meditation on the intricacy of exchange between history and autobiography" (174). Still other critics of Munro write from other positions, from other places, in other voices, cultivating their own deeply personal responses.

Much is to be learned from studying the variety of arguments, methods, and styles found in different critics of Munro. Canadian writer and critic John Metcalf, in an introduction to "Royal Beatings" and "Meneseteung" in the anthology *Canadian Classics*, observes of Munro:

[S]he often writes stories now which have the intensity of dreams and something of the same mysteriousness. Some of these stories resist logical or interpretive approaches; we must give ourselves up to their imagery and event, enter into them as into a dream. The section of "Meneseteung," for example, where Almeda Roth discovers the "dead" body has an intensity which, if we are to experience the story fully, must not simply "mean" but must oppress us like that nightmare from which we cannot wake. (102)

Furthermore, an ever-increasing number of critics are choosing to write entire essays exploring the subtleties of single Munro stories, as seen in Pam Houston's and Dermot McCarthy's analyses of "Meneseteung." This, too, it would seem, is a mark of the maturation and the maturity of Munro criticism, as readers keep peering into that mysterious river whose deep holes—those darkly luminous images in her mind—Alice pictures so perfectly and so compellingly.

ANALYSIS

For Alice Munro, as she observed in the aforementioned brief essay, her own personal landscape and region and home, the very special world of southwestern Ontario, "will provide whatever myths you want, whatever adventures," because, as she understands so well, "This ordinary place is sufficient, everything here touchable and mysterious" (33). Munro's first short-story collection, *Dance of the Happy Shades*, published in 1968 and the product of a fifteen-year to twenty-year apprenticeship, is characterized by the use of what she prefers to call not exactly autobiographical material but rather personal material. The stories in *Dance of the Happy Shades* present what she has described as a "closed rural society," a place populated by individuals who share Munro's Scotch-Irish background, a world "going slowly to decay" (Munro in Stainsby 29–30). It is a world, nonetheless, whose detail and texture and voices have taken hold—have taken life—in Munro's imagination, a world, therefore, perhaps not so different from Emily Brontë's mythological world of Gondal, a source for what was Munro's favorite novel during and, it would appear, long after her adolescence, *Wuthering Heights*. It is a world, we immediately feel, that is magical, folkloric, gothic, and intensely real—intensely real, we ultimately understand, not only because it has been so vividly recollected but also, and more importantly, because it has been so brilliantly imagined.

Dance of the Happy Shades contains fifteen stories, beginning with "Walker Brothers Cowboy," "The Shining Houses," "Images," "Thanks for the Ride," and "The Office." The order of these stories, Munro explains, represented an effort at emphasizing variety, typically by alternating between first-person stories that used material drawn from Munro's own experience and knowledge of southwestern Ontario—"Souwesto," as painter Greg Curnoe and poet/playwright James Reaney have termed it—and stories that seemed to back off from her most characteristic ways of handling personal material. *Dance of the Happy Shades*, in Munro's own judgment, contains a number of stories, such as "Walker Brothers Cowboy" and "Images" (which, along with the story "Postcard," were the last to be finished for the collection), that she considers "real" and a number of stories, including "The Shining Houses," "Thanks for the Ride," and "The Office," that she considers "exercise stories" (Munro in Struthers, "The Real Material" 21–23). Yet each of these stories can tell us a good deal about what Alice Munro, early in her career, thought the language of story, the technique of story, the form of story can do and be. Indeed, the "exercise stories" are themselves important, distinctive, even unusual. A story like "The Shining Houses," set in Vancouver, British Columbia, is interesting because it is so seemingly unusual—like each of the stories, in fact, that Munro places second in each of her subsequent collections.

Written in the middle 1950s, produced on CBC Radio in the early 1960s, and unpublished until it was collected in 1968 in *Dance of the Happy Shades*, "The Shining Houses" represents a fascinating perception of the West Coast of Canada as that place might be understood by someone with the deep feeling for time, landscape, and folklore that Alice Munro acquired through her rural southwestern Ontario upbringing. "The Shining Houses" is a story of conflict between opposing discourses, conflict between the new and the old, conflict between different people, and conflict within the focal character of the story, a young suburban housewife and mother named Mary. Munro's heroine takes pleasure in listening to her neighbour Mrs. Fullerton—someone not unlike the strong, eccentric heroines in the fiction of the older Canadian writer Ethel Wilson, who was living in Vancouver when Munro moved there and whose work Munro began to read avidly, she explains, because Wilson's writing presented "so elegant a style," because Wilson provided Munro with an example "that a point of view so complex and ironic was possible in Canadian literature" (Munro in Struthers, "The Real Material" 18). Most importantly, however, Mrs. Fullerton is a storyteller, an aged character occupying an aged house and belonging to an even more ancient world of folklore, an individual to be considered both literally and metaphorically as the egg lady. And so the story begins:

Mary sat on the back steps of Mrs. Fullerton's house, talking—or really listening—to Mrs. Fullerton, who sold her eggs. . . . And Mary found herself exploring her neighbour's life as she had once explored the life of grandmothers and aunts—by pretending to know less than she did, asking for some story she had heard before; this way, remembered episodes emerged each time with slight differences of content, meaning, colour, yet with a pure reality that usually attaches to things which are at least part legend. She had almost forgotten that there are people whose lives can be seen like this. (19)

At the climax, the turning point, of "The Shining Houses," Mary—in an action that recalls Stephen Dedalus's famous repudiation of authority in James Joyce's *A Portrait of the Artist as a Young Man*—chooses to withhold her signature, both literally and metaphorically, from a petition prepared by others from the same neighborhood, including her own husband, who want to invoke a by-law that would rid their community of Mrs. Fullerton, her "shack" (27), and her chickens. But Mary fears that "she had no argument. She could try all night and never find any words to stand up to their words, which came at her now invincibly from all sides: *shack, eyesore, filthy, property, value*" (27). It is interesting to note the order of words in Munro's original list, to note how the final word, *"value,"* is limited, made to seem misused, out of place, by the succession of words that precedes it. As a result, the reader is led to participate in the making of the story by imagining, or inferring from other passages in the story, what words—what time-honored and timeless words—might be used to counter those Mary has heard: *place, home, tradition, loyalty, value*, perhaps? "The Shining Houses" represents a conflict between opposing discourses, between opposing forms of word-magic: between the language of commerce or self-interest or economics and the language of art or human feeling or the imagination.

A story such as "The Shining Houses" attests to the range, the variety, and therefore an element of surprise in Munro's work, particularly for the reader whose first exposure to Munro is through a single anthology piece that is somehow intended to convey something essential about Munro rather than what is different about each story by her. A story like "Labor Day Dinner," written in the early 1980s, published in The *New Yorker*, and collected shortly thereafter in Munro's fifth book, *The Moons of Jupiter*, attests to the power, profundity, and complexity of her writing, qualities that grow from one book to the next but that also grow as we reread each Munro story, however early or however late in her writing career it belongs. "Labor Day Dinner" is the story chosen by American short-story writer and novelist David Leavitt for the anthology *You've Got to Read This: Contemporary American Writers Introduce Stories That Held Them in Awe*. Leavitt remarks in part: "Munro's sensitivity to the nuances of family life humbles me, as does the elegant simplicity of her prose; the seeming effortlessness with which she alternates points of view; the delicacy of her humor; above all, the craftsmanly skill with which she resolves a panoply of elements into a denouement that makes the reader (like the heroine) quite literally catch his [or her] breath" (380). Leavitt testifies: " 'Labor Day Dinner' . . . suggested to me vast possibilities, novelistic possibilities, of which I had not previously imagined the short story capable" (380).

We might go further. Alice Munro's "Labor Day Dinner," like any number of other stories by her, brings us—in the ancient, ritualistic, measured, and inevitable way of great art like Sophocles' *Oedipus Rex* or Shakespeare's *King Lear* or Hardy's *Tess of the D'Urbervilles* or Chekhov's "Heartache"—to our knees. "Shut up together, driving over the hot gravel roads at an almost funereal pace, they are pinned down by a murderous silence" (136), Munro writes of George and Roberta in this story as the couple heads over for dinner with their friends—a description that conveys a great deal, too, about the compressed power of the form of the short story. As "Labor Day Dinner" proceeds to its conclusion, we find ourselves overwhelmed, exhausted, a good deal wiser and humbler, feeling as if we have very narrowly escaped not just actual death, the dark form of a speeding car, but a more terrible death of the spirit, the death of a relationship. We are brought to a point where we know we are in the presence not only of great art, but also of a greater presence suggested by the appearance near the story's end of "a gibbous moon" (158), to which the only appropriate response may be to raise our voices in prayer and, as Munro writes, "thanksgiving" (159).

"Labor Day Dinner" takes the reader through numerous agonizing emotional responses: as Munro writes, "What they feel is not terror or thanksgiving—not yet. What they feel is strangeness" (159). But "Labor Day Dinner"—perhaps like the earlier story "Tell Me Yes or No" from *Something I've Been Meaning To Tell You*, a story that Canadian short-story writer and novelist Hugh Hood considers to be addressed to God, and certainly like the provocatively titled story "Providence" from *Who Do You Think You Are?*—operates also on another plane. "Labor Day Dinner" represents an extended meditation on, or extended confrontation with, the principle of balance in the world, a balance between absence and presence, a balance between tragedy and comedy. At the same time, "Labor Day Dinner" presents a "tension" (Munro in Struthers, "The Real Material" 15) that is precisely what Munro explains is most attractive to her, indeed a necessity for her, in the very form of the short story: an epiphanic moment when characters and readers alike may lose or find, as Munro phrases it in the story "Simon's Luck" from *Who Do You Think You Are?*, "a private balance spring, a little dry kernal of probity" (170). "Labor Day Dinner"—like "Tell Me Yes or No" from *Something I've Been Meaning To Tell You*, like "Simon's Luck" from *Who Do You Think You Are?*, like "White Dump" from *The Progress of Love*, and like "Oranges and Apples" from *Friend of My Youth*—clarifies just how far from relatively innocent, albeit wonderful, Genesis or Revelation stories (as represented by the opening and closing stories, the two framing stories, "Walker Brothers Cowboy" and "Dance of the Happy Shades," in her first collection) Munro has moved.

Munro, it would seem, has come to situate her work more in the tradition of the Book of Job, though she of course writes in a way, in a style, that is all her own. What, Munro has asked, can be more important than "the intensity and colour of perception and the quality of writing" (Munro in Boyce and Smith 230)? Not politics: Alice Munro is certainly not a writer who deals in abstractions or dogma, but rather a genuinely religious writer—if we define "religious" as a mode of perception that attends so precisely, so intensely, to the details of our lives in this world that these come to be seen as filled with the sometimes dark, sometimes luminous image, the sense of ultimate possibility, that some people name "God."

For a final example of Munro's extraordinary achievement, one might turn to the story "Oranges and Apples," written in the late 1980s, published in the *New Yorker*, and collected shortly thereafter in Munro's seventh book, *Friend of My*

Youth. The story concerns the marriage of Murray and Barbara and the threats to that marriage, including their deep fear that Barbara may have cancer:

The doctor said that the lump could be a floater—malignant cells that had their origin somewhere else in the body. A sealed message. And they could remain a mystery—bad cells whose home base could never be found. If indeed they proved to be bad cells at all. "The future is unclear till we know," said the doctor. (112)

What is most interesting about this passage is its metafictional dimensions, the way it subtly emphasizes Munro's own concerns as a short-story writer with all that is knowable and unknowable—with sealed messages, with mysteries, with origins, with everything from the malignant to the benign. "Oranges and Apples" is a story about second chances that finishes with a gorgeously written and deeply moving scene as Murray, terrified at the prospects of his wife's test results, waits for her on the beach below the Sunset Steps overlooking Lake Huron. Both Murray and the reader watch closely as Barbara descends the Sunset Steps; then, as Barbara and Murray approach each other on the boardwalk running along the beach, she suddenly stops and picks up a white balloon. Time stops; both Murray and the reader feel their hearts catch. The intensely subtle feeling for landscape and metaphor and ritual here is unsurpassed, I believe, in contemporary writing. But notice also the lightness, a tone that anticipates the very ending of the story:

"Look at this," Barbara says as she comes up to him. She reads from a card attached to the string of the balloon. " 'Anthony Burler. Twelve years old. Joliet Elementary School. Crompton, Illinois. October 15th.' That's three days ago. Could it have flown over here in just three days?

"I'm O.K.," she says then. "It wasn't anything. It wasn't anything bad. There isn't anything to worry about."

"No," says Murray. He holds her arms, he breathes the leafy, kitchen smell of her black-and-white hair.

"Are you shaking?" she says.

He doesn't think that he is.

Easily, without guilt, in the long-married way, he cancels out the message that flashed out when he saw her at the top of the steps: *Don't disappoint me again.*

He looks at the card in her hand and says, "There's more. 'Favorite book—*The Last of the Mohicans.*' "

"Oh, that's for the teacher," Barbara says, with the familiar little snort of laughter in her voice, dismissing and promising. "That's a lie." (135–36)

What terror, what heart-rending poignancy, what jollity: who else besides Alice Munro could manage this? Story as floater, story as sealed message, story as lie: can we find anything more challenging, anything more fulfilling, than this?

There is in "Oranges and Apples" and in so many stories by Munro from "Royal Beatings" onwards, in her collections *The Progress of Love, Friend of*

My Youth, Open Secrets, and *The Love of a Good Woman* in particular, a terrible but beautiful honesty of vision, an unrelenting desire for truthfulness, that we recognize and accept in the work of Samuel Beckett but do not seem to want to recognize or accept in Alice Munro, even when we are confronted violently with it. Yet, as in Beckett, there is also, and always, the comedy—or, we may say in Munro's case, celebration. For in the story "Spelling" from *Who Do You Think You Are?*, when Rose goes out to the old-age home to see Flo and meets a seemingly ruined soul named Aunty, the final word that Aunty heroically succeeds in articulating to Rose is " 'C-E-L-E-B-R-A-T-E' " (183).

WORKS CITED AND CONSULTED

Primary

Munro, Alice. *Dance of the Happy Shades*. Toronto: Ryerson, 1968; New York: McGraw-Hill, 1973; London: Allen Lane, 1974.

———. "Everything Here Is Touchable and Mysterious." *Weekend Magazine* [Globe and Mail] May 11, 1974: [33].

———. *Friend of My Youth*. Toronto: McClelland & Stewart, 1990; New York: Knopf, 1990; London: Chatto & Windus, 1990.

———. *Lives of Girls and Women*. Toronto: McGraw-Hill Ryerson, 1971; New York: McGraw-Hill, 1972; London: Allen Lane, 1973.

———. *The Love of a Good Woman*. Toronto: McClelland & Stewart, 1998; New York: Knopf, 1998; London: Chatto & Windus, 1998.

———. *The Moons of Jupiter*. Toronto: Macmillan of Canada, 1982; New York: Knopf, 1983; London: Allen Lane, 1983.

———. *Open Secrets*. Toronto: McClelland & Stewart, 1994; New York: Knopf, 1994; London: Chatto & Windus, 1994.

———. *The Progress of Love*. Toronto: McClelland & Stewart, 1986; New York: Knopf, 1986; London: Chatto & Windus, 1987.

———. *Selected Stories*. Toronto: McClelland & Stewart, 1996; New York: Knopf, 1996; London: Chatto & Windus, 1996.

———. *Something I've Been Meaning To Tell You*. Toronto: McGraw-Hill Ryerson, 1974; New York: McGraw-Hill, 1974; Harmondsworth: Penguin, 1985.

———. *Who Do You Think You Are?* Toronto: Macmillan of Canada, 1978. Rpt. as *The Beggar Maid: Stories of Flo and Rose*. New York: Knopf, 1979; London: Allen Lane, 1980.

Secondary

Besner, Neil K. *Introducing Alice Munro's Lives of Girls and Women: A Reader's Guide*. Canadian Fiction Studies 8. Toronto: ECW, 1990.

Blodgett, E. D. *Alice Munro*. Twayne's World Authors Series 800. Boston: Twayne/G. K. Hall, 1988.

Boyce, Pleuke, and Ron Smith. "A National Treasure: An Interview with Alice Munro." *O Canada 2*. Ed. Cassandra Pybus. *Meanjin* 54 (1995): 222–32.

Carrington, Ildikó de Papp. *Controlling the Uncontrollable: The Fiction of Alice Munro*. DeKalb: Northern Illinois University Press, 1989.

Carscallen, James. *The Other Country: Patterns in the Writings of Alice Munro*. Toronto: ECW, 1993.

Dahlie, Hallvard. "Alice Munro and Her Works." *Canadian Writers and Their Works*. Fiction Series. Vol. 7. Ed. Robert Lecker, Jack David, and Ellen Quigley. Toronto: ECW, 1985. 215–56. Rpt. as *Alice Munro and Her Works*. Toronto: ECW, 1985.

Gadpaille, Michelle. "Alice Munro." *The Canadian Short Story*. Perspectives on Canadian Culture. Toronto: Oxford University Press, 1988. 57–81.

Heble, Ajay. *The Tumble of Reason: Alice Munro's Discourse of Absence*. Toronto: University of Toronto Press, 1994.

Houston, Pam. "A Hopeful Sign: The Making of Metonymic Meaning in Munro's 'Meneseteung.' " *Kenyon Review* 14.4 (1992): 79–92.

Hoy, Helen. "Alice Munro: 'Unforgettable, Indigestible Messages.' " *Journal of Canadian Studies* 26.1 (1991): 5–21.

———. " 'Dull, Simple, Amazing and Unfathomable': Paradox and Double Vision in Alice Munro's Fiction." *Studies in Canadian Literature* 5 (1980): 100–15.

———. " 'Rose and Janet': Alice Munro's Metafiction." *Canadian Literature* 121 (1989): 59–83.

Keith, W. J. *Literary Images of Ontario*. Ontario Historical Studies Series. Toronto: University of Toronto Press, 1992.

Leavitt, David. " 'Labor Day Dinner' by Alice Munro." *You've Got to Read This: Contemporary American Writers Introduce Stories That Held Them in Awe*. Ed. Ron Hansen and Jim Shepherd. New York: HarperCollins, 1994. 380.

MacKendrick, Louis K., ed. *Probable Fictions: Alice Munro's Narrative Acts*. Downsview, Ontario: ECW, 1983.

———. *Some Other Reality: Alice Munro's Something I've Been Meaning To Tell You*. Canadian Fiction Studies 25. Toronto: ECW, 1993.

Martin, W. R. *Alice Munro: Paradox and Parallel*. Edmonton: University of Alberta Press, 1987.

McCarthy, Dermot. "The Woman Out Back: Alice Munro's 'Meneseteung.' " *Studies in Canadian Literature* 19.1 (1994): 1–19.

McCulloch, Jeanne, and Mona Simpson. "Alice Munro: The Art of Fiction CXXXVII." *Paris Review* 131 (1994): 226–64.

Metcalf, John. "Casting Sad Spells: Alice Munro's 'Walker Brothers Cowboy.' " *Writers in Aspic*. Ed. John Metcalf. Montreal: Véhicule, 1988. 186–200. Rpt. in his *Freedom from Culture: Selected Essays 1982–92*. Toronto: ECW, 1994. 173–87.

———. "A Conversation with Alice Munro." *Journal of Canadian Fiction* 1.4 (1972): 54–62.

Metcalf, John, and J. R. (Tim) Struthers. "Alice Munro." *Canadian Classics: An Anthology of Short Stories*. Ed. John Metcalf and J. R. (Tim) Struthers. Toronto: McGraw-Hill Ryerson, 1993. 101–3, 144–45.

———, eds. *How Stories Mean*. Critical Directions 3. Erin, Ontario: Porcupine's Quill, 1993.

Miller, Judith, ed. *The Art of Alice Munro: Saying the Unsayable*. Waterloo, Ontario: University of Waterloo Press, 1984.

Moore, Jean M., comp. *The Alice Munro Papers Second Accession: An Inventory of the*

Archive at the University of Calgary Libraries. Ed. Apollonia Steele and Jean F. Tener. Calgary: University of Calgary Press, 1987.

Moore, Jean M., and Jean F. Tener, comps. *The Alice Munro Papers First Accession: An Inventory of the Archive at the University of Calgary Libraries.* Ed. Apollonia Steele and Jean F. Tener. Calgary: University of Calgary Press, 1986.

Pfaus, B[renda]. *Alice Munro.* Ottawa: Golden Dog, 1984.

Rasporich, Beverly J. *Dance of the Sexes: Art and Gender in the Fiction of Alice Munro.* Edmonton: University of Alberta Press, 1990.

Redekop, Magdalene. *Mothers and Other Clowns: The Stories of Alice Munro.* London: Routledge, 1992.

Ross, Catherine Sheldrick. "Alice Munro." *Canadian Writers since 1960: First Series.* Ed. W. H. New. *Dictionary of Literary Biography.* Vol. 53. Detroit: Gale Research, 1986. 295–307.

———. *Alice Munro: A Double Life.* Canadian Biography Series 1. Toronto: ECW, 1992.

———. " 'At least part legend': The Fiction of Alice Munro." *Probable Fictions: Alice Munro's Narrative Acts.* Ed. Louis K. MacKendrick. Downsview, Ontario: ECW, 1983. 112–26.

———. "Calling Back the Ghost of the Old-Time Heroine: Duncan, Montgomery, Atwood, Laurence, and Munro." *Studies in Canadian Literature* 4.1 (1979): 43–58.

———. "An Interview with Alice Munro." *Canadian Children's Literature* 53 (1989): 14–24.

Smythe, Karen. *Figuring Grief: Gallant, Munro, and the Poetics of Elegy.* Montreal: McGill–Queen's University Press, 1992.

Stainsby, Mari. "Alice Munro Talks with Mari Stainsby." *British Columbia Library Quarterly* 35.1 (1971): 27–31.

Struthers, J. R. (Tim). "Alice Munro and the American South." *Canadian Review of American Studies* 6 (1975): 196–204. Rpt. with revisions in *Here and Now.* Ed. John Moss. *The Canadian Novel.* Vol. 1. Toronto: NC, 1978. 121–33.

———. "Alice Munro's Fictive Imagination." *The Art of Alice Munro: Saying the Unsayable.* Ed. Judith Miller. Waterloo, Ontario: University of Waterloo Press, 1984. 103–12.

———. "Reality and Ordering: The Growth of a Young Artist in *Lives of Girls and Women.*" *Essays on Canadian Writing* 3 (1975): 32–46. Rpt. with corrections in *Modern Canadian Fiction.* Comp. Carole Gerson. Richmond, British Columbia: Open Learning Institute, 1980. 166–74.

———. "The Real Material: An Interview with Alice Munro." *Probable Fictions: Alice Munro's Narrative Acts.* Ed. Louis K. MacKendrick. Downsview, Ontario: ECW, 1983. 5–36.

Thacker, Robert. "Alice Munro: An Annotated Bibliography." *The Annotated Bibliography of Canada's Major Authors.* Vol. 5. Ed. Robert Lecker and Jack David. Downsview, Ontario: ECW, 1984. 354–414.

———. "Alice Munro and the Anxiety of American Influence." *Context North America: Canadian/U.S. Literary Relations.* Ed. Camille La Bossière. Ottawa: University of Ottawa Press, 1994. 133–44.

———. "Alice Munro's Willa Cather." *Canadian Literature* 134 (1992): 42–57.

———, ed. *Alice Munro Writing On. . . . Essays on Canadian Writing* 66 (1998). Rpt. as *The Rest of the Story: Critical Essays on Alice Munro.* Toronto: ECW, 1999.

———. " 'Clear Jelly': Alice Munro's Narrative Dialectics." *Probable Fictions: Alice Munro's Narrative Acts.* Ed. Louis K. MacKendrick. Downsview, Ontario: ECW, 1983. 37–60.

———. "Conferring Munro." *Essays on Canadian Writing* 34 (1987): 162–69.

———. "Connection: Alice Munro and Ontario." *American Review of Canadian Studies* 14 (1984): 213–26.

———. "Go Ask Alice: The Progress of Munro Criticism." *Journal of Canadian Studies* 26.2 (1991): 156–69.

———. "Introduction: Alice Munro, Writing 'Home': 'Seeing This Trickle in Time.' " *Alice Munro Writing On . . .* Ed. Robert Thacker. *Essays on Canadian Writing* 66 (1998): 1–20. Rpt. in *The Rest of the Story: Critical Essays on Alice Munro.* Ed. Robert Thacker. Toronto: ECW, 1999.

———. " 'So Shocking a Verdict in Real Life': Autobiography in Alice Munro's Stories." *Reflections: Autobiography and Canadian Literature.* Ed. K. P. Stich. Reappraisals: Canadian Writers 14. Ottawa: University of Ottawa Press, 1988. 153–61.

———. "What's 'Material'?: The Progress of Munro Criticism, Part 2." *Journal of Canadian Studies* 33.2 (1998): 196–210.

Wallace, Bronwen. "Women's Lives: Alice Munro." *The Human Elements: Critical Essays.* Ed. David Helwig. Ottawa: Oberon, 1978. 52–67.

Weaver, John. "Society and Culture in Rural and Small-Town Ontario: Alice Munro's Testimony on the Last Forty Years." *Patterns of the Past: Interpreting Ontario's History.* Ed. Roger Hall, William Westfall, and Laurel Sefton MacDowell. Toronto: Dundurn, 1988. 381–402.

York, Lorraine M. *"The Other Side of Dailiness": Photography in the Works of Alice Munro, Timothy Findley, Michael Ondaatje, and Margaret Laurence.* Toronto: ECW, 1988.

R. K. NARAYAN
(October 10, 1906–   )

Britta Olinder

BIOGRAPHY

Rasipuram Krishnaswami Narayan was born in Madras, the son of a school-teacher. When his father took up a position as headmaster in Mysore, the rest of the family followed him and settled there, while the future writer stayed in his grandmother's care. His autobiography *My Days* relates many of his experiences and impressions during this period and depicts his life in these conditions. At school, Narayan was not a success but got his B.A. degree in 1930 at the Maharaja College, Mysore. After trying his hand at several professions, he decided to become a writer. In his autobiography, he mentions the many rejection slips he received before the publication of his novels of childhood, *Swami and Friends*, of young adulthood, *The Bachelor of Arts*, and of the precarious situation of Indian wives, *The Dark Room*.

The most crucial period of Narayan's personal life appears to encompass years of courtship and marriage that ended with his wife's sudden death and his own subsequent mourning for her. For seven years he could not publish any novel. Then he put his experience on paper in *The English Teacher*, his most autobiographical but also his most fantastic novel. From then on he published a number of novels, the titles of which often indicate various professions, such as *Mr. Sampath* or *The Printer of Malgudi*, *The Financial Expert*, *The Guide*, *The Sweet-Vendor*, and *The Painter of Signs*. They are all, like most of his short stories, set in or around Malgudi, a fictitious community similar to Mysore and possessed of features recognizable in many south Indian towns.

Narayan's tendency to use the same material in different ways is reflected in the fact that his Gandhian novel *Waiting for the Mahatma* has a later parallel in *The Painter of Signs*. Similarly, there are significant likenesses between *Mr. Sampath* and *The Man-Eater of Malgudi*, between *The Financial Expert* and

The Sweet-Vendor, as well as between *The Guide* and *A Tiger for Malgudi*. His latest two novels are *Talkative Man* and *The World of Nagaraj*.

Before any of his novels, Narayan wrote short stories for the Madras daily *The Hindu*. We may note, however, that it was not until the period between *The Dark Room* and *The English Teacher* that he published his first three collections in book form. Throughout his career he has taken recourse to writing short stories as a relief from the more demanding and time-consuming work of novels. The result is thirteen collections; the later ones, however, often reprint stories from earlier collections.

Apart from his autobiography and fiction, long and short, Narayan has published versions of Hindu myths, essays, and travel books. In the 1940s, Narayan became editor of a journal, *Indian Thought*, and created Indian Thought Publications in order to get his works distributed in his own country. Narayan has a house in Mysore but spends most of his time with his granddaughter's family in Madras.

CRITICISM

On the one hand, Narayan has been called India's most accomplished author, one of the most admired writers in English today. On the other, his simplicity and his naïveté have been emphasized. He has been regarded as a small-town ironist presenting the human comedy without the disturbance of philosophical considerations. To some extent, Narayan himself has pointed in this direction and led his critics astray by disclaiming profundity and artistic ambitions. There are, however, other voices, such as that of Keith Garebian, who acknowledges the structure and "sense of shape" of Narayan's novels, or M. K. Naik, who has studied the ironic vision in Narayan's fiction, or Fakrul Alam, who reveals the subtlety of Narayan's narrative strategies.

The overwhelming majority of critical works on Narayan concern his novels. Only a handful of critics have found it worthwhile to look into the short stories. Among them, Perry Westbrook (1968) points out that while the novels have been more appreciated in the West, Narayan's fellow countrymen seem to prefer his short stories, which, first published in newspapers, may appear more like reports of Indian life. In a chapter mostly devoted to the short stories, another scholar, P. S. Sundaram (1973), demonstrates how some of them illuminate or complement the novels. Like other critics, he affirms that Narayan is primarily interested in characters rather than plot or atmosphere. Syd Harrex (1978) underlines the social aspects of the stories as well as the capacity of the characters for both compassion and wild exaggeration.

The "workmanliness and finish" of Narayan's stories are praised by M. K. Naik (1983) rather than "the quality of the reading of life they offer" (93). Compared with the novels, Naik argues, the stories lack depth, complexity of experience, and subtlety of response. He goes so far as to sum them up as a "museum of minor motifs" (104). This line of argument may seem quite convincing until the reader realizes how cursory Naik's accounts of Narayan's plots are. Moreover, we must be aware of the great distance between Indian storytelling methods and Western critical criteria, even as applied by an Indian critic. We may note in this context that stories are told all over the world, while the novel is a Western genre. Individual Narayan stories are always entertaining but may sometimes seem trivial. Taken together, however, they will, as Viney Kirpal has shown, offer both complexity and an understanding of the human condition with its latent vulnerability. As John Updike (1983) says in a review of a collection of Narayan stories, "His social range and his successful attempt to convey, in sum, an entire population shame most American authors, who also . . . could do worse than emulate Narayan's Hindu acceptance and vital, benign fellow-feeling" (722).

ANALYSIS

The central characters of Narayan's novels mostly belong to the lower middle class, with Margaya of *The Financial Expert* and Raju of *The Guide* moving both higher up and lower down the social scale. His short stories, in contrast, mainly turn around animals, children and students, beggars, servants, and office slaves, each depending on others and mastered by them. Some are mentally simple or retarded people who are abused by others. With over a hundred stories, Narayan covers a considerably larger panorama of Indian society in them than in his fifteen novels.

We find a development from very short stories of only a couple of pages to later ones in *Grandmother's Tale: Three Novellas* of up to sixty-five pages. Sometimes the stories, particularly the early ones, provide merely a passing glimpse of a life that may seem insignificant. It is the impact of a number of them together, however, that allows us to perceive the vitality and richness of the universe that Narayan has created: Malgudi with its busy crowds of people and the single individuals amid them, with its streets and shops, with the ever-present Sarayu River, and the Mempi Hills over looking it all. We get acquainted with this world in Narayan's novels, but we find its full breadth only when we add the short stories.

As an introduction to his collection of stories from the great Indian epics, *Gods, Demons, and Others*, Narayan writes about the "World of the Storyteller." This is the man in the village whose duty it is to carry on the oral tradition, and who, as the center of the community, provides the others with a framework, a perspective, and a meaning for their lives. This is Narayan's place and function in his society at the same time as he also writes "out of the impact of life and persons around me" (10)

In another introduction, this time to *Malgudi Days* (1982), he claims, "I discover a story when a personality passes through a crisis of spirit or circumstances" (ix). He says that his central character either resolves the crisis "or lives with it. But some stories may prove to be nothing more than a special or significant moment in someone's life or a pattern of existence brought to view" (ix).

Because there are well over a hundred stories in Narayan's thirteen collections, this analysis can only address a few of them. A good place to start is with the first *Malgudi Days* (1941) and the story "A Career," partly because its narrator, the Talkative Man, appears in about a dozen other stories and, with a slightly different function, in one of Narayan's later novels called precisely *Talkative Man*. In the short stories, he acts as an intermediary between writer and reader, conveying the puzzlement at seeing what people are and what they do. He creates a certain distance from the action while at the same time being involved in it. He has the double role of observer and actor.

In "A Career," the Talkative Man entrusts the deceitful Ramu with handling his affairs and, as a result, loses his shop and all his possessions. After years of misery, he finally gets help to make a fresh start. Meanwhile, Ramu, who after ten years has squandered his ill-gotten gain, is glimpsed as a blind beggar, observed by the main character but deprived of the capacity to look back. The moral of the story is almost over obvious. If, however, we relate it to Narayan's other stories, long or short, we find many examples of greed and exploitation of other people or their money as the key failing in human relationships, a dehumanizing factor.

From *Dodu* (1943), the title story will serve to exemplify Narayan's understanding of children. Like several other stories about schoolboys, it can be related to the author's first novel, *Swami and Friends*, which itself may be read as a collection of stories. In this case, Dodu investigates different ways of acquiring money in spite of all the obstacles created by teachers, parents, and elder brothers. He shows ingenuity and courage, but in the end, it is the understanding and generosity of an adult that allow him to succeed.

Here, in just five pages, we enter the eight-year-old's world. We learn significant little details along with the history of his earlier attempts at making money in spite of his elders. Through direct and indirect dialogue as well as through Dodu's reactions and thoughts contrasted with the older generation's insensitivity, the reader sees clearly the slyness of the child and the open-mindedness of the professional man.

The inhumanity of an incomprehensible school and examination system is more or less directly criticized in Narayan's first two novels, in his autobiography, and in many of his essays. Among the stories that address this issue, "Iswaran" from *Cyclone and Other Stories* (1944) stands out. Here the young protagonist Iswaran has been trying to pass his exam for the tenth time. His own doubts about the result, other people's certainty of his failure, the experience of being laughed at behind his back, and the general feeling of being "a sort of outcast" make him prepare for suicide by drowning. With his feet already in the water, he yet musters the courage to check the results alone in the middle of the night. He finds his name not in the third-class list but among the second classes. The shock of success deranges his mind. He imagines riding a horse and making it swim across the river, where his body is found next day, as well as his suicide note. In this story, Narayan's irony, so often gentle, has strongly tragic dimensions.

"An Astrologer's Day" had appeared earlier but furnished the title of Narayan's fourth collection (1947). The story is a model of economy without leaving out relevant detail. There are elements here foreshadowing both *The Financial Expert*, particularly the setting, and *The Guide*, notably the power of attracting people's trust. The story concerns what some might interpret as pure chance and others as fate. At the same time, the central character's assumed profession as an astrologer while he is "as much a stranger to the stars as his innocent customers" reveals the profound irony of the conception. The story ends with the main character's immense relief at being set free from the threat of physical danger by means of a lie, and, not least, at having evidence that he is not guilty of manslaughter.

In "Lawley Road," another title story, it is again the Talkative Man who is the narrator, this time as a journalist and house owner. It is a highly enjoyable satire of the scant wisdom and integrity with which states and municipalities are governed. It depicts the comic confusion that results from community tributes to independence. In particular, it focuses on the immense statue of Sir Frederick Lawley, supposedly a colonial tyrant. The narrator is asked to remove the obnoxious statue, a task that requires superhuman effort. With some dynamite, a large working force, and a carriage drawn by several bullocks, the monument is finally lodged in the narrator's house with its legs stretched out into the street. At this point, however, it is discovered that Sir Frederick had in fact founded the town, had done a lot of good, and had even declared anticolonial ideas. The general demand then is to have him reinstated. But how? The solution finally proposed is for the Municipal Chairman to win fame by buying the house along with the statue and making it a National Trust. This is why the street is renamed Lawley Road. Both road and statue frequently appear in Narayan's stories.

One other element of this story deserves mention as typical of Narayan's world view as well as his sense of humor: the smallness of human beings and the enormity of their tasks, the size and massiveness of objects or machines they have to deal with. The scale seems to be on a par with the Lilliputians in relation to Gulliver. An obvious parallel among Narayan's stories is "Engine Trouble," in *Dodu, An Astrologer's Day*, and *Malgudi Days* (1982).

"A Horse and Two Goats" is a story that appears in two versions, one of four pages and the other of twenty-three. While the longer version indulges in circumstantial background presenting full and detailed portraits, the shorter excels in artistic economy. Both of them set off characteristic attitudes and reactions of representatives of East and West.

A red-faced American tourist stops with his car close to an old Indian villager resting at the foot of a horse statue while watching his two goats. They begin a conversation, each in his own language without understanding the other's. The irony is brought out in their different associations and resulting misunderstandings. Admiring the old sculpture, the foreigner immediately wants to buy it. As he discusses its commercial value, the villager talks about its religious meaning and importance. In the end, the red-faced man pays a hundred rupees for the piece while the Indian accepts this unexpected payment for his two goats. Seeing a religious monument in commercial terms is totally inconceivable to him.

Another demonstration of the clash of the perceptions of East and West is provided by "God and the Cobbler," one of the stories in the second *Malgudi Days* (1982). Here a hippie observes a cobbler sitting composed, self-contained, and without demands under a branch of a margosa tree showering flowers over him. At once the hippie sees an Eastern mystic in the cobbler and admires him. When he asks him to fix his sandals, the latter looks up at him and is reminded of God Shiva. In the midst of the traffic and the crowds of people passing, they begin to talk about God, existence, and the next birth. The conversation leads them both to recall episodes that they would rather forget: the Indian admits that he has set fire to his enemy's hut with a family inside, and the hippie confesses that he, too, has set fire to villages, flying over them without even knowing the people he destroyed. While the cobbler suspects the hippie of having stolen the little silver figure that he offers to give him, he still thinks of him as a god.

This, then, is a story in which different attitudes toward life and death, crime and guilt, gods and religion are set side by side, in which secrets of yogis and knowledge of wonder workers in India seem no more or less remarkable than a moon walk. Similarity serves to emphasize difference, and vice versa. It is an example of a passing episode that assumes artistic and philosophical dimensions.

Narayan's early short stories, written for publication in periodicals and hence limited by specific requirements, are usually only a few pages long. Later works, uninhibited by such restrictions, tend to grow longer, as we can see in his later collections, but particularly in *The Grandmother's Tale: Three Novellas* (1993), which employs both "tale" and "novella." The title story of this collection begins in autobiographical detail of Narayan's early life with his grandmother in Madras and of his visits with her in later years. This is the framework for her telling stories, particularly of her own mother's adventurous early life. What ensues then is Narayan's version of his great-grandmother's marriage when only a small child, of her husband's leaving when he was still a mere boy, and of her following in search of him. It is like a picaresque tale or a story out of *The Arabian Nights*. After several years, the strong-willed young woman manages to find her husband, to become a servant to his new wife, and finally to make him accompany her, leaving his second wife. When she has achieved her goal, she turns into the most dutiful, obedient wife until her death.

Here, however, grandmother's tale goes on to relate her father's further destiny, ending with his death much later and the division of his property. Apart from its length, the epic character and structure as well as the shifting points of view of this work distinguish it very clearly from the single-episode short story that Narayan usually writes.

Modern experimentation and new techniques in writing seem to have very little appeal for Narayan. As he sees it, there are too many good stories waiting to be discovered. The sheer enjoyment in the telling of stories is his aim and his driving force. Whether we consider Narayan's novels or his short stories, or any of his other works, for that matter, the abiding impression is of his rich sense of comedy, often mixed with sadness and alive with irony, a combination that reveals a profound wisdom. He is a sensitive interpreter not only of India and Indians, but in many ways of the whole of humanity.

WORKS CITED AND CONSULTED

Primary

Novels

Narayan, R. K. *The Bachelor of Arts: A Novel.* London: Nelson, 1937; Chicago: University of Chicago Press, 1980.
———. *The Dark Room: A Novel.* London: Macmillan, 1938; New Delhi: Hind Pocket Books, 1979.
———. *The English Teacher.* London: Eyre & Spottiswoode, 1945. Rpt. as *Grateful to Life and Death.* East Lansing: Michigan State College Press, 1953; Mysore: Indian Thought Publications, 1989.
———. *The Financial Expert: A Novel.* London: Methuen, 1952; East Lansing: Michigan State College Press, 1953; Chicago: University of Chicago Press, 1981.
———. *The Guide: A Novel.* Madras: Higginbothams, 1958; London: Methuen, 1958; New York: Viking Press, 1958; New York: Penguin, 1980.
———. *The Man-Eater of Malgudi.* New York: Viking Press, 1961; London: Heinemann, 1962; New Delhi: Hind Pocket Books, 1979.
———. *Mr. Sampath.* London: Eyre & Spottiswoode, 1949. Rpt. as *The Printer of Malgudi.* East Lansing: Michigan State College Press, 1957; Mysore: Indian Thought Publications, 1957; New Delhi: Hind Pocket Books, 1979.
———. *The Painter of Signs.* New York: Viking Press, 1976; London: Heinemann, 1976.
———. *Swami and Friends: A Novel of Malgudi.* London: Hamish Hamilton, 1935; Mysore: Indian Thought Publications, 1983.
———. *The Sweet-Vendor.* London: Bodley Head, 1967; Mysore: Indian Thought Publications, 1967; Rpt. as *The Vendor of Sweets.* New York: Viking, 1967; London: Heinemann, 1980; Harmondsworth: Penguin, 1983.
———. *Talkative Man.* Sketches by R. K. Laxman. Mysore: Indian Thought Publications, 1986; New York: Viking, 1987.
———. *A Tiger for Malgudi.* London: Heinemann, 1983.
———. *Waiting for the Mahatma: A Novel.* London: Methuen, 1955; East Lansing: Michigan State University Press, 1955; Mysore: Indian Thought Publications, 1960.

———. *The World of Nagaraj*. London: Heinemann, 1990; Mysore: Indian Thought Publications, 1990; New York: Viking, 1990.

Short Stories

Narayan, R. K. *An Astrologer's Day and Other Stories*. London: Eyre & Spottiswoode, 1947.
———. *Cyclone and Other Stories*. Mysore: Indian Thought Publications, 1944.
———. *Dodu and Other Stories*. Mysore: Indian Thought Publications, 1943.
———. *Gods, Demons, and Others*. New York: Viking, 1964; London: Heinemann, 1965.
———. *The Grandmother's Tale: Three Novellas*. London: Heinemann, 1993.
———. *The Grandmother's Tale and Selected Stories*. New York: Viking, 1994.
———. *A Horse and Two Goats and Other Stories*. London: Bodley Head, 1970.
———. *Lawley Road: Thirty-two Short Stories*. Mysore: Indian Thought Publications, 1956.
———. *Malgudi Days*. Mysore: Indian Thought Publications, 1941.
———. *Malgudi Days*. London: Heinemann, 1982.
———. *Old and New*. Mysore: Indian Thought Publications, 1981.
———. *Salt and Sawdust: Stories and Table Talk*. New Delhi: Penguin, 1993.
———. *A Story-Teller's World*. With an introduction by Syd Harrex. New Delhi: Penguin, 1989.
———. *Under the Banyan Tree and Other Stories*. London: Heinemann, 1985.

Other

Narayan, R. K. *The Emerald Route*. Sketches by R. K. Laxman. Bangalore: Director of Information and Publicity, Government of Karnataka, 1977; Mysore: Indian Thought Publications, 1977.
———. *The Mahabharata*. London: Heinemann, 1978.
———. *My Dateless Diary*. Mysore: Indian Thought Publications, 1960.
———. *My Days*. London: Chatto & Windus, 1975.
———. *Mysore*. Mysore: Indian Thought Publications, 1944.
———. *Next Sunday*. New Delhi: Orient Paperbacks, 1956.
———. *The Ramayana*. London: Chatto & Windus, 1973.
———. *Reluctant Guru*. New Delhi: Orient Paperbacks, 1974.
———. *A Writer's Nightmare: Selected Essays, 1958–1988*. New Delhi: Penguin, 1988.

Secondary

Albertazzi, Silvia. "The Story-Teller and the Talkative Man: Some Conventions of Oral Literature in R. K. Narayan's Short Stories." *Commonwealth Essays and Studies* 9.2 (Spring 1987): 59–64.
Gilra, Shiv K. *R. K. Narayan: His World and His Art*. Meerut: Saru Publishing House, 1984.
Goyal, Bhagwat S., ed. *R. K. Narayan's India: Myth and Reality*. New Delhi: Sarup & Sons, 1993.
Hariprasanna, A. *The World of Malgudi: A Study of R. K. Narayan's Novels*. New Delhi: Prestige Books, 1994.

Harrex, Syd. *The Fire and the Offering: The English-Language Novel of India, 1935– 1970.* 2 vols. Calcutta: Writers Workshop, 1977–78.

Kain, Geoffrey, ed. *R. K. Narayan: Contemporary Critical Perspectives.* East Lansing: Michigan State University Press, 1993.

Kirpal, Viney Pal Kaur. "An Analysis of Narayan's Technique." *Ariel* 14.4 (October 1983): 16–19.

McLeod, A. L., ed. *R. K. Narayan: Contemporary Critical Perspectives.* New Delhi: Sterling, 1994.

Naik, M. K. *The Ironic Vision: A Study of the Fiction of R. K. Narayan.* New Delhi: Sterling, 1983.

Olinder, Britta. "Irony in R. K. Narayan's Short Stories." *Short Fiction in the New Literatures in English.* Ed. J. Bardolph. Nice: Faculté des Lettres, 1989. 183–187.

———. "R. K. Narayan's Short Stories: Some Introductory Remarks." *Commonwealth Essays and Studies* 8.1 (Autumn 1985): 24–30.

Pontes, Hilda. *R. K. Narayan.* A Bibliography of Indian Writing in English 1. New Delhi: Concept, 1983.

Raizada, Harish. *R. K. Narayan: A Critical Study of His Works.* New Delhi: Young Asia, 1969.

Sundaram, P. S. *R. K. Narayan.* New Delhi: Arnold-Heinemann, 1973.

Updike, John. "India Going On." Rev. of *Malgudi Days. Hugging the Shore: Essays and Criticism.* New York: Knopf, 1983. 716–22.

Venugopal, C. V. *The Indian Short Story in English: A Survey.* Bareilly: Prakash, 1975.

Walsh, William. *R. K. Narayan.* Writers and Their Work no. 224. London: British Council; Longman, 1971.

———. *R. K. Narayan: A Critical Appreciation.* London: Heinemann, 1982.

Westbrook, Perry D. "The Short Stories of R. K. Narayan." *Journal of Commonwealth Literature* 5 (1968): 41–51.

TIM O'BRIEN
(October 1, 1946–   )

Brady Harrison

BIOGRAPHY

Born in Austin, Minnesota, Tim O'Brien grew up in Worthington—the "Turkey Capital of the World"—and attended Macalester College. In 1968, a month after graduating summa cum laude in political science, O'Brien was drafted into the U.S. Army and shipped to Vietnam as a foot soldier. During his tour with the 198th Infantry Brigade, he achieved the rank of sergeant and received the Purple Heart. After his return from Vietnam in 1970, O'Brien went on to graduate work in government at Harvard University, taking time off to work as a reporter for the *Washington Post*. At Harvard, O'Brien began concentrating on writing, and he has worked successfully in a number of genres.

O'Brien's first book, *If I Die in a Combat Zone* (1973), grew out of a number of magazine and newspaper pieces on his experiences in the war and has been labeled "autofiction," a narrative that combines autobiography with the techniques of fiction. After his combat memoir, O'Brien produced *Northern Lights* (1975), an out-of-print novel that the author has described as "a terrible book" (Naparsteck 2). O'Brien's next work, *Going after Cacciato* (1978), won the National Book Award and is considered by many critics to be one of the best novels about the Vietnam War. A lesser novel, *The Nuclear Age* (1985), tells the story of a 1960s radical who becomes consumed with the threat of a nuclear apocalypse. With the highly praised short-story collection *The Things They Carried* (1990), O'Brien returned to Vietnam fiction. *In the Lake of the Woods* (1994) tells the story of John Wade, a politician whose career is ruined by revelations of his involvement in the massacre at My Lai in 1968. O'Brien's latest novel, *Tomcat in Love* (1998), explores the desires and humiliations of Thomas Chippering, a punning, randy linguistics professor. Throughout his career, O'Brien has published short fiction in popular and literary magazines such as the *New Yorker, Esquire*, the *Massachusetts Review*, and the *Quarterly*, and a number of his stories have been included in *The Best American Short Stories* (1977, 1987), *Prize Stories: The O. Henry Awards* (1976, 1978, 1982), and *The Pushcart Prize* (vols. 2 and 10).

CRITICISM

For O'Brien, the short story is both an end in itself and the building block of longer, more complicated fictions. Just as *If I Die in a Combat Zone* grew out of magazine pieces, *Going after Cacciato* evolved from short stories into a complex fictional meditation on courage, responsibility, and the imagination. In *The Things They Carried*, O'Brien further develops this technique: the interwoven stories (some of which are more like commentaries on stories than actual stories) collectively form a dramatic and discursive novel.

In *Understanding Tim O'Brien*, Steven Kaplan observes that O'Brien "approaches writing novels as if he were working on a collection of short stories": "O'Brien tries to make all of his chapters into independent stories, which have their own beginning, middle, and end. This approach to individual chapters reflects his concern with the tightness and compression of his writing" (12). We can see this in the first chapter of *Going after Cacciato*, a piece that works both as a short story (which has been anthologized) and as the opening of a novel. On its own as it was first published, "Going after Cacciato" is a story about a dumb kid who decides to walk away from the war—we don't know why, but we can supply our own answers—and about another soldier who becomes engaged with the idea of walking to Paris. As an opening chapter, it sets the reader on a course to discovering why Cacciato walks away and leaves us wondering if Paul Berlin will follow. While the two pieces are very similar, O'Brien revised the story stylistically to sharpen it and to bring it more into accord with the rest of the novel. Numerous sections of O'Brien's novels have been published on their own, and of those, many, like "Going after Cacciato," stand as superb short stories. For a fuller consideration of the relationship between O'Brien the short-story writer and O'Brien the novelist, see Catherine E. Calloway's excellent essay "Pluralities of Vision: *Going after Cacciato* and Tim O'Brien's Short Fiction." For the most recent book-length study of O'Brien's work, see Tobey C. Herzog's *Tim O'Brien*.

ANALYSIS

O'Brien's mastery of the short story can be seen best in *The Things They Carried*. He uses this short-story collection/novel as an occasion to reprise and extend some of his deepest themes and to comment on the purpose and art of fiction. Writing with considerable humor and sympathy, O'Brien offers his stories as a kind of history of the war because "story-truth is truer sometimes than happening-truth" (203); as O'Brien remarks in one of his commentary chapters, "What stories can do, I guess, is make things present" (204).

"The Things They Carried," the frequently anthologized title story to the collection, is, like many of O'Brien's works, a literary hybrid that defies easy classification; but above all, it is a moving narrative about the physical, emotional, and psychological burdens a soldier must bear. Part story (it has characters, a setting, and something of a plot), part military training manual, and part hardware list, the story investigates the "weight" of the different "tangibles" and "intangibles" the soldiers "hump," or carry. At times, depending upon the mission, the soldiers carry a host of tangible objects. They carry a variety of weapons, from M-16s all the way down to a slingshot, "a weapon of last resort" (8), and pounds and pounds of standard gear: flak jackets, dog tags, can openers, toothbrushes, and countless other items. As O'Brien details these objects and gives their weight—"they all carried steel helmets that weighed 5 pounds" (4)—the story reads like lists or excerpts from a survival guide. But among the inventories of concrete things, O'Brien often includes in half a sentence a thing that has no physical mass but that nonetheless weighs heavily on the grunts: "Some carried CS or tear gas grenades. Some carried white phosphorus grenades. They carried all they could bear, and then some, including a silent awe for the terrible power of the things they carried" (9). The true weight of the things they carry is the purpose for which they were designed: to kill other people.

If the tangibles burden the soldiers, the intangibles press down upon them even more: "They carried all the emotional baggage of men who might die. Grief, terror, love, longing—these were intangibles, but the intangibles had their own mass and specific gravity, they had tangible weight" (20). Ted Lavender, a soldier who is shot in the head after urinating, carried the standard gear, plus tranquilizers and marijuana to help ease "the unweighed fear" of being maimed or killed. As the narrator remarks, "They all carried ghosts" (10); not only do they remember their comrades who have died, but they carry fear of the elusive Viet Cong who lurk somewhere in the jungle, out of sight, ghostlike. Amid all the violence and death, "they carried their own lives" (15). As in many of his works, O'Brien also examines what keeps soldiers fighting even when—as was often the case in Vietnam—they did not understand the reasons for the war: "They carried the common secret of cowardice barely restrained, the instinct to run or freeze or hide, and in many respects this was the heaviest burden of all. . . . Men killed, and died, because they were embarrassed not to" (20–21). According to O'Brien, the weight of family and country, obligation and honor, and the fear of being labeled a coward press down upon the men. It is a weight so heavy they risk their own lives and destroy others to ease the strain. By blending long lists with characters and moments of action, O'Brien creates a powerful story that makes present for us the terrible burdens we ask soldiers to carry on our behalf.

"The Things They Carry" also examines the senselessness and pointlessness of the Vietnam War. When Ted Lavender gets *"zapped while zipping,"* Lt. Jimmy Cross blames himself. Freighted with "the responsibility for the lives of his men" (19), Cross believes that because he continually thinks about Martha, a girl he knows back in the States, he failed to secure the perimeter and thus exposed his men to danger: "He had loved Martha more than his men, and as a consequence Lavender was now dead" (16). Despite his self-recriminations, there is no evidence that Cross did anything wrong; a sniper picked a target and fired, and there was nothing any of them could have done. In retaliation for Lavender's death, however, the squad destroys the nearby village of Than Khe: "They burned everything. They shot chickens and dogs, they trashed the village well, they called in artillery and watched the wreckage" (16). They never capture or kill the sniper; their vengeance is a hollow act that harms the lives of non-combatants trapped between the warring sides. The senseless destruction of the village fits into the larger pattern of pointlessness that the men participate in: "By daylight they took sniper fire, at night they were mortared, but it was not battle, it was just endless march, village to village, without purpose, nothing won or lost" (15). Neither the war nor the soldiers' actions make military or ethical sense. O'Brien, a writer with a keen sense of irony, sums up the meaninglessness in the standard, existential grunt phrase "there it is": when the squad comes upon a dead VC, one says, "there's a definite moral here" (13); after debating back and forth, another concludes, "Yeah, well . . . I don't see no moral." The first responds, "There it *is*, man." There is no morality at work here, only death.

In "On the Rainy River," another story in the collection, O'Brien reprises one of his themes from "The Things They Carried"; it is also a crucial theme in *If I Die in a Combat Zone* and *Going after Cacciato* (and *The Nuclear Age* and *In the Lake of the Woods*). Indeed, the theme of flight, of fleeing from war, could be O'Brien's chief preoccupation as a writer. In the summer of 1968, the young narrator of "On the Rainy River"—a guy named "Tim O'Brien"—receives his draft notice and must decide whether he will go to war or become a draft dodger: "I was drafted to fight a war I hated. I was twenty-one years old. Young, yes, and politically naive, but even so the American war in Vietnam seemed to me wrong. Certain blood was being shed for uncertain reasons" (44). Face to face with the war, O'Brien begins "thinking seriously about Canada" (47–48). O'Brien's fictional alter ego wrestles with the same question the author wrestled with in *If I Die*; on leave from advanced infantry training, O'Brien does some research in a public library: "I knew Canada harbored draft dodgers, but I couldn't find anything on their policy toward deserters, and I doubted our northern neighbors went that far" (60). In *Going after Cacciato*, Cacciato takes off for Paris after the squad frags its lieutenant, and Paul Berlin imagines his own flight and weighs the potential consequences of such an act.

O'Brien returns again and again to questions of responsibility and obligation to one's family, to one's nation, and, most importantly, to one's self and sense of right and wrong. In "On the Rainy River," Tim takes off for the Canadian border but cannot commit himself to turning his back on everything he has known. In one sentence, the narrator says simply and painfully what O'Brien has tried to say over and over again: "I would go to war—I would kill and maybe die—because I was embarrassed not to" (62). The weight of society works against the self's ethical sense and wins. A kind of prose-poet, O'Brien distills feelings of shame and regret into the sparest sentences: "I was a coward. I went to the war" (63). By casting himself as a character, he personalizes the anguish many soldiers felt; this is not just a character, or an anonymous soldier, but a thoughtful, decent (and public) individual who admits that he made a mistake in consenting to an ill-conceived war. There may be, despite O'Brien's disclaimer that a war story does not "suggest models of proper human behavior" (76), a moral or two lurking in his work.

"The Sweetheart of the Song Tra Bong," another frequently anthologized story in the collection, is a comic, yet harrowing rewrite of Joseph Conrad's *Heart of Darkness*. In Conrad's tale, Marlow, on board a yawl anchored in the Thames, tells of his journey upriver into Africa's ivory country. Once "in country" (to borrow a Vietnam War phrase), Marlow learns of Mr. Kurtz, the company's most successful agent; when he reaches the Inner Station, he finds a row of severed heads and discovers that Kurtz rules over the "natives" with acts of barbarism. In O'Brien's tale, Mary Anne Bell, a seventeen-year-old graduate of Cleveland Heights Senior High, comes to Vietnam at her boyfriend's request. Once in country, however, Mary Anne exchanges her "white culottes and . . . sexy pink sweater" (102) for combat fatigues and begins going out on ambush missions with a squad of Green Berets. Like Kurtz, she comes under the spell of violence and the jungle. When her boyfriend tries to reclaim her from the "Greenies," he finds her in their hootch, a place that seems "to echo with a weird deep-wilderness sound—tribal music—bamboo flutes and drums and chimes" and that smells like an animal's den, filled with "a mix of blood and scorched hair and excrement and the sweet-sour smell of moldering flesh—the stink of the kill" (119). When he confronts her, Mary Anne, wearing "a necklace of human tongues" (120), refuses to leave: "Sometimes I want to *eat* this place. Vietnam. I want to swallow the whole country—the dirt, the death—I just want to eat it and have it there inside me" (121). Mary Anne transforms from a "cute blond" to a kind of ghost in the landscape; she eventually abandons the Greenies to set out on her own—rumors suggest that she lives "up in one of the high mountain villas, maybe with the Montagnard tribes" (124). Mary Anne becomes Kurtz. O'Brien mimics Conrad so thoroughly that just as Conrad frames Marlow's narrative through an anonymous narrator, O'Brien makes Rat Kiley the witness and his fictional self the frame narrator.

Both chilling and funny—the story works so well as a black comedy that further analysis risks contaminating the sheer weird pleasure of the tale—"The Sweetheart of the Song Tra Bong" also points to serious issues about the effects of a violent environment on the individual and about U.S. involvement in the war. What happened to Mary Anne, for all its comic improbability and exaggeration, happened to a lesser extent to many of the young soldiers sent to Vietnam. Many of them changed from the kid next door to people who unleashed violence against both the enemy and the defenseless. As Rat Kiley remarks with a Hemingwayesque precision, "You come over clean and you get dirty and then afterward it's never the same" (123). Vietnam and the Vietnamese, however, did not somehow invite such a response; U.S. involvement in the war fostered an environment where moral confusion and the strain of guerrilla warfare led to atrocities. The history of U.S. engagement in colonialism and imperialism is too involved to go into here; nonetheless, this history haunts O'Brien's comic retelling of Conrad.

If the tale of Mary Anne Bell works in part through humor, "Speaking of Courage," "Notes," and "In the Field," a trilogy of stories about bravery and death, sound a much more somber note. Norman Bowker, a veteran who has returned to Iowa, finds himself driving around and around a lake thinking about how he almost won the Silver Star for Valor, but failed at the last moment to save a friend. As Bowker drives, he imagines telling his father about the night they inadvertently camped in "a shit field" (a phrase that serves as an ugly metaphor for the war). During the night, they came under mortar fire and one of the squad, wounded, got sucked into the muck—he became part of the "waste" of the war. Bowker's father, however, had his own war and prefers not to discuss their combat experiences; Norman has no one to speak to, no one to tell about how he had a grip on his friend, but let him go. We learn in "Notes," one of the chapters that is as much commentary as story, that Norman Bowker was an actual veteran who wrote to O'Brien about his feelings of dislocation after returning home; a few years after receiving the letter, the author learned that Norman had committed suicide. As Walter H. Capps reminds us in *The Unfinished War: Vietnam and the American Conscience*, as many veterans have taken their own lives as died in combat in Vietnam.

O'Brien is not so much concerned with bringing the terrible fact of veteran suicide to our attention as he is with dramatizing the weight of ghosts upon one's memory and with contemplating the power of stories. In "Notes," he realizes that "the act of writing had led [him] through a swirl of memories that might otherwise have ended in paralysis or worse" (179). In his stories, he confronts his ghosts and organizes his experiences in a manner that allows him to go on with life. Stories might also do the same for others. As O'Brien remarks, he hopes that " 'Speaking of Courage' makes good on Norman Bowker's silence' " (181). If others can read (or write) a story that illuminates their own condition, then perhaps that story can be a way for them to begin confronting their ghosts. O'Brien rather remarkably argues that "stories can save us" (255).

O'Brien mulls over this profound claim for the power of stories in the last piece in the collection, the brilliantly titled "The Lives of the Dead." Throughout *The Things They Carried*, in sections such as "Spin," "How to Tell a True War Story," "Ambush," "Notes," and "The Lives of the Dead," the author explores his ideas about what it means to be a writer and about the purpose of stories: whatever else it is, the book is also a work of metafiction. As O'Brien explained in an interview, the book "is sort of half novel, half group of stories. It's part nonfiction, too" (Naparsteck 7): "It's a new form, I think. I blended my own personality with the stories, and I'm writing about the stories, and yet everything is made up, including the commentary" (Naparsteck 8). The collection represents O'Brien's mastery of his art. It is a mature piece by a mature artist that not only extends his own themes and techniques, but also maps out new terrain in literature: he offers a fusion of the artist with his art form. At least part of the purpose of this fusion is to allow O'Brien to ask what the use of stories is, to inquire of his art what it is for. In "The Lives of the Dead," he gives a provisional answer. Stories bring the dead to life: "The thing about a story is that you dream it as you tell it, hoping that others might then dream along with you, and in this way memory and imagination and language combine to make spirits in the head. There is the illusion of aliveness" (259–60). With stories, the intersection of memory and imagination, you not only add to your sum of experience, but you participate in a process that salvages some measure of people, places, and events from the dust.

In "The Lives of the Dead," O'Brien dramatizes the conviction that we keep "the dead alive with stories" (267). He does so through two interwoven narrative strands. One revisits some of the war deaths described earlier in the book; the other recalls the death of a girl, Linda, that "Timmy" knew when he was a boy. Linda and Timmy, Tim tells us, were in love even though they were only nine years old. On their first date, a trip to the movies with Tim's parents, Linda wears a red cap; later we learn that she wears the cap to cover the scars left by an operation to remove a brain tumor. She dies. As a forty-three-year-old man, O'Brien brings her back to life in his fiction: "And as a writer now, I want to save Linda's life. Not her body—her life" (265). In a similar manner, the grunts eased the shock of death by telling stories that make the dead seem less dead— Ted Lavender, in their stories, "wasn't dead, just laid-back" (267). For O'Brien, stories keep individuals—small, ordinary people and the things they did, and thought, and wished for—alive. Stories are a kind of history and a way to bring forward emotions and events that may otherwise be lost, and it does not matter if most of it is made up. As O'Brien remarks, almost everything is made up: the events, the stories, even his thoughts on the meaning of stories—eelish does not begin to describe how slippery he can be. At the same time, O'Brien's point is that it doesn't matter if most of it is made up; what fiction does is heighten, sharpen, compress, and rearrange experience into a form that communicates some kind of truth. Whether it is war stories—and O'Brien would say that he is writing more than war stories—or stories about cats, if they reach into us, change us, make us feel or think, tell us about what something was like, then the difference between "happening-truth" and "story-truth" does not matter. We have learned; maybe we have helped keep the dead alive.

WORKS CITED AND CONSULTED

Primary

O'Brien, Tim. *Going after Cacciato*. New York: Delta, 1978.
————. *If I Die in a Combat Zone, Box Me Up and Ship Me Home*. New York: Dell, 1973.
————. *In the Lake of the Woods*. Boston: Houghton Mifflin, 1994.
————. *Northern Lights*. New York: Delacorte, 1975.
————. *The Nuclear Age*. New York: Knopf, 1985.
————. *The Things They Carried*. New York: Penguin, 1990.
————. *Tomcat in Love*. New York: Broadway, 1998.

Secondary

Bates, Milton J. "Tim O'Brien's Myth of Courage." *Modern Fiction Studies* 33 (Summer 1987): 263–79.
Beidler, Philip D. *American Literature and the Experience of Vietnam*. Athens: University of Georgia Press, 1982.
Calloway, Catherine E. "Pluralities of Vision: *Going after Cacciato* and Tim O'Brien's Short Fiction." *America Rediscovered: Critical Essays on Literature and Film of the Vietnam War*. Ed. Owen W. Gilman, Jr., and Lorrie Smith. New York: Garland, 1990. 213–24.
————. "Tim O'Brien (1946–   ): A Primary and Secondary Bibliography." *Bulletin of Bibliography* 50.3 (September 1993): 223–29.
Capps, Walter. *The Unfinished War: Vietnam and the American Conscience*. Boston: Beacon Press, 1982.
Herzog, Tobey C. *Tim O'Brien*. Boston: Twayne, 1997.
Kaplan, Steven. *Understanding Tim O'Brien*. Columbia: University of South Carolina Press, 1995.
Naparsteck, Martin. "An Interview with Tim O'Brien." *Contemporary Literature* 32.1 (1991): 1–11.
Nelson, Marie. "Two Consciences: A Reading of Tim O'Brien's Vietnam Trilogy: *If I Die in a Combat Zone, Going after Cacciato*, and *Northern Lights.*" *Third Force Psychology and the Study of Literature*. Ed. Bernard J. Paris. Rutherford, NJ: Fairleigh Dickinson University Press, 1986. 262–79.
Wilhelm, Albert E. "Ballad Allusions in Tim O'Brien's 'Where Have You Gone, Charming Billy?' " *Studies in Short Fiction* 28 (Spring 1991): 218–22.

MICHAEL ONDAATJE
(September 12, 1943–   )

Allan Weiss

BIOGRAPHY

Michael Ondaatje is extremely shy about revealing details of his personal life; as far as we know, he was born on September 12, 1943, in Kegalle, Ceylon (now Sri Lanka), near his family's tea estate. His father, Philip Mervyn Ondaatje, was an alcoholic who enjoyed living the good life; also, he was determined to emulate the lifestyle of the British colonial aristocracy. The combination of excessive spending on alcohol and entertainment, his failings as a businessman, and his oldest son Christopher's expensive education at a private school in England led to huge debts and the loss of the estate. No longer able to tolerate his increasingly serious drinking problem and inability to support their growing family, Ondaatje's mother, Doris (née Gratiaen), divorced him in 1945 and moved to Colombo. There she worked at a hotel and in 1949 enrolled Michael Ondaatje at St. Thomas College Boys' School. That same year she moved to England and opened a boardinghouse. Michael joined her in 1952 and was placed in Dulwich College, a private school. The British education he received in Colombo and England provided him with a strong sense of the British cultural heritage, while the de facto loss of his father had more profound, less easily measurable effects on his personality and, ultimately, his writing.

Ondaatje joined his brother in Canada in 1962 to attend Bishop's College (later Bishop's University). At Bishop's, he met writers and teachers who inspired him with a love of literature and encouraged him to write. Financial problems forced him to live with poet Doug G. Jones and his wife Kim, whose marriage was deeply troubled. Kim Jones eventually left Doug for Ondaatje, and they were married in 1964. They moved to Toronto, where Ondaatje continued his studies at the University of Toronto, receiving his B.A. in English in 1965. That year, his father died in a drunken accident at home. Ondaatje continued to meet and befriend influential fellow writers, particularly those associated with Coach House Press: bpNichol, Frank Davey, Victor Coleman, and others. He pursued his graduate studies at Queen's University and completed his M.A. in 1967 with a thesis on mythology in the poetry of Edwin Muir. His scholarly work reflected and enhanced his growing interest in the role of myth in literature and popular culture.

During his university days, he began to publish his poetry in literary magazines and the anthology *New Wave Canada* (1966). In 1967, his first book of poetry was published, *The Dainty Monsters*. Later poetry publications included *The Man with Seven Toes* (1969), *The Collected Works of Billy the Kid* (1970) (which also contained prose), and *Rat Jelly* (1973). His contact with the writers at Coach House Press encouraged him to explore various media, including film (*Sons of Captain Poetry* [1970] about bpNichol) and drama. He supported himself by teaching at the University of Western Ontario (1967–71) and Glendon College, York University (1971–   ). His first novel was *Coming through Slaughter* (1976), about jazz musician Buddy Bolden; soon afterward he edited the short-story anthology *Personal Fictions: Stories by Munro, Wiebe, Thomas, and Blaise* (1977). His works received numerous awards, and his critical success continued with his novels *In the Skin of a Lion* (1987) and *The English Patient* (1992), winner of the Booker Prize and the Governor General's Award.

In 1978 and 1980, Ondaatje, who had always felt rootless, took trips to Sri Lanka to discover and come to terms with the homeland he barely remembered and the family, particularly the father, he had never known. The result of his trips and searches into his past was the fictionalized portrait of his parents and other family members, *Running in the Family* (1982). While the book is based on fact, it is an imaginative reconstruction of their lives.

CRITICISM

Because Ondaatje has written so little short fiction, analyses of his work have understandably focused on his poetry and novels. Leslie Mundwiler's *Michael Ondaatje: Word Image, Imagination* (1984) provides a biographical and critical overview emphasizing the importance of language and politics as themes in Ondaatje's work. The critics in *Spider Blues: Essays on Michael Ondaatje*, edited by Sam Solecki (1985), examine Ondaatje's poetry and fiction from various perspectives but seem to agree that paradox is a major structural and thematic feature of all his work. The domestic and violent, mythic and mundane, fictional and historical, inner and outer, natural and artificial often collide, producing a violent energy that drives the work forward. Indeed, critics have long debated the role of violence in Ondaatje's work; some see it as merely a reflection of his dualistic vision, while others—notably Christian Bök (1992)—question whether its presence is so benign, especially its possibly sexist features. In any case, critical studies like Douglas Barbour's *Michael Ondaatje* (1993) and Ed Jewinski's biographical *Michael Ondaatje: Express Yourself Beautifully* (1994) are almost unanimous in describing Ondaatje as a postmodernist who seeks to challenge the boundaries between genres and states of being; he portrays the arbitrary nature of those boundaries by blurring them, and portraying the violent clash of opposites.

ANALYSIS

Running in the Family is illustrative of Ondaatje's characteristic blending of fact and fiction, of genres, of modes and approaches. Ondaatje has long sought to break down the barriers between the real and the fictional, showing how these two apparently divergent areas of experience actually merge with each other. As part of this project, he has sought the mythic in the everyday, and vice versa; he will raise vulgar realities (like his father's drinking) to mythic proportion while attempting to find the commonplace reality behind the events and people (like Billy the Kid) that popular culture has turned into myth.

Ondaatje has written little short fiction; most of his prose has been either of novel length or in the form of brief narratives that are part of longer works. Only one of these works can be classified as a short story (contradicting the claim in his introduction to his short-story anthology, *From Ink Lake*: "I have never written a short story, and probably never will" [xvi]). His early efforts at prose were inspired by his reading of Leonard Cohen's novel *Beautiful Losers* (1966) in preparation for a short critical study of Cohen's work (published in 1970).

The Collected Works of Billy the Kid includes a number of short narratives, often in Billy's own voice, portraying key moments in the outlaw's life. The first prose passage concerns an early shoot-out with Pat Garrett told from Billy's point of view. But the poet's own voice is unmistakably present as well: "Garrett fired at O'Folliard's flash and took his shoulder off. Tom O'Folliard screaming out onto the quiet Fort Sumner street, Christmas night, walking over to Garrett, no shoulder left, his jaws tilting up and down like mad bladders going" (7). Like all his works, *The Collected Works of Billy the Kid* is ultimately about Ondaatje himself—the title of the book makes it clear that such passages are by a poet, not a "real" gunslinger. Ondaatje becomes one with his subject and sees through Billy's eyes as Billy might see through a poet's: "It was the colour and light of the place that made me stay there, not my fever. It became a calm week. It was the colour and the light" (17). In this hideout, where Billy recuperates from a bout of fever, he finds refuge from his violent life: "When I walked I avoided the cobwebs who had places to grow to, who had stories to finish. The flies caught in those acrobat nets were the only murder I saw" (17).

The book includes idyllic scenes of lovemaking interspersed with violent episodes; like his poetry, Ondaatje's fiction combines the domestic and the brutal, again to show that our conventional boundaries are just that: merely conventions. The scene of Billy's drunken sexual encounter with Angie D ends: "On the nail above the bed the black holster and gun is coiled like a snake, glinting also in the early morning white" (71). Also challenged are our notions of heroes and villains—Sheriff Pat Garrett is an "ideal assassin" who had "the ability to kill someone on the street walk back and finish a joke" (28). We are told of Garrett's alcoholism and its effects: "He stole and sold himself to survive. One day he was robbing the house of Juanita Martinez, was discovered by her, and collapsed in her living room. In about six months she had un-iced his addiction. They married and two weeks later she died of a consumption she had hidden from him" (29). This is hardly the stuff of popular mythology or legend. We are told about the Chisums, John and Sallie, who provided Billy with a safe haven, and the lives of those in Billy's gang—accounts of mindless brutality and sudden bursts of violence, such as the story of Tom O'Folliard (50–51). Billy and Garrett, much like Billy and the poet, are mirrors of each other.

Most of the short prose pieces Ondaatje published in the literary magazines were excerpts from *Running in the Family* and his novels, but a few scattered stories—if they can be called such—appeared as well. His one true short story is "Austin," which appeared in the first issue of the prose journal *Periodics*. Austin is a car mechanic who, along with relatives and a few friends, is staging a drunken wake in the garage after having just returned from the funeral of an unidentified friend or relative. The unnamed narrator appears to be another friend who joins the wake; through his participation we learn that Austin considers himself an expert blaster, capable of safely detonating dynamite. He says, "Ok say you're standing on 8 feet of limestone I can, I can crank out 3 feet from under you and you wouldn't feel a thing not a thing" (45). Despite his boasts, we wonder if the wake is for a victim of an accident he has caused. The possibility is suggested by the sharp contrast between his confident assurances that he can easily make himself and others rich and his two bankruptcies in five years (45). His friends and family leave him one by one, until only the narrator and Austin's horse are left—and even the horse races away at the sound of his voice.

"Lunch Conversation," which was published in the same journal in 1979, appears to be an early form of the sort of story that would later make up *Running in the Family*. The mother in this dialogue is named Doris, the sister is Gillian, and the grandmother is Lala (a slight variation on Ondaatje's real grandmother's name); how "true" the conversation is, however, can of course never be known for sure. The characters, the period being discussed, and the details of the events portrayed are kept deliberately obscure—for the reader and the narrator, who is attempting to piece together the story being told by Barbara about a drowning. In fact, we are never quite sure who is the true "narrator," since the one telling the story to us (the author of "Lunch Conversation") acts primarily as a listener, and a confused one at that. We learn here that Lala "nearly drowned too" and "[c]laimed she passed ships" (29), further suggesting the autobiographic roots, if not facts, of the story. Stories covering at least three periods intertwine, and at last the narrator takes over the story, making it his own: "So an hour later my grandmother, Lala, comes back and entertains everyone over how she passed ships out there and they tell her John Grenier is dead" (31). In fact, we get the sense that virtually everyone in the story tells stories about everyone else—even a lie about the dead man (" 'He's fine,' Lala says. 'He is in the next room having a cup of tea.' " [31]).

The meshing of fact and fiction, as noted earlier, dominates *Running in the Family*. The book is a collection of stories about Ondaatje's parents and grandparents, some entirely true, others richly embellished. Perhaps the most thoroughly "fictional" is the story of Ondaatje's maternal grandmother, called "The Passions of Lalla." This prominent story purports to present Lalla's vibrant and romantic life and death. It is difficult to know how colorful Lalla really was; we can be certain, however, that her death was nothing like what is described at the end of the story. Floods have washed over the region of Ceylon where she lived:

Lalla took one step off the front porch and was immediately hauled away by an arm of water. . . . It was her last perfect journey. The new river in the street moved her right across the race course and park towards the bus station. As the light came up slowly she was being swirled fast, "floating" . . . alongside branches and leaves, the dawn starting to hit flamboyant trees as she slipped past them like a dark log, shoes lost, false breast lost. . . . In the park she floated over the intricate fir tree hedges of the maze . . . its secret spread out naked as a skeleton for her. The symmetrical flower beds also began to receive the day's light and Lalla gazed down at them with wonder . . . she went under for longer and longer moments coming up with a gasp and then pulled down like bait, pulled under by something not comfortable any more, and then there was the great blue ahead of her, like a sheaf of blue wheat, like a large eye that peered towards her, and she hit it and was dead. (127–29)

In fact, Lalla died when she got drunk with her brother and, according to Christopher Ondaatje, "simply never woke up" (qtd. in Jewinski 118).

"Escarpment" was published in *Island* in 1985. The unnamed protagonist and his lover are enjoying the landscape and each other's company, and their communion with nature becomes a metaphor for their lovemaking: "He slips under the fallen tree holding the cedar root the way he holds her forearm. He hangs a moment, his body being pulled by water going down river. He holds it the same way and for the same reasons. Heart Creek? Arm River? he writes, he mutters to her in the darkness" (72). Clearly, then, past and present meld, as do experience and the writing about it. Ondaatje has developed a postmodernist focus on the writing process itself. Just as he has long challenged the boundaries between truth and fiction, prose and poetry, writer and subject, he has come to challenge those between writing and subject. Novels like *In the Skin of a Lion* and *The English Patient* seek to tell previously unknown stories—about those who have been forgotten by traditional history. In his short fiction, Ondaatje seems to have similarly tried to raise questions about the nature of writing and its relationship to what is being written about. "Escarpment" is as much about the gaps, the areas of missing knowledge and connection, as it is about communion: "Sun lays its crossword, litters itself, along the whole turning length of this river. . . . He has gone far enough to look for a bridge and has not found it" (73).

Ondaatje's short fiction, then, defies labels and conventions. His is an art of paradox and tensions between opposites: fact and fiction, history and myth, heroism and villainy, domestic peace and sudden, horrifying violence, narrator and subject, narrator and story. His greatest innovation in the short-fiction form is in his refusal to separate it clearly from family or public history, from poetry, or from his explorations of his past and his self.

WORKS CITED AND CONSULTED

Primary

Ondaatje, Michael. "Austin." *Periodics* 1 (Spring, 1977): 44–46.
————. "Bessie Smith at Roy Thomson Hall." *Now Magazine* December 1–7, 1983: 15.
————. *The Collected Works of Billy the Kid.* Toronto: House of Anansi Press, 1970.
————. *Coming Through Slaughter.* Toronto: House of Anansi Press, 1976.
————. *The Dainty Monsters.* Toronto: Coach House Press, 1967.
————. *The English Patient.* Toronto: McClelland & Stewart, 1992.
————. "Escarpment." *Island* 15–16 (1985): 72–73.
————, ed. *From Ink Lake: Canadian Stories.* Toronto: Lester & Orpen Dennys. 1990.
————. *In the Skin of a Lion.* Toronto: McClelland & Stewart, 1987.
————. "Lunch Conversation." *Periodics* 5 (1979): 29–31.
————. *The Man with Seven Toes.* Toronto: Coach House Press, 1969.
————. "The Passions of Lalla." *Canadian Forum* 62 (October 1982): 17–21.
————. "The Passions of Lalla" (excerpt). *Rubicon* 1 (Spring 1983): [1].
————, ed. *Personal Fictions: Stories by Munro, Wiebe, Thomas, & Blaise.* Toronto: Oxford University Press, 1977.
————. *Rat Jelly.* Toronto: Coach House Press, 1973.
————. *Running in the Family.* Toronto: McClelland & Stewart, 1982.
————. *Running in the Family* (excerpts). *Capilano Review* 16–17 (1979): 5–43; *Camrose Review* 1 [1982], 23; *Island* 11 (1982): 5.

Secondary

Barbour, Douglas. *Michael Ondaatje.* New York: Twayne, 1993.
Bök, Christian. "Destructive Creation: The Politicization of Violence in the Works of Michael Ondaatje." *Canadian Literature* 132 (1992): 109–24.
Clarke, George Elliott. "Michael Ondaatje and the Production of Myth." *Studies in Canadian Literature* 16.1 (1991): 1–21.
Heighton, Steven. "Approaching That Perfect Edge': Kinetic Techniques in the Poetry and Fiction of Michael Ondaatje." *Studies in Canadian Literature* 13.2 (1988): 223–43.
Jacobs, Naomi. "Michael Ondaatje and the New Fiction Biographies." *Studies in Canadian Literature* 11.1 (1986): 2–18.

Jewinski, Ed. *Michael Ondaatje: Express Yourself Beautifully*. Toronto: ECW Press, 1994.

Kertzer, Jon. "Ondaatje." *Canadian Literature* 106 (1985): 163–66.

Mundwiler, Leslie. *Michael Ondaatje: Word, Image, Imagination*. Vancouver: Talonbooks, 1984.

Solecki, Sam, ed. *Spider Blues: Essays on Michael Ondaatje*. Montreal: Véhicule Press, 1985.

CYNTHIA OZICK
(April 17, 1928–   )

Allan Weiss

BIOGRAPHY

Cynthia Ozick was born in New York City and spent her early years in the Bronx. Her parents were Russian immigrants who were steeped in the culture of the shtetl; her father, William, was an avid scholar and ensured that his daughter received a parochial as well as public education. Also contributing to Ozick's literary background was the fact that Abraham Regelson, a prominent Yiddish poet, was her mother's brother. After suffering anti-Semitism in public school (an experience reflected in her novel *The Cannibal Galaxy* [1983]), she attended Hunter High School in Manhattan, where her intelligence and talent were finally recognized and encouraged.

Ozick attended Washington Square College, New York University, from 1946 to 1949, graduating with a B.A. in English. She went to Ohio State University intending to pursue a doctorate in English, but after receiving an M.A. in 1950 with a thesis on Henry James, she cut her studies short and married Bernard Hallote in 1952. After working for a time as an advertising copywriter, she taught briefly at New York University (1964–65). Her first novel, *Trust*, appeared in 1966, but it was her work in the short story that earned her the greatest critical acclaim. Many of her stories have won prizes and have been included in volumes of *The Best American Short Stories* and *Prize Stories: The O. Henry Prize Winners*. Thanks to grants and awards, she has been able to devote herself largely to her writing. She has published four novels—*Trust* (1966), *The Cannibal Galaxy* (1983), *The Messiah of Stockholm* (1987), and *The Shawl* (1989)—and, more important for our purposes, three collections of shorter fiction: *The Pagan Rabbi and Other Stories* (1971), *Bloodshed and Three Novellas* (1976), and *Levitation: Five Fictions* (1982).

In addition to her fiction, Ozick has also published a number of essays, many of them very significant studies and arguments in the field of Jewish and Jewish-

American thought and literature. Her most important essays were collected in *Art and Ardor: Essays* (1983) and *Metaphor and Memory: Essays* (1989).

CRITICISM

Ozick's reputation as one of the premier short-story writers of the United States has not meant that she has always received due attention from critics. In fact, the first book-length study of her work did not appear until 1987, when Sanford Pinsker published *The Uncompromising Fiction of Cynthia Ozick*. Few serious articles were published before this; most can be found in the Modern Critical Views volume about her edited by Harold Bloom (published in 1986). The early studies engaged in a debate over the place of Ozick in the traditions of Jewish thought and Jewish-American writing. The view of many critics, such as Joseph Lowin in his Twayne study (1988), is that she expresses a very traditional (in fact, religious) Jewish perspective. Many critics seem to assume that her fiction takes a clear side in the many debates it portrays between characters who represent traditional and more assimilated North American Judaism.

It was not until the work of Elaine M. Kauvar, particularly in her detailed study *Cynthia Ozick's Fiction: Tradition and Invention* (1993), that Ozick's dual vision was fully explored. Ozick strikes a far greater balance between the various dichotomies she presents than is acknowledged by earlier critics. Also, Kauvar (intentionally or not) cautions us to be very skeptical about Ozick's beliefs and fictional intentions as expressed in her essays and the preface to *Bloodshed and Three Novellas*. While Ozick is clearly a traditionalist, she is also a satirist, and so her works seldom permit easy interpretation. One should note the recent study by Sarah Blacher Cohen, *Cynthia Ozick's Comic Art* (1994), a useful corrective to the portrait of the very serious writer painted by earlier critics.

ANALYSIS

As mentioned, Ozick's fiction depends heavily on dualities, and these dualities often appear in balance. Among the oppositions usually cited are Hellenic/ Hebraic (following Matthew Arnold's distinction), ancient/modern, religious/ secular, individual/social, and Pan/Moses. These dual perspectives reflect the position of a writer who belongs to a culture that challenges and is even opposed, in some ways, to that of the larger community. The culture clash experienced by first- , second- , and even third-generation immigrants can be traced in such areas as language, religion, ideology, and practices. For Ozick, the key problem is writing Jewish stories in a Gentile language and country.

The comic element of Jewish literature and culture prevents her from taking any one position too seriously. Thus she is prone to undercutting characters with which she might otherwise have identified fully. It may be that her intention has been to portray the more traditional, liturgical, Talmudic, Mosaic view as the correct one, the one that more truly reflects the Jewish soul, but her comic impulse produces quite the opposite response in the reader. Thus in the novella "Envy; or, Yiddish in America," we do sympathize with Edelshtein's traditionalism at an intellectual level, but we cannot help laughing at his petty jealousy, and that undercuts our identification with his philosophy. As Cohen demonstrates, Ozick's characters are too human—too humanly complex—to become ideal spokespeople for particular points of view. In any case, the world itself is too complex to sustain simple moral judgments.

Discussing her short stories is made difficult by the various ways in which her works have been categorized. Many shorter works that have been described as short stories by critics are far too long to fit the definition, and some of these (particularly the ones published in *Bloodshed and Three Novellas*) are quite clearly not short stories in the author's own mind. This analysis will be limited to those works that are unarguably short stories.

Duality as theme and structural principle dominates Ozick's fiction from the earliest stories to the most recent. Her first collection, *The Pagan Rabbi and Other Stories*, portrays characters struggling to reconcile or choose between conflicting imperatives. The title story, one of Ozick's best and best known, concerns Rabbi Isaac Kornfeld, a friend of the narrator and by all accounts a devout and scholarly Jew. But Kornfeld has hanged himself from a tree, committing one of the worst sins in Judaism, and the narrator visits his widow to try to learn why.

The story embodies some of Ozick's most common themes, particularly the clash between paganism and Judaism. The narrator learns that Kornfeld has become a paganist and sought to achieve spiritual communion with Nature, following the tenets of Hellenism rather than Hebraism. Kornfeld believed that the body restricts the soul, and he sought freedom for his soul through actual as well as symbolic copulation with a tree. Ozick feels, in keeping with traditional Jewish thought, that one of Judaism's most fundamental attributes is its rejection of idol worship (consider Abraham's iconoclasm); the deification of Nature in this way is to her a form of idolatry. In the journal he leaves upon his death, Kornfeld denies that his love of Nature is idolatry since he believes that Nature is the creation and embodiment of God. Nevertheless, it is clear that he has become a pagan, and in his worship of the tree, he encounters (if we are to accept his word) a dryad named Iripomooi. He succeeds in splitting his soul from his body, only to discover that his soul takes the form of an old Talmudic scholar—in other words, it is profoundly Jewish. His suicide, then, is the result of his recognition that he can never reconcile his pagan desires with his Jewish identity.

The symbolism of the story is typical of Ozick's work. She associates nature with sexual desire, idol worship, and the free—and very private—imagination. Thus Kornfeld is a very creative man who composes fantastic bedtime stories for his daughters. The fact that his pagan impulses and behavior are unknown until after his death demonstrates how private they are, as opposed to the social duties imposed by his calling. For Ozick, the asocial indulgence of such an asocial and amoral philosophy directly contradicts Jewish thought and practice. It is a denial of tradition and the self and is therefore ultimately self-destructive.

On the other hand, we should be careful not to exaggerate Ozick's criticism of Kornfeld. For one thing, Ozick's suspicion of the creative imagination, as expressed in her fiction and essays, is contradicted by her very art. Second, she establishes sympathy for Kornfeld by giving us his story from his own point of view. The image of the Talmudic scholar who represents his soul is hardly prepossessing: he is old, dusty, with his nose buried in a book, and seemingly lacking in any joy of life or in God's creation. It was from this very book-centered, apparently life-denying existence that Kornfeld sought to free his soul. It may be that Ozick sees this soul as his truer self, one he must learn to accept, but it is difficult to see such a dry-as-dust pursuit as a happier choice for Kornfeld. His suicide is therefore rendered more tragic as we see him trapped as well as defined by his heritage.

The story operates on a base of oppositions and dualities. The narrator is a mirror image of Kornfeld: not as good a scholar, but a better Jew. Both men's fathers engage in a battle of filial comparisons, with Kornfeld's father winning the bragging war—until the very end; again, they are doubles and opposites of each other. As Kornfeld's story unfolds, we move back and forth between arguments for and against Pan and Moses, individual desire and social and moral responsibility, and so on.

Similar flirting with paganism appears in "The Dock-Witch." The narrator is a lawyer from the Midwest who moves to New York to work for a firm specializing in shipping contracts; he thereby violates the family tradition of being tied to the land rather than the sea. He meets a woman named Undine who, like many characters in Ozick's fiction, lives a double life. As Sylvia, she is married to a pharmacist who happens to have the same name as the narrator, George; when she is not a dutiful wife, she spends hours at the dock seeing off steamship passengers she does not know. She becomes the narrator's lover and reveals herself to be a sea nymph. The narrator is irresistibly attracted to her and, since she appears more and more in the form of a siren, is destroyed by her. More exactly, he is destroyed by his obsession for her and for the sea and his determination to renounce everything in his past. The story is richly symbolic, packed with classical allusions and water imagery, right up to its final scene, in which the two Georges meet and find out who she really is. "The Dock-Witch" is a doppelgänger story, a fantasy, and a tale about split identities and competing impulses. Once more, Ozick seems to suggest, even for her Gentile characters, that loyalty to one's cultural heritage is the only path to salvation and survival. Yet the narrator's life beyond the Calypso that Undine constructs for him is so empty and "dry" that it is hard not to sympathize with his paganist impulses.

The power of one's cultural heritage is revealed in "The Suitcase." The story concerns an art show being attended by the artist's father, Mr. Hencke—a German immigrant—and the artist's Jewish mistress, Genevieve Lewin. Mr. Hencke was in the German air force during World War I and immigrated to

the United States before the rise of Nazi Germany. Nevertheless, when he encounters her, their initial conflict over her status as mistress descends into a
clash over the Holocaust. Mr. Hencke was not personally implicated in the
Holocaust in any way, yet Genevieve seems to suggest that he has an inescapable
cultural responsibility merely by virtue of being German. It is difficult to tell
what Ozick's own position on the issue is, since as Hans Borchers has shown
in his article "Of Suitcases and Other Burdens," her portrayal of Germany and
Germans is designed for thematic purposes rather than historical accuracy. The
convention in Jewish-American writing, he demonstrates, is to present Germany
and Nazism as inextricably linked. It is not fair to blame every German for what
happened, yet the very fact that Mr. Hencke was in America at the time makes
the resolution of the story problematic. He clearly feels guilt for what is perhaps
a racial sin, the warlike element of German culture. His dreams and memories
of Germany haunt him, and when Genevieve's purse is stolen, he very defen-
sively opens his suitcase to prove that he was not responsible for the crime.
Jews and Germans may not be reconcilable until the Mr. Henckes accept the
lessons of history rather than attempt to deny their relevance. Once again, Ozick
is able to evoke the reader's sympathy for a character whose amorality and
desire to deny his past make him philosophically objectionable. In terms of the
story's structure, Mr. Hencke is in many ways a double of his son, and the
dialectical structure is embodied in the clash between Mr. Hencke and Genevieve.

"The Doctor's Wife" concerns a character who lives in a world of illusion.
Dr. Pincus Silver has long imagined achieving great things, but has not had the
courage to realize his dreams. He is a mediocre figure preferring fantasy to
reality. He is also a bachelor; his "wife" is the photographic image of a woman
in a biography of Chekhov, known only as "Unknown Friend." Because she is
merely a photo, she is timeless, imaginatively manipulable, perfect, and quite
dead. Consequently, for Silver, she is preferable to a real woman like Gerda
Steinweh, whom his sisters invite to his fiftieth-birthday party in an attempt at
matchmaking. The sisters' own marriages are deeply flawed (one sister is having
an affair with the husband of another), and so we are not expected to see Gerda
or the prospect of marriage as ideal. Ozick is careful to balance the unpleasant
reality with the deluding fantasy of "Unknown Friend"; while we have a moral
obligation to live and play a moral role in the real world, that is not always a
pleasant and certainly never a perfect choice.

Ozick's most overtly feminist tale is "Virility," about a young poet named
Elia Gatoff who tries to become a respected and famous poet by basing his
works entirely on the dictionary. His attempt to impress the critics with linguistic
erudition fails. Suddenly, however, his poetry improves markedly, and he gains
fame, honor, and fortune with a series of marvelous collections all entitled *Virility*. Ironically, these poems are not his, either; he has plagiarized them from
letters he has been getting from his aunt, who escaped with him from Russia
and settled in Liverpool. He is fully an impostor, even to the extent of writing

under an assumed name, Edmund Gate, based in part on the narrator's own first name. Poems praised for being "seminal and hard," "robust, lusty, male," are in fact the products of a woman. Guilt overtakes Gate/Gatoff, and he brings out the final volume with Tante Rivka's name on them. Suddenly, her imaginative creations are treated with much less respect. They are described as "limited, as all domestic verse must be. Flat. The typical unimaginativeness of her sex," and "distaff talent, secondary by nature. Lacks masculine energy." Judging art by the sex of the artist is as wrong for the male establishment as for the feminists who challenge it.

The title story of Ozick's next collection of tales, *Bloodshed and Three Novellas*, ranks with "The Pagan Rabbi" among Ozick's best and most widely anthologized. Bleilip is a lawyer visiting his cousin Toby, who has married, and become, a Hassidic Jew. Bleilip's motivation for visiting her is obscure, but apparently he wishes to see for himself what it is like to have strong faith. He himself is a secular Jew living the North American way; he is a rationalist who rejects the Hassidic approach of strict adherence to the law of the Torah and of what he believes is total faith in God. He debates the issues with Toby and her husband, Yussel, but agrees to accompany them to evening services. There he meets the Rebbe and finds himself singled out for debate by this more formidable opponent. What we discover is that Bleilip and the Rebbe are, typically, mirror images of each other. The Rebbe, being human, occasionally experiences religious doubt; Bleilip, despite his skepticism, experiences religious curiosity and spiritual emptiness. He has abandoned his Jewish heritage, and the result is a great internal loss. Once more the Holocaust becomes the focus of cultural and individual questioning; here the main question is, as the Rebbe says, "How is it possible to live?" In a world of suffering and meaningless death, so different from the redemptive death of the scapegoat as described in the the day's Bible reading, how can Jews live and not succumb to despair?

Bleilip's own spiritual suffering is revealed only when the Rebbe asks him to empty his pockets (which are described early in the story as mysteriously heavy). Bleilip is carrying two guns, one a toy and the other real. Clearly, his despair—the product of living among the Gentiles without the foundation of his Jewish traditions and faith—has become so deep that he is contemplating suicide. The two guns symbolize the two goats used in the ancient scapegoat ceremony, the two worlds of Jew and Gentile in which Bleilip barely lives, and the two choices he has: life, reality, and a Jewish past and future, or death, deception, and lack of cultural foundation and identity. The story is built around debate, the clash of opposing views, in keeping with its Talmudic themes and Ozick's general technique.

Levitation: Five Fictions contains three works that are clearly short stories and one that is a satirical fiction. The title story concerns the Feingolds, a married couple who are both second-rate novelists. They share certain assumptions about their "art": they will eschew the trendy practice of writing about writers (a position Ozick would clearly agree with, given her disdain for "art for art's sake"—fiction with no social function). But other than this, Jimmy and Lucy are quite different. He is immersed in history; she rejects such a complete involvement in it. In fact, she is a Jewish convert and therefore lives without a clear religious or cultural tradition. The Feingolds throw a cocktail party, hoping that members of New York's cultural elite will attend; unfortunately, the most famous and prestigious writers never come, and the guests who do arrive are as mediocre as the Feingolds themselves. One of the guests is a Holocaust survivor and begins to tell his story. Because his tale is based on truth rather than pretension or an uncertain cultural heritage, he is able to affect an audience in ways Lucy will simply never be able to do. All the Jews in the room levitate—whether literally or figuratively is not made entirely clear—but Lucy is left on the ground. Life means putting down strong cultural roots and in this way being able to reach for the sky; Lucy, however, has avoided such complete involvement, preferring to gain a phony measure of freedom from all religious and cultural attachment. The result is that she is left behind by those whose historical consciousness and clear sense of self render them able to rise far above her.

The problem of the artist is further explored in "Shots." Here the artist is a photographer. Her goal is that of the artist who designed Keats's Grecian urn: use art to freeze life, preserve history, and make the past permanent. But as Keats has shown, the attempt to preserve life in art also removes its vitality, killing that which it attempts to make eternal. The unnamed narrator's art is thus associated with death; her photographic "shots" are like the shot taken by an assassin at a Chilean diplomat. The assassin's shot misses but kills the translator instead, and since the photographer is herself a translator—of reality into image—the suggestion is made that she will be the real victim of her work. Indeed, she begins a futile affair with Sam, a professor married to a "terrific" woman named, somewhat baldly, Verity. Verity and the narrator are direct opposites: one represents real life, domesticity, and history as the passage of time, while the other represents art, the idolatry of the creative imagination and its products, and history as something dead and well preserved. One of the narrator's most treasured possessions is a photograph of the "Brown Girl," an inmate of the Home for Elderly Female Ill. The Brown Girl is much like Dr. Silver's "Unknown Friend": a static, lifeless, perfect image. At the end of the story, the narrator is made into the Brown Girl by Verity, who insists on dressing her up in some old clothes she has found. The narrator learns that time cannot be stopped, whether by art or by mere wishing; the real world is in time, and she cannot deny this fundamental truth. By trying to deny time, she betrays life itself, and her art can thus never be honest or true.

"From a Refugee's Notebook" is a pair of explorations on the same theme of the denial of life. The first part, "Freud's Room," is a fiction about what Ozick sees as Freud's antilife examination of the Unconscious, something that, to her, is a self-aggrandizing myth. She dismisses Freud as an idolater, with the idol being the self. In "The Sewing Harem," women on a planet called Acirema (America backwards) sew up their own genitals to prevent childbirth. They are seeking to increase their freedom by denying their role in procreation; they are therefore rejecting the whole concept of heritage, tradition, the passing down of life and culture. The story has been seen as a satire on radical feminists and an affirmation of women's role in achieving continuity of culture and the species.

"Puttermesser: Her Work History, Her Ancestry, Her Afterlife" is, as the title suggests, a three-part fictional biography of an independent woman. It describes her two jobs—in a law firm and in the New York City bureaucracy—where she faces anti-Semitism and sexism. Her bosses are out to achieve and exercise power, and they show disdain for Jewish moral and cultural values. In response, Ruth Puttermesser searches for her Jewish roots by getting Hebrew lessons from her Uncle Zindel—except that the narrator interrupts the story to inform us that Zindel had died before her birth. The story is an excellent example of the meta-fictional approach Ozick often takes, an approach her critics have not acknowledged. Puttermesser's search for her heritage is an imaginative rather than "real" quest, but no less valid for it.

Indeed, the apparent contradiction in Ozick's expressed view of literature as idol and her work as a writer can in part be explained by her dual approach to the imagination. When writers turn literature into their entire focus, emphasizing form over content and the life of the artist over life itself, they do indeed make an idol of it. Literature is not to be worshipped; instead, it should be used as an imaginative means to explore the questions of heritage, culture, faith, and the self: in sum, the subjects of Jewish study and debate. Ozick's is thus a literature of ideas, but at the same time it reflects the humanism of Judaism, and therefore her characters, while frequently self-deluding, are always worthy of our sympathy.

WORKS CITED AND CONSULTED

Primary

Ozick, Cynthia. *Art and Ardor. Essays.* New York: Knopf, 1983.
———. *Bloodshed and Three Novellas.* New York: Knopf, 1976.
———. *The Cannibal Galaxy.* New York: Knopf, 1983.
———. *Levitation: Five Fictions.* New York: Knopf, 1982.
———. *The Messiah of Stockholm.* New York: Knopf, 1987.
———. *Metaphor and Memory: Essays.* New York: Knopf, 1989.
———. *The Pagan Rabbi and Other Stories.* New York: Knopf, 1971.
———. *The Shawl.* New York: Vintage Books, 1989.
———. *Trust.* New York: New American Library, 1966.

Secondary

Bloom, Harold, ed. *Cynthia Ozick.* Modern Critical Views. New York: Chelsea House, 1986.

Borchers, Hans. "Of Suitcases and Other Burdens: The Ambiguities of Cynthia Ozick's Image of Germany." *Centennial Review* 35 (1991): 607–24.

Chertok, Haim. "Ozick's Hoofprints." *Modern Jewish Studies Annual* 6 (*Yiddish* 6.4 [1987]): 5–12.

Cohen, Sarah Blacher. *Cynthia Ozick's Comic Art: From Levity to Liturgy*. Bloomington: Indiana University Press, 1993.

Kauvar, Elaine M. *Cynthia Ozick's Fiction: Tradition and Invention*. Bloomington: Indiana University Press, 1993.

Lowin, Joseph. *Cynthia Ozick*. Boston: Twayne, 1988.

Pinsker, Sanford. *The Uncompromising Fictions of Cynthia Ozick*. Columbia: University of Missouri Press, 1987.

GRACE PALEY
(December 11, 1922–   )

Ann Charters

BIOGRAPHY

Grace Paley, writer and social activist, was born in the Bronx, New York, the third child of the physician Isaac Goodside (Gutseit) and his wife Manya. In 1906, both of her parents had immigrated as a young married couple from Russia after waves of pogroms against the Jews swept Eastern Europe. Their first daughter and son were born shortly after their arrival in the United States. Later, Paley felt that "as the youngest, I was cherished" (Arcana 22).

In New York, Isaac Goodside quickly earned his degree in medicine and began his practice in an office in the family's home in the Bronx. He worked long hours every day to support his wife, his three children, his mother, and his two sisters, all of whom lived together in the house at 1538 Hoe Street. In this nest of adults, Paley remembered that she was both "let alone a lot, and . . . over-cared for" (Arcana 19). A headstrong teenager, she did poorly in high school, much to her family's disappointment. After graduation, she briefly attended New York City College, but dropped out and worked at a series of office jobs after her father insisted that she must learn secretarial skills in order to support herself.

On June 20, 1942, while still a teenager, Grace married her first husband, Jess Paley, the son of German Jews who had immigrated to America many generations before. In the early years of their marriage, he served in the Signal Corps in the South Pacific. Like many veterans returning home at the end of World War II, he suffered psychologically from his war experience and could only work sporadically as a photographer to support Grace and their two children, Nora (born in 1949) and Danny (born in 1951). The family lived in cramped apartments in Greenwich Village, where Grace was fully occupied as the primary caretaker of the children, managing the household on her husband's uncertain income.

In the 1950s, Paley lived what she later considered a laid-back bohemian or "Beat" lifestyle (Arcana 77), but at the time, she had no friends among younger Beat women writers in the Village like Diane DiPrima or Hettie Jones. Later Paley said that she regarded what she called "fifties fiction" as a "masculine fiction, whether traditional, avant-garde, or—later—Beat" (*Collected Stories* x). Before her marriage, she had taken a course in writing poetry at the New School from W. H. Auden, who encouraged her to write in the language she actually heard and spoke, instead of in stilted English. After her marriage, she wrote letters and poems and "thought about language a lot. That was important to me. That was my teacher. My fiction teacher was poetry" (Charters 1484).

As the mother of young children, Paley gradually became aware that what was going on in her own life could become the subject of fiction rather than poetry. Like many of the Beat writers, when she began to create fiction, she wrote autobiographically, the chosen form of many marginalized writers. Later she told an interviewer that she "began to think of certain subject matter, women's lives specifically, and what was happening around me. . . . All sorts of things began to worry me, and I began to think about them a lot. I couldn't deal with any of this subject matter in poetry" (Charters 1485).

Eighteen months after the birth of Paley's second child, she became pregnant again and decided to have an abortion. Confiding her situation to friends among the other mothers watching their young children in Washington Square Park, Paley recalled, "There wasn't anything that we didn't talk about together. I had my two and they were both in one carriage and I said, 'You know, I just can't have this baby.' And the woman I was talking to said, 'Yes.' She told me about this guy. And I went there with Jess; we went there together and we did it" (Arcana 59). In the introduction to her volume of collected stories, Paley explained how recuperating from her abortion in 1953 gave her the opportunity to begin writing short fiction: "I became sick enough for the children to remain in Greenwich House . . . but not so sick that I couldn't sit at our living-room table to write or type all day. I began the story 'Goodbye and Good Luck' and to my surprise carried it through to the end. So much prose" (ix).

Paley completed her first story out of the need "to speak in some inventive way about our female and male lives in those years" and feeling "a real physical pressure, probably in the middle of my chest—maybe just to the right of the heart," which she attributed to "the storyteller's pain: Listen! I *have* to tell you something!" (ix). She wanted to write a story "about lots of older women I knew who didn't get married," and she began by quoting six words that echoed in her mind, a phrase spoken by her husband's unmarried aunt while visiting them: "I was popular in certain circles" (Charters 1485).

Putting her children in daycare, Paley gained possession of quiet afternoons for her own creative work. She followed her first story, "Goodbye and Good Luck," with two others, "The Contest" and "A Woman, Young and Old." Paley realized that she could tell stories based on her own life in a distinctively personal narrative voice, mingling "the street language and the home language with its Russian and Yiddish accents, a language my early characters knew well, the only language I spoke" (*Collected Stories* x). Relying on autobiographical material as the basis of her fiction, she developed a tone as a writer that reflected her own ebullient personality, what critic Judith Arcana has described as a "nurturant sensibility that dictates fierce pacifism and stubborn, intense personal attachments" (58).

In the next six years, Paley produced only eight more stories. She sent them out to magazines, and after many rejections, "Goodbye and Good Luck" and "The Contest" were accepted by *Accent: A Quarterly of New Literature*. She was offered a contract for a short-story collection when Doubleday editor Ken McCormick, the father of two of her children's playmates, liked her first three stories and said that he would publish a book if she would write more stories like them. Her first book, *The Little Disturbances of Man*, was published in 1959 to considerable critical acclaim. In 1961, Paley was awarded a Guggenheim Fellowship; in 1966, she was the recipient of a National Endowment for the Arts award. *The Little Disturbances of Man* was reprinted in a second hardcover edition by Viking Press in 1968 and in a paperback edition by the New American Library in 1973.

The following year her second story collection, *Enormous Changes at the Last Minute*, was published by Farrar Straus Giroux, which followed it with Paley's third collection, *Later the Same Day*, in 1985. A volume of *The Collected Stories* appeared in 1994, forty-five stories written over more than thirty years. As Paley told an interviewer, "There is a long time in me between knowing and telling" (Charters 1102).

The reason for the "long time" between stories in Paley's productivity may be found in her commitment to social activism. Interviewer Mickey Pearlman found that as "the consummate peace activist," Paley had "lost track of how many times she was arrested in the sixties during protests against American involvement in Vietnam, at marches against the use of nuclear power, and at rallies for women's rights" (24). At a dinner party celebrating her sixty-fifth birthday in 1987, six months before her retirement from teaching in the writing program at Sarah Lawrence College, Paley was presented with a scroll inscribed "To Grace, who made getting arrested a creative act, and going to jail an education" (Arcana 217). Ironically, in the following year, she was designated the first official New York State author by an act of the state legislature.

In hindsight, it is clear that Paley's life as a mother of young children became the source of both her art and her politics (Arcana 64). Beginning with a demonstration in Greenwich Village to get a fenced playground around her children's public school, Paley escalated her activities to help in the struggle for civil rights. Later, with neighborhood and women's groups, she demonstrated against the Vietnam and Gulf wars and traveled to political meetings in Sweden, Russia, Central America, and China. Since her second marriage in 1972 to the landscape architect, playwright, and pacifist Robert Nichols, Paley has divided her time between her apartment on West Eleventh Street in Greenwich Village

and Nichols's farm in Vermont, involving herself in environmental issues, especially the antinuclear movement. She defines her political stance as "pacifist
anarchism," believing that "your politics is where your life is" (Arcana 94). In
1994, in Paley's introduction to her collected stories, she also acknowledged her
debt as a writer to the women's movement:

I was a woman writing at the early moment when small drops of worried resentment
and noble rage were secretly, slowly building into the second wave of the women's
movement. I didn't know my small drop presence or usefulness in this accumulation.
Others like . . . Tillie Olsen, who was writing her stories through the forties and fifties,
had more consciousness than I and suffered more. (xi)

CRITICISM

In translating her life into works of short fiction, Paley has created what
Arcana has recognized as

a community of characters within a complex of evolving themes: a story cycle . . . neither
so fully integrated nor so deliberately constructed as [Sherwood Anderson's] *Winesburg,
Ohio*, Grace Paley's stories, written over a thirty-five year period, are perhaps more like
the cycle of Faulkner's Yoknapatawpha tales; they describe and populate—with few
exceptions—a neighborhood of characters who share and exchange knowledge of their
mutual history. (87–88)

Thirty-one of Paley's forty-five stories are told in the first person, often in the
voice of a persona named "Faith," who reappears in later stories that recall
characters, continue episodes, or refer to conversations in earlier stories. The
progression of the stories reflects the narrator's maturing social and ethical consciousness as she gains perspective on her family and surroundings. Paley believes that "the attempt to distinguish between right and wrong is essentially the
attempt to see clearly," and her characters, who are often representatives of
different ideas and social movements, strive to define a moral base in their own
chaotic lives (Arcana 112).

Paley's use of her own direct experience to suggest incidents for her stories
sometimes misleads readers expecting a literal translation of her life into her
fiction. Naïve readers who believe that the fictional character named Faith is
actually Grace Paley are surprised to learn that in "real life" the author has a
daughter named Nora and a son named Danny, instead of the two fictional sons
named Tonto and Richard who reappear as Faith's children in various stories.
Paley bases her fiction on the events and people in her own life, but she uses
poetic license in creating works of literature. Nonetheless, her stories can be
read as the responses of a woman with an active social conscience representative
of other radicalized women of her time. She accepts her responsibility as a writer
to "write as damn well as I can" (Arcana 101) to help secure the future of

literature. In her writing, she has also said that she tries to foster the idea that "people ought to live in mutual aid and concern, listening to one another's stories" (Arcana 101).

Paley's narratives primarily dramatize her relationships with the men in her life and the shifting tensions evoked by the demands of her different roles of daughter, lover, wife, and mother. Loosely linked incidents portray the female protagonist's experiences from childhood to middle age. Paley's stories cohere as a unity through the agency of her narrative voice. Language is the key to her art, allowing her to eschew sentimentality in her sketches of a mid-twentieth-century woman's domestic life in New York City. As the novelist Jonathan Baumbach recognized, "The voice of Paley's fiction—quirky, tough, wise-ass, vulnerable, bruised into wisdom by the knocks of experience—is the triumph and defining characteristic of her art" (23).

ANALYSIS

Paley's most frequently anthologized story, "A Conversation with My Father," from her second collection, *Enormous Changes at the Last Minute*, illustrates her fictional method and emphasizes the importance of her distinctive narrative voice. Told by a first-person narrator, it is a story-within-a-story in which a dutiful middle-aged daughter attempts to please her eighty-six-year-old dying father by writing a conventional story at his request in the manner of Maupassant or Chekhov. Since her father criticizes her unconventional stories, she creates a story in a short single paragraph that is an unadorned vignette about one of her neighbors in Manhattan, a mother who joined her son in his addiction to heroin and was left alone to grieve when he finally gave up his drug habit.

This grim example of social realism leaves her father unimpressed. After he criticizes her story, she rewrites it, lengthening it into seven paragraphs with more physical details about the characters and the neighborhood setting, a smattering of dialogue, and a barrage of descriptive adjectives. Her father is still not satisfied, and the narrative ends with him arguing with the narrator, who considerately allows him to have the last word.

While the inner story in "A Conversation with My Father" is told as a plot summary in simple standard English declarative sentences, the frame story proceeds mostly through a colloquial dialogue between the father and the daughter. In the contrast between the two ways of telling a story, Paley is showing the reader what she considers essential to memorable fiction—the sound of spoken English expressed in a lively exchange between two characters. Both stories contain clearly delineated plots and characters, but only Paley's frame story seems to have sufficient dimensionality as fiction. In it, she allows her readers what she calls "enough space to move around" on the printed page (Arcana 101), so they can interact imaginatively in the story she is telling. When Paley lengthens the inner story at her father's request by adding more physical details

about the characters' appearances and behavior, her narrative assumes an even
more opaque texture. It gains in humor but continues to lack the poetic resonance that makes her frame story come to life.

In "A Conversation with My Father," the narrator's father complains that she
cannot write a plain, ordinary story: "I object not to facts but to people sitting
in trees talking senselessly, voices from who knows where" (162). Paley's fictional father is referring to an earlier story also appearing in *Enormous Changes
at the Last Minute*, her story "Faith in a Tree." There, in the first person, she
describes her protagonist on an afternoon in Washington Square Park "sitting
on the twelve-foot-high, strong, long arm of a sycamore, my feet swinging"
(78), conversing with a group of other mothers and "Saturday fathers" watching
their children.

"Faith in a Tree" ends with a description of an anti–Vietnam War protest
march through the park led by a group of grownups "a few years behind me in
the mommy-and-daddy business, pushing little go-carts with babies in them, a
couple of three-year-olds hanging on" (97). After a policeman turns up to stop
them—"No parades in the park"—Faith's older son Richard becomes furious
that his mother and her friends "didn't just stand up to that stupid cop and say
fuck you" (97). He takes a piece of pink chalk and copies onto the playground
blacktop the slogan on the protesters' placards showing a napalmed Vietnamese
child: "WOULD YOU BURN A CHILD? WHEN NECESSARY" (97).

In her earliest story collection, Paley's narratives are perhaps most poignant
when her young abandoned wives describe the behavior of their husbands, portrayed as irredeemably irresponsible fathers but irresistible friends and lovers.
(When this collection was reprinted in 1968, Paley was angry to see that the
book's subtitle had been changed by Viking Press from *The Little Disturbances
of Man: Stories of Women and Men at Love* to *The Little Disturbances of Man:
Stories of Men and Women in Love*.) Stories like "The Pale Pink Roast," "The
Used-Boy Raisers," and "A Subject of Childhood" dramatize the fragile emotional link between wives, husbands, and lovers and the much stronger, unbreak-
able link between mother and son. The strength of family bonding helps
immigrant parents (who do not enjoy the luxury of divorce, unlike first-
generation Faith) to survive the rough passage of their children's assimilation
into mainstream American culture in stories like "The Loudest Voice." This
story, one of Paley's funniest, examines the "tra-la-la for Christmas" in a public
grammar school where a little girl from a Jewish family is chosen to narrate the
Christmas play celebrating the virgin birth of Jesus Christ.

Paley's second collection, *Enormous Changes at the Last Minute*, is her
strongest. In choosing the order of the stories, she subtly emphasized the brutality of urban life and its cost to the children in the inner city, whether a young
Negro boy killed after fooling around with his friends on the platform between
trains in the subway ("Samuel") or a teenage runaway girl murdered (or driven
to suicide) after sexual molestation in the apartment of a junky ("The Little
Girl"). Her most ambitious story, "The Long-Distance Runner," concludes the

book, a bravura account of Faith's return to her childhood home (located in this piece of short fiction in Brooklyn's Brighton Beach instead of the factual Bronx). In the story, Faith is introduced jogging to stay in shape after turning forty-two, intent on investigating "the old neighborhood streets a couple of times, before old age and urban renewal ended them and me" (179).

In "The Long-Distance Runner," Faith finds that African Americans are now living in her old neighborhood, and after young toughs hanging out on the sidewalk give her a hard time, she runs up the stairs to what had been her parents' apartment when she was a little girl. Regressing to childhood, she pounds on the door and cries out, "Mama! Mama! let me in!" It is opened by Mrs. Luddy, "a slim woman whose age I couldn't invent" (187), a single mother with four young children who allows Faith to stay in the apartment. Three weeks later, when Faith returns home to her second husband, Jack, and her two grown sons, they welcome her casually while going about their usual activities. She tries to tell them where she has been, but her critical son Richard replies, "What are you talking about? Cut the baby talk" (198). Finally she explains to her husband what she has learned from the experience: "A woman inside the steamy energy of middle-age runs and runs. She finds the houses and streets where her childhood happened. She lives in them. She learns as though she was still a child what in the world is coming next" (198).

Paley published her first book of poetry, *Leaning Forward*, the same year as her third story collection, *Later the Same Day* (1985). The stories in this volume reflect her increasing absorption in writing poetry. They are often short poetic sketches, like "Mother" (two printed pages), an autobiographical fragment dramatizing Paley's memory of her mother's unhappiness making "worried preparations for death" from cancer as a middle-aged woman. In a brilliant juxtaposition of dialogue and narrative summary, Paley evokes her mother's concern for her daughter's future, since she (the mother) "would not be present, she thought, when I was twenty." This classic Paley story "is shorter than most short fiction; its language is unusual in its quickly executed images and occasionally bizarre sentence structure; and both the framing and the phrasing of the story remind the reader, visually and rhythmically, of poetry" (Arcana 145).

Paley's sensitivity to the emotional lives of women and children is always apparent in *The Collected Stories* (1994). Now past the storms of her own life with her husbands, sons, and parents, she acknowledges in the last story, "Listening," that she is free to give her full response to the claims on her attention of her close women friends. In this sense, Paley's fiction chronicles her radicalization as a feminist. She has stated that she does not want to create works of art in her poetry and fiction, but "works of truth" (Arcana 102). For Paley, "writing the lives of women *is* politics" (Pearlman 26).

WORKS CITED AND CONSULTED

Primary

Paley, Grace. *The Collected Stories*. New York: Farrar Straus Giroux, 1994.
―――. *Enormous Changes at the Last Minute*. New York: Farrar Straus Giroux, 1974.
―――. *Just As I Thought*. New York: Farrar Straus Giroux, 1998.
―――. *Later the Same Day*. New York: Farrar Straus Giroux, 1985; New York: Penguin, 1986.
―――. *Leaning Forward: Poems*. Maine: Granite Press, 1985.
―――. *The Little Disturbances of Man*. Garden City, N.Y.: Doubleday, 1959; New York: Meridian, 1960; New York: Viking, 1968; New York: New American Library, 1973; Penguin, 1985.
―――. *New and Collected Poems*. Maine: Tilbury House, 1992.

Secondary

Arcana, Judith. *Grace Paley's Life Stories*. Urbana: University of Illinois Press, 1993.
Baumbach, Jonathan, ed. *Writers as Teachers/Teachers as Writers*. New York: Holt, Rinehart, & Winston, 1970.
Charters, Ann. "A Conversation with Grace Paley." *The Story and Its Writer*. 4th ed. Boston: Bedford Books of St. Martin's Press, 1995. 1102, 1484–1487.
Isaacs, Neal D. *Grace Paley: A Study of the Short Fiction*. Boston: Twayne, 1990.
Pearlman, Mickey. *Listen to Their Voices*. (Interview with Grace Paley.) Boston: Houghton Mifflin, 1993. 26.

VELMA POLLARD
(1937–   )

Pierre-Damien Mvuyekure

BIOGRAPHY

Velma Pollard was born at Comfort Hall, St. Andrew, Jamaica. She has studied in Jamaica, the United States, and Canada. She holds a Ph.D. in English education and is a senior lecturer at the University of the West Indies in Kingston, Jamaica, where she is involved in creative writing and research on both the language of Caribbean literature and the language of the Rastafari. Her research is primarily focused on the teaching of English in a Creole environment. Velma Pollard has taught English in high schools in Trinidad, Canada, and the United States. As a writer, she is famous for her poems, short stories, a novella, and a novel, all deeply rooted in the tradition of the Creole language of Jamaica. In 1988, she published *Crown Point and Other Poems,* a volume of poetry, followed by *Considering Woman* (1989), her first collection of short stories. Her next works were *Shame Trees Don't Grow Here* (1992), a collection of poems, and *Homestretch* (1994), a novel. In 1994, she published *Karl and Other Stories*, a novella and a collection of short stories.

Velma Pollard's stories have appeared in numerous regional and international journals, including *Caribbean Quarterly, Bim, Jamaica Journal, Arts Review*, and in an anthology, *Over Our Way*; in addition, she has been published by prestigious presses such as Longman in its Caribbean Writers series. Velma Pollard has participated in the International Short Story Conferences held in Iowa and New Orleans and won the Casa de las Americas literary award for her novella *Karl*.

CRITICISM

Although Velma Pollard is a prolific and well-published poet, novelist, and short-story writer who has been compared to Erna Brodber, Zora Neale Hurston,

and Jamaica Kincaid, critical studies on her work are not yet available (at least
in the United States), except for a three-paragraph entry by Evelyn O'Callaghan
in *Encyclopedia of Post-colonial Literatures in English*, published in 1994. The
short biographical notes included in her work emphasize the fact that she is
particularly interested in Creole languages of the Anglophone Caribbean region,
the language of Caribbean literature, as well as Caribbean women's writing.
These themes demand critical attention for a better understanding and appreciation of Pollard's contribution to the short-story genre. Perhaps with more scholarly attention, Pollard will be recognized for her shifting in language use or code
switching from standard English to Jamaican Creole (which she calls JC) without warning to the reader.

ANALYSIS

   In *The Empire Writes Back: Theory and Practice in Post-colonial Literatures*
(1989), the necessity of re-placing language as a textual strategy in postcolonial
writing emerges as a primary concern. Because language functions as a means
of power, it is perceived as imperative that "post-colonial writing define itself
by seizing the language of the center and re-placing it in a discourse fully
adapted to the colonized place" (Ashcroft, Griffiths, and Tiffin 38). Elsewhere
the study identifies a Creole literary presence whereby Caribbean writers such
as Wilson Harris, George Lamming, Derek Walcott, and others employ "code-
switching and vernacular transcription" in order to "achieve the dual result of
abrogating the Standard English and appropriating an english [*sic*] as a culturally
significant discourse" (46). Such postcolonial thinking toward the English language permeates Velma Pollard's *Considering Woman* and *Karl and Other Stories*.
   Evelyn O'Callaghan has argued that although the striking feature of Velma
Pollard's writing is "the exploitation of the resources of Jamaican language
varieties," the writing does not simply transpose oral Creole, but "juggles and
juxtaposes registers of English and Creole and styles, including biblical and
proverbial, in a manner both casual and semantically complex" (1285). As is
further illustrated in her afterword to *Considering Woman*, Pollard is conscious
of language as an issue in her writing. She preempts harsh criticism from her
readers and critics by apologizing for any confusion that might have resulted
from the use of both English and Creole languages, especially when the latter
are related to the former. Moreover, she defines the language she uses in her
stories as Jamaican Creole or JC, "an English related creole, the result of the
interaction of English and several West African languages in a plantation situation" (73). Additionally, she relates that fiction writers use Jamaican Creole
and other native languages to achieve "greater accuracy in their representation
of character" (74). In other words, Jamaican Creole is used as an element of
verisimilitude in characterization and setting. A close analysis of *Considering
Woman* and *Karl and Other Stories* reveals this crucial function of language.

Considering Woman contains nine stories divided into three sections, "Parables," "Cages," and "Tales of Mothering," prefaced by two poems, "Women Poets (with Your Permission)" and "Version." The two poems set the tone of the stories by showing a woman's creative writing being challenged or ridiculed by the "little man" of "Women Poets" and Adam of "Version." In "Version," Eve implores Adam not to make her a woman-poet, but simply a poet, because she wants to be free and genderless. The stories in "Parables" display the world of folklore, mystery, and fantasy, coupled with everyday life such as the role and presence of the woman in society. The "Cages" stories consider female-male relationships in marriage, while those in "Tales of Mothering" showcase the bonds between sisters, a daughter and a mother, and a grandchild and a grandmother.

"Parable I" tells the story of a grandmother's log that one day metamorphosed into a snake after having fooled people for many years into thinking that it was a log. Instead of leaving the snake alone, someone called the police, who came and took the snake to the zoo. Thereafter, a man was seen walking with his wife's head tucked under his arm, dripping blood. On the surface, the story seems to suggest that the people should have respected the snake as they do the snake of Damballah, the Voodoo god of fecundity. For Pollard, however, this story has deeper implications. In an unpublished interview with Alisha Faciane, the author relates that she is "partly talking about the fact that people are making noise about women doing this and doing that when women were always there, just as the snake was always there but if people thought it was a log that is their problem" (1).

"Parable I" introduces us gently to Pollard's use of both Jamaican Creole and English. Throughout the narrative, the pronoun "we" is substituted for its possessive form "our," as in "invited we friends." Similarly, there is an alternating absence and presence of the pronoun "it" in the story: "is true the snake didn't threaten anybody; is true nobody even try to find out if is a poison snake; and it didn't run, it only moved ve-e-r-y slowly" (2). The representation of Jamaican Creole speech, however, is more apparent in "Parable II." Here we encounter a story about Auntie, a woman who used to walk with her right hand cupped halfway, supposedly holding a tiny child. One day, after the small child changed into a little boy and jumped into a sinkhole, her niece saw her walking with a straight right hand: "My heart leap, but you know, a didn't cry, is like I know that sink-hole didn't go to the sea. I followed my mind. Just as if somebody was guiding me. And a walk clear cross the town to where I think the sink-hole come out. . . . I find the spot but not a sign of the child" (4). In this short excerpt, "a" and "I" are used interchangeably in a code-switching mode. In her afterword, Pollard explains that when she uses Creole speech forms, she writes them as she herself speaks when she speaks Jamaican Creole. "Sometimes, for example I write 'a' and sometimes 'I' to express the equivalent of the English 'I.' That is the way I speak. I know for example that you can't be emphatic with 'a' in the way you can with 'I' " (74). Even with this theory in mind, it is difficult to decide whether or not, "I" in "I know that sink-hole" is more emphatic than "a didn't cry." It is clear, however, that the speech pattern fits the character of Auntie and her folkloric tale. Elsewhere, the story replaces "my hand" with "me hand," "my" with "me," and "me" with "mi" to the point of confusion, as in the sentence "Now you know how many years I been walking with that little one in my hand and a never had a mishap; and now this one, so much bigger, got lost from mi now. I sit down at the street side with me hand at mi chin" (4), but this confusion does not obfuscate the understanding of the text.

In contrast to the "Parable" stories, the "Cages" stories use Jamaican Creole only rarely, perhaps because the characters seem to be more educated. The structure of these stories is woven around women's quest for satisfaction and freedom in marriage. Interestingly, the title of the stories comes from Derek Walcott's play *The Joker of Seville* (1978), an adaptation of the seventeenth-century Spanish play *El bulador de Sevilla* by Tirso de Molina. The stories in this section are prefaced by an epigraph from Walcott's play, "You beasts must love your cages after all" (8). This is a line from Don Juan Tenorio, a knight, to Tisbea, a fishergirl of Spain, toward the end of the fifth scene of the first act in *The Joker of Seville*. After a shipwreck, Don Juan finds himself on a beach in the New World and, true to his seductive nature, tells Tisbea to walk naked as "an unremorseful Eve" (Walcott 47). Tisbea answers that she will give whatever he is looking for as any good wife should, after which Don Juan bursts into insults and calls Tisbea heartless and calculating. By calling women beasts who love their cages, it is clear that Don Juan sees marriage as a cage in which he cannot freely seduce every woman who comes his way. One can argue that in these stories Pollard challenges the images of women in writings by male writers. As analysis shows, however, the three women of the three stories, Jean, Joan, and Joy, are all beasts in cages; only Joan escapes from the cage.

"Cage I" is rich in metaphors of beast and cage. Jean laments that in the zoo there is enough space for animals occasionally to leap forward and assumes that a "bird of Hugh's size would have a very large cage with enough space for a good whirl now and then. And even so they show claustrophobic tendencies" (9). In this excerpt, Jean refers to the fact that her husband is always longing for a space to sit quietly, read, and have nothing to do with his wife. Hugh compares Jean to "an octopus trying to hold him in a sort of multiple embrace" (11). Yet marriage is not a cage for Hugh: as we learn in "Cage III," he has a mistress, Joy. Unfortunately, Joy is as trapped in the cage as Jean is in "Cage I," to the extent that the narrator concludes the story by saying, "Perhaps when the door is open, you can't really feel the cageness of the cage" (20).

In "Cage II," Pollard returns to the myth of the cave to present Joan as a woman trapped inside with her children, washing and cooking, and "the original cave-man coming home every night and moving the stone a little so you just glimpse the light of day and grunting and getting into bed" (15). In stark contrast to Jean and Joy, Joan leaves her husband for another man. Just as it is impossible for Plato's caveman to return to his cave once he is aware of the world outside, so it is impossible for Joan to go back to Jim's cage.

Except for "My Mother," in which people attending a funeral break into Jamaican Creole, the stories in "Tales of Mothering" consistently use standard English. In "Gran," the longest story of the collection, Pollard brings lyrical and pastoral poetry to the short story. Nursery rhymes and Christian hymns shared between a mother and her children evoke the narrator's memory of her grandmother. In the process of remembering, the narrator compares women to tangerine trees: not only do both have wombs and some have babies, but also their babies look exactly like their mothers. She sees in the tangerine trees an affirmation that "Nature is birth repeated a hundred times" (41). In other words, she sees in her own inception a repetition of her grandmother's birth, a parallel made explicit when she describes how her grandmother now depends on her for fulfillment, while she depends on her grandmother for "an ego inflation" she did not earn but "was heir to—first child of her eldest child with her face written on me; each feeding the other in a re-enactment of the creation pattern again" (58). In a sense, this story sharply contrasts with the "Cages" stories in that Gran is portrayed as an independent woman whom her granddaughter calls a matriarch, "some kind of founder of a line, some large female inspirer marking off a crossroads on some time map in a family" (51).

Karl and Other Stories, a collection that includes a novella and seven stories, is consistently written in Jamaican Creole and standard English, and contains international themes about Jamaicans in the United States, Jamaican students in Canada, and Jamaican ex-servicemen of European wars. In "Karl," a novella that takes place in Jamaica and Canada, the eponymous protagonist receives a scholarship to study in Canada and develops high hopes for the future. But when he returns to Jamaica, Karl is unable to adjust to the system and eventually commits suicide. In marked contrast, Kenneth, another young man who succeeds academically, breaks with the establishment and runs his own business. Pollard has argued that the message in this story is that Jamaican society "is so complex that it is not enough to be academically bright. There are a lot of things that you are asked to be" (Faciane 3).

This pessimism also runs through the successive stories "A Night's Tale," "Rainbow Corner," and "Altamont Jones." These narratives return to the theme of husbands and wives. In "Altamont Jones," Jones is forced out of the house when his wife suspects that he is having an affair with a "red gal." Here characters speak Jamaican Creole whenever they are angry: " 'Yes, you nat answerin'," the high-pitched female voice continued. 'I know dih trick; so dat everybody will seh I am a virgo an you are a nice quiet man' " (133). When tempers cool, standard English returns.

The theme of internationalism is evident in "Georgia and Them There United States" and "Betsy Hyde." "Georgia and Them There United States" comments on the lives of Jamaicans in the United States around 1953. It begins with a letter from Schenectady, New York, in which Aunt Teach informs her sister in Jamaica that Georgia's visa will come through, and that she is celebrating her American citizenship. In this story, we encounter opposing pictures of the United States. Some Jamaicans think that the United States is paradise, so glamorized that no one ever "questioned whether America was a great place to be" (99). But Aunt Teach's niece describes ugliness and depression in the Bronx, "a place that could not be complimented: burnt out, dirty, dingy, waste" (96).

"Betsy Hyde" is the only story in which Pollard directly confronts the scars of colonialism and postcolonialism. Here the main character, Betsy, endures abuses from her husband, Jed, an ex-serviceman who fought in Europe and came back a changed man "with an American twang" (115). When Betsy consults a seer-man, she is told that it is "the quicksilver in his head that was responsible for some of the craziness he would do. Blame the war for that" (126). As this short excerpt suggests, Pollard is not only writing of the colonial history of her people, but also is writing back to the empire. In her interview with Faciane, she revealed that when she and other female writers from the Commonwealth were asked to contribute to a collection called *Unbecoming Daughters of the Empire*, most of their remarks about "being the children of the Empire, of Britain" were negative (9).

WORKS CITED AND CONSULTED

Primary

D'Costa, Jean, and Velma Pollard, eds. *Over Our Way: A Collection of Caribbean Short Stories for Young Readers*. 2nd ed. Kingston, Jamaica: Longman Caribbean, 1994.
Pollard, Velma. *Considering Woman*. London: Women's Press, 1989.
———. *Crown Point and Other Poems*. Leeds, UK: Peepal Tree Press, 1988.
———. *Dread Talk: The Language of Rastafari*. Kingston, Jamaica: Canoe Press, 1994.
———. *Homestretch*. Burnt Mill, Harlow, Essex, UK: Longman, 1994.
———. *Karl and Other Stories*. UK: Longman, 1994.
———. *Personal Interview by Alisha Facaine*. October 1996.
———. *Shame Trees Don't Grow Here*. Leeds, UK: Peepal Tree Press, 1992.

Secondary

Ashcroft, Bill, Gareth Griffiths, and Helen Tiffin. *The Empire Writes Back: Theory and Practice in Post-colonial Literatures*. New York: Routledge, 1989.
O'Callaghan, Evelyn. "Pollard, Velma (1937)." *Encyclopedia of Post-Colonial Literatures in English*. Vol. 2. Ed. Eugene Benson and L. W. Conolly. New York: Routledge, 1994. 1285.
Walcott, Derek. *The Joker of Seville and O Babylon!* New York: Farrar Straus Giroux, 1978.

VICTOR SAWDON PRITCHETT
(December 16, 1900–March 20, 1997)

Karen Tracey

BIOGRAPHY

V. S. Pritchett has not yet become the subject of extended critical dialogue, yet he is among the most highly respected of twentieth-century short-story writers. Pritchett was born in London in 1900 into a family that moved frequently as his father changed jobs and struggled with debt. He was educated sporadically at several different schools and was apprenticed into the leather trade in 1916 when he would have preferred a university education. But Pritchett persisted in educating himself and left London in 1920 for France to pursue his dream of becoming a writer. Though his move paralleled that of Hemingway and other "Lost Generation" writers, his life never became interwoven with theirs. He developed his craft from his wide reading in fiction and supported himself by working as a correspondent for the *Christian Science Monitor* in France, Spain, and Ireland. He began publishing apprenticeship work after losing that job in 1928: a travel book, a novel, and his first collection of short fiction, the *Spanish Virgin and Other Stories* (1930).

Throughout a long and productive career, Pritchett wrote journalism, travel books, criticism, autobiography, and reviews along with short stories and novels, compiling a daunting collection of work. He was honored repeatedly with awards, honorary degrees, visiting professorships, and prestigious positions in national and international literary societies; he was knighted in 1975. He is best known for his short fiction, collected over the years in several volumes: *You Make Your Own Life* (1938), *It May Never Happen* (1945), *When My Girl Comes Home* (1961), *The Saint and Other Stories* (1966), *Blind Love and Other Stories* (1969), *On the Edge of the Cliff* (1979), and *A Careless Widow and Other Stories* (1989). *The Complete Collected Stories*, containing eighty-two stories, was published in 1991. After his death in March 1997, he was celebrated with a collection of stories, novel excerpts, and criticism entitled *The Pritchett Century* (1997).

CRITICISM

In 1981, Walter Allen anointed Pritchett the "outstanding English short-story writer" after the death of D. H. Lawrence (268), but discussed his work for only seven pages. This combination of lavish praise and stinting discussion typifies Pritchett's fate in academic circles. Except for the 1982 French work by Alain Theil, *Les nouvelles de V. S. Pritchett*, no full-length book or substantive article had been published on Pritchett until fifteen years ago, when the tide began to turn. Both 1985 Twayne volumes on the *The English Short Story* (one covering 1880–1945 and the other 1945–80) include discussions of Pritchett, a tribute to his longevity. In the spring of 1986, the *Journal of the Short Story in English* devoted a special issue to Pritchett; in 1987, Dean Baldwin published a book on Pritchett in the Twayne English Authors Series; and in 1992, John J. Stinson published a full-length study of Pritchett's short stories in the Twayne Studies in Short Fiction series. Such a surge of scholarship should bode well for Pritchett's academic fate, but after all, were it not for Twayne, he would still be noticed primarily with exclamations about his undeserved neglect.

Why has Pritchett's work failed to fire the critical imagination? Each study of Pritchett faces this question. Baldwin is frankly puzzled: "The vagaries of literary politics are impossible to comprehend, but perhaps his failure to produce a major novel lies at the heart of his undeserved obscurity" (28). Thinking along similar lines, Stinson attributes some of Pritchett's neglect to the general lack of attention to the short-story form, Pritchett's specialty (xi). Some reviewers have found Pritchett too simple; others find him too ambiguous. Stinson concludes that "Pritchett provides fewer interpretive clues than most writers; consequently, neither critics nor general readers can arrive at tidily definitive interpretations of many of his stories" (3). We could take Stinson's insight further and note that Pritchett also frustrates a critic's desire to discover dominant themes or messages in an author's work as a whole, a distinctive and consistent vision, or some avenue by which one could carve out a unifying label to attach to Pritchett's art. His work simply does not invite one to form and defend critical hypotheses.

Pritchett further stymies critics because he avoided self-promotion. Despite his two autobiographies and the granting of occasional interviews, Pritchett did not project a public persona one could use as a basis for a reading of his art. He drew some stories from his own life, but many from imagination and observation as well. Furthermore, Pritchett cannot be categorized as belonging to any particular artistic "school"; he was influenced by wide reading, and while his work fits under the broad rubric of social realism, he is not closely identified with any particular group or distinctive style.

We are driven, then, to celebrate the variety and ambiguity offered by Pritchett's short fiction. First place in Pritchett's stories usually goes to characters, and what an astounding variety of characters! Pritchett's stories are written from a range of points of view, from first and third person, usually from a male but sometimes from a female perspective, sometimes from the main character's consciousness, and sometimes from an observer's stance. Characters are drawn freely from the English middle or lower-middle classes, and occasionally from other nationalities and classes as well. The main characters are of all ages, from a seven-year-old child to an elderly gentleman. Because Pritchett's career spans so much of the century, his characters, too, populate at least six different decades.

ANALYSIS

We begin our analysis of Pritchett's short fiction by turning to the final story in one of his last published collections, "The Image Trade" from *A Careless Widow and Other Stories* (1989). Photographer Zut comes to take writer Pearson's picture. In a psychological game of one-upmanship, Pearson attempts to control the photographic session by offering himself with apparent openness, while Zut tries to strip Pearson down to his essentials. Pearson denies that he can be thus stripped: "If you take me naked, you will miss all the et cetera of my life. I am all et cetera," he thinks to himself (*Complete Collected Stories* 1214; all page references to Pritchett's stories are from *Complete Collected Stories*). Yet Pearson has also noted the similarity between his work and Zut's: "As a writer, in the news too and in another branch of the human-image trade, Pearson depended on seeing people and things as strictly they are not." But Pearson is disturbed and astounded by the image Zut chooses to display in the exhibition: "No sparkling anemone there but the bald head of a melancholy frog, its feet clinging to a log, floating in literature." Pearson concludes that Zut "by a mysterious accident of art had portrayed his soul instead of mine" (1218). The reader is left to conclude whether Pearson's image of Zut or Zut's image of Pearson, if either, is accurate.

One could end an analysis of any Pritchett story with a sentence beginning, "The reader is left to conclude." Pritchett loves to render characters, to explore human absurdities and insights, to touch up epiphanic moments with twists of irony, yet not to strip characters bare. Pearson admires Zut's wife because she refuses to allow Zut to take her photograph, "fearing perhaps the Evil Eye" (1218). Perhaps the author Pritchett fears to damn his characters with the Evil Eye, or to portray his own soul rather than theirs, and so he typically stops short of stripping them bare of "all the et cetera" of their lives.

This ambivalent attitude toward characters is demonstrated particularly well by "The Marvellous Girl" from *The Camberwell Beauty* (1974). The story is told in third person through the consciousness of a young artist named Francis who has been separated from his wife for two years but who has been unable to disentangle his life from hers, "for if marriages come to an end, paraphernalia hangs on" (898). The "paraphernalia" is both literal, as in the stained rug his wife wants returned to her, and emotional, as both Francis and his wife interest themselves in one another's love affairs. The narrative tracks the illogical yet realistic emotional process by which Francis falls in love with his wife's secretary, the "marvellous girl": he has mistakenly thought that she was in hospital, but she is not, and he is moved; he thinks that she is going to Canada to marry, and he bewails the thought of her sleeping in a "continent of flies and snow" (902). They both attend a dull ceremony during which a blackout leaves the crowd in the dark; he and the girl push through the crowds and darkness and find one another, maintaining a conspiracy of silence to avoid discovery by the woman who is both his estranged wife and the girl's employer. They then feel their way to a dark office where they are engaged in a passionate embrace when the lights come back on: "They got up, scared, hot-faced, hot-eyed, hating the light." Pritchett reveals their embarrassment, but he allows them to escape, to hurry "from the lighted room to get into the darkness of the city" (907).

Just so does Pritchett typically allow his characters to escape full exposure. We have a glimpse of them in moments of vulnerability, but are not allowed to dissect them thoroughly, to satisfy ourselves that we understand all there is to know about a character's response to a situation; in story after story, Pritchett concedes a privacy to his characters. When we attempt to reduce a story to a clear message about an identifiable theme, ambiguity if not obscurity is introduced. It is hard to answer with certainty even the most basic of questions of a Pritchett story: How did Francis change or what did he learn? What does the story say about marriage and love? What do the motifs of darkness and light suggest? Stinson notes that the story "causes the reader to think about modern relationships between the sexes vis-à-vis the old questions about delusion, compatibility and incompatibility, and romantic attraction," and that furthermore, it "maintains a successful double-edged effect. Readers can share the excitement of Francis's romantic infatuation, or they can view it ironically" (57).

This quality of openness, or of ambiguity, or of incompleteness, was evident in "Sense of Humour" (*You Make Your Own Life*, 1938), generally agreed to be "Pritchett's first major story" (Stinson 4). William Peden terms it "relatively simple in narrative, decidedly complex in its implications" (145); Stinson says that it "both teases and entertains" (4); Julia Boken concludes that it "underscores one of Pritchett's favorite techniques: peeling away at the character with grim irony and even then not providing enough details to see the character's inner self" (1933). The story is a rendering of a common-enough love triangle: a glib and self-confident traveling salesman (Arthur) comes to a small town and successfully courts the attractive girlfriend (Muriel) of an inarticulate country boy (Colin). But each character is more complex than such a story line might lead one to expect.

One way to read the story is to understand Muriel, rather than the narrator Arthur, as the controlling character. She is an Irish girl stuck working in a hotel in a small English town, and she wants out. She enjoys Colin's possessiveness—

"He's sloppy about me"—and admires the speed of his driving, described suggestively by the narrator, "[His motorcycle was] a red roaring thing and he opened it full out" (6); yet she also wants the relative financial security and change of scene offered by Arthur. The crisis occurs when Arthur and Muriel visit Arthur's parents to announce their engagement. Colin, who has followed them as he often does, crashes his motorcycle and is killed. Arthur sits by Muriel for hours while she sobs for Colin, and then Muriel's grief and Arthur's sympathy evolve into a passion associated with Colin and with engines: "It was like being on the mail steamer and feeling engines start under your feet, thumping louder and louder" (12). Arthur puzzles over the strange fact that Colin's death somehow ignited their passion, for "she would hardly let me touch her before that" (12); he worries whether she loved Colin all along, or even thought he was Colin. Arthur is more excited than offended by being called "Colin," as he realizes. What is "funny" in this tale about "Sense of Humour"? Arthur has this answer:

Then I kept thinking it was funny her saying "Colin!" like that in the night; it was funny it made her feel that way with me, and how it made me feel when she called me Colin. I'd never thought of her in that way, in what you might call the "Colin" way. . . . the smiles kept coming to both of us. (15–16)

By naming Arthur "Colin," Muriel gains both the material security offered by Arthur and the sexual passion offered by Colin, and at the close of the story, she is riding triumphantly with Arthur in the hearse conveying Colin's casket to its final resting place. It is difficult to know whether to condemn Muriel and Arthur for hypocrisy, to sympathize with them because of the loss of Colin, or to congratulate them on their engagement. It is a funny story, in both senses of the word.

"The Saint" and "The Fly in the Ointment," two of Pritchett's most compelling stories, were collected in *It May Never Happen and Other Stories* (1945). Both tales present young men who recognize foolishness and limitation on the part of their elders but yet do not wish to strip those elders of all dignity. Within the fictional world, they demonstrate Pritchett's attitude toward character: analyze honestly, yet restrain any judgment. They also provide outstanding examples of Pritchett's style, of his technique of allowing detail and incident inherent in the story to point toward possibilities of multiple meanings. Rarely does he impose a symbol on a story.

"The Fly in the Ointment" explores the strained relationship between a son who scrapes a living teaching at a provincial university and a father whose business has failed. The opening paragraph sets the mood of loss and alienation:

It was the dead hour of a November afternoon. Under the ceiling of level mud-coloured cloud, the latest office buildings of the city stood out alarmingly like new tombstones, among the mass of older buildings. And along the streets, the few cars and the few people appeared and disappeared slowly as if they were not following the roadway or the pavement, but some inner, personal route. (297)

The rhythms of the language support the description. The term "alarmingly" jumps from the middle of the sentence, while the final sentence wanders like the slowly moving people. The "new tombstone" in this commercial neighborhood is the father's failed business, and the traveler of the "inner, personal route" is the son who comes to offer consolation. The father "despises" the son for his lack of worldly ambitions, while the son distrusts the father he hopes to comfort. The loss and tension are evoked through the story in two images drawn from concrete detail in the story and imbued with additional meanings: the fly buzzing in the room and the son's perception of his father's two faces.

The title figure of speech invites one to consider the fly whose presence in the room irritates the father. The fly, heralded by its "small dying fizz," has been "deceived beyond its strength by the autumn sun" (302); it is doomed by the lateness of the year, if not by the father's attacks, and could represent the failing business, the failing relationship, or the failures of either or both of the characters. After climbing atop a table in a fruitless attempt to swat the fly, the father "put a heavy hand on his son's shoulder and the son felt the great helpless weight of his father's body" (303). The son longs to see his father in a positive light, yet he does not trust him, and the father's weight is literal and figurative: "He was ashamed to think how he, how they all dreaded having the gregarious, optimistic, extravagant, uncontrollable, disingenuous old man on their hands" (304).

A second, more dominant image is the son's perception of the father's two faces: "His father had two faces. There was the outer face like a soft, warm and careless daub of innocent sealing wax and inside it, as if thumbed there by a seal, was a much smaller one, babyish, shrewd, scared and hard" (300). When the innocent outer face is evident, the son is sympathetic; when the calculating inner face peers out, the son is angry and embarrassed. At one moment, "A glow of sympathy transported the younger man. He felt as though a sun had risen," but at the next, he is in "a panic of embarrassment," fearing that the father is going to confess his shortcomings (303).

At length, the son offers to give his father money should his father ever be in real need; the father misunderstands, and the little face "suddenly became dominant": "Why didn't you tell me before you could raise money? How can you raise it? Where? By when?" (305). The ironic kick most obviously targets the father, who has just been proclaiming his newfound freedom from money concerns. Yet it also suggests a faint admiration for the fighting spirit of this defeated old man.

The first-person narrator of "The Saint" is recalling his seventeenth year, during which, he announces in the opening sentence, he lost his religious faith. Together with his uncle and aunt, he had joined the Church of the Last Purification, a sect whose defining doctrine was that nothing unpleasant could possibly be real, since God loves his children and would not allow harm to befall them. The narrator, although he wishes to retain his faith, finds himself wondering about the origin of evil, reasoning that even if evil was only illusion, the illusion itself must have had an origin. The sincerity and intelligence of the narrator give Pritchett a means to pillory a ridiculous doctrine while protecting the dignity of the characters.

The narrator's uncle arranges for Mr. Timberlake, a visiting church dignitary, to reason his doubts away. If any character were ever set up to be ridiculed, that character would be Timberlake, who has "one of those torpid, enamelled smiles which were said by our enemies to be too common in our sect" (189), who has supposedly performed many miracle healings, and yet who has not sense enough to be careful while punting on the river. Refusing to follow the boy's good advice, Mr. Timberlake is swept off the punt and is left hanging by a willow branch that slowly gives way and dunks him into the river. The language in which the fallen saint is described draws out the connections in the boy's consciousness between Mr. Timberlake, saints, and idols:

One seam of shirt with its pant-loops and brace-tabs broke like a crack across the middle of Mr. Timberlake. It was like a fatal flaw in a statue, an earthquake crack that made the monumental mortal. . . . He was a declining dogma. . . . The head resting on the platter of water had the sneer of calamity on it, such as one sees in the pictures of a beheaded saint. (195)

An epiphany occurs: "The final revelation about man and society on earth had come to nobody and . . . Mr. Timberlake knew nothing at all about the origin of evil" (195); however, this relatively simple conclusion is not the primary insight offered by the story. When the narrator learns of Mr. Timberlake's death from heart disease sixteen years after this incident, he recalls the day of the punting accident and realizes that Mr. Timberlake had never talked to him about the origin of evil because he was "honest," and that for the same reason he had "made for himself a protective, sedentary blandness, an automatic smile, a collection of phrases" (199). The "ape" of doubt, which only followed the narrator, had been "inside Mr. Timberlake eating out his heart" (199). The narrator links literal heart disease with metaphorical heart disease and blames both on the ape of evil. "The Saint" finally invites the reader not merely to ridicule or to pity Mr. Timberlake, but to respect him.

Pritchett believes that each individual hopes to overcome the anonymity imposed by a "mass society," that "we look for the moment in which our privacy breaks through and reveals its significance in our comedies and disasters" (qtd. in Stinson 102). Drawing on this philosophy, Pritchett is able to write sympathetically and insightfully about characters quite unlike himself. For example, "The Sniff" from *Collected Stories* (1956) is written primarily from the point of view of a woman whose husband has recently returned from the war. Mrs. N. "has what she calls 'a woman's life,' " and she feels "that her heart has become a cage and that she cannot get out of it" (391). Mr. N. takes up painting, and although this hobby delights their children and seems preferable to the vices taken up by other returning veterans, Mrs. N. is disturbed by it: "The smell made her sniff, but he took no notice of that; he simply grunted . . . that was their only conversation" (396).

Longing to get Mr. N's attention, Mrs. N. volunteers to pose nude for him. She finds it "terrible" to be assessed by his cool artist's eye, but he does talk to her, sympathetically, about her "hard life. . . . Shut up with three children, always at the stove or at the sink" (398). She realizes that "he had a life, a life she couldn't share, a secret life she could not enter. Wonderfully kind he sounded—wonderfully kind, just like a man who is being unfaithful to you. . . . She sat there, naked, ironical, muttering her thoughts." Mr. N. seems to believe that she can also get a life, while she is limited by her notions of what a woman's life consists of: "A woman's life is a man, a child, another person" (399).

Mr. N. sees that his wife needs a life of her own, but he cannot free her from her house and child-care chores; on the contrary, he wants to quit his job to paint full-time. Mrs. N. is conscious of living in a cage, boxed in by her "woman's life" and, ironically, by her inability to imagine for herself a fulfilling life like the one her husband has found for himself. In fact, at the close of the story, she has "enslaved" herself to her husband's mistress, the painting, and she takes him dinner trays and keeps the children away. The story deftly sketches a cultural dilemma playing out in the lives of these characters that Pritchett does not venture to resolve: "It is hard to say what the present situation is, whether it is improving or whether it is becoming one of those everlasting situations that mark the characters and memories of children" (391). The "situation" is both the impasse between Mr. and Mrs. N. and the impasse between men and women as Pritchett sees it in the years following World War II.

Pritchett's work offers rich material for a critic with a historical or cultural perspective, for a scholar who could respond to and interpret the rich texture of social detail. No work exploring such intriguing possibilities has yet appeared. Meanwhile, his stories continue to reward thoughtful reading, to provoke discussion and contemplation even though, or rather because, they rarely offer a hook on which to hang a thesis. In a 1975 interview, Pritchett offered this view: "Literature enlarges our knowledge and possibilities of human nature to an extraordinary degree. It makes us aware of people, emotions, and ideas of which we are normally unaware or which we take for granted. It's really a secret communication" (qtd. in Stinson 98).

WORKS CITED AND CONSULTED

Primary

Pritchett, V. S. "Agranti, for Lisbon." *Fortnightly Review* August 1930: 235–46.
———. "The Ape Who Lost His Tail." *New Writing* n.s. 1 (Autumn 1938): 233–40.

————. *Blind Love and Other Stories*. London: Chatto & Windus, 1969.

————. *The Camberwell Beauty and Other Stories*. London: Chatto & Windus, 1974; New York: Random House, 1974.

————. *A Careless Widow and Other Stories*. London: Chatto & Windus, 1989; New York: Random House, 1989.

————. "The Chimney." *New Statesman and Nation* December 26, 1936: 1061–63.

————. *Collected Stories*. London: Chatto & Windus, 1956.

————. *Collected Stories*. London: Chatto & Windus, 1982; New York: Random House, 1982.

————. *Complete Collected Stories*. New York: Random House, 1990.

————. *The Complete Short Stories*. London: Chatto & Windus, 1990.

————. "Cup Final." *New Statesman and Nation* December 18, 1943: 398–99.

————. "Doctor's Story." *New Statesman and Nation* January 3, 1948: 8–9.

————. "The Educated Girl." *Transatlantic Review* 5 (December 1960): 51–56. Rpt. in *Stories from the Transatlantic Review*. Ed. Joseph F. McCrindle. New York: Holt, 1970.

————. "Father and the Bucket Shop." *Night and Day* September 23, 1937: 12–15.

————. "Goldfish." *New Statesman and Nation* December 26, 1942: 422–23.

————. "Hiawatha Complex." *New Statesman and Nation* December 29, 1956: 835–36.

————. "In Autumn Quietly." *John o'London's Weekly* February 4, 1933: 713–15.

————. "The Invader." *New Statesman and Nation* January 11, 1941: 34–35.

————. "I Passed by Your Window." *London Mercury* December 1938: 131–44.

————. *It May Never Happen and Other Stories*. London: Chatto & Windus, 1945; New York: Reynal, 1947.

————. "Jury." *Fortnightly Review* March 1937: 321–27.

————. *The Key to My Heart*. London: Chatto & Windus, 1963; New York: Random House, 1964.

————. *More Collected Stories*. London: Chatto & Windus, 1983; New York: Vintage, 1985.

————. "New World." *John o'London's Weekly* December 22, 1939: 373–74.

————. *On the Edge of the Cliff and Other Stories*. London: Chatto & Windus, 1980; New York: Random House, 1979.

————. *The Pritchett Century: A Selection of the Best by V. S. Pritchett*. New York: Random House, 1997.

————. "A Public Benefactress." *Bystander* August 17, 1938.

————. *The Sailor, Sense of Humour, and Other Stories*. New York: Knopf, 1956.

————. *The Saint and Other Stories*. Harmondsworth, UK: Penguin, 1966.

————. *Selected Stories*. New York: Random House, 1978.

————. "Serious Question." *Fortnightly Review* February 1931: 209–17.

————. "Slooter's Vengeance." *New Statesman and Nation* March 28, 1931: vi–vii.

————. *The Spanish Virgin and Other Stories*. London: Ernest Benn, 1930.

————. "The Truth about Mrs. Brown." *Nash's Pall Mall* March 1936: 111–27.

————. "Uncle for Christmas." *News Chronicle* April 12, 1939.

————. "Upstairs, Downstairs." *Night and Day* July 1, 1937: 13–15.

————. *When My Girl Comes Home*. London: Chatto & Windus, 1961; New York: Knopf, 1961.

————. "Woolly Gloves." *Fortnightly Review* June 1931: 804–16. Rpt. in *Best British*

Short Stories of 1932. Ed. Edward J. O'Brien. Boston: Houghton Mifflin, 1933.
    209–222.
———. *You Make Your Own Life*. London: Chatto & Windus, 1938.

Secondary

Allen, Walter. *The Short Story in English*. Oxford: Clarendon Press, 1981.
Baldwin, Dean R. *V. S. Pritchett*. Boston: Twayne, 1987.
Boken, Julia B. "V. S. Pritchett." *Critical Survey of Short Fiction*. 1929–1939. Rev. ed.
    Ed. Frank N. Magill. Vol. 5. Pasadena, CA: Salem Press, 1993.
Journal of the Short Story in English 6 (Spring 1986). Special V. S. Pritchett issue.
Peden, William. "V. S. Pritchett." *The English Short Story, 1880–1945*. Ed. Joseph M.
    Flora. Boston: Twayne, 1982. 143–51.
Stinson, John J. *V. S. Pritchett: A Study of the Short Fiction*. New York: Twayne, 1992.
Theil, Alan. "Les nouvelles de V. S. Pritchett." *The English Short Story 1880–1945*. Ed.
    Joseph M. Flora. Boston: Twayne, 1982.
Vanatta, Dennis, ed. *The English Short Story, 1945–1980*. Boston: Twayne, 1985.

JEAN RHYS
(August 24, 1890–May 14, 1979)

Paul Kotrodimos

BIOGRAPHY

Jean Rhys was born Ella Gwendolyn Rhys Williams in August 1890 (some sources claim that she was born in 1894) in Roseau, Dominica, West Indies. Rhys lived in Dominica with her parents, a Welsh doctor named William Rhys and a Dominican Creole named Minna Lockhart Williams, until the age of sixteen, when she moved to England to live with her aunt Clarice Williams. In 1909 Rhys, then an aspiring actress, entered the Academy of Dramatic Art. Unfortunately, the death of her father left her destitute, and she was forced to leave the academy.

To support herself, Rhys worked with a traveling chorus group for two years. She supplemented her income by performing odd jobs like posing for advertisements and modeling for artists. In 1917, she met a French-Dutch artist named Jean Lenglet, whom she married in 1919. After a short stay in Holland, the two traveled to Paris, Brussels, Budapest, and elsewhere. However, Lenglet's illegal activities eventually landed him in prison, and Rhys found herself again destitute, now with a daughter, Maryvonne, who was born in 1922. It was in this condition that she first encountered Ford Madox Ford; in 1923, she entered into a dubious living arrangement with him and his mistress. Though Ford exploited her precarious situation, he also facilitated her career as a writer by introducing her in the "proper" literary circles and helping her to publish.

In 1927, Rhys published a volume of short stories entitled *The Left Bank, and Other Stories*. Although the book was not a great success, its garnered some generous reviews. The collection is characterized both by its terse, conservative language and its use of episode or situation in place of a linear plot structure. In 1928, Rhys published her first novel, *Quartet*, which focuses on the abusive relationship she had with Ford and the mental strain caused by a fruitless affair some years earlier with a man named Lancelot Smith. The year 1931 saw the publication of Rhys's second novel, *After Leaving Mr. Mackenzie*. In this novel, Rhys draws heavily on her childhood in the West Indies: it portrays ambivalent family relations and the process of a woman slowly losing her grip on reality.

Rhys married Leslie Tilden Smith in 1934. That was also the year her third novel, *Voyage in the Dark*, was published. This novel, the author's favorite work, again explores the mundane existence of a young, destitute, single female fighting to retain her sanity and repel the forces that threaten to overwhelm her. Rhys's fourth novel, *Good Morning, Midnight* (1939), depicts a young woman trying to cope with loneliness and psychological instability in a Paris that preys on such women. A radio adaptation of this story was broadcast by Selma Vaz Dias in 1957.

Wide Sargasso Sea, Rhys's most acclaimed novel, was published in 1966; in 1967, she won the W. H. Smith literary award. Two more collections of short stories were published before her death in 1979: *Tigers Are Better-Looking*, a collection of eight new stories and nine previously published stories from *The Left Bank, and Other Stories*, was published in 1968, and *Sleep It Off, Lady* appeared in 1976. Perhaps her finest collection of stories, *Sleep It Off, Lady* departs from the conventional Rhys story in terms of its characterization and plot development. These stories, no longer episodic situations but coherently structured short stories, still focus on the outsider, the typical Rhys heroine struggling to retain sanity and control.

CRITICISM

Rhys's first collection of stories, *The Left Bank, and Other Stories* did not receive the praise that it deserves. Though reviewers were kind, the collection was for the most part dismissed. Still, the bizarre nature of the stories caught the attention of some critics who, while not necessarily praising the collection, were able at least to acknowledge the author's prowess in presenting the chaotic, terrifying, psychologically debilitating nature of the female postcolonial and ex-patriate. In the December 11, 1927, issue of The *New York Times Book Review*, an anonymous critic claims, "For the most part Miss Rhys's stories and sketches are very brief. Her method is to reject the descriptive and the expository, to reject for the most part structural plot, and even to reject fullness of character-ization as we understand it" (28). However negative this response to *The Left Bank, and Other Stories* may sound, the reviewer does qualify his statements by adding, "For all its frequent fumbling . . . sketchiness . . . [and] fiascoes of experimentalism, 'The Left Bank' . . . is proof of a fresh and personal talent. Miss Rhys is worth keeping an eye on" (30).

But it is the strange nature of these situation pieces, coupled with the psy-chologically distraught characters, that catches the attention of readers and critics alike. Rosalind Miles, as quoted in *Jean Rhys* by Peter Wolfe, "in 1974, inter-prets the Left Bank as 'that shabby fringe of society' peopled by 'the sinister, the frightening, the out of order' " (33). Peter Wolfe focuses heavily on the structure of the stories to show that the collection has "a flow or curve, if not a linear structure" (34). This point is important, for through the use of structure and strange characterization, Rhys accomplishes her task of entrenching her motifs, what Wolfe calls "the mood of creativity and exile" (33).

Another subject of interest to Rhys critics is the autobiographical nature of her stories. Some critics "in the early 1970's seemed to find the autobiographical sources of her subject matter a distraction, if not an outright embarrassment" (Hite 19). For some feminist critics, though, the autobiographical nature of Rhys's work gives it importance and power. Teresa O'Connor, for example, states that Rhys's main theme is a certain "malaise: the dislocation and alienation that comes from [not] having a true home, metaphorically and literally" (35). She states later that "it is [Rhys's] heroines' statelessness, homelessness and lack of familial and deep ties that lead to their malaise" (35).

Although critics cannot agree on every aspect of Rhys's short-story collections, they do concur on one point: the themes of psychological instability, the inability to identify with a specific culture, loneliness, despair, and a lack of familial bonds are the focal points of her work. Moreover, though critics assign these themes varying degrees of importance, many would argue that Rhys uses them to better effect than any other female writer of the twentieth century. Rhys, despite criticism to the contrary, uses both autobiographical material and artistic prowess to address the challenges faced by a variety of women who, despite differences in age and cultural background, are quite similar (Hite 22).

ANALYSIS

Although Jean Rhys published three collections of short stories, only two will be discussed here, *The Left Bank, and Other Stories* and *Sleep It Off, Lady*. The third, *Tigers Are Better-Looking*, includes many stories already collected in *The Left Bank*, along with several new episodic situation pieces with minimal (if any) plot structure and character development. The stories contained in *The Left Bank*, then, are sufficient to explicate the main elements of theme and structure inherent in Rhys's early short fiction.

Perhaps the most distinguishing feature of Rhys's earlier short fiction is her use of terse, episodic narrative as opposed to more fully developed plots. At first glance, inexperienced readers may be inclined to dismiss these pieces as trite or perhaps even meaningless snippets in the lives of characters whose degenerate and marginal states can have no interest or worth. Yet this is precisely what gives Rhys's short fiction its meaning, power, and depth. As Peter Wolfe writes in the preface to his book *Jean Rhys*, "Jean Rhys has performed in her fiction the rare feat of writing good books about dull characters trapped in numbing routines" (9).

Indeed, Jean Rhys captures the essence of the marginalized character, especially female, who lives a ghostlike existence between the camps of the colonizer and the colonized. Already dispossesed by virtue of their sex, Rhys's women protagonists suffer under the strain of mixed cultural identity and no means of survival except natural beauty and wit.

In a very short story titled "Trio," Rhys explores this problem of mixed identity and cultural affiliation. In this story, a man, a woman, and a young girl eating dinner in a restaurant are described by the narrator as "simple-hearted people who like their neighbors to see and know their pleasures" (83), a description evocative of established stereotypes of West Indians. Within the two-and-one-half-page scope of this story, however, Rhys undermines such preconceptions. Broadly distinguishing degrees of race, the narrator explains, "The man was black—coal black. . . . The woman was coffee coloured and fat. Between them was the girl. . . . There was evidently much white blood in her veins" (83). Demonstrating an overtly affectionate relationship with the young girl, the man "would stop eating to kiss her . . . long, lingering kisses, and, after each one she would look round the room as if to gather up a tribute of glances of admiration and envy" (84). In any such trio, age would suggest a familial relationship. Yet here the sexual relationship between the young girl and the man subverts the notion of "normal" or acceptable familial ties.

This story, then, critiques the reality- and normalcy-distorting effects of colonialism, a system that imposes standards of one culture onto those of another. For example, when the narrator sees the man kissing the young girl with "long, lingering kisses," she is not repulsed, nor does she even think to comment on it. Instead, she responds by saying, "You cannot think what home-sickness descended over me" (84). "It was because these were my compatriots that in that Montparnasse restaurant I remembered the Antilles," she says (85). In other words, the narrator straddles the fence dividing two worlds. Like the trio that combines a range of different cultures and skin shades, she herself is a mixture of identities, aligned with the other restaurant patrons but also with the West Indians. But what are the consequences of such divided loyalties?

"Mixing Cocktails" also considers the dichotomies that emerge when disparate cultures combine. The story begins with a description of an ugly house in the hills, "perched oddly on high posts" (87). However, the verandah is the most important feature of the house. It is from the verandah with its "wooden table with four stout legs" that one is able to view the natural West Indian countryside, paradoxically peppered with evidence of modernity, like the French steamers at the coast. This combination of "savage" reality and European industrialism presents a strange contrast that serves to inform the conflict of the plot.

Rhys's narrator, a young colonial girl, explains the scene exquisitely. By describing the house on its high posts and the table with stout legs, she emphasizes the nature of a colonial society where colonizers try to stand apart from their new territory by placing themselves above it, isolating themselves from it. Yet the young narrator takes this further by setting up the distance between reality and dreaming. She implies that her most important activity each day is dreaming, going so far as to divide her day into morning dream, afternoon dream, and so on. But these distinctions between dream and reality perform a distinct function, one that explicates social differences.

Her morning dream, "A very short dream, the morning dream—mostly about what one would do with the endless blue day" (88), sets up a dichotomy between the "civilized" European countries and the "pagan, savage" West Indian culture. When she first mentions the morning dream, she says that it is the best one but does not immediately explain herself. Instead, she describes the sea and sky with the fishing boats: "The sea was then a very tender blue, like the Virgin Mary, and on it were little white triangles" (88). Then, in contrast to the reverent description of the landscape, the following paragraph describes a fantasy of finding treasure purportedly buried in "a wild place, Dominica. Savage and lost. Just the place for Morgan to hide his treasure in" (88). But the nature of dreaming goes much further in the story. It is an activity that carries its own reality, its own validity.

The afternoon dream is also pleasurable, but it is interrupted often, usually under the guise that "one was not to sit in the sun. One would one day regret freckles" (89). It is strange that dark blemishes on the skin would be reason to refrain from engaging in a pleasant activity, but here the story offers a subtle comment on "going native." Dreaming and engaging in native or savage activities is something to be avoided; it is taboo. Although this is not explicitly stated, the narrator leaves no doubt in the reader's mind that it is the case.

The best time to retire to the verandah, says the narrator, is late afternoon. At this time of day, however, the inevitable presence of other people will ruin the experience. She comments, "So soon does one learn the bitter lesson that humanity is never content just to differ from you and let it go at that. Never. They must interfere, actively and grimly, between your thoughts and yourself— with the passionate wish to level up everything and everybody" (89). This short statement, clearly the climax of the story, reflects the underlying tension between the colonizing mentality and that of the colonized. The two cultures contain a disparity that, instead of being accepted, is consciously pushed away and discarded.

Some critics have failed to notice this story's political and social implications. They have determined instead that the story is about a "young girl's vague awakening into the adult world amid the contrast of British colonial upbringing and the lush, sensuous world of Dominica" (Staley 28). This reading, while it contains elements of truth, limits the scope of the story to the narrator's individual circumstance and downplays the importance of the contrast of the two cultures. But the scope of the story goes beyond the narrow confines of a colonial girl's experience in Dominica.

Recognizing the significance of dreaming to the narrator is key to understanding the story. The narrator, castigated by her elders for being absent-minded— for, in essence, acting like a native—chooses to dream in validation of her "culture" despite their warnings. With biting insight, she observes: "In spite of my absentmindedness I mix cocktails very well and swizzle them better . . . than anyone else in the house. Here then is something I can do. . . . Action, they say, is more worthy than dreaming" (91–92). The irony here is unmistakable. The high-minded colonial culture that prizes material over imaginative productivity devalues the girl's exquisite gift of dreaming. It measures her worth only by her ability to "act" her part. Yet despite her success at finding "something [she] can do," she remains a product of both native and imperial cultures and hence a member of neither. Relegated to the position of outcast, she is isolated, ordered about, and cast aside at any moment. Her task of mixing cocktails with a swizzle stick, an eroticized activity, ultimately serves the men who make up the established social and power structure.

Such tension appears in many of Rhys's stories. "Pioneers, Oh, Pioneers" from the collection *Sleep It Off, Lady*, for example, invests the motif of duality with heady resonance. In this story, Rhys moves away from her usual female protagonist and tells instead of a young man newly arrived in the West Indies named Mr. Ramage. Ramage comes to the islands to acquire a plantation, but, the reader is quick to learn, he is no ordinary colonizer.

The story begins with two young girls, Irene and Rosalie, the daughters of Ramage's friend Dr. Cox, discussing an eccentric old lady. When Irene says to her sister that the lady should be ashamed of her eccentricities, Rosalie does not understand why. " 'Oh, you," Irene jeers in response to her sister's confusion, "You like crazy people. You liked Ramage, nasty beastly horrible Ramage' " (11). Immediately, then, Ramage emerges as a person of complex character. On the one hand, he is seen as a "horrible," "crazy" man, while on the other, he is seen as worthy of a certain amount of pathos.

This dual view of Ramage is not limited to the two girls; rather, it persists within the society at large. The young girls' father, for example, is sympathetic to Ramage. He "had liked the man, had stuck up for him, laughed off his obvious eccentricities, denied point blank that he was certifiable" (12). He is a doctor with unique status and influence on the island, and his view of Ramage reflects a side of the society that is understanding. But not all the upper-class colonists have such a sympathetic view of the newcomer. Another symbolic figure, Mr. Eliot, the owner of a large, productive plantation called Twickenham, has little patience with Ramage or his peculiarities. In fact, it is Mr. Eliot "who started the trouble" that eventually leads to Ramage's downfall.

Ramage, atypical among the colonists, moved to the islands in search not of prosperity, but of peace. His blatant disregard for capital, along with his eccentric behavior—including a scandalous marriage to a native—set him apart and made him the target of hatred. When he encountered Mr. Eliot and his wife having tea in a field one day, his shocking countenance and demeanor sealed his fate: "[Ramage] was burnt a deep brown, his hair fell to his shoulders, his beard to his chest. He was wearing sandals and a leather belt, on one side of which hung a cutlass, on the other a large pouch. Nothing else." To Mrs. Eliot he exclaimed, "What an uncomfortable dress—and how ugly!" (16).

Fanned by Mr. Eliot's indignation, the awkward situation escalates to a fren-
zied pitch until the citizens of the island ultimately kill Ramage. Yet here Rhys
makes a subtle commentary on human nature. Mr. Eliot's hatred of Ramage,
the reader learns, does not stem directly from the fact that he was rude to Mrs.
Eliot. As the wealthy planter explains, "We got home and my wife locked herself
in the bedroom. When she came out she wouldn't speak to me at first, then she
said that he was quite right, I didn't care what she looked like, so now she
didn't either. She called me a mean man. A mean man. I won't have it" (16).

Mr. Eliot inadvertently admits that although he is upset by Ramage's indecent
behavior, he is even angrier that the honest statement made about his wife's
clothes brings her to the realization that Mr. Eliot is a cold, unfeeling man.
Moreover, as Ramage seems increasingly more "native" than colonist, the insult
to Mr. Eliot takes on the gravity of a conquered people "being so bold and
presumptuous" as to place judgment on the ruling class. It is in this way that
Rhys shows her expertise. In effect, Ramage lives precariously between two
worlds: one privileged but restricted, one underprivileged but free. It is this
dichotomy that surfaces in much of Rhys's short fiction.

WORKS CITED AND CONSULTED

Primary

Rhys, Jean. *After Leaving Mr. Mackenzie.* New York: Perennial, 1931.
————. *The Collected Short Stories.* New York: W. W. Norton, 1987.
————. *Good Morning, Midnight.* New York: Harper & Row, 1970.
————. *The Left Bank, and Other Stories.* Freeport, NY: Books for Libraries Press,
    1970.
————. *My Day: 3 Pieces.* New York: N.Y.F. Hallman, 1975.
————. *Quartet.* New York: Harper & Row, 1957, 1971.
————. *Sleep It Off, Lady.* New York: Harper & Row, 1976.
————. *Smile Please: An Unfinished Autobiography.* New York: Harper & Row, 1979.
————. *Tales of the Wide Caribbean.* London: Heinemann, 1985.
————. *Tigers Are Better-Looking: With a Selection from The Left Bank: Stories.* New
    York: Harper & Row, 1974.
————. *Voyage in the Dark.* London: Constable, 1934.
————. *Wide Sargasso Sea.* New York: W. W. Norton, 1966, 1992.

Secondary

Hite, Molly. *The Other Side of the Story: Structures and Strategies of Contemporary
    Feminist Narrative.* Ithaca, NY: Cornell University Press, 1989.
O'Connor, Teresa F. *Jean Rhys: The West Indian Novels.* New York: New York Uni-
    versity Press, 1986.
Rev. of *The Left Bank, and Other Stories. New York Times Book Review* December 11,
    1927.
Staley, Thomas F. *Jean Rhys : A Critical Study.* Austin: University of Texas Press, 1979.
Wolfe, Peter. *Jean Rhys.* Boston: Twayne, 1980.

SALMAN RUSHDIE
(June 19, 1947–   )

Farhat Iftekharuddin

BIOGRAPHY

Salman Rushdie was born in Bombay in June 1947 to a business family that originally hailed from Kashmir and later moved to Karachi. Rushdie grew up speaking both Urdu and English in this family of businesspeople. His education started off at the Cathedral School in Bombay. In 1961, he was sent to Rugby, and following that, he attended King's College, Cambridge, majoring in history. Rushdie excelled in education at all levels, something that brought him more grief in the already racist environment of Rugby. Although literature is not his background (neither is creative writing), Rushdie read profoundly, basically training himself in the literary field. He claimed that he spent his student life under the influence of "Buñuel, Godard . . . Bergman . . . Dylan, Lennon, Jagger, and, inevitably, the two-headed fellow known to Grass readers as Maryangels" (*Imaginary Homelands* 276). Rushdie's seething denunciation of the British, particularly in such works as *The Satanic Verses*, derives partly from this leftist influence and greatly from his experience with racism. It is clear from his essay "Günter Grass" (from *Imaginary Homelands*) that Rushdie was determined to be a writer:

And then there are readers who dream of becoming writers; . . . [for] these would-be migrants from the World to the Book, there are (if they are lucky) books which give them permission . . . to become the sort of writer they have it in themselves to be. . . . This is what Grass's great novel said to me in its drumbeats: Go for broke. . . . Be bloody-minded. Argue with the world. And never forget that writing is as close as we get to keeping a hold of the thousand and one things—childhood, certainties, cities, doubts, dreams, instants, phrases, parents, love . . . and one more. . . . When you've done it once, start all over again and do it better. (276–77)

Rushdie was not "lucky" with his first novel, *Grimus* (1975), written for the Gollancz's Science Fiction Prize that he did not win. However, he remained undaunted, gave up working as an advertising copywriter, and produced his second novel, *Midnight's Children*, in 1980. This won him the Booker Prize and launched his career as a significant writer. *Midnight's Children* is a complex postmodern text that, besides accounting for significant historical and political events regarding India between 1947 and 1978, reveals the dark, Jacobean side of human nature with all its intrigue, corruption, conspiracy, and revenge. Rushdie followed this masterpiece with his next novel, *Shame* (1983). Using Pakistan as its historic platform, this work catalogs the concept of shame that tarnishes the history of this country. In July 1986, Rushdie visited Nicaragua, then in the midst of revolution. *The Jaguar Smile: A Nicaraguan Journey* (1987) is a product of that visit. More a chronicle than a novel, it presents an admiring portrait of the Sandinistas and a vengeful indictment of American foreign policy and imperialism. Because of this, *The Jaguar Smile* lacks the artistic wizardry that Rushdie had already demonstrated with *Midnight's Children* and *Shame*.

In 1988, the publication of *The Satanic Verses* set off political effects the magnitude of which not even Rushdie anticipated. This novel offended and outraged Muslims and launched the Islamic world into a frenzy culminating in a *fatwah* (Islamic religious legal judgment) from Ayatollah Khomeini:

In the name of Him, the Highest . . . only one God, I inform all zealous Muslims . . . that . . . all those involved in its publication . . . are sentenced to death. I call on all zealous Muslims to execute them quickly. In addition, anyone who has access to the author . . . but does not possess the power to execute him, should report him to the people so that he may be punished for his actions. (Pipes 27)

A multimillion-dollar reward for his execution still threatens Rushdie's life. Ironically, Syed Shahabuddin, a member of the Indian Parliament who is credited for stirring the Muslims into agitation, has never read the book. In a letter to Rushdie published in the *Times of India*, he stated, "You are aggrieved that some of us have condemned you without a hearing, and asked for a ban without reading your book. I have not read it, nor do I intend to. I do not have to wade through a filthy drain to know what is filth" (Appignanesi and Maitland 4). Rushdie lamented that "this is the saddest irony of all. . . . That after working for five years to give voice and fictional flesh to the immigrant culture of which I myself am a member, I should see my book burned, largely unread, by the people it's about" (4). At one level, at least, *The Satanic Verses* parodies Islamic republics and their leaders, particularly Khomeini, and moreover denounces the British government. Artistically, the text is an extremely complicated postmodern work; Rushdie himself explains that "the book itself was metamorphosing all the time" (Appignanesi and Maitland 8).

Rushdie's subsequent works have all been written while he has been in hiding. His 1990 novel *Haroun and the Sea of Stories* addresses the issue of censorship and stifling artistic imagination. In 1991, Granta Books, in association with Penguin Books, published Rushdie's *Imaginary Homelands: Essays and Criti-*

cism, 1981–1991. In this collection of seventy-five essays written over a period of ten years, Rushdie comments on politics, religion, and race, as well as on a variety of authors such as Günter Grass, Gabriel García Márquez, Italo Calvino, V. S. Naipaul, and Raymond Carver. *East, West: Stories*, his first collection of short stories, appeared in 1994; *The Moor's Last Sigh* followed in 1995; and *The Ground beneath Her Feet*, Rushdie's latest work, was published in 1999.

Six of the nine stories in *East, West* have been published elsewhere in, as Rushdie states, "somewhat different form." "Good Advice Is Rarer than Rubies" appeared in the *New Yorker*, "The Free Radio" in *Atlantic Monthly*, "The Prophet's Hair" in *London Review of Books*, "Yorick" in *Encounter*, "At the Auction of the Ruby Slippers" in *Granta*, and "Christopher Columbus and Queen Isabella of Spain" in the *New Yorker*. The last three stories have not been published before.

Salman Rushdie has given numerous interviews and has recently ventured out of hiding to promote his books, risking a now-years-old Iranian death threat. In spite of this threat, Rushdie continues to write, producing works that may appear to many no less satanic than *The Satanic Verses*.

CRITICISM

Salman Rushdie has already established his literary prowess through his novels, essays, and criticism. Among scholars, his novels have generated significant research and publication. However, with *East, West: Stories*, Rushdie has provided evidence that his literary forte is not limited solely to the novel. In this collection of stories, Rushdie, the master postmodern artist, is still at work, and the deftness of his transition from one genre (the novel) to another (the short story) is remarkable.

Since the publication of *East, West: Stories*, two significant reviews of the collection have appeared: Henry Louis Gates, Jr.'s, "The Empire Writes Back" and Hilary Mantel's "Real Magicians." Gates states that Rushdie, as "the Pandora of postmodernism, has forever dispelled any doubt about the potency of the modern fairy tale" (91) and, as such, has put together a collection of these fairy tales in *East, West*. According to Gates, in these stories, Rushdie "reminds us that borders crossed aren't merely the kind drawn in dirt. His restless intelligence is forever challenging the lines between East and West" (91), and "if Rushdie's persecutors have made the experience of rootless nomadism all too literal for him, he is still teaching the rest of us why we can't go home again" (92).

Mantel observes that in *East, West*, Rushdie pursues the theme of his novel *Haroun and the Sea of Stories*, where cult master Khattam-Shud is bent on terminating human imagination since he is "the Arch-enemy of all stories, even of language itself" (*Haroun* 79). This tyrant fails because "fiction creates . . . a multiplicity of worlds he can never command: stories are outside rules and creeds" (Mantel 9). Mantel notes that the stories in *East, West* "are written with a wariness and a gentle humor that one associates more with Narayan than with Rushdie. Exuberant, flamboyant prose is not much on display, and some of Rushdie's admirers will regret this; others will believe that his genius shines brighter through plain words" (9). Because of his novels, Rushdie has been compared to such powerful writers as Mario Vargas Llosa, Gabriel García Márquez, and Isabel Allende. *East, West: Stories* gives further credence to that comparison.

ANALYSIS

Rushdie's contribution to the short story is that in a compact form, he has managed to include the multitudinous levels of narrative for which his novels are famous. In each story, multiple realities function simultaneously, complicating the process of linear comprehension. The central theme in Rushdie's stories appears to be the struggle to maintain inalienable human rights in the face of social and religious taboos, cultural biases, and political agendas. It is often difficult to locate this theme because its central idea emerges through refracted realities in oftentimes-parallel worlds. The versatility with which he captures a singular moment in each of the stories in *East, West* is a result of his dexterity with language itself. By infusing the English language with the dialectal variants of the Asian immigrants, Rushdie has forged a new language that requires etymological reconfiguration to comprehend not only his texts but also the characters that inhabit them. Postmodernism is Rushdie's umbrella; in telling his stories in this mode, he creates myths both magical and real. The driving motive behind this storyteller can best be described in this line from "Interminable Life" in Isabel Allende's *The Stories of Eva Luna*: "To exorcise the demons of memory, it is sometimes necessary to tell them as a story." This he does in *East, West: Stories*.

East, West: Stories is a collection of nine stories grouped under three sections: "East," "West," and "East, West." These divisions are superficial separations only. The stories of the East are also about the West. Those grouped under "East, West" are at once about both and neither.

The first story, "Good Advice Is Rarer than Rubies," under the section "East" focuses on a corrupt industry peripheral to the British consulate that embodies its own form of corruption. The central issue is immigration and a British passport that is imperative. The applicants who crowd the British consulate on Tuesdays are uneducated women who live on the verge of poverty; they are the "Tuesday women" (5). To these women, the passport officials at the British consulate are the impediment to their perceived chance at freedom and affluence. The intrusive nature of British investigation has bred a black-market industry for British passports, an industry of exploitation of like by like.

Muhammed Ali is an "old gray-haired fraud" (7) who, classifying himself as an "advice expert" (5), specializes "in advising the most vulnerable-looking of these weekly supplicants" (6). The Tuesday women he preys upon come from hundreds of miles away—he usually makes certain of this before swindling them, so if they discover his trick, they are not likely to return (10). Muhammed Ali, uneducated and poor himself, has found his own source of riches in these women; his rationalization of his trade shows a parasitic side of the economically disadvantaged: "Life is hard, and an old man must live by his wits" (10).

Rehana, with her youth, beauty, and independence, is the hopeful antidote in this degenerate circle of corruption. She deliberately mishandles her interview with the passport official, choosing dignity over perversion, and turns down Muhammed Ali's "genuine" passport, opting for acceptance of her lot over falsity. The story ends with Muhammed Ali experiencing a virtual epiphany: "Her last smile . . . was the happiest thing he had ever seen in his long, hot, hard, unloving life" (16).

The second story under "East," titled "The Free Radio," once again involves individuals who are uneducated and economically strapped. The protagonist is a young rickshaw puller who manages a living through sweat and grind; however, when he dares to dream, his desires do not comfortably package themselves to meet conformities to society, economics, or politics. Ramani, the rickshaw wallah, follows his passion and falls in love with a thief's widow with five children. He thus exceeds his own economic abilities as well as violates a multifaceted cultural taboo that prohibits association with a female of a questionable background or an affair with a widow, particularly one with children. The tragicomic tone of the story is set in the opening observation of the narrator that Ramani was "an innocent, a real donkey's child" (19). These qualifiers serve not only to describe the general, large, uneducated population of the Indian subcontinent, but also as foreshadowing and irony. Ramani's "innocence" represents not only sexual innocence but also political innocence. He acquiesces to the widow's demands that he not add to the existing five children and agrees to a vasectomy. This draws him into the political claws of the government. Residents of the Indian subcontinent (because of their actual experience or knowledge of like incidents) can readily recognize the multiple levels of irony in Ramani's situation. With the promise of a free radio that never arrived, the Indian government actually performed countless numbers of vasectomies not only on "innocents" like Ramani, but also on the poor elderly who at their age could hardly have contributed to the overpopulation of India. The government accomplished this task with the aid of thugs from the youth movement, a further irony. These ironies multiply almost endlessly and contribute to the tragedy of countries known to the Western world as Third World nations. The most tragic irony is that the "vasectomy" that renders Ramani impotent also represents the impotence of a government that has failed in its economic and educational plans for the country.

Ironies in this story move the plot along into postmodern realities. Ramani, who never gets the radio, imagines it into existence by cupping his hand over his ears and yelling out the news from All India Radio as he peddles on the streets. This same "act of will" enables Ramani to escape into another "conjured reality," his romantic world, Bombay, to become a film star. Ironically and tragically, he attempts to replace his own sterilization with another sterile world, one "filled with light and success and no-questions-asked alcohol" (32).

The last story under this section, "The Prophet's Hair," involves a money-lender, Hashim, and his surreal experience following his finding the Prophet's hair. A strand of the prophet Muhammed's hair stored in a vial had been stolen from Hazratbal mosque. The thieves, "alarmed" by the "unprecedented . . . pandemonium" that they created, tossed the vial into a lake, and it came to rest at Hashim's dock. Hashim, a collector of curios, justifies not returning the hair to the mosque by interpreting religion in his favor. But keeping the Prophet's hair sets off a devastating set of events. Intrinsically embodying the truth and honesty of the Prophet, the hair evokes Islamic truth out of Hashim. He turns from a loving husband and father to a tyrant expounding religious dictates: " 'An end to politeness!' . . . 'An end to hypocrisy!' " (45). In converting from the secular to the spiritual, Hashim replaces one tyrannical exploit, moneylending, with another, religious fundamentalism.

To remedy matters, Hashim's children, Atta and Huma, decide that the vial must be stolen back and returned. They hire a master criminal whose name, Sheikh Sín, carries an obvious metaphor. However, there is no escaping the cleansing avalanche of religion. The hair takes on a life of its own and avenges its displacement, leaving behind a litter of dead bodies comparable to Kydian tragedy. Atta dies from a blood clot in his brain, the result of a beating at the hands of the very criminals he wanted to hire to steal the vial from his father. Huma dies when her father mistakes her for a thief and runs her through with a sword. Hashim kills himself with the same sword that accidentally killed his daughter; his wife turns insane; and Sheikh Sín, the master criminal, dies from a bullet to his belly. His four sons, crippled at birth by their father to ensure their lifelong trade in begging, recover through the miracle of the Prophet's hair; their recovery, however, ruins them financially, leaving no handicap to justify begging.

"The Prophet's Hair" is an illusive story. It raises issues concerning religion, but allows no resolutions that can gratify either the agnostic or the religious zealot. The story does, however, point to the fact that contemporary life, particularly in places like the subcontinent, offers few options, and those that are available are in themselves treacherous: moneylending is a corrupt trade, and crippling one's children, even if its intent is to ensure sustenance, is a heinous act. On the other hand, religion, particularly a fanatical one, carries its own element of tyranny.

Although the venue shifts westward in the stories under "West," the focus here is on concepts rather than on geography. The first story, "Yorick," is a patchwork of fiction and drama. Beginning with an observation of the human need to destroy, the story moves to a rewriting of Hamlet, employing both Elizabethan language and Laurence Sterne punctuation (dashes and asterisks). In this tour de force, Sterne's parson Yorick marries Ophelia and later kills the

King of Denmark, who has fornicated with her. Claudius detects the crime and executes Yorick. Yorick as ghost visits Hamlet and convinces him that Claudius is guilty of fratricide. Hamlet kills Claudius, mistreats his own Ophelia, and finally dies from a drink of poison himself. "Yorick" is a postmodern pastiche of parody, word games, and merged literary allusions. The story introduces "Yorick's saga" as having begun when the "ancient text" came into the possession of "Tristram, who . . . was neither triste nor ram, the frothiest, most heady Shandy of a fellow" (64). The game ends with the subtitle of *Tristram Shandy*, stating that "such a cock-and-bull story is by this last confession brought quite to its conclusion" (83).

Entirely self-reflexive in form, "Yorick" is self-critical as it parodies sixteenth and eighteenth-century texts. The story's narrator is a jester merging with Yorick the court jester and ultimately with Rushdie the archjester. However, Rushdie's humor is, as always, a "cryptic key" to hidden meanings (65). Thus "Yorick" is also a parable for the plight of migrants. The "cryptic key" ultimately unlocks Rushdie's own predicament: "I can no longer keep the great World from my pages" (72).

In the second story, "At the Auction of the Ruby Slippers," the auction draws a microcosmic gathering. Present are memorabilia junkies, exiles, political refugees, religious fundamentalists, and even orphans. Here the Auctioneer assesses not so much the value of the ruby slippers as the accounting of ourselves: "the value of our past, of our futures, of our lives" (101). Rushdie's postmodern game becomes clearer as each layer of the story gives way to the next in rapid succession. "At the Auction of the Ruby Slippers" is a compilation of sketches illustrating each of the representational groups present. As each sketch presents a voyeuristic depiction of the absurdities of contemporary affluence-driven, agenda-oriented irrationalities, Rushdie makes the point that contemporary life is tenuous and fragile, like the ruby slippers. The slippers themselves are the obvious symbol of intangibility, of the unreal, the fictional.

These sketches of contemporary Western absurdities inevitably point to the central concern of the story (and even of Rushdie's work as a whole): finding a home for the émigrés who, like the Latino janitor of this story, clean up the metaphorical "pools of saliva" around the "shrine of the ruby-sequined slippers" left behind by the affluence-driven Western culture, or, like the "orphans," the "untouchables," and the "outcasts," come seeking reunion with deceased loved ones. To the émigrés, " 'home' has become . . . a scattered, damaged various concept" (93). Rushdie points out that in the true sense of "home"—a place for setting roots—there is no place for émigrés. Contrary to Frosts' assertion in "The Death of the Hired Man" that home is where "they have to take you in," the only security today is money, with which anyone can become *"somebody"* (103).

The last story in the "West" section, "Christopher Columbus and Queen Isabella of Spain Consummate Their Relationship (Santa Fé, AD 1492)," further explores the concerns of the immigrant. In this narrative, Rushdie, while maintaining a fairly traditional structure with a main plot—Columbus seeking support for his travels from the Queen—provides a slight twist by inserting authorial monologues that, while running concurrently within the narrative, actually comprise the real story. "Christopher Columbus" is a modern allegory supposed to illustrate the plight of foreigners, but the story soon ends up cataloging, almost polemically, the position that many immigrants occupy in a displaced environment. As it proceeds, its tone becomes confrontational, and "Columbus, a foreigner," in essence all foreigners, takes on the appearance of a con man, a rogue, and a nuisance. Throughout the story, there is little relief from this tension. In fact, the authorial monologue forces the issue even further, suggesting that foreigners are obstinate and insubordinate.

The surface story of "Columbus" ratifies these authorial observations. This polemical cataloging of immigrant behavior and the attitude of acceptance by the natives is based on real perceptions of one about the other. Christopher Columbus, the traveler, the adventurer, the seeker of fortunes, symbolizes immigrants with the same dreams and aspirations who are caught in the illusion that a voyage westward will invest their lives with meaning. Herein lies the irony of their condition. The immigrants arrive chasing a dream and, like Columbus, seeking "preferment," equity, and equality, only to experience "unrequited love" and hear the "echo" of their own "annihilated past[s]" (115).

Parodying the form of cheap television sequels, this story is a snapshot rewrite of the trials and travails of Christopher Columbus, complete with hope, shattered dreams, an imagined scenario in which Columbus makes the Queen wait on him following her realization of his true potential, and a return to reality as foreigner again. The title of this story contains the very irony that permeates it: the word *consummation*, an act that takes place neither in the story nor in reality. Consummation suggests oneness, equality in partnership, in this case partnership with the West; however, the reality of dislocation proscribes such joining. The story reiterates this point: it opens and closes not around the word *consummation*, but around the word *supplicant*.

The collection's final section, "East, West," is set in England and contains three stories, "The Harmony of Spheres," "Chekov and Zulu," and "The Courter." The concept of home in its various shifting definitions is still the overt concern in this last section. The two spheres, East and West, achieve proximity only in the printed form "East, West," but remain otherwise awkwardly distant. The three stories in this section comment on both the East and the West and reveal a third grotesque existence, fragmented selves that never seem to coalesce. The comingling of immigrants with the native white Anglo-Saxon British results only occasionally in superficial tolerance but mostly verges on the dystopic.

The title of the first story, "The Harmony of Spheres," is a cynical misnomer. A young Indian student, Khan, in search of "balance" in his life befriends a Welsh writer, Eliot, who introduces him to the zeitgeist of diverse cultures toward spiritualism and hypnotic states that can release soul from body. Khan's wife, "lonely Mala from Mauritius," had been "propelled in [his] direction by

Eliot Crane" (129). What appears to be a bond among three individuals of diverse origins that leads Khan to believe in acceptance turns out to be a betrayal on multiple levels. After Eliot's genius turns to insanity and he commits suicide, Khan finds among Eliot's countless typed papers not only lunatic rants against the world, but also a perverse accounting of Eliot and Mala. It is only after he relates his discovery to Mala that Khan sees the greater betrayal: As his wife turns her back on him, Khan experiences the cruelest of all epiphanies: " 'Those weren't fantasies,' she said" (146). This final act of betrayal from within, from one who like himself is a foreigner, provides Khan with the answer to the questions that he was struggling with: "Home, like Hell, turned out to be other people" (139).

The story "Chekov and Zulu" appears to be completely zany as Asian diplomats fantasize exploratory missions and impersonate *Star Trek* officers. In the background of this story are actual political events such as the assassination of Prime Minister Indira Gandhi by a Sikh and the Tamil uprising. Political turmoil in their homeland forces Chekov and Zulu, who are both Sikhs, into a defensive posture, running surveillance and antisurveillance to test the security or the insecurity of their positions. Thus their fantasy *Star Trek* game concocted in Dehra Dun, India, becomes real in this fictional narrative. Beneath the story's overt absurdity, however, lies a darker issue: the loss of identity and the Indian subcontinent's view of England. "Their museums are full of our treasures," Chekov laments. "They have stolen us" (156).

In this story, the tentative existence of Indians on the political landscape parallels their turmoil-ridden existence at home. Major political shifts generate random violence that destabilizes social order. Heads of state meet tragic ends, and this loss of leadership demands constant rebuilding and renewal. Whether at home or abroad, the struggle for Asian peoples has centered on maintaining stability. Chekov knows this as he comments, "The tragedy is not how one dies . . . it is how one has lived" (170).

The last story of this collection, "The Courter," is the most haunting of all the stories, perhaps because it reveals the most sinister and cruel face of the English and because it accounts for both the defeat of the immigrant and the instinctive, furtive unacceptance of that defeat. It is a story of recollection, a young Indian remembering the family flat in London in the 1960s and his Aya, "Certainly-Mary," who "never said plain yes or no; always this O-yes-certainly or No-certainly-not" (176). Certainly-Mary, akin to her name, lives in a hyphenated world in England, trying to cope with both culture and language. Thus Certainly-Mary, through accidental transposition of letters and with "unintentional but prophetic overtones of romance" (178), renamed Mecir, the East European porter, "the courter." Mecir, prior to his immigrant status in London, was a chess grand master. Certainly-Mary developed a loving kinship with Mecir, and soon chess became "their private language" (195) and a means of covert flirtation.

Hatred of immigrants shatters this tranquillity when the Aya and the narrator's mother, as victims of mistaken identity, experience a barrage of profanities from a pair of British youngsters. Mecir, knifed by one of these youngsters, goes back to work for a while; however, defeated by racial hatred, both Mecir and Certainly-Mary lose their smile and turn inward. Homesick, Certainly-Mary returns to Bombay, and Mecir, who has no family, disappears into uncertainty. Despite the racial attack on Mecir, Certainly-Mary, and his mother, the young narrator carries on the immigrant struggle to survive in a foreign land. At sixteen, eager to break free from his father's control, he awaits his British passport. The passport does arrive, and although he acknowledges that "in many ways [it] set me free" (211), he also has to confess to a dilemma that haunts all immigrants: "I . . . have ropes around my neck . . . pulling me this way and that, East and West, the nooses tightening, commanding, *choose, choose*" (211). This realization, however, is not entirely acquiescent: "I buck, I smart, I whinny, I roar, I kick. Ropes . . . I choose neither of you, and both. Do you hear? I refuse to choose" (211). Ironically, the ropes and horses in this last act of refusal are an allusion to a movie titled *The Misfits*.

East, West: Stories is about Rushdie's "grotesques," whether they are set in the East or the West. It is also about beliefs that expose human perversion in both Indians and the British. Except for two stories, "The Free Radio" and "The Prophet's Hair," this collection also documents the peripatetic journey of Rushdie's nomads, the immigrants who fight an endless battle for recognition, for definition, for equity and balance, but in the end remain suspended between the East and the West. Rushdie, who revels in the art of nonlinear and fragmented narrative, has here crafted stories that are traditional at the surface level. At the core, however, they embody a complex menagerie of concepts that trouble, challenge, and sometimes enrage his two audiences, East and West.

WORKS CITED AND CONSULTED

Primary

Rushdie, Salman. *East, West: Stories*. New York: Pantheon Books, 1994.
———. *Grimus*. London: Granada, 1977.
———. *The Ground beneath Her Feet: A Novel*. New York: Henry Holt, 1999.
———. *Haroun and the Sea of Stories*. London: Granta Books, 1990.
———. *Imaginary Homelands: Essays and Criticisms, 1981–1991*. New York: Penguin, 1992.
———. *The Jaguar Smile: A Nicaraguan Journey*. New York: Viking, 1987.
———. *Midnight's Children*. New York: Avon Books, 1980.
———. *Mirrorwork: 50 Years of Indian Writing, 1947–1997*. New York: Henry Holt, 1997.
———. *The Moor's Last Sigh*. New York: Knopf, 1996.
———. *The Satanic Verses*. New York: Viking, 1988.
———. *Shame*. New York: Vintage, 1983.

Secondary

Amanuddin, Syed. "The Novels of Salman Rushdie: Mediated Reality as Fantasy." *World Literature Today* 63.1 (Winter 1989): 42–45.

Appignanesi, Lisa, and Sara Maitland, eds. *The Rushdie File*. Syracuse: Syracuse University Press, 1990.

Birch, David. "Postmodernist Chutneys." *Textual Practice* 5.1 (Spring 1991): 1–7.

Cook, Rufus. "Place and Displacement in Salman Rushdie's Work." *World Literature Today* 68.1 (Winter 1994): 23–28.

Edmundson, Mark. "Prophet of a New Postmodernism: The Greater Challenge of Salman Rushdie." *Harper's Magazine* December 1989: 62–66, 68–71.

Fenton, James. "Keeping Up with Salman Rushdie" (interview). *New York Review of Books* March 28, 1991: 26–34.

Gates, Henry Louis. "The Empire Writes Back: Worlds Collide in Rushdie's New Collection." *New Yorker* January 23, 1995: 91–92.

Mantel, Hilary. "Real Magicians." *New York Review of Books*, February 16, 1995.

SAMUEL DICKSON SELVON
(May 20, 1923–April 6, 1994)

Hermine Lee

BIOGRAPHY

Samuel Dickson Selvon was horn in San Fernando, Trinidad, in 1923. His father was a descendant of Indian immigrants, and his mother was part Indian and part Scottish. As a young man during World War II, he enlisted as a radio operator in the British Royal Naval Reserve in 1940—Trinidad then being a British colony. He was even then writing and experimenting. After the war, he worked for the *Trinidad Guardian*, and between 1946 and 1950, he was editor of the literary section of the *Sunday Guardian*. During these years, Selvon contributed several essays, poems, and stories to the *Guardian*'s afternoon paper, the *Evening News*.

Selvon went to England in 1950. One of the thousands of West Indians who hoped to improve their prospects there after the war, he lived for the first few years among the kind of immigrants he wrote about and worked at odd jobs. Some of Selvon's stories were published in journals and newspapers, and two years after his arrival, his first book was published. He received several fellowships and scholarships, including two Guggenheim Fellowships.

Samuel Selvon left England to live in Canada in 1978. In December 1993, he returned to Trinidad for a visit. He died there in April 1994.

CRITICISM

Although the several books and articles written on the works of Samuel Selvon mostly discuss his novels, some criticism applies to his short stories as well, especially comments regarding his treatment of peasant characters, the humorous bent of his storytelling, and his innovative use of a modified dialect. Gordon Rohlehr, in "The Language of the People," makes the connection between Selvon's style and the oral tradition of the West Indies—the calypso and the trickster, Brer Anansi, of folktales. The characters of the short stories are "con artists" like Anansi, Rohlehr explains, and the stories carry a lyricism reminiscent of calypso rhythms. In "Samuel Selvon and the West Indian Literary Renaissance," Frank Birbalsingh discusses what he perceives to be the lack of in-depth characterization in Selvon's short stories. Praising his skill as a novelist, Birbalsingh suggests that Selvon's work lacks "intellectual interest" but has "humour, compassion and ultimately pathos" (157). In contrast, however, Louis James refers to Selvon's short stories as "sensitive, and perhaps a unique achievement. . . . they catch the jaunty/insecure stance of the uprooted West Indian in suspended tragi-comedy as has nothing else in this literature" (132).

ANALYSIS

The stories in the collection *Ways of Sunlight* are arranged in two groups, "Trinidad" and "London." As they differ significantly in the types of characters they depict, the issues they consider, and the styles they employ, this discussion will limit its analysis to the latter group only.

Set in London in the 1950s, these stories depict the lives of islander immigrants who left their homes to settle in England. Filled with dreams of a better life, the newcomers did not envision the cold and dreary days, the difficulties of adjusting to a different and complex way of life, and the discrimination they would endure living in a predominantly white, class-conscious society. Many were not equipped psychologically to handle these pressures, nor had they the skills to compete for jobs. Hence they found themselves outside the mainstream of English life, clinging together for survival.

In constructing these stories, Selvon draws upon the oral tradition of the West Indies, in particular that of Trinidad, his homeland. Traditional West Indian stories are based on folktales: stories of witchcraft, ghosts, and devils and tall tales that were brought to the region by slaves (Ramchand, *Best* 2). A recurring figure in these tales is Anansi, a cunning but lazy spider-man, who relies on his wits alone to survive. Whether he succeeds or fails in his schemes, he always tries again. Some of the characters in the "London" stories possess this combination of optimism, wit, and humor. Some are lazy and conniving, and, sometimes, like Anansi, they become objects of ridicule when their schemes backfire.

Selvon's works also echo another traditional form of "storytelling" from the West Indies: calypso music. The lyrics of the calypso typically address topical concerns, such as economic inflation and unemployment. Some convey messages of political dissent, at times addressing politicians directly with angry protests. Such songs evoke the rhythm and "feel" of West Indian life, especially the laugh beneath the cry. Their despairing, aggressive, or even violent sentiments are softened by the medium used and the festive setting in which the songs are sung. Selvon, who frequently embeds his message in an entertaining and lyrical mode, borrows heavily from this form. One may easily read his stories for their humor alone and fail to perceive a deeper "message" in the texts. Selvon acknowledged his debt to the music by referring to his stories as "ballads" and even naming a character "Calypso."

Samuel Selvon was not the first West Indian writer to use dialect in writing. He was, however, the first to use it to narrow the gap between the peasant characters and the "implied author" (Ramchand, *West* 102). In these stories, the narrator's syntax echoes the speech patterns of the people he portrays. The narrator of "Calypso in London," for example, explains that "one winter a kind of blight fall on Mangohead in London" (125), echoing the native dialect spoken by his characters. Rather than observing from a distance, he is clearly among his subjects, his voice mingling with theirs seamlessly: "All right, Hotboy say grudgingly, let we go in the back of the shop" (128). The narrator of "Working the Transport" also emerges from the community he describes. "One time a fellar named Small Change get a job with London Transport" (132), he tells us, while his character asks, "What happening boy, which part you working?" (136). The narrator's affinity with his characters, then, casts him as a sympathetic onlooker and ultimately invites the reader to enter into the community as well.

The dialect as used by Selvon lends itself to the dramatic: like his methods and his characters, it is colorful and vibrant. In "Calypso in London," for example, Mangohead has lost his job and needs to borrow money from his friends. He approaches his friend Hotboy for a loan, but Hotboy stops him before he can say a word:

"Yes, I know what you come round here for, since you borrow ten shillings from me last week, you lose the address and you only come now to tell me that you expecting a work next week, and if I could lend you another ten please God until you start to work. But Mangohead you lie you hear? I telling you in front, no, no, no. I ain't lending you a nail till you pay me back that ten." "But look at my crosses!" Mango rose to the occasion fast. "Me borrow money from you!" (127)

The long first sentence carries the breathlessness and indignation of the speaker as he anticipates Mangohead's many excuses. Mango's response is that of the "con man's" bristling. As Gordon Rohlehr observes, his is "the language of the small-time confidence-trickster, the Brer Anansi figure . . . whose method is to spin words fast enough to ensnare his victim" (158). Despite Hotboy's protests, then, the trickster ultimately gets his money.

Beneath its humor, however, the story unobtrusively depicts a character lost in this environment. The imagery of fog and smog in the following passage is indicative not just of London weather but of the psychological condition of characters like Mangohead:

This time so I don't have to tell you how the winter grim in London—I mean I don't think it have any other place in the world where the weather powerful, and Mangohead drifting through the fog and the smog and the snow getting in his shoes and the wind passing right through him as if he ain't have on any clothes at all. (126)

The characters of the "London" stories are narrowly drawn, fragmented per-sonalities. When these stories are compared with his "Trinidad" stories, the differences in development are obvious. While the latter have characters of some depth and examine a variety of issues and emotions, the London characters are all fun-loving "fellars" who have no familial attachments or responsibilities. They spend their free time either with each other or picking up English girls. Even their greatest disappointments barely change their outlook. Their attitude toward life is childlike; Selvon's reference to them as "boys" emphasizes their naïveté as well as their camaraderie.

"Working the Transport" presents such a figure in the character Small Change. His "true name," the narrator tells us, is unknown to those around him, a con-dition that emphasizes his displacement in the foreign "mainland." Yet with a cunning suggestive of the folkloric man-spider's antics, Small Change outwits his interviewers and convinces them that he went to the best college in Barbados and that he could drive a bus. He, in fact, had never been to school. While the situation is ironic—the small-island peasant outsmarts the British official—Change is doomed to failure because he is not equipped to survive in this society. His ruse ultimately fails, he is fired, and he "went to mourn with the boys what happen" (138).

Similarly, "Waiting for Aunty to Cough" expresses the discomfort of the islander immigrant within a humorous tale. Brackley, the main character of the story, accompanies his girl, Beatrice, to her home outside central London. It is the first time he has ventured to such parts, and he is scared of getting lost. The narrator laughs with Brackley about the event:

Though Brackley living in England for eight years, is as if he start to discover a new world. . . .
    "You sure we on the right train?" Brackley frighten like hell the first time feeling like they going to Scotland or something.
    "How far you say this place is?"
    "It is London, I keep telling you," the girl say patiently.
    "All of this is London?" (140)

Later, when he has overcome his fear, he brags about his knowledge of London to his friends, again invoking the spirit of Anansi. " 'Man,' he boasting, 'you all don't know London! You think London is the Gate and the Arch and Tra-falgar Square, but them places is nothing. You ever hear about Honor Oak Rise?' "(141).

Another story, "Brackley and the Bed," has a character similar to the Anansi figure of the previous stories, except that here a woman's determination forces him to change his way of life. Teena is a Trinidadian with a purpose in life, and Brackley is part of it. (It needs mentioning here that women do not play an important role in most of these stories.) Teena, though domineering, seems to be the force needed to stir Brackley from his lethargy. In fact, it is the prospect of getting married to her in Trinidad that sends Brackley scurrying to England. When he hears, therefore, that she is on her way to meet him, he is desperate to escape her. He refuses to sleep with her when she arrives in London, and as there is only one bed between them, Brackley takes to sleeping on the floor. Later, however, in order to get use of the bed, he proposes marriage. Teena agrees on condition that he come straight home from work each day and that he "doesn't look at white girls" (155). After the wedding, as Brackley savors the pleasure of sleeping in his bed, Teena springs another surprise: her Aunt is arriving that very day. Brackley returns to sleeping on the floor.

"If Winter Comes" describes the effects of the harsh London weather on the immigrants who come to England from the islands. The "grim days of winter when night fall on the city from three o'clock in the after-noon" (156) mark a time of loneliness, suspicion, and depression for "the boys." Without sunshine and flowers to brighten their outlooks, the misery of their circumstances grows more pronounced. This story sums up the plight of the men: the cold and dreary winters that they are not accustomed to, the scarcity of money, the distrust of native Londoners and even of the "fellars," and their utter despair.

"The Cricket Match" and "Obeah in the Grove" are stories that use two cultural practices as their anchor. The game of cricket is common to both England and the islands, but the practice of obeah (a form of witchcraft practiced under other names in other islands) is Jamaican. Though cricket was originally an Englishman's game, the West Indians have often played it more skillfully than their imperialist instructors; "The Cricket Match" centers around this irony. A West Indian, Algernon, who does not play the game at all, boasts to the "Englishers" about how good he is at the sport. Invited to play a match, he manages, in unorthodox fashion and with a lot of luck, to maintain his ruse until rain halts the game.

"Obeah in the Grove" explores a more serious issue, housing discrimination. People of color, it relates, have difficulty renting lodging except when landlords want to sell their houses. As the "spades" move in, the tenants say, "Gracious me! I can't stay in this house any longer! and they hustle to get another room while the landlord laughing. Next thing he give the spades notice" (168). In this story, however, when the men realize how they are being used, they cause the house to fall apart. They may not have a voice in how they are treated, but at times they can take care of themselves. The narrator, of course, relates the story in the voice common to these stories and does not pass judgment on the practice of obeah. It is up to the reader to decide if it works or not.

The last story in the collection, "My Girl and the City," is very different from the others in that it is written completely in English and is a beautiful lyrical piece. A lover reminisces about the special times he had with his girl and his love for London.

As a West Indian living in London, Samuel Selvon understood many of the problems faced by islander immigrants. He understood living through grim winters and feeling alienated from English society. Although his mixed race and social position may have protected him from some of these difficulties, he used his voice to bring attention to the plight of disadvantaged new Londoners. It is a voice that indulges in the belly laugh as well as in the chuckle, but the humor is never pursued at the expense of his characters. He is at one and the same time distanced from the pain and a part of it.

WORKS CITED AND CONSULTED

Primary

Selvon, Samuel. *A Brighter Sun*. London: Allan Wingate, 1952; New York: Viking, 1953; Trinidad and Jamaica: Longman Caribbean, 1971.

———. *Carnival in Trinidad*. Wellington, New Zealand: Department of Education, 1964.

———. *A Cruise in the Caribbean*. Wellington, New Zealand: Department of Education, 1966.

———. *A Drink of Water*. London: Nelson, 1968.

———. *Eldorado West One*. Leeds, UK: Peepal Tree, 1988.

———. *Foreday Morning: Selected Prose, 1946–1986*. Ed. Kenneth Ramchand and Susheila Nasta. London: Longman, 1988.

———. *Highway in the Sun and Other Plays*. Leeds UK: Peepal Tree, 1991.

———. *The Housing Lark*. London: MacGibbon & Kee, 1965.

———. *I Hear Thunder*. London: MacGibbon & Kee, 1963; New York: St. Martin's, 1963.

———. *An Island Is a World*. London: Allan Wingate, 1955.

———. *The Lonely Londoners*. London: Allan Wingate, 1956; New York: St. Martin's, 1956; Longman Caribbean, 1972. Also published as *The Lonely Ones*. London: Brown, Watson, 1959.

———. *Moses Ascending*. London: Davis-Poynter, 1975.

———. *Moses Migrating*. Harlow, UK: Longman, 1983; Washington, DC: Three Continents, 1991.

———. *The Plains of Caroni*. London: MacGibbon & Kee, 1970.

———. *Those Who Eat the Cascadura*. London: Davis-Poynter, 1972.

———. *Turn Again Tiger*. London: MacGibbon & Kee, 1958; New York: St. Martin's, 1959; St. Andrews, Jamaica: Longman Caribbean, 1978.

———. *Ways of Sunlight*. London: MacGibbon & Kee, 1957; New York: St. Martin's, 1957; St. Andrews, Jamaica: Longman Caribbean, 1973.

Secondary

Baugh, Edward, ed. *Critics on Caribbean Literature*. London: Allen & Unwin, 1978.

Birbalsingh, Frank. "Samuel Selvon and the West Indian Literary Renaissance." *Critical Perspectives on Sam Selvon*. Ed. Susheila Nasta. Washington, DC: Three Continents Press, 1988. 142–59.

James, Louis. "Fragmentation of Experience." *Critical Perspectives on Sam Selvon*. Ed. Susheila Nasta. Washington, DC: Three Continents Press, 1988.

Nasta, Susheila, ed. *Critical Perspectives on Sam Selvon*. Washington, DC: Three Continents Press, 1988. 132–133.

Ramchand, Kenneth, ed. *Best West Indian Stories*. London: Faber & Faber, 1979.

———. *The West Indian Novel and Its Background*. London: Faber & Faber, 1970.

Salkey, Andrew, ed. *West Indian Stories*: Faber & Faber, 1979.

OLIVE SENIOR
(December 23, 1941–   )

Mary Gravitt

BIOGRAPHY

Olive Senior, born in 1941 in the Cockpit country of western Jamaica, is a contemporary Caribbean short-story writer, poet, and social critic in the C.L.R. James tradition of Caribbean national identity. An award-winning author, she received the Institute of Jamaica Centenary Medal in 1980, the Commonwealth Writers Prize in 1987, and the Silver Musgrave Medal for Literature in 1989 and was made a fellow at the Hawthornden International Retreat for Writers in 1990. Further, she has served as a guest lecturer and writer-in-residence in both the Caribbean and abroad. She is a cultural historian and a philanthropist who supports fellow writers—this, too, in line with the Jamesian concept of establishing and maintaining a West Indian identity.

To date, Senior has written three collections of short stories: *Summer Lightning and Other Stories* (1986), *Arrival of the Snake-Woman and Other Stories* (1989), and *Discerner of Hearts* (1995). All of her works involve an element of autobiography. This is not unusual in works by writers of the African Diaspora. She weaves into her narrative structures the stories of children or young adults, mostly females, who are alienated from their communities because they have dared to be different. Such plots reflect on her own childhood.

Senior was born into a culture that granted status based on skin color and the ownership of property. As with any society of color that was colonized by Europeans, the lighter the complexion of the subjugated individual, the more beautiful or handsome and the closer to human the subject was thought to be. If the subjugated beings had a modicum of wealth or property, they were automatically made part of the mulatto social elite. Olive was beautiful, but poor. In order to compensate, her family sent her to live with wealthy, landed relatives at the age of four. She traveled back and forth between her native countryside and the home of her wealthy relatives for the better part of her young life. This travel alienated her from both her parents and her adopted family. She was caught between two worlds, "village life [that] was largely African in character with a rich folk culture and storytelling tradition, [and] the world of her landed relatives [that] was closer to European norms" (Narain 341).

Senior was also influenced by a Calvinistic religion that she describes "as the most oppressive force in her childhood." This religion, she says, is "a very restricted, narrow kind of Christianity combined with poverty . . . a ruthless combination, in that they both attack the spirit, they are both anti-life, they are both anti-freedom, soul-destroying as far as I am concerned" (Narain 341). Thus the theme of religion as oppression, rather than human salvation, permeates Senior's works in both prose and poetry.

CRITICISM

Senior, like many other African Diaspora authors (her predecessor in West Indian letters, C.L.R. James, among them), could find no model for her writing in the Western literary tradition and turned instead to the "native oral cultural tradition" of the folk—"preaching, praying, testifying, concerts, and storytelling sessions"—for inspiration. She narrated *Summer Lightning and Other Stories* and *Discerner of the Hearts*, consequently, mostly in the Creole of the common folk. *Arrival of the Snake-Woman and Other Stories*, however, is narrated mostly in standard English because it is mainly an urban text.

With few exceptions, West Indian authors have not been able to reproduce authentically Jamaican Creole in their written works. Olive Senior is one such exception. She successfully combines, as Ramchand states, standard English and native dialect into a linguistic binary. The two registers of the standard and the patois then become open to influences from each other (Patteson 14). With this technique, Senior breaks the linguistic hegemony of the West over narrative voice.

Expressing her freedom to use the vernacular in her short stories and verse, Senior sets her plots in both rural and urban Jamaica. Her stories typically concern issues of identity and the perversion of individual and communal personality through "miseducation." Moreover, they emphasize that the personal is always a result of the political, and that no social problem in the West Indian context is apolitical. Stylistically, Senior's stories employ the Greek tradition of the chorus—here, the chorus of commentary on issues from the community (Narain 348). Additionally, all of her stories are told by narrators who emerge as three-dimensional characters who tell their own stories in their own particular, and sometimes peculiar, Caribbean way.

ANALYSIS

Many of the young protagonists in *Summer Lightning and Other Stories* are females who tell other people's stories, only to have their own emerge. In "Ballad," for example, Lenora reveals the quality of her own character in the process of describing the local harlot, Miss Rilla. Like Miss Rilla, she refuses to co-operate in her own enslavement and feels alienated from her community. "The Boy Who Loved Ice Cream," in contrast, presents the story of a boy caught between two competing adult perspectives on "authentic" West Indian identity. Ice cream in the story is a symbol for "obsessive jealousy and possessiveness" (Narain 348). "Christian child abuse" is the theme of "Do Angels Wear Bras-sieres?" while "Country of the One Eye God" explores the issue of cultural and theological imperialism, exemplified by Pentecostal practices among natives. Class struggle is addressed in both "Ascot" and "Real Old Time T'ing": Ascot moves up in class because of his light skin color, while Patricia ascends through marriage.

Senior's second collection of short stories, *Arrival of the Snake-Woman and Other Stories*, is narrated mostly in standard English and focuses predominantly on the middle class. The title story, "Arrival of the Snake-Woman," demands reader participation by leaving gaps in the narrative that encourage the reader to give the "snake-woman," Miss Coolie, a past and thus a presence in the story. A mysterious East Indian woman, Miss Coolie introduces modern changes to the rural village, then assumes a West Indian Creolized identity. Ultimately, she becomes the most prominent and wealthy citizen of the rural shire. Narrated from the end to the beginning by Ish, a physician, who was a young boy when Miss Coolie arrived, this story explores the consequences of introducing an alien presence into an indigenous culture.

"Tears of the Sea" and "See the Tiki-Tiki Scatter" address the subject of juvenile schizophrenia. Both works feature female protagonists abandoned by their parents. "The Two Grandmothers" presents a series of monologues spoken by a young protagonist who compares and contrasts living with her maternal and paternal grandmothers: Grandma Del and Grandma Elaine. Critic Denise deCaires Narain states that in this story, "Senior uses the child's visits to Grandma Del in her rural village and Grandma Elaine in town as a way of exploring the cultural values associated with environment" (347).

Assuming the moral middle ground in this story, Senior neither sanctions nor judges the narrator's view of poverty or wealth. Rather, she uses "Miami" as the signifier for materialism. In fact, as Richard F. Patteson observes, the author seldom chooses sides: "Rarely does Senior present Western influence as an un-alloyed evil, or even as a factor wholly extraneous to Caribbean experience. Although she clearly recognizes the destructive potential in headlong assimila-tion of Western (especially American) ways, she also implicitly acknowledges the interpenetration of the cosmopolitan and the insular as an essential element in the process of Creolization" (18). In spite of its colonial affinities, then, English emerges for Senior as a useful vehicle of communication between the Anglophone West Indians and the rest of the world.

In "View from the Terrace," Senior writes about an extreme case of inter-nalized racism. Mr. Barton, a black man who sings a cold European colonial song while sitting in the warm West Indian sun, agonizes over his ethnic identity. In contrast to his servant, Marcus, a West Indian who embraces his native culture, Barton abhors his heritage and aspires to be more European. When Marcus fathers a child with the black woman whose shack blocks the scenic view from Mr. Barton's European-style mansion on the hill, the Eurocentric master drops dead from shock. In his mind, he is an English country squire or colonial master employed with the task of visiting and inspecting his plantation and his natives, yet his frequent trips to England show him, to his self-disgust, that he is neither British nor, therefore, civilized.

"The Tenantry of Birds" presents a young, married, light-skinned, female protagonist who gradually begins to understand that color and class do not automatically grant eternal happiness. Because of her color and class, she has almost forgotten that she must be a strong woman and mother, and not an empty-headed showpiece to be ordered about and taken for granted. Nolene awakens to the conclusion that she must, like the pecharies, drive out the "rough uncouth chattering and uncaring" (47) kling-klings that have attempted to take over her space and home.

The final story in the collection, "Lily-Lily," is a tale of incest and hypocrisy. It presents the respectable middle-class couple, Mr. and Mrs. DaSilva, who adopt a supposedly illegitimate child, Lily. When Mr. DaSilva begins to sexually abuse Lily, the child runs away for protection to her Aunt Lily, and a disturbing series of family secrets are revealed. This is the most antineocolonialist story in *Arrival of the Snake-Woman and Other Stories*. In it, Senior addresses feminist and social issues in the Caribbean context.

Senior's *Discerner of Hearts* is a collection "marked by a juxtaposition of lively voices, rigid class lines and competing societies" (Garb 32). Employing an anachronistic arrangement of eras in Jamaican history, the stories, Michael Thorpe suggests, "regardless of chronology, [reflect] a constricted society whose relationships are over-determined by class and color; caste-power, or the lack of it, is constantly felt" (455). The story "Theresa," for example, is about a young girl caught between the old African-centered and new neocolonial cultures of Jamaica. Similarly, "The Glass-Bottom Boat" characterizes a midlife crisis that sets its male protagonist adrift.

The voices in *Discerner* are mostly female and marginal, and they speak in both standard English and the Creole of Jamaica. Senior uses language to denote class stratification and to differentiate between servants and masters. This is done most obviously in "The Case against the Queen" and "Zig Zag." Cissy, a servant, narrates "The Case against the Queen" in patois. In "Zig Zag," on the other hand, Saddie is a genteel, meaning poor, white girl whose narration is in standard English. Her story is based in a West Indian world on the brink of change where "being white or light-skinned is a depreciating asset, an outmoded recipe for success in the world" (Thorpe 455); that recipe is being replaced by a materialism where it is no longer the color of the skin that matters, but the content of the pocketbook.

Postcolonial changes bring with them all the afflictions that plague the West, including "coke and the crack and all them sinting" (Thorpe 455) in "The Lizardy Man and His Lady." As the modern world intrudes into "The Islands," the West Indian increasingly struggles to confirm her or his identity in a system that "offers him no true self-consciousness." Human rights in Senior's stories—the rights to life, liberty, and the pursuit of happiness—depend on disposable income.

Senior does not manufacture her plots in the relationships she writes about. She simply comments on the culture she "knows" and in so doing comments on the universal. Her stories frequently present characters who yearn for "self-actualization." The colonial superstructure is collapsed in Senior's fiction, when the "native" seeks freedom.

These stories of postcolonial colorism and class conflict mark Senior as the premier contemporary critic of the relationships that determine the West Indian identity. Senior's use of the outsider/insider strategy allows her to see and write without judging or preaching, while always offering empowering messages in her works.

WORKS CITED AND CONSULTED

Primary

Senior, Olive. *Arrival of the Snake-Woman and Other Stories*. Burnt Mill, Harlow, Essex, UK: Longman, 1989.
———. *Discerner of Hearts*. Toronto: McClelland & Stewart, 1995.
———. *Gardening in the Tropics*. Toronto: McClelland & Stewart, 1996.
———. *Summer Lightning and Other Stories*. Essex, UK: Longman, 1986.

Secondary

Fenwick, M. J. *Writers of the Caribbean and Central America: A Bibliography*. Vol. 1. New York: Garland, 1992.
Garb, Maggie. "Books in Brief: Fiction." *New York Times* October 1, 1995, sec. 7: 32.
Gates, Henry Louis, Jr. ed. *The Classic Slave Narratives*. New York: Penguin, 1987.
———. *The Signifying Monkey: A Theory of Afro-American Literary Criticism*. New York: Oxford University Press, 1988.
Henry, Paget, and Paul Buhle, eds. *C.L.R. James's Caribbean*. Durham: Duke University Press, 1992.
Herdeck, Donald E., ed. *Caribbean Writers: A Bio-Bibliographical–Critical Encyclopedia*. Washington, DC: Three Continents Press, 1979.
James, C.L.R. *The Future in the Present: Selected Writings*. Westport, CT: Lawrence Hill, 1977.
———. *Spheres of Existence: Selected Writings*. Westport, CT: Lawrence Hill, 1980.
Narain, Denise deCaires. "Olive Senior." *Twentieth-Century Caribbean and Black Afri-

  can Writers. Third Series. *Dictionary of Literary Biography.* Vol. 157. Detroit: Gale Research, 1996. 340–48.

Obradovic, Nadezda. "Jamaica." *World Literature Today* 64.3 (Summer 1990): 514.

Patteson, Richard F. "The Fiction of Olive Senior: Traditional Society and the Wider World." *Ariel: A Review of International English Literature* 24.1 (January 1993): 13–33.

Smith, Raymond T. "Working Miracles: Women's Lives in the English-speaking Caribbean." *Man* 27.4 (December 1992): 890.

Thorpe, Michael. "Discerner of Hearts." *World Literature Today* 70.2 (Spring 1996): 455.

Webster, Roger. *Studying Literary Theory: An Introduction.* London: Edward Arnold, 1992.

LESLIE MARMON SILKO
(March 5, 1948–   )

Neil Nakadate

BIOGRAPHY

Leslie Marmon Silko was born in Albuquerque, New Mexico, in 1948, and is of mixed Laguna, Mexican, and white ancestry; she grew up at Laguna Pueblo, in west central New Mexico. While Laguna Pueblo itself has a mixed population that also includes Hopi, Zuni, Navajo, Jemez, Acoma, and other residents, Silko has always identified most closely with the Laguna. At the same time, she has long been aware that being of mixed blood and from a locally prestigious family over several generations gave her problematic status and at times distanced her from others in the community.

Silko's formal education included girlhood years at a private day school in Albuquerque, fifty miles from home; college education at the University of New Mexico, from which she graduated with honors in 1969; and a brief attempt to study law, also at New Mexico. All of these experiences separated Silko physically and emotionally—but not imaginatively—from Laguna, where her schooling began and where her informal education in storytelling started. On numerous occasions, both orally and in print, Silko has stressed that her roots in Laguna landscape, experience, and culture are at the core of her being as a person and a writer.

While Silko was growing up, many of those who conveyed to her a sense of her heritage were women, among them her grandmother, Marie Anaya Marmon, and her Aunt Susie (actually her father's aunt). Aunt Susie, in particular, seems to have served simultaneously as a role model and a crucial link to the long tradition of Native American oral narrative. Removed from Laguna and educated at Carlisle Indian School in Pennsylvania and at Dickinson College, Aunt Susie returned to raise a family, to teach, to write, and to tell stories. In *Storyteller*, the 1981 collection of her work, Silko describes Aunt Susie as from "the last generation here at Laguna, / that passed down an entire culture / by word of mouth / an entire history / an entire vision of the world / which depended upon memory / and retelling by subsequent generations" (4, 6).

The legacy of Aunt Susie and others informed Silko's first attempts at fiction writing while she was an undergraduate and her publication of "Tony's Story" and "The Man to Send Rain Clouds" in 1969. This early success gained her the recognition of a National Endowment for the Humanities Discovery Grant in 1971 and was reconfirmed by Silko's dominating presence in *The Man to Send Rain Clouds* (1974), an anthology subtitled *Contemporary Stories by American Indians* and edited by Kenneth Rosen. In that volume, Silko is represented by seven of the nineteen selections. *Laguna Woman*, a collection of poetry, appeared the same year and was followed by the novel *Ceremony* (1977), largely written while Silko was living in Ketchikan, Alaska. *Ceremony* was immediately recognized and praised for its incorporation of Indian storytelling elements into a novel that focuses on the alienation and reintegration into traditional Indian life of a young veteran of World War II. The widespread recognition and critical praise of *Ceremony* no doubt contributed to Silko's being awarded a 1981 MacArthur Foundation Fellowship, the support of which enabled her to suspend teaching at the University of Arizona and focus her attention on *Almanac of the Dead* (1991), a long and in some ways experimental novel inspired by ancient Mayan almanacs. In addition to her teaching appointment at the University of Arizona, Silko has had academic associations with Navajo Community College in Tsaile, Arizona, and the University of New Mexico.

CRITICISM

The reception of Silko's work as a short-story writer has grown since the initial recognition provided by the Rosen collection in 1974. Rosen's volume, containing a variety of stories by a range of accomplished authors from various tribes, constituted a key moment of recognition for Native American short-story writers, but particularly for Silko. In subsequent years, Silko's work has given rise to numerous critical essays and conference papers and has won her firm standing as an important writer of contemporary American fiction. Silko's best readers recognize that her skill in crafting narratives in the Western (that is, Western European-American) tradition of the short story as a genre is always modified by content, conventions, and qualities of the oral tradition. For example, some critics have taken particular note of Silko's ability to implicate traditional legends in contemporary situations, and her blending or interpolation of transcribed versions of Indian oral genres. In addition, several others have brought contemporary interpretive theory to bear on Silko's work, typically with an eye toward addressing that work on its own terms and avoiding the imposition of culturally and intellectually prescriptive expectations.

In reading Silko, it is particularly crucial to resist the casual application of the terminology and habits of mind most familiar to readers of fiction in English. That is, terms such as "novel" and "short story," "narrator" and "point of view" should be recognized as necessary and useful in the discussion of Silko's short fiction, but inconsistent with its roots in the oral tradition. Similarly, readers of Silko should resist a dependence on such familiar, fundamental Western concepts as text, author(ity), narrative closure, "meaning," and a sharp distinction between fact and fiction. A preoccupation with any of these concerns can be a distraction that results in misunderstanding and misinterpretation. The most useful and responsible criticism of Silko's fiction keeps in mind the difference between told-to-the-people stories and told-to-the-page stories (as Paula Gunn Allen calls them in her introduction to *Spider Woman's Granddaughters*), the difference between an oral performance for a live audience and writing for a reader of a printed text, and the difference between meaning and value derived, to a significant extent, from a specific audience and storytelling situation versus meaning and value vested in a written or printed text. Simply put, a radically un-Western set of fiction-making attitudes and conventions operates in her writing, as reflected (for example) in this observation regarding the open-ended, less-than-definitive nature of any given story: "I know Aunt Susie and Aunt Alice would tell me stories they had told me before but with changes in details or descriptions. The story was the important thing and little changes here and there were really part of the story. There were even stories about the different versions of stories and how they imagined these differing versions came to be" (*Storyteller* 227).

The range of critical work on Silko is typified by the contributions of A. LaVonne Ruoff, Linda Danielson, and Arnold Krupat. Ruoff's "Ritual and Renewal: Keres Traditions in the Short Fiction of Leslie Silko" clarifies the roles of adaptability and variation in the storytelling tradition as keys to its resilience and vitality, and her overview essays provide a necessary general context for understanding Silko's relationship to native traditions, literary and oral. Like Ruoff, Danielson advocates the application of feminist consciousness and critical strategies to Silko's writing and sees the mythic tradition as essentially female (circular, cyclical, clustering) rather than male (linear). In "*Storyteller*: Grandmother Spider's Web," Danielson asserts that Silko's book "represents . . . a revision of the world from her vantage point as a Laguna Indian woman" (327). Krupat's "The Dialogic of Silko's *Storyteller*" applies the work of Mikhail Bakhtin and others to a reading of the 1981 collection. In addition, valuable work that sheds light on Silko's stories has been done by Paula Gunn Allen, also of Laguna heritage and an accomplished writer of poetry and fiction, and by Kenneth Lincoln in "Grandmother Storyteller: Leslie Silko," which includes a long reading of "Storyteller." Finally, Silko herself has been generous with interviews and essays, and these should not be overlooked for insights into her sense of short-story writing in relation to the native tradition.

ANALYSIS

In the tradition of oral storytelling that informs all of Silko's writing, sacred chants, ceremonies, and rituals make up the larger context of songs and narratives and of various special styles and applications of language. That is, the Indian way of storytelling should be seen as part of an inclusive cultural consciousness that is tied to spirituality and its expressions in ceremony, ritual, and myth. Among the key values of Indian spirituality are harmony and balance, kinship and community, civility and decorum, and a reverent appreciation of the interrelatedness of all aspects of the natural world. Among the defining characteristics of Indian literatures are cyclical patterns, recurring figures and themes, variations and departures from previous versions, and a general acceptance of the tentative and open-ended in narrative performances and presentations.

Silko's work as a writer of the short story, then, should be seen as an extension of this tradition; in her, formal education and training in Euro-American literary forms (she majored in English at the University of New Mexico) are complemented by an even longer informal education in Native American storytelling. For this reason, her short fiction might well be best understood if it is read along with the accompanying chants, songs, poems, biographical and autobiographical notes, and photographs of *Storyteller*, all of which function intertextually (that is, provide an interacting context for each other). Notable in this collection for their deft blend of oral-traditional and Western short-story conventions are "Storyteller," "Lullaby," "Tony's Story," "Yellow Woman," "The Man to Send Rain Clouds," and "A Geronimo Story" (all quotations from the stories are taken from the versions printed in *Storyteller*).

"Storyteller" is notable for its explicit acknowledgment of the fierce imperatives of storytelling and the power of storytelling to bear witness to everything human beings must endure. It is also notable because it is set not in the American Southwest, as are Silko's other stories, but in the Arctic; in fact, "Storyteller" is an outgrowth of her interlude in Alaska in the mid-1970s. Nevertheless, its themes and issues resonate in Silko's work. The young Eskimo woman at the story's center is one of many Silko characters driven by anger at the brutality and exploitation visited on native peoples and land by greedy outsiders, in this case the "Gussucks" or white men. She has been angry since enduring the outrages of the English-only Gussuck school, learning how the occupation of native territory was motivated first by the hunt for fur and fish and later by the search for oil, and experiencing sexual abuse, first at the hands of the old man who lives with her grandmother and then from crude and perverted Gussuck workers. In inspired anger she salvages the red tin and uses it to mark her dwelling and reassert her presence in the face of withering affliction—cultural more than that of the natural world. Her hostility toward the invaders is expressed as ridicule of the pathetic efforts of the whites to fend off the arctic winter with insulation-stuffed metal buildings and to extract oil from the ground with big yellow machines and a giant drill that freezes and shatters in the cold, ending up in a tundra graveyard. Her need for revenge for the alcohol killing her parents is expressed in her well-planned seduction of the Gussuck storeman onto the unstable river ice.

Here, as elsewhere in Silko, the natural world is accepted by native people on its own terms, but is thought of by outsiders only in terms of conflict—as something to be fought and conquered. So when the young woman runs onto the ice, the river and the freezing cold become her allies and the storeman's doom: "She was familiar with the river, down to the instant ice flexed into hairline fractures" (30). After the storeman's death, nonnative auditors who have power over Eskimo lives refuse either to listen to or act on the testimony offered by a native speaker, dismissing it because it does not fit their view of the world. The white authorities do not understand intimate affinities between nature and human beings, and they do not understand that in native cultures storytelling is itself crucial testimony regarding how and why things happen and how events fit together: "I will not change the story, not even to escape this place and go home. I intended that he die. The story must be told as it is" (31). The authorities find it difficult to believe that for this woman truthtelling is more important than freedom, and they either deny or try to get her to misrepresent what took place. "The Gussucks did not understand the story; they could not see the way it must be told . . . without lapse or silence" (31–32).

The old man's story of the giant polar bear stalking the lone hunter reveals his anticipation and acceptance of his own impending death, but it also echoes and reinforces the larger story of the inexorable approach of an overwhelming arctic winter—the sun "frozen, caught in the middle of the sky" (18) and draped by heavy frost, the boundaries between river and land and sky "swallowed by the freezing white" (30). There is an apocalyptic quality to the bear in the old man's story, but because the bear is the color of glacier ice and, after all, a living part of the arctic world, its coming signals not "the end of things," but only the end of some things, In the long view, all that is natural will go on.

"Lullaby" also addresses the emotional costs of the conflict between native and Euro-American cultures. Its focus on a Navajo family rather than a Laguna one is a reminder of Silko's involvement in the Indian tradition of storytelling give-and-take across tribal boundaries and the fact that the decline of native culture in the face of oppressive forces has been shared by all indigenous groups. In "Lullaby," the manifestations of white cultural hegemony are numerous, and the consequences catastrophic. Ayah, whose life "had become memories" (43), embodies the story's devotion to traditional ways; she grieves for a lost life that was protected and sustained by the shelter of a hogan, handwoven blankets, and buckskin leggings and elkhide moccasins. Decades later, she mourns the death of her oldest child, taken by the army and the war. She mourns the loss of her two younger children, Danny and Ella, taken by force and placed in the "protective" custody of white policemen, doctors, and teachers—that is, the debilitating paternalism of white institutions and the culturally hostile policies of the Bureau of Indian Affairs.

It is worth noting that the family was made vulnerable by Chato's naïve trust in the integrity of the white rancher who employed him, and by his willingness to learn and use Spanish and English, languages of the cultures that have oppressed the Indians since the moment of their first contact. In fact, one of the recurring motifs in the story is that of paper as a sign of deception, betrayal, and death, and this is closely linked to the white man's use of English, in particular (just one element of a formal education that represses rather than enables), as a tool of cultural oppression. To adopt the oppressors' language is to endanger oneself, the old ones have said, and Ayah learns that it was a mistake to learn how to sign her name. The independence and integrity of Navajo life have been compromised almost to extinction by the paternalistic welfare (rice, sugar, peaches) of the government and the debilitating presence of alcohol and Spanish music. At the end, it seems that only in the pure vision made possible by the crystalline light of a clearing sky can Ayah achieve a sense of peace, and only through the ancient lullaby can she find consolation for her losses and a sense that they are not permanent.

Starker and more dramatically confrontational than "Lullaby," "Tony's Story" also affirms more aggressively the power of Indian spirituality. The essential conflict is between Leon, who has been angered and alienated by his hitch in the military, and the sadistic, arbitrarily violent state cop. Tony, the narrator, is both a mediating voice and an alternative consciousness. Like Chato in "Lullaby," Leon is betrayed in his willingness to believe the claims and promises of those who hold power over the Indians, and he tries to obtain justice through the appropriate conventional channels. In response to his efforts to stand up for himself (and, by extension, for Indians in general), Leon is labeled a troublemaker by his own tribe and held to blame for his own beating.

Tony, with a less compromised sense of traditional beliefs (represented by his wearing of an arrowhead on a string as a talisman), associates the cop's destructive presence with darkness and witchery; Tony's sense of good and evil as constantly active spiritual forces results in his dream-state transmogrification of the cop's billy club into a long human bone and his sunglasses into "little, round, white-rimmed eyes on a black ceremonial mask" (125). By the time the cop gets around to threatening Tony and Leon again, Tony's imagination has confirmed him as a witch to be dispatched through the use of Leon's .30-30 and finally exorcised by burning. It is clear here that, in part because he has not been as strongly influenced in and by the world of the dominant culture, Tony rather than Leon is the one who understands the essential meaning of their relationship to the cop and how the spiritual world can be manifested in everyday life. For him, the killing of the cop is natural and consistent with fundamental beliefs and the ongoing struggle between good and evil, and thus hardly illegal or wrong.

Silko conveys a similar sense of an alternate Indian world view in "Yellow Woman," her best-known and most often reprinted story, in which the central figure cooperates with the man who spirits her away from the pueblo rather than resist him, as might be expected. "Yellow Woman" is Silko's version of a traditional abduction tale and demonstrates her conviction that "you should understand / the way it was / back then, / because it is the same / even now" (94). The story should be seen as extending a cycle of traditional narratives that concern a woman ("Kochininako" or "Kochinnenako") whose association with the river and water (sometimes rain) is linked to her seduction and abduction (perhaps both simultaneously), an interlude of lovemaking with an ambiguous commitment to the trickster-kidnapper, and an eventual return to her former way of life. Because of the traditional identification of the color yellow with the very concept of "woman," the title itself constitutes a reiteration of its mythic and symbolic significance. In reading this story, then, it is important not to impose on the abducted woman who narrates it the moral expectations of another time and culture or of other circumstances. Yellow Woman's vitalizing interlude of lovemaking, like Silva's stealing of cattle, transcends the imposed boundaries and moral strictures of any individual tribe; her nonconformist behavior is less to be judged than understood in the larger context of the long life and survival of the people.

Crucially, and in a manner that typifies her development not only of short stories but also of longer fiction and the *Storyteller* collection as a whole, Silko literally embeds the core story in the contemporary one: "Yellow Woman went away with the spirit from the north and lived with him and his relatives. She was gone for a long time, but then one day she came back and brought twin boys" (56). It is important to Silko's contemporary version of this story that the abducted woman's resistance is not so much to her abductor as to the possibility that he is more than a cattle thief ("Arrow Boy," perhaps, or maybe Coyote) and that she might be Yellow Woman. Even as she denies the seducer-abductor's contention that the two of them are (re)living ancient roles, she capitulates to Silva's imperatives and to the likelihood that her abduction has in fact constituted a kind of salvation from the modern world and an induction, in spirit as much as in body, into the ongoing life of her culture. In returning to the pueblo, she makes no apologies for her actions or her absence and offers no logical explanation: "I did not decide to go. I just went" (59), she says. She no longer wonders "if Yellow Woman had known . . . that she would become part of the stories" (55).

"The Man to Send Rain Clouds" is another widely anthologized Silko story, and another story concerned with the individual's significance within a larger context. Like "Storyteller" and "Lullaby," it conveys a sense of the threat presented by the imposition of non-Indian traditions and beliefs. But where "Storyteller" expresses anger and "Lullaby" conveys transcendent grief, "The Man to Send Rain Clouds" is infused with humor. The death of Teofilo (whose name means "lover of God") becomes the occasion for a battle of wills and strategies between the local priest and the old grandfather's family and friends. The Indians' successful insistence on the primacy of traditional rituals (cornmeal, pollen, face painting, and so on) over the Catholic sacraments undercuts the priest's "missionary magazine" preoccupation with salvation and sustenance. The Indians' verbal jockeying for the priest's capitulation to their wishes is a reminder, frequent in Silko's work, that humor is one of the sustaining elements of Native American life. That the Indians ask the priest for holy water as an afterthought and to ease the old man's journey is, of course, only consistent with their own as well as Catholic beliefs and is connected with the old man's larger purpose of entering the spirit world and sending the people rain.

In fact, the Indians' conviction that any water used to send Teofilo on his way will return in the form of rain reinforces their belief in the circularity (rather than linearity) of life, and that the old man's passing is part of a familiar and constantly repeating pattern, a universal ritual, rather than the end of something. The humorous elements of "The Man to Send Rain Clouds" complement this theme by displacing the grim solemnity of the priest and his concern for "Last Rites."

"A Geronimo Story" is a blend of humor and satire. Longer than most of Silko's stories, it shares with many of them a sense of undetermined moment and location, part of a constantly lived and seamless reality; it is, for example, *a* Geronimo story, one of many that have occurred and might again take place. Silko's Geronimo, then, should be read as a universal rather than a historical figure, for the Indians as representative of admirable and awe-inspiring qualities and exploits as were Cochise, Crazy Horse, and Chief Joseph. Like Silva-Coyote in "Yellow Woman," the Geronimo of Silko's story seems to defy the restrictions of space and time, and the Indian searchers are sure from the outset that he cannot be found, let alone captured. In fact, the story's humor derives largely from the significant gap between Major Littlecock's premise that they are in urgent pursuit of a renegade and the Indian scouts' assumption that they are only engaged in a leisurely hunt, with expenses paid by the government. The manic and ineffectual Littlecock, satirized throughout by Silko in broadly rendered strokes, is contrasted to Captain Pratt, who always has "plenty of time for some tea" (215) and prefers the company of Indians and horses to that of any self-important, glory-seeking officer.

At the same time, the story's center of consciousness, the young boy Andy, comes to understand the fundamental contrasts between the Indians and the whites, as evidenced in differences between Indian and white ways of doing virtually anything. Andy sees the affinity between Geronimo and Siteye—and their respective abilities to thwart and ridicule Littlecock. As a singer and storyteller, as well as a smart hunter who knows when and what not to hunt, Siteye is Andy's mentor. Siteye's hope is not to catch Geronimo, but rather that the hunt be "a beautiful journey" (214). He teaches Andy how to roll cigarettes, make a warm bed, and remember the trail he has traveled, but also that "we don't have to listen to white men" (216). He helps Andy realize that "anybody can act violently—there is nothing to it; but not every person is able to destroy his enemy with words" (222). At the same time, it might be safest to read Andy's journey as less a coming-of-age or initiation story than as (in the Indian tradition of narrative) just one more significant episode in the ongoing process of life and of storytelling. The final verbal contest between the insensitive Littlecock and the irreverent Siteye ("mediated" by a bemused Captain Pratt) gives way to humorous commentary by the other Indians, a kind of gloss on the whole (mis)adventure, undoubtedly to be invoked at future renderings of this and other hunting stories.

Finally, "A Geronimo Story," like the others cited here, conveys Silko's sense not only of something important happening, but also of storytelling itself as an important process, and beyond that, of the Indian belief in thinking and using the Word wisely as a crucial human endeavor and a source of remarkable power. That is, the telling and reception of stories are enabling acts that acknowledge the potential of words to affect the relations of things. "It was beautiful to hear Siteye talk; his words were careful and thoughtful, but they followed each other smoothly to tell a good story. He would pause to let you get a feeling for the words; and even silence was alive in his stories" (215). The same, of course, might be said of Silko's own work. As she herself pointed out in an interview, "The best thing, I learned, the best thing you can have in life is to have someone tell you a story" (Coltelli 145).

WORKS CITED AND CONSULTED

Primary

Rosen, Kenneth, ed. *The Man to Send Rain Clouds: Contemporary Stories by American Indians*. New York: Viking, 1974. Includes Silko's stories "The Man to Send Rain Clouds," "Yellow Woman," "Tony's Story," "Uncle Tony's Goat," "A Geronimo Story," "Bravura," and "From Humaweepi, the Warrior Priest," published together for the first time.

Silko, Leslie Marmon. *Almanac of the Dead: A Novel*. New York: Simon & Schuster, 1991.

———. *Ceremony*. New York: Viking, 1977.

———. *Laguna Woman: Poems*. Greenfield Center, NY: Greenfield Review Press, 1974. 2nd ed. Tucson, AZ: Flood Plain Press, 1994.

———. "Landscape, History, and the Pueblo Imagination." *Antaeus* 57 (Autumn 1986): 83–94.

———. "Language and Literature from a Pueblo Indian Perspective." *English Literature: Opening Up the Canon*. Ed. Leslie A. Fiedler and Houston A. Baker, Jr. Baltimore: Johns Hopkins University Press, 1981. 54–72.

———. *Sacred Water: Narratives and Pictures*. Tucson, AZ: Flood Plain Press, 1993. Limited edition of 750 copies.

———. *Storyteller*. New York: Seaver Books, 1981; New York: Little, Brown/Arcade, 1981. Contains most of the stories previously published in *The Man to Send Rain Clouds* (some in slightly different versions) and "Storyteller," "Lullaby," and "Coyote Holds a Full House in His Hand."

———. *Yellow Woman and a Beauty of the Spirit: Essays on Native American Life Today*. New York: Simon & Schuster, 1996.

Wright, Anne, ed. *The Delicacy and Strength of Lace: Letters between Leslie Marmon Silko and James Wright*. Saint Paul: Graywolf Press, 1986.

———. *Gardens in the Dunes*. New York: Simon & Schuster, 1999.

Secondary

Allen, Paula Gunn, ed. *Spider Woman's Granddaughters: Traditional Tales and Contemporary Writing by Native American Women.* Boston: Beacon, 1989.

Barnes, Kim. "A Leslie Marmon Silko Interview." *Journal of Ethnic Studies* 13 (Winter 1986): 83–105.

Barnett, Louise K., and James L. Thorson, eds. *Leslie Marmon Silko: A Collection of Critical Essays.* Albuquerque: University of New Mexico Press, 1999.

Buell, Lawrence. *The Environmental Imagination: Thoreau, Nature Writing, and the Formation of American Culture.* Cambridge, MA: Belknap Press of Harvard University Press, 1995. 285–96.

Coltelli, Laura, ed. "Leslie Marmon Silko" (interview). *Winged Words: American Indian Writers Speak.* Lincoln: University of Nebraska Press, 1990. 134–53.

Danielson, Linda. "*Storyteller*: Grandmother Spider's Web." *Journal of the Southwest* 30.3 (Autumn 1988): 325–55.

———. "The Storytellers in *Storyteller.*" *Studies in American Indian Literatures* 1 (Fall 1989): 21–31.

Evers, Larry, and Denny Carr. "A Conversation with Leslie Marmon Silko." *Sun Tracks* 3 (Fall 1976): 28–33.

Fisher, Dexter. "Stories and Their Tellers: A Conversation with Leslie Marmon Silko." *The Third Woman: Minority Women Writers of the United States.* Ed. Dexter Fisher. Boston: Houghton Mifflin, 1980. 18–23.

Graulich, Melody, ed. *Yellow Woman.* New Brunswick, NJ: Rutgers University Press, 1993.

Jaskoski, Helen. *Leslie Marmon Silko: A Study of the Short Fiction.* New York: Twayne, 1998; London: Prentice Hall, 1998.

Krupat, Arnold. "The Dialogic of Silko's *Storyteller.*" *Narrative Chance: Postmodern Discourse on Native American Indian Literatures.* Ed. Gerald Vizenor. Albuquerque: University of New Mexico Press, 1989. 55–68.

Lincoln, Kenneth. "Grandmother Storyteller: Leslie Silko." *Native American Renaissance.* Berkeley and Los Angeles: University of California Press, 1983. 222–50.

Ruoff, A. LaVonne Brown. *American Indian Literatures: An Introduction, Bibliographic Review, and Selected Bibliography.* New York: Modern Language Association, 1990.

———. "Ritual and Renewal: Keres Traditions in the Short Fiction of Leslie Silko." *MELUS* 5 (Winter 1978): 2–17.

Salyer, Gregory. *Leslie Marmon Silko.* New York: Twayne, 1997; London: Prentice Hall, 1997.

Seyersted, Per. *Leslie Marmon Silko.* Boise, ID: Boise State University, 1980.

Velie, Alan R. *Four American Indian Literary Masters: N. Scott Momaday, James Welch, Leslie Marmon Silko, and Gerald Vizenor.* Norman: University of Oklahoma Press, 1982.

AMY TAN
(February 19, 1952–   )

Elias Ellefson

BIOGRAPHY

Amy Tan was born in Oakland, California, the daughter of John and Daisy Tan. Her Chinese immigrant parents arrived in the United States two and a half years prior to her birth. John Tan worked as an electrical engineer and served as a minister for a Chinese-American Baptist congregation. Tan's mother held a position as a vocational nurse and participated as a member of a Joy Luck Club.

Like many Chinese immigrants, John and Daisy set high expectations for their daughter, placing a strong emphasis on education. They envisioned for Amy a career as a neurosurgeon and a part-time concert pianist. In spite of her parents' dream, Tan pursued both bachelor's and master's degrees in English and linguistics at San Jose State University. Upon completing her studies at San Jose, she undertook postgraduate studies at the University of California at Berkeley.

Tan's literary career stemmed from her frustration with her work as an educational administrator and free-lance technical writer. Hoping to curtail her workaholic habits and career dissatisfaction, she sought psychological counseling. However, counseling proved to be unsuccessful because her therapist fell asleep during her sessions. Undaunted, Tan took it upon herself to spend fewer hours working and more hours playing jazz piano and writing fiction. Eventually, her early stories won her a place in the Squaw Valley Community of Writers. Tan's association with this writers' workshop honed her storytelling talents and, with the publication of *The Joy Luck Club* in 1989, gave rise to a new career.

The Joy Luck Club was an immediate success; it remained at the top of the best-seller list for several months. Though *The Joy Luck Club* was published as a novel, it is a short-story cycle comprised of separate and complete short stories that cohere around major characters and themes. The reading public, as well as critics, hailed Tan's first publication for its poignancy and stirring use of language. Additionally, *The Joy Luck Club* attracted attention from Hollywood, as Tan later collaborated with Ronald Bass to write an adaptation of the novel for Oliver Stone.

Tan's success continued with the publication of her second book, *The Kitchen God's Wife* (1991), and two children's books, *The Moon Lady* (1992) and *The Chinese Siamese Cat* (1994). In addition to her fiction, Tan has contributed her essay "Mother Tongue" to *Best American Essays 1991*. Her popularity as a writer has enabled her to enjoy a celebrity's life. She has made an appearance on *Sesame Street* in addition to singing in a rock band with Stephen King. She currently lives in San Francisco with her husband, Lou DeMattei.

CRITICISM

Tan quickly found praise as a gifted storyteller who merges Chinese folklore with her personal recollections of her family history. Tan learned to appreciate her ethnicity as a result of her writing career. Her fiction often demonstrates how her cultural legacy is at times subverted by the pressure to assimilate into a rootless American society. Drawing a great deal on her personal experiences as a second-generation Chinese American, Tan describes with sensitivity the pressure of conforming to mainstream American values while realizing the importance of honoring her ancestral legacy.

Tan's contribution to the contemporary short story is her implementation of what Robert M. Luscher (1993) calls the short-story sequence (or short-story cycle). *The Joy Luck Club* is an example of how Tan creates a unifying theme throughout several stories. Although each story in *The Joy Luck Club* possesses a sense of wholeness, their ordering creates a context that transcends the limits of a single short story. In spite of their autonomy and compression, Tan's stories complement each other by expanding characters and providing different points of view.

Charlotte Painter, however, expresses some reservations about Tan's ability to maintain distinct voices. According to Painter, Tan's narrators are so similar in voice that readers may not be able to distinguish between them (16). David Gates agrees with Painter, adding that Tan's male characters lack depth and ultimately are indistinguishable from each other (68).

Many critics note Tan's talent for creating realistic dialogue. Valerie Miner praises Tan's skill for dialogue in which she captures the "choppy English of the mothers and the sloppy California vernacular with sensitive authenticity" (567). Tan's stories are marked by a California brand of frankness that stretches across the Pacific to China. Additionally, Tan's narrative style remains uncomplicated and straightforward as it presents highly emotional and moving stories.

ANALYSIS

As a collection of distinct stories in a successive order, *The Joy Luck Club* allows the reader to enjoy repetitive themes, motifs, and characters as when reading a novel. Yet each story in this collection can be enjoyed as a single entity in itself. The sixteen stories of *The Joy Luck Club* are divided into four sections. Tan divides these sections equally between the mothers and daughters, with each woman narrating two stories. However, Tan does not conform to a strict symmetry because there are only seven voices telling sixteen stories. Jing-mei acts as the voice of her deceased mother and thus plays a dual role in Tan's short-story sequence. In relaying Suyuan's story, Jing-mei becomes the link between the generations.

In the first story, "The Joy Luck Club," Tan reveals her theme of maintaining the ties between generations. The aunties

see their own daughters, just as ignorant, just as unmindful of all the truths and hopes they have brought to America. . . . They see that joy and luck do not mean the same to their daughters, that to these closed American-born minds "joy luck" is not a word, it does not exist. They see daughters who will bear grandchildren born without any connecting hope passed from generation to generation. (31)

The sequence of stories revolves around the generational conflict between the Chinese immigrant mothers and their American-born daughters. Jing-mei describes the China that the mothers (Suyuan Woo, An-mei Hsu, Lindo Jong, and Ying-Ying St. Clair) have left behind. Although they have come from different parts of China, the mothers form a club that serves as a support group as they begin their new lives in America. The Joy Luck Club preserves its Chinese identity by enabling the mothers to share familiar food, stories, and customs around a mah-jong table.

The stories unfold around the mission of Suyuan's daughter, Jing-mei (June May) Woo, to inform her half sisters in China that their mother has passed away. Jing-mei is invited to assume her mother's place at the mah-jong table. Despite her reluctance to join her "aunties," Jing-mei learns to honor both her deceased mother and her cultural legacy. She becomes a foil for the other daughters (Rose Hsu Jordan, Waverly Jong, and Lena St. Clair), who reject their Chinese heritage and, consequently, become distanced from their mothers.

Tan pursues the importance of ethnic identity throughout the sequence by shifting narrators. Each story reflects how differently the mothers and daughters regard Chinese values. Yet Tan does not maintain a tight order. Jing-mei's mother is not present to tell her story. Her absence allows Jing-mei to bridge the generations. Walter Shear points out that Tan's description of shifting cultural values is reminiscent of Sherwood Anderson's story cycle *Winesburg, Ohio* and William Faulkner's *The Unvanquished*. Tan arranges her stories to illustrate the differing thinking of the generations. Although each of the stories sustains a sense of internal wholeness, together, they portray the contrast between the Chinese-born mothers and their American-born daughters (193).

The mother-daughter tensions stem from the differences between the Old World and the New World. Walter Shear notes that the stories focus on either a mother or a daughter. If the focus is on a mother, she has come to an understanding of her world; if it is on a daughter, she is caught in "cultural traps," never knowing answers, always posing questions, trying to live in what seems an "ambivalent world" (195). Unlike Maxine Hong Kingston's *The Woman Warrior*, Tan's *The Joy Luck Club* provides several points of view, establishing a "broader canvas" and "multiplicity of personal narratives" (199).

The two points of view in the mother-daughter pairs illustrate the contrasts between generations. Jing-mei's stories, "The Joy Luck Club" and "A Pair of Tickets," are the framework for the entire sequence. In "The Joy Luck Club," Jing-mei gives details that will shed light on the stories that follow. For example, Jing-mei explains the origins of the Joy Luck Club and the relationships between the mothers. A key passage centers on Suyuan Woo's great tragedy of being forced to abandon her twin daughters during World War II. Jing-mei is given traveling money for a trip to meet her half sisters. However, this trip will enable Jing-mei to learn her mother's true identity, as well as her own. "A Pair of Tickets" describes Jing-mei's mission, one that leads her to a deeper understanding of her ethnic identity.

The story "Half and Half" illustrates how Tan merges the past with the present. In this story, Rose Hsu Jordan describes three events in her life: first, the "present" situation in which she faces a divorce; second, the memory of her response to a family crisis—the tragic event of a brother drowned during a family picnic at an ocean beach; third, a reflection of the factors that lead to the disintegration of her marriage. The contrast between the mother and the daughter in their responses to the loss of a beloved one centers around the fact that the mother draws her strength from her belief that fate cannot cheat faith. However, one must be willing to have faith before fate can be altered. The mother demonstrates her strength by refusing to accept her son's death despite the reality. The daughter believes that her divorce cannot be avoided.

In Tan's stories, the mothers exhibit stronger personalities, tempered by their experiences. Unfortunately, the daughters are often embarrassed by their mothers and fail to appreciate their wisdom. Furthermore, the daughters are so swept up in the middle-class, white American mindset that they cannot comprehend what the mothers wish to teach them. In "The Red Candle," Tan contrasts the mother's selflessness with the daughter's selfishness. Lindo Jong laments, "I once sacrificed my life to keep my parents' promise. This means nothing to you, because to you a promise means nothing" (42). At the age of sixteen, Lindo marries the son of a wealthy family. As one can expect, Lindo is disappointed in her new husband. Nevertheless, she honors the commitment her parents made in order to protect her family's honor. Although Lindo Jong is forced to enter an arranged marriage, she discovers the means of empowering herself. Her husband is a pampered boy who has always been under his mother's control. In order to placate her demanding mother-in-law Huang Taitai, Lindo Jong strives to act as a model wife. Despite her diligence, Lindo does not meet Huang Taitai's expectations because she fails to bear a grandson. Finding her marriage arrangements intolerable, Lindo tricks her mother-in-law into believing that ill fortune will prevail unless her marriage is dissolved. In taking control of her situation, Lindo demonstrates how the mothers refuse to accept adversity without a struggle.

In "Four Directions," Tan further illustrates the rift between mothers and daughters. The difference in character creates the central conflict in "Four Directions," which is both internal and external. Lindo Jong's daughter, Waverly, tells about her frustrations with her mother, her difficulty in understanding her mother's character, and her mother's expectation of her growing up in America. Lindo wanted her children to have "the best combination: American circumstances and Chinese character" (254). Waverly blames her mother for not understanding that "these two things do not mix" (254) until years later, after much struggle and defeat in her life, she begins to miss the kind of power and resistance, the kind of confidence, self-esteem, and resourcefulness that she used to derive from her mother. Lindo's comments about her daughter are very comic and rich with irony: "But now she wants to be Chinese, it is so fashionable. And I know it is too late. All those years I tried to teach her!" (253).

In her article "Daughter-Text/Mother-Text: Matrilineage in Amy Tan's *Joy Luck Club*," Marina Heung stresses the role of language in Tan's stories. As the primary instrument of subjectivity, language illustrates the cultural variances of Tan's characters. For example, the mothers' broken English places them between cultures. Furthermore, Heung states that Tan's stories argue for "reclaiming language as an instrument of intersubjectivity and dialogue, and as a medium of transmission from mothers to daughters" (604). The concluding story of *The Joy Luck Club*, "A Pair of Tickets," illustrates Amy Tan's awareness of how culture and especially language shape individuals. As she travels to meet her lost half sisters, Jing-mei becomes immersed in her mother's mother tongue. Consequently, she reclaims her mother's cultural identity that she had rebelled against as a child immersed in mainstream America.

WORKS CITED AND CONSULTED

Primary

Tan, Amy. *The Chinese Siamese Cat*. New York: Macmillan, 1994.
———. *The Joy Luck Club*. New York: Ballantine, 1989.
———. *The Kitchen God's Wife*. New York: Ballantine, 1992.
———. *The Moon Lady*. New York: Macmillan, 1992.
———. "Mother Tongue." *The Best American Essays 1991*.

Secondary

Gates, David. "A Game of Show Not Tell." *Newsweek* April 17, 1989: 68–69.
Heung, Marina. "Daughter-Text/Mother-Text: Matrilineage in Amy Tan's *Joy Luck Club*." *Feminist Studies* 19 (1993): 597–616.

Luscher, Robert M. *John Updike: A Study of the Short Fiction*. New York: Twayne, 1993.

Miner, Valerie. "The Daughters' Journeys." *Nation* April 24, 1989: 566–69.

Painter, Charlotte. "In Search of a Voice." *San Francisco Review of Books* Summer 1989: 15–17.

Shear, Walter. "Generational Differences and the Diaspora in *The Joy Luck Club.*" *Critique: Studies in Contemporary Fiction* 34.3 (Spring 1993): 193–99.

Souris, Stephen. "Only Two Kinds of Daughters: Inter-Monologue Dialecticity in *The Joy Luck Club.*" *MELUS* (Summer 1994): 97–99.

WILLIAM TREVOR
(May 24, 1928–   )

Miriam Marty Clark

BIOGRAPHY

William Trevor was born William Trevor Cox in Mitchelstown, County Cork, of what he calls "smalltime protestant stock, far removed from the well-to-do Ascendancy of the recent past" (xiii). His father, James William Cox—"a big, healthy-looking man with a brown bald head" (*Excursions in the Real World* 19)—was a fairly successful banker; he was also, by Trevor's account, a drinker, a gambler, an avid storyteller, and an occasional moviegoer, though not much of a reader. Trevor's mother, Gertrude Davison Cox, was, Trevor writes, "tiny, capricious and beautiful, firm of purpose, fiery and aloof, with a sharp tongue, and an eccentric sense of humour that often took you by surprise" (19). Increasingly dissatisfied with her own life, she read widely, borrowing books from the nuns at the convent and the circulating library in the many provincial Irish towns where the family lived.

Several early circumstances of Trevor's life have left a permanent stamp on his writing. The first is the accident of having been born Protestant in Ireland, "into a minority that all my life has seemed in danger of withering away" (*Excursions* xiii). The second is the family's frequent moves, associated with his father's career, which gave Trevor both a wide experience of Irish provincial life and schooling and (largely by way of his mother) a pervasive sense of uprootedness. A third circumstance is the gradual disintegration of his parents' marriage and their eventual estrangement. Trevor traces these developments in his 1994 memoir, *Excursions in the Real World*.

At thirteen, Trevor left home for the Sandford Park School in Dublin and the boarding-school experiences that would recur in his fiction. From there he went to St. Columba's College and to Trinity College, Dublin, where he received a B.A. in history in 1950. Though he had once envisioned himself in commerce, a grocer or a draper, Trevor taught history and art and established himself as a sculptor; he continued sculpting until about 1960, when his work had become "wholly abstract" and no longer satisfying to him. Meanwhile, during the 1950s, he had married Jane Ryan, had settled in Devon, England (where they still live), and had begun to write. His first novel, *A Standard of Behaviour*, was published in 1958.

Since that time, Trevor has published ten novels, twelve collections of stories and novellas, several dramas, a photo essay (*A Writer's Ireland*), a memoir, and numerous prose pieces. In 1965, he won the Hawthornden Prize for his second novel, and since then he has won many awards, fellowships, and honorary degrees, including a Royal Society of Literature Award (for *Angels at the Ritz and Other Stories*) and two Whitbread Awards (for *The Children of Dynmouth* and *Fools of Fortune*).

Trevor has given a number of interviews over the years and has recently begun to use the memoir as a way of returning to the raw materials of his stories. Meanwhile, he continues to publish new stories (many of these in the *New Yorker* and other American periodicals) and novels; these have met with strongly positive reviews and sustained interest in the United States as well as in Britain.

CRITICISM

The appearance of *The Collected Stories* in 1992 provided an occasion for new and substantial writing on the author's short fiction, both in the popular press and in academic journals. Useful reassessments of Trevor's stories over thirty years come from Richard Tillinghast in *New Criterion*, Bruce Allen in *Sewanee Review*, Stephen Schiff in the *New Yorker*, and Brian Moore in the *New York Review of Books*. Sustained scholarly consideration of the stories appeared in articles by Jim Haughey, Richard Bonaccorso, and Miriam Marty Clark.

The 1990s have seen the publication of three books on William Trevor's work, including Suzanne Morrow Paulson's study of Trevor's short fiction. Paulson begins with a hundred-page study that places Trevor in a "serious modernist tradition" and looks closely at "the divided self struggling for a secure identity in a complex world" (102). Paulson treats the stories in clusters, looking at themes of trauma (political and personal), alienation, and courtship; she concludes with a discussion of comic stories, arguing that Trevor's brilliant wit has gone unacknowledged in earlier criticism. Part 2 of her book brings together interviews and short prose pieces under the heading "The Writer." Part 3 provides a selection of reviews and critical excerpts on the stories.

Gregory A. Schirmer's *William Trevor* (1990) includes a chapter-long survey of the short fiction. Schirmer explores Trevor's "dark moral vision" and his attunement to alienation and aloneness; he looks as well at Trevor's sustained craftsmanship, particularly his use of juxtaposition, parallelism, and irony. Kristin Morrison's *William Trevor* (1993) draws on stories and novels alike to illustrate the importance of a "system of correspondences" as the intellectual framework for Trevor's fiction. Under this system, past and present converge, as do public and private, political and domestic realms, space and time; at these points of convergence, Trevor explores metaphorically the problem of evil and its origins.

ANALYSIS

Like his high modernist predecessors, most notably James Joyce (who comes not only to be felt but to be talked about in some late stories, including "Music"), Trevor takes as the primary subject for his short stories the human mind, its subtle shifts of perception, its dawning self-knowledge, and its epiphanic and sometimes annihilating insights. The settings of his stories range far and wide, from cramped London flats to crumbling provincial estates, from Dublin pubs to Italian *pensiones*; the stories' concerns also range widely, from brooding youth to embittered age, from marital discord to political turmoil, from slowly dimming prospects to staggering ruin. Nevertheless, the stories hold in common a passionate and minute interest in human knowing and its enveloping, seductive other, unknowing.

This interest has its expression in the stories' pervasive, almost obsessive attentiveness to lies. Scarcely a story of the eighty-five in *Collected Stories* passes without a lie, pointedly observed; many could be said to be about lying and its consequences. Some are simple deceptions—a boy's lie about his age, a young maid's invention of a flat tire to explain her delayed return after a day of freedom—but many others are complex and far-reaching. Lies are told to spare or to exploit, in self-protection, or (like the petty thefts that often go along with them) in childish desperation. Large or small, however motivated, they are almost invariably symptomatic, distortions and concealments that unfold into dark disclosures about the human condition.

Some are outright lies, often about sex, money, or property. One man keeps occasional company with a Dublin prostitute who becomes "Mr. McNamara," a friend and business associate in the stories he tells his wife and children on his returns to the countryside. A single man in "The Forty-seventh Saturday" invents a wife and two children so that on Saturdays when he meets his working-class mistress, "no dawdling would be required of him after he had exacted what he had come to look upon as his due" (183). In "Widows," a workman presents a grieving woman with a bill her late husband has already paid. Some of these lies detonate within the stories, doing fearful damage: the discovery of the Dublin whore after his father's sudden death in "Mr. McNamara" destroys a boy's comfortable sense of the past and isolates him from his unenlightened mother and sisters. Others release a kind of slow poison: at twenty-seven, Mavie is beginning to be deformed by longing for a real life with her "married" lover. Still others, like that in "Widows," provide occasion for a grave reckoning with the ways of the world and one's aloneness in it.

Concealments and half-truths represent a different kind of falsehood, more important for Trevor, particularly in the middle stories. These include the most benign lies—a disappointment unspoken, a harsh reality softened. At other times, they represent a threshold, carefully preserved, between the public world and the private; these are often sexual secrets—impotence in "Cocktails at Doneys," homosexuality in "Bodily Secrets," forbidden love in "Music" and "The Printmaker."

But they also include the most malignant deceptions, those concerning perversion, greed, madness, or murder. In "The Bedroom Eyes of Mrs. Vansittart," for example, a woman's flagrant unfaithfulness to her husband earns her the disapproval of others in her wealthy circle—making her, in one man's words, "The Wife Whom Nobody Cares For" (704)—but her seductive behavior conceals, as it is carefully calculated to, the pedophilia of her well-liked husband. A man's apparent success at teaching difficult boys in "O Fat White Woman" conceals the fact that he "derives sexual pleasure from inflicting pain on children" (329), as an unsparing servant informs his wife after one boy has died of it. In "Mulvihill's Memorial," a man's ordinariness belies—until his death—his penchant for pornography and voyeurism. A woman's household staff in "Last Wishes" conspires to conceal her death and go on living on her estate and her income. In "The Blue Dress," a middle-aged man smitten by a sense of his own surprising good fortune in love comes to understand that his young fiancée Dorothea was, as a child, implicated in the death of an envied playmate.

Often, too, even the benign shades into the malignant. In "Death in Jerusalem," one of Trevor's finest stories, two men embark on a long-anticipated tour of the Holy Lands. One is a worldly, well-traveled priest, Father Paul; the other is his younger brother Francis, a single man of thirty-seven who has devoted himself to his aging mother and the family hardware business. For Francis, the trip, though deeply desired, is fraught from the beginning with guilt, nervousness, and disappointment. At the end of their first day in Jerusalem, Father Paul receives a telegram informing him of their mother's death; he wires back that the funeral should be postponed until the following Monday and decides to withhold the news from Francis until they have had time to enjoy at least part of their trip, to take in Nazareth and Galilee. A day later, unable to withstand the strain of his lie, Father Paul tells Francis, urging his younger brother not to fly home immediately but to go with him to Galilee the next morning. Father Paul's lie—which was at once well intended and profoundly selfish—crystallizes Francis's disappointment in the present, his sense of his own circumstances, and his vision of a lonely future. "I'll always hate the Holy Land now," Francis tells Paul. "No need for that, Francis," his brother replies.

But Francis felt there was and he felt he would hate, as well, the brother he had admired for as long as he could remember. . . . His brother's deceit and the endless whiskey in his brother's glass, and his casualness after a death seemed like the scorning of a Church which honoured so steadfastly the mother of its founder. . . . his own mother's eyes reminded him that they'd told him he was making a mistake, and upbraided him for not heeding her. Of course there was mockery everywhere. . . . He'd become part of it himself, sending postcards to the dead. (625–26)

Concealments and half-truths may be preserved in the stories, or else they are slowly chipped away or laid bare in an act of brutal exposure. Or they may open, as Father Paul's deception does for Francis, onto bleak epiphany. A similar thing happens to Justin Condon in "Music" as a result of a dying confession by the aunt who from his childhood has cultivated his musical gifts and caused him to think of himself as an artist. When she tells him that she did so only to be able to spend time with the priest who gave him the piano lessons at her house on Sundays and Wednesdays, only so that they might be for a little while a kind of "family," his whole sense of himself is exposed as a lie.

The self-deceptions and lived lies that are brought to light in such epiphanies as Francis's and Justin's are another very important kind of falsehood in Trevor's stories from early to late. Occasionally an epiphany of self-knowledge carries a faint promise of liberation, even happiness. Sarah Machaen, plain and unloved at forty-seven, is much taken aback by a younger woman's sexual advances in "Flights of Fancy" but finally glimpses in them—perhaps already vanished—a new possibility for friendship and affection.

Much more often, however, truth comes ungently and unwelcome to self-deceivers, leaving them cruelly disillusioned about themselves and their prospects. Near the end of "Music," sitting with the penitent old woman, Justin tries not to hear her story,

to convey through his agitation that he did not want to hear; that once she had spoken, the words could not be undone. For a long time now he had known he could play the piano in a tidy, racy way, that possibly he possessed no greater gift. . . . And yet his fantasy sprang from a lingering sliver of hope, from words that had once been spoken in his Aunt Roche's sitting room. (1084)

Often the truth is more brutal and less anticipated than this, and it comes not from old friends but from indifferent acquaintances and strangers bent on "home truths." In "Raymond Bamber and Mrs. Fitch," for example, a woman who declares herself unable to lie corners Raymond Bamber at a party and disrupts his quiet life by quizzing him about his "perversions" and loudly declaring him a homosexual. "She gets tight," explains another man, unwilling to dismiss Mrs. Fitch's claims, "She's liable to tell a home truth or two. . . . *In vino veritas*" (347).

Her victim, like Francis Conary in "Death in Jerusalem" and Justin Condon in "Music," returns—stripped of illusions, home truths echoing in his ears—to his quiet life. But elsewhere, and particularly for some of the women in Trevor's stories, the end of self-deception is cataclysmic. Mrs. Digby-Hunter of "O Fat White Woman" finds both her past life and her present self destroyed by the schoolboy Wraggett's death. Determined to make a successful marriage, Trevor explains early in the story, "and to come up to scratch as a wife, she had pursued a policy of agreeableness. . . . In a bedroom of a Welsh hotel she had disguised, on her wedding night, her puzzled disappointment when her husband had abruptly left her side" (317). Mrs. Digby-Hunter grows fat and complacent, overlooking obvious abuses at Milton Grange, the school her husband runs for wayward boys. As the story opens, she dozes in a deck chair on the lawn, a box of Terry's All Gold chocolates on her lap and a paperback novel by her side. "White fat slug," one of the resentful young maids remarks at the sight of her. "She can't think. . . . Was she human once?" (321). After the boy's death from a head injury, the same two maids force her to hear their accounts of blows and pinches and perversions at the school. "She tried to speak the truth about Milton Grange, as she saw it," Trevor writes, but she is drowned out by their litany of horrors.

Finally a new conviction takes hold, that it was all her fault. She imagines a different past, one in which she would deride her husband for his failures and force an end to his brutal ways with the boys. "The tragedy had temporarily unhinged her," the sergeant thinks when she comes into the kitchen weeping and babbling. "Her voice continued in the kitchen, the words pouring from it, repetitiously and in a hurry" (332).

In "The Grass Widows," Mrs. Angusthorpe, another headmaster's wife, tries earnestly to disillusion a young bride and persuade her to leave her marriage in the midst of a disappointing honeymoon. In trying to get Daphne to turn her back on Jackson Major, a cruel, ruthless, and dull boy she has known from his school days, Mrs. Angusthorpe confronts the loss of her own illusions about herself and her marriage: "Quite suddenly, she had seen her state of resignation as an insult to the woman she once, too long ago, had been" (228). For Mrs. Angusthorpe, as for fat, white Mrs. Digby-Hunter, there is no turning away from this new knowledge and no refuge from it. In their stories, as in so many others, self-deceptions have given shelter, have given shape to existence. To be undeceived is to go without in the world.

Almost to a one, Trevor's stories drive toward such clarity, however painful, even annihilating. They do not brood long on things beyond themselves; religion, history, and politics exist in ruined, human forms and no other. The writer, Trevor suggests in *Excursions in the Real World*, "attempts to extract an essence from the truth by turning it into what John Updike has called 'fiction's shapely lies' " (xii). Lying becomes meaningful in fictions where truth is possible; at the same time, truth makes its way—hidden, resisted, changing, and dangerous—in fictions, among lies.

WORKS CITED AND CONSULTED

Primary

Trevor, William. *After Rain*. New York: Viking, 1996.
———. *Angels at the Ritz and Other Stories*. New York: Viking, 1976.

————. *The Ballroom of Romance and Other Stories*. New York: Viking, 1972.

————. *Beyond the Pale and Other Stories*. New York: Viking, 1982.

————. *Boarding House*. New York: Viking, 1965.

————. *The Children of Dynmouth*. New York: Viking, 1977.

————. *Collected Stories*. New York: Viking, 1992.

————. *The Day We Got Drunk on Cake and Other Stories*. New York: Viking, 1967.

————. *Death in Summer*. New York: Viking, 1998.

————. *The Distant Past and Other Stories*. Dublin: Poolbeg, 1979.

————. *Elizabeth Alone*. New York: Viking, 1974.

————. *Excursions in the Real World: Memoirs*. New York: Knopf, 1994.

————. *Family Sins and Other Stories*. New York: Viking, 1990.

————. *Felicia's Journey*. New York: Viking, 1994.

————. *Fools of Fortune*. New York: Viking, 1983.

————. *Going Home: A Play*. New York: French, 1972.

————. *Ireland: Selected Stories*. New York: Penguin, 1998.

————. *Juliet's Story*. New York: Simon & Schuster, 1994.

————. *The Last Lunch of the Season*. London: Covent Garden Press, 1973.

————. *The Love Department*. New York: Viking, 1967.

————. *Lovers of Their Time and Other Stories*. New York: Viking, 1979.

————. *Marriages: A Play*. New York: French, 1973.

————. *Miss Gomez and the Brethren*. London: Bodley Head, 1971.

————. *Mrs. Eckdorf in O'Neill's Hotel*. New York: Viking, 1969.

————. *The News from Ireland and Other Stories*. New York: Viking, 1986.

————. *A Night with Mrs. da Tanka: A Play*. New York: French, 1972.

————. *Nights at the Alexandra*. Harper Short Novel Series. New York: Harper & Row, 1987.

————. *The Old Boys: A Novel*. Viking, 1964.

————. *Other People's Worlds*. Viking, 1981.

————. *Scenes from an Album*. Dublin: Co-op Books, 1981.

————. *The Silence in the Garden*. Viking, 1988.

————. *The Stories of William Trevor*. Harmondsworth: Penguin, 1983.

————. *Two Lives: Reading Turgenev and My House in Umbria*. New York: Viking, 1991.

————. *A Writer's Ireland: Landscape in Literature*. London: Thames & Hudson, 1984.

Secondary

Allen, Bruce. "Collected Stories." *Sewanee Review* 101 (1993): 138–44.

Bonaccorso, Richard. "William Trevor's Martyrs for Truth." *Studies in Short Fiction* 34.1 (1997): 113–19.

Clark, Miriam Marty. "The Scenic Self in William Trevor's Stories." *Narrative* 6.2 (May 1998): 174–87.

Haughey, Jim. "Joyce and Trevor's Dubliners: The Legacy of Colonialism." *Studies in Short Fiction* 32.2 (Summer 1995): 355–66.

Moore, Brian. "No Other Life." *New York Review of Books* 40 (October 21, 1993): 3.

Morrison, Kristin. *William Trevor*. New York: Twayne, 1993.

Paulson, Suzanne Morrow. *William Trevor: A Study of the Short Fiction*. New York: Twayne, 1993.

Schiff, Stephen. "The Shadows of William Trevor: Cultural Pursuits." *New Yorker* 68.45
    (December 28, 1992): 158+.
Schirmer, Gregory A. *William Trevor*. London: Routledge, 1990.
Tillinghast, Richard. "They Were as Good as We Were: The Stories of William Trevor."
    New Criterion 11 (February 1993): 10–17.

SELECTED ANNOTATED
BIBLIOGRAPHY

Allen, Walter. *The Short Story in English*. New York: Oxford University Press, 1981.
Like Mary Rohrberger, Allen argues that there is a "dual tradition"; stories bifurcate into two kinds: the formulaic and the experimental.

Anderson, Sherwood. *A Story Teller's Story*. New York: Huebsch, 1924. Central to the development of the short story in the United States, Anderson rejected the linear plot line, labeling it the "poison plot."

Baldeshwiler, Eileen. "The Lyric Short Story: The Sketch of a History." *Studies in Short Fiction* 6 (1969): 443–54. Baldeshwiler makes a distinction between two narrative modes, the epical and the lyrical—respectively distinguished by a focus on external or internal action. The author sketches a history of the lyrical short story, identifying key writers and their special contributions to the form.

Bayley, John. *The Short Story. Henry James to Elizabeth Bowen*. Brighton: Harvester Press, 1988. Bayley concentrates on British, Anglo-American, and Anglo-Irish writers from the late nineteenth century to World War II. The book contains one of the few discussions on the merits of Elizabeth Bowen as a short-story writer.

Birbalsingh, Frank, ed. *Frontiers of Caribbean Literature in English*. New York: St. Martin's, 1996. A collection of interviews with writers from diverse backgrounds, this volume seeks to give "an impression" of developments on the frontiers of postcolonial English literature.

Bonheim, Helmut. *The Narrative Modes: Techniques of the Short Story*. Cambridge, UK: D. S. Brewer, 1982. Principally structuralist, Bonheim's theory divides the genre of the short story into five modes or structural patterns, focusing on openings and closings. His work presents a valuable introduction to the structural aspects of the genre.

Brown, Suzanne Hunter. " 'Tess' and *Tess*: An Experiment in Genre." *Modern Fiction Studies* 28.1 (Spring 1982): 25–44. Brown applies the idea of spatial (as opposed to temporal) narrative form to short stories, contending that unlike novels, short stories deal primarily in spatial form as part of their epiphanic nature.

Condé, Mary, and Thorunn Lonsdale, eds. *Caribbean Women Writers: Fiction in English*.

New York: St. Martin's, 1999. The stated purpose of this volume, which includes both theory and criticism, is to consider the work of Caribbean women seriously.

Crowley, Donald. *The American Short Story, 1850–1900*. Boston: Twayne, 1989. This volume is more a critical history than a speculative work on the nature of the short story; it is especially useful for the beginning student.

Current-Garcia, E. *The American Short Story before 1850*. Boston: Twayne, 1985. Current-Garcia traces the roots of the American tale and legend from the Puritans through Washington Irving and the beginning of the American Renaissance.

Dance, Daryl Cumber. *New World Adams: Conversations with Contemporary West Indian Writers*. Leeds, Yorkshire: Peepal Tree, 1992. This text contains candid interviews with twenty-one of the most prominent West Indian writers.

Exjenbaum, Boris. "O. Henry and the Theory of the Short Story." Trans. I. R. Titunik. *Readings in Russian Poetics*. Ed. L. Matejka and K. Pomorska. Cambridge, MA: MIT Press, 1971. Although it was ignored for many years after its publication, Exjenbaum's text is now considered one of the major formalist statements of its time. O. Henry's stories, neatly plotted as they are, often ending on a twist of fate, are easy to assimilate in terms of structural patterns.

Ferguson, Suzanne. "Defining the Short Story: Impressionism and Form." *Modern Fiction Studies* 28.1 (Spring 1982): 13–23. Ferguson has spent much of her academic career trying to discover whether the short story is in fact a distinct genre from the novel. Here she argues that impressionism is characteristic of both novels and stories, but in the literary world, impressionistic effects are heightened to a greater degree in the short story than in the novel. She concludes that it is the reduced emphasis on physical action in the plot of the impressionistic short story that most distinguishes it from novels in that genre.

Fusco, Richard. *Maupassant and the American Short Story*. University Park: Pennsylvania State University Press, 1994. Fusco traces what he considers to be the influence of Maupassant on American writers such as Henry James and Stephen Crane. He argues that Maupassant demonstrated that a story may contain a compound of significant moments that may or may not coincide with a character's moment of illumination. He says of this development that it offered American writers an alternative to Poe's concept of single effect.

Gerlach, John. *Toward the End: Closure and Structure in the American Short Story*. University: University of Alabama Press, 1985. This influential work manages to study a wide range of stories in depth by limiting its focus to the moment of closure, which is regarded as the most distinctive feature of the genre.

Gordimer, Nadine. *Writing and Being*. Cambridge, MA: Harvard University Press, 1995. Gordimer's metaphor and definition of the short story is often referred to—"as instantaneous as the flash of fireflies."

Gullason, Thomas. "Revelation and Evolution: A Neglected Dimension of the Short Story." *Studies in Short Fiction* 10 (1973): 347–56. Gullason uses works by Steinbeck and Lawrence to argue that the short story works not only through revelation, but also through evolution, a feature of the novel sometimes opposed to revelation as a distinguishing trait of the short story.

———. "The Short Story: An Underrated Art." *Studies in Short Fiction* 1 (1964): 13–31. Gullason describes the short story as a "private art," one that, because of its intrinsic brevity, allows the reader to form an immediate and intimate relationship with the story.

————. "The Short Story: Revision and Renewal." *Studies in Short Fiction* 19 (1982). 221–30. Gullason takes stock of the distance the short story has traversed in the twentieth century and argues that its vitality as a working genre has not been lost.

Hanson, Clare, ed. *Re-reading the Short Story*. New York: St. Martin's, 1989. This text discusses formal aspects of the short story, such as disjunction, and their potential relationships to countercultural ideologies. Hanson argues that the form of the short story makes it ideal for expressing varieties of knowledge repressed in mainstream culture.

————. *Short Stories and Short Fictions, 1880–1980*. London: Macmillan, 1985. Hanson argues that the modern short story gained wide acclaim in the late nineteenth century largely because of the surge in magazine publication. This wide-ranging book pays particular attention to writers such as Gertrude Stein, Saki, and O. Henry who have often been overlooked due to the formulaic aspects of their stories. She also uses Freud's theory of humor to discuss the process of pleasure involved in reading the short story.

Head, Dominic. *The Modernist Short Story*. Cambridge: Cambridge University Press, 1992. Head approaches the works of several important writers, including Mansfield, Joyce, and Woolf, from the point of view of deconstructionist and Bakhtinian critical theory. This is one of the most theoretically challenging studies of the genre to date.

Hemingway, Ernest. *Death in the Afternoon*. New York: Scribner, 1932. Issuing perhaps the best-known theoretical statement based on metaphor, Hemingway presents the so-called iceberg theory, the idea that a story reveals at the surface only the tip of the iceberg. Readers must find the iceberg's hidden body to experience a story's total meaning and realize its significance.

Iftekharuddin, Farhat, Mary Rohrberger, and Maurice Lee, eds. *Speaking of the Short Story*. Jackson: University Press of Mississippi, 1997. This unique collection of interviews with both writers and theorists discusses many facets of the short story from multicultural and individualistic points of view. The introduction includes a valuable overview of postmodernism, magic realism, and minimalism in relation to the short story.

Ingram, Forrest. *Representative Short Story Cycles of the Twentieth Century: Studies in a Literary Genre*. The Hague: Mouton, 1971. This volume includes extensive theoretical discussions of cycles by Kafka, Faulkner, and Sherwood Anderson as well as a history of cycle genre theory, definitions, reviews of previous criticism, and a new theoretical system for approaching short-story cycles.

James, Louis. *Caribbean Literature in English*. New York: Longman, 1999. James examines problems in defining Caribbean literature and describes the modern cultural history of the Caribbean, focusing on the evolution of its distinctive aesthetic and pluralism.

King, Bruce. *The New English Literatures: Cultural Nationalism in a Changing World*. New York: St. Martin's, 1980. King presents a comparative study of new English literatures and major authors, discussing origins, themes, contexts, and cultural change.

————, ed. *New National and Post-colonial Literatures: An Introduction*. Oxford: Clarendon Press, 1996. This collection discusses issues such as literature and language, creolity, colonialism, and cultural pluralism. It includes a comparative examination of theories, significant writers, and contexts. It is useful to both beginners and specialists.

———. *West Indian Literature*. Hamden, CT: Archon Books, 1979. This collection of essays provides a survey of the history of West Indian literature, comprehensive introductions to major authors, assessments of recent works, and connections with social and political contexts.

Lane, Dorothy F. *The Island as Site of Resistance: An Examination of Caribbean and New Zealand Texts*. New York: Lang, 1995. Lane presents a postmodern examination of the island as a metaphor for the bounding of discursive and narrative patterns in (cultural) imperialism. She uses a variety of texts to discuss strategies of resistance to colonialist island discourses.

Levy, Andrew. *The Culture and Commerce of the American Short Story*. Cambridge: Cambridge University Press, 1993. Levy offers an examination of the role that "how-to" manuals played in the writing of short stories.

Lohafer, Susan. *Coming to Terms with the Short Story*. Baton Rouge: Louisiana State University Press, 1983. A ground-breaking structuralist study of the genre, this work considerably heightened the level of theoretical sophistication applied to the short story.

Lohafer, Susan, and J. E. Clarey, eds. *Short Story Theory at a Crossroads*. Baton Rouge: Louisiana State University Press, 1989. An interlinked series of essays with connecting introductions by Lohafer, this work contains theories by the major scholars of the short story. The collection of essays and the bibliography created much of the impetus for a reawakening of scholarly interest in the short story as a genre.

Lounsberry, Barbara, Susan Lohafer, Mary Rohrberger, Stephen Pett, and R. C. Feddersen, eds. *The Tales We Tell: Perspectives on the Short Story*. Westport, CT: Greenwood, 1998. These essays divide into four major sections: form, history, genre, and cognition. Departing from the genre defensiveness that threatens to narrow the field of short-story theory, this collection of interdisciplinary and speculative essays appreciatively highlights both the primacy of the short story in human discourse and its potential for new directions.

Mann, Susan Garland. *The Short Story Cycle: A Genre Companion and Reference Guide*. New York: Greenwood, 1989. More critical and historical than theoretical, Mann discusses a variety of well-known cycles by Joyce, Sherwood Anderson, Hemingway, Faulkner, Updike, Welty, and others. Other sections cover the composition process, history, and generic characteristics of the form. Mann asserts that the cycle is unified and similar to the novel but for the lack of a continuous plot. Her annotated list of cycles includes over 120 twentieth-century titles.

Mansfield, Katherine. *Journal of Katherine Mansfield*. Ed. J. Middleton Murry. New York: Knopf, 1946. Katherine Mansfield expressed her vision of stories as focused on single moments; past, present, and future merge in a moment of illumination.

Markham, E. A. Introduction. *The Penguin Book of Caribbean Short Stories*. Ed. E. A. Markham. London: Penguin, 1996. Markham's discussion of the sources, influences, and history of Caribbean short stories is energetic, well documented, and socially concerned. It is indispensable for beginners.

Matthews, Brander. *Philosophy of the Short-Story*. New York: Longmans, 1901. A short-story writer himself, as well as a critic and theoretician, Matthews was the first

writer after Poe to give serious sustained attention to the art of the short story.
He is credited with announcing the "birth" of a new genre. Matthews must also
be credited with the statement that the short story deals with a single character
in a single situation at a single moment in time.

May, Charles E. *Edgar Allan Poe: A Study of the Short Fiction*. Boston: Twayne, 1991.
A discussion of Poe's literary theories and the application of those theories in his
own work.

———. "The Nature of Knowledge in Short Fiction." *Studies in Short Fiction* 21 (1984):
327–38. May argues that the short story offers an epistemology that is distinct
from that of the novel and that is more reliant on revelation and knowledge of
the sacred.

———, ed. *The New Short Story Theories*. Athens: Ohio University Press, 1994. May
offers this volume as an update and sourcebook for future study of the form. The
most prominent issue remains definition of the genre; May says that he supports
"family resemblance" categorization, although others have cast him as looking
for a "single characteristic." The modernity of the collection shows in a new
emphasis on rhetoric and ideas from language theory. The annotated bibliography
is extensive and valuable.

———, ed. *Short Story Theories*. Athens: Ohio University Press, 1976. This early collection of diverse and sometimes-provocative theoretical articles called fresh attention to the field of short-story theory.

———. *The Short Story: The Reality of Artifice*. Boston: Twayne, 1995. An important
study, this volume explores the theoretical roots of the short story while tracing
the genre's development from realism to formalism to postmodernism, minimalism, and experimentation. The book also contains an extensive bibliographic
essay.

———. *Twentieth Century European Short Story: An Annotated Bibliography*. Pasadena,
CA: Salem, 1989. In this study, May takes a critical approach to the European
short story; a bio-bibliographical work, it is not especially theoretical. The book
introduces to the American reading public many important European writers such
as Isaac Babel, Halo Calvino, and Isak Dinesen.

McClave, Heather, ed. *Women Writers of the Short Story*. Englewood Cliffs, NJ: Prentice-
Hall, 1980. More interpretive than theoretical, these essays, penned by a variety
of well-known thinkers, constitute a series of new critical readings of particular
works by such authors as Welty, Katherine Anne Porter, and Frank O'Connor.

O'Connor, Frank. *The Lonely Voice*. London: Macmillan, 1963. O'Connor argues that
the short story, more than any other genre, involves a protagonist who is an
outsider and operates on the periphery of society. O'Connor's volume is concerned more with theme than with structure.

Pascoe, Allan H. "On Defining Short Stories." *New Literary History* 22.2 (Spring 1991):
406–22. Pascoe argues that a short story has an "undefinable set of characteristics
which each age and each author deploys in different ways and with different
variables" (407).

Pattee, Fred Lewis. *The Development of the American Short Story*. New York: Biblo &
Tannen, 1970. For many years, this volume was considered the standard text for
understanding the emergence of the short story, ranging from Irving's *Sketchbook*
to the magazine stories of the late nineteenth century.

Poe, Edgar A. *The Complete Works of Edgar Allan Poe*. Ed. J. A. Harrison. New York:

AMS, 1965. Poe's review of Nathaniel Hawthorne's *Twice Told Tales* is often cited as the beginning of short-story theory. In that review and in his essay "Philosophy of Composition," Poe stresses that a well-made tale should create "a single effect" and be readable in "one sitting."

Reid, Ian. *The Short Story*. London: Methuen, 1977. This brief history of the short story is especially useful with regard to modernist critical and theoretical approaches to the short story. Reid raises the controversial question of whether the genre of the short story is truly distinct from that of the novel.

Rohrberger, Mary. *Hawthorne and the Modern Short Story*. The Hague: Mouton, 1966. This ground-breaking theoretical treatment of the short story makes a distinction between "simple narrative" and the "short story proper." Rohrberger argues that the short story has a greater depth of detail and symbolic resonance than the simple narratives of writers such as O. Henry. Her distinction seems to form the basis for differences noted by subsequent critics and theoreticians between the anecdotal and symbolic aspects of the genre.

Rohrberger, Mary, and Dan Burns. "Short Fiction and the Numinous Realm: Another Attempt at Definition." *Modern Fiction Studies* 28.1 (1982): 5–13. Rohrberger and Burns argue that from Hawthorne to Donald Barthelme, the line of development of the short-story genre has become less plot motivated and more image directed.

Shaw, Valerie. *The Short Story: A Critical Introduction*. London: Longman, 1983. This book focuses on British writers and deals with character, setting, and subject. Shaw seems to stand against the attempt to define the short story in a unified way, asserting the insufficiency of criteria such as writers' devices and characteristics such as singleness of effect.

Shklovsky, Viktor. *Theory of Prose*. Trans. Benjamin Sher. Elmwood Park, IL: Dalkey Press, 1990. Shklovsky states that the modern novel was preceded by the short-story collection. Making the statement as a chronological fact, Shklovsky does not necessarily imply a causal relationship between the two forms, but he does discuss the cyclic or episodic construction of many modern novels, relying in part on the works of Anton Chekhov.

Smitten, Jeffrey R., and Ann Daghistany, eds. *Spatial Form in Narrative*. Ithaca, NY: Cornell University Press, 1981. Here "spatial form," a metaphor for the atemporal ordering of a narrative and a distinctive characteristic of the short story, is discussed relative to a number of genres.

Tallack, Douglas. *The Nineteenth-Century American Short Story*. London: Routledge, 1993. This volume is one of the few works to engage in theoretical questioning of the nineteenth-century American short story. Tallack's stated purpose is to combine two levels of analysis: a metatheoretical critique both of the ways in which the short story has been monopolized by modernist theory and of how modernist theory has been applied to the nineteenth-century American short story. The volume includes a thorough critical bibliography.

Voss, Arthur. *The American Short Story: A Critical Survey*. Norman: University of Oklahoma Press, 1973. Voss presents a simple introduction to the American short story, historically arranged.

Welty, Eudora. "The Reading and Writing of Short Stories," *Atlantic Monthly* February 1949: 54–58; March 1949: 46–49. Welty writes about the mystery of the story, describing how, with atmosphere, the story resists easy definition and analysis.

Wright, Austin. *The American Short Story in the Twenties*. Chicago: University of Chicago Press, 1961. Wright's book covers one of the most impressive decades in the genre of the short story by weaving together critical and theoretical questions with close readings of works by Hemingway and other American short-story writers.

INDEX

ABOUT THE EDITORS AND CONTRIBUTORS

Erica Benson graduated from the University of South Carolina with a master of arts in linguistics and a graduate certificate in teaching English as a foreign language. She has taught a variety of English, linguistic, and ESL/EFL courses at universities in the United States and Europe, including Franklin University, the University of Northern Iowa, the University of South Carolina, the University of Warsaw, Poland, and the University of Bamberg, Germany. She is currently a Ph.D. candidate at Michigan State University.

Ann Charters is Professor of American Literature at the University of Connecticut. Among other publications, she is the editor of *The Story and Its Writer* and *Major Writers of Short Fiction*.

Miriam Marty Clark is Associate Professor of English at Auburn University, where she teaches courses in twentieth-century literature. Her published work includes recent essays on Alice Munro, Ann Beattie, and Raymond Carver as well as more broadly focused discussions of the short story. She is currently working on a book-length study of the American short story at the end of the twentieth century.

Charles Dameron is Associate Professor of English at the University of Texas at Brownsville and Texas Southmost College. His publications include essays and reviews of such contemporary writers as Italo Calvino, Derek Walcott, Wole Soyinka, Nadine Gordimer, and Kofi Awoonor. His own poetry has been published in a number of literary magazines, and he is the author of two collections of poems.

Brian Dibble is Professor of Comparative Literature and Foundation Head of Curtin University's School of Communication and Cultural Studies in Western Australia. With Barbara Milech, he is researching and writing a biography of Elizabeth Jolley. He has written extensively on Jolley.

Mary Ellen Doyle has served as Chair of Humanities and Associate Professor of English at Divine Word College, Epworth, Iowa. Her book on the fiction of Ernest Gaines, whom she has studied since meeting him in 1983 and later touring his home territory in Louisiana is forthcoming from LSU Press. Other published works on Gaines include a recently republished interview, a biographical essay, an annotated bibliography, and several articles. She currently teaches African American literature at Spalding University, Louisville, Kentucky.

Elias Ellefson teaches English at Aplington-Parkersburg High School, Parkersburg, Iowa. He has a master's degree from the University of Northern Iowa and earned his B.A. at Luther College. He currently resides in Wisconsin.

Gayle Elliott is Assistant Professor of Creative Writing at St. Lawrence University in upstate New York, where she teaches beginning and advanced fiction workshops as well as literature courses. She also publishes both fiction and literary criticism.

Erin Fallon is a graduate student at the University of New Orleans. She has worked as assistant coordinator for the International Conference on the Short Story in English and recording secretary of the Society for the Study of the Short Story. She currently serves as assistant editor for the journal *Short Story*.

R. C. Feddersen holds a master's degree from the University of Northern Iowa. He has worked as an assistant editor and criticism editor for *Short Story* and is currently completing a doctorate at Oklahoma State University.

Carol Franko is Associate Professor of English at Kansas State University. Her research interests include utopian science fiction and fiction by contemporary women writers.

Mary Gravitt earned an M.A. in African studies and an M.L.S. in library and information science from the University of Iowa, as well as an M.A. in English literature and language from the University of Northern Iowa. Her recent research interests include issues of postcolonialism and American-ethnic literature.

Larry D. Griffin serves as Professor of English and Dean of Arts and Sciences at Dyersburg State Community College in Dyersburg, Tennessee. He has published critical articles, short stories, and poetry, including such works as *Airspace* and *The Blue Water Tower*. He has also exhibited several paintings and photographs.

Brady Harrison is Assistant Professor of English at the University of Montana. His work on literatures of Vietnam and the American empire have appeared or are forthcoming in *American Studies, Southwestern American Literature*, and a collection, *The Vietnam War and Postmodernity*.

Farhat Iftekharuddin is Associate Professor of English and Dean of the College of Arts and Sciences at the University of Texas at Brownsville. He is the editor of the literary journal *Short Story*. His research interests include post-modernism, minimalism, magic realism, and feminist issues in contemporary literature. He has published articles and papers on such authors as Salman Rushdie, Isabelle Allende, Bharati Mukherjee, and Rudolfo Anaya.

Jerome Klinkowitz is Professor of English and University Distinguished Scholar at the University of Northern Iowa. Among his many published books are *Literary Disruptions* (1975), *Donald Barthelme: A Comprehensive Bibliography and Annotated Secondary Checklist* (1977, with Asa Pieratt and Robert Murray Davis), and *Donald Barthelme: An Exhibition* (1991).

Paul Kotrodimos received his B.A. and M.A. from the University of Northern Iowa. He has worked as assistant editor for *Short Story* and assistant coordinator for the International Conference on the Short Story in English.

James Kurtzleben received an M.A. in American literature at the University of Northern Iowa, where he taught freshman composition and worked as assistant editor for *Short Story* and *Literary Magazine Review*, as well as assistant coordinator for the International Conference on the Short Story in English. His research focuses on feminist psychoanalytic theory.

Hermine Lee is a teacher of special education in the Madison, Wisonsin, Metropolitan School District. She has also taught a course in American literature for the Department of Continuing Education at the University of Northern Iowa. She has degrees from Micro Teachers College and the University of the West Indies, Mona, both in Jamaica.

Maurice A. Lee is Professor of English and Dean of the College of Liberal Arts at Central Arkansas University. He received his doctorate from the University of Wisconsin at Madison. His specialties include American literature, African-American literature, and Caribbean literature. He is founder and editor of the *Journal of Caribbean Literatures* as well as the director of the biennial International Conference on the Short Story in English.

L. M. Lewis is Professor of English at the University of Texas at Brownsville. He has written about basic writing, critical thinking, university administration, Wallace Stevens, country music, and the Vietnam War. Currently, he is concentrating on Sandra Cisneros's work, revising a book-length manuscript that attempts to sort out the influences of gender, class, race, and ethnicity.

Christine Loflin teaches African, Caribbean, and other literatures in English at Grinnell College. She has published essays on Ngugi wa Thiong'o, Flora Nwapa, and Zaynab Alkali; her book *African Horizons: The Landscapes of African Fiction* was published in 1998 by Greenwood Press.

Terry J. Martin is Associate Professor of English at Baldwin-Wallace College. He received his Ph.D. from the State University of New York at Buffalo in 1988. He regularly teaches courses in nineteenth-century American Literature and African-American literature and has published essays on short fiction by Poe, Hawthorne, Melville, and Nabokov.

Sherry Morton-Mollo is a graduate of the University of California at Los Angeles and California State University at Fullerton. She is currently completing a doctoral program at Claremont Graduate School and hopes to pursue further studies in immigrant literature.

Pierre-Damien Mvuyekure is Associate Professor of English, American, and African-American Literature at the University of Northern Iowa. He is also a poet and fiction writer. He is currently working on a book on Ishmael Reed and the poetics of multiculturalism.

Neil Nakadate is Professor of English at Iowa State University, where he teaches courses in contemporary American literature. He is coeditor of *A Rhetoric of Doing: Essays on Written Discourse in Honor of James L. Kinneavy* (1992), coauthor of *Writing in the Liberal Arts Tradition* (1985, 1990), editor of *Robert Penn Warren: A Reference Guide* (1977) and *Robert Penn Warren: Critical Perspectives* (1981), and author of *Understanding Jane Smiley* (1999).

Rick Oehling is finishing a doctoral degree at the University of Wisconsin at Madison. He currently resides in Iowa.

Britta Olinder is Senior Lecturer in English Language Literatures at Göteborg University. She has published essays on seventeenth-century drama and Irish and Indian literature and has hosted several conferences on postcolonial literatures.

Cheryl Roberts is Associate Professor of TESOL at the University of Northern Iowa. Her interests include first- and second-language acquisition, children's literature, and short fiction, particularly of the Vietnam generation.

Susan Rochette-Crawley is Assistant Professor and Director of Creative Writing at the University of Northern Iowa, where she teaches fiction writing, short-story theory, and literary editing. Her publications have appeared in *Short Story, Sou'wester, Literary Magazine Review*, and *Contemporary Literature*, among other journals. She recently won a fellowship from Inkwell International through Hamilton College, New York.

Mary Rohrberger is Professor of English in Residence at the University of New Orleans. She is the founder of the International Conference on the Short Story in English, the Society for the Study of the Short Story, and the journal *Short Story*. Her best-known books include *Story to Anti-Story* and *Hawthorne and the Modern Short Story: A Study in Genre*.

Minoli Salgado is a lecturer in English at the University of Sussex. She holds a doctorate in postindependence Indian women's writing from the University of Warwick and currently teaches courses on postcolonial literature.

Selina Samuels teaches at the University of New South Wales in Sydney, Australia. She received her Ph.D. at Queen Mary and Westfield College, University of London, with a dissertation on the postcolonial short story by women writers. She is the editor of three volumes on Australian literature for the *Dictionary of Literary Biography* and the fiction editor of *HEAT* magazine.

Scharron A. Shy-Clayton is Associate Professor of Ethnic and Cultural Studies in the Department of Philosophy and Religion at the University of Northern Iowa. She has also served as Associate Dean in the College of Humanities and Fine Arts. Her recent research interests include the culture and philosophy of African-American life and the developmental psychological factors that impact white behavior and race relations.

Hilary Siebert is Associate Professor of English at Radford University in Virginia, where he teaches courses in oral and written storytelling traditions. He is currently on leave, completing a manuscript titled *The Poetic Space of the Short Story*. Previous publications have focused on the short stories of Carver, Paley, and others.

Begoña Sío-Castiñeira is a scholar of Jewish-American literature, with particular interest in questions of identity as they manifest themselves in immigrant literature. Her publications include *The Short Stories of Bernard Malamud: In Search of Post-Immigrant Identity* (1998). She has taught at various universities in the United States and currently lives in Vigo, Spain.

Wayne B. Stengel is Professor of English at the University of Central Arkansas. He has published a book on Donald Barthelme and essays on Ernest Hemingway, John Cheever, Robert Coover, Sam Shepard, Alfred Hitchcock, Brian DePalma, and Jonathan Demme. He teaches American modernism, postmodernism, and film studies and is currently researching a book on the concept of history in the American postmodern novel.

Linda H. Straubel is Assistant Professor of English (Creative Writing Concentration) at the University of Montana. She has been teaching English composition, creative writing, and literature courses since the summer of 1994. She has several publications and is currently working on an anthology, *The New Western Revisited*.

J. R. (Tim) Struthers has won wide recognition for his work as a bibliographer, interviewer, critic, editor, and publisher in his chosen field, the Canadian short story. He has been teaching at the University of Guelph since 1985 and is the coeditor, with John Metcalf, of the landmark collection *How Stories Mean*. He has published extensively on Alice Munro.

Troy Thibodeaux received his master's degree from Louisiana State University. He has published articles on W. B. Yeats and Gerard Manley Hopkins. He is currently pursuing a Ph.D. at New York University with a specialization in twentieth-century American literature.

Grant Tracey, editor of *Literary Magazine Review* and the on-line magazine *Images*, is Assistant Professor of English at the University of Northern Iowa, where he teaches film and creative writing. He has also written a number of short stories.

Karen Tracey is Assistant Professor of English at the University of Northern Iowa. She has contributed entries on Sarah Orne Jewette, Harriet Beecher Stowe, and Constance Fenimore Woolson to other bio-bibliographical sourcebooks and has published an article on teaching revision in the National Council of Teachers of English *Classroom Practice* series. Her book *Plots and Proposals: American Women's Fiction, 1850–1890* was published in 2000.

Michael Trussler teaches English at the University of Regina. He has published articles on Raymond Carver, Donald Barthelme, Richard Ford, and short-story theory.

Jennie Wang is Associate Professor of English at the University of Northern Iowa. Her article "Tripmaster Monkey: Kingston's Postmodern Representation of a New China Man" was published in the spring 1995 issue of *MELUS*. Since then, she has published a critical study of romantic love in Nabokov and is currently completing a book on Maxine Hong Kingston's works.

Allan Weiss is a Toronto free-lance writer and university instructor, currently teaching at York University and Woodsworth College. His stories have been published in various journals and anthologies, including *Short Story, Fiddlehead*, and most recently *Prairie Fire*. He was cocurator of the National Library of Canada's recent exhibit on Canadian science fiction and fantasy and is working on a book-length study of Canadian fantastic literature.

Robin Werner is a Ph.D. candidate in English at Tulane University. Her major fields of study are Victorian literature and gender performance.

Norma C. Wilson is Professor of English at the University of South Dakota, where she specializes in American and Native American literature. Her publications include essays on the work of Walt Whitman, N. Scott Momaday, Leslie Marmon Silko, and Linda Hogan as well as poetry, articles, and reviews in magazines. She and her husband, Jerry Wilson, cowrote the script for the film *South Dakota: A Meeting of Cultures* (1985). She has served as chair of the South Dakota Humanities Council.

Michael W. Young teaches in the Department of Communications at Robert Morris College in Pittsburgh. His publications include original short fiction and poetry, along with work in American and Canadian literature, Shakespeare, and writing pedagogy.